Beyond Behavior Modification

A Cognitive–Behavioral Approach to Behavior Management in the School

THIRD EDITION

Beyond Behavior Modification

A Cognitive–Behavioral Approach to Behavior Management in the School

THIRD EDITION

Joseph S. Kaplan

with Jane Carter

Illustrated by Nancy Cross

pro·ed

8700 Shoal Creek Boulevard
Austin, Texas 78757-6897

pro·ed

© 1995 by PRO-ED, Inc.
8700 Shoal Creek Boulevard
Austin, Texas 78757-6897

Base charts in Figures 8.6, 8.8–8.15, 8.21, 8.28–8.37, 8.39, and on pp. 317 and 319 (6-cycle chart);
base charts in Figures 8.16, 8.19, 8.20, 8.24–8.26, 8.38, 8.40, 14.3, 14.5, and on pp. 311, 315, 321, 323, 325, 326, 331, and 338 (4-cycle chart); and
base charts in Figures 8.17, 8.18, 8.23, 8.27, and on pp. 313, 316, 329, 333, 337, 339, and 340 (2-cycle chart) are adapted from charts produced by Behavior Research Company, Kansas City, KS, and Graphics for Behavior Measurement, Eugene, OR.

Library of Congress Cataloging-in-Publication Data

Kaplan, Joseph S.
　　Beyond behavior modification / Joseph Kaplan—3rd ed.
　　　　p.　　cm.
　　Includes bibliographical references and indexes.
　　ISBN 0-89079-663-7
　　1. Classroom management.　2. Behavior modification.　3. Cognitive
　therapy.　I. Title.
LB3013.K33　1995
371.1'024—dc20　　　　　　　　　　　　　　94-40188
　　　　　　　　　　　　　　　　　　　　　　CIP

This book is designed in Cheltenham Book and Syntax.

Production Manager: Alan Grimes
Production Coordinator: Karen Swain
Art Director: Lori Kopp
Reprints Buyer: Alicia Woods
Editor: Tracy Sergo
Editorial Assistant: Claudette Landry
Project Manager: Adrienne Booth

Printed in the United States of America

1　2　3　4　5　6　7　8　9　10　　99　98　97　96　95

*To my greatest
source of reinforcement—
my children—
Ross, Kim, and Hannah*

Contents

CHAPTER 13

Stress Management Strategies • 449

CHAPTER 14

Changing Teacher Behavior • 473

APPENDIX A

Interest Inventory • 499

APPENDIX B

Legal Rights Checklist • 503

APPENDIX C

Relaxation Script for Children • 507

APPENDIX D

Commercially Available Programs and Materials • 511

Preface

This second revision of *Beyond Behavior Modification* was supposed to take "just a matter of months" to finish. As it turned out, it *has* been only a matter of months—but 16 of them! I didn't realize when I started writing in June of 1993, with an August '93 deadline, that I would be rewriting virtually the entire text. Before going any further, I must thank the people at PRO-ED for their patience (indulgence, actually); for me, writing is difficult enough without guilt, and with guilt it is darn near impossible.

Now that I'm finally finished, I feel pretty good about this book, much better than I did about editions one and two. There are major differences between this edition and its predecessor. For one thing, the material on the ecological model (two chapters in the Second Edition) has been reduced to make room for a more detailed treatment of data collection and the cognitive behavior modification strategies. There is a new chapter on data displays and data analysis written from a Precision Teaching perspective. Another new chapter looks at proactive behavior management with an emphasis on effective instruction. There is also new material contrasting models of behavior management including the psychoeducational, biophysical, and ecological approaches as well as discussing the behavioral and social learning theory models upon which this book is based.

The material on cognitive strategies has been expanded to two chapters: one chapter on cognitive restructuring and one on problem solving, verbal mediation, and self-instructional training. There is new material on the ethical use of behavior reduction procedures in the chapter on weakening behaviors. The chapter on social skills training has been completely rewritten by Jane Carter, an expert in this area.

In addition to all of the new material described above, I have tried to make the old material easier to understand. Much of it has been reorganized and rewritten. The chapters are now sequenced according to *what is changed*—behavior first; then cognitions; and, finally, emotions—*not who changes it* (i.e., teacher or student). In an effort to help you assess your understanding of the material, several brief assessments called *checkpoints* now appear in each chapter. These within-chapter checkpoints are designed to assess your knowledge and comprehension of the material as it is presented, while the new end-of-chapter assessments are intended to measure your performance at the application level. The acceptable responses to the end-of-chapter assessments have been moved from the appendixes at the end of the book to a more logical and convenient position at the end of each chapter, immediately following the assessment. I can't stress enough the importance of the end-of-chapter assessments: The best way to learn how to design a token economy, write a shaping program, or plot and analyze data is to *do it*; the end-of-chapter assessments provide you with this opportunity, and the acceptable responses provide you a model with which to compare your efforts. In fact, you might want to photocopy the acceptable responses section for each chapter and keep them in a looseleaf binder for easy reference. They serve as excellent models for many of the strategies covered in the text.

In closing, I want to thank the many people who made this new edition possible. First, thanks to everyone who bought the second edition; your comments and suggestions have been invaluable, and I can honestly say that without you there never would have been a third edition. Thanks also to my editor at PRO-ED, James Patton, for not losing faith in me or the book. A special thank you to my wife, Betsy Davenport, who was virtually without a husband for months at a time. She could have made things harder but, as usual, she made them easier for me. Thanks to Karna Nelson and Jane Carter for their honest and accurate reviews of the second edition. All I can say is, maybe next time. Thanks to my old friend and Precision Teaching mentor, Owen White, for taking the time (while writing a grant) to review the chapter on data display and analysis. Thanks also to my colleague at PSU, Elisa Slee, for reviewing the material on social learning theory.

And thank you for taking the time to read this—prefaces typically do not come under the heading of assigned reading. I like reading them because they remind me that behind all the facts and figures and tables, there are real people. I sincerely hope you find this book worth the time and money you spend on it. If you do like it, tell a friend. If you don't like it, please tell me. I can be reached by writing Joe Kaplan, Department of Special and Counselor Education, PO Box 751, Portland State University, Portland, OR 97207 or calling (503) 725-4637.

June, 1995
Portland, Oregon

CHAPTER ONE

Behavior Management

An Introduction

Upon successful completion of this chapter, the learner should be able to:

1. Demonstrate knowledge of proactive approaches to behavior management as well as an understanding of the importance of preventive behavior management

2. Suggest a possible diagnosis and intervention for a given behavior problem according to each of the major approaches to behavior management

A PROACTIVE APPROACH TO BEHAVIOR MANAGEMENT

For the most part, the practices discussed in this text are reactive; that is, they were designed to be used *in response to* a behavior problem. Before we look at these practices, let's look at what can be done to prevent behavior problems from occurring in the first place. Whenever I am asked by teachers what they can do to prevent behavior problems in their classrooms, I tell them the best proactive approach is to do a good job of teaching. This typically elicits the response, "What does that have to do with behavior problems?" Well, think about it: The better job you do of teaching academic content, the more time your students will spend *on task*. By on task, I mean the student is engaged in the seatwork or recitation lesson to the extent that he is doing whatever he needs to do to learn the skill or knowledge being taught. The more time students spend on task, the less time they have to get into trouble.

There are two ways you can increase your students' on-task behavior and, in the process, prevent a number of behavior problems from occurring. One is to make your curriculum intrinsically rewarding and the other is to effectively manage your classroom while you teach. Let's examine each strategy.

Teaching an Intrinsically Rewarding Curriculum

While most teachers recognize the importance of keeping students on task, they tend to rely on extrin-

sic motivation to accomplish this. (See Figure 1.1.) They use contrived extrinsic rewards to get students to stay on task, instead of making the task itself so rewarding the student will be intrinsically motivated to attend. By "contrived," I mean tangible rewards such as tokens or prizes a student might be encouraged to work for. I do not include praise in this category since I believe praise functions to provide far greater benefits than that of merely keeping students on task. Praise contributes to the development of rapport between teacher and student, and enhances the student's self-esteem. It also functions as a model

Figure 1.1. It is important to provide students with intrinsically motivating instruction rather than using contrived extrinsic rewards.

of prosocial behavior for the student and his peer group. Unfortunately, praise alone is often not enough to keep students on task. For a task itself to be intrinsically rewarding it must be stimulating, relevant, or relatively easy to learn, or all three.

Stimulating

I use the term *stimulating* as synonymous with arousing or exciting. When students are aroused or excited, they are more alert to what is going on in their environment. Tasks can be inherently stimulating; for example, tasks that are related to controversial issues such as sex, drugs, and rock 'n' roll are inherently stimulating to adolescents. I'm not suggesting that you build your curriculum around *Rolling Stone* magazine or MTV. I'm simply suggesting that when students are stimulated by what they are doing, they are more likely to keep doing it.

Unfortunately, we can't teach inherently stimulating content all the time. Eventually we have to teach stuff like who fought in the Civil War, what a preposition is, and how to compute percentages. Even though this content, by itself, might not arouse and excite, it is still possible to teach such content in a stimulating manner so that students will want to learn it and stay on task. (See Figures 1.2 and 1.3.) A classic example of this may be seen in the movie *Teachers* starring Nick Nolte and Judd Hirsch. Most of the movie takes place in a high school where a substitute teacher, played by Richard Mulligan, has been hired to teach history to a class of bored adolescents. Instead of feeding his students a dry mix of names, dates, and places, Mulligan dresses up as historical characters. He delivers the Gettysburg Address while wearing a black frock coat, stovepipe hat, and beard. In another scene, he's dressed as George Washington exhorting his troops (i.e., his students) as they cross the Delaware (the classroom) in a boat (their desks). The way Mulligan's character teaches history, none of his students are off task. But that is Hollywood; in the real world, you don't usually have costumes or special effects at your disposal. Still, there are other things you can do to make your teaching more stimulating.

Try to put some enthusiasm into your lessons. Teaching is a rewarding and exciting job; try to convey this to your students. Be animated. Use humor. Students are more likely to stay on task if you reinforce their expectation that something funny could happen at any moment and make it clear that the teacher (rather than their peers) will provide the humor. Do the unpredictable. Use fooler games. Make mistakes on purpose and challenge your

Figure 1.2. Low stimulation results in a high rate of off-task behavior.

Figure 1.3. High stimulation leads to a lower rate of off-task behavior.

students to catch you at it; it can be fun to see the *teacher* "mess up" for a change. Be aware of your pacing—go too fast and they won't understand you, too slow, and they will lose interest. Watch the local newscaster on TV or a particularly interesting speaker or teacher, and try to emulate them. Involve your students in your lessons; avoid lecture. Ask questions and encourage your students to answer them. Asking questions not only engages your students and is more stimulating for them, it keeps you from talking too much, which can have a sedating effect (just ask my students). Encourage student participation in class discussions. Be accepting of different points of view; students who feel they can't voice their opinions will keep quiet and eventually tune you out.

Relevant

Even when you are not able to teach something in a stimulating manner, you can still help your students stay on task by teaching relevant content. Content is relevant if it is something your students want to learn: It is useful to them; it has value for them. For instance, learning to feed oneself has inherent value for an infant. Learning to dress oneself has inherent value for a preschooler. Learning to read has inherent value for a primary student. Other types of learning that have inherent value include getting along with others; driving a car; studying for or taking tests, or both; learning one's telephone number and how to use the telephone; solving interpersonal problems; learning the alphabet or the days of the week; learning how to fill out a job application, how to use a computer, a can opener, or public transportation; learning how to make purchases in a store or how to change a light bulb; learning what city, state, and country you live in. The list is endless and there is something for everyone. When students understand why it is intrinsically advantageous to learn a skill or knowledge, they are less likely to need extrinsic motivation to stay on task.

Look at your curriculum content and try to come up with reasons for why you are teaching what you teach. If you can't think of a reason for teaching something, you might want to discuss this with your curriculum supervisor or building principal. Poll your students at the beginning of the school year or periodically during the year to find out what they want to learn. Do your best to accommodate them. Be creative. If a student wants to learn how to drive an automobile, you might not be able or equipped to teach him driver education—but you can still teach many things related to driving that will eventually help him obtain his driver's license. You can, for instance, teach him to read and comprehend the driver's manual or to recognize traffic signs. You can help him learn how to be a safe, responsible driver by discussing substance abuse and seat belt use. Newspapers typically report whether or not accident victims were wearing seat belts; you can cut out and discuss newspaper articles regarding automobile accidents. You can invite a representative from the local police department to your classroom to discuss automobile safety.

Ask your students to try to think of reasons why you are teaching them some skill or knowledge (e.g., "Can anybody tell me why we need to learn multiplication?"). Have them brainstorm reasons for learning whatever you are teaching them. No matter how aversive their questions seem, always try to answer them when they ask, "Why do I have to do this?" You don't have to spend a lot of time answering these questions or get into arguments, but students (as well as instructors) often need to be reminded about the relevance of the curriculum. Students also need to know that there is a more meaningful reason to do something than "just to please you" or "to keep you off their backs."

Effective instruction

If you can't teach relevant content in a stimulating manner, you can still make your curriculum intrinsically rewarding by programming for success. This means teaching in a way that ensures your students will be successful at learning. It means using teaching methods and materials that are effective. Fortunately, you can draw from a large body of research on effective instruction (see Brophy, 1979; Brophy & Evertson, 1977; Brophy & Good, 1986; Englert, Tarrant, & Mariage, 1992; Good, 1979; Rosenshine, 1978; Rosenshine & Stevens, 1986). The following is a list of instructional practices with empirically demonstrated efficacy in increasing student achievement.

1. *Time spent teaching correlates positively with achievement (i.e., learning).* The more time spent on instruction, the greater the achievement. This does not necessarily mean longer lessons but, rather, more exposure to an effective program. In other words, *two* effective fifteen-minute lessons per day are better than *one* effective fifteen-minute lesson.

2. *Teacher emphasis on content covered correlates positively with achievement.* Place more emphasis on (i.e., attach more importance to) content areas that students are having difficulty with. The more teacher emphasis given to specific content, the greater the achievement in that area.

3. *Teach in small groups (N = 2 to 6) whenever possible.* Small group instruction correlates more

highly with achievement than one-to-one or large group instruction.

4. *Modeling is a powerful teaching tool, and vicarious reinforcement (i.e., watching a peer being rewarded for a correct response) is better than no reinforcement at all.* Try to include at least one student in the group who has acquired or mastered the skill or knowledge being taught.

5. *More task-related cues (i.e., questions or directives) result in more learning.* Teacher cues that are task related correlate positively with achievement.

6. *Program as many stimulus* ➔ *response units into your lesson as time allows.* Each S ➔ R unit should consist of a stimulus in the form of a teacher cue (e.g., "How much is two plus two?"), a student response (e.g., "four"), and feedback (e.g., "That's right!"). The more task-related S ➔ R units there are in a given lesson, the greater the achievement.

7. *Use direct instruction whenever possible.* Direct instruction requires the active involvement of the teacher giving task-related cues and feedback without delay.

8. *Fast-paced instruction is more effective than slow- or even moderately-paced instruction for most learners.* Fast-paced instruction keeps the learner on task for longer periods of time, and more on-task behavior (i.e., more attention given to teacher cues and/or feedback) means more achievement.

9. *The more student responses that are task related, the more learning takes place.* Task-related student responses correlate positively with achievement. Try to ignore off-task comments in response to task-related cues. For example:

TEACHER: How much is two plus two?

STUDENT: I got a bike for Christmas.

TEACHER: How much is two plus two?

STUDENT: Don't you want to hear about my bike?

TEACHER: We can talk about that later. Now it's time for math. So how much is two plus two?

Some of you may consider the teacher in the above exchange to be rather insensitive, and you may view this as a wasted opportunity to establish rapport. I am in no way suggesting that teachers should be cold-blooded teaching machines concerned only with the number of S ➔ R units. I'm simply saying that when it is time to teach, you teach, and when it is time to establish rapport, you establish rapport. I also know from personal experience that rapport can be developed and even enhanced through effective teaching. I can think of many teachers I had over the years who were warm, caring individuals who placed a high premium on rapport-building but who were not particularly effective instructors. I did not particularly enjoy being in their classes. I associated my failure in their classes with their ineffective instructional strategies, and eventually what little rapport there was between us evaporated. On the other hand, I developed a strong and lasting rapport with teachers who were effective instructors first and rapport-builders second; I associated my success in their classes with their effective teaching and enjoyed attending their classes.

10. *Rely more on novel prompts in giving feedback, rather than simply repeating the cue and/or modeling the desired response.* Use modeling and cue repetition only when other prompts are not successful. For example:

TEACHER: How much is two plus two?

STUDENT: (says nothing)

TEACHER: Two plus two is . . . (holds up four fingers)

STUDENT: (says nothing)

TEACHER: Two plus two is . . . (holds up four fingers and says 'ffff')

STUDENT: (says nothing)

TEACHER: Two plus two is four. How much is two plus two?

11. *Avoid giving praise for student responses or behavior that is not task related.* The more praise given for student behavior that is unrelated to the task, the less achievement is likely to occur.

While these practices are effective with most students most of the time, there are always going to be exceptions to the rule. Never assume anything. Be accountable. Determine the efficacy of an instructional practice through direct and continuous measurement of student progress. This means testing your students daily on the same content you are teaching them. I know daily data collection is difficult but the research does indicate that teachers who collect continuous data on their students' performance and make data-based decisions regarding instruction typically have the most successful learners (White, 1986).

☑ **Checkpoint 1.1**

[pages 1–5]

Fill in the answers to the following items (1–15). Check your responses by referring to the text; relevant page numbers appear in brackets.

The difference between reactive and proactive behavior management is **(1)**

_____

_____

_____

_____[1].

Two ways to prevent behavior problems are **(2)**

_____

_____ and **(3)**

_____

_____[1].

The three ways you can make your curriculum more reinforcing are **(4, 5, 6)**

_____

_____

_____

_____

_____

_____[2].

Three things you can do to make your teaching more stimulating are **(7, 8, 9)**

_____

_____

_____

_____

_____

_____ [2–3].

(continues)

CHECKPOINT 1.1, continued

Three things you can do to make your teaching more relevant are **(10, 11, 12)**

_____

_____

_____

_____

_____

_____[3].

Three things you can do to make your teaching (and learners) more successful are **(13, 14, 15)**

_____

_____

_____

_____

_____

_____ [3–5]

Redo any items you missed. If you missed more than 3 of the items, you should probably reread the material. Otherwise, continue on to the next section.

Using Effective Classroom Management Strategies

In addition to making your curriculum more reinforcing, another way to strengthen your students' on-task behavior is to practice effective classroom management. Not behavior management—*classroom* management; they are two distinctly different strategies. The term *behavior management* is often used as a code for *behavior modification,* since it comes in handy when discussing interventions with people who get hostile at the very mention of the words "behavior modification." I prefer to use the term behavior management generically to mean any practice or group of practices used in an intervention on a behavior problem. It is typically used with individuals or groups of students for whom classroom management is ineffective.

For the most part, teachers work with groups, not with individuals. They typically work with a large group of learners such as a classroom of students, or with small groups such as a reading group within a classroom. Classroom management refers to those practices best suited for teaching groups of learners curriculum content in recitation or seatwork settings.

The key differences between behavior management and classroom management are:

1. Classroom management is used primarily with groups of students while behavior management may be used with any number of students, although most behavior management interventions tend to be designed for individuals;

2. classroom management is used primarily to facilitate the learning of curriculum content while behavior management is used primarily for the modification of maladaptive behavior; and

3. classroom management is used in the classroom during recitation and seatwork sessions while behavior management may be used in or out of the classroom in any setting.

Because their purpose is to keep students on task and thereby facilitate learning, classroom management practices indirectly function as a form of preventive behavior management. Why? The better the job of classroom management teachers do, the less likely it is that they will have to use behavior management. Good classroom management means that your students will be spending more time on task and less time engaging in maladaptive behavior. While it goes without saying that teachers should be competent at both classroom management and behavior management, if you are not good at classroom management you had better be very good at behavior management! Teachers who are not good at classroom management tend to have students who are off task more often and who achieve less and, typically, engage in higher rates of maladaptive behavior (Kounin, 1970).

Teachers who are good at classroom management exhibit the teaching behaviors described by Jacob Kounin (1970). Kounin studied videotapes of teachers in 80 elementary school classrooms and found, among other things:

a. Teachers who frequently used classroom management practices had students who exhibited high frequencies of on-task behavior and low frequencies of misbehavior;

b. conversely, teachers who used classroom management practices had students who exhibited low frequencies of off-task behavior and low frequencies of misbehavior;

c. the teachers' classroom management styles had an effect not only on individual students but on the classroom as a whole (Kounin referred to this as the "ripple effect"); this was the case for both regular education students and students with emotional/behavioral disorders; and

d. there was more work involvement and less deviancy in the recitation settings, where the teacher actively conducted an instructional session, than in the seatwork settings, where students worked on their own. (Kounin, 1970)

Kounin (1970) identified the dimensions of teacher classroom management styles that correlated significantly with students' behavior in learning settings. He labeled these as: (1) withitness; (2) overlapping; (3) movement management (i.e., smoothness and momentum); (4) group alerting and accountability; (5) valence and challenge arousal; and (6) seatwork variety and challenge. Let's take a look at each.

1. *Withitness* is demonstrating that you know what's going on (i.e., "having eyes in the back of your head"). This is communicated through the teacher's behavior rather than by simply announcing, "I know what's going on." To demonstrate withitness, the teacher must use a *desist*

Figure 1.4. This teacher is not displaying withitness.

(a term Kounin uses to describe whatever intervention the teacher makes to stop a behavior) with the correct student before the deviancy spreads or increases in seriousness or does both. For example: A student is purposely trying to get his peers off task by making crude noises. The teacher who is withit intervenes quickly, before the peer group starts imitating the student's behavior. Note that she aims her desist at the student. This communicates to the class that she knows what's going on and puts them on notice that it will be difficult to get away with such behavior in her classroom. (See Figures 1.4 and 1.5.) Again, Kounin found that teachers who exhibit withitness in their classrooms are more likely to have students who are on task and less likely to have behavior problems.

2. *Overlapping* is what you do when you successfully deal with two or more matters at the same time. This is a particularly important skill in view of all the interruptions the average teacher must manage. Without it there are times when teachers become completely immersed in a behavior problem and drop the ongoing activity. For example: A teacher is conducting a group lesson on current events. While she asks who knows the name of the vice president, a student makes a crude sound to disrupt the lesson. Not only is his teacher withit—she immediately aims her desist at this student—she keeps the class focused on the lesson by repeating the question regarding the vice president. While looking at the student and pointing to a seat in the back of the

classroom (to indicate he will have to take a time-out if the behavior continues), she asks, "So who knows who the vice president is?" This communicates to the class that she knows what is going on and that she will not be distracted from the business at hand. (See Figure 1.6.) Kounin's research indicates that teachers who are able to overlap are more likely to have students who are on task and who are less likely to engage in misbehavior.

3. *Smoothness and momentum* refers to the ease and quickness of the teacher's management of topic movement during recitations and transitions. Some teachers display "jerkiness," episodes in which they induce stops or jarring breaks in the activity flow. These breaks may be short or long in duration and include dangles, truncations, flipflops, and stimulus boundedness. *Dangles* occur when the teacher suddenly stops an activity and leaves it hanging. For example, the teacher says, "Let's all take out our math workbooks and open them to page fifteen. Does anybody know where Mary is? (long pause) Diane, do you know where Mary is? (long pause) OK. Let's look at our math workbooks." *Truncations* are extended or permanent dangles. The

Figure 1.5. This teacher is displaying withitness.

Figure 1.6. An example of overlapping in the extreme.

teacher in the preceding example eventually returned her attention to the math workbook. In a truncation, the teacher would not return—she would continue her quest for the missing student until time ran out or the student showed up. *Flipflops* are when the teacher terminates one activity, begins a second activity, and then suddenly returns to the first activity again. For example, Joey's teacher says, "Let's all put our spelling lists away and take out our math workbooks and open them to page fifteen. (pause) OK, I want you to do the first ten examples on page fifteen. So who got all their spelling words correct? (pause) Never mind. Let's concentrate on math now. (pause) Anybody get *all* of their spelling words right?" *Stimulus boundedness* refers to the teacher's ability to stay focused on the activity at hand. For example, the teacher is conducting a group lesson on multiplication and notices some paper on the floor. She interrupts the lesson and asks, "Who put this paper on the floor?" and spends the next ten minutes trying to determine who the culprit is. (All of you obsessive-compulsive teachers out there, take notice.)

In addition to jerkiness, you also need to be aware of *slowdowns,* actions which keep an activity from moving quickly. We all know how important pacing is in learning. When the activity slows down, student attention strays, learning suffers, and there is an increased opportunity for behavior problems. Examples of slowdowns are overdwelling and fragmentation. *Overdwelling* occurs when the teacher goes on and on about an issue or a student's behavior (e.g., "Joey, that kind of behavior is rude. You'll never have any friends if you insist on making sounds like that. Blah, blah, blah. . . ."). *Fragmentation* is the unnecessary breaking down of a task or activity and requiring one person or group to perform it at a time (e.g., "All right. Row one may get out their readers. . . . Now row two . . . Now row three . . ."). This is not only boring, it is over-controlling and can invite rebellion. Kounin (1970) found that teachers who manage movement quickly and smoothly are more likely to have students who are on task and less likely to engage in misbehavior.

4. *Group Alerting* refers to the degree to which the teacher attempts to involve the nonreciting students in the recitation task, maintain their attention, and keep them alerted or "on their toes." For example, one way to effectively keep nonre-

citers on their toes while another child is reciting, or before the selection of a new reciter, is to pick reciters randomly. Calling on reciters in a predictable order allows your students the luxury of being off task until it is their turn to be called on. If they don't know when they are going to be called on, they have to pay attention all of the time. Remember, anything the teacher does that reduces the involvement of nonreciters—such as changing the focus of attention from the group to the individual, forgetting there is a group, prepicking the reciter before asking the question (e.g., "Joey, here's a question for you," signals that now everybody but Joey can be off task), or having reciters perform in a predetermined sequence—can lead to increased off-task behavior and, eventually, to the increased probability of misbehavior.

5. *Accountability* is the degree to which the teacher holds students accountable and responsible for their task performances. When you ask students to produce or demonstrate work by turning in a completed assignment or showing you their work, or ask students to recite in unison, you are holding them accountable for their actions. Accountability may also be achieved by bringing other students into the performance (e.g., "Joey, you watch Ellen do that problem and then tell me what she did right or wrong"); asking to see the hands of students who are prepared to demonstrate the performance; or circulating among your students and checking the products of the nonreciters. Keeping your students accountable puts them on notice that you expect something from them and that they had better stay on task in order to meet those expectations. Kounin (1970) found that teachers who keep their students accountable during recitation or seatwork are more likely to have students who are on task and who are less likely to engage in misbehavior.

6. *Valence* is the power to attract. Applied to the classroom, it refers to what the teacher does to attract and hold her students' attention and prevent satiation from occurring. *Satiation* occurs when a reinforcing activity loses its power to attract through overuse. Kounin (1970) found that repetition (doing the same thing over and over again without getting anywhere) can quickly lead to satiation. Symptoms of satiation include decreased work quality, increased errors, dedifferentiation (e.g., a student required to write a sentence over and over chooses to write

the first word several times, then the second word, and so on, instead of writing the complete sentence each time), broken attention or focus, and avoidance/escape behaviors which are incompatible with working on the task. All of these lead to lower work production and more deviancy. Ways to avoid satiation include letting students know that progress and accomplishment are occurring (e.g., "When you started, you were only able to do one problem. Now you can do ten problems in the same amount of time. Let's see how many you can do today."), showing enthusiasm, setting students up (e.g., "This next one is going to be fun" or "This is going to be hard, think you can do it?"), and by using selective attention activities. An example of the latter is the fooler game in which the teacher purposely makes mistakes so that students will pay attention and try to catch her. Teachers who program for high valence have students who are more likely to be on task and less likely to engage in misbehavior.

7. *Seatwork variety and challenge* will also result in more on-task behavior in your students. This is accomplished by programming learning activities with enough variety and intellectual challenge (especially in seatwork settings) to stimulate learning. Kounin (1970) found that programming learning-related variety significantly correlated with improved work production and reduced behavior problems. I know from personal experience that my most productive teaching occurs when I combine lecture with group activities, discussions, media, and the like.

Behavior management, done right, is a time-consuming venture. If you want to save yourself some time, you should plan on doing whatever is necessary to reduce the opportunity for behavior problems in your classroom. This can be accomplished by being an effective teacher of academic content. By making your curriculum reinforcing (i.e., stimulating, relevant, and easy to learn) and following Kounin's (1970) classroom management practices, you will increase the effectiveness of your instruction and eventually decrease the time you spend on behavior management.

✔ Checkpoint 1.2

[pages 5–9]

Fill in the answers to the following items (1–11). Check your responses by referring to the text; relevant page numbers appear in brackets.

The key differences between behavior management and classroom management are

(1, 2, 3) _____

_____

_____

_____

_____

_____

_____ [5–6].

State the relationship between behavior management and classroom management (i.e., why it is important to be good at classroom management).

(4) _____

_____

_____

_____ [6].

Explain what Kounin means by each of the following terms.

(5) withitness: _____

_____

_____

_____ [6–7].

(6) overlapping: _____

_____

_____

_____ [7].

(continues)

CONCEPTUAL MODELS OF BEHAVIOR MANAGEMENT

Let's assume that your proactive approach doesn't work with all of your students, and eventually you have to use some type of behavior management to deal with a behavior problem. Which type of behavior management should you use? Most of the behavior management practices currently used are derived from the following models: (1) a psychoedu-cational or insight-oriented model, (2) a biophysical or medical model, (3) a behavioral model, (4) a social learning theory or social–cognitive model, and (5) an ecological model. In the following pages, I provide a brief description of each approach. As you read this material, pay particular attention to what each says about the cause(s) of a behavior problem. More than anything else, etiology is what separates one model from the others, and it is usually etiology that dictates treatment.

Psychoeducational Model

The psychoeducational model is an outgrowth of Freud's (1938) psychoanalytical or psychodynamic approach. Purists might argue that a psychoeducational approach to *behavior* management is a contradiction in terms. In fact, the psychoeducational model was originally an attempt by Alfred Adler (1962) to adapt Freud's ideas to devise practical solutions to the everyday behavior problems encountered by teachers, students, parents, and children. More recent contributors include Rudolf Dreikurs (1968; 1971), Fritz Redl (Redl, 1959; Redl & Wineman, 1952), and Nicholas Long and William Morse (Long, Morse, & Newman, 1965). An important underlying assumption of this approach is that behavior problems are typically the result of unconscious motivations being acted upon by the student. Dreikurs, Grunwald, and Pepper (1971) described these motivations as the need for attention, revenge, power, and assumed disability (i.e., the desire to be left alone), or any of these together.

Let's apply the psychoeducational approach to a school-based problem of a disruptive student. This particular student shouts out in class, usually during individual seatwork sessions when the teacher is helping another student. Although the target student is not the only one who shouts out in class, she is usually the most vocal and certainly the most disruptive. The teacher's response to the shouting-out behavior is scolding—for example, "Cut that out!" or "Be quiet!" A proponent of the psychoeducational model assumes that the student's behavior is the result of an unconscious motivation and asks the student a series of questions such as "Are you trying to get me to pay attention to you?" (attention goal); "Do you want to show me that nobody can make you do anything?" (power goal); "Are you trying to hurt me (or others)?" (revenge goal); and "Do you want me to leave you alone?" (assumed disability goal). Upon asking these questions he observes the student's reactions in order to determine which of the unconscious motivations is driving her behavior. Let's assume that the unconscious goal of the disruptive student is to get attention. The teacher, again through questioning, helps the student gain insight into her motivations and identify other, more prosocial, ways of reaching her goal (e.g., "What else could you do to get my attention besides yelling out in class?") *Insight* is the key word here. The teacher never tells the student what he thinks her unconscious motivation for behavior is; the student must discover this for herself, albeit with the help of the teacher.

Although this approach has been out of favor for a number of years, it is making a comeback of sorts. Professionals working with students with emotional/behavioral disorders are rediscovering the insight-oriented approach (see Jones, 1992). Although a major criticism is the lack of supportive research, in all fairness, this does not necessarily mean the approach is ineffective. It simply means there have been few, if any, studies with adequate controls that attempted to measure the efficacy of this approach. Does the approach work? It can be effective under the following conditions: (a) if the student is verbal and has average intelligence and is willing to sit and discuss the problem with the teacher; (b) if the teacher can get away with being a judgmental teacher one minute and nonjudgmental "therapist" the next (or at the very least, convey this to the student); and (c) if the teacher has insight into his own unconscious motivations for behavior (e.g., Is he acting out of a need to gain positive regard from his students?; Is he acting out of a need to control his students?; Is he acting out of a need to hurt his students for making his job difficult?; Is he acting out of a need to be left alone because the demands of the job are too much for him?). It also helps if the teacher has time to sit with the student and discuss the problem and is in no rush for results; insight does not occur overnight.

If it achieves nothing else, the psychoeducational approach does humanize the behavior management process by improving communication between teachers and students. While the biophysical and behavioral approaches often regard the student as comparable to a lab rat to be experimented on (with or without his consent), the psychoeducational approach, with its emphasis on communication and insight, maintains the human—and humane—quality of teaching.

Figure 1.7 is a diagram illustrating the etiology of the behavior problem according to the psychoeducational approach. The **P** in the diagram stands for *personal variables,* or what the student brings to the

situation that contributes to the behavior problem. In this case, it happens to be unconscious motivation (e.g., need for attention). The **B** stands for *behavior* (e.g., shouting out). The arrow drawn from **P** to **B** suggests that it is the student's unconscious need for attention that leads to (i.e., causes) the behavior problem.

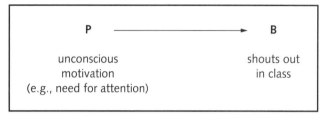

Figure 1.7. Etiology of disruptive behavior according to the *psychoeducational* approach to behavior management.

Biophysical Model

Proponents of the biophysical approach such as Bernard Rimland (1964) believe that all behavior problems have a physical origin. Such problems are the result of: (a) a dysfunction of the central nervous system due to heredity or trauma, (b) an allergy, (c) a faulty metabolism, (d) a difficult temperament, or any of these together. Applying this approach to the problem of the disruptive student discussed above, the teacher probably defers to a medical person regarding etiology. Let's assume that the diagnosis is impulsivity caused by attention deficit hyperactivity disorder (ADHD). In this case, the biophysical intervention consists primarily of administration of stimulant medication (e.g., Ritalin).

One advantage of the biophysical approach is that it tends to get all the adults "off of the student's back." That doesn't mean that we no longer hold the student responsible for her behavior; it does mean we don't *blame* her or damn her for her behavior—a student with a "bump on the brain" elicits more sympathy than one who willfully misbehaves, and teachers seem more willing to go the extra mile for her. Instead of getting angry at the student for shouting out, the teacher exhibits patience in dealing with the disruptive behavior. Also, let's not forget the "placebo effect." Putting the student on meds and telling the teacher to watch for improvement in her behavior often leads to a change in the *teacher's perception* of the student's behavior. Knowing that she "can't help it" somehow makes the student's behavior less disturbing.

Another advantage of this model is that physical (i.e., medical) interventions often work faster than educational or psychological interventions. Unfortunately, some people consider the relative ease with which the intervention can be implemented as an advantage: You simply give the student a pill and step back and watch. I use the term "unfortunately" for two reasons. First, I think it sad that where the welfare of children is concerned, adults would want to take the easy way out. Second, the drug doesn't do everything. It doesn't make the disruptive student raise her hand and wait to be called on. What it does do is help the student control her impulsivity, thereby providing the teacher with a window of opportunity during which he might teach the student how to obtain attention in an appropriate manner.

Figure 1.8 illustrates the etiology of the disruptive behavior according to the biophysical model. In this case, the personal variables of impulsivity associated with ADHD lead to (i.e., cause) her shouting-out behavior.

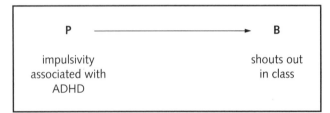

Figure 1.8. Etiology of disruptive behavior according to the *biophysical* approach to behavior management.

Behavioral Model

Following on the work of John Watson (1913) and Edward Thorndike (1921), B. F. Skinner (1938) developed and successfully tested his theories of operant conditioning. Applied to real-world situations, Skinner's laboratory-tested theories have become known (and either loved or loathed) as behavior modification. The underlying philosophy of the behavioral model is that all behavior is shaped and maintained by its consequences. "Bad" behavior is learned, and can therefore be unlearned. The behaviorist would say that behavior problems are primarily the result of the environment inadvertently conditioning the wrong behaviors. Applying this model to the problem of the disruptive student, the behaviorist would say that she has *learned* to shout out in class for attention. The teacher may think he is punishing the student's disruptive behavior by telling her to "cut it out" and "be quiet"; however, since this is the only time the teacher pays any attention to the student—and negative attention is better than no attention at all—she continues to misbehave in order to get

teacher attention. Instead of *punishing* her disruptive behavior, the teacher is actually *positively reinforcing* it! According to the behavioral model, the proper intervention requires that the teacher withhold the known reinforcer (in this case, attention) by ignoring all shouting behavior and by positively reinforcing hand-raising and waiting behavior instead.

Figure 1.9 diagrams the etiology of the disruptive behavior. Notice that environment, **E**, has replaced personal variables. In the psychoeducational and biophysical approaches, the primary cause of the behavior problem lies within the student; in the behavioral model, the primary cause of the behavior problem is in the environment.

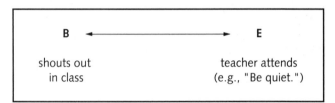

Figure 1.9. Etiology of disruptive behavior according to the *behavioral* approach to behavior management.

The good news about the behavioral approach is that it is effective. It may not work as quickly as medication, but it does work and it produces results faster than the psychoeducational approach. The bad news is that these results don't necessarily maintain over time or generalize across settings (Marholin & Steinman, 1977; O'Leary, Becker, Evans, & Sandargas, 1969; Walker & Buckley, 1972). Another shortcoming of the behavioral model is that it leaves so many unanswered questions. For example, if behavior is shaped and maintained by its consequences, why do some children continue to engage in undesirable behavior despite powerful aversive consequences? Conversely, why do some children refuse to engage in desirable behavior even though it means giving up powerful rewards? For that matter, why do some children behave in a desirable manner without any environmental consequences? For the answers to these and similar questions, we need to turn our attention to the work of Albert Bandura and social learning theory.

Social Learning Theory Model

The models we have looked at so far either stress the internal (psychoeducational and biophysical) or external (behavioral) causes of behavior problems. According to social learning theory (SLT; also known as social cognitive theory), "man is neither driven by inner forces nor buffeted helplessly by environmental influences" (Bandura, 1973, p. 43). Human behavior is more complicated than that. SLT views behavior as the result of reciprocal influences among: (1) *the personal variables* (internal) of the individual, (2) *the environment* (external) in which the behavior occurs, and (3) *the behavior* itself. Bandura refers to this interaction as reciprocal determinism (1974, 1977, 1986) and, along with modeling (1965, 1971, 1972), it is a central feature of the SLT approach to behavior management. Figure 1.10 is a diagram of reciprocal determinism with a listing of the most common personal (*P*) and environmental (*E*) variables that influence behavior (*B*). For a detailed discussion of how each variable influences behavior and how it is assessed, refer to Chapter 4.

SLT suggests that human behavior is learned through social exchanges, either through people interacting directly with people or through people observing these interactions second hand (i.e., observational learning). Behaviorists also examine social exchanges, but they focus only on external events (that is, what they can see). To the behaviorist, the social exchange between the disruptive student and her teacher is a relatively simple case of stimulus–response–stimulus (S–R–S): The student sees the teacher attending to peers (preceding stimulus); the student shouts out (response); the teacher attends (consequent stimulus). While SLT recognizes the importance of the environment in influencing behavior, it goes beyond the environment—beyond behavior modification—in explaining and treating behavior problems.

To the social learning (SL) theorist, the social exchange between the teacher and his disruptive student is much more complex than S–R–S. Because internal variables are considered as important as external variables, the SL theorist attempts to determine what, if any, personal variables might be influencing the student's behavior. Using a variety of assessments including, but not limited to, interviews, direct observations, and pencil and paper

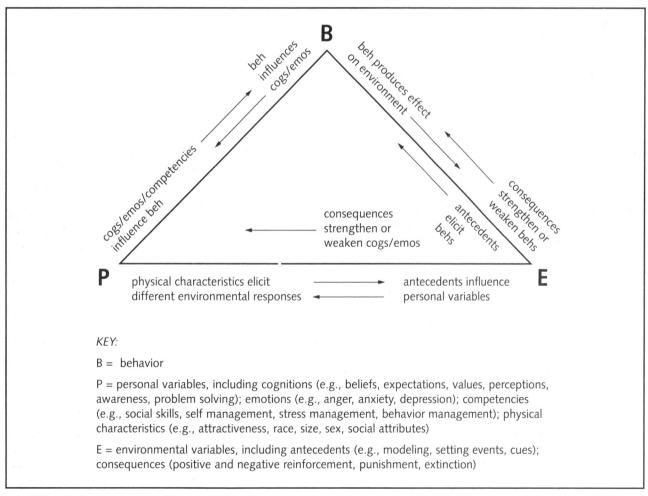

Figure 1.10.   Reciprocal determinism applied to behavior problems.

measures, the SL theorist manages to collect the following data:

a. The student has a strong need for adult attention but receives little or no attention from her teacher unless she misbehaves;

b. the student believes her worth as a person is tied to the attention she receives (i.e., the more attention, the more self-worth; the less attention, the less self-worth);

c. the student gets anxious when she thinks she might not get the attention she wants from the teacher;

d. the student has poor behavior management and stress management skills; and

e. the student has witnessed shouting for adult attention modeled by her sibs at home and her peers at school and has seen that it can produce successful results.

The SL theorist uses this information to formulate a hypothesis regarding the cause of the behavior problem. A schematic display of this hypothesis may be seen in the diagram in Figure 1.11.

The setting events, or contextual stimuli, that set the exchange in motion include any situation in the classroom in which the teacher attends to one or more of the student's classmates. "Attending" in this case requires that the teacher go to the student's desk and talk and/or listen to the student. The target student perceives (i.e., interprets) the latter as a signal (i.e., invitation) to compete for the attention of the teacher. The student's need for attention is driven by her irrational belief that her self-worth is tied exclusively to the amount of attention she receives from others, especially adults. The student becomes anxious when she sees her peers getting the attention she wants and thinks how awful it is that this attention has not been directed toward her. This anxiety combined with the expectation that shouting will get her what she wants causes her to call out. This behavior has two significant effects. First, it provides the student with an immediate, albeit brief, respite from the stress of anxiety. Second, it causes the teacher to scold (i.e., attend to) her. Because it provides attention, the teacher's scolding reinforces the student's shouting. The teacher's response (scolding) also reinforces the student's expectation that shouting will get her what she wants.

What happens to the student is only half the story. This is, after all, a social *exchange;* it is a mutual transaction. The other half of the story describes what happens to the teacher. Focusing a second round of assessments on the teacher, the SL theorist determines that:

a. The teacher does not pay attention to the student unless she misbehaves;

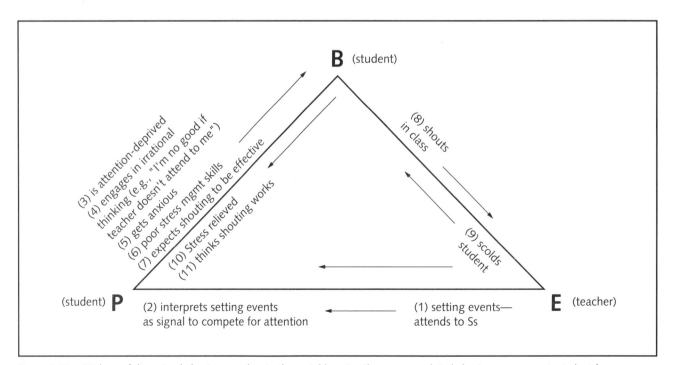

Figure 1.11. Etiology of disruptive behavior according to the *social learning theory* approach to behavior management; student focus.

b. the teacher equates quiet and conforming students with teacher control, and shouting out in class with anarchy;

c. students who shout in class make the teacher nervous;

d. the teacher doesn't know how to consequate shouting out any way other than scolding;

e. the teacher has poor stress management skills; and

f. because scolding has the immediate effect of interrupting the student's shouting, the teacher believes that scolding is effective at weakening shouting.

Given the above information, the SL theorist expands the original hypothesis. The expanded hypothesis is diagrammed in Figure 1.12. The teacher's personal variables (e.g., his irrational thinking regarding a student revolt, the resultant anxiety, his poor self-management and behavior-management skills) all serve to influence his scolding behavior. In turn, his scolding influences his personal variables since it results in the reduction of stress. His scolding also influences the environment (i.e., the student) by weakening, or at least interrupting, the student's behavior. The environment reciprocally influences both the teacher's behavior by negatively reinforcing his scolding, and his personal variables

by making him think that scolding is effective and that he is still "in control" of his class.

The social exchange described above is a classic example of what SL theorist Gerry Patterson (1973) refers to as "pain control." The student experiences the psychological and physiological pain of anxiety and learns to use pain (in the form of shouting) to control her own anxiety as well as to control her teacher's behavior. The teacher, meanwhile, experiences similar pains and learns to control them along with the student's behavior by using *what he believes* to be painful for her.

Given all of the above, it is easy to see why an SLT intervention is much more comprehensive than a behavioral intervention. The latter simply involves changing the teacher's scolding behavior in response to the student's shouting. On the other hand, recommendations for an SLT intervention would include:

1. Training in cognitive restructuring for the student to help her identify and dispute irrational thinking (e.g., equating attention from others with her self-worth);

2. appropriate modeling of the target behavior (e.g., how to access adult attention in a prosocial manner) by peers who are successful at accessing teacher attention;

3. training in basic behavior modification for the teacher so that he can consequate disruptive student behavior more appropriately;

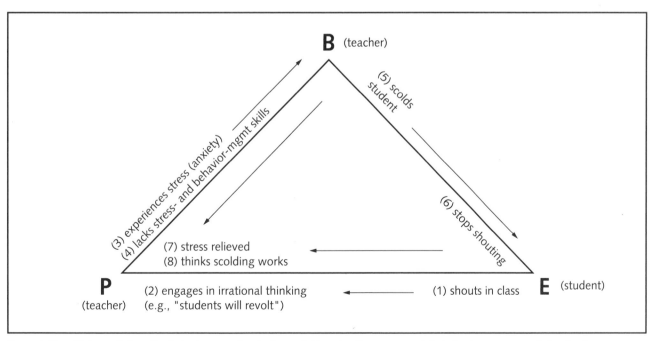

Figure 1.12. Etiology of disruptive behavior according to the *social learning theory* approach to behavior management; <u>teacher focus.</u>

4. a self-management program for the teacher with the goal that he increase the amount of positive attention he pays to the student; and

5. a stress inoculation program (combining cognitive restructuring, relaxation, and behavioral rehearsal) to help him control his anxiety in dealing with difficult students and a similar program for the student to help her control her anxiety associated with attention seeking.

An obvious disadvantage of the SL approach is that it is more difficult to put into practice than a simple behavior modification program. Changing cognitions and emotions is much more complicated than changing behaviors. In addition, you are not simply focusing your intervention on a single student but on all of the individuals involved in the faulty social exchange. And because many of the strategies in this approach require normal or near-normal cognitive functioning in the student, the SL approach is not as effective as behavior modification in dealing with the problems of students with severe handicaps. Still, one of the many things I find appealing about SLT is its holistic nature. We are, after all, more than trained seals doing tricks for pieces of herring; we have thoughts and feelings that influence our behavior as much as, and in some cases more than, environmental consequences.

Another advantage of the SLT approach over the traditional behavioral model is its emphasis on self-regulated behavior. While the behavioral approach tends to promote a reliance on the environment for remediation of behavior problems, the SLT model emphasizes self-reliance. Power to the person!

Most important, the SLT approach to behavior management provides answers for those questions behaviorism ignores. Some children persist in engaging in undesirable behavior, even in the face of powerful aversive consequences, because of strong convictions (i.e., beliefs) or because of undeveloped skills or powerful emotions that have more control over their behavior than external events. Also, these same personal variables may keep some children from engaging in desirable behavior despite the promise of powerful rewards. And other children engage in behavior without rewards simply because they are imitating what they see other children (or adults) doing.

Ecological Model

Drawing on ideas from many fields including cultural anthropology, ethology, psychology, sociology, and natural or animal ecology, the ecological approach to behavior problems was pioneered primarily by William Rhodes (1967) and Nicholas Hobbs (1966). The underlying assumption of the ecological model is that the cause of the behavior problem does not reside within the student, but rather is the lack of goodness of fit between the personal variables of the student and the ecosystem in which the behavior problem occurs. Proponents of the ecological model argue that when goodness of fit is lacking, a behavior problem is likely to occur. The ecological intervention always begins with a thorough examination of the ecosystem (including the target student), sometimes referred to as an ecobehavioral analysis (Rogers-Warren, 1984). The purpose of the ecobehavioral analysis is to determine which characteristics require modification. For example, in the case of the disruptive student, an ecobehavioral analysis might yield the following information:

1. The *student needs attention* desperately but is in a classroom where the *teacher seldom gives attention* to students unless they are misbehaving;

2. the *student shouts out* in class to get teacher attention but has a *teacher* who, because of his poor behavior management skills, *responds inappropriately* (i.e., by attending instead of ignoring);

3. the *student shouts out* in class but has a *teacher* who happens to be most *stressed by students shouting out,* making it particularly difficult for him to ignore this behavior;

4. the *student has trouble waiting* for individual attention but is in a classroom where the *student–teacher ratio is too high* for her to receive appropriate attention quickly;

5. the *student has trouble learning academic content* but is in a classroom where the *academic curriculum* (i.e., content and materials) is *inappropriate* for her (i.e., is too difficult and doesn't match her learning styles); and

6. the *student shouts out* in class but is in a classroom with *peers* who *model shouting-out behavior.*

When one takes into consideration all of the above, it is easy to see how the lack of goodness of fit between the characteristics of the student and the characteristics of the ecosystem has resulted in the problem behavior. The ecological intervention attempts to modify as many of these characteristics as possible in order to achieve goodness of fit, which might result in the elimination of the behavior problem. For example, the teacher can be provided with an instructional assistant whose primary responsibility is to attend to the target student when necessary. The teacher can also receive training in basic behavior management to help him consequate student behavior more appropriately. Stress management for the teacher is also indicated. The student should get a new set of instructional materials that are at her level of functioning and more in line with her particular learning style. These are but a few of the recommendations possible.

If this all sounds familiar, it should. The ecological approach is similar to the SLT approach in that it examines the reciprocal relationships typical of behavior problems. Where the ecological model differs from SLT is in its broadness of scope. The ecologist considers a wide variety of interactive factors including the physical environment (e.g., seating, room size, temperature, lighting, furniture) and the curriculum (e.g., what is being taught, and when and how it is taught).

The obvious problem with the ecological approach is that because it is systems centered, it is often difficult to act on all of the recommended modifications. Some ecological interventions require changes in physical setting, curriculum, building (or school district) policy, family behavior, and even community factors. Implementing these interventions can be quite daunting. Another drawback is the amount of time required to conduct the ecobehavioral analysis. In an era when most school districts are experiencing budgetary constraints, the ecological approach may not be cost-effective in the short term. Still, the approach *can* be effective; and, as the saying goes, you either pay now or you pay later.

CONCLUSIONS

All of the approaches described above have something to offer, and as I suggested earlier, the field is moving toward a multifaceted approach to behavior management. We need to be more eclectic—there is no one way to solve all behavior problems. Unfortunately, I can't do justice to all of the approaches to behavior management in one textbook. I have chosen to write about the behavioral and social learning approaches because I firmly believe they have the most to offer the classroom teacher. They can be learned easily, and while they don't come with guarantees, there is a large body of research attesting to their efficacy in treating behavior problems of all types. More than anything else, they are founded upon sound etiologic explanations for behavior. While some behavior problems may be the result of unconscious motivation or a lack of neurotransmitters in the brain, most of the typical behavior problems teachers encounter in schools can be explained by the theoretical principles of behaviorism or social learning theory. Finally, this textbook is intended primarily for teachers. It is only fitting, therefore, that it feature practices designed for teachers to use.

☑ **Checkpoint 1.3**

[pages 10–17]

Identify each of the characteristics listed in Items 1–18 using the following labels: **PE** for psychoeducational, **BIO** for biophysical, **BEH** for behavioral, **SLT** for social learning theory, and **ECO** for ecological. Check your responses by referring to the answers shown following Item 18.

(1) Emphasizes communication between student and teacher with the latter playing role of therapist. _____

(2) Typically requires medical doctor (e.g., pediatrician or psychiatrist) to determine cause of behavior problem. _____

(3) The goal is for the student to *gain insight* into his or her unconscious motivations. _____

(4) Primary intervention is psychopharmacology (i.e., medication). _____

(5) Underlying assumption is that behavior is shaped and maintained by its environmental consequences. _____

(6) Treatment typically achieves results faster than other approaches. _____

(7) An underlying assumption is that behavior problems are the result of unconscious motivations being acted upon by the student. _____

(8) Although effective, its results do not typically generalize or maintain over time. _____

(continues)

CHECKPOINT 1.3, continued

(9) Reciprocal determinism is central to this behavior management approach. _____

(10) Assumes all behavior problems have physical origin (e.g., allergy, faulty metabolism, or dysfunction of CNS). _____

(11) Cognitions and emotions in both the student and the teacher are considered along with behavior in determining the etiology of a behavior problem. _____

(12) A lack of goodness of fit between the personal variables of the student and the characteristics of the environment is considered the cause of a behavior problem. _____

(13) A systems-centered approach to behavior management. _____

(14) Lacks research data to support its efficacy. _____

(15) Stresses the influence of modeling in behavior problems. _____

(16) Personal (internal) variables and environmental (external) variables are both considered important in causing behavior problems. _____

(17) Based on Skinner's operant conditioning and popularly known as behavior modification. _____

(18) Considers environmental variables most important in causing behavior problems. _____

ANSWERS (1–18): (1) PE, (2) BIO, (3) PE, (4) BIO, (5) BEH, (6) BIO, (7) PE, (8) BEH, (9) SLT, (10) BIO, (11) SLT, (12) ECO, (13) ECO, (14) PE, (15) SLT, (16) SLT, (17) BEH, (18) BEH

State one advantage and one disadvantage for each of the following approaches to behavior management. Check your responses by referring to the text; relevant page numbers appear in brackets.

Psychoeducational:

advantage: **(19)** _____
_____[11].

(continues)

CHECKPOINT 1.3, continued

disadvantage: **(20)** _____
_____[11].

Biophysical:

advantage: **(21)** _____
_____[11-12].

disadvantage: **(22)** _____
_____[12].

Behavioral:

advantage: **(23)** _____
_____[12].

disadvantage: **(24)** _____
_____[12].

Social Learning Theory:

advantage: **(25)** _____
_____[16].

disadvantage: **(26)** _____
_____[16].

Ecological:

advantage: **(27)** _____
_____[17].

disadvantage: **(28)** _____
_____[17].

Redo any items you missed. If you missed more than 6 of the items, you should probably reread the material. Otherwise, continue on to the Chapter Assessment.

ASSESSMENT / CHAPTER 1

A list of acceptable responses appears following the Assessment.

1.0 *A Reinforcing Curriculum.* You get a job as a substitute teacher in a middle school social studies class for one week in a building with a bad reputation for behavior problems. You are required to teach a unit on Mexico. Describe what you would do to make this experience more intrinsically rewarding for your students. Try to list as many ideas as possible.

2.0 *Classroom Management.* In each of the following hypothetical situations, the teacher did something wrong and lost the attention of his students. Read each situation and decide what type of classroom management error the teacher made and explain what he or she should have done instead and why.

> **2.1** Mr. Washington is teaching a social studies lesson to his class. During the lesson one of his students passes a note to a student in the seat next to him. The student receiving the note reads it and starts to laugh. Other students nearby turn toward the laughing student. They want to see the note. Eventually, the whole class is off task and Mr. Washington is yelling at them to be quiet. According to Kounin, what classroom management error did Mr. Washington make? What should he have done instead and why?

2.2   Ms. Munitz has just finished giving a spelling test to her class. After she collects their papers she tells them to take out their math workbooks and turn to the lesson on decimals. After her students find the lesson on decimals in their workbooks, Ms. Munitz asks them how they think they did on the spelling test. Several students shout out comments, e.g., "I failed it," "I aced it," "*what* spelling test?" Many of the students are distracted by the comments and Ms. Munitz has a difficult time trying to get them back on task (i.e., the lesson on decimals). According to Kounin, what type of classroom management error did Ms. Munitz make? What should she have done instead and why?

2.3   While dictating words on a spelling test, Mr. Ellis walks up and down the aisles of his classroom. He notices a reader on the floor and picks it up. Looking at the reader, while his students turn their attention from their papers to him, he notices several pages have gum sticking to them. Mr. Ellis asks one of the students nearby, "Is this your reader?" When the student nods yes, Mr. Ellis begins to lecture him (e.g., "Is this the way you take care of school property?"). During this time, several of the students begin whispering to one another and showing each other their spelling papers. According to Kounin, what type of classroom management error did Mr. Ellis make? What should he have done instead and why?

2.4   While teaching a lesson on the U.S. Civil War to her students, Ms. Walkup asks them questions to make sure they are paying attention. The only problem is she keeps calling on the only student who volunteers an answer. As a result, few of Ms. Walkup's students are paying attention to the lesson. The others are either daydreaming or visiting. According to Kounin, what type of classroom management error did Ms. Walkup make? What should she have done instead and why?

2.5   During a social studies lesson, Ms. Robinson has her students each take a turn reading out loud from their social studies textbook. They each take a turn according to their seating (e.g., the first person in row one reads first; then the second person in row one; then the third person in row one; and so on). While a student is reading out loud, many of the other students are off task and have to be told to be quiet. The result is that Ms. Robinson keeps interrupting the students who are reading. To make matters worse, after reprimanding the offending student, Ms. Robinson has the student who had to stop reading begin over again. Eventually, the students who were paying attention get bored and are off task. According to Kounin, what two types of classroom management errors did Ms. Robinson make? What should she have done instead and why?

2.6   Mr. Tibbs wants his students to get dictionaries from the bookshelf in the back of the classroom. He has students leave their seats two at a time to get a dictionary. Students are called on according to their seating (e.g., the first two students in row one go first; then the next two; and so on). In each case, Mr. Tibbs waits for the students to return before sending the next pair. This takes a long time and a few of the students who went first and already have their dictionaries get into trouble and have to be disciplined. According to Kounin, what type of classroom management error did Mr. Tibbs make? What should he have done instead and why?

2.7   Ms. Maggio doesn't like to teach math but she has to, so she gives her students dittoed math sheets to do every day. At first, her students like the dittos; but after doing the same ones day after day, they begin to lose interest and are frequently off task. Ms. Maggio spends a lot of her time disciplining her students for being off task and not getting their work done. According to Kounin, what type of classroom management error did Ms. Maggio make? What should she have done instead and why?

2.8   Mrs. Baxter is teaching her students a health lesson on the human body. Whenever she asks a question of her students, they break off eye contact with her and look away. Usually, after a count of "one Mississippi, two Mississippi," Mrs. Baxter answers her own question. Having learned they don't need to pay attention to what she is saying, many of her students are off task and Mrs. Baxter has to deal with some behavior problems. According to Kounin, what error in classroom management did Mrs. Baxter make? What should she have done instead and why?

2.9   Whenever Mr. Vargas has to deal with deviant (i.e., off-task) behavior in the classroom, he stops teaching and focuses all of his attention on the offending student. The result is usually more deviant behavior from other students. According to Kounin, what classroom management error did Mr. Vargas make? What should he have done instead and why?

2.10   Mr. Vargas also tends to lecture any student he catches engaging in deviant behavior. "Why are you doing that? Don't you want to learn?" You'll never learn if you don't pay attention. Why can't you pay attention? Blah, blah, blah, blah, blah." The result is that the offending student tunes him out after the first sentence while the other students use this opportunity to get off task and misbehave. Mr. Vargas is so focused on his sermon, he typically forgets about the rest of the class. According to Kounin, what classroom management error did Mr. Vargas make? What should he have done instead and why?

3.0 *Approaches to Behavior Management.* Rudy is a thirteen-year-old student in Mr. Shapiro's math class. He is called "Rude Dude" by his peers because he is always "in your face." Rudy engages in unprovoked verbally aggressive behavior including threats ("I'm gonna kick your butt"), swearing ("----off, ---hole"), and mocking ("how'd you get to be so stupid, pizza face?").

After referring Rudy (and himself) for a pre-referral intervention, Mr. Shapiro is visited by not one, not two, but five different specialists. Unfortunately, each has a different orientation or approach to behavior management and, therefore, a different opinion of why Rudy behaves the way he does and what should be done about his behavior. Put yourself in the position of each of the five specialists and write a possible diagnosis and recommendation for treating Rudy's behavior problem. Be specific in referring to Rudy's behaviors.

    3.1 *Specialist #1 (psychoeducational orientation)*

    3.2 *Specialist #2 (biophysical orientation):*

    3.3 *Specialist #3 (behavioral orientation):*

    3.4 *Specialist #4 (social learning orientation):*

    3.5 *Specialist #5 (ecological orientation):*

ACCEPTABLE RESPONSES

1.0 *A Reinforcing Curriculum.* Your response should include *at least ten* of the following:

- Decorate room with Mexican art.

- Ask students what they want to learn about Mexico.

- Bring in children and/or adults of Mexican heritage to speak to class.

- Play Mexican music; sing Mexican songs.

- Contrast lifestyle of Mexicans and Americans.

- Put on a Mexican fiesta.

- Bring in a piñata.

- Prepare and/or eat Mexican food.

- Teach Spanish; label things in room; teach simple Spanish phrases and require students to use them (e.g., "necesito usar el baño"—"I have to use the bathroom").

- Teach Mexican folk dances.

- Make a video (e.g., commercial to travel/visit Mexico).

- Plan and "take" an imaginary journey (keep travel log; create student passport).

- Assign small group research project regarding Mexico; students share information with class.

- "Choose your own adventure in Mexico trip": Take an imaginary plane trip with popcorn and a movie introducing the country; pass out crayon packets and maps to color; each day, give students a choice of destinations and plan culturally appropriate adventures for each.

- Put on a play about Mexico.

- Have students brainstorm activities.

- Plan a Mexican costume party: Each student comes dressed as an important person in Mexico's history; they introduce themselves and tell why they are important.

- Set up a trading post or bank and exchange American and Mexican money.

- Find out what your students already know about Mexico.

- Create a time line in pictures—a pictorial history of Mexico from the Aztecs to NAFTA.

2.0 *Classroom Management.* Identify the classroom management error by name (e.g., "flipflop" or "overdwelling"); explain why you think it is that particular error and describe what the teacher should have done instead.

2.1 Mr. Washington displayed a lack of WITHITNESS because he waited too long to intervene and he wound up intervening with the entire class instead of the individuals who started the problem. He should have intervened immediately to communicate his withitness.

2.2 Ms. Munitz committed the dreaded classroom management error known as the FLIPFLOP because she ended one activity (spelling), started a new activity (math), and suddenly returned to the first activity. She should have gone on with math and waited for another time to ask her students about their spelling tests.

2.3 Mr. Ellis is guilty of a lack of STIMULUS BOUNDEDNESS because he was not able to stay focused on the activity at hand. He let the gum in the book distract him from the spelling test. He should have either ignored the paper or picked it up and kept on dictating spelling words. He could have discussed it with his students after he was finished dictating.

2.4 Ms. Walkup has made a GROUP ALERTING error. Because she always calls on the same student, her other students feel they can be off task. She should have tried to ask questions of different students in her class.

2.5 Ms. Robinson has made two classroom management errors. The first is a GROUP ALERTING error. Because she calls on students to read in the order of their seating, many of the students feel they can be off task. Her second error is a SLOW DOWN. After Ms. Robinson interrupts a reader in order to reprimand students who are talking, she has the reader start all over again from the beginning. First of all, Ms. Robinson should have called on her students randomly when she wanted them to read. This way, they all would have paid attention to the reader. If she did have to interrupt a reader, she should have had him start reading where he left off instead of making him start all over from the beginning.

2.6 Mr. Tibbs has committed the classroom management error known as FRAGMENTATION by having his students access the dictionaries in the back of the room only in pairs. This takes too long and many of his students get bored with the waiting and the inactivity. He should have had them access the dictionaries by rows or any way that would speed up the process.

2.7 Ms. Maggio's seatwork lacks VARIETY AND INTELLECTUAL CHALLENGE. Doing the same thing (dittos) over and over again has become boring for her students and has led to satiation. She needs to provide her students with seatwork that has enough variety and intellectual challenge to keep them interested and on task.

2.8 Mrs. Baxter is not keeping her students ACCOUNT-ABLE. By answering her own questions, she allows the students to be off task if they choose. She needs to keep her students accountable by requiring them to answer her questions. If she gets few volunteers, or the same ones over and over, she should start calling on other students.

2.9 Mr. Vargas lacks STIMULUS BOUNDEDNESS. He appears to be unable to keep his focus on the lesson. By focusing instead on off-task behavior, he pulls the other students off task. He should either ignore the off-task behavior (as long as it is not disruptive) or try to do two things at once and proceed with his lesson.

2.10 Mr. Vargas is also guilty of OVERDWELLING. When he lectures an offending student, he not only loses the attention of that student (who tunes him out within the first few minutes), he loses the attention of the rest of the class. If he needs to reprimand an offending student, he should do so quickly and without diverting attention away from the lesson.

3.0 *Approaches to Behavior Management.* I haven't given you very much information about Rudy and his class, so feel free to invent in order to support your responses; the important thing is that you get the focus right.

3.1 *Psychodynamic.* Focus: on unconscious motivation and gaining insight. Rudy's aggression is caused by an unconscious motivation (e.g., probably a need for power); specialist interviews Rudy to better determine this motivation; recommends psychotherapy sessions for Rudy at local mental health clinic to help him gain insight into his problem; talks with teacher and Rudy about prosocial (i.e., behaviorally sublimated) ways Rudy can realize his goal such as being given more authority over peers (peer tutor, monitor).

3.2 *Biophysical.* Focus: on neurological or physiological factors and involvement of medical profession in diagnosis and/or treatment. Rudy needs to undergo medical examination to determine cause of aggression; possible causes may be neurological problem, fetal alcohol syndrome, drug abuse, food allergy, among others; once cause is determined, Rudy can be treated with medication and/or diet.

3.3 *Behavioral.* Focus: on relationship between Rudy's behavior and the environment (i.e., how peers and teacher consequate his behavior). Rudy's behavior is learned; his aggressive behavior has been reinforced positively when it helps him get what he wants, and negatively when it helps him escape from or avoid aversive situations; teacher and peer group need to change their responses to Rudy's aggressive behavior; aggressive behavior will be punished and prosocial (nonaggressive) behavior will be rewarded.

3.4 *Social Learning Theory.* Focus: similar to behavioral, with addition of cognitive and affective factors; analysis of social exchange between Rudy and environment. Rudy's behavior is result of reciprocal relationships between his *personal variables* (e.g., fact that aggressive behavior has been modeled for him at home; his contempt for his peers and authority; his expectation that aggression gets him what he wants; his anger; poor social skills), his *behavior,* and the *environment* (e.g., his aggressive behavior is rewarded); in addition to changing environmental consequences, Rudy's problem requires a more comprehensive solution including anger management, cognitive restructuring, and social skills training; Rudy's teacher and his peers need to be reinforced for standing up to him when he's aggressive and for rewarding him when he engages in prosocial behavior (in other words, the focus can't be only on *Rudy's* behavior).

3.5 *Ecological.* Focus is on ecosystem in which aggression occurs instead of looking strictly at Rudy. Aggression in ecosystem is the result of a lack of goodness of fit between characteristics in Rudy and characteristics of ecosystem. For example, Rudy is aggressive and teacher and peer group are easily intimidated by aggressive behavior (need to do something about Rudy's aggression *and* teacher's and peer group's fear of aggression); physical environment is conducive to aggression since class is large with only one adult and lack of supervision—makes students easy victims for "predator" like Rudy (need to provide teacher with more adult supervision or fewer student).

CHAPTER TWO

Behavior Modification

Upon successful completion of this chapter, the learner should be able to:

1. Write a rebuttal to each of the myths (i.e., misconceptions) regarding behavior modification

2. Correctly identify examples of positive and negative reinforcement, punishment, and extinction

MISCONCEPTIONS

Behavior modification is probably one of the most misunderstood concepts in education today. It never ceases to amaze me that so many people can have such strong feelings concerning a topic about which they know so little. At the beginning of each class I teach in behavior modification I ask my students to complete the sentence "Behavior modification is. . . ." On the basis of their responses, I have drawn up a list of the most common misconceptions regarding behavior modification. Let me now present that list.

Figure 2.2. Myth: Behavior modification is using aversive controls.

Figure 2.1. Myth: Behavior modification is ignoring the bad and praising the good.

Myth #1: Behavior modification is when you ignore all student misbehavior and only reward good behavior. (See Figure 2.1.)

Nonsense! Who in his right mind would suggest that a teacher ignore a student hitting another student or a student disrupting the learning environment? Behavior modification teaches that the only time a teacher should ignore a student's misbehavior is when that behavior is being reinforced by the teacher's attention.

Myth #2: Behavior modification is the use of aversive controls such as nausea-inducing drugs and cattle prods. (See Figure 2.2.)

I can't really blame people for believing this, considering the popularity of novels and films such as *Brave New World, The Manchurian Candidate,* and *A*

Clockwork Orange. It is true that Behavior Therapy, a form of behavior modification, does employ aversives in the control of certain behaviors; but I hasten to add that aversive controls have been used in such cases only with the informed consent of the client receiving the treatment. Behavior modification as it is (and should be) used in the schools has nothing to do with brainwashing, post-hypnotic suggestion, electro-convulsive (shock) therapy, or the application of physically painful aversives.

Myth #3: Behavior modification is token reinforcement. (See Figure 2.3.)

I wish I had an M&M for every graduate student who requested a waiver of my behavior management course on the basis of "already being competent" in behavior modification. As it usually turns out, their idea of being competent is having used a token economy at one time or another, as though behavior modification is nothing more than token reinforcement. Did they collect data on student behavior? No—they didn't have the time. Even if they had, they wouldn't have known how to monitor student behavior, and besides, they wouldn't have seen the value in doing so. Had they ever used other behavior modification techniques such as shaping, chaining, or fading? No—they had never heard of them. Did they reinforce on a schedule of reinforcement? No—they reinforced whenever they remembered to. These individuals were not competent in behavior modification, because behavior modification encompasses much more than token reinforcement.

Myth #4: Behavior modification is M&Ms (or Big Macs or Twinkies).

Given the average American's addiction to junk food, I can understand the origin of this myth. But primary (food) reinforcers are not necessarily used in every behavior modification program. Their use is usually the exception rather than the rule in programs for learners with mild to moderate handicaps. It is often more appropriate to use token reinforcers, activity reinforcers, or social reinforcement. Second, if it is necessary to use primary reinforcers with a particular student, there are plenty of nutritious treats available to use instead of junk food. Raisins, yogurt, and fresh fruit are all superior to candies; reinforcing with candies will often work against a behavioral program by producing mood swings in children that ultimately lead to more undesirable behavior.

Myth #5: Behavior modification is for animals (e.g., rats, pigeons, monkeys, seals) or for "subhumans" such as the institutionalized retarded or mentally ill. (See Figure 2.4.)

The truth is that behavior modification has demonstrated its effectiveness in ameliorating a myriad of dysfunctions across a wide range of subjects. One need only peruse the literature (or the last section in this chapter) to recognize the many applications and documented successes of behavior modification.

Figure 2.3. Myth: Behavior modification is providing token reinforcement.

Figure 2.4. Myth: Behavior modification is for animals.

Myth #6: Behavior modification is a philosophy (or a religion or way of life). (See Figure 2.5.)

The very premise behind this book is that while behavior modification can explain much about student behavior, it does not go far enough. The professional educator who is sincerely committed to helping children would do well to study all of the approaches to behavior management discussed in chapter one. I become very suspicious when I hear a so-called "expert" describing his or her system as the "only way." Behavior modification is just one of many tools which can help children learn. It is not a religion, and simply using it does not make you a behaviorist.

Myth #7: Behavior modification is dangerous because it can eventually lead to a population of adults susceptible to mind control and the ultimate take-over of a foreign power.

Shades of Joe McCarthy! First of all, behavior modification is all around us. Anybody who watches television or goes shopping has been exposed to it. Behavior modification is a form of behavior influence; the latter occurs when one person attempts to exert a degree of control over another. Society attempts to influence the behavior of its citizens by requiring them to attend schools and study a curriculum that largely reflects the values of that society. Parents use behavior influence on their children. Businesses try to influence the purchasing behavior of potential customers through commercials and advertisements. Politicians attempt to influence the voting behavior of their constituents. What we think, how we dress, what we eat, and much of what we say are all products of behavior influence. It begins the minute we are born and does not stop until the day we die. I would submit, then, that whether we like it or not (or even know it or not), we have been exposed to behavior modification for a long time and our democracy is still intact.

Myth #8: Behavior modification doesn't work because of symptom substitution.

Critics charge that behavior modification doesn't get to the real reason the child is misbehaving—it only deals with the symptoms and not the underlying cause. An analogy would be trying to fix an apparently leaky car radiator by plugging the leaks when the underlying cause of the problem is actually a faulty thermostat. To a certain extent, this criticism is warranted: It *is* ludicrous to attempt to modify an angry student's fighting behavior through the application of extrinsic rewards or punishers without doing anything about the underlying anger. While symptom substitution is the exception rather than the rule, it can easily occur if we take the simplistic behaviorist view that all behavior problems are the result of inappropriate consequences.

Myth #9: Behavior modification is nothing more than bribery.

Webster defines bribery as "anything, especially money, given or promised to induce a person to do something illegal or wrong" (1958, p. 181). Following directions and learning one's lessons can be intrinsically rewarding to those of us who have no difficulty following directions and learning our lessons. However, there are many children in school who have a great deal of difficulty learning any lessons. I don't see anything wrong in rewarding these children for their efforts by using grades or other reinforcers until such time as the effort to learn becomes rewarding in and of itself. This is not to say that behavior modification can never be bribery; for me, the key is whether the change agent is acting in his own best interest or that of the child. When in doubt, ask yourself if you are rewarding behavior that is in the child's best interest (e.g., learning to get along with others, staying on task, completing assignments) or your own best interest (e.g., leaving you alone, never questioning your authority).

Figure 2.5. Myth: Behavior modification is a way of life

Myth #10: Behavior modification is not humanistic because it takes away the individual's freedom of choice.

Skinner said, "To refuse to control is to leave control not to the person himself, but to other parts of the social and non-social environments" (1971, p. 84). Bandura expressed the same idea when he wrote that the "basic moral question is not whether man's behavior will be controlled, but rather by whom, by what means, and for what ends" (1969, p. 85). The point is, no one is completely free of controls, and freedom is a matter of degrees—some of us are more "free" than others. I tend to equate freedom with choices; the more choices you have available to you, the more freedom you have. Students who fail in school have fewer choices than those who succeed. Therefore, I would argue that any practice that helps students succeed, such as behavior modification, actually increases rather than decreases their freedom in the long run.

☑ **Checkpoint 2.1**

[pages 27–30]

List as many of the common misconceptions about behavior modification as you can. Check your responses by referring to the text; relevant page numbers appear in brackets.

1.

2.

3.

(continues)

CHECKPOINT 2.1, continued

4.

5.

6.

7.

8.

9.

(continues)

CHECKPOINT 2.1, continued

10.

Redo any items you missed. If you missed more than 2 of the items, you should probably reread the material. Otherwise, continue on to the next

OPERANT CONDITIONING

So far I have told you what behavior modification is not. Now let's talk about what it is. Behavior modification is the systematic application of the principles of *operant conditioning* (Skinner, 1938) such as positive reinforcement, negative reinforcement, punishment, and extinction, for the expressed purpose of strengthening or weakening behavior. Skinner's operant conditioning should not be confused with Pavlov's *respondent conditioning* (Pavlov, 1897). Respondent behaviors are controlled by the autonomic nervous system and the involuntary muscles. Examples of respondent behaviors are the eyeblink reflex, the knee-jerk reflex, the heartbeat, the salivation response, and many other physiological and/or somatic responses of the body which characterize emotional states such as anger, anxiety, and the like. Respondent behaviors are elicited *in response to* the presentation of a stimulus. That is, respondent behaviors occur only after a stimulus appears. An example of this is the dog salivating in Pavlov's classic conditioning experiments: Meat powder was the stimulus that elicited the salivation response in the dog. The sequence may be seen in Figure 2.6.

Operant behaviors are controlled by the central nervous system and the voluntary muscles. Operants usually occur first and are later modified (i.e., changed) or maintained (i.e., kept the same) by the presentation of a stimulus. Since this stimulus occurs after the operant, it is often referred to as a consequent stimulus event (CSE). The term *operant* means to operate, and *operate* means to produce an effect. Hence, operant behavior got its name because it is behavior that produces an effect on the environment. The environmental effect produced by an operant will cause the operant to change in some way or, conversely, keep the operant from changing. This sequence is illustrated in Figure 2.7.

Examples of operants are walking, talking, writing, hitting, hugging, and reading. Behaviors such as talking or hitting produce an effect on the environment which will either change or maintain that behavior. For example, you talk to someone and the effect of your talking is that someone listens to you. Having a person listen to you while you talk will probably strengthen, or at least maintain, your talking behavior. If you hit someone, the effect of your hitting might be to make someone hit you back, harder. Having someone hit back after you hit him will probably weaken *your* hitting behavior. Notice that I used the word "probably" in each example. Human beings are more complex organisms than rats or pigeons; they have cognitions (e.g., beliefs, expectations, perceptions) and emotions (e.g., anger, fear), and these can influence their operant behavior every bit as much as CSEs. See Figure 2.8.

Operants can also be influenced by environmental events that precede them. In other words, something in the environment can stimulate, or elicit, an operant. An event that elicits an operant is usually referred to as an antecedent stimulus event (ASE). Operant behavior such as talking is often elicited by another person asking a question. In this instance, the ASE is being asked a question, the operant is answering the question, and the CSE is having the person listen to the answer and giving feedback. This sequence may be seen in Figure 2.9.

Positive Reinforcement

There are two kinds of CSEs: Those that strengthen operants and those that weaken them. CSEs that strengthen the operants they follow are called reinforcers. Reinforcement is the strengthening of an operant. There are two kinds of reinforcement: positive and negative. Positive reinforcement (R+) is the strengthening of an operant by immediately following it with a designated reward or the presentation of something a person likes. An everyday example of this may be seen in the work world. A person works hard (i.e., behaves or emits certain desirable operants) and this work is followed by the presentation of something the person likes, his pay-

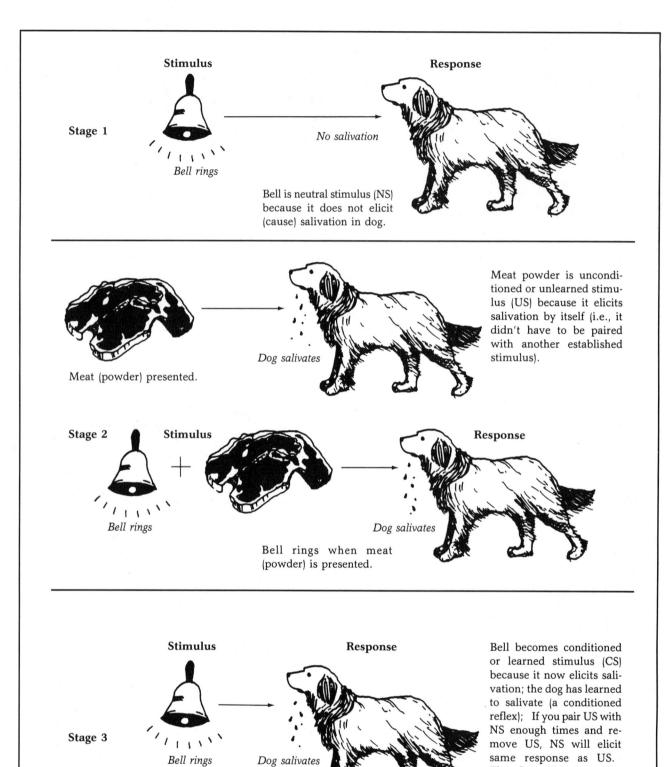

Figure 2.6. Pavlov's salivating dog.

Figure 2.7 Operant conditioning sequence.

Figure 2.8 An example of operant conditioning, with sequence expanded to include thoughts and feelings.

check. The result is that the person continues to work hard. We may then say that the hard-working behavior was positively reinforced because: (a) it was followed by a reward or the presentation of something the worker liked (i.e., money), and (b) it got stronger (or was maintained) as a direct result. Other examples of R+ may be seen in Figure 2.10.

Negative Reinforcement

Negative Reinforcement (R–) is the strengthening of an operant by immediately following it with the removal or avoidance of something the person doesn't like. An example of this commonly seen in the classroom is as follows. A student who refuses to

Figure 2.9. Operant sequence beginning with stimulus.

Contingency	Operant	CSE	Effect
Students who raise their hand without calling out will be called on by the teacher.	Jerry raises his hand and waits to be called on.	Teacher calls on Jerry.	Jerry continues to raise his hand and wait to be called on.
Only students who are in their seats will get finger paints.	Mary Beth stays in her seat.	Teacher gives finger paints to Mary Beth.	Mary Beth continues to stay in her seat.
Students will only be allowed to use power tools if they wear safety goggles.	Bart puts on safety goggles when he uses power tools.	Teacher continues to let Bart use power tools.	Bart continues to put on safety goggles when he uses power tools.
Students who ask good questions in class will be told so.	Mr. G. asks a good question in class.	Professor X. says, "That's a good question, Mr. G."	Mr. G. continues to ask good questions in class.
People who write to me will receive an answering letter within two weeks of the receipt of their letter.	Aunt Eleanor writes me a letter.	I send an answering letter to Aunt Eleanor within 2 weeks of receiving hers.	Aunt Eleanor continues to send me letters.

Figure 2.10. Examples of positive reinforcement (R+).

do his work is told that he will have to complete it after school if he doesn't finish the assignment by dismissal time. The thought of detention is aversive enough to the student to motivate him to start working. He finishes before dismissal and is allowed to leave at that time. We may say that the student's working behavior was negatively reinforced because: (a) it was followed by the removal or avoidance of something aversive to him (i.e., detention), and (b) it got stronger as a direct result. Figure 2.11 provides more examples of R–.

Negative reinforcement is sometimes confused with positive reinforcement, so let's compare them. How are they alike? Both R+ and R– serve to strengthen a behavior. How are they different? In R+, the behavior is strengthened as a result of presenting a pleasing CSE or reward. In R–, the behavior is strengthened as a result of removing an aversive CSE.

For example: Because you like someone, you want her to pay attention to you. Therefore, whenever you see this person, you will want to greet her. If your greeting results in the presentation of a pleasing CSE (i.e., she greets you in return), the chances are that in the future you will continue to greet your friend when you see her. We may say that the operant greeting has been strengthened because it resulted in the presentation of a pleasing CSE (i.e., being attended to by someone we like). On the other hand, if you dislike someone, you don't want her to pay attention to you. We try to avoid people we dislike. Therefore, whenever you see a person you dislike, you might avoid making eye contact with her, turn away, walk away from her, or even try not to let her see you. If these avoidance behaviors work, the chances are that in the future you will continue to use them to avoid the attention of a person you do not wish to see. We may say that the operant behaviors of looking away, turning away, walking away, and/or hiding have been strengthened because they resulted in the removal or avoidance of an aversive CSE (i.e., being attended to by someone we dislike). In addition to the technical differences between R+ and R–, there is also a philosophical difference which is discussed at length in Chapter 5.

Extinction

Since reinforcers are CSEs that strengthen operants, it becomes possible to weaken an operant by withholding a known positive reinforcer. This proce-

Contingency	Operant	CSE	Effect
Students who finish their work will not have to stay in after school.	Ken finishes his work.	Ken is dismissed when the bell rings.	Ken continues to finish his work to avoid detention.
Drivers who obey the speed laws will not lose their licenses.	Mrs. Y. obeys the speed laws (i.e., does not exceed posted limits).	Mrs. Y. does not get a speeding ticket.	Mrs. Y. continues to obey the speed laws to avoid getting a ticket and losing her license.
Charlene will not have to go out with Gomer if she makes excuses.	Charlene tells Gomer she has leprosy whenever he calls her for a date.	Gomer says, "Gee, Charlene, I sure hope you get better soon. I'll call again next week."	Charlene continues to lie about her health whenever Gomer calls.
Bobby's pain will go away if he puts ice on a bad bump.	Bobby puts ice on his forehead after he bangs it.	The pain goes away.	Bobby continues to put ice on bad bumps.
Students who study for tests will not fail them.	Sissy studies for her test in English.	Sissy passes her English test.	Sissy continues to study for her tests.

Figure 2.11. Examples of negative reinforcement (R–).

dure is referred to as extinction. Let's go back to the example of the worker being reinforced for his hard-working behavior. Suppose instead of paying him at the end of 5 days, the worker's boss tells him that because business has been bad lately, she won't be able to pay him until the following week. However, after 5 more days of working, the worker gets no pay and the same excuse. How long do you think his hard-working behavior will last? If there are no other rewards being presented for hard-working behavior that are as desirable as money, his behavior will weaken and eventually cease—that is, it will become extinct. We may say that extinction of hard-working behavior has occurred because: (a) the behavior was followed by the removal of a known reward (wages), and (b) the behavior got weaker as a direct result.

Remember that extinction has not occurred unless the withholding of the known positive reinforcer results in the weakening and subsequent elimination of the operant. If the worker continues to work hard even though he is not being paid, we cannot say that extinction has occurred. We can only assume that another positive reinforcer (e.g., plea-

sure derived from doing the job or from interacting with his co-workers) is present, or it could be a negative reinforcer (e.g., wanting to avoid looking for another job). While in this case the worker's boss did not want to weaken his employee's hard-working behavior, there are times when extinction is deliberately used to eliminate an undesirable behavior.

For example, let's say that whenever Aaron wants his parents' attention, he whines. The consequence of his whining is that he is picked up and held by one of his parents. We may say that Aaron's whining behavior has been positively reinforced by his parents' attending behavior. However, as Aaron gets older and continues this behavior in front of others, his parents become embarrassed by it and decide to ignore him when he whines for attention. Does Aaron stop whining? Probably not right away; don't forget, this behavior has been reinforced for a long time. In fact, the whining will probably get worse before it gets any better. One reason for this result is that Aaron will probably become frustrated and angry over the removal of the reinforcer and this may generate more intense whining. Second, depending upon

Contingency	Operant	CSE	Effect
Babies who cry for their parents' attention after they are put to bed will be ignored.	Baby Ruth cries when she is put to bed.	Baby Ruth's mother and father ignore her.	Baby Ruth stops crying and after a few more days, Baby Ruth does not cry when she is put to bed.
Students who call out in class without raising their hands will be ignored.	Todd calls out in class without raising his hand.	Todd's teacher ignores him whenever he calls out in class without raising his hand.	Todd stops calling out in class without raising his hand.
Children who swear in order to get the attention of adults will be ignored.	Sandy swears in front of her mother while her relatives are visiting.	Sandy's mother and her relatives all ignore Sandy when she swears.	Sandy stops swearing in the presence of adults.
Customers who want soda and put money into a vending machine will get nothing.	Kim puts a quarter into a vending machine.	The quarter drops down to the coin return slot and no soda appears.	After two or thre more tries, Kim stops putting coins into the machine.
A person who works for pay will not receive any checks.	Mitchell comes to work and does his assigned tasks.	Mitchell receives no paychecks.	Mitchell stops coming to work.

Figure 2.12. Examples of extinction.

how intelligent Aaron is, he may conclude that more intense whining is necessary to get the old response from his parents and he will, therefore, escalate his whining behavior. Third, Aaron's whining may simply be *perceived* by his parents as "worse" because they have never let it last this long before, and they are now having to deal with their frustration, guilt, anxiety, or anger, or the combination of any of these emotions. Eventually, however, the whining will stop, once Aaron learns that no matter how intense the whining gets or how long it lasts, it won't produce the old CSE. When he stops whining for parental attention, we may say that extinction has occurred as a result of removing the known positive reinforcer (i.e., being picked up). Other examples of extinction may be seen in Figure 2.12.

Punishment

CSEs that serve to weaken behavior are called punishers. Punishment is the weakening of an operant by following it with an aversive CSE. For example, let's say that Sandy curses in front of her mom and then gets her mouth washed out with soap. If the consequence is aversive enough, it will weaken Sandy's cursing behavior (at least in front of her mom). We may say that Sandy's cursing behavior has been punished because: (a) the behavior was followed by the presentation of an aversive, and (b) it got weaker as a direct result. If, however, Sandy continued to curse in front of her mom, we could not say that her mom had punished her swearing behavior; she had merely presented a CSE that wasn't aversive enough to Sandy to weaken the cursing behavior. A CSE is not a punisher unless it is aversive enough to weaken the behavior it follows. Teachers often use CSEs that they believe are aversive to their students (e.g., imposing detention, sending notes home, sending a student to the office) simply because those CSEs would have been aversive to most teachers when they were students. Therefore, it warrants repeating that *you have not punished a student's behavior unless the CSE weakens the behavior.* The same may be said of reinforcement. Don't think that you are going to positively reinforce a student's behavior simply by using a CSE that is pleasing to you. What may be pleasing to you might be aversive to the student; in that case, you might actually be punishing the student's behavior instead of reinforcing it. Figure 2.13 shows how punishment works.

Contingency	Operant	CSE	Effect
Children who touch a flame will be burned.	Baby Ruth touches a lit match in her father's hand while his attention is elsewhere.	Baby Ruth burns her finger.	Baby Ruth never touches a lit match again.
People who walk down dark streets in rough neighborhoods will be mugged.	Joey walks through a rough neighborhood one night.	Joey is mugged.	Joey never walks through a rough neighborhood at night again.
Children who say curse words will have their mouths washed out with soap.	Garbage-Mouth curses in front of an adult.	The adult washes his mouth out with soap.	Garbage-Mouth never curses in front of an adult again.
Unpopular people who call Charlene for a date will be refused in a nasty manner.	Gomer calls Charlene for a date.	Charlene tells Gomer, "Bug off, you creep!" and hangs up.	Gomer never calls Charlene for a date again.
Students who ask "dumb" questions in class will be made fun of.	Mr. G. asks a question in class.	Professor X. laughs at Mr. G.'s question and so does the rest of the class.	Mr. G. never asks a question in class again.

Figure 2.13. Examples of punishment.

People often confuse punishment with R–. Remember, to *reinforce* means to *strengthen*. Since to *punish* means to *weaken*, it should be easy to see the difference between the two. Punishment is the weakening of behavior by presenting an aversive CSE after the behavior occurs. R– is the strengthening of behavior by removing an aversive CSE after the behavior occurs. Here's an example: Let's say that you have a student who is off task by talking to his peers instead of doing his work. If you wanted to weaken talking to peers, you might scold him (e.g., "Stop your talking!") every time you caught him off task. Assuming he stops talking, we may say that you punished his talking by presenting an aversive CSE (i.e., scolding) immediately following the behavior (i.e., talking). Unfortunately, the effects of punishment typically do not last long and you have a student who is not talking now but will probably start talking again the minute your back is turned. Maybe you will have better luck if you concentrate on his working instead of his talking. This time, you tell him that he will have to complete all of his work before the scheduled dismissal time if he wants to go home on the school bus. Otherwise, he will have to call his parents to pick him up after he has completed his work during after-hours detention. The prospect of detention and having to call his parents for a ride is aversive to the student. Since he can avoid this aversive CSE by doing his work, he gets back on task, completes all of his work before dismissal and is able to ride the bus home with his peers. You may now say that you negatively reinforced the student's on-task behavior by removing an aversive CSE

(detention). Other comparisons of punishment, extinction, R+, and R– may be seen in Figure 2.14.

Reciprocal Relationships

In Chapter 1, I explained that social learning theorists look for reciprocal relationships between behaviors, environments, and personal variables. The behaviorist version of reciprocal determinism is limited to behaviors and environments. You should be aware that when you attempt to condition another person's behavior through R+, R–, punishment, or extinction, the result of that attempt may serve to condition your behavior as well. Let's go back to the example of Aaron, who whined for attention. Remember, Aaron whined to get attention and his parents attended to him when he whined. What did Aaron learn? Any time he wanted his parents' attention, he should whine. Therefore, we may say that Aaron's whining behavior was positively reinforced by parent attention. Now let's look at the parents' behavior. Aaron's whining was aversive to them and when they picked him up, he stopped whining. What did Aaron's parents learn? Any time they wanted to stop the child's whining, all they had to do was pick him up. Therefore, we may say that the parents' attending behavior was negatively reinforced by removing the aversive whining. This is an example of the behavioral concept of reciprocal determinism; we teach our children and they, in turn, teach us. Figure 2.15 shows other examples of reciprocal relationships.

Principle	Implementation	Result
Positive Reinforcement (R+)	Follow behavior with presentation of pleasing CSE (e.g., praise)	Strengthens behavior
Negative Reinforcement (R–)	Follow behavior with removal of aversive CSE (e.g., stop nagging, let student leave detention)	Strengthens behavior
Punishment	Follow behavior with presentation of aversive CSE (e.g., nagging, detention)	Weakens behavior
Extinction	Follow behavior with removal of known reinforcer (e.g., attention)	Weakens behavior

Figure 2.14. Comparison of positive reinforcement, negative reinforcement, punishment, and extinction.

Operant #1: Mary gets out of her seat without permission.

CSE: Mary's teacher yells at her to sit down.

Effect: Mary sits down.

Operant #2: Mary's teacher yells at her when she is out of her seat without permission.

CSE: Mary sits down.

Effect: Mary's teacher continues to yell at her whenever she is out of her seat without permission.

We may say that Mary's out-of-seat behavior (operant #1) has been punished by her teacher's yelling. We may also say that the teacher's yelling behavior (operant #2) has been negatively reinforced by Mary's sitting down.

Operant #3: Gilbert's teacher calls on him to answer a question.

CSE: Gilbert answers the teacher's questions correctly.

Effect: Gilbert's teacher continues to call on him to answer questions in class.

Operant #4: Gilbert attempts to answer a question in class.

CSE: Gilbert's teacher calls on him.

Effect: Gilbert continues to attempt to answer questions in class.

We may say that the teacher's calling-on-Gilbert behavior (operant #3) has been positively reinforced by Gilbert's answering questions correctly. We may also say that Gilbert's attempting-to-answer-questions behavior (operant #4) has been positively reinforced by the teacher calling on him.

Operant #5: Tony's mom nags him to do his chores.

CSE: Tony does his chores.

Effect: Tony's mom continues to nag him when he doesn't do his chores.

Operant #6: Tony does his chores.

CSE: His mother stops nagging him.

Effect: Tony continues to do his chores when he is nagged.

We may say that Tony's mom's nagging behavior has been positively reinforced by Tony's doing his chores. We may also say that Tony's chore-doing behavior has been negatively reinforced by his mother stopping her nagging.

Figure 2.15 *Examples of reciprocal relationships in operant conditioning.*

☑ **Checkpoint 2.2**

[pages 31–39]

Fill in the answers to the following items (1–18). Check your responses by referring to the text; relevant numbers appear in brackets.

Behavior modification is **(1)** _____

_____

_____

_____

_____

_____[31].

The difference between operant conditioning and respondent conditioning is **(2)** _____

_____

_____

_____

_____

_____[31].

Five examples of operants are:

(3) _____

(4) _____

(5) _____

(6) _____

(7) _____ [31]

Five examples of respondents are:

(8) _____

(9) _____

(10) _____

(continues)

CHECKPOINT 2.2, continued

(11) _____

(12) _____ [31]

CSEs are **(13)** _____

_____[31].

Positive reinforcement is **(14)**_____

_____

_____[31].

Negative reinforcement is **(15)** _____

_____

_____[33].

Extinction is **(16)** _____

_____

_____ [35–36].

Punishment is **(17)**_____

_____

_____[37].

Reciprocal relationship in behavior modification is **(18)** _____

_____

_____[38].

Redo any items you missed. If you missed more than 4 of the items, you should probably reread the material. Otherwise, continue on to the next section.

THE CHANGING SCENE

In this section, we take a look at the past, present, and future of behavior modification. The material presented here represents some of the most significant accomplishments and events in the history of behavior modification. It is not necessary for you to commit them to memory. My purpose in listing them in chronological order is to give you an idea of how behavior modification has changed over the years. In the beginning, its application was limited to animals. Then its use moved into institutions, where it was applied to problems of people with severe and profound handicaps. Eventually, it crept into the public schools (sounds insidious, doesn't it?) and was used with learners who had mild to moderate handicaps. More recently, we have seen a change in the focus of the research. Whereas work done in the early and middle years focused on change in behaviors through operant practices, the focus of work done in recent years indicates a movement toward changing cognitions and emotions using strategies more common to social learning theory than to behavior modification. Will this trend continue? It's hard to say, but one thing is certain: The field of behavior management has moved beyond behavior modification and there is no going back.

Early Years, 1890s–1930s

Pavlov (1897) writes a book entitled *Lectures on the Work of Digestive Glands,* in which he describes his famous classical conditioning experiments which serve as an impetus for future research.

American psychologist John Watson (1913) publishes his treatise entitled *Psychology as a Behaviorist Views It.*

Watson and Raynor (1920) publish their famous "Albert and the White Rat" study in which they pair a loud noise with a white rat to condition fear of the rat in an eleven-month-old boy who previously had no fear of the animal.

While a doctoral student at Teachers College, Columbia University, Thorndike (1921) conducts his famous puzzle box research and "discovers" the Law of Effect: When a behavior is followed by a satisfying (rewarding) consequence, it is likely to be learned; when followed by punishment or failure, it is less likely to occur. When he places a cat inside a box, Thorndike discovers that it is able to escape from the box much faster on successive trials, thus indicating that learning has taken place. The cat learned the escape behavior because it was followed by a reward (escape). It did not continue to emit any "escape" behavior that was not successful.

Jones (1924) conducts his equally famous "Peter and the White Rabbit" study using behavioral techniques such as counter-conditioning, extinction, and shaping to eliminate a 3-year-old's fear of a white rabbit.

Mowrer and Mowrer (1938) use an apparatus of their design to eliminate enuresis in young children. A liquid-sensitive pad on the child's bed has a buzzer which is activated when the child begins to urinate. Awakened by the buzzer, the child's parents immediately take him to the toilet. In the original study, all 30 subjects treated reach criterion of 14 consecutive dry nights within 2 months.

B. F. Skinner (1938) writes *The Behavior of Organisms,* in which he introduces operant conditioning and the Law of Reinforcement: If an operant behavior occurs, and is followed by a reward, its probability of occurring again increases.

Middle Years, 1940s–1960s

Dunlap (1942) uses the behavioral technique of negative practice to eliminate stammering and tic behavior in youngsters with athetoid cerebral palsy. By purposely practicing the grimacing and blinking behavior over and over again, it eventually comes under the child's control and is eliminated.

Fuller (1949) shapes the arm-raising behavior of an institutionalized 18-year-old who was profoundly retarded and who had not learned anything prior to this. Using a syringe filled with a sugar and milk solution for reinforcement, Fuller shapes behavior never before emitted by the subject.

Sheehan (1951) applies behavioral techniques with people who stutter and decreases disfluent speech.

Azrin and Lindsley (1956) teach cooperative behavior to children 7 to 12 years old using principles of operant conditioning.

Gewirtz and Baer (1958) study the effects of deprivation and satiation of adult attention on children with regard to the adult's later reinforcement power. They find that when children are deprived of adult attention, it is easier for that adult to reinforce them later.

Premack (1959) discovers what becomes known as the Premack principle: If a high frequency behavior is made contingent upon a low frequency behavior, the low frequency behavior will increase in frequency. I also refer to this as Grandma's Rule: "You can't have your dessert until you eat all your vegetables" (Grandma Kaplan, personal communication circa 1945).

Williams (1959) demonstrates that the tantrums of a 21-month-old infant can be eliminated by withholding attention when they occur.

Lazarus (1959) eliminates car phobia in a child by reinforcing him with candy, first whenever he mentions cars, later when he sits in cars, and finally when he rides in them.

Staats, Staats, Schutz, and Wolf (1962) use M&Ms with kids in a tutorial program at Arizona State University and find that kids tire of M&Ms (i.e., experience satiation) but do not tire of tokens.

Bandura, Ross, and Ross (1963) conduct a series of studies on modeling, and demonstrate that watching aggressive acts performed in cartoons and by peers and adults makes children more aggressive. Modeling becomes a powerful behavioral technique.

Schwitzgebel (1964) significantly changes frequency of arrests and incarcerations of juvenile delinquents in Boston. By paying them $1 an hour simply to tape record their delinquent experiences, he manages a 50% reduction in arrests and incarcerations among the experimental group. After a 3-year follow-up study, the behavioral change is shown to have been maintained.

Birnbrauer and Lawler (1964) make the first attempt to apply a token reinforcement system in a classroom for retarded children in Rainier, Washington. They are successful in getting students to work for tokens and delay the receipt of primary reinforcers. The token system improves the studying behavior of children previously thought to be uneducable.

Hewett (1964) at UCLA uses operant principles to teach reading to a 13-year-old autistic boy who literally has no speech. Cards and pictures are used.

Lindsley (1964) develops precision teaching model for use in monitoring behaviors and predicting behavior change.

Lovaas, Schaeffer, and Simmons (1965) use behavior modification techniques to eliminate self-injurious behavior in autistic children in addition to developing speech, self-help, and academic skills.

Patterson (1965) demonstrates that behavior modification can successfully control the hyperactive behavior of a 9-year-old diagnosed with minimal brain dysfunction (i.e., brain damage). Out-of-seat behavior is brought under control by a box on the student's desk that lights at varying intervals when he is in his seat and produces candy which he shares with his peers. The results suggest that organically-induced hyperactivity may be brought under control without medication.

Ayllon and Azrin (1968) publish *The Token Economy* based on their experiences in designing and running a token economy with psychotic adults in a state hospital in Illinois.

Hall, at the University of Kansas, develops inservice teacher-training programs designed to change the behavior of teachers. Professionals begin to recognize the need for behavior change in adults in children's environments as well as in the children themselves (Hall, Panyan, Rabon, & Broden, 1968).

Homme applies Premack principle to kids in the classroom, calling it "contingency contracting" (Homme, Csanyi, Gonzales, & Rechs 1969).

At Oregon Research Institute in Eugene, Patterson (1969) trains observers to monitor the behavior of high-risk antisocial adolescents and their parents. Again, the need to modify the environment the child comes from (as well as the child) is recognized.

Recent Years, 1970s–1990s

Becker, Engelmann, and Thomas (1971) develop DISTAR learning programs for use with disadvantaged children. Their materials are based on operant principles of learning. Follow-Through Project (1973) research indicates children on DISTAR increased reading levels by 4.1 grades in 3 years, whereas the typical gain without DISTAR is 0.6 of a grade per year (i.e., 1.8 grades in 3 years).

Wolf, now at the University of Kansas, starts Achievement Place with eight delinquent boys and two teachers who also function as surrogate parents. Successful program leads to inservice training programs (Phillips, Phillips, Fixsen, & Wolf, 1971).

Cohen's CASE Project at the National Training School for Boys in Washington, D.C. is described in his book, *A New Learning Environment* (Cohen & Filipczak, 1971). A token economy is used with delinquent adolescents in a detention setting. Cohen finds that his students made academic gains that are 3 times greater than the standard gains expected of public school students.

Meichenbaum and Goodman (1971) use a form of cognitive behavior modification called self-instruction training to prove that hyperactive–impulsive children can be taught to think before they act.

Goldfried (1973) uses cognitive behavior modification to reduce anxiety in adults.

Gottman, Gonso, and Rasmussen (1974) use cognitive behavior modification strategies successfully to treat socially withdrawn third graders.

Ulrich demonstrates that an entire school can run on principles of behavior modification (Hren, Mueller, Spates, Ulrich, & Ulrich, 1974). His Learning Village in western Michigan is a 75-student private facility where infants up through upper elementary-age students attend school on a year-round basis.

Others apply similar cognitive behavioral techniques effectively to treat speech anxiety (Meichenbaum, Gilmore, & Fedoravicius, 1971), test anxiety (Sarason, 1973), anger (Novaco, 1975), social incompetence (Christensen, 1974; Glass, 1974; Kazdin, 1973; Shmurak, 1974), and asthma in children (Renne & Creer, 1976). Cognitive behavior modification strategies (e.g., cognitive restructuring, problem solving, self-instruction, and verbal mediation) as well as other interventions incorporting cognitive or behavioral strategies or both, such as social skills training, stress management, and self-management are used successfully to treat a wide range of problem behaviors including: poor hygiene and grooming habits (Miller, Osborne, & Burt, 1987), off-task behavior (Argulewicz, Elliott, and Spencer, 1982; Miller et al.), phobias (Bornstein & Knapp, 1981), impulsivity (Schlesser & Thackwray, 1982; Zakay, Bar-El, & Kreitler, 1984), aggression (Camp, 1980; Kennedy, 1982; Kettlewell & Kausch, 1983; Schlichter & Horan, 1981; Wilson, 1984), anger (Feindler & Fremouw, 1983; Fleming, 1983; Garrison & Stolberg, 1983; Hinshaw, 1984), disruptive behavior (Allen, 1980), poor motivation (Pearl, 1985), poor academic skills (Bowers, Clement, Fantuzzo, & Sorensen, 1985; Leon & Pepe, 1983; Wong, 1985), and poor social skills (Gresham, 1981; 1985).

ASSESSMENT / CHAPTER 2

A list of acceptable responses appears following the Assessment.

1.0 Write a rebuttal for each of the myths or misconceptions about behavior modification listed below.

1.1 "Behavior modification is when you ignore all student misbehavior and only reward good behavior."

1.2 "Behavior modification is the use of aversive controls such as nausea-inducing drugs and cattle prods."

1.3 "Behavior modification is token reinforcement."

1.4 "Behavior modification is M&Ms."

1.5   "Behavior modification is for animals."

1.6   "Behavior modification is a philosophy (or a religion or way of life)."

1.7   "Behavior modification is dangerous because it can eventually lead to a population of adults susceptible to mind control and the ultimate take-over by a foreign power."

1.8   "Behavior modification doesn't work because of symptom substitution."

1.9   "Behavior modification is nothing more than bribery."

1.10 "Behavior modification is not humanistic because it takes away the individual's freedom of choice."

2.0 Read each of the hypothetical cases below and decide whether it describes positive or negative reinforcement, punishment, or extinction, and underline the correct label inside the parentheses. Explain your answer. *See sample item below.*

Sample Item
Benny doesn't like to do homework but he does like to eat pizza. His parents promise to take him for pizza on the weekend if he does all of his homework for the week. Benny finishes all of his homework for the week and gets to go out for pizza on the weekend.

We may say that Benny's doing-homework behavior was modified by (<u>positive reinforcement</u>, negative reinforcement, extinction, punishment) because <u>doing homework was followed by the presentation of a reward (pizza) and it got stronger.</u>

Most drivers will tell you that they stop at stop signs because they don't want to get into an accident or get a ticket.

> **2.1** We may say that their stopping-at-stop-signs behavior has been modified by (positive reinforcement, negative reinforcement, extinction, punishment) because

_____

_____

Margaret likes to have a soft drink during her break at work. She goes to the Pepsi machine on her office floor, puts in the correct change and makes her choice. Nothing happens. She hits the coin return button and gets her money back. She tries once more, and again nothing happens. She gets her money back and tries once more. No drink. Margaret stops putting money in the Pepsi machine.

> **2.2.** We may say that Margaret's behavior of trying to get a drink from the Pepsi machine has been modified by (positive reinforcement, negative reinforcement, extinction, punishment) because

_____

_____

Margaret tries to get a drink from the Coke machine on the next floor. She puts in the correct change and makes her choice. Nothing happens. She hits the coin return button but only gets a nickel and a dime back. She tries once more and this time the Coke splashes out without a cup. She gets some Coke on her new dress. Margaret doesn't like this. She stops putting money in the Coke machine.

> **2.3**   We may say that Margaret's behavior of trying to get a drink from the Coke machine has been modified by (positive reinforcement, negative reinforcement, extinction, punishment) because

> _____

> _____

Jim is taking a graduate course in education. Each time he tries to ask a question during the first night of class, the instructor ignores him. This happens again during the second and third class sessions. Finally, Jim gives up and doesn't ask any questions for the remainder of the term.

> **2.4**   We may say that Jim's question-asking behavior has been modified by (positive reinforcement, negative reinforcement, extinction, punishment) because

> _____

> _____

Darlene is taking a different course than Jim. Every time she tries to ask a question in class, the instructor not only answers it but often compliments her on her question. This makes Darlene feel good. She continues to ask questions in class for the rest of the term.

> **2.5**   We may say that Darlene's question-asking behavior has been modified by (positive reinforcement, negative reinforcement, extinction, punishment) because

> _____

> _____

Reggie is taking a different course than either Jim or Darlene. Every time he tries to ask a question, his instructor makes a sarcastic remark such as "Oh, you can't be serious." Reggie decides not to risk embarrassment again and stops asking questions in class.

> **2.6**   We may say that Reggie's question-asking behavior has been modified by (positive reinforcement, negative reinforcement, extinction, punishment) because

> _____

> _____

When her teacher asks Beth if she made the mess in the girl's lavatory, Beth lies and says she didn't. She gets away with it. The next time her teacher asks her if she did something wrong, Beth lies again. And again she gets away with it. Beth continues to lie to avoid punishment.

> **2.7.** We may say that Beth's lying behavior has been modified by (positive reinforcement, negative reinforcement, extinction, punishment) because

_____

_____

Perry engages in self-injurious behavior. He punches himself in the face when he gets upset. Whenever Perry does this, his teachers grab his hands and shout "No!" in his face. Perry hates being grabbed and yelled at. After a while, he stops punching himself.

> **2.8** We may say that Perry's face-punching behavior has been modified by (positive reinforcement, negative reinforcement, extinction, punishment) because

_____

_____

When Benny is standing on line in the cafeteria, an older boy cuts in front of him. Benny tells his teacher and the boy is told to go to the end of the line. Later that day in the school yard, the boy pushes Benny down and kicks him. The next time someone cuts in front of Benny he doesn't do anything about it.

> **2.9** We may say that Benny's assertive behavior has been modified by (positive reinforcement, negative reinforcement, extinction, punishment) because

_____

_____

Jerzy doesn't care if he gets into trouble and has to stay after school. However, none of Jerzy's classmates share his fondness for detention. When Jerzy tries to make his peers laugh by making rude noises and silly faces during a quiet study period, his teacher starts to write on the blackboard under the word "detention" the names of those students who are laughing and encouraging Jerzy. Jerzy's peers quickly stop attending to him and get back on task. After several futile attempts to get their attention, Jerzy gives up and puts his head down on the desk and goes to sleep.

> **2.10** We may say that Jerzy's disruptive behavior has been modified by (positive reinforcement, negative reinforcement, extinction, punishment) because

_____

_____

> **2.11** We may also say that Jerzy's peers' on-task behavior has been modified by (positive reinforcement, negative reinforcement, extinction, punishment) because

_____

_____

When Michelle answers questions in class, her classmates usually laugh at her speech impediment. When this happens, Michelle usually puts her head down and sobs, to the delight of her peers. After a while, Michelle stops speaking altogether.

> **2.12** We may say that Michelle's peers' teasing behavior has been modified by (positive reinforcement, negative reinforcement, extinction, punishment) because
>
> _____
>
> _____
>
> **2.13** We may also say that Michelle's speaking behavior has been modified by (positive reinforcement, negative reinforcement, extinction, punishment) because
>
> _____
>
> _____

Mary wants some attention from her teacher but the only time her teacher attends to her is when she does something the teacher doesn't like. Each time Mary calls out in class or gets out of her seat without permission, her teacher scolds her (e.g., "Mary, be quiet" or "Mary, sit down"). The immediate effect is that Mary stops doing whatever it is her teacher doesn't like, but this doesn't last for long. Eventually, she calls out or gets out of her seat again. Mary's teacher continues to scold her.

> **2.14** We may say that Mary's calling-out and out-of-seat behavior have been modified by (positive reinforcement, negative reinforcement, extinction, punishment) because
>
> _____
>
> _____
>
> **2.15** We may also say that her teacher's scolding behavior has been modified by (positive reinforcement, negative reinforcement, extinction, punishment) because
>
> _____
>
> _____

After taking an inservice workshop on behavior modification, Mary's teacher decides to ignore Mary's calling-out and out-of-seat behavior and attend to her only when she raises her hand or is in her seat. Eventually, Mary stops calling out and begins raising her hand and staying in her seat more often.

> **2.16** We may say that Mary' calling-out and out-of-seat behaviors have been modified by (positive reinforcement, negative reinforcement, extinction, punishment) because
>
> _____
>
> _____
>
> **2.17** We may also say that Mary's hand-raising and in-seat behaviors have been modified by (positive reinforcement, negative reinforcement, extinction, punishment) because
>
> _____
>
> _____

Leon is at a party where everyone is smoking grass. Leon doesn't like to smoke grass but he is afraid he won't be accepted by his peers if he refuses to join in. When someone passes a joint to him, he takes a hit and passes it on. He does this several times during the evening until he gets stoned and passes out. Leon gets so sick from this experience that he never smokes grass again.

2.18   We may say that before he got sick, Leon's grass-smoking behavior was modified by (positive reinforcement, negative reinforcement, extinction, punishment) because

_____

_____

2.19   We may also say that after he got sick, Leon's grass-smoking behavior was modified by (positive reinforcement, negative reinforcement, extinction, punishment) because

_____

_____

Polly is extremely shy. She is so shy that she doesn't talk to any of her classmates at school unless they talk to her first, and even then she won't look at them. Eventually, Polly's classmates stop talking to her altogether.

2.20   We may say that Polly's classmates' talking to her has been modified by (positive reinforcement, negative reinforcement, punishment, extinction) because

_____

_____

ACCEPTABLE RESPONSES

1.0 *Rebuttals to Myths and Misconceptions.* Instead of writing out examples of rebuttals, I decided to provide you with the key ideas that should be included in an acceptable rebuttal.

1.1 BMod says: "Ignore maladaptive behavior only when it is reinforced by your attention."

1.2 BMod says: "Use aversives only as last resort and with informed consent of client."

1.3 Token reinforcement is one of many BMod techniques; is not all there is to BMod.

1.4 Primary reinforcement (in form of food) is sometimes necessary; always better to use nutritional foods; BMod is not M&Ms.

1.5 BMod has demonstrated efficacy with wide range of subjects, from handicapped to gifted learner.

1.6 Idea behind this book: BMod is not the indisputable "only way"; it is simply one of many tools; using BMod does not make you a behaviorist.

1.7 BMod was around long before Skinner; no evidence that BMod in schools makes us susceptible to foreign takeover; opposite may be true—educated citizenry is less vulnerable to indoctrination and BMod can help students be more successful in school.

1.8 Symptom substitution is not an automatic side effect of BMod; however, it can occur if underlying emotions are ignored and focus is only on behavior.

1.9 Bribery is "inducement to commit illegal or immoral act"—in best interest of briber; not same as teacher using BMod to induce student to learn to read or get along with peers.

1.10 Freedom may be equated w/choices (more choices = more freedom); use of BMod in schools can lead to more (not less) choices; therefore, use of BMod can lead to more (not less) freedom; some element of society will try to control student in or out of school (e.g., peer group, police, family, media, government, church); exposure to BMod can make student less (not more) vulnerable to this manipulation.

2.0 *Terminology.* Don't forget to state *why* you chose your response.

2.1 negative reinforcement, because they want to *avoid an aversive* stimulus (e.g., accident or ticket) and the behavior got stronger

2.2 extinction, because the *known reinforcer* (Pepsi) was *withheld* and the behavior got weaker

2.3 punishment, because an *aversive stimulus* (Coke splashed on her new dress) was *presented* and the behavior got weaker

2.4 extinction, because the *known reinforcer* (teacher calling on him) was *withheld* and the behavior got weaker

2.5 positive reinforcement, because a *pleasing stimulus* (teacher calling on her and complimenting her) was *presented* and the behavior got stronger

2.6 punishment, because an *aversive stimulus* (sarcastic remark) was *presented* and the behavior got weaker

2.7 negative reinforcement, because she wants to *avoid an aversive stimulus* (punishment for making a mess) and the behavior got stronger

2.8 punishment, because an *aversive stimulus* (being grabbed and yelled at) was *presented* and the behavior got weaker

2.9 punishment, because an *aversive stimulus* (being beaten up) was *presented* and the behavior got weaker

2.10 extinction, because the *known reinforcer* (peer attention) was *withheld* and the behavior got weaker

2.11 negative reinforcement, because they want to *avoid an aversive stimulus* (detention) and the behavior got stronger

2.12 positive reinforcement, because a *pleasing stimulus* (Michelle's crying) was *presented* and the behavior got stronger

2.13 punishment, because an *aversive stimulus* (peers laughing) was *presented* and the behavior got weaker

2.14 positive reinforcement, because a *pleasing stimulus* (teacher attention) was *presented* and the behavior got stronger

2.15 negative reinforcement, because she wants to *escape from an aversive stimulus* (Mary's out-of-seat behavior) and the behavior got stronger

2.16 extinction, because the *known reinforcer* (teacher attention) was *withheld* and the behavior got weaker

2.17 positive reinforcement, because a *pleasing stimulus* (teacher attention) was *presented* and the behavior got stronger

2.18 negative reinforcement, because he wants to *avoid an aversive stimulus* (peer rejection) and the behavior got stronger

2.19 punishment, because an *aversive stimulus* (getting sick) was *presented* and the behavior got weaker

2.20 extinction, because the *known reinforcer* (Polly's talking to or looking at them) was *withheld* and the behavior got weaker

CHAPTER THREE

Identifying and Specifying Behaviors

Upon successful completion of this chapter, the learner should be able to:

1. Describe behavior by writing pinpoints that pass the stranger test

2. Judge behaviors by citing reasons why they should or should not be changed

3. Target behaviors by producing fair-pair behaviors and performance objectives

This is perhaps the most critical chapter in the text because the competencies discussed here will help you decide whether or not you should undertake an intervention in the first place. The competencies covered in this chapter include: describing precisely what the student does now that is undesirable; judging whether or not the behavior should be changed; and, if a change is necessary, targeting new behavior. Let's begin by learning how to describe behavior precisely.

DESCRIBING BEHAVIOR

Before you can judge whether or not a behavior should be changed, you have to know *precisely* what that behavior is. Unfortunately, people often think they are describing behavior precisely when in fact they are not. Consider the following.

Constructs—The Story of Jack

Many years ago, while attending a graduate-level course in special education, I had an interesting experience which relates to the description of behavior. One evening, about fifteen minutes into the instructor's lecture, a student named Jack entered the room and noisily walked to his seat. He then took out a newspaper and proceeded to read it out loud. Needless to say, this behavior created much consternation among his peers, and eventually the instructor stopped lecturing. After being asked to put away the newspaper, Jack began a long harangue about

"student rights" and "boring lectures." Then, directing an obscene gesture at the instructor, he walked out of the room, slamming the door behind him. After a brief period of stunned silence, the instructor asked each of us to write a short statement describing the incident because he intended to report Jack's behavior to the dean of the graduate school. We were told to "write down what happened" and to turn these descriptions in to the instructor without signing our names. After collecting all of the statements, the instructor glanced briefly at each of them. Eventually he put the statements down, and opening the door of the classroom he called out, "You can come in now." At this point, our old friend Jack walked back into the room and quietly took his seat. While the rest of us sat with open mouths, the instructor proceeded to read aloud excerpts from a number of the statements we had written. As it turned out, there were few objective accounts of what had happened. Although a few students had stated what they had seen and heard (the facts), most of us had resorted to making value judgments (our interpretation of the facts). Jack's behavior had been labeled "menacing," "awful," "dumb," and "disgraceful," while Jack had been called "drunk," "a jerk," and "inconsiderate." As I recall, one person suggested that Jack might be a "Commie pervert" (this was, after all, 1960) while others described him as a "psycho" (Hitchcock's movie had just come out).

After reading these exerpts from our statements while we squirmed in our seats, the instructor tossed them all into the wastebasket. He then explained that he had asked Jack to behave that way on purpose because he wanted to see how objective we could be in reporting the incident. He had hypothesized that very few of us would be objective and, as it turned out, he was correct. Naturally, many students were angry and embarrassed, and told him what they thought of his "cheap trick." He replied by asking them if Jack had a right to be angry or embarrassed by their comments. Although some students felt that Jack had relinquished any rights he had as a student because of his behavior, most of us eventually agreed that we hadn't been exactly fair to him in our descriptions of his behavior. The instructor then read aloud some statements about student behavior written by teachers, which he had collected over the years. Words such as "brain damaged," "hostile," "mean," "bad," "lazy," and "no good," among others, were used to describe student behavior. There were few, if any, verbs or verb phrases used—such as "hits," "reads," "looks out of the window," "is out of seat," "makes funny faces," "starts fights," "refuses to work," "cries," or "calls out." The instructor asked how we would feel if, as parents of these students, we had heard or read these statements about our children. By the end of the evening most of us were convinced that we needed to be more precise in describing the behavior of others.

This little story illustrates very well the difficulty intelligent and well-meaning people often have in doing something as simple as describing another person's behavior. Over the years I have experienced countless situations in which professional educators simply could not describe a student's behavior in a precise manner. The one thing they all did wrong was to use *constructs* instead of verbs. Since the use of constructs seems to be so common, I think it is worth discussing.

Constructs are broad descriptive terms that are open to interpretation such as "good," "bad," "smart," "dumb," "brave," "clean," and "reverent." Constructs are easy to use. Too easy. It is much easier, for example, to describe someone's behavior with a single word such as "good" or "bad" than to state precisely what they did that led you to think of "good" or "bad" in the first place. Constructs are also easy to use because they help us give expression to our feelings about the student and his behavior. If we are angry at a student for not doing his school work, we may describe him as "lazy." Calling him lazy makes us feel better than simply saying "he completes less than 25% of his assignments." Constructs may be easy to use and they may help us vent our emotions, but they have some serious drawbacks.

In the long run, constructs make communication *less*, not more, economical. Even though it is easier to say a student is lazy than to say he completes less than 25% of his assignments, not everyone knows what you mean by "lazy." By lazy, do you mean that the student never does anything at all, or that he only does what he wants to do, or that he only does easy things and will not do hard things? Or do you mean that he won't do anything without prodding, or that he won't do anything without a reward? Even your own concept of lazy can get a little fuzzy and take on a different meaning over time. Therefore, while it may be easier initially to describe a student as lazy, in the long run it is not very economical because we may have to explain what lazy means over and over again.

Constructs tell us more about how we interpret a factual event than they do about the event itself. In the story of Jack, the instructor asked us to "write what happened." In other words, we were asked to describe a factual event. What did we see? What did we hear? Instead of describing the event, we interpreted it. Instead of "Jack read a newspaper out loud during the instructor's lecture" (a description of the event), we wrote "Jack's behavior was disgraceful" (our interpretation of the event). We used constructs to express the meaning of the event instead of behavioral terms to simply describe what happened. When we describe a student's behavior as "lazy," "crazy," or "stupid" (all constructs), we aren't really stating what the behavior is; we are stating our opinion of what the behavior means. The student doesn't do his work, and to us that means he is lazy. The student screams in class, and to us that means he is crazy. The student answers questions incorrectly, and to us that means he is stupid. But describing behavior precisely requires that we state the facts *without editorializing*.

Using constructs to describe student behavior changes our focus from what the student *does* to what the student *is*. Let's suppose that in discussing a student who rarely does his schoolwork, we use the construct "lazy" to describe his behavior. After a while, we begin to use the word lazy whenever we discuss the student. "Oh, *he's* lazy!" Subtly, but surely, we have changed our focus from what the student does to what the student is. There are **several** problems with this. First of all, the term *lazy* implies an etiology, and perhaps even a diagnosis. This may not be our intention, but others (e.g., teachers, parents, the student himself) may perceive it as suggesting a reason for the student's behavior. However, the truth is that there could be any number of reasons for the student's behavior. Maybe he lacks the prerequisite academic skills to successfully complete the work we give him and, finding it aversive, chooses not to do it. Maybe he doesn't find the work relevant and sees little value in doing it. Maybe he has difficulty concentrating on tasks to the extent that he has trouble finishing anything he starts. Any one of these could be the real reason for the student's behavior. Unfortunately, we won't discover any of them unless we spend the necessary time and energy on assessment. It is so much easier to forgo the assessment and simply assume the student is lazy.

Second, thinking of the student as lazy can have a negative influence on how we behave towards him and, conversely, how he behaves toward us. If, for example, we believe that the student rarely does his school work because of a trait fixed at birth which makes it highly unlikely he will do anything requiring much effort, we might find it daunting to try and change his behavior. We might stop making any expectations of him. We might become frustrated and angry with the student. Even worse, if we communicate our feelings to the student, we run the risk of damaging his self-esteem (which can't be too high to begin with) or providing him with an excuse (rationalization) for his behavior, or both.

Third, thinking of the student as lazy can lead to a self-fulfilling prophecy. If we call the student lazy enough times, we may begin to believe he actually is lazy. If we believe the student is lazy, we may begin to treat him as lazy. If we treat the student is lazy, *he* may begin to believe he is lazy and behave accordingly. Why should he bother trying if people expect him not to? At this point, the student's behavior serves to validate our initial description of him as lazy.

Using constructs to describe behavior makes it difficult to measure progress. For example, if we describe the student's behavior simply as lazy, how will we be able to tell whether or not his behavior is improving, staying the same, or getting worse? If, on the other hand, we describe his behavior as "completes less than 25% of his assigned work," we can always use the amount of assigned work completed to determine if change has occurred. If he completes 25% of his work during the first few days of our intervention and more than 25% after the first week, we will know that the behavior is changing for the better. Simply describing his behavior as lazy will not help us detect change.

Let's suppose that instead of using constructs, we make a conscientious effort to precisely describe this student's behavior. Focusing on what he does (instead of what he may or may not be), we simply say that "he completes less than 25% of his assignments." Can you see how this would help us avoid all of the negative consequences discussed above? This

is not a rhetorical question. It begs an answer. If your answer is "no," go back and reread the section on constructs. If your answer is "yes," go on to the next section on pinpointing.

✔ **Checkpoint 3.1**

[pages 53–55]

Fill in the answers to the following items (1–9). Check your responses by referring to the text; relevant page numbers appear in brackets.

Constructs are **(1)** _____

_____

_____ [54].

Five examples of constructs are:

(2) _____
(3) _____
(4) _____
(5) _____
(6) _____ [54].

When we use a construct such as "lazy" to describe a student's behavior, we often change our focus from what the student does to what the student is. Three problems with this are

(7, 8, 9) _____

_____

_____

_____

_____ [54–55].

Redo any items you missed. If you missed more than 3 of the items, you should probably reread the material. Otherwise, continue on to the next section.

Pinpointing

Describing behavior precisely is referred to as pinpointing and, as you might have guessed, the end result is a pinpoint. From now on, when I talk about "describing behavior precisely," I will instead use the term *pinpointing*. I have included a number of examples and "not-examples" of pinpoints in Figure 3.1. Notice that verbs are always used in pinpoints. Words such as "hits," "smiles," "cries," and "talks" are less open to interpretation than are "rough," "happy," "sad," or "motormouth." Also notice that non-specific adverbs (e.g., "talks *a lot*," "hits *hard*," "smiles *inappropriately*," "laughs *loudly*") are not used, since they are open to interpretation. What seems "hard" to one person may seem "light," "moderate," or "soft" to another.

The stranger test

The best way to determine whether or not you have written a pinpoint is to apply the *stranger test*. This means that anyone not familiar with the student could read your description of the student's behav-

---

MALADAPTIVE PINPOINTS

Not-Example	Example
1. is aggressive (construct)	1. hits peers
2. is lazy (construct)	2. does not complete assignments
3. is immature (construct)	3. plays with children much younger
4. is anxious (construct)	4. says "I'm afraid"
5. cannot accept criticism (what does "accept" mean?)	5. cries when corrected by teacher
6. is out of seat (open to interpretation)	6. no part of anatomy touching seat
7. is dumb (construct)	7. fails tests
8. uses backtalk (what is backtalk"?)	8. says "I don't have to" when given a directive
9. calls out inappropriately ("inappropriately" open to interpretation)	9. calls out without raising hand and waiting to be called on
10. is off task (open to interpretation)	10. looks away from work on desk

TARGET PINPOINTS

Not-Example	Example
1. is mature (construct)	1. plays with children his own age
2. is considerate of others (what does "considerate" mean?)	2. offers to help others without being told
3. accepts criticism (what does "accepts" mean?)	3. asks teacher what he can do to make it better when criticized
4. is compliant (construct)	4. follows directive first time given
5. is responsible (construct)	5. completes work assigned
6. exercises self-control (open to interpretation)	6. sits next to peers without poking them
7. is on task (open to interpretation)	7. looks at work on desk
8. is smart (construct)	8. passes tests
9. is in seat (open to interpretation)	9. hips, buttocks, and/or legs touching seat
10. uses socially appropriate language (open to interpretation)	10. communicates without cursing (e.g., "f--k")

Figure 3.1. Examples and not-examples of pinpoints.

ior and interpret it the same way as you do. If a description of a behavior passes the stranger test, you may consider it a pinpoint. If it doesn't pass the stranger test, it is not a pinpoint. For example, "hostility" is not a pinpoint because it doesn't pass the stranger test. Assume that you ask a stranger to come into your classroom and monitor (i.e., observe, count, and record) all acts of "hostility" in a given student. Could the stranger do this? He probably could—but only if his interpretation of hostility is the same as yours. But what if the stranger interprets hostility differently than you? What if the stranger interprets hostility as "hits, bites, shoves, and kicks," while you interpret hostility as "using provocative language (e.g., verbal threats or profanity) with peers"? What if you both interpret hostility as "a form of physical aggression (e.g., hits, bites, shoves, kicks)" but the stranger interprets it as any instance of physical aggression, provoked or unprovoked, while you interpret it strictly as unprovoked aggression? Given these differences in interpretation between you and the stranger, it is easy to see why "hostility" does not pass the stranger test and therefore is not a pinpoint.

Let's suppose that instead of using the construct "hostility" to define the student's behavior, you tell the stranger that your student "hits without provocation, where 'with provocation' means 'in response to an obvious physical or verbal attack from a peer.'" Because this description would result in both of you observing, counting, and recording the exact same behavior, you would both get the same data. Therefore, you may say that your description of the student's behavior passes the stranger test and is a pinpoint. Keep in mind, you don't have to have the stranger actually monitor the student's behavior and compare results in order to apply the stranger test. You can simply provide the stranger with your description (either verbally or in writing) of the student's behavior and ask him to tell you what he would count if he were actually going to monitor the student. If his description of what he would count is the same as yours, then you may say that you have pinpointed the student's behavior.

✔ Checkpoint 3.2

[pages 56–57]

Fill in the answers to the following items (1–20). Check your responses by referring to the text; relevant page numbers appear in brackets.

Describing behavior precisely is called

(1) _____ [56],

the resulting descriptive statement is called a

(2) _____ [56].

A statement about a student's behavior is a pinpoint if it passes the

(3) _____ test [56].

We would know that a statement about a student's behavior passed the stranger test if

(4) _____

_____

_____ [57].

Label each of the following statements about behavior (items 5–20) **P** for pinpoint or **NP** for not pinpoint, on the line next to the number. For each **NP,** write a brief explanation of why it is not a pinpoint. Check your responses by referring to the answers following Item 20.

(5) _____ the student swears (i.e., says four-letter words such as f--k, s--t, d--n)

_____

(6) _____ the student is withdrawn _____

_____

(7) _____ the student laughs inappropriately

_____

(8) _____ the student is manipulative _____

_____

(9) _____ the student acts crazy_____

_____

(continues)

CHECKPOINT 3.2, continued

(10) _____ the student says school sucks _____

_____

(11) _____ the student is obnoxious _____

_____

(12) _____ the student is negative about school

_____

(13) _____ the student hits peers _____

_____

(14) _____ the student has a poor self-image

_____

(15) _____ the student completes assignments

_____

(16) _____ the student shouts out without raising his hand _____

_____

(17) _____ the student tries hard _____

_____

(18) _____ the student speaks only when spoken to _____

_____

(19) _____ the student is responsible _____

_____

(20) _____ the student is in his seat when the tardy bell rings_____

_____

(continues)

CHECKPOINT 3.2, continued

ANSWERS (5–20): (5) P; (6) NP ("withdrawn" is open to interpretation); (7) NP ("inappropriately" is open to interpretation); (8) NP ("manipulative" is open to interpretation); (9) NP ("crazy" is open to interpretation); (10) P; (11) NP ("obnoxious" is open to interpretation); (12) NP ("negative" is open to interpretation); (13) P; (14) NP ("poor" and "self-image" are open to interpretation); (15) P; (16) P; (17) NP ("tries hard" is open to interpretation); (18) P; (19) NP ("responsible" is open to interpretation); (20) P

Redo any items you missed. If you missed more than 4 of the items, you should probably read the material over again. Otherwise, continue on to the next section.

JUDGING BEHAVIOR

Rule Violating

After pinpointing what the student does, you are now ready to judge the behavior. Judging behavior, in this context, simply means deciding whether or not the behavior should be changed. Sometimes this decision is easy to make. For example, any time the student's behavior is a direct violation of a school rule (i.e., a standard or expectation of how students should behave, enacted by teachers or administrators or by both) and there is a clear consensus (i.e., most educators and/or parents and/or students agree) that the rule is reasonable (necessary) and fair (does not discriminate), your decision should be to change the offending behavior. This does not mean that all rule-violating behavior should be changed. I am not suggesting you adopt a rule of rules, or "meta-rule," such as "all rule-breaking behavior is bad and therefore must be changed." There is no clear consensus on the reasonableness and fairness of *all* rules enacted by educators. Every term I teach a course in behavior management, I have my graduate students list five classroom rules they want their students to obey. I then have them meet in groups and discuss their rules. I encourage them to play devil's advocate and question the reasonableness and fairness of each other's rules. Figures 3.2 and 3.3 represent those rules for which there is consensus and those for which there is no clear consensus among hundreds of teachers and teachers-in-training.

Students shall not deliberately cause others physical harm.

Students shall attend all classes.

Students shall arrive to class on time.

Students shall not disrupt the learning environment.

Students shall complete work assigned.

Students shall not cheat.

Students shall not destroy school property.

Students shall not steal.

Students shall comply with teacher directives.

Students shall not threaten, intimidate or attempt to coerce others.

Figure 3.2. Examples of school rules for which there is a clear consensus.

Students shall not chew gum or eat food during class.

Students shall raise hand to access teacher attention.

Students shall not leave seat during class.

Students shall not wear hats in class.

Students shall pay attention during class.

Students shall not sleep during class.

Students shall not address teacher by first name.

Students shall not question teacher directives or openly disagree with teacher.

Students shall not express anger or displeasure in class.

Students shall not talk in class without permission.

Figure 3.3. Examples of school rules for which there is no clear consensus.

Control

One cautionary note regarding rule violating. My experience in education tells me that teachers spend far too much time enacting and enforcing rules. Most teachers to this whether they want to or not. Their first day on the job they are handed a list of umpteen-hundred rules and feel they have to enforce them if they want to keep their jobs. There are also, however, some teachers who have their *own* need to control their environments, and they manifest this need by enacting and enforcing as many rules as they can. This practice has several negative consequences. First of all, it produces a high number of conflicts per day. The more rules you have, the more opportunities there will be for students to break them, thus creating more conflicts between you and your students. Second, the more rules you try to enforce, the more time and energy you will expend. This not only takes *time* away from your primary responsibility of teaching, it also saps your *energy* for teaching. Third, you are modeling *controlling* behavior for your students—this is not what they need to learn. Finally, trying to control your classroom by enacting and enforcing rules often puts you in the difficult position of having to defend rules that may be indefensible. Why can't we wear our hats in school? Why can I only go to the lavatory once in the morning and once in the afternoon? Why can't I listen to my radio if I've finished my work? Why are we doing this work anyway? What do you tell your students—"Because I said so!"? The point to remember is: When you have a violation of a rule for which there is no clear consensus regarding its reasonableness and fairness, you should not pass judgment until, like a judge in a court of law, you have completed a careful deliberation of the situation.

The So What? Test

Deciding whether or not to fix (i.e., change) a student's behavior when that behavior is a violation of a questionable rule, or when there is no rule violation, can be difficult. A simple but practical test I have found useful in the past is the So what? test. I call it the So what? test because one applies it by looking at the student's behavior and asking, "So what?" So what if she calls out without raising her hand? So what if he frequently gets out of his seat? To apply the So what? test, one must determine whether or not there is any evidence that the student's behavior is maladaptive. Maladaptive behavior may be defined as any behavior that interferes with the physical, emotional, social, or academic well-being of a student or of any other person. For example, let's say you have a student who calls out in class, and you want to determine whether or not her behavior warrants changing. Apply the So what? test by asking yourself whether her calling out in class interferes with her (or another person's) physical, emotional, social, or academic well-being. Let's assume that, in this particular instance, the result of the student's calling-out behavior is that her peers get angry and hold her in contempt and that she suffers from low self-esteem. Given this situation, we can say there is compelling evidence that this student's behavior does, in fact, interfere with her social and emotional well-being. The behavior may be considered maladaptive because it passes the So what? test and therefore it should be changed. What if you have a student who frequently gets out of his seat without permission? Let's assume in this case that there is no direct evidence of his behavior interfering with anyone's physical, emotional, social, or academic well-being. His out-of-seat behavior does not put him at risk for physical trauma and it does not disrupt the learning environment. He is functioning academically at the appropriate grade level and is well liked by his peers. So what if he frequently gets out of his seat. Because there is no evidence that the student's behavior is harmful, the behavior does not pass the So what? test.

A critical question, of course, is: Will it always be obvious when a student's behavior is interfering with someone's physical, emotional, social, or academic well-being? (See Figure 3.4.) In some cases, yes, it will be obvious, especially if you have been with a student over a long period of time. However, if you are

not sure, look for empirical (i.e., directly observable) evidence. For example, if a student engages in frequent noncompliant behavior (i.e., not following a directive the first time it is given), you might want to look for empirical evidence that the noncompliance interferes with the student's academic well-being. Common sense tells us that students who do not follow teacher directions typically have a difficult time achieving academically. Based on your past experience with this particular student, have you noticed that he is having difficulty achieving academically? If the answer is yes, the chances are his academic difficulties can be traced to his noncompliance. Given that his noncompliance interferes with his academic well-being, we may say that it passes the So what? test and should be changed. Since common sense also suggests that noncompliance might interfere with the student's physical well-being, we should also look for evidence of this. For example, has the student's noncompliance ever placed him in a dangerous situation (e.g., refusing to leave the school during a fire drill, using power tools without supervision)? Again, if the answer is yes, the behavior should be changed. It is also possible that noncompliance might have a negative effect on the student's social well-being, especially if it infringes upon the rights of his peers. We need to look for any evidence of this, too. We might have to observe the student in class for several days to get the evidence we need, especially if our recollections are vague or if we have had little or no prior experience with the student. We might also have to rely on others who have had more experience with the student—don't be shy about asking others to tell you about their experiences with the student. This can include other teachers, students, family members, and even the target student herself. Most of the behaviors listed in Figure 3.2 would probably pass the So what? test. Ask yourself why each one might pass the So what? test.

Sociocultural Considerations

When dealing with students from diverse cultures, we need to do more than simply apply the So what? test. It is not enough to decide a particular behavior is maladaptive in a given student simply by asking whether or not it interferes with his physical, emotional, social, or academic well-being. If this particular behavior is culture bound, we need to ask whether or not we have the right to change it or, for that matter, even to consider it maladaptive. Students from minority-group cultures may find it difficult if not impossible to always follow school rules,

Figure 3.4. Deviancy is in the eyes of the beholder.

because these rules are established by the majority-group culture, often without regard for the diversity of students. This situation can often lead to behaviors such as noncompliance, rule breaking, social isolation, defiance, and even aggression. Because such behavior can interfere with the student's physical, emotional, social, and academic well-being, it passes the So what? test and gets labeled maladaptive. The question is, does the behavior interfere with the student's physical, emotional, social, or academic well-being only because it disturbs the majority-group teacher, or would it also be considered maladaptive in the student's own culture? Figure 3.5 is a list of culture-bound behaviors in minority-group students that majority-group teachers might consider maladaptive. Instead of judging such culture-bound behaviors to be maladaptive and in need of modification, we might want to reconsider; it might be more appropriate to change some aspect of the environment (e.g., teacher expectations) instead of changing the student's behavior.

Sociocultural considerations when referring culturally and linguistically different children for special education

General Area	Selected Indicating Behaviors	Sociocultural Considerations[a]
Withdrawn Behaviors	Not responding when spoken to. Fails to talk though has skill. Prefers to be alone.	Normal stage in second language acquisition and adaptation to new culture. Culturally appropriate to native culture.
Defensive Behaviors	Losing belongings. Exhibits "I don't care" attitude. Lack of responsibility. Wastes time. Arrives late. Cheating. Blames others. Difficulty in changing activities.	Presupposes familiarity with having belongings. Adapting to new culture may cause anxiety and resistance to change. Concepts of time vary considerably from culture to culture. External locus of control may be taught or encouraged in some cultures. External vs. interal locus of control confusion results from adapting to new culture. Concepts of cheating/stealing vary from culture to culture.
Disorganized Behaviors	Confused in terms of time. Poor living skills. Extreme social withdrawal. Poor interpersonal relationships and adaptation to new culture.	Concepts of time vary considerably from culture to culture. Culturally appropriate to native culture. Normal stage in second language acquisition.
Agressive Behaviors	Talks out in class. Fights or harasses others. Impulsive behavior. Talks back to teacher. Does not follow class rules.	Culturally appropriate in native culture. Presupposes familiarity with appropriate school behavior and language.

[a]Further explanation may be found in Berry (1976), Nazzaro (1981), Padilla (1980), and Pepper (1976).

Figure 3.5. Culture-bound behaviors in minority-group students that majority-group teachers might consider maladaptive. *Note.* From "Referring Culturally Different Children: Sociocultural Considerations," by J. J. Hoover and C. Collier, 1985, *Academic Therapy, 20,* pp. 504–505. Reprinted with permission.

✔ Checkpoint 3.3

[pages 58–61]

Fill in the answers to the following items (1–17). Check your responses by referring to the text; relevant page numbers appear in brackets.

Judging behavior means **(1)** _____

_____ [58].

Five rule-violating behaviors that should definitely be changed are:

(2) _____

_____

(3) _____

_____

(4) _____

_____

(5) _____

_____

(6) _____

_____[59].

Four negative consequences of over-enacting or over-enforcing rules are:

(7) _____

_____

(8) _____

_____

(9) _____

_____

(10) _____

_____ [59].

The So what? test is **(11)** _____

_____

_____

_____ [59–60].

(continues)

CHECKPOINT 3.3, continued

Maladaptive behavior is **(12)** _____

_____

_____

_____

_____

_____ [59–60].

Five examples of culture-bound behaviors in minority-group students that might be considered maladaptive by majority-group teachers are:

(13) _____

_____

(14) _____

_____

(15) _____

_____

(16) _____

_____

(17) _____

_____[61]

Redo any items you missed. If you missed more than 3 of the items, you should probably reread the material. Otherwise, continue on to the next section.

TARGETING BEHAVIOR

Behaviorists traditionally refer to undesirable behavior (i.e., behavior that needs fixing) as the "target behavior." For example, if a student is noncompliant (i.e., does not follow directives the first time given), we say that the target behavior is "not following directives the first time given." This implies that the target or primary focus of an intervention is the elimination of an undesirable behavior. To me, the primary focus of any intervention is not the elimination of an undesirable behavior but the replacement of undesirable behavior with desirable behavior. For a child who fights when teased, the target of the intervention is not the elimination of fighting but the replacement of fighting with assertive behavior in response to teasing. Therefore, I choose to break with tradition and use the term *target behavior* synonymously with *desirable behavior*. If the undesirable behavior is no longer called the target behavior, let's agree to call it the maladaptive behavior. The term "undesirable" simply means that somebody (typically other than the student) doesn't like the student's behavior. This doesn't always mean there is something wrong with the student's behavior and that it should be changed. The maladaptive behavior is simply what the student currently does that needs changing and the target behavior is what we want the student to do instead of the maladaptive behavior. Now that we have gotten those definitions out of the way, here are some guidelines to follow when deciding on an appropriate target behavior.

The target behavior should replace the maladaptive behavior. Teachers spend an inordinate amount of time focusing on the negative. We tend to notice kids being "bad" and tend to ignore them when they are being "good" (i.e., doing what we want them to). At an education conference a number of years ago, teachers were asked to list behaviors they wanted to work on with their students. The result was that the teachers as a group listed twice as many "bad" behaviors as "good". Teachers frequently ask me for advice on how to change a negative behavior. "How can I stop him from hitting?" "What should I do about her calling out in class?" The focus always seems to be on getting the student to stop doing something "bad." The problem with always focusing on negative behaviors is that once we get rid of them, the student is left with nothing in their place. Eliminating a negative behavior without replacing it with an incompatible positive behavior usually results in the return of the negative behavior. If we punish a student every time he hits a peer when he is provoked, we will eventually weaken his hitting behavior. However, if we don't teach him how to handle the provocations in a positive manner, assuming that the provocations continue, we will find that the student may do one of three things. He might return to his hitting behavior since he has nothing else to use in its place, or he might resort to less physical forms of retaliation such as threats or name calling, or he might try to hit

without getting caught. If, instead of just punishing the student every time he engages in provoked hitting, we teach him a positive response to provocation such as ignoring or being verbally assertive, the chances are the student will not go back to his old behavior or substitute any new negative responses. Not only are the maladaptive behaviors eliminated, the student now has adaptive behaviors he didn't have in his repertoire at the beginning of the year.

The Dead Man's Test

To keep from falling into the trap of simply weakening or eliminating maladaptive behavior without replacing it, try applying a simple test known affectionately as the "dead man's test." The question posed by the dead man's test is: Can a dead man do it? When you decide on a target behavior, apply the dead man's test—ask yourself if this is behavior you could observe in a dead man. If the answer is yes, you could observe this behavior in a dead man, the target behavior does not pass the dead man's test and is not a replacement behavior. If the answer is no, you could *not* observe this behavior in a dead man, the target behavior passes the dead man's test and is a replacement behavior.

Consider the following example. Suppose we have a student who swears at peers. Let's say that we decide the target behavior should be "does not swear at peers." Does this pass the dead man's test? Is *not swearing* behavior you could observe in a dead man? Yes. Not swearing is behavior you could observe in a dead man. Since "does not swear at peers" is behavior you could observe in a dead man, it does not pass the dead man's test and is not a replacement behavior. How about "speaks to peers without swearing." Does this pass the dead man's test? Can you observe *speaks to peers without swearing* in a dead man? No. A dead man cannot speak to peers. The target behavior of "speaks to peers without swearing" is behavior a dead man could not engage in. Therefore it is a replacement behavior and passes the dead man's test. Essentially, what we are saying is that if we only focus on eliminating the student's maladaptive behavior without replacing it with an adaptive behavior, and take this approach to extremes, we leave the student no better off than a dead man—unable to do anything. (See Figure 3.6.) Figure 3.7 includes a number of examples of target behaviors that pass the dead man's test, as well as a number of "not-examples," which do not pass the test.

Figure 3.6. If no adaptive behavior is taught to replace an eliminated maladaptive behavior, the student may feel "no better off than a dead man."

The Fair Pair

The replacement or target behavior should create a fair pair. It is not enough to replace a maladaptive behavior with behavior a dead man cannot engage in. An appropriate replacement behavior should also be incompatible with, or should at least compete with, the maladaptive behavior it is supposed to replace. This is easy to remember if you think of the maladaptive and target behaviors as a *fair pair.* The "pair" is obvious; we are talking about

two behaviors. The "fair" refers to the notion that it is only fair to weaken a student's maladaptive behavior if we strengthen an adaptive behavior in its place. Thus "fair pair" refers to a student's maladaptive behavior we intend to weaken plus an incompatible or competing target behavior we intend to strengthen in its place. Choosing a target behavior that is incompatible with or competes with the maladaptive behavior is important because strengthening the former will lead to the weakening and eventual elimination of the latter. Some examples of fair pairs may be seen in Figure 3.8. Notice that by strengthening in-seat behavior we are also weakening out-of-seat behavior, because these behaviors are incompatible: a student can't be in and out of her seat at the same time. As long as a person has two hands, eating with fingers is not incompatible with eating with a fork and spoon—when socially permissible, we often pick up food with our fingers while using a fork or spoon with the other hand. However, for a student who indiscriminately eats all foods with his hands, the strengthening of fork or spoon use should discourage and eventually weaken eating with his hands. An example of a pairing of behaviors that is *not* a fair pair would be strengthening hand-raising behavior to weaken out-of-seat behavior; the strengthening of hand-raising behavior *does not lead to* the weakening of the other behavior. The next time you have to decide on a target behavior, use the fair pair concept as a guide. Simply ask yourself if, when you strengthen the target behavior, you are also weakening the maladaptive behavior. If the answer is yes, your target behavior is appropriate. If the answer is no, think again.

Students' Interests Versus Teachers' Interests

The target behavior should be in the student's best interest. Ask yourself whose interests are best served by the change in behavior, your interests or the student's interests. Teachers often feel threatened by students who question their authority by asking "Why?" whenever they are told to do something. Teachers also may feel threatened by noise and movement in their classrooms that they consider excessive or that they have not initiated. Students who question authority or who are noisy or active probably elicit anxiety in a teacher because their behavior suggests that the teacher is not in control of the class. Losing control of one's class is a most frightening prospect for a teacher to contemplate. As teachers we have been conditioned over

---

Dead Man's Test

1. *swears (says four-letter words, e.g., "s--t", "f--k")*

   Not-Example: does not swear (a dead man can do this)

   Example: talks to others without swearing (a dead man cannot do this)

2. *hits peers*

   Not-example: does not hit peers (a dead man can do this)

   Example: interacts with peers without hitting (a dead man cannot do this)

3. *destroys property of others*

   Not-Example: does not destroy property of others (a dead man can do this)

   Example: uses property of others without destroying it (a dead man cannot do this)

4. *calls out without raising hand*

   Not-Example: does not call out without raising hand (a dead man can do this)

   Example: raises hand and waits to be called on (a dead man cannot do this)

5. *tantrums (i.e., cries and screams) when his demands are not met*

   Not-Example: does not tantrum when demands are not met (a dead man can do this)

   Example: asks "Why not?" when demands are not met, without crying or screaming (a dead man cannot do this)

Figure 3.7.   Examples and not-examples of target behaviors that pass the dead man's test.

the years to believe that noise, movement, and questioning authority are the three warning signs of an impending revolt in the classroom. Conversely, when students comply without question, sit still, and stay quiet, we teachers perceive ourselves as being in control. Perhaps this is why we are so quick to punish noncompliance or any questioning of our authority. Unfortunately, punishing such behavior in our students can create a classroom full of passive conformists who are afraid to assert themselves with any adults or authority figures. This kind of grooming of young citizens will hardly prepare them to meet the challenges of the real world. Teachers must recognize that schools are primarily for the students, not for the adults who work there. This means that in any behavior-management situation, the child is the individual of primary concern, and that "any appropriate target behavior must be one which is justifiable in terms of the demonstrable long-term well-being of the target child or population" (Harris & Kapche, 1978, p. 27).

Instead of only reinforcing behaviors such as "stays in seat," "raises hand," and "is quiet," we should strengthen behaviors such as "makes positive comments to peers," "engages in assertive behavior with peers and adults (when appropriate)," and "uses spontaneous audible language in group discussions." Again, many teachers are going to be threatened by these behaviors in their students. I recall an incident I observed a number of years ago which is a perfect example of a teacher who obviously felt threatened by spontaneous loud verbal exchanges in her students, even though this behavior was actually positive and represented no threat to the teacher's control. A colleague and I were teaching gymnastics to a class of students with emotional/behavioral disabilities. On this particular occasion, we were teaching some basic vaults on a gymnastic apparatus called the buck, which is a smaller version of the pommel horse without the pommels. The teacher of the class, a devout follower of behavior modification, was watching the lesson in

---

Maladaptive Behavior → Target Behavior

is out of seat (no part of anatomy on chair) → is in seat (hips, buttocks and/or legs touching chair)

eats with fingers → eats with fork and spoon

bites fingernails → makes fist (when has urge to bite nails)

teases or makes fun of peers → compliments peers

steals (takes property of others without asking) → requests permission to use others' property

lies → tells truth

cries when criticized → when criticized, asks what he can do to improve

does not complete assignments → completes assignments

does not follow directions first time given → follows directions first time given

is off task (looks away from work on desk) → is on task (looks at work on desk)

calls out to get attention → raises hand and waits to get attention

hits peers when provoked → acts assertive when provoked (says "No" or "Stop it!")

punches self in face when upset → tells others when upset

makes bowel movements in pants → makes bowel movements in toilet

picks nose → blows nose with handkerchief

cheats (turns in work of others as his own) → turns in own work

disrupts learning environment (causes peers to look away from their work by making animal sounds) → completes task quietly

destroys property of others → uses property of others without destroying it

---

Figure 3.8. Examples of fair-pair behaviors.

the gym. She had earlier warned the class (without our knowledge) that talking out would not be allowed during the gymnastics lesson. If they had something to say, they had to raise their hands. As the lesson wore on in silence, all of the students were experiencing success except for one overweight youngster I'll call Ralph, who continuously had difficulty getting over the buck. Each attempt would end in frustration and Ralph would walk dejectedly back to the end of the line of students. However, near the end of the period, Ralph finally succeeded in getting his body over the buck. This precipitated a number

of excited congratulatory comments from his peers, e.g., "Atta way, Ralph!" There was also applause and much cheering. In the next instant, the teacher was telling each student who called out that they were losing ten points for each of their talk outs. We couldn't believe it! Ralph hardly ever did anything in his life that resulted in cheers from his peer group. His peers, who usually heaped verbal abuse on him, seldom, if ever, made any positive comments to anyone. In this instance their talk-outs should have been rewarded, not punished. This is an example of a teacher acting in her own best interest instead of that of her students. Talk-outs in the classroom may have been maladaptive, because they disrupted the learning environment and lowered academic achievement. However, talk-outs in the gym were not maladaptive. On the contrary, in this case they were more likely representative of adaptive behavior. If this teacher had taken the time to ask herself in whose interests she was acting, she might have acted differently.

Ecological Considerations

Changing a student's behavior often has an effect on the ecosystem in which the student behaves. For example, let's suppose we have a student who is constantly being picked on and manipulated by his peers. Because of his passivity, he is the perfect victim. Changing this student's passivity and replacing it with assertiveness could actually put him at risk. If this student, who used to give in to his peers' demands, suddenly becomes uncooperative and refuses them, they might take out their frustration on him with physical aggression. I'm not saying that we shouldn't try to help this student become more assertive. I'm simply saying that we should try to predict the effects of this change in behavior on the student's ecosystem and act accordingly. In this particular case, it would certainly be important to teach the student to pick his spots and use his new assertive skills in those situations which would be least likely to put him at risk for physical reprisals. It would also be prudent to attempt some form of intervention (e.g., anger management) with those peers who abuse him.

☑ Checkpoint 3.4

[pages 62–67]

Fill in the answers to the following items (1–4). Check your responses by referring to the text; relevant page numbers appear in brackets.

According to the author, target behavior refers to

(1) _____

_____

_____

_____

_____ [62–63].

One reason why we should focus our intervention on strengthening a target behavior in place of the maladaptive behavior is:

(2) _____

_____

_____

_____ [63].

The dead man's test is

(3) _____

_____

_____

_____

_____ [64].

The fair pair is defined as

(4) _____

_____

_____

_____

_____ [65].

(continues)

CHECKPOINT 3.4, continued

Label each of the following **FP** (for fair pair) or **NFP** (for not fair pair) on the line next to the number. For each **NFP**, write a brief explanation of why it is not a fair pair. Check your responses by referring to the answers following Item 14.

(5) _____ hits peers when teased / tells peers to stop when teased

_____

(6) _____ bites self / pinches self

_____

(7) _____ eats food with fingers / eats food with fork and spoon

_____

(8) _____ bites self / bites peers

_____

(9) _____ calls classmates names / does not speak to classmates

_____

(10) _____ out of seat / stays in seat

_____

(11) _____ makes negative comments about school / makes negative comments about family

_____

(12) _____ does not do assignments / copies assignments from peers

_____

(13) _____ does not speak unless spoken to / initiates conversation

_____

(continues)

CHECKPOINT 3.4, continued

(14) _____ says swear words / does not say swear words

_____

ANSWERS (5–14): (5) FP; (6) NFP (neither behavior is in student's best interest); (7) FP; (8) NFP (neither behavior is in student's best interest); (9) NFP ("does not speak to classmates" does not pass dead man's test and is not in student's best interest); (10) FP; (11) NFP (neither behavior is in student's best interest); (12) NFP (neither behavior is in student's best interest); (13) FP; (14) NFP ("does not say swear words" does not pass dead man's test and is not in student's best interest)

Redo any items you missed. If you missed more than 2 of the items, you should probably reread the material. Otherwise, continue on to the next section.

PERFORMANCE OBJECTIVES

Once we decide that a behavior needs changing and we decide on what that change will be, we need to describe what the student will do to demonstrate that the change has occurred. This description is called a *performance objective*. The performance objective tells us when we should terminate our intervention. If we think of the target behavior as our "destination," we must be very clear about where we are going so that we will know when we have arrived. As Mager says, "if you're not sure where you're going, you're liable to end up someplace else, and not even know it" (1962, p. vii).

Teachers often assume that they already know exactly what they want from students in terms of target behavior. For example, they want their students to "do their work," "look at me when I talk to them," "come to class prepared," "obey the rules," and "be on time," among other things. How much work must a student do, and under what conditions must this work be done, before the teacher may say that the target behavior has been reached? Must the student always look at the teacher when she's talking? Is eye contact really a valid measure of attentiveness in the first place? What does "come to class prepared" actually mean? Does it mean "bring the textbook, pencils and paper," or does it mean "behave with a willingness to work and a 'sunny disposition'"? What rules must be followed? How often and under what conditions? Until all of these questions are answered, the teacher may not really know where she's going. Without this knowledge, she might stop her behavior modification program too soon or continue using it too long. Neither situation benefits the student. Stopping a program before the target behavior is reached may result in an unsuccessful intervention program which "turns off" both the student and the teacher. Continuing a program after the target behavior has been reached wastes time and may inhibit internalization by making the student overly dependent upon extrinsic reinforcement.

Teachers routinely write performance objectives for academic behaviors such as reading and math. It is every bit as important for us to write objectives for social behaviors as well. Up until now, many teachers have not had to write objectives for social behaviors because they were not expected to provide formal instruction in social behaviors. This has changed dramatically with the growth of social skills training programs for use in special education classrooms. Students are now receiving formal instruction in social behaviors and we need to determine how well they have learned the behaviors taught. According to Mager, "if you are teaching skills which cannot be evaluated you are in the awkward position of being unable to demonstrate that you are teaching anything at all" (1962, p. 47). Unless target behaviors—academic or social—are written as performance objectives, they cannot be evaluated, and if they cannot be evaluated, we may never know if we have taught them.

If you have little or no experience writing objectives or if you need a refresher course, take a look at Mager (1962) or Howell, Kaplan, and O'Connell (1979), or simply use the objectives provided in Figure 3.9. Notice that the behavior is always stated as a verb and, if necessary, is described, defined, or amended with an example. This leaves little to the imagination. Also note that it is important to state any limiting conditions as well. It is not enough just to say that a student will do something. You should say when or where or under what circumstances he will do it. For example, the student will do it (the behavior) "the first time asked" or "when angry" or "when talking to peers" or "without being prompted" or "on the school bus." All of these conditions serve as descriptors that make the behavior in the performance objective easier to define and, thus, to measure change in.

When you write objectives, it is also important to establish criteria for acceptable performance (CAP).

These criteria go beyond the immediately limiting conditions discussed above. It's not enough to say that the student will "stay in his seat." How long must he stay in it? One minute? Ten minutes? One hour? Ten percent of the time observed? How do you decide which of these CAPs is most appropriate for a given student? How do you decide how long a student should stay on task, or decide what is an adequate rate of spontaneous speech from a student who never speaks unless he is spoken to? One method is essentially the same as choosing CAP for an academic objective: You simply find a student or group of students who are already engaging in the target behavior and measure their performance in order to get a minimum standard to use with the target child. Instead of choosing students at random, which constitutes a normative approach, use the criterion-referenced approach of monitoring a small sample of those students who regularly engage in the target behavior. The specific methods used to monitor such behavior are discussed in detail in Chapter 7. Another way of determining appropriate CAP is to base your assessment on the individual student's need. For example, if you wanted to determine how long the student should stay in his seat, you could simply ask, "How long does he need to?" If his longest in-seat assignment takes him 15 minutes to complete, he needs to stay in his seat for a minimum of 15 minutes at a time.

Many teachers would argue that it is unnecessary to go to such lengths to determine appropriate CAP. They contend that a teacher should be able to arbitrarily determine the CAP for certain target behaviors. In some instances, I would agree. For example, no one would disagree that the CAP for self-injurious behavior should be zero. The same can be said of unprovoked physically or verbally aggressive behavior if it appears to be maladaptive. Any teacher who has to deal with these behaviors doesn't need to conduct an ecological baseline to determine CAP. However, there are other behaviors for which the arbitrary determination of CAP is questionable. For example, most teachers want a CAP of 100% for compliance—they want a student to comply with a request every time he is asked. Teachers also tend to want students to be in their seats (when that behavior is appropriate) 100% of the time observed. They usually want talk outs (i.e., calling out without raising hand) to occur at a rate of zero per minute. Are these CAP realistic? More important, are they in the student's best interests? Do we really want a room full of robots who move and speak only when we push a button? Do we want to stifle the spontaneous reaction of a student who experiences success for the

Maladaptive Behavior	Target Behavior	Performance Objective
calls out w/o raising hand	raises hand and waits	Beh: student will raise hand and wait Cond: when he wants teacher's attention CAP: 80% of the time over 3-day period
does not follow directives	follows directives	Beh: student will follow directive first time given Cond: given a directive CAP: 100% of the time over 5-day period
hits peers w/o provocation	interacts with peers w/o hitting	Beh: student will interact without hitting Cond: when interacting with peers CAP: rate of zero hits per minute over a 10-day period
swears when talking to others	talks to others without swearing	Beh: student will talk without swearing Cond: when talking to others CAP: rate of 2 swears per 100 minutes over a 10-day period
does not complete assignments	completes assignments	Beh: student will complete assigned work Cond: given assignments CAP: 80% of assignments over a 5-day period
steals others' property	asks for others' property	Beh: student will ask for others' property Cond: when he wants to use CAP: 90% of the time over 5-day period
lies	tells the truth	Beh: student will answer in a truthful manner Cond: given a query from the teacher CAP: 100% of the time over 5-day period
off task (looks away from work on desk)	on task (looks at work on desk)	Beh: student will look at work on desk Cond: given work on desk CAP: 90% of times observed over 2-day period
bites self when angry	tells person he is angry w/o biting self	Beh: student says "I'm angry" without biting self Cond: when angry CAP: 100% of time over 5-day period

Figure 3.9. Examples of performance objectives.

first time? Do we want to inhibit students from encouraging each other? Is it always necessary for one student to raise his hand, wait to be called on, and then ask for permission to express encouragement or praise to a peer? Do we want to curb a student's assertiveness with his peers or with adults? Should students believe everything we tell them, or can we be secure enough in ourselves to let them question us openly without fear of anarchy? There are already enough sheep in the world. What we need are more leaders, or, at the very least, more citizens who are not afraid to question the wisdom of those who lead. All potential change agents must consider these questions before they arbitrarily decide how "well" a child should behave.

☑ Checkpoint 3.5

[pages 68–71]

Fill in the answers to the following items (1–7). Check your responses by referring to the text; relevant page numbers appear in brackets.

The performance objective is

(1) _____

_____

_____

_____

_____ [68].

We need to write a performance objective because

(2) _____

_____

_____

_____

_____ [68–69].

(continues)

CHECKPOINT 3.5, continued

The three components of a performance objective are

(3, 4, 5) _____

_____

_____

_____

_____

_____ [69].

Two ways to establish criteria for acceptable performance are

(6, 7) _____

_____

_____

_____

_____

_____ [69].

Redo any items you missed. If you missed more than 1 of the items, you should probably reread the material. Otherwise, continue on to the next section.

PUTTING IT ALL TOGETHER

In case I've lost you along the way, here is a list of steps to follow when deciding what changes to make.

1. Pinpoint the undesirable behavior the student currently engages in. Apply the stranger test to determine whether or not you have pinpointed the behavior. If the answer is no (you did not pinpoint the behavior), try again. If the answer is yes (you did pinpoint the behavior), move on to step 2.

2. Apply the So what? test to the pinpoint to determine whether or not it is maladaptive and needs changing. Look for evidence based on your (or another's) past experience with the student or based on data from direct observation of the student's behavior, that indicates whether the behavior is interfering with the student's or another person's physical, emotional, social, or academic well-being. If there is no evidence that the behavior is interfering, abort the process. If there is evidence that the behavior is interfering, consider the behavior maladaptive. Assuming the student is not a member of a cultural minority group, move on to step 3. If the student is a member of a cultural minority group, consider whether or not the behavior in question is culture bound and if it should be changed or even considered maladaptive. If you don't know, ask someone who does. If it turns out that the behavior is culture bound and it appears that change

is not in the student's best interest, consider a change in the ecosystem rather than the student. If the behavior is not culture bound or if change is determined to be in the student's best interest, proceed to step 3.

3. Pinpoint the target behavior. Refer to #1 above.

4. Apply the So what? test to the target pinpoint to determine whether or not it meets the following criteria:

   a. it must make a fair pair (i.e., a replacement behavior which, when strengthened, will lead to the weakening or elimination of the 'maladaptive behavior) when paired with the original behavior;

   b. it must be in the student's best interest (i.e., will foster his physical, emotional, social, or academic well-being); and

   c. the change must not have any adverse effect on the ecosystem.

   If the target pinpoint does not pass the So what? test, make changes as necessary. If it does pass the So what? test, move on to step 5.

5. Write a performance objective for the target pinpoint that includes the behavior, the conditions under which the behavior will occur, and criteria describing how well the student will perform the behavior. If you are not sure what the CAP should be, identify and observe students who already engage in the target behavior.

ASSESSMENT / CHAPTER 3

A list of acceptable responses appears following the Assessment.

1. *Describing Behavior*
Write a pinpoint that passes the stranger test for each of the following:

    a. off task:

    b. is punctual:

    c. talks out:

    d. uses leisure time wisely:

    e. is considerate of others:

    f. lies:

g. steals:

h. talks loud:

i. comes to class prepared:

j. out of seat:

k. laughs inappropriately:

l. is responsible:

m. accepts criticism:

n. is clean:

o. acts mature:

p. is withdrawn:

q. tantrums:

r. does good work:

s. has poor self-image:

t. is hostile:

2. *Judging Behavior*
For each of the following behaviors, present an argument that states reasons why the behavior should be changed. Also present a counter-argument that states reasons why the behavior should not be changed.

    a. *hits peers when teased*

change:

don't change:

    b. *hits peers when hit*

change:

don't change:

c. *chews gum in class*

change:

don't change:

d. *wears hat in class*

change:

don't change:

e. *sleeps in class*

change:

don't change:

f. *uses racist terms (e.g., "nigger," "kike," "spic") when talking to peers*

change:

don't change:

g. *gets out of seat without permission*

change:

don't change:

h. *no eye contact (i.e., does not look at person speaking to him/her)*

change:

don't change:

i. *lets peers copy work*

change:

don't change:

j. *questions authority (i.e., wants to know why he/she has to follow directive)*

change:

don't change:

3. *Targeting Behavior*
Write a fair-pair target pinpoint for each of the following:

    a. out of seat (e.g., bottom on chair w/body facing front):

    b. does not complete asignments:

    c. calls out without raising hand:

    d. is late to class:

    e. hits peers when provoked:

    f. makes disparaging remarks to peers (e.g., "You're stupid."):

    g. gives up (e.g., stops working) when frustrated:

    h. directs attention away from task:

    i. does not speak unless spoken to:

    j. tantrums (e.g., screams, cries) when request is denied:

k. does not follow directives given:

l. destroys property of others:

m. is disruptive (e.g., makes noises during lesson):

n. acts passive when teased by peers (e.g., gets anxious; looks to others for help):

o. makes incorrect responses to questions:

p. acts impulsively (e.g., starts responding before teacher has given all directions):

q. eats food with hands:

r. makes bowel movements in pants:

s. bangs head when upset:

t. picks nose:

4. Write a performance objective for each of the following (make up your own CAP):

    a. shares belongings with peers:

    b. raises hand without calling out:

    c. asserts himself with peers:

    d. is on time to class:

    e. tells the truth:

f.   accepts criticism:

g.   gets along with peers:

h.   uses socially appropriate language:

i.   stays in seat:

j.   finishes work:

ACCEPTABLE RESPONSES

1. *Describing Behavior.* Appropriate responses are anything approximating the following examples of pinpoints.

a. looks away from work for more than ____ seconds; head turned away from task; looks at peer(s) instead of work

b. is in seat (or room) when late bell rings

c. calls out without raising hand and waiting to be called on; addresses the teacher without permission

d. given free time, S. engages in task (or behavior) acceptable to teacher

e. talks about others without making disparaging remarks; gives others a turn first; helps peers when they ask for it

f. makes statements that are obviously untrue

g. takes things that do not belong to him without permission; takes property of others without their consent or knowledge

h. talks in a voice audible in all parts of the room; uses a voice that can be heard all over the room

i. brings pencil, paper and book(s) to class; brings whatever is required by teacher to class

j. buttocks not in contact with seat; no part of body in contact with seat

k. laughs when he sees someone hurt; laughs when he is told something others consider sad

l. finishes work without being reminded; successfully runs errands; follows directions as they are given

m. when work is corrected, makes necessary changes without dissent or complaint

n. comes to school wearing clean clothes; washes hands before eating without being told; brushes teeth after meals without being reminded

o. plays with children her own age; engages in behavior indicative of age group

p. speaks only when spoken to; speaks spontaneously only to one peer

q. cries, screams, curses to get his way; shouts and curses when things don't go his way

r. gets "B" or better on all assignments; has "B" average in all subjects

s. often makes self-deprecating remarks (e.g., "I'm stupid" or "I'm no good at that"); refuses to try tasks he has performed successfully in past

t. hits, kicks, pushes peers without provocation; threatens peers without provocation (e.g., "I'm gonna beat you up!")

2. *Judging Behavior.* Should have at least one argument *for* changing and one argument *against* changing; since I haven't thought of every possible argument, you may have one that is not listed below—this is OK. You may want to check out your argument with a friend or colleague.

a. *hits peers when teased*

CHANGE:

—being teased is part of going to school; if every student hit somebody who teased them at school, teachers would be doing nothing but breaking up fights all day long

—students need to learn that fighting is a behavior that is typically not tolerated in society and that people who fight (in school, home, or workplace) are usually not as successful as people who resolve their differences without fighting

—fighting is dangerous; students can get hurt badly and teachers who let them fight can get sued

—people who fight usually don't have many friends, and school is supposed to be a place where students develop social skills and friendships

—fighting when teased is usually not an effective way of stopping the teasing; there are better ways to stop others from teasing

DON'T CHANGE:

—some students won't learn to stop teasing others unless they are hurt physically; unfortunately, they have to learn the hard way; therefore, it is in the best interest of the teasing student that teachers not interfere

—everyone has the right to defend him or herself as best they can

—it's a cruel world and children need to learn how to stand up for themselves; only the strong will survive

—being hit by someone is a logical consequence of having insulted them; the student who did the insulting is the one who should be punished rather than the person who was insulted

—people who insult others are despicable and deserve whatever they get

b. *hits peers when hit*

CHANGE:

—essentially the same arguments as above

DON'T CHANGE:

—same as above, although people tend to use the self-defense argument more often in cases of provocation by hitting than in cases of teasing (i.e., you shouldn't hit someone just because they teased you but it's OK to hit them if they hit you first)

c. *chews gum in class*

CHANGE:

—chewing gum is an unseemly behavior that makes people look like they have no manners, or worse, like animals (cows chewing their cud); it has no place in polite society

—letting students get away with chewing gum in class will ultimately lead to more serious rule infractions

—chewing gum can be dangerous in some teaching situations (e.g., physical education class)

—chewing gum can interfere with a student's performance in some teaching situations (e.g., oral recitations)

—chewing gum can lead to unsanitary situations in school, such as students sticking gum on furniture or throwing it on the floor or inside wastebaskets and can create more work for building maintenance staff

DON'T CHANGE:

—chewing gum never hurt anyone

—chewing gum might help some students concentrate better in class

—the no-gum-chewing rule is too hard for teachers to enforce and leads to unnecessary conflict and confrontation

—chewing gum is better than using smokeless tobacco

—there are too many other, more important rules to enforce than no-gum-chewing

d. *wears hat in class*

CHANGE:

—is disrespectful for students (especially males) to wear hats inside a building

—doesn't look good to see students wearing their hats in class; makes teacher look like a lax disciplinarian

—letting students get away with wearing their hats in class will ultimately lead to more serious rule infractions

—could lead to a hygiene or health problem

DON'T CHANGE:

—rules regarding social etiquette have changed and more people (especially males) are wearing hats

inside a building now than before

—there are more important rules to enforce

—will lead to power struggles

—may be culture-bound behavior (common to certain religious groups)

e. *sleeps in class*

CHANGE:

—student won't learn anything if he sleeps in class

—makes teacher look bad (boring, poor instructor, no discipline)

—what will students who are on task think?; won't they resent it?; will they complain to parents or, worse yet, start imitating the behavior?

DON'T CHANGE:

—student may need the rest; sleep may be more important for his physical and emotional well-being than learning curriculum

f. *uses racist terms*

CHANGE:

—no place in schools for racist terms

—is in violation of student's civil rights

—could lead to violence, perhaps on large scale (race riots)

DON'T CHANGE:

—students' free speech is guaranteed by U.S. Constitution

—isn't it OK if used by members of same group (e.g., African Americans calling each other "nigger")?

—prejudices run too deep for school to do anything about them; besides, prejudices are "values" learned in the home and it's not the school's role to teach values, especially where they conflict with those taught at home

g. *gets out of seat without permission*

CHANGE:

—somebody could get hurt if enough students are moving about the room without supervision

—makes teacher look bad (no control)

—most learning in school typically occurs at student's desk; how will students learn if they are away from their desks?

—typically leads to disruption of the learning environment; if left unchecked, others will imitate

DON'T CHANGE:

—too confining for students to stay at their desks all day; need to move about

—enforcing the in-seat rule will disrupt the learning environment more than out-of-seat students will

h. *no eye contact*

CHANGE:

—is an important social skill all students need to learn

—is disrespectful for a person (student) not to look at person (teacher) when that person is speaking to them

DON'T CHANGE:

—may be a culture-bound behavior (actually a sign of respect in some cultures)

i. *lets peers copy work*

CHANGE:

—is cheating, pure and simple

DON'T CHANGE:

—may be a culture-bound behavior (i.e., sharing what you have with others is not looked on as cheating or collusion)

j. *questions authority*

CHANGE:

—students (children and youth) should never question the authority of teachers (adults)

—students are too young (immature, irresponsible) to know what's best for them; therefore, all decisions involving students need to be made by adults (teachers, parents, administrators) and should never be questioned

—letting students question authority at school will ultimately lead to student rebellion and anarchy

DON'T CHANGE:

—do we want to raise a generation of "sheep" who blindly follow whatever someone in authority tells them, even though that authority figure may not have their best interests in mind?

—don't teachers question the authority of administrators and school boards?; why else would they belong to a teachers' union?; why should there be a double standard (i.e., it's OK for educators to question the authority of other educators but not OK for students to question the authority of educators)?

3. *Targeting Behavior*
Fair Pairs [should be incompatible or competing behavior]

a. buttocks in contact with seat

b. completes assignments

c. raises hand and waits to be called on

d. is in room before late bell rings

e. is assertive when provoked (e.g., says "No" or "Stop it")

f. compliments peers (e.g., "That's a good answer")

g. perseveres (e.g., keeps working) or asks for help when frustrated

h. is on task (i.e., works at task without drawing peers' attention)

i. initiates conversation with others

j. accepts denied request without screaming or crying

k. complies with directive first time given

l. uses property of others without destroying it

m. attends school on regular basis

n. acts assertive when teased by peers (e.g., tells them to stop)

o. answers questions correctly

p. waits until teacher gives all directions before responding

q. uses utensils to eat food

r. makes bowel movements in toilet

s. tells person how he feels when upset

t. use tissue or handkerchief to blow nose

4. *Performance Objectives* [Must have all three components: B–behavior; C–conditions; and CAP–criteria for acceptable performance]

a. Given an object of his own (C), the student will, when asked (C), share the object with a peer (B). He will do so 80% of the time over a 3-day period (CAP).

b. Given a situation in which it is appropriate for the student to raise his hand and wait to be called on before speaking (C), s/he will do so (B) 90% of the time over a 5-day period (CAP).

c. When teased (C), the student will act assertive by telling his peers to stop and by stating his feelings (B). He will do this 100% of the times he is teased over 3-day period (CAP).

d. The student will be in his seat (B) before the late bell rings (C) 9 out of 10 days (CAP).

e. Given a query from the teacher or peer (C), the student will answer in a truthful manner (B) 100% of the time over a 2-week period (C).

f. When told that she did something incorrectly (C), the student will accept this by not crying, and by asking how she can correct her mistake(s) (B). She will do this 100% of the time over a 2-week period (CAP).

g. Given all situations where the student is interacting verbally with peers (C), she will talk to them without making any (CAP) negative comments (e.g., "You're stupid!") (B) for 1 week (CAP).

h. When speaking to others (CAP), the student will use language without profanity (B) 90% of the time observed over a 2-week period (CAP).

i. Given situations when it is inappropriate to be out of seat (C), the student will be in his seat (i.e., buttocks in contact with seat) (B) 90% of the times observed over a 5-day period (CAP).

j. The student will finish (B) 100% (CAP) of assigned work (C) over a 3-day period (CAP).

CHAPTER FOUR

Diagnosing Behavior Problems

Upon successful completion of this chapter, the learner should be able to demonstrate knowledge of when and how to use functional analysis and Pre-Mod analysis to diagnose the cause of behavior problems.

WHY ASK WHY?

I hesitated to use the word "diagnosing" in the title of this chapter—or anywhere else in this book, for that matter. Not only is it a medical term suggesting a disease state, it seems out of place in a book about behavior modification. I think behaviorists have always been uncomfortable with the notion of diagnosis. To diagnose means to ask why. I remember once asking a psychologist, who was an advocate of the behavioral approach, why a particular student behaved as he did. The psychologist answered, "Who cares *why*?" This response, for me, sums up the behaviorist attitude toward diagnosis: The "why" of a behavior problem isn't necessary. Behavior is shaped and maintained by its consequences. Period. Simply change the consequences and you'll change the behavior. This makes diagnosis, in the traditional sense, superfluous. There is only one problem with these assumptions: Not all behavior is shaped and maintained by its consequences. Consider the following example.

Imagine a teacher with ten students in his class who seldom, if ever, turn in any completed homework. Imagine also that, unlike the teacher, we know the actual reasons these students do not do their homework. For example, the reason the *first* student doesn't do his homework is because he doesn't know how to do it. It's too hard for him. The *second* student, who is able to do the work, refuses to do it because she doesn't see any intrinsic value in doing it; she passes all of the tests at school without doing homework. The *third* student comes from a home environment where caring for six younger siblings while his mother is at work is considered more important than homework. Consequently, he never

has the time to do school assignments. The *fourth* student hates school and all of her teachers. She also believes that they hate her (some actually do) and that homework is their way of making her life miserable; therefore, she refuses to do any. The *fifth* student simply can't remember to do it. This fellow sometimes has trouble remembering where his classroom is. Despite having the ability, the *sixth* student doesn't expect to succeed at the tasks she's given for homework. Since she also believes that it's awful when you don't succeed, she tends to give up easily and consequently completes few homework assignments. The *seventh* student is so disorganized that he often loses his homework assignments, while the *eighth* student spends so much of the time daydreaming in school she doesn't even know she's supposed to do any homework. Since the *ninth* student considers doing homework "uncool" ("only nerds do it"), he never does any. Finally, the *tenth* student is such a perfectionist that she does her homework assignments over and over until she gets so frustrated and confused that she quits in disgust. Consequently, she turns in assignments late or unfinished or tries to avoid doing homework altogether.

As you can see, all of these students engage in the same behavior for different reasons. However, their teacher doesn't know this. When he complains to his colleagues in the faculty room, they tell him he isn't being tough enough. They tell him he needs to implement some powerful aversive consequences such as failing grades, detention, and phone calls home. While his colleagues may not be card-carrying behaviorists, they are looking at the problem from the same point of view: They believe that behavior is shaped and maintained by its consequences. They may not even know what negative reinforcement is, but they are certainly advocating it as the intervention of choice. They believe that if you make the consequences of not doing homework aversive enough, the students will do the homework in order to avoid the aversive consequences.

Let's imagine that our teacher is desperate enough to take his peers' advice and decides to get tough. He announces to his class that from now on, students will receive a zero for each homework assignment not turned in and that the zeros will be included in determining their final grade. Since this situation is hypothetical, I can make it come out any way I want. Still, I feel safe in predicting that the teacher's "get tough" policy won't solve his problem with this group of students. To begin with, all the zeros in the world won't motivate the first student to turn in his homework as long as he doesn't know how to do it. What it does do is motivate him to copy another student's homework on the school bus and turn it in as his own. This student really needs remedial instruction for his academic weaknesses and/or some adaptation of his homework assignments to take advantage of what academic strengths he has.

The second student will probably change her behavior now that homework counts towards the final grade. Still, it wouldn't hurt to make the homework assignments more interesting so she would be intrinsically motivated to do them. Nothing is going to help the third student as long as he doesn't have the time to do school work at home. Survival is the major motivator here. His single-parent mom has to work so the family can survive, and child care is too expensive. This student is another casualty of poverty. If arrangements can't be made at home, arrangements need to be made at school such as allowing him an extra study hall or letting him do homework during homeroom or in this teacher's class. The fourth student views the zeros as proof that "school sucks" and that "teachers are the enemy." She continues to boycott homework and suffers the zeros in silent rage. Rather than punishment, she needs a program in cognitive restructuring to help her challenge and dispute her irrational and counterproductive thinking about school and teachers.

The zeros might motivate the fifth student, but only if his memory problem is related to a lack of motivation. We all have selective memory on occasion—we remember to do the things we like doing and conveniently forget the nasty stuff. Student number five enters his house after school, gets a Coke from the fridge, goes to the family room, turns on the TV, and spaces out for six hours. When he finally acknowledges he has homework to do, it's too late. Is this loss of memory or loss of motivation? Maybe the

threat of failure is enough to motivate him; maybe not. Maybe he needs a self-management program. What he definitely needs is a new behavior chain. Instead of enter house → go to kitchen → get Coke from fridge → go to family room → turn on TV → lie down on couch, he needs to: enter house → go to designated study area (e.g., kitchen table) → set timer → work on homework until timer rings → reward self with snack from fridge → reset timer → work on homework until timer rings → reward self with brief free time, and so on until the homework is completed. We don't want him anywhere near the TV until his homework is done.

Something has to be done about the sixth student's "I stink" thinking if she is going to do any homework. Because she believes she is stupid and is so afraid of failing, she procrastinates until it is too late to start her homework. The zeros only serve to confirm her beliefs. She needs some encouragement and a program in cognitive restructuring that will help her challenge and dispute her irrational thinking. The seventh student would be better off if he learned how to be more organized. As much as he wants to avoid those zeros, he won't be very successful as long as he keeps misplacing his assignments. He needs to be taught a system that will help him stay on top of his school work. At the very least, he should be given an assignment book to keep track of assignments. The eighth student needs some positive reinforcement for being on task *in school.* The zeros aren't going to motivate her to do schoolwork at home as long as she spaces out at school. She needs a self-management program to use at school that will help her pay attention in class. She could even use brief periods of daydreaming as a reward.

As long as the ninth student considers it uncool to succeed—or even try—at school, he won't change. He "wears" his zeros with pride. He needs a program in cognitive restructuring to help him challenge and dispute the irrational belief that acting like a student is uncool. Like some of the other students, he suffers from low self-esteem and, consequently, feels he needs to go along with the herd mentality at school that says you have to fail to be popular. The tenth student doesn't need the threat of a failing grade to motivate her. If anything, she is overly motivated. She could benefit from some cognitive restructuring as well as some stress management to help alleviate the anxiety and frustration she experiences in trying to be perfect.

The moral of this story is: Don't assume all behavior has a common cause, and never try to fix something if you don't know what's wrong with it. Behavior modification is very effective but it is not a panacea. More often than not, if you want to solve a behavior problem, some form of diagnosis is necessary.

☑ **Checkpoint 4.1**

[pages 89–91]

Fill in the answers to the following items (1–8). Check your responses by referring to the text; relevant page numbers appear in brackets.

According to the author, behaviorists tend to be uncomfortable with diagnosis because

(1) _____
_____
_____
_____[89].

The author tends to be critical of the behaviorist view of diagnosis because

(2) _____
_____
_____
_____
_____[89].

Assume that you are a high school English teacher and that several of your students come to class late. List six different reasons why students might be tardy to your class.

(3) _____
_____

(4) _____
_____

(5) _____
_____

(continues)

CHECKPOINT 4.1, continued

(6) _____
_____

(7) _____
_____

(8) _____
_____

Redo any items you missed. If you missed more than 2 of the items, reread the material. Otherwise, continue on to the next section.

BEST DIAGNOSTIC PRACTICES

There are many ways to diagnose a behavior problem. What's the best way? While that question is open for debate, in my opinion the best methods are those used easily by teachers with little or no special training in assessment. Teachers should not have to refer their students to a higher authority every time they need to diagnose a behavior problem. This takes time, and teachers are sometimes self-conscious about how many students they refer for help. We want our students to be self-reliant; why shouldn't we expect the same from ourselves? In addition to being easy to use, the best diagnostic methods provide teachers with reasonably reliable data they can use to design effective interventions. (Test data that tell you what is wrong but give no clues as to how to fix it are, in my judgment, worthless.) Functional analysis (O'Neill, Horner, Albin, Storey, & Sprague, 1990; Sugai & Colvin, 1989b) and prerequisite modification (Pre-Mod) analysis (Kaplan & Kent, 1983) are two diagnostic methods that can be used by teachers with very little training. They also provide reliable data that can be used to design interventions. Let's take a closer look at each method.

Functional Analysis

Functional analysis is based on applied behavioral analysis (ABA). ABA is defined as "the extension of experimental methods to applied settings" (Kazdin, 1994, p. 25). The primary focus of ABA is on overt behavior rather than "covert" behavior such as thoughts and feelings. Therefore, the primary focus of a functional analysis is on the behavior of the target student and those observable environmental stimuli that precede and follow it.

The first step in completing a functional analysis is to observe the student engaging in the offending behavior so you can identify the antecedents and consequences of that behavior. You want to know what happens immediately before and after the behavior occurs. Second, you hypothesize which antecedent and/or consequence is most likely influencing the behavior. Sugai and Colvin (1989b) refer to such a hypothesis as the "testable explanation"— you *think* it is the cause but you need to test it to be sure. Third, you test this hypothesis by making changes in one or more of the antecedents and/or consequences and watching for any concomitant change in the offending behavior. If a desired change in behavior occurs, you know you manipulated the correct variable. If a desired change does not occur, you manipulate a different set of antecedents and/or consequences. While this may sound like simple trial and error, functional analysis is actually quite effective when used by someone who has a thorough understanding of behavioral principles (i.e., positive and negative reinforcement, punishment, and extinction). The following are examples of how the process might work.

Joey is a student in Mr. Howell's class who calls out whenever he wants attention. This usually works because whenever Joey calls out, Mr. Howell looks at him, listens to him, and/or speaks to him. Sometimes the attention is as brief as a glance and sometimes Mr. Howell talks to Joey. Either way, Joey gets Mr. Howell's attention. Mr. Howell finds Joey's calling-out behavior aversive but doesn't know what to change or how to change it. He believes there is something wrong with Joey and refers him for special education evaluation. A member of the pre-referral team attends Mr. Howell's class and completes an S-R-S form on Joey's behavior during independent seatwork when the calling out seems to be the worst (see Figure 4.1). After analyzing the data on the S-R-S form, it is hypothesized that Mr. Howell is positively reinforcing Joey's calling-out behavior by consequating it with his attention. To test this hypothesis, Mr. Howell is told to ignore Joey's calling out: no looking, no listening, no speaking. Data are subsequently collected on Joey's behavior and they indicate that the calling out has gotten worse instead of better. Joey's calling out not only increased in frequency, it got louder. Since this is what typically happens when a *known reinforcer* is withheld, it appears that the hypothesis has been validated. Joey's calling-out behavior is caused by Mr. Howell's attending to it. The intervention requires that Mr. Howell ignore Joey when he calls out and attend to him only when he raises his hand and waits to be called on. After several days of the intervention, Joey's calling-out behavior begins to weaken and is slowly but surely replaced by hand raising and waiting.

Not all behavior is shaped and maintained by its consequences. Some behavior is triggered by its antecedents. For example, Nicole is a severely handicapped student in Mr. Ross' class who often engages in self-stimulating ("stimming") behavior such as rocking, head tapping and hand flapping. On occasion, this behavior occurs with greater frequency and with more intensity. In order to eliminate this behavior, Mr. Ross needs to determine what, if any, environmental events are maintaining it. He completes an S-R-S form (see Figure 4.2), and after analyzing the data hypothesizes that the self-stimming is caused by staff requests to terminate one activity and begin another; transitions appear to be stressful for Nicole and the stress is manifested in her rocking, head tapping, and hand flapping. To test his hypothesis, Mr. Ross conducts the following experiment. For one hour, he lets Nicole engage in whatever activities she wishes without any directives to terminate and begin a new activity. He monitors the frequency and intensity of her self-stimming during this first sixty minutes without any imposed transitions. During the second sixty minutes, Mr. Ross imposes transitions on Nicole every ten minutes. Again, he monitors the frequency and intensity of her rocking, head tapping, and hand flapping, and the data validate his hypothesis. The frequency and intensity of Nicole's self-stimming during the second hour is significantly greater than that of the first hour. Mr. Ross uses this information to design an intervention. He teaches Nicole, who has limited expressive language, how to sign her displeasure ("No. I don't want to.") and provides her with early warnings so she has time to adjust to the idea of a transition. The initial results of his intervention are encouraging.

Functional analysis requires the following teacher competencies:

1. be able to observe and record the behavior in a given situation in which there is a behavior problem on an S-R-S form;

2. be able to analyze the situation and identify antecedents, behaviors, and consequences;

Student: Joey	Teacher: Mr. Howell	Date: March 1995

Behavior: calling out without raising hand and waiting to be called on

Setting Events: in classroom during social studies lesson; rule is to raise hand and wait for permission to speak

S	R	S
T asks, "what is the capital of Oregon?"	J calls out "Portland"	"No. It's not Portland."
C (consequence)	J calls out "Beaverton?"	Looks at J and shakes head no
C	J calls out "Washington"	Looks at J; puts finger to lips; says "Shhh. Joey, raise your hand."
C	J raises his hand	T calls on Mary who raised her hand and gives correct answer ("Salem"); T praises Mary
C	J calls out "I was gonna say Salem. You didn't call on me."	"Joey. Please raise your hand."
C	"I did raise my hand."	"I'm talking about right now."
C	"I did raise my hand."	"Now just be quiet. I don't want to hear another word."

Figure 4.1. S-R-S form completed for Joey.

Student: **Nicole**	Teacher: **Mr. Ross**	Date: **Feb. 1995**

Behavior: **self-stimming (e.g., rocking, head tapping, hand flapping)**

Setting Events: **in classroom with teacher or aide present; Nicole working on task at her desk**

S	R	S
	N puts puzzle pieces together; no self-stimming	T watches
C	N continues working on puzzle; no self-stim	T asks N to put puzzle away
C	N begins to self-stim	T repeats request
C	more self-stimming	T takes away puzzle
C	more intense self-stimming	T watches
C	self-stimming continues	T presents peg board
C	self-stimming continues	T watches
C	self-stimming decreases	T watches
C	N "sifts" pegs	T puts few pegs on peg board
C	N picks up peg; sniffs it; tastes it	T puts peg in peg board
C	N puts peg in peg board	T watches

Figure 4.2. S-R-S form completed for Nicole.

3. be able to produce a testable explanation or hypothesis that might explain the cause of the behavior problem;

4. be able to manipulate the variables (e.g., antecedents and/or consequences) in order to test the hypothesis; and

5. be able to interpret the results of the test (i.e., evaluate the effects on behavior).

Two of the better resources on functional analysis are *Environmental Explanations of Behavior: Conducting a Functional Analysis* (Sugai & Colvin, 1989b) and *Functional Analysis of Problem Behavior: A Practical Assessment Guide* (O'Neill, Horner, Albin, Storey, & Sprague, 1990).

Functional analysis can often be a valid and efficient method for diagnosing the cause of a maladaptive behavior. However, the success of functional analysis is still predicated on the theory that all maladaptive behavior is caused by inappropriate antecedents and/or consequences. We know that human behavior is more complex than that. Let's go back to the case of Joey and Mr. Howell. What if Joey's calling-out behavior is not the result of inappropriate consequences? What if it actually is caused by impulsivity which he currently has difficulty controlling? If Joey acts on impulse, without reflecting on the consequences of his actions, changing the consequences is not likely to influence his behavior. People who act impulsively typically have difficulty reflecting on the consequences of their actions. They act first and think about the consequences afterward. The question is, would a functional analysis like the one conducted by Mr. Howell tell him whether or not Joey is impulsive? Probably not. What if, instead of (or in addition to) being impulsive, Joey is anxious and feels he needs constant assurance that everything is OK? What if he believes that he should be the center of attention and doesn't want to share Mr. Howell's attention with anyone else? What if he enjoys disrupting the learning environment? What if Joey doesn't know any other way to obtain teacher attention than to call out? Each of these could be a testable explanation for Joey's behavior. Unfortunately, the functional analysis simply tells you what happens before and after a behavior. It doesn't tell you anything about internal states or traits in the target student or in anyone else involved. Do you remember Bandura's theory of reciprocal determinism—personal variables, behavior, and environment? The functional analysis tells you about the behavior (response) and the environment (antecedent and consequence) but it tells you

nothing about the personal variables of the individual(s) involved in the behavior problem. What cognitions and emotions influence Joey's behavior? What cognitions and emotions influence Mr. Howell's response to Joey's behavior?

Functional analysis may not provide you with information regarding the personal variables that contribute to a behavior problem, but it is still a good place to begin your diagnosis. Because it is relatively easy to use, I recommend that you start with a functional analysis and, if you are not satisfied with the results, go on to a more comprehensive approach such as Pre-Mod analysis. (Pre-Mod techniques are described in the following section.) A good way to compare the two is to think of the following analogy: Functional analysis is to Pre-Mod analysis as behaviorism is to social learning theory.

☑ Checkpoint 4.2

[pages 91–95]

Fill in the answers to the following items (1–12). Check your responses by referring to the text; relevant page numbers appear in brackets.

According to the author, the best methods for diagnosing behavior problems meet the following criteria:

(1) _____

_____

(2) _____

_____ [91]

Describe each of the steps in the functional analysis:

(3) _____

_____

(4) _____

_____

(5) _____

_____ [92]

(continues)

Pre-Mod Analysis

Several years ago, my colleagues and I wrote a book called *Evaluating Exceptional Children: A Task Analysis Approach* (Howell, Kaplan, & O'Connell, 1979). As the title implies, a major portion of the text is devoted to an educational diagnostic process we refer to as the task analytical model. The underlying premise of this model is: If a student does not engage in behavior deemed desirable by the school, he probably lacks one or more of the prerequisites necessary to engage in that behavior. For example, if a student has difficulty computing a simple addition problem correctly, you might assume he is unable to (a) comprehend operation signs, (b) read numerals, (c) demonstrate knowledge of add facts, (d) write numerals, or (e) perform any of these tasks combined. Once you determine which, if any, of these prerequisites the student is lacking, you will then know why he is experiencing difficulty with the task and what you need to do to remediate the deficit.

In a follow-up text, *Diagnosing Basic Skills: A Handbook for Deciding What to Teach* (Howell & Kaplan, 1980), we extended the application of the task analytical model to social as well as academic behavior problems. For example, if a student has difficulty interacting with peers without fighting, we might assume that she (a) doesn't understand the rule regarding fighting with peers, (b) isn't aware of when she is interacting with or without fighting, (c) is unable to control her anger to the extent that she can't stop herself from fighting, (d) doesn't know how to interact without fighting, (e) considers the consequences of fighting more rewarding (or less aversive) than the consequences of not fighting, and/or (f) engages in a style of thinking that is incompatible with interacting without fighting. Just as you did for the academic (computation) problem discussed above, you try to determine which, if any, prerequisites the student is lacking. Once you know which prerequisites are lacking, you know why the student is unable to interact with peers without fighting and you are in a position to remediate the problem.

The difficulty with applying the task analytical model to social behavior problems is obvious. It is much more difficult to task analyze a social behavior problem than an academic problem. What I have done is to identify six generic prerequisites that I believe are necessary to enable the student to engage in any social (target) behavior. Before going any further, let's examine each of these prerequisites with regard to its rationale, assessment, and modification. Think of each prerequisite as a personal variable of the student (or teacher or peer) that, interacting with behavior and environment, contributes to the behavior problem.

The Pre-Mod prerequisites

1. The student understands what behavior is expected of him. In other words, the student must understand the rules. Students with low cognitive ability, deficits in receptive language, or both may not understand all of the rules regarding classroom conduct, especially if they have not been carefully explained. In addition, some teachers may be inconsistent in enforcing their rules and provide students with mixed messages. Students who are confused about what behavior is expected of them are likely to have difficulty engaging in the expected behavior. (See Figure 4.3.)

To assess whether or not the student understands what behavior is expected of him, ask the student to tell you the rule regarding the behavior in his own words. For example, "What is the rule about doing your own work?" If the student has difficulty expressing himself verbally, have him identify the students in the class who are following the rule. If he does not know their names, point to a student and ask, "Is she following the rule?" He can simply nod yes or no. Do this without alerting the students in your classroom so that you have both examples and

not-examples of students who are following the rules. If necessary, use pictures (take Polaroids) of students who are and are not following the rules. The student should respond quickly and correctly, with little or no prompting. If he cannot do so, assume he is lacking this prerequisite and modify the deficit.

To modify the deficit to fulfill Prerequisite 1, simply teach the student the rule. Explain and model the maladaptive behavior as behavior he may not engage in and the target behavior as the behavior he is expected to engage in. Quiz the student when he enters your room or immediately prior to those situations when the maladaptive behavior is likely to occur (e.g., "What are you supposed to do if you want to answer a question?"). Remind the student (verbally) about the rules from time to time. Keep the rules posted somewhere in the classroom or on the student's desk to serve as reminders. Teach the rule until the student can meet the following objective: When asked what behavior is expected of him, the student will quickly and correctly state the behavior rule in his own words. He will do so with little or no prompting on at least two separate trials.

2. The student is aware of his behavior. Sometimes students become so habituated to their own behavior that they are often unaware of when they engage in it. (See Figure 4.4.) Students who frequently use profanity, talk out, or touch others inappropriately are often unaware of this behavior when they are engaging in it and it is only after someone else has brought the behavior to their attention that they become aware of it. Unfortunately, by that time, it is too late. In order for a student to consciously change his behavior he must be aware of it at the time he is engaging in it.

To assess the student's awareness of his behavior, have him self-monitor the behavior(s) in question. You monitor the student's behavior(s) at the same time. A detailed description of this procedure may be found in Chapter 9. There should be at least 80% agreement between data collected by the student and data collected by the teacher.

If there is less than 80% agreement, assume that the student is lacking this prerequisite and attempt to modify it.

The procedure for *modifying* Prerequisite 2 is the same as the procedure used for assessing it. Have the student monitor his own behavior while you do the same. Continue the intervention until the student is able to meet the following objective: When the student and the teacher monitor his behavior over a period of 3 days (trials), there should be no less than 80% agreement between them on each of the trials.

Figure 4.3. Does the student understand what behavior is expected?

Figure 4.4. Is the student aware of his behavior?

3. The student is able to bring his behavior under his control. There should be no factors such as intense emotions or impulsivity, currently beyond the student's control, that make it difficult (or impossible) for him to engage in the target behavior. (See Figure 4.5.) For example, poorly managed anger can contribute to verbally and physically aggressive behaviors, noncompliance, destruction of property, and disruption, among other behaviors. Students who experience situational or diffuse anxiety have difficulty being assertive. Poorly managed anxiety can also contribute to social isolation (fear of rejection) and noncompliance (fear of failure). Depression makes it difficult for students to attend school, complete assigned work, stay on task, comply with directives, and interact socially. Students with poor impulse control have difficulty engaging in a number of target behaviors that require reflection. Impulsivity can contribute to many behavior problems including noncompliance, aggression, off task, and destruction of property, among others.

To determine if there are any intense emotions (e.g., anger, anxiety, depression) currently beyond the student's control that might influence his behavior, you can use one of the standardized self-report measures cited in Chapter 13, collect data via direct observation of the student's behavior, or do both. Using both assessment methods provides more reliable data. However, if you are only able to use one of the approaches, I recommend direct observation of student behavior. This requires collecting data on the frequency and/or intensity of the behavioral correlates of an emotional state. For example, if you suspect poorly managed anxiety is making it difficult for the student to engage in the target behavior, monitor (i.e., observe and record) the frequency and intensity of the behavioral correlates (i.e., characteristics or symptoms) of anxiety. These correlates are listed along with those for anger and depression in Figure 4.6. Monitor the correlates of anxiety in the target student and in a few randomly selected peers. (Refer to Chapter 7 for a detailed description of the procedures used to monitor both the frequency and intensity of behaviors.) After collecting the data, compare the target-student data with peer data to see if the target student displays correlates of anxiety with greater frequency and/or greater intensity than his peers. If anxiety is not contributing to the target student's behavioral problem, there should be no appreciable difference between the target student and his peers.

Remember that neither the direct observation nor the self-report measure alone is nearly as reliable as using both forms of assessment. If possible, begin with the direct observation of behavioral correlates over a 3-day period and, if the data suggest a problem, follow up with the self-report measure. If one or both of these measures suggest a problem with anxiety, assess whether or not the target student currently has the coping skills and knowledge necessary to manage his anxiety. Ask him to describe two things he does (or could do) to keep his anxiety under control. He should be able to describe two acceptable coping strategies quickly and with little or no prompting. Acceptable strategies include, but are not limited to, activities such as talking to oneself or others, engaging in an alternative activity, thought stopping, or somatic relaxation (e.g., deep breathing). You should be trying to determine if (a) the student doesn't know how to manage his emotions or (b) he knows how but chooses not to. If he doesn't know how, he needs to be taught stress management skills (see Chapter 13). If he knows how to manage his anxiety but chooses not to, he might profit from a self-management program (see Chapter 9). An

Figure 4.5. Is the student able to control his behavior?

example of a performance objective for this prerequisite is: There will be no significant difference between the target student and his peer group with regard to the frequency and/or intensity of anxiety when both the target student and peers are monitored for the behavioral correlates of anxiety.

The assessment procedures discussed above can also be used to measure impulse control. Again, begin by monitoring the behavioral correlates of impulsivity (see Figure 4.6) in the target student and in randomly selected peers. With impulsivity, I would be more concerned about frequency than intensity of response. You may want to follow up your direct observation with a pencil and paper measure such as the *Self-Control Rating Scale* (Kendall & Wilcox, 1979), the revised *Conners Parent Rating Scale* (Goyette, Conners, & Ulrich, 1978), or the Matching Familiar Figures Test (Kagan, 1966). If one or both measures suggest a problem with impulsivity, interview the target student to determine whether or not he knows how to manage his impulsive behavior. If he doesn't know how, teach him (the cognitive-behavioral strategies in Chapter 11 would be most appropriate). If he knows how to manage his impulsivity but chooses not to, consider putting him on a self-management program (see Chapter 9).

Impulsivity and emotions such as anxiety, anger, and depression are two types of "control" factors

that can influence student behavior. They are not the only ones. Sensory impairment such as hearing or vision loss can also influence behavior. A student with hearing loss may have difficulty complying with directives if she doesn't always hear them, and a student with a vision problem may have difficulty completing tasks. Students with neurological conditions such as Tourette's syndrome or Attention Deficit Disorder also typically have difficulty controlling their behavior. Other control factors include health problems (e.g., asthma, allergies, hypo- or hyperglycemia) as well as the effects of medication taken by the student. Fetal alcohol syndrome certainly makes it difficult for students to control their behavior as does direct substance abuse. Most of these factors can be assessed through a careful interview with family and/or physician, perusal of the student's health records, direct observation of behavior, or a combination of any of these methods. Interventions will typically require the involvement of individuals outside of the classroom such as the school nurse, the student's physician, the student's family, or professional counselors, among others.

4. The student knows how to engage in the target behavior. If the target behavior is completing work assignments, the student must know how to do the work. If the target behavior is being assertive with

Anger

heightened frequency or intensity of aggressive behavior (e.g., punching, slapping, pushing, kicking, spitting, cursing, yelling, teasing, threats)

temper tantrums

changes in speech (e.g., disfluencies) or quality and tone of voice (e.g., shrill or low)

facial expressions (looks angry)

verbalizations ("I'm angry!")

movement of extremities (e.g., arm and hand waving)

gestures and posture (e.g., hand banging, table banging, fist clenching, hands on hips, arms folded across chest)

Anxiety

speech disturbances/speech disfluencies (e.g., corrections, "ahs," "uhs," mispronunciations, incomplete words)

quality and tone of voice (e.g., shrill or low)

rate of speech (e.g., marked acceleration or deceleration)

synchrony between verbal and nonverbal behaviors (occur simultaneously)

verbalizations (e.g., "This is scary")

movement (e.g., pacing back and forth)

orientation of eyes or head (e.g., changes frequently)

self-manipulations (e.g., touching face, wringing hands)

facial expressions (looks scared or anxious)

gestures and posture (e.g., "defensive" movements of hands)

number of questions asked regarding performance or security of individual increases

Depression

slowed rate of speech

number of verbal behaviors directed toward others (decreases)

verbalizations (e.g., "This is hopeless")

range of interactions with others decreases

number of positive reactions versus negative reactions

action latency—speed with which the student responds to another's reaction is slow

activity level (decreases)

voice volume (decreases)

eye contact (less)

affect—facial expression (flat or sad)

head aversions (head oriented away from person speaking)

smiling (limited)

Impulsivity

acts without reflecting on his/her actions (student shows sincere remorse after engaging in maladaptive behavior)

starts tasks before getting all directions/relevant information from teacher

action latency—speed with which student responds to another's reaction is quick

tendency to perseverate on tasks with select-response format (selects same answer over and over again)

manifests obvious impatience when required to wait

Figure 4.6. Behavioral correlates of emotional states that typically contribute to maladaptive behavior.

his peers, he must know what to say and do to be assertive. If the target behavior is asking for help instead of giving up or having a tantrum when he becomes frustrated, the student must know how to ask. Whatever it is that you want the student to do, he must know how to do it. Don't be too quick to say, "Oh, he knows how." If he has been engaging in the maladaptive behavior for years, it is likely that he hasn't had much practice in engaging in the target behavior. Students come from different environments and have different skills. Teachers cannot make the assumption that all students know how to engage in the same wide variety of behaviors. If students don't do what you want them to, they may not know how.

If the target behavior is a social skill, you can assess prerequisite four using the methods described in Chapter 10 and/or use the informal role-play procedure described below. Have the student role play the behavior in question. Say "Let's pretend I walk up to you on the playground and start calling you names. You are supposed to act assertive with me. *Show me* how you would act assertive." Then commence the role play. Encourage the student to act out (demonstrate) the social skill in question rather than merely explaining to you what he would do. Use more than just one or two different scenarios, so the student has the opportunity to demonstrate the social skill under different conditions. Figure 4.7 describes three role plays that might be used to assess a student's assertive behavior. The student should be able to demonstrate the social skill quickly and correctly, without prompting, in each role play. If he cannot do so, assume he is lacking this prerequisite and modify the deficit. Strategies for the modification of deficits involving Prerequisite 4 may be found in Chapter 10. The performance objective for this prerequisite is: When given a role play test, the student will correctly demonstrate the target behavior in three separate role plays. He will do so quickly and with little or no prompting.

5. *The student must consider the consequences of engaging in the target behavior more rewarding or less aversive than the consequences of engaging in the maladaptive behavior.* Some students engage in the target behavior so seldom (if ever) that they are virtually unaware that the target behavior can elicit positive consequences. Others might have engaged in the target behavior on occasion but their teachers, parents, or peer group have been inconsistent in rewarding them when they did. For this reason they may be unsure of the consequences of engaging in the target behavior.

Name _____ Date _____

Directions: Read everything in upper case to students. I WANT YOU TO ROLE PLAY WITH ME WHAT YOU SHOULD SAY AND DO FOR EACH OF THE FOLLOWING SITUATIONS. Encourage the student to *show you* (i.e., model)—rather than explain to you—what s/he should say and do. *In each case,* the student should model either ignoring behavior (e.g., he does not look at or speak to you but continues doing whatever he was doing at the time he was teased) or assertiveness (e.g., he tells you to "stop it" using a level but firm voice). Repeat your teasing several times and see if the student can continue to ignore or be assertive without being aggressive.

1. YOU ARE ON THE PLAYGROUND AND I COME UP TO YOU AND SAY, "HI, RETARD." SHOW ME WHAT YOU SHOULD DO. (Begin the role play)

2. YOU ARE WALKING IN THE HALL AND I PASS YOU AND MAKE FUN OF THE WAY YOU WALK. SHOW ME WHAT YOU SHOULD DO. (Begin the role play)

3. YOU ARE IN THE CLASSROOM AND YOU ASK THE TEACHER A QUESTION AND I SAY FOR EVERYBODY TO HEAR, "WHAT A DUMB QUESTION." SHOW ME WHAT YOU SHOULD DO. (Begin the role play)

Figure 4.7. Example of role play test to use in assessing Prerequisite 4 ("student knows how to").

In other cases, the student may know what happens when he engages in the target behavior but he doesn't consider the consequences particularly rewarding. His teachers, parents, or peer group may have a different perception than he does about what constitutes a reward. For example, gushing praise on an adolescent may actually be aversive to him. The opportunity to go out to recess after work is completed may not be rewarding to a student who is uncomfortable with his peers. If the student doesn't know the consequences of engaging in the target behavior or doesn't consider them rewarding, it is possible that he may not see any reason to behave as expected.

Conversely, it is important that the student know the consequences for engaging in the maladaptive behavior and that she consider them aversive. If she doesn't know what happens when she misbehaves, how can these consequences have any effect on her behavior? Teachers may be inconsistent in consequating misbehavior, or a particular student may be functioning at such a low developmental level that she has difficulty making the connection between what she does and what happens to her. Again, what seems aversive to the teacher may not seem aversive to the student. Therefore, it is possible that even if the student knows the consequences of her misbehavior, she may not consider them aversive enough to discontinue the behavior.

If you want the student to engage in the target behavior, she should not consider it aversive to do so. Or at least she should not consider the target behavior more aversive than engaging in the maladaptive behavior. For example, a student may be "punished" with a failing grade for not turning in her work assignments. However, because these assignments are too difficult for the student, she experiences a great deal of frustration in doing them. Each time she tries one, she gives up, thinking she's stupid. After a while, she simply stops doing them altogether. In this instance, the failing grade is not as aversive to the student as doing the work. Because the teacher considers the failing grade an aversive stimulus, the teacher thinks that the student is either lazy, crazy, or stupid because this stimulus seems to have no effect on her; the teacher doesn't realize that there may be something even more aversive to the student than the failing grade. There is also the possibility that the student finds the maladaptive behavior more rewarding than the target behavior. For example, a student may know that when she stays on task she earns tokens which she considers rewarding. However, she may also consider it rewarding to talk to her peers; because the reward of turning in the tokens earned is delayed until the end of the day and the reward of talking to peers is immediate, the latter often has more power to reinforce her behavior.

To assess Prerequisite 5, use a technique known as the *cue sort* (Howell, Fox, & Morehead, 1993; Stephenson, 1980). Begin by having the student tell you the consequences of the target behavior ("What happens when you raise your hand and wait to be called on?") and the maladaptive behavior ("What happens when you shout out without raising your hand and waiting?"). Write these down on 3" × 5" cards. Shuffle the cards and have the student sort the consequences (i.e., cards) into two piles: those consequences he likes and those he dislikes. If teacher and student share the same views about what is aversive and what is rewarding, the student can be expected to sort all of the consequences of the target behavior into the "like" pile and all of the consequences of the maladaptive behavior into the "don't like" pile. If the results of the cue sort indicate that the student doesn't consider all of the consequences of the target behavior more rewarding or less aversive than the consequences of the maladaptive behavior, assume he is lacking this prerequisite and attempt to modify the deficit.

First, teach the student the consequences of the maladaptive and target behaviors until he is able to name all of them quickly and with little or no prompting. Then use one of the techniques described in Chapter 5 (e.g., interest inventory, interview, observation) to identify the consequences of the target behavior. Refer to Chapter 6 for information regarding consequating maladaptive behavior. The performance objective for Prerequisite 5 is: Given a cue-sort exercise, the student will correctly name the consequences of the maladaptive and target behaviors. He will then sort (i.e., identify) all of the consequences of the target behavior as "like" and all of the consequences of the maladaptive behavior as "dislike" on two separate trials.

6. The student should not hold any belief that is incompatible with the target behavior.

Cognitive psychologists have long held the view that cognitions (particularly cognitive structures or beliefs) play an important role in influencing behavior. For example, if you want the student to complete his work assignments or to persist in the face of adversity instead of giving up, he must believe that there is a relationship between his behavior and what happens to him. If, instead, he believes that what hap-

pens to him is controlled by fate or chance, he may simply consider himself unlucky and give up.

The degree to which an individual believes he is able to influence the outcome of situations is referred to by social learning theorists as *locus of control* (Rotter, 1966). Students who believe they have little or no influence over the outcome of the situations in their lives are referred to as having an external locus of control; that is, the control comes from outside themselves. Such students believe that if something good happens to them they are favored by the teacher or lucky, and if something bad happens it's the teacher's fault or they are unlucky—"I don't do too good in her class 'cause she don't like me." Students who have external locus of control (and who are therefore referred to as "externals") may not only fail to internalize target behaviors, they may not even respond to extrinsic consequences since they are convinced that they have little control over the rewards and punishment they receive.

Locus of control is not the only belief that can influence the target behavior. Students who believe that "it's terrible if things don't go my way" may never learn to accept criticism. Others who believe that "school work is dumb" or "school is dumb" may continue to be truant or tardy, may come to class unprepared, and may simply not do their work.

The student who believes "it's terrible when I fail" may not do his work either. The student who believes "it's terrible if everybody doesn't like me" may continue to be the class clown and find it difficult to refrain from calling out or making faces during a group discussion. The student who believes "if people do things to me that I dislike, then they must be bad people" will have a hard time learning how to get along with his peers without acting physically or verbally aggressive toward them. Likewise, the student who believes "it's not macho to walk away from a fight" or "it's cool to beat up on guys" will have trouble staying out of fights. All of these students will have difficulty engaging in the target behavior because they hold a belief that is incompatible with it—a belief that either encourages them to engage in the maladaptive behavior or prevents them from engaging in the target behavior.

To assess the student's beliefs, you can use one or more of the standardized beliefs assessments cited in Chapter 11 or construct your own beliefs assessment based on the maladaptive and target behaviors for a specific student. The construction, standardization, and validation of beliefs assessments is discussed in detail in Chapter 11. Figure 4.8 is an example of a teacher-constructed beliefs assessment for a student who is noncompliant. To

Name _____ Date _____

Directions: Read each statement below and decide whether it is true or false. If you believe the statement is true, write the letter T on the line next to the number of the statement. If you think the statement is false, write the letter F. It is not necessary to think about each one for very long. Be honest. You are not going to be graded on this and no one but you and your teacher will ever see it. Don't answer the way you think your teacher might want you to or the way you think you are supposed to. You won't get into any trouble because of your answers so *answer the way you really believe.*

_____ 1. I'm a pretty good person.

_____ 2. I like school.

_____ 3. I have very little control over what happens to me at school.

_____ 4. My classmates like me.

_____ 5. School is hard.

_____ 6. It's important to learn how to follow directions.

_____ 7. Whether you like it or not, teacher is boss at school.

_____ 8. If at first you don't succeed, try, try again.

_____ 9. Everybody in this world has to follow directions sometimes.

_____ 10. School sucks.

_____ 11. I should not have to do anything I don't want to.

_____ 12. Rules are made to broken.

_____ 13. I hate being bossed around.

_____ 14. Getting an education is important.

_____ 15. Nobody should have the right to tell others what to do.

_____ 16. I have lots of friends.

_____ 17. People who do things I don't like are mean and should be punished.

_____ 18. All teachers are on a power trip.

_____ 19. It's cool to disobey the teacher.

_____ 20. It's OK to make mistakes.

_____ 21. Teachers usually want what is best for their students.

_____ 22. The rules at my school are not fair.

_____ 23. I'm old enough to do what I want.

_____ 24. I don't trust my teachers.

Figure 4.8. Example of beliefs assessment for student who is noncompliant.

pass this assessment, the student must answer "true" to all of the statements that are compatible with following a directive the first time it is given and "false" to all of the statements that are incompatible with this target behavior.

If a written beliefs assessment is inappropriate for use with your student, try a verbal approach. Ask

the student questions based on an appropriate beliefs assessment. He may be candid with you and reply honestly, but if he does not, try a third-person approach. Discuss a hypothetical student who engages in similar behavior and ask him questions about that student. If he won't cooperate, try having someone else ask the questions. And if he *still* won't cooperate, it is reasonable to assume he endorses a belief that is incompatible with the target behavior. If the student does cooperate but his responses suggest that he endorses even one belief that is incompatible with the target behavior, you should assume he is lacking this prerequisite and attempt to modify the deficit. Strategies for modification of Prerequisite 6 are discussed in depth in Chapter 11. The performance objective for this prerequisite is: When a beliefs assessment is administered, the student will label as *true* all beliefs that support the target behavior and will label as *false* all beliefs that support the maladaptive behavior. Assessment will be done using a test–retest format with alternate forms of the beliefs assessment administered over a 2-day period.

☑ **Checkpoint 4.3**

[pages 96–104]

Fill in the answers to the following items (1–7). Check your responses by referring to the text; relevant page numbers appear in brackets.

The underlying philosophy of the task analytical model, upon which Pre-Mod analysis is based, is:

(1) _____

_____

_____

_____

_____

_____ [96].

Name the six generic prerequisites necessary for most, if not all, social (target) behaviors along with a rationale for each prerequisite.

(2) _____

_____

_____

_____ [97].

(3) _____

_____

_____

_____ [97].

(continues)

CHECKPOINT 4.3, continued

(4) _____

_____

_____

_____

_____ [98–99].

(5) _____

_____

_____

_____

_____ [99–100].

(6) _____

_____

_____

_____

_____ [100–102].

(7) _____

_____

_____

_____

_____ [102–104].

Redo any items you missed. If you missed more than 1 of the items, reread the material. Otherwise, continue on to the next section.

How Pre-Mod works

There are four basic steps in Pre-Mod: (1) targeting, (2) task analyzing, (3) evaluating, and 4) interpreting. Figure 4.9 is a flowchart diagramming the steps in the process. Let's examine each step in more detail.

1. Targeting. The first step in the model is to identify and specify the target behavior. Techniques for doing this are explained in Chapter 3. Let's suppose you have a student named Rosario who hits peers when teased. Your fair-pair target behavior is "ignores peer teasing, or responds assertively (e.g., tells peers to stop and tells peers how he feels)." Figure 4.10 is an example of a Pre-Mod worksheet we will use with the hypothetical student.

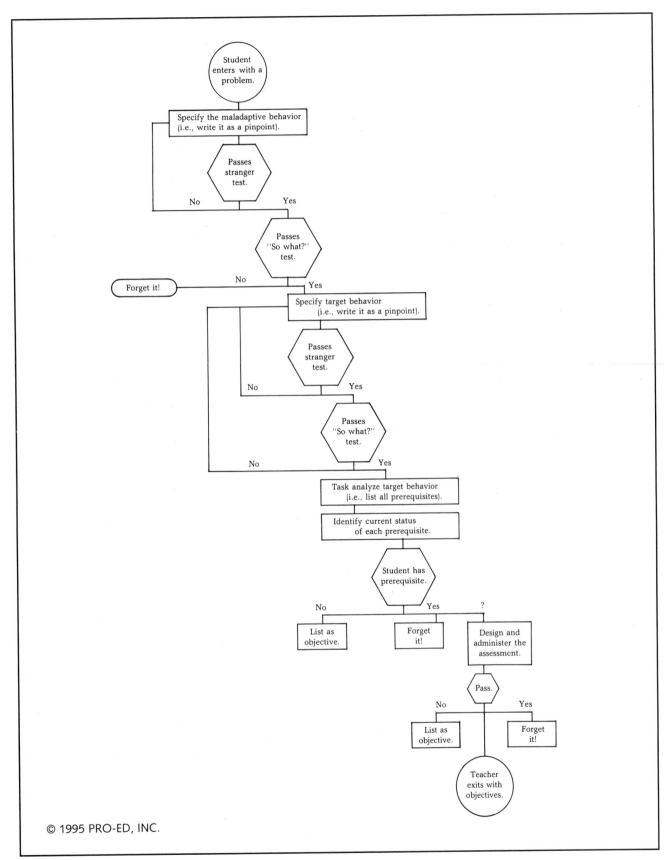

Figure 4.9. Flowchart outlining steps in prerequisite modification (Pre-Mod) analysis.

© 1995 PRO-ED, INC.

2. *Task Analyzing.* Once you have decided what behavior you want the student to engage in, task analyze it by listing all of the essential knowledge, skills, perceptions, expectations, values, and beliefs the student needs to successfully engage in the target behavior. Using the six generic prerequisites described above, you need to restate each prerequisite so that it is specific to your target behavior. For example, the first generic prerequisite is "knows and understands what behavior is expected." This is restated as "Rosario knows and understands that he is supposed to ignore peer teasing or respond to it assertively." The second generic prerequisite, "is aware of own behavior," is restated as "Rosario is aware of when he is responding to peer teasing by fighting, ignoring, or being assertive." The third prerequisite, "is able to control own behavior," is restated as "there are no emotional factors (e.g., anger) currently beyond Rosario's control that prohibit him from ignoring peer teasing or responding to it assertively."

Restate Prerequisite 4, "knows how to behave," as "Rosario knows how to ignore peer teasing or respond to it assertively." The fifth prerequisite, "considers consequences of target behavior more rewarding (or less aversive) than consequences of maladaptive behavior," is restated as "Rosario considers consequences of ignoring peer teasing or responding to it assertively more rewarding (or less aversive) than consequences of responding to peer teasing aggressively." Restate the sixth prerequisite, "engages only in thinking that is compatible with the target behavior," as "Rosario engages only in thinking that is compatible with ignoring peer teasing or responding assertively to peer teasing." These prerequisites have been written on Rosario's worksheet in Figure 4.11. More examples of generic prerequisites restated for specific target behaviors are shown in Figure 4.12.

Checkpoint 4.4 follows Figures 4.10, 4.11, and 4.12, on p. 110.

Student: **Rosario**   Evaluator: **Mr. Howell**   Date: **Jan. '95**

Maladaptive Pinpoint: **hits peers when teased**

Target Pinpoint: **ignores peer teasing or responds assertively (e.g., tells them to stop and how he feels)**

Prerequisites	Status	Assessments	Results

Figure 4.10.   Pre-Mod worksheet for Rosario: the targeting stage.

Student: __Rosario__   Evaluator: __Mr. Howell__   Date: __Jan. '95__

Maladaptive Pinpoint: __hits peers when teased__

Target Pinpoint: __ignores peer teasing or responds assertively (e.g., tells them to stop and how he feels)__

, Prerequisites	Status	Assessments	Results
1. R understands he is supposed to ignore peer teasing or respond assertively			
2. R is aware of when he is responding to peer teasing by fighting, ignoring, and being assertive			
3. There are no emotional factors currently beyond R's control that prohibit him from ignoring or responding assertively to peer teasing			
4. R knows how to ignore teasing or respond assertively			
5. R considers the consequences of ignoring or responding assertively to peer teasing to be more rewarding (or less aversive) than responding aggressively			
6. R engages only in thinking that is compatible with ignoring or responding assertively to peer teasing			

Figure 4.11.   Pre-Mod worksheet for Rosario: the task analyzing stage.

Maladaptive Behavior: Does not comply with request; has to be told several times to do something before she complies.

Target Behavior: Complies with request first time given.
1. student understands she is supposed to comply with a request first time given
2. student is aware of when she is complying with a request first time given and when she is not
3. there are no emotional factors currently not under the student's control that prohibit her from complying with a request first time given
4. student knows how to comply with all requests given by teacher (i.e., she understands all requests and is able to follow them)
5. student considers the consequences of complying with a request first time given more rewarding (or less aversive) than the consequences of noncompliance
6. student only endorses beliefs that are compatible with complying with a request first time given

Maladaptive Behavior: Grabs/takes objects belonging to and/or being used by others without asking for and receiving permission first.

Target Behavior: Obtains objects in prosocial manner (i.e., with permission of owner/user).
1. student understands he is not supposed to take an object from owner/user unless he asks for and receives permission from that person first
2. student is aware of when he is obtaining object in prosocial and in antisocial manner (i.e., taking without asking and receiving permission first)
3. there are no emotional factors currently not under the student's control that prohibit him from obtaining objects in prosocial manner
4. student knows how to obtain objects in prosocial manner (i.e., knows who to ask and how to ask and wait for permission)
5. student considers consequences of obtaining objects in prosocial manner more rewarding (or less aversive) than the consequences of taking without asking/receiving permission first
6. student only endorses beliefs that are compatible with obtaining objects in prosocial manner

Maladaptive Behavior: Off task (i.e., looks away from work and/or engages in non–work-related activity).

Target Behavior: On task (i.e., looks at work, does work, talks to others about work).
1. student understands she is supposed to be on task (i.e., looking at or doing work or talking to others about work)
2. student is aware of when she is engaging in on- and off-task behavior
3. there are no emotional factors currently not under the student's control that prohibit her from being on task
4. student knows how to do work assigned and how to access help if needed
5. student considers consequences of being on task more rewarding (or less aversive) than being off task
6. student only endorses beliefs that are compatible with being on task

Maladaptive Behavior: Tantrums (e.g., screams, cries, hits self) to get own way.

Target Behavior: Negotiates to get what he wants but will accept "No" for an answer when negotiation is not an option.
1. student understands he is supposed to negotiate (and not tantrum) to get what he wants and to accept "No" when negotiation is not an option
2. student is aware of when he is negotiating, accepting "No," and when he is tantrumming
3. there are no emotional factors currently not under the student's control that prohibit him from negotiating without tantrumming and accepting "No"
4. student knows how to negotiate to get what he wants
5. student considers the consequences of negotiating to get what he wants or accepting no without tantrumming more rewarding (or less aversive) than the consequences of tantrumming
6. student only endorses beliefs compatible with negotiating to get what he wants or accepting "No" when negotiating is not an option

Figure 4.12.   Generic prerequisites restated for specific target behaviors.

✔ Checkpoint 4.4

[pages 104–109]

Fill in the answers to the following items (1–10). Check your responses by referring to the text; relevant page numbers appear in brackets.

Restate each of the generic prerequisites listed below so that it is specific to the following target behavior: "Student will attend school on a regular basis."

(1) student knows what he is supposed to do:

_____

_____

_____

(2) student is aware of his behavior:

_____

_____

_____

(3) student is able to control his behavior:

_____

_____

_____

(4) student knows how to engage in target behavior:

_____

_____

_____

_____

(continues)

CHECKPOINT 4.4, continued

(5) student considers consequences of target behavior more rewarding (or less aversive) than consequences of maladaptive behavior:

_____

_____

_____

_____

(6) student only engages in thinking compatible with target behavior:

_____

_____

_____

_____ [106, 108, 109].

Restate each of the generic prerequisites listed below so that it is specific to the following target behavior: "Student will obtain property of others only after asking for and receiving permission to do so."

(7) student knows what she is supposed to do:

_____

_____

_____

_____.

(8) student is aware of her behavior:

_____

_____

_____

_____.

(continues)

CHECKPOINT 4.4, continued

(9) student is able to control her behavior:

_____

_____

_____

_____.

(10) student knows how to engage in target behavior:

_____

_____

_____

_____.

(11) student considers consequences of target behavior more rewarding (or less aversive) than consequences of maladaptive behavior:

_____

_____

_____

_____.

(12) student only engages in thinking compatible with target behavior:

_____

_____

_____

_____[106, 108, 109].

Redo any items you missed. If you missed more than 2 of the items, reread the material. Otherwise, continue on to the next section.

---

3. Evaluating. This stage of Pre-Mod analysis requires that you determine whether or not the student currently has the prerequisites you identified in Stage 2. This can be based on your past experiences with the student (assuming you know her well enough) without formal assessment or, when in doubt, it can be based on an informal assessment. *Remember, you need to use an informal assessment only if you are in doubt about the current status of the*

prerequisite. The following are some basic assessment rules to be aware of.

a. If your student refuses to cooperate on an assessment or if you have reason to suspect the validity of his responses, assume that he lacks the prerequisite in question and act accordingly.

b. If your student has any difficulty responding to any assessment using a supply-response format (i.e., where he must *produce* the answer from memory), try switching to a select-response format (i.e., where he must *identify* the answer from among a group of answers). This way, all he has to do is answer "yes" or "no," give one- or two-word responses, or simply nod or shake his head. On the other hand, if the student has difficulty with receptive language (e.g., a reading deficit), try having him listen to the question(s) instead of reading them. Again, be flexible and don't hesitate to improvise when necessary.

c. Try to impress upon the student the importance of responding honestly (i.e., telling how he really feels), especially on the subjective measures used in assessing some of the prerequisites (e.g., Prerequisites 5 and 6). Be sure he knows he will not be penalized in any way for his responses, and be sure you stick to that promise. Remember, your objective is to find out why the student behaves the way he does, not to lecture or sermonize. You are testing, not teaching. If you have any reason to believe your student is not responding honestly to an assessment in your presence, let him complete it on his own or have someone else administer it to him. Because attitudes are often influenced by mood, I suggest you assess Prerequisites 5 and 6 on more than one occasion with at least 24 hours between trials; since the student's moods are subject to change over time, you can increase the probability of collecting valid data by assessing his attitudes across time.

d. Always make sure the student understands the directions for an assessment by having him paraphrase them (not simply repeat them) before he participates in the assessment.

e. While there are no specific time limits (i.e., minutes or seconds) for many of the assessments, spontaneous responses are preferred over responses the student has time to think out; spontaneous responses are apt to be a more accurate reflection of how the student really thinks. Therefore, decide on an appropriate time limit based upon what you know about the student's ability to read, write, listen, etc.

f. Remember, the assessment methods and materials described in this chapter are offered as suggestions for those of you who might not have the time, experience, or inclination to develop your own. Use them as they are, or with modifications, or not at all. You may decide to use them simply as models to develop your own assessment methods and materials. The choice is yours.

g. Two things you can do to improve the validity of your student's responses are to give an assessment more than once and use as many different types of assessments as you can to evaluate the same prerequisite. This will not always be possible, due to time constraints and the lack of valid assessments available. Still, if there is more than one way to assess a prerequisite, and if you have the time, try using more than one assessment procedure. This is particularly important if you are assessing emotional states (Prerequisite 3). While you don't want to make this a long, drawn-out project, you do want valid assessment data; invalid data will lead to an unsuccessful intervention and you will inevitably need to use Pre-Mod again to diagnose the same maladaptive behavior at a later date.

h. Administering these assessments obviously requires cooperation from the target student. In cases where you are assessing the status of prerequisites for a student who is noncompliant, you may not get the cooperation needed to acquire valid data. By all means, try to enlist this cooperation. However, if the student does not cooperate, assume he does not have the prerequisite.

Now let's look at the specific methods and materials for assessing each of the Pre-Mod prerequisites. Again, we'll use Rosario as an example. Let's assume that, based on your experience with Rosario, you know he definitely has Prerequisite 1: He knows and understands that he is either supposed to ignore teasing or respond to it assertively. You know this because he has told you what he is supposed to do in the past when you have questioned him after a fight. (Teacher: "What are you supposed to do when somebody teases you?" Rosario: "Walk away or tell 'em to stop it.") You also know, based on your experience, that Rosario definitely is aware of his behavior. He knows when he is fighting and when he is walking away (ignoring) and telling them to stop it

(being assertive). This means he definitely has Prerequisite 2. You also know, based on your experience, that Rosario has an anger management problem. You have observed him display many of the behavioral correlates of anger frequently and with a high level of intensity. You also know that he does not know what to do to manage his anger. (Teacher: "What can you do to keep from getting angry?" Rosario: [shrugs shoulders] "I can't help it.") This means that Rosario is definitely lacking Prerequisite 3. What you don't know yet is whether or not Rosario has prerequisites 4, 5, and 6. At this point your worksheet should look like Figure 4.13.

To assess Prerequisite 4 ("knows how"), give Rosario a role play test. "Show me how you would ignore (or be assertive with) a classmate who is teasing you. I'll be the classmate. Ready?" Involve Rosario in at least three separate role plays where you require him to demonstrate (not just explain) how he would ignore or respond assertively to teasing. To adequately demonstrate ignoring, he should, with minimal prompting, exhibit any of the following behaviors: not look at you, not speak to you, walk away from you, or engage himself in another activity. To adequately demonstrate assertiveness, Rosario should, with minimal prompting, tell you to stop teasing him and/or say how he feels (e.g., "I don't like it when you do that."). Let's assume that, to your surprise, Rosario is able to demonstrate both skills for each role play. So far, Rosario has Prerequisites 1 ("knows rule"), 2 ("is aware"), and 4 ("knows how") but lacks Prerequisite 3 ("can control").

To assess Prerequisite 5 ("considers consequences rewarding," or "wants to"), use a cue sort technique. First, ask Rosario to name all the consequences of responding to teasing by fighting (e.g., "Tell me all the things that happen when you get into a fight with someone who teases you."). Write each consequence he names on a 3" × 5" card. He should name all relevant consequences; prompt him if necessary (e.g., "What else happens?"). Let's suppose he names "I get hurt," "they get hurt," "I get in trouble," "I get sent to the office," "you yell at me," and "I get detention." Next, ask him to name all the consequences of ignoring teasing or being assertive. After some prompting, he names "nobody gets hurt," "I don't get into trouble," and "I get my work done." You have a total of nine cards, each with a consequence on it. After shuffling the deck, you have him sort the cards into two piles: things he wants to happen, and things he doesn't want to happen. Assume that Rosario puts all the consequences of fights when teased into the pile of things he does not want to happen and all the consequences of ignores or

Student: **Rosario**   Evaluator: **Mr. Howell**   Date: **Jan. '95**

Maladaptive Pinpoint: **hits peers when teased**

Target Pinpoint: **ignores peer teasing or responds assertively (e.g., tells them to stop and how he feels)**

Prerequisites	Status	Assessments	Results
1. R understands he is supposed to ignore peer teasing or respond assertively	Y— has told me when questioned after a fight		
2. R is aware of when he is responding to peer teasing by fighting, ignoring, and being assertive	Y— same as above		
3. There are no emotional factors currently beyond R's control that prohibit him from ignoring or responding assertively to peer teasing	N— appears to have anger management problem; based on past observation		
4. R knows how to ignore teasing or respond assertively	?		
5. R considers the consequences of ignoring or responding assertively to peer teasing to be more rewarding (or less aversive) than responding aggressively	?		
6. R engages only in thinking that is compatible with ignoring or responding assertively to peer teasing	?		

Figure 4.13.   Pre-Mod worksheet for Rosario: the evaluation stage, without assessments.

responds assertively into the pile of things he wants to happen. So far, Rosario has Prerequisites 1, 2, 4, and 5 but lacks Prerequisite 3.

To assess Prerequisite 6 ("he believes"), give Rosario the pencil and paper beliefs assessment shown in Figure 4.14. Rosario's answers should not reflect any beliefs incompatible with ignoring or being assertive. He does not pass this assessment. When you administer the assessment again after a 24-hour delay, his answers are the same. You conclude that he endorses beliefs incompatible with ignoring or being assertive which, in fact, probably contribute to his anger (e.g., "people who do things I don't like are bad and should be punished," "I am the way I am and I can't change."). The final tally shows Rosario has Prerequisites 1, 2, 4, and 5 but is lacking Prerequisites 3 and 6. The completed evaluation form is shown in Figure 4.15 (see p. 116).

Your evaluation yielded the following facts: Rosario understands that he is supposed to ignore, or respond assertively to, teasing; he is aware of when he is fighting, ignoring, or being assertive in response to teasing; he knows how to ignore and respond assertively to teasing; and he considers the consequences of ignoring or responding to teasing more rewarding than the consequences of fighting. On the other hand, Rosario is not able to manage his anger when he is teased and he engages in thinking that is incompatible with ignoring or responding assertively. Now you are ready for the last step in the Pre-Mod analysis.

Checkpoint 4.5 follows Figures 4.14 and 4.15, on p. 117.

PA/PROV

Name _Rosario_   Date _January 1995_

Directions: Read each statement below and decide whether it is true or false. If you believe the statement is true, write the letter T on the line next to the number of the statement. If you think it is false, write the letter F on the line. It is not necessary to think about each one for very long. Be honest. You are not going to be graded on this and no one but you and your teacher will ever see it. Don't answer the way you think your teacher might want you to or the way you think you are supposed to. You won't get into any trouble because of your answers so answer the way you really believe.

__T__ 1. I like school.

__T__ 2. People who do things I don't like are bad and should be punished.

__T__ 3. If at first you don't succeed, try, try again.

__T__ 4. Anybody who lets people make fun of them is a wimp.

__F__ 5. The best thing to do when somebody teases you is to tell them how you feel about it.

__F__ 6. I hate school.

__F__ 7. The best thing to do when somebody teases you is to ignore it.

__F__ 8. I am the way I am and I can't change.

__T__ 9. The best thing to do when somebody teases you is to fight with them.

__T__ 10. I never get into trouble at school.

__F__ 11. The worst thing to do when somebody teases you is to tell them how you feel about it.

__F__ 12. Nobody likes me.

__T__ 13. If you ignore somebody when they tease you, they'll think you're afraid and keep on teasing you.

__F__ 14. The worst thing to do when somebody teases you is to fight with them.

__T__ 15. As long as I like myself, it doesn't matter what other people say about me.

__F__ 16. If you ignore somebody when they tease you, they will probably get tired of teasing you and stop.

__F__ 17. If you tell somebody who is teasing you how you feel about it, they will probably stop doing it.

__T__ 18. The worst thing to do when somebody teases you is to ignore it.

__F__ 19. If people say bad things about me, they must be true.

__T__ 20. Two wrongs don't make a right. Just because somebody picks on you is no reason to pick on them.

__T__ 21. People should try to get along with each other instead of fighting.

__F__ 22. Lots of people like me.

__T__ 23. Not fighting is a sign of weakness.

__T__ 24. It's OK if somebody doesn't like you. Not everybody is going to like you.

__F__ 25. I like to fight.

Figure 4.14. Beliefs assessment: Rosario's responses regarding physical aggression with provocation.

Student: **Rosario**   Evaluator: **Mr. Howell**   Date: **Jan. '95**

Maladaptive Pinpoint: **hits peers when teased**

Target Pinpoint: **ignores peer teasing or responds assertively (e.g., tells them to stop and how he feels)**

Prerequisites	Status	Assessments	Results
1. R understands he is supposed to ignore peer teasing or respond assertively	Y— has told me when questioned after a fight		
2. R is aware of when he is responding to peer teasing by fighting, ignoring, and being assertive	Y— same as above		
3. There are no emotional factors currently beyond R's control that prohibit him from ignoring or responding assertively to peer teasing	N — appears to have anger management problem; based on past observation		
4. R knows how to ignore teasing or respond assertively	? Y	role play test; 3/3 correct	3/3 correct [pass]
5. R considers the consequences of ignoring or responding assertively to peer teasing to be more rewarding (or less aversive) than responding aggressively	? Y	cue sort; 100%	100% [pass]
6. R engages only in thinking that is compatible with ignoring or responding assertively to peer teasing	? N	beliefs assessment; answers all items correctly	endorses "You stink!' beliefs [no pass]

Figure 4.15. Pre-Mod worksheet for Rosario: the evaluation stage, with assessment descriptions and results.

☑ Checkpoint 4.5

[pages 97–104, 111–116]

Fill in the answers to the following items (1–11). Check your responses by referring to the text; relevant page numbers appear in brackets.

List at least five basic assessment rules you should follow if you have to evaluate the status of a prerequisite using assessments:

(1) _____

_____

_____

_____[111–112].

(2) _____

_____

_____

_____[111–112].

(3) _____

_____

_____

_____[111–112].

(4) _____

_____

_____

_____[111–112].

(5) _____

_____

_____

_____[111–112].

(continues)

CHECKPOINT 4.5, continued

Briefly describe the methods and materials you would use to assess each of the six generic prerequisites:

(6) knows rule:_____

_____

_____

_____ [97].

(7) is aware: _____

_____

_____

_____ [97].

(8) can control:_____

_____

_____

_____[98–99].

(9) knows how: _____

_____

_____

_____[99–100].

(10) wants to: _____

_____

_____

_____[102].

(11) believes: _____

_____

_____

_____[102].

Redo any items you missed. If you missed more than 2 of the items, reread the material. Otherwise, continue on to the next section.

4. Interpreting Results. This final step in Pre-Mod requires that *for each missing prerequisite,* you (a) choose an appropriate intervention to be used to modify the deficient prerequisite (thus the name prerequisite modification, or Pre-Mod) and (b) write a performance objective statement that describes what the student must do to demonstrate that the prerequisite has been successfully modified to correct the deficiency. In Rosario's case, you need to modify Prerequisites 3 and 6.

To modify Prerequisite 3 ("can't control"), implement an anger management program. Some commercially available anger management programs are listed in Appendix D. A stress inoculation program, as described in Chapter 13, might also serve to manage anger. The performance objective for this prerequisite is: When the teacher observes anger responses (ARs) in Rosario and his peers, there will be no significant difference in the rates of ARs between them over a 3-day period.

Modifying Prerequisite 6 ("beliefs") requires a cognitive restructuring program such as the one described in Chapter 11. You can combine this with the stress inoculation program, if one has been implemented, because stress inoculation also has a cognitive component. The performance objective for this prerequisite is: When a beliefs assessment is administered on at least two separate occasions, Rosario's answers will not reflect any thinking that is incompatible with ignoring or responding assertively to peer teasing.

So far, we have focused our diagnosis on the target student, Rosario. Remember, the problem behavior in this case is a social exchange—a mutual transaction between Rosario and his peers. They tease; he fights; they tease some more. It is therefore also necessary to diagnose those peers who do the teasing. The procedure is basically the same whether applied to a single individual or to a group. Let's say that you identify three peers who do most of the teasing: Larry, Moe, and Curly, also known as "The Three Teasers." First, you identify and specify the maladaptive behavior: The Three Teasers tease Rosario (i.e., call him names he does not like such as "tardo" and "punk"). Then you identify and specify the target behavior: The Three Teasers will communicate with (i.e., talk to) Rosario without calling him names he does not like. Next, restate the six generic prerequisites in a way that is specific to the target behavior. The restated prerequisites are as follows:

1. Each of The Three Teasers understands that they are supposed to communicate with Rosario without teasing him;

2. each of the teasers is aware of when they are communicating with Rosario with and without teasing him;

3. there are no emotional/physical factors currently beyond the control of any teaser that prohibit them from communicating with Rosario without teasing him;

4. each of the teasers knows how to communication with Rosario without teasing him;

5. each of the teasers considers the consequences of communicating with Rosario without teasing him more rewarding (or less aversive) than teasing him; and

6. none of the teasers engage in thinking that is incompatible with communicating with Rosario without teasing him.

After listing your prerequisites, begin your evaluation. You already know that each of The Three Teasers definitely knows the rule regarding teasing, because they have each paraphrased it in the past. You also know that there are no control factors prohibiting any of them from engaging in the target behavior; none of them appears to be angry, anxious, or depressed, nor are any of them especially impulsive. In addition, each of them is able to communicate with others without teasing. You know this because you have seen each of them do this with Rosario and with other students on several occasions. Since you are not sure about the status of their awareness, motivation, or beliefs, you decide to assess each area. To assess awareness, you show the teasers how to self-monitor their talking to others (with and without teasing) behavior. You also monitor this behavior. After 3 days, there is enough agreement between your data and theirs to indicate they are aware of their behavior. So far, they have Prerequisite 1 ("knows rule"), 2 ("is aware"), 3 ("can control"), and 4 ("knows how").

To assess Prerequisite 5 ("wants to"), use the cue sort technique and have each student name all of the consequences of their teasing ("Rosario fights me and gets into trouble"; "sometimes I get into trouble"; "I get to beat up Rosario"; "I feel good"; "my friends think I'm tough"; "Rosario knows I don't like him") and the consequences of not teasing ("I don't get into trouble"; "I get bored and I don't have any fun"; "my friends think I'm a goody-goody.") After sorting these consequences into "like" and "dislike" or "want" and "don't want" piles, you find that the teasers consider the consequences of teasing more rewarding than the consequences of not teasing. Now you know that they have Prerequisites 1 through 4 but lack Prerequisite 5. To assess Prerequisite 6, administer a beliefs assessment on a test–retest basis with a 24-hour latency to each of the teasers individually. (See Figure 4.16 for a sample peer beliefs assessment.) Each of the teasers fails the assessment—they answer "true" to beliefs such as "It's fun to get people upset" and "People should be able to take a little teasing."

After interpreting the results of the Pre-Mod analysis of the teasers, you determine that each of them: understands the rule about teasing; is aware of when they are teasing and when they are not; is able to control their teasing; and knows how to communicate without teasing. Unfortunately, each of them considers the consequences of teasing Rosario more rewarding than the consequences of not teasing him and they engage in thinking that is incompatible with not teasing. Figure 4.17 is the Pre-Mod worksheet completed for Larry, Moe, and Curly. Performance objectives for the missing prerequisites are: (5) when a cue sort exercise is administered, each teaser will identify all consequences of teasing as "dislike" and all consequences of not teasing as "like," and (6) when given a beliefs assessment on two separate occasions, all teasers will indicate by their responses that they do not endorse any thinking incompatible with communicating without teasing.

The intervention for Prerequisite 5 requires that you identify a new set of consequences for communicating without teasing. These consequences should be more rewarding (or less aversive) than the consequences for teasing. Chapter 5 describes the strategies you might use to identify a new set of consequences. Cognitive restructuring is the strategy of choice for modifying the Prerequisite 6 deficit. This is discussed in Chapter 11. Until you modify the deficient prerequisites for Rosario and his three tormentors, you should not expect any real progress toward the target behaviors for either Rosario or the teasers. Rosario will not ignore or respond assertively to teasing until he has all of the necessary prerequisites, and until Larry, Moe, and Curly have all of the prerequisites necessary to communicate without teasing, they will not do so on a regular basis.

GOOD NEWS, BAD NEWS— PRE-MOD ADVANTAGES AND DISADVANTAGES

As you have already surmised, Pre-Mod is not a perfect system. Like most things in life, it has some advantages and some disadvantages. One definite disadvantage is its reliance on the cooperation of the student during the assessment phase. If the student doesn't cooperate, you either get invalid data or no data at all. Some might argue that it is unrealistic to expect students to participate in activities such as the cue sort, beliefs assessment, role play test, self-monitoring, and others. What if you attempt a Pre-Mod analysis on a student who is noncompliant? Even if they willingly participate in the process, can you really be certain they are not faking their responses? These are good questions. Still, such questions could (and should) be asked about *any* diagnostic procedure. Who is to say that a student will cooperate on an intelligence test or a projective measure? As a rule, students—especially those with learning or behavior problems—don't particularly care for tests of any kind. But even when a student does not fully cooperate, all is not lost. If you encounter a student who refuses to participate or if you have reason to believe he is not doing his best or responding truthfully, you can always throw out the results and operate under the assumption that he does not have the prerequisite(s) you were attempting to assess. You will find out soon enough whether or not he really has the prerequisite, when you attempt to modify the deficit. On the other hand, if you assume that he has the prerequisite without knowing for sure, you will be setting up the both of you for future failure.

Another criticism leveled against Pre-Mod is its reliance on informal, teacher-made and -administered assessments. Based on my experience as a school psychologist, and having taught evaluation courses and written textbooks on evaluation, I believe that informal teacher-made tests are every bit as reliable and valid as the standardized commercial kind; in many cases, they are better than the store-bought variety. For one thing, the norms or criteria teachers use on their assessments are more representative of the students they give the tests to than are those of many commercial tests. For example, if you wanted to assess the frequency and intensity of a student's anger responses to see if they are significantly different from that of his peer group,

TSNG

Name *Larry*   Date *Jan. '95*

Directions: Read each statement below and decide whether it is true or false. If you believe the statement is true, write the letter T on the line next to the number of the statement. If you think it is false, write the letter F on the line. It is not necessary to think about each one for very long. Be honest. You are not going to be graded on this and no one but you and your teacher will ever see it. Don't answer the way you think your teacher might want you to or the way you think you are supposed to. You won't get into any trouble because of your answers so answer the way you really believe.

F   1. I like school.

T   2. There is nothing wrong with making fun of people.

T   3. If there is something wrong with somebody, it's OK to tease them about it.

T   4. Fighting is cool.

T   5. School is dumb.

F   6. Teasing doesn't hurt anybody.

T   7. I am the way I am and I can't change.

F   8. If you tease somebody and they can't take it, the best thing to do is stop teasing them.

F   9. Fighting is dumb.

F   10. It's not OK to make fun of people.

T   11. If at first you don't succeed, try, try again.

T   12. If people are different than I am, it's OK to tease them about it.

F   13. I have little control over what happens to me.

T   14. If you tease somebody and they can't take it, the best thing to do is tease them some more.

F   15. I like all my classmates.

T   16. People who are different than I am are no good and deserve whatever they get.

T   17. If you don't like somebody, it's OK to pick on them.

F   18. All my classmates like me.

T   19. Everyone should treat me fairly.

T   20. Hurting people is a good way to control them.

F   21. You should treat others the same way you want to be treated.

T   22. With a little effort, you can change the way you are.

T   23. The best part of teasing somebody is to watch them suffer.

F   24. Most people won't like me anyway, so it doesn't matter how I treat them.

T   25. I like to get people mad at me.

T   26. People will either like you or they won't. There isn't much you can do about it.

T   27. People who are not as good as I am deserve whatever they get.

F   28. Whether or not people like you depends on how you treat them.

T   29. People who try to be nice to others are pathetic.

T   30. Calling somebody a name can't hurt them. It's not like you're hitting them over the head with a stick.

T   31. People should treat each other with respect.

Figure 4.16. Peer beliefs assessment: Teasing.

Student: _Larry, Moe, Curly_ Evaluator: _Mr. Howell_ Date: _Jan. '95_

Maladaptive Pinpoint: _teasing classmate Rosario (calling him derogatory names, e.g., "tardo," "punk")_

Target Pinpoint: _will communicate with peers without teasing_

Prerequisites	Status	Assessments	Results
1. 3 teasers understand they are supposed to communicate with R without teasing him	Y — have paraphrased it in the past		
2. 3 teasers are aware of when they are communicating with R with and without teasing	? Y	T monitors / 3 teasers monitor teasing behavior; should be 80% agreement	80% agreement [pass]
3. 3 teasers are able to control their teasing (i.e., there are no physical/emotional factors that make it difficult or impossible for them to do so)	Y — no evidence of anger or impulsivity; have demonstrated control on occasion		
4. 3 teasers know how to communicate with R w/o teasing him	Y — have observed them doing so in past		
5. 3 teasers consider consequences of communicating with R w/o teasing him more rewarding (or less aversive) than consequences of teasing him	? N	cue sort; CAP = 100%	< 100% [no pass]
6. 3 teasers only endorse beliefs compatible with communicating with R w/o teasing him	? N	beliefs assessment; CAP = 100%	< 100% [no pass]

Figure 4.17. Pre-Mod worksheet for three peers who tease Rosario.

you would be better off establishing your own set of norms on the target student's peer group, rather than using norms from a commercial measure that was standardized on a sample of students completely different from yours. Anger responses can be culturally influenced, and the frequency and intensity of anger responses among one ethnic, racial, or socioeconomic group may differ from those of another group. It therefore becomes important to compare the target student with students from *his own group* if you want to determine whether or not he really exhibits an anger response. Commercially available assessments are typically standardized on majority-group populations. However, many of the students you may use Pre-Mod assessments with are from minority-group and/or low SES populations—all the more reason to use your own test instruments. Also, there is currently a movement in education (at least in special education) away from summative (pre- and post-) measurement using normative commercially standardized assessments. The current trend is toward more formative curriculum-based measurement using teacher-made informal assessments. (You can consider yourself quite trendy!)

Pre-Mod is not easy. It requires some time and energy. If you are in short supply of either, you can always do a functional analysis instead and ignore the personal variables, or you can get someone else (e.g., the school psychologist or behavior specialist) to do a Pre-Mod analysis for you. Keep in mind that you need not do a Pre-Mod analysis for every student with a behavior problem. Just do it for those students who don't respond to your regular behavior management program. If you are using a token economy in your classroom and it works for all of your students, you don't need to use Pre-Mod with the entire class. Just use it with the students who are giving you fits. You should also know that a number of teachers who have used Pre-Mod say it gets easier the more they use it, because they are able to use the same assessments (with some modifications) over and over again with different students and for different behaviors. If Pre-Mod still seems like a lot of work, consider this: You can either pay now or pay later. Either you spend the time and energy doing Pre-Mod and use the results to design effective interventions now, or you can skip the diagnosis and wind up with ineffective interventions later. The choice is yours.

Pre-Mod does have some advantages over the more traditional systems for diagnosing behavior problems. First, it doesn't rely on strangers such as psychiatrists and psychologists to make the diagnosis. Instead, the diagnosis is made by the one person who knows the student better than anyone else: the student's teacher. Most teachers know more than any psychiatrist, psychologist, or even the student's parents about why a student misbehaves at school. The advantage of having the teacher conduct the diagnosis is that it probably will be more valid, it will be completed sooner, and the person ultimately responsible for the intervention will have ready access to the data.

Another advantage of Pre-Mod is that it focuses directly on student behavior. This is important because the parties involved (i.e., the student and the teacher) do not lose sight of the original problem. Too often, when a student's behavior problem is diagnosed via one of the traditional systems, there is a tendency for everyone concerned to forget about the specific behavior(s) that precipitated the diagnosis in the first place. Labels and technical terms are often used by students as excuses for their behavior ("I act that way on account of my nervous disorder") and by teachers as excuses for not modifying those behaviors ("My God, how do you expect me to deal with a kid who manifests schizoid tendencies?") By focusing the diagnosis on the student's behavior instead of on the student, both the teacher and the student remain mindful of the central issue: what the student *does,* not what the student "is." This makes possible a much more optimistic and positive intervention program.

I get a lot of calls from teachers about behavior problems. When it is obvious that (a) the teacher has a behavior management program in place, (b) she is using behavior management techniques consistently and effectively with her students, and (c) she has made several unsuccessful attempts at manipulating environmental events (i.e., antecedents and consequences) with the target student, I start asking Pre-Mod's "six sacred questions" (i.e., knowing the rule, being aware, having self-control, etc.). The typical response I get is "You know, I never thought about any of those things as possible reasons for a behavior problem." To me, the most significant advantage of Pre-Mod is that it helps teachers realize there are more reasons for a student's misbehavior than emotional disturbance, bad genes, faulty parenting, inappropriate schedules of reinforcement, or a rotten disposition. I find that after they do a Pre-Mod analysis, teachers often view their students in a new light: They are seen less as "nuts," "spoiled," or "bad," and more as simply human and fallible.

☑ Checkpoint 4.6

[pages 118–122]

Fill in the answers to the following items (1–6). Check your responses by referring to the text; relevant page numbers appear in brackets.

State three criticisms of Pre-Mod analysis and write a rebuttal for each.

(1) _____

_____

_____

_____

_____

_____

_____[119, 122].

(2) _____

_____

_____

_____

_____

_____

_____[119, 122].

(continues)

CHECKPOINT 4.6, continued

(3) _____

_____

_____

_____

_____

_____

_____

_____[119, 122].

State three advantages of Pre-Mod analysis as a diagnostic tool in determining the cause of behavior problems.

(4) _____

_____

_____

_____[119, 122].

(5) _____

_____

_____[119, 122].

(6) _____

_____

_____[119, 122].

Redo any items you missed. If you missed more than 1 of the items, reread the material. Otherwise, continue on to the Chapter Assessment.

ASSESSMENT / CHAPTER 4 ▰▰▰▰▰

A list of acceptable responses appears following the Assessment.

1.0 *Functional Analysis*
For both of the following situations,

a. fill in the antecedents, behaviors, and consequences on the S-R-S form below;

b. state a testable explanation (i.e., hypothesis) as to what you think is causing the behavior problem; and

c. state what you would do to test your hypothesis.

    1.1 *Situation:* When Judy sits next to Jerry, she pokes him. His response is to call out "Teacher, Judy's bugging me again." Judy immediately stops poking Jerry when he calls out to the teacher and says "No, I'm not!" This sequence occurs over and over again until the teacher separates them.

        Target Student: *Judy*   **Behavior:** *Poking Jerry*

        Setting Events: *In classroom, sitting next to Jerry*

S	R	S

    Explanation:

    Test:

1.2 *Situation*: Betsy is a low achiever and poor reader. Whenever she is asked to read aloud in reading group and she makes mistakes, the other children in the group snicker and whisper to each other. One day, Betsy shouts a profanity at her peers for laughing at her. Her teacher makes her stand outside the classroom for swearing. After that, Betsy swears at her peers whenever they laugh at her reading. She keeps getting put in "time-out."

Target Student: *Betsy* **Behavior:** *Shouting profanities at peers*

Setting Events: *7 students (including B) in reading group in seats in circle back of classroom taking turns reading aloud*

S	R	S

Explanation:

Test:

2.0 *Pre-Mod Analysis*

Situation: Joey destroys school property. He tears pages from and scribbles in nonconsumable materials (e.g., textbooks and workbooks). He breaks crayons, chews pencils, and scratches desk tops with scissors. You have completed a functional analysis but it does not yield any significant information you can use to design an intervention.

2.1 Fill out the following Pre-Mod worksheet. Write the student's name, your name, the date, and the maladaptive and target behaviors. Write each of the six generic prerequisites specific to the target behavior in the "prerequisite" column. Assume that all of the prerequisites are in doubt and enter a ? (question mark) next to each prerequisite in the "status" column. Next, describe the methods and materials you would use to evaluate the status of each prerequisite in the "assessment" column. Be sure to include CAP for each assessment.

Student _____ Evaluator _____ Date _____

Maladaptive Behavior _____

_____

Target Behavior _____

_____

Prerequisites	*Current Status*	*Assessments*	*Results*

. . . .

2.2 Refer to the following filled-in Pre-Mod worksheet and assume these are the evaluation results from the hypothetical case of "Joey." In the space following the worksheet, write your interpretation of the results. Be sure to include (a) a statement regarding the prerequisites the subject does and does not have (i.e., why he engages in the maladaptive behavior), (b) a recommended intervention for each of the prerequisites he is lacking, and (c) a performance objective for each of the missing prerequisites.

Student _____ Joey _____ **Evaluator** _____ Kaplan _____ **Date** _Jan '95_

Maladaptive Behavior _____ destroys school property—tears pages from and scribbles in nonconsumables (e.g., books), breaks crayons, chews pencils, and scratches desk tops with scissors

Target Behavior _____ will use school property appropriately (i.e., will use crayons, paper, books, pencils, desks, as prescribed without breaking, tearing, chewing, marking)

Prerequisites	Current Status	Assessments	Results
1. knows he is supposed to use school property appropriately (i.e., pencils are used to write with, not to chew; scissors are used to cut paper with, not scratch desktops with; etc.)	?	ask to paraphrase rule CAP = immediate and accurate, w/o prompting	able to paraphrase rule [pass]
2. aware of when he is using school property appropriately and inappropriately	?	both T and J monitor J's beh (i.e., using school mtls appropriately or inappropriately); CAP = min. 80% agreement	30% agreement [no pass]
3. there are no emotional factors currently not under J's control that prohibit him from using school property appropriately	?	a. T monitors beh. correlates of anger in J and in peers; CAP = no signif. difference in %age of ARs	%age of ARs for J = >60; avg for peers = <40 [no pass]
		b. interview J to see if has coping skills	Cannot name one skill [no pass]

(continues)

(Item #2.2, continued)

Prerequisites	Current Status	Assessments	Results
4. knows how to use school property appropriately	?	ask J to demonstrate appropriate use of school property (e.g., "Show me how you are supposed to use these crayons")	able to use appropriately [pass]
5. considers consequences of using school property appropriately more rewarding than consequences of handling inappropriately	?	cue sort (with all positive and negative consequences); 100% CAP	100% [pass]
6. holds beliefs compatible with using school property appropriately	?	paper and pencil beliefs assessment; 100% CAP	100% [pass]

Interpretation:

Recommendations for Intervention:

ACCEPTABLE RESPONSES

1.0 *Functional Analysis* Your responses should include the S-R-S form filled out, as well as the explanation (hypothesis) and a statement about how you intend to test your hypothesis. The answers shown here are provided merely as examples; your responses do not have to match mine exactly.

1.1 *Judy and Jerry*

Target Student: *Judy*   **Behavior:** *Poking Jerry*

Setting Events: *In classroom sitting next to Jerry*

S	R	S
	Judy pokes Jerry	Jerry calls out "Teacher, Judy's bugging me again."
c	Judy stops poking Jerry; she says "No, I'm not"	Jerry stops calling out
c	Judy pokes Jerry	Jerry calls out
c	Judy stops poking Jerry; she says "No, I'm not"	Jerry stops calling out

Possible Explanation (#1): Judy's poking behavior is positively reinforced by Jerry's calling-out behavior.

Test: Reinforce Jerry for ignoring Judy's poking behavior (if Jerry doesn't call out, Judy doesn't get what she wants and she stops poking him).

Possible Explanation (#2): Judy doesn't like Jerry (i.e., she would poke him whether he called out or not).

Test: Have Judy sit next to a different student each day (if Judy doesn't poke other students, we know it's Jerry and not what Jerry does, that maintains her poking behavior).

1.2 *Betsy*

Target Student: *Betsy*   **Behavior:** *Shouting profanities at peers*

Setting Events: *7 students (including B) in reading group in seats in circle back of classroom taking turns reading aloud*

S	R	S
	Betsy reads and makes mistakes	peers in group snicker and whisper
C	Betsy shouts profanity	teacher sends her to time-out
C	Betsy reads and makes mistakes	peers in group snicker and whisper
C	Betsy shouts profanity	teacher sends her to time-out

Possible Explanation: Betsy's swearing behavior is negatively reinforced because it helps her escape from an aversive situation (i.e., peers laughing at her reading).

Test: Don't send Betsy to time-out when she swears (when she sees that swearing doesn't help her escape reading group, she will stop swearing).

2.0 *Pre-Mod Analysis/Joey*   In addition to a completed Pre-Mod analysis worksheet (showing prerequisites, status, assessment, and assessment results), your response should include an interpretation (i.e., prerequisites student has and doesn't have; performance objectives for all prerequisites student lacks; and recommended interventions for each). Again, your response need not match my examples word for word.

(An example of a completed Pre-Mod worksheet appears on p. 132; see interpretation, below.)

Interpretation: Joey currently understands what behavior is expected of him, knows how to engage in the target behavior, considers the consequences of the target behavior more rewarding than the maladaptive behavior, and holds beliefs compatible with using school property appropriately. He is not, however, aware of when he is using school property appropriately and he has an anger management problem that makes it difficult for him to use school property without destroying it. Recommended interventions are self-monitoring to develop awareness and an anger management program such as stress inoculation. Performance objectives are (a) When the teacher and Joey monitor Joey's awareness of whether or not he is using school property appropriately, there will be at least 80% agreement between data collected over a 3-day period; and (b) When the teacher monitors behavior correlates of anger in Joey and his peers, there will be no significant difference in percentage of anger responses between Joey and his peers over a 3-day period

2.1 and **2.2** *Joey*

Student _____ Joey _____ Evaluator ____(your name)____ Date _(today's date)_

Maladaptive Behavior __Joey destroys school property (i.e., tears pages from books and scribbles in nonconsumable__

___materials); breaks crayons, chews pencils, scratches desk tops with scissors___

Target Behavior __Joey will use school property (e.g., books, workbooks, crayons, pencils, etc.) as they were intended__

___to be used without destroying them___

Prerequisites	*Current Status*	*Assessments*	*Results*
1. knows he is supposed to use school property appropriately (i.e., pencils are used to write with, not to chew; scissors are used to cut paper with, not scratch desktops with; etc.)	? Y	ask to paraphrase rule; CAP = immediate and accurate, w/o prompting	able to paraphrase rule [pass]
2. aware of when he is using school property appropriately and inappropriately	? N	both T and J monitor J's beh (i.e., using school mtls appropriately or inappropriately); CAP = min. 80% agreement	30% agreement [no pass]
3. there are no emotional factors currently not under J's control that prohibit him from using school property appropriately	? N	a. T monitors beh. correlates of anger in J and in peers; CAP = no signif. difference in %age of ARs	%age of ARs for J = >60; avg for peers = <40 [no pass]
		b. interview J to see if has coping skills	cannot name one skill [no pass]
4. knows how to use school property appropriately	? Y	ask J to demonstrate appropriate use of school property (e.g., "Show me how you are supposed to use these crayons")	able to use appropriately [pass]
5. considers consequences of using school property appropriately more rewarding than consequences of handling inappropriately	? Y	cue sort (with all positive and negative consequences); 100% CAP	100% [pass]
6. holds beliefs compatible with using school property appropriately	? Y	paper and pencil beliefs assessment; 100% CAP	100% [pass]

CHAPTER FIVE

Strengthening Behaviors

Upon successful completion of this chapter, the learner should be able to: design interventions utilizing strategies such as positive reinforcement, negative reinforcement, shaping, fading, chaining, the Premack principle, contingency contracting, token economy, the level system, and modeling.

CAVEAT EMPTOR

I should mention at the outset that this chapter—for that matter, this whole book—focuses primarily on general strategies rather than specific behavior problems. I don't tell you what you "should" do to modify specific disruptive or noncompliant or aggressive behavior. I have no compunction about sitting down with a teacher to help them design an intervention for a specific behavior problem in a specific student; I just happen to believe that, in the long run, it is more beneficial for teachers to learn some basic intervention strategies they can apply to a wide variety of behaviors instead of relying on someone to tell them exactly what to do in each special case. I am a firm believer in the old adage, "Give a person a fish and he can eat for a day; teach him to fish and he can eat for a lifetime." I also believe (as I have already stated in Chapter 4) that several students can engage in the same behavior for different reasons. This makes it difficult to suggest a specific intervention for a specific behavior problem that will work for all students. If you want this kind of information, three excellent resources are *The Solution Book: A Guide to Classroom Discipline* (Sprick, 1981), *Discipline in the Secondary Classroom: A Problem-by-problem Survival Guide* (Sprick, 1985), and *Problem Behavior Management: Educator's Resource Service* (Algozzine, 1992).

STRENGTHENING BEHAVIOR

When I use the term *strengthening behavior,* I am referring to any of the following situations:

1. when a student learns a new behavior (e.g., a student who never looks at anyone learns to establish eye contact);

2. when a student engages in an existing behavior more than he did before (e.g., a student who goes from 50% on task up to 90% on task); and

3. when a student continues to use an existing behavior that is already strong (i.e., getting a student who is 90% on task to continue at that level).

Specific reinforcement strategies typically used to strengthen behavior include shaping, fading, chaining, modeling, contingency contracting, token reinforcement, and level systems. Before examining each of these strategies, let's take a look at reinforcement in general.

POSITIVE VERSUS NEGATIVE REINFORCEMENT

As I stated in an earlier chapter, according to operant theory there are two ways you can strengthen behavior: *positive* and *negative reinforcement.* In positive reinforcement, behavior is strengthened by presenting a pleasing stimulus, or reward, after the behavior occurs. In negative reinforcement, behavior is strengthened by removing an aversive stimulus after the behavior occurs.

The following examples illustrate how positive and negative reinforcement are typically used in the classroom. Two teachers—we'll call them Mr.

Positive and Mr. Negative—have students who seldom complete assigned work without constant supervision (e.g., repeated directives to "get busy"). Mr. Positive knows that free time is rewarding to his students, so he tells them they can "earn" time to do what they want as soon as their work is done. The result is his students finish their work with very little supervision and receive free time. We may say that Mr. P positively reinforces his students' working behavior because getting a reward (free time) for finishing work causes his students to work harder. I should point out that, technically, the students' working behavior gets stronger as a result of the students' *expectation* (i.e., belief) that they will receive a reward when they finish their assignments. This is an example of the influence of cognitions on behavior. If Mr. P's students do not believe they can finish the work on time or they do not trust him to reward them, they will probably not complete their work.

Meanwhile, in the classroom next door, Mr. Negative decides to use negative reinforcement to strengthen his students' working behavior. Knowing that his students hate detention, he tells them they

will have to stay after school to finish their work if they don't get it done by dismissal. The result is that Mr. Negative's students finish their work without supervision in order to avoid detention. We may say that Mr. N negatively reinforces his students' working behavior because removing an aversive (i.e., avoiding detention) for finishing work causes them to work harder. (See Figure 5.1.) Again, to be technically correct, we should say that Mr. N's students' working behavior is influenced to a large extent by their expectation that they can avoid detention by finishing their work. If Mr. N's students do not believe they can finish the work on time or if they do not believe Mr. N will actually keep them after school (or that he will keep them after school whether they finish their work or not), they probably will not finish it.

So much for how positive and negative reinforcement work. Let's turn our attention to which type of reinforcement you should use. Both teachers in the example above got their students to do what they wanted them to. If both strategies work, does it really matter whether you use positive reinforcement or negative reinforcement? Yes, I believe it does matter.

Figure 5.1. Contrasting techniques for strengthening behavior: positive vs. negative reinforcement.

Let me put it this way: Which teacher would you rather be? Mr. Positive or Mr. Negative? Before you answer, consider the following questions. Which would you rather do: (a) Tell a student she may have free time to do whatever she wants because she did a good job of completing her work, or (b) tell a student she must stay after school to complete her work? Which situation would produce more stress for you as the teacher? Which situation would provide you with more satisfaction? Which of these models would you rather provide for your students: (a) Someone who focuses on the good in others and rewards it, or (b) someone who focuses on the bad and punishes it? In short, do you want to be a positive model or a negative model? I have to believe most of you would rather be like Mr. Positive than Mr. Negative. Unfortunately, we are all, to a large extent, products of our environments, and as children many of us were routinely exposed to negative reinforcement either in the home, in school, or in the world at large. Think about it. Most of us learn to obey society's laws not necessarily because they are good laws that should be obeyed or because we will be rewarded if we obey them, but because of the bad things that might happen to us if we disobey them. For example, the Internal Revenue Service does not give out rewards to people who file their income tax returns on time or without error; most of us simply pay our taxes on time to avoid getting in trouble with the IRS. The police do not reward drivers who obey the traffic laws; most of us obey traffic laws to avoid getting fines, losing our license, or getting injured or killed in a traffic accident. Most of the world's major religions threaten us with eternal damnation, excommunication or, at the very least, censure, if we don't behave as proscribed—if we do not do as we are told, something bad will happen to us in this life or the next. Our governments manage the behavior of other governments by threatening military or economic actions against them; smaller and weaker countries comply with the demands of larger, stronger countries to avoid being attacked or

invaded. On a more personal level, many of us learn to comply in order to avoid rejection or the loss of a love that is conditional upon our being "good" (i.e., doing what another person wants us to). It is no different in the schools—students obey the rules in order to avoid aversives (e.g., detention, failing grades, negative attention, suspension), not to receive rewards. Those students who don't obey the rules have learned how to lie, sneak, and cheat to avoid the negative consequences—more negative reinforcement. With so much exposure to negative reinforcement throughout our lives, is it any wonder there are so many Mr. Negatives teaching in the schools?

To be sure, there are times when positive reinforcement is inappropriate or ineffective, and when negative reinforcement is the better strategy to use. For example, you cannot reinforce behavior unless it occurs. If you have a student who is off task 80% to 100% of the time, it becomes extremely difficult—given that you have other things to do than watch him all day—to catch him on task and reward him. In this situation, positive reinforcement may not be the best strategy to use. You may also find that some students respond better to the threat of an aversive than the promise of a reward. In fact, research regarding the efficacy of positive versus negative reinforcement indicates that both strategies are equally effective at strengthening target behaviors (Iwata & Bailey, 1974; Kaufman & O'Leary, 1972). I am not saying that negative reinforcement should never be used. I am saying that positive reinforcement is more humane, more healthy, and much more fun. Although we may never be able to reverse the widespread use of negative reinforcement in our society, as teachers we can surely do something about its use in our schools. Toward this end, I would leave you with the sage advice of that great philosopher, Mr. Hoagie Carmichael, who said, "You gotta accentuate the positive, eliminate the negative, . . . and don't mess with Mr. Inbetween."

(Checkpoint 5.1 follows, on p. 136.)

✔ Checkpoint 5.1

[pages 133–135]

Fill in the answers to the following items (1–10). Check your responses by referring to the text; relevant page numbers appear in brackets.

By "strengthening behavior," the author means

(1) _____

_____

_____

_____

(2) _____

_____

_____

_____

(3) _____

_____

_____

_____ [133].

In *positive* reinforcement, behavior is strengthened by

(4) _____

_____

_____ [133].

In *negative* reinforcement, behavior is strengthened by

(5) _____

_____

_____ [133].

(continues)

CHECKPOINT 5.1, continued

Three real-life examples of how negative reinforcement is used in our society to strengthen behavior are

(6) _____

_____

_____

(7) _____

_____

_____

_____

(8) _____

_____

_____ [135].

Two reasons why teachers should use positive reinforcement, rather than negative reinforcement, to strengthen the behavior of their students are

(9) _____

_____

_____

(10) _____

_____

_____

_____[135].

Redo any items you missed. If you missed more than 2 of the items, reread the material. Otherwise, continue on to the next section.

POSITIVE REINFORCEMENT

Rules Regarding Reinforcement

Before getting into the "nuts and bolts" of positive reinforcement, it is important that we first discuss some basic rules of the game.

Rule 1: Tell your students exactly what they must do in order to receive reinforcement. Don't assume that your students know what behavior is expected of them or that they know they will be reinforced for it. Students who know exactly what behavior is expected of them as well as the consequences of that behavior are more likely to engage in the behavior than those students who don't know what to do or what the consequences of their actions are. Simply tell your students up front: This is what I want you to do and this is what happens if you do it.

Rule 2: Only reward behavior that is acceptable to you. Remember Mr. Positive? He told his class they could have free time if they finished their work. Students who finished their work got free time and those who didn't finish their work did not get free time. If Mr. Positive rewarded all of his students with free time whether they finished their work or not, he would be teaching his students that working hard is not important; whether you work hard or not, you still get a reward. If it doesn't make any difference whether you work hard or not to get a reward, why bother working hard? The technical term for what the student has to do to get a reward is called *the contingency.* When teachers reward students even though the students have not done what they are supposed to, this is called *non-contingent reinforcement.* It is easy to engage in non-contingent reinforcement if you feel sorry for a student or you are intimidated by a student or you just happen to be in good mood. Non-contingent reinforcement is not in the best interest of the student. Non-contingent reinforcement teaches students that you don't mean what you say, that you should not be taken seriously, and that you are not worthy of respect. Worst of all, non-contingent reinforcement teaches students that you don't respect them—that you don't really care whether they learn and improve or not. It also has the effect of confusing them: You say they will be reinforced for paying attention but you also reinforce them when they are off task, so what is it you really want?

Rule 3: Keep the latency (time elapsed) between the student's response and your reinforcement as short as possible. Older and more developmentally able students can usually make the association between their response and the reward even when the latter is delayed; for example, my graduate students make the connection between their studying behavior and the passing grade they receive on a test even though a week might intervene between the two. On the other hand, very young students or students with disabilities must receive positive reinforcement immediately following a response in order to understand that they are being rewarded for it. See Figure 5.2.

Rule 4: Reinforce behavior according to a schedule. This is one of the reasons why behavior modification is referred to as the *systematic* application of rewards and punishers. New (unlearned) behavior cannot be randomly reinforced or it may never be learned. Instead, it must be reinforced on a continuous schedule. Conversely, behavior that has been learned and is fairly well established should no longer be reinforced continuously, or the student may become satiated or so dependent upon the extrinsic reward that he never internalizes the behavior; instead, learned behaviors should be randomly reinforced on a variable schedule. Because the change from the continuous to the variable schedule often must be gradual, a fixed schedule of reinforcement should be used as a bridge (i.e., transition) between the two. These three schedules of reinforcement—continuous, fixed and variable—are discussed in detail later in this chapter.

Rule 5: Reinforce behavior that is a step in the right direction. If you wait until the student emits the exact response you want before you reinforce him, you may be waiting a long, long time. For example, if

Figure 5.2. Reinforce immediately whenever possible.

you want a student who never turns in assignments to complete all of his work, you should begin your reinforcement program by rewarding him for turning in parts of assignments. Reinforcing behavior that is a step in the right direction is called *shaping,* and it should be used whenever there is a wide gap between the student's present level of functioning and the terminal (i.e., target) behavior. Shaping is also discussed in detail later in this chapter.

Rule 6: Model the behavior you want from your students.   A great deal of human behavior is learned by watching and imitating significant others in the environment. Children learn by modeling their parents, peers, and teachers. It has also been said that we teach more by our deeds than by our words. Therefore, if you want a student to persevere at a difficult task, you should not just tell him to "hang in there." You should demonstrate perseverance by your actions or point out examples of perseverance in the environment. The worst thing you can do when you want to reinforce a behavior in a student is to model the opposite of that behavior. You don't help a screaming student learn self-control by yelling at him to be quiet.

Rule 7: Try to maintain enough of a state of deprivation in the student so that the reinforcer will maintain its reinforcing properties.   In order for a reinforcer to be effective in strengthening a student's behavior, the student has to want the reinforcer enough to emit the behavior for it. The more he wants the reinforcer, the more inclined he will be to engage in the contingent behavior. The intensity of this desire is related to the student's state of deprivation. If he feels deprived (i.e., lacking the reinforcer), he will work harder to overcome this deficit. From a practical standpoint, this will require the teacher to create a situation in which the student always feels deprived of the reinforcer so that he will constantly work to get it. Imagine that you were using a token economy in which students earned tokens such as chips or points for work completed or socially acceptable behavior. Then, imagine that a student earned more than enough tokens to "buy" a favored activity at the end of the day. It is entirely possible that she might stop working or behaving properly an hour or more before the favored-activity

period. She might quit working or behaving properly because she does not feel deprived of the tokens if she does not need any more of them to purchase her reward. In order to avoid this situation, the teacher must create a state of deprivation by removing some of the tokens which the student had previously earned. More will be said about this practice later, in the section on token economies.

Rule 8: Use rewards because they are reinforcing to your students, not because they are reinforcing to you. Looking at old copies of *National Geographic* or *Boy's Life* may have been fun for you when you were younger, but your students may not enjoy this activity. To find out what your students do enjoy, follow the directions in the following section on reinforcers.

Rule 9: Program for generalization and maintenance of newly learned behavior.   Don't assume that the newly learned behavior will last or transfer to other settings and situations simply because the student is now doing it; chances are he is doing it now because he is reinforced for doing it now. What happens when he stops getting reinforced? The research on generalization and maintenance of behavior suggests that newly learned behaviors do not maintain or generalize on their own; rather, this requires procedures specifically designed to enhance generalization and maintenance (Marholin & Steinman, 1977; O'Leary, Becker, Evans, & Sandargas, 1969; Walker & Buckley, 1972). More about these procedures later.

Rule 10: Combine social reinforcement with other forms of reinforcement.   Social reinforcement in the form of a compliment or smile can be a very powerful reinforcer. It is also inexpensive compared to most tangible reinforcers and is quick and easy to give. Using social praise along with other forms of reinforcement makes the latter more effective. Details about social reinforcement are presented later.

Rule 11:   Try to use the least-artificial, least-intrusive type of reinforcer or system of reinforcement possible. You don't need an elaborate token economy when a simple "good boy" will do the job. You don't need to use edibles when a pat on the back can achieve the same effect. Keep it simple. More on this later, too. Right now, let's review what we have learned so far.

✔ Checkpoint 5.2

[pages 137–138]

Fill in the answers to the following items (1–11). Check your responses by referring to the text; relevant page numbers appear in brackets.

State a reason for each of the following rules of reinforcement:

Tell students exactly what they must do to receive reinforcement

(1) _____
_____
_____ [137].

Only reward behavior that is acceptable

(2) _____
_____ [137].

Keep latency between behavior and reinforcement brief

(3) _____
_____ [137].

Reinforce behavior according to a schedule

(4) _____
_____ [137].

Reinforce behavior that is a step in the right direction

(5) _____
_____[137–138].

(continues)

CHECKPOINT 5.2, continued

Model behavior you want from students

(6) _____
_____
_____ [138].

Maintain a state of deprivation

(7) _____
_____ [138].

Use rewards that are reinforcing to students

(8) _____
_____
_____ [138].

Program for generalization and maintenance

(9) _____
_____
_____ [138].

Combine social reinforcement with other forms

(10) _____
_____
_____ [138].

Use least-artificial, least-intrusive reinforcement

(11) _____
_____
_____ [138].

Redo any items you missed. If you missed more than 2 of the items, reread the material. Otherwise, continue on to the next section.

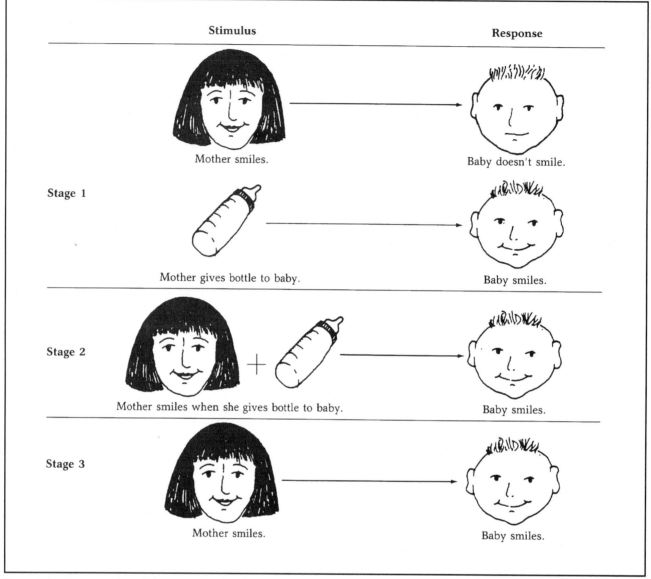

Stimulus		Response

Stage 1

Mother smiles. → Baby doesn't smile.

Mother gives bottle to baby. → Baby smiles.

Stage 2

Mother smiles when she gives bottle to baby. → Baby smiles.

Stage 3

Mother smiles. → Baby smiles.

Figure 5.3. How secondary reinforcers are developed.

Reinforcers

Types of reinforcers

There are two classes of reinforcers: unlearned (primary, or unconditioned) and learned (secondary, or conditioned). Unlearned reinforcers do not have to be paired with other reinforcers for learning to take place. Examples are food, the air we breathe, sunshine (for Oregonians), sex, warmth, and the like. Because all of these produce pleasure by themselves, they do not have to be paired with other reinforcers to have the power to reinforce. Learned reinforcers, on the other hand, must be paired with an unlearned reinforcer in order to develop reinforcing properties. For example, a smile (a learned rein-

forcer) must be paired with the food (an unlearned reinforcer) a mother gives her child when the child is hungry. As the child grows and experiences the pairing of the smile and the food, the child learns that "good," or pleasing, things are usually associated with smiles, and eventually smiles come to have their own reinforcing properties (see Figure 5.3). Smiles eventually can reinforce behavior without being paired with a primary reinforcer; they remain, however, secondary (learned) reinforcers.

The most commonly used primary reinforcer is food. Unfortunately, the type of food most often used as a primary reinforcer is junk! I have a strong aversion to the use of candy, cookies, cupcakes, doughnuts, potato chips, and Kool-Aid as primary reinforcers—kids do not need all of the sugar, salt, and artificial ingredients in these foods. There are plenty of natural and nutritious foods available, such as fresh fruits and vegetables, unsalted nuts (dry toasted in the oven instead of being roasted in oil), granola, yogurt with fruit, popcorn, raisins, apple sauce, milk or fruit juice, sweetened herbal tea, and carob (a substitute for chocolate). Using junk foods with high sugar content as reinforcers can have negative side effects. First, it reinforces your students' poor eating habits. They get enough of this junk outside of school. Second, you are setting them (and subsequently yourself) up for the maladaptive behavior that usually accompanies the drop in blood sugar after the "quick high." M&Ms may appealingly "melt in your mouth and not in your hand," but if you really have the student's best interests at heart, you'll find something better to use as a primary reinforcer. It is also extremely important that you determine whether or not your students are diabetic, hypoglycemic, or have any food allergies. Since food reinforcers are so powerful, be careful to ensure that your students do not have easy access to them. When using them, keep them out of sight and present them only contingent upon the desired behavior. Keeping a box of raisins on the table in front of a student you intend to reward for establishing eye contact is not a good idea; the student may focus attention on the reward rather than on the behavior you are trying to reinforce. Keeping the raisins in your pocket or holding one raisin next to your eye makes better sense. Also, don't forget the rule about deprivation—your student will not work for food if he has just finished lunch or if he has had his fill of raisins. To keep this state of deprivation, use food reinforcers long after the student has finished a meal and either keep the number of reinforced trials to a minimum, give small amounts of the food reinforcer (e.g., a small piece of a cracker rather than one whole cracker), and/or provide the student with the opportunity to earn food reinforcers for later consumption.

Social reinforcement is by far the cheapest kind to give, and it is one of the most effective. Examples are verbal praise, smiles, attention (e.g., looking at someone when they are speaking), nodding your head (as if in agreement with the speaker), and physical contact such as hugs, pats, and touches. While praise should be dispensed freely, be careful not to satiate your students. Too much praise tends to lose its importance. Also, try to sound sincere. Don't be unctuous or patronizing. Kids who can't read a word can spot an insincere person a mile away! Try to avoid making comments about the student; instead, praise his behavior. Many students have heard nothing but derisive remarks from their teachers, and by the time they get to your class, they are convinced that they are lazy, crazy, stupid, or just plain no good. However, they can still tell when they have done something correctly. By confining your praise to their response, you are merely stating the obvious. If you start generalizing, making statements such as "Boy, are you smart!" your credibility will suffer. If you program for success so that they have many opportunities to respond correctly and so that they often receive praise for their correct responses, eventually the student's self-image may improve enough so that you can make some value judgements without losing any credibility. It's really very simple. Instead of saying, "Boy, you're smart!" simply say, "You're right! That was a good answer." Even if you don't like the student, try to give praise with some feeling. Think of it this way: You are actually praising *yourself*—if you weren't such a good teacher, your students wouldn't be giving you all those opportunities to praise them. Also, try to vary your comments from time to time so that they don't get repetitive and lose their power to reinforce. Make sure your students understand you. Be aware of your vocabulary; don't use comments that are too babyish or too adult for your students. You wouldn't want to reward a high school student with "Good boy!" or a first grader with "Now you're cooking!" Refer to the list of approval responses found in Figure 5.4 if you find yourself running out of things to say.

Tangible reinforcers are like those little prizes you get in cereal or Cracker Jack boxes. They are relatively inexpensive and easy to give. Students from low-SES (i.e., poor) backgrounds often may especially enjoy earning tangibles. However, be careful that the tangibles don't become too distracting to the student and interfere with the behavior you are trying to strengthen. Some students will play with these items to the extent that they do little else. The teacher then winds up in a power struggle trying to take the distracting item away. For this reason, tangibles should be dispensed so that the student can see what he's earned but can't handle it until his work is finished or the school day is over. Also, try to use tangibles that serve a constructive purpose. Pencils, pens, writing and drawing pads, loose-leaf notebooks, paperback books, modeling clay, inexpensive puzzles, games, shoelaces, toothbrushes, and combs all serve a more constructive purpose as tangible rewards than do water pistols, cap guns, fake spiders, and rubber knives. If you find you must use tangibles as reinforcers, try not to get trapped into buying them yourself. Many of these items can be donated by the school store or one of the local mer-

Verbal or Written

yes	oh boy	delicious	neato
good	correct	fabulous	very good
neat	excellent	splendid	well done
nice	that's right	smart thinking	nicely done
OK	perfect	right on	congratulations
great	how true	wow	superior
uh-huh	absolutely right	good choice	yeh
positively	keep going	on target	
go ahead	good responses	now you're cooking	
yeah	beautiful	that's the way	
all right	wonderful job	keep it up	
exactly	fantastic	thank you	
of course	terrific	fine	
cool	super	I like it	
wonderful	swell	I love it	
outstanding	tasty	the best yet	
exciting	marvelous	bravo	

Nonverbal

smiling	widening eyes	signaling OK with fingers	touching nose
winking	wrinkling nose		patting back
nodding	whistling	giving thumbs up	giving quick squeeze
grinning	cheering	shaking head	touching arm
raising eyebrows	licking lips	circling hand	hugging
forming kiss	rolling eyes	touching head (student's)	putting hand on hand
opening eyes wide	clapping hands		shaking hands
slowly closing eyes	raising arms	patting head	giving "high five"
laughing	shaking fist	pinching cheek	

Figure 5.4. Social reinforcers—responses indicating approval.

chants. The parents (or PTA/PTO group) in your school or district are another likely funding source. If you can't find anyone to subsidize your tangible-reinforcement program, change to another type of reinforcer. In my opinion, social reinforcement and favored activities (see next paragraph) are preferable to tangible reinforcers.

Activity reinforcers actually provide double benefits because the participation in the activity often gives the student an opportunity to receive bonus reinforcement in the form of verbal praise. For example, when a student earns free time to draw a picture, he not only gets to enjoy the activity of drawing but has the opportunity to receive social reinforcement from the environment when his picture is hung up on the bulletin board. Aside from giving the student an opportunity to develop life-long skills and interests, activity reinforcers also allow him to experience intrinsic reinforcement. Everybody enjoys doing things at which they are good. The average school setting provides many opportunities for a variety of activity reinforcers such as helping the building maintenance people, working in the kitchen or helping in the office, serving as a messenger or peer tutor, working in the machine shop or playing in the gym (in addition to regularly scheduled times), taking over as teacher of the class, listening to recorded music, reading material from the school library, and being a school monitor. The list of activities can be as long as the teacher's imagination and resources and the cooperation of the rest of the school will permit. Also, don't be afraid to use activity reinforcers that *you* would normally consider undesirable so long as they are harmless. Many years ago, I let some of my students write on a "graffiti board" in the classroom as a payoff for low-frequency (desirable) behavior. Usually they spent more time writing outside of class, on walls, than they did in class writing on paper. These students were mostly low achievers from the inner city who lived in buildings with graffitied walls, rode on graffitied subway trains, and walked on graffitied sidewalks—see what I mean about the power of modeling? After numerous com-

plaints from the school maintenance people and several ineffective attempts at punishing this behavior, I decided that if they liked writing on walls so much, I would let them do it in class—provided they earned the privilege by first writing on paper. This practice not only increased the number of written assignments completed, it resulted in a marked decrease in graffiti-writing outside of class. This is merely one example of a seemingly undesirable activity being used as a payoff for a desirable low-frequency behavior. I have listed others in Figure 5.5. Don't be afraid to use them if the more conventional reinforcers don't work. You can't expect all of your students to work for a smile or a Twinkie.

Token reinforcers are dispensed in place of actual reinforcers such as primaries, tangibles, or favored activities. Some examples of token reinforcers are points, stars, checkmarks, and chips. Students seldom tire of getting tokens because the tokens can be turned in for a variety of reinforcers. This allows the tokens to keep their reinforcing properties. Token reinforcers, like most social reinforcers, tangibles, and favored activities, are considered secondary (i.e., learned or conditioned) reinforcers because the student has to learn the connection between the token and the "real" reinforcer before the token can acquire any reinforcing properties. Much more will be said about tokens and token reinforcement later in the chapter.

One more thing about reinforcers. A good rule of thumb to follow, whenever possible, is to try to use the least artificial reinforcer you can get away with. Artificial reinforcers are different from the reinforcers typically used in the public schools. They are contrived, unique, elaborate, and markedly less effective than those naturally occurring reinforcers typically used in the learner's environment (see Figure 5.6). While a young student with severe disabilities may need to be rewarded with food or toys, an older, more able student would probably work for a reward in the form of a more common school activity (e.g., playground equipment monitor) or for social praise. Figure 5.7 displays a hierarchy of contrived and naturally occurring reinforcers. Naturally occurring reinforcers have many advantages over contrived reinforcers. They are generally easier to access. They usually cost less in terms of time and money. Naturally occurring reinforcers are also more likely to be used by change agents other than the teacher; many of them are more likely to be used outside of the student's classroom and are also easier to wean the student off of than are contrived reinforcers. Right now, let's examine how to go about choosing the right reinforcer.

---

1. Sleeping (i.e., allowing student to put head down on desk to rest)

2. Graffiti board (should be covered when not in use to avoid distracting students)

3. Reading comic books

4. Playing cards or rolling dice (acceptable as long as no money changes hands)

5. Eating in class (as long as students clean up after themselves)

6. Chewing gum (as long as it isn't stuck on chairs, tables, or desks)

7. Listening to portable radio (as long as it doesn't disrupt learning environment)

8. Wandering around room (same as number 7)

9. Talking to peers (same as number 7)

10. Daydreaming

11. Taking things apart (as long as they are put back together)

12. Passing notes to peers

13. Making a mess (as long as it is cleaned up)

14. Playing with puzzle or game (e.g., Rubik's Cube)

15. Ignoring teacher when she or he is talking (not attending)

16. Talking loudly

17. Singing or whistling

18. Leaving the classroom (to go to another supervised area)

Figure 5.5. Acceptable "undesirable" behaviors for use as reinforcers.

Figure 5.6. Contrived reinforcement.

1. verbal, nonverbal and written approval responses (e.g., "good," thumbs up, smiling face drawn on paper)

2. public recognition (e.g., sharing approval responses with others)

3. activity reinforcers typically found in schools (e.g., extra recess, free time)

4. grades

5. high-frequency behavior—behavior that may be undesirable but is not necessarily maladaptive (e.g., sleeping, daydreaming, talking to peers) and is contingent upon low-frequency behavior

6. primary reinforcement (e.g., food)

7. token reinforcement (points, stars, chips)

8. tangible reinforcers (e.g., prizes)

9. activity reinforcers not typically found in schools (e.g., trips to McDonald's)

Figure 5.7. Hierarchy of reinforcers, from most natural (1) to most contrived (9).

Choosing reinforcers

First, you won't know whether or not you have chosen the right reinforcer until after you have used it with your student. If the behavior you wish to strengthen gets stronger, you may say that you chose the right reinforcer. On the other hand, if the behavior stays the same or weakens, you might not have chosen the right reinforcer. I say "might not" because there are other things that can cause a behavior to weaken besides using the wrong reinforcer, and these will be discussed at the end of the chapter.

Basically, there are two ways to choose a reinforcer. The first is simply to observe the student during his free time to see what he enjoys doing. This is especially helpful when you are planning to use an activity reinforcer. Watch the student to see if he spends his free time daydreaming, coloring, talking to peers or to you or to himself, sleeping, listening to music, reading comics or magazines, writing novels, or composing symphonies. (See Figure 5.8.) Try to provide him with as many activities as possible from which to choose during his free time. If you limit the choices to coloring, playing with puzzles, or looking at magazines, you won't necessarily know what *the student* considers reinforcing. All you will know is which of the three activities *available to him* he considers the most reinforcing (or the least boring).

A second method for choosing a reinforcer is to ask the student what she likes. Assuming that she can read and write, have her complete an interest inventory such as the one in Appendix A. If she can't read or write, ask her the questions and let her dic-

tate the answers. If possible, consult with her parents, siblings, past teachers, and friends to find out what the student considers reinforcing in the way of activity, primary, tangible, or social reinforcers. It goes without saying that the items on the interest inventory should be appropriate for the student's age and developmental level. If you feel that they are too babyish or too sophisticated for her, make the necessary modifications. Once you determine what the student will work for, it is time to place her on a schedule of reinforcement.

Figure 5.8. Observing students during their free time to identify potential reinforcers.

✔ Checkpoint 5.3

[pages 140–144]

Fill in the answers to the following items (1–19). Check your responses by referring to the text; relevant page numbers appear in brackets.

Two classes of reinforcement are *primary* and *secondary.* The difference between them is **(1)**

_____

_____

_____

_____ [140].

Two examples for each of the following types of reinforcers are:

Token **(2)** _____

and **(3)** _____

Primary **(4)** _____

and **(5)** _____

Tangible **(6)** _____

and **(7)** _____

Activity **(8)** _____

and **(9)** _____

Social **(10)** _____

and **(11)**_____[140–143].

(*continues*)

CHECKPOINT 5.3, continued

Give three examples for each of the following:

artificial reinforcers **(12, 13, 14)**_____

_____

_____

_____

_____ [143].

natural reinforcers **(15, 16, 17)** _____

_____

_____

_____

_____ [143].

Two methods used to choose reinforcers are:

(18) _____

_____

(19) _____

_____ [144].

Redo any items you missed. If you missed more than 4 of the items, reread the material. Otherwise, continue on to the next section.

Schedules of Reinforcement

A *continuous* schedule of reinforcement should be used whenever you are beginning to introduce or modify a new (i.e., not yet learned) behavior. In order for the student to learn this behavior, he will have to be reinforced every time he engages in it. Diagrams of continuous reinforcement schedules may be seen in Figures 5.9 and 5.10. Of all the schedules, continuous reinforcement is the least resistant to extinction. This means that if you were to forget to reward the student from time to time, it is likely that extinction would occur.

A *fixed* schedule of reinforcement should be used when the student has demonstrated that he is capable of engaging in the new behavior and you want to begin to wean him off of continuous reinforcement. Simply move from rewarding every single desired response to every second, third, fourth, or more. While your reinforcement pattern is still predictable, you are making the student work harder to get the same reward. Diagrams of fixed schedules of reinforcement may be seen in Figures 5.11 and 5.12.

A *variable* schedule of reinforcement is similar to the fixed schedule except that it is not predictable. Because the student never knows when he is going to get a reward, he needs to behave appropriately all the time if he wants the reinforcer. This type of schedule is used as a maintenance schedule after the behavior has been learned and after the student has been sufficiently weaned off the continuous reinforcement through use of the fixed schedule. A diagram of a variable schedule of reinforcement may be seen in Figure 5.13. Of the three schedules, it is by far the most resistant to extinction. This means that if you were to forget to reinforce the student from time to time, extinction probably would not occur (i.e., the student would continue to behave appropriately).

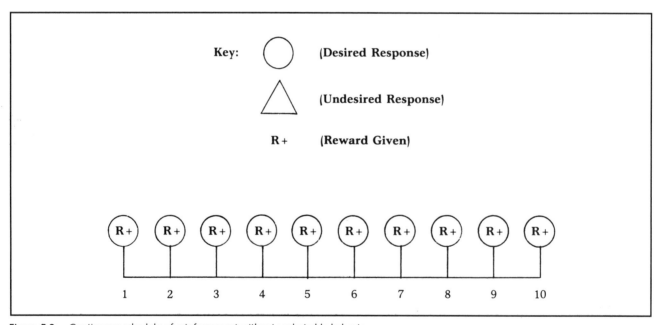

Figure 5.9. Continuous schedule of reinforcement without undesirable behavior.

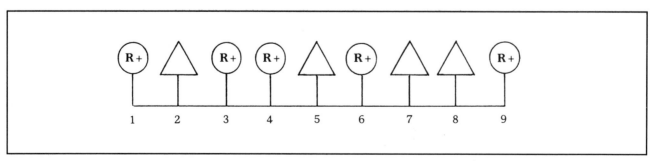

Figure 5.10. Continuous schedule with undesirable behavior.

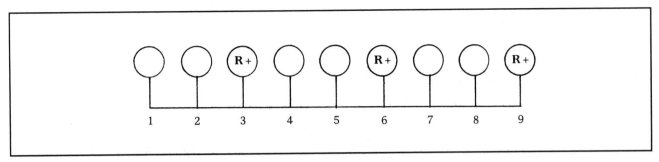

Figure 5.11. Fixed schedule without undesirable behavior.

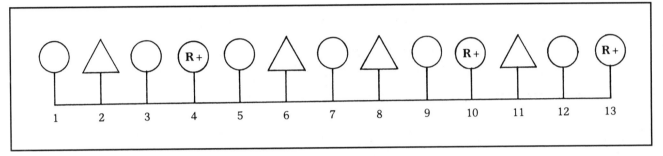

Figure 5.12. Fixed schedule with undesirable behavior.

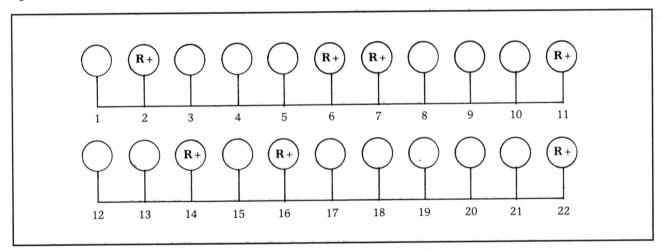

Figure 5.13. Variable schedule without undesirable behavior.

Reinforcing response frequency and duration: ratio and interval schedules

Two aspects of behavior that the teacher can reinforce are frequency and duration of response. For example, the teacher can reinforce a certain behavior according to the number of times it occurs (frequency) or how long it lasts (duration). It is possible to reinforce frequency or duration of response for each of the three schedules of reinforcement discussed above. Response (frequency) schedules are referred to as *ratio schedules*. For example, there are continuous-, fixed-, and variable-ratio schedules. Duration (time) schedules are called *interval sched-*

ules. There are continuous-, fixed-, and variable-interval schedules.

In Figure 5.14 the student is being reinforced on a fixed-ratio (FR) schedule. The number of consecutive correct responses necessary for presenting the reinforcer is known as the *arrangement*. In Figure 5.14 the arrangement is two. In other words, the student has to make two consecutive correct responses before the teacher will present the reinforcer. Note that I said *consecutive* responses. Figure 5.15 is also an FR schedule with a 2:1 arrangement. However, in this example, the student is still occasionally engaging in some undesirable behavior. Notice that the student was not reinforced for her third response even though it was her second correct response. This was

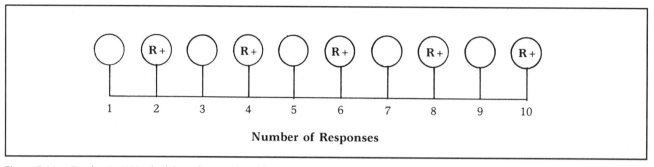

Figure 5.14. Fixed-ratio (FR) schedule without undesirable behavior and with 2:1 arrangement.

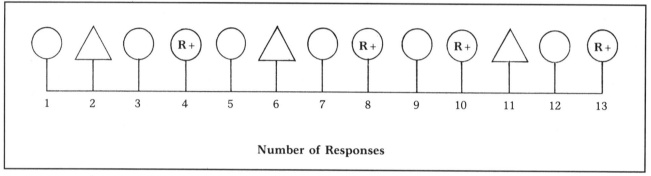

Figure 5.15. Fixed-ratio (FR) schedule with undesirable behavior and with 2:1 arrangement.

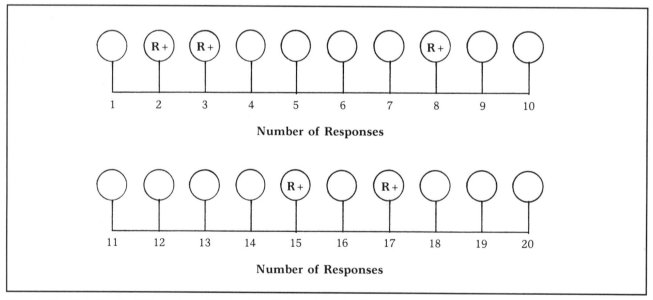

Figure 5.16. Variable-ratio (VR) schedule without undesirable behavior and with average of 4:1 arrangement.

because it was not her second consecutive correct response. Don't think that all FR schedules of reinforcement call for the student to be reinforced after only two consecutive correct responses; some require three, four, five, and more. The number of consecutive correct responses required may change as the student's behavior changes.

Figure 5.16 is an example of a variable-ratio (VR) schedule with a 4:1 arrangement. This means that the student is reinforced once on the average of every four consecutive correct responses. In this case, the teacher knew ahead of time that she wanted the student to make twenty responses so she gave her twenty cues, or opportunities, to respond. Because she also wanted her on a VR schedule of 4:1, she divided the average (4) into the number of opportunities to respond (20) to get the number of times she would have to reinforce her (5). Then she presented the reinforcer five times on a random (unpredictable) basis.

An example of a fixed-interval (FI) schedule may be seen in Figure 5.17. Notice that I have arbitrarily made the "sticks" (i.e., vertical lines) in this diagram stand for minutes instead of responses. The arrangement is 4:1. In other words, the student is being reinforced once at the end of each four-minute block of time. As in the FR schedule, the contingency is consecutive behavior. In Figure 5.18, where the arrangement is 2:1, the student is not reinforced for his second minute of on-task behavior because it wasn't the second *consecutive* minute on task.

Finally, Figure 5.19 shows an example of a variable-interval (VI) schedule of reinforcement. In this case the student is being reinforced once on the average of every five consecutive minutes that he engages in the target behavior. In this case the teacher knows ahead of time that the student's assignment would take him 20 minutes if he stayed on task all of the time. Because she wanted him on a VI schedule of 5:1, she divided the average (5 min.) into the total number of minutes to behave (20 min.) to get the number of times she would need to reinforce him (4). Then she presented the reinforcer four times on a random (unpredictable) basis.

Although I have already discussed when you should use each of the three schedules of reinforcement, I have not talked about moving from one schedule to the next. There is no universal rule that would apply to every student with whom you work. In general, you should be guided by the student's behavior. For example, if you are reinforcing hand-raising behavior on a ratio schedule and baseline data indicate that the student seldom raises his hand and almost always calls out, you should assume that hand-raising behavior is new and reinforce it on a continuous schedule (i.e., every time it occurs). When the intervention data show that the student is beginning to raise his hand more often than he calls out, try moving from the continuous schedule to an FR schedule with a 2:1 arrangement and see what happens. If the subsequent data show any regression, you can always go back to your continuous schedule. If, however, the level of desirable behavior continues to improve, change the contingency for reinforcement by increasing the arrangement from 2:1 to 3:1, and so on. Do this until the data show that the student *always* raises his hand. At this point, begin using a VR schedule and gradually increase the average in the arrangement. If you have done everything you were supposed to in the way it was supposed to be done, eventually the student's hand-raising behavior should maintain even if you don't attend to him on all occasions.

Although the transition from schedule to schedule is the same when you are reinforcing behaviors based on duration (i.e., interval), you don't have to make your reinforcement contingent upon minutes passed. For example, baseline data might show that the longest period of time that student is able to stay on task is 30 seconds. In this case, you would begin with a continuous interval schedule and reinforce the student for every 30 seconds of sustained on-task behavior.

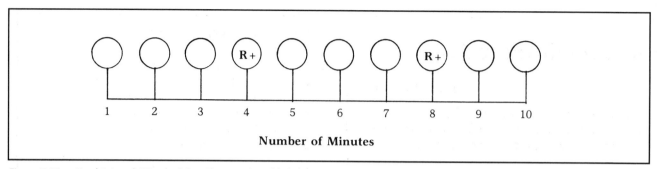

Figure 5.17. Fixed-interval (FI) schedule without undesirable behavior and with 4:1 arrangement.

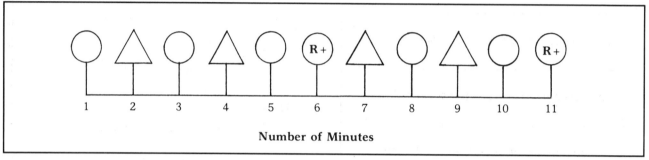

Figure 5.18. Fixed-interval (FI) schedule with undesirable behavior and with 2:1 arrangement.

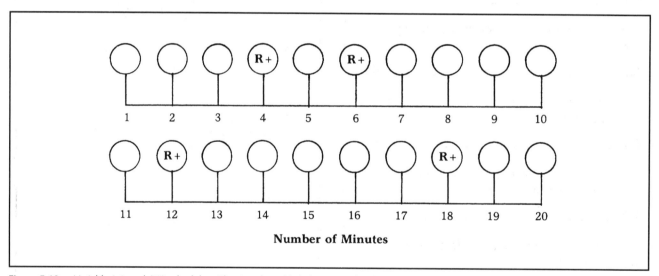

Figure 5.19. Variable-interval (VI) schedule without undesirable behavior and with average of 5:1 arrangement.

☑ Checkpoint 5.4

[pages 146–150]

Fill in the answers to the following items (1–15). Check your responses by referring to the text; relevant page numbers appear in brackets.

The best schedule to use when you are first starting to build a new behavior is the

(1) _____[146].

The best schedule to use for maintenance is the

(2) _____.

The best schedule to use as a transition is the

(3) _____[146].

The schedule that is most resistant to change is the

(4) _____[146].

The schedule that is least resistant to change is the

(5) _____ [146].

The schedule used when behavior is reinforced over time is the

(6) _____[147].

The schedule used when behavior is reinforced according to responses is the

(7) _____[147].

An intermittent schedule of reinforcement that is predictable is the

(8) _____[146].

An intermittent schedule of reinforcement that is unpredictable is the

(9) _____[146].

(continues)

CHECKPOINT 5.4, continued

Look at the schedules of reinforcement diagrammed here and label each continuous, fixed, or variable. Be sure to include whether it is a ratio or interval schedule and what the arrangement is. Check your answers; the correct answers are shown following Item 10.

Key: ◯ desirable behavior

△ undesirable behavior

R+ reinforcement presented

(10)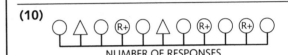
NUMBER OF RESPONSES

(11)
NUMBER OF MINUTES

(12)
NUMBER OF MINUTES

(13)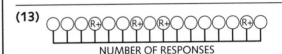
NUMBER OF RESPONSES

(14)
NUMBER OF MINUTES

(15)
NUMBER OF RESPONSES

ANSWERS: (10) fixed-ratio (2:1); (11) continuous; (12) variable-interval (3:1); (13) variable-ratio (4:1); (14) fixed-interval (3:1); (15) continuous

Redo any items you missed. If you missed more than 3 of the items, reread the material. Otherwise, continue on to the next section.

Shaping

Shaping should be used when there is a wide gap between a student's present level of functioning and the target behavior. It is unrealistic to expect a student who has been misbehaving for years to suddenly change overnight. Similarly, since students need to be positively reinforced for desirable behavior, you cannot always wait until a student's behavior is exactly the way you want it before reinforcing it. Therefore, you must reinforce *change in the right direction* (i.e., improvement). A shaping program has three basic components: successive approximations, differential reinforcement, and shifting criteria for reinforcement. Let's examine each.

Successive approximations

The word *approximation* means "something like." In shaping, you choose a target behavior that you want the student to engage in and reward each successive approximation of the behavior until the student is able to engage in the target behavior. While the student may not be able to engage in the target behavior in the beginning, she will most likely be able to engage in behavior that is something like (i.e., an approximation of) the target behavior. As the student progresses through the conditioning (i.e., learning) process she will be able to engage in behavior that is a closer approximation of (more like) the target behavior. Each of these behaviors that are closer and closer to the target behavior is referred to as a *successive approximation;* an *approximation,* because neither is the target behavior but only something like it, and *successive* because each new behavior is more like the target behavior than the one that preceded it.

For example, let's suppose that you have a student who is always near his seat but is seldom in it. Because he is so seldom in his seat and you are busy with teaching, it is virtually impossible to catch him in his seat and reward him on a continuous schedule. The fair-pair target behavior for this student is to stay in his seat for ten minutes at a time. However, if you waited until he stayed in his seat for ten minutes at a time before you rewarded him, you would probably never reward him. The gap between where he is now (i.e., seldom in his seat) and where you want him to be (i.e., in his seat for ten minutes) is too great. However, you could start by rewarding him for being *near* his seat. You might simply put a small rug or carpet remnant under his desk, and whenever he's on the rug you could reward him for being near his seat. Eventually, you could reward him for being *next to* his seat. After that, for being in physical contact with his seat. Then, for sitting in his seat in any fashion. Next, for sitting in his seat properly (i.e., with both legs under his desk). After that, for sitting in his seat properly for one minute. Then you could reward behavior of two minutes, five minutes, and finally, of ten minutes duration—the target behavior. Beginning with "being near his seat" up through "sitting properly for five minutes," you would have rewarded eight successive approximations of the target behavior. Notice that each approximation was more like the target behavior than the preceding one. This is critical. If you are merely rewarding several different behaviors that are not successive approximations of the target behavior, you are not actually doing any and you may never reach your goal.

Differential reinforcement

When you reward a student for an approximation of a target behavior, it is likely that she will repeat the approximation. However, if you reward the student randomly, or for all approximations of the target behavior, you will probably confuse her because she won't know which specific approximation you want her to make. If you are careful to only reinforce the desired approximation and not earlier approximations the student will eventually learn what it is you expect from her. This process is referred to as *differential reinforcement.* It is called differential because it is used to help the student to be able to differentiate between behavior that results in the presentation of a reward and behavior that does not.

In the out-of-seat example used above, if you want to strengthen being next to seat (approximation #2) instead of being near seat (approximation #1), you should only reinforce the student when he is next to his seat and not when he is just near it. When you strengthen both behaviors, the student may assume (correctly) that he can do either and still get reinforced. Since approximation #1 is probably easier for the student than approximation #2, it is likely that if you reinforce him for both approximations he will revert back to the easier behavior (#1). If the student engages in a more difficult (i.e., closer) approximation such as #3 (physical contact with seat) when you were looking for approximation #2, reinforce him for the more difficult behavior. There is no rule that requires the student to go through the successive approximations one at a time. If he can successfully skip some along the way, more power to him!

Shifting criteria for reinforcement

Remember, the teacher should reward successive approximations of the target behavior. The question is, how will you know when a student has performed one approximation long enough and needs to move on to the next? One rule to follow, especially with cognitively slow students, is to move on to the next approximation when the student is able to successfully engage in the current approximating behavior on a variable schedule of reinforcement. For example, in the out-of-seat example used above, the student would be reinforced for being near his seat on a continuous schedule, then on a fixed schedule, and finally on a variable schedule of reinforcement. When he was able to stay near his seat on a variable schedule, for however long you deem necessary, you would shift criteria for reinforcement and move to the next approximation. Again, you would first use a continuous schedule to reinforce him for being next to his seat, then use a fixed schedule, then variable, and so on. The reason you want the student doing one approximation on a variable schedule before moving to the next (closer) approximation is that cognitively slow students may not understand that the contingency for receiving reinforcement has changed, and they may not emit the next approximation for a while. Since you are practicing differential reinforcement, you will no longer be reinforcing the "old" approximation when it occurs; you no longer reinforce approximation #1 while you wait for the student to engage in approximation #2. In this case, extinction of approximation #1 may occur while you wait for the student to engage in approximation #2. But by waiting until approximation #1 is well established (on a variable schedule) before moving on to approximation #2, you can lessen the probability of extinction.

Another rule, more appropriate for cognitively able students, is to simply spend an arbitrary amount of time at a given approximation and at some point inform the student that the contingency for receiving reinforcement is going to change. Let's say that you were shaping the number of assignments completed. You could shift from one approximation to the next when your student is able to perform an approximation for two consecutive days. In this instance, it doesn't matter whether or not the student is being reinforced on a variable schedule before moving on to the next approximation. You can assume that the student understands that the contingency for receiving reinforcement will change.

How to shape behavior

Here are the specific steps you will need to use in any shaping program. The first step is to decide on the target behavior. This is the "goal"—the point at which you want to stop intervening. Let's suppose you have a student who doesn't speak at all unless she is spoken to by one particular student in your class, and even then she only makes one-word responses (e.g., "Yes" or "No") and never establishes eye contact. The target behavior you specify might be for her to initiate conversations with her peers.

The second step in the program is to decide where to start. This means establishing which behavior the student has in her present repertoire that you are going to reinforce now. For example, in our hypothetical case of the withdrawn student, you would probably begin the shaping program by reinforcing the student when she is talking to her one friend whenever her friend asks a question, without requiring eye contact.

The third step is to decide what you are going to use to reward the student. Let's suppose that after using the interest inventory or observation method you decide to reinforce the shy student with tokens to be turned in later in exchange for time spent coloring.

The next step is to make a list of successive approximations. For example, let's list the first approximation of the target behavior as "Verbally responds to questions from her friend requiring one-word answers, e.g., `Yes' or `No' without eye contact." This is the behavior you chose in step two above. A list of successive approximations of this target behavior appears in Figure 5.20, where I have outlined the entire shaping program for this hypothetical case.

After implementing a program, you may find that the approximations are too far apart (i.e., require rather severe jumps). There is no law saying you can't add new approximations in between those originally listed.

After you have listed the chosen approximations, you may begin implementing the program by rewarding the first approximation. Whenever the student talks to her friend she is given a token; when she is not talking to her friend, she receives no tokens. This is differential reinforcement. When the student is

Where To Stop: When student initiates conversations (i.e., is able to get a student's attention by calling his or her name and asking a question while maintaining eye contact with that person) with all classmates

Where To Start: When she verbally responds to questions from her friend requiring one-word answers (e.g., "yes" or "no") without eye contact

Reward: Token dispensed by peers, to be turned in for time spent coloring

Approximations:

1. When she verbally responds to questions from her friend requiring one-word answers (e.g., "yes" or "no") without eye contact

2. When she verbally responds to questions from her friend requiring two- or three-word answers without eye contact

3. Same as approximation 2 with brief eye contact

4. Same as approximation 3 maintaining eye contact while speaking

5. When she initiates verbal communication with her friend by calling her name to get her attention

6. When she gets her friend's attention and asks her a question

7. Same as approximation 6 with a second student (other than her friend)

Continue adding students until target student is able to initiate conversation with all classmates.

Shift criterion for reinforcement when she is able to perform an approximation on a variable-ratio schedule for one full day.

Figure 5.20.   Shaping program.

able to talk to her friend on a variable schedule of reinforcement or she is able to demonstrate this behavior over a prespecified period of time (e.g., 1 day, 1 week), you may decide to go on to the next approximation. This move entails shifting the criteria for reinforcement. You continue to move through each successive approximation until the student is able to engage in the target behavior on a variable schedule of reinforcement or demonstrate each approximate behavior over a prespecified period of time. If the student has difficulty performing at any one of the approximation stages, you can always return to an earlier (preceding) approximation and continue to work on it or add a new approximation that is harder than the old one but not as hard as the new one with which the student is having trouble.

☑ Checkpoint 5.5

[pages 152–154]

Fill in the answers to the following items (1–13). Check your responses by referring to the text; relevant page numbers appear in brackets.

Shaping should be used when **(1)** _____

_____

_____

_____

_____[152]

List and describe the three basic components in a shaping program:

(2) _____

_____

_____

_____

(3) _____

_____

_____

_____

(4) _____

_____

_____

_____ [152–153]

The steps in writing a shaping program are:

(5) _____

_____

(6) _____

_____

(continues)

CHECKPOINT 5.5, continued

(7) _____

_____

(8) _____

_____[153–154]

List five successive approximations in a shaping program for a student who can pick up a pencil (start behavior) with the goal that she write her name from memory (stop behavior). Check your responses against the answers shown following Item 13.

(9) _____

_____

(10) _____

_____

(11) _____

_____

(12) _____

_____

(13) _____

ANSWERS: While your approximations do not have to match mine exactly, they should represent change in behavior (not the environment) and each should be a closer approximation of the stop behavior *without being the stop behavior*. For example: (9) picks up pencil; (10) makes controlled marks with pencil; (11) makes straight and curved lines with pencil; (12) copies letters with pencil; (13) copies name with pencil.

Redo any items you missed. If you missed more than 3 of the items, reread the material. Otherwise, continue on to the next section.

Fading

Fading is often confused with shaping. According to Mikulas (1978), fading involves "taking a behavior that occurs in one situation and getting it to occur in a second situation by gradually changing the first situation into the second" (p. 85). Notice that the definition states that the *situation* is gradually changed, not the student's behavior. This is in marked contrast to shaping, where the student's behavior is gradually changed. In other words, shaping involves approximations of responses and fading involves approximations of stimuli. Shaping provides an effective means of changing behavior from one response to another, while fading helps facilitate the generalization of that behavior change from one setting to another. See Figure 5.21 for examples of shaping and fading.

Suppose you are teaching in a resource room for learners with disabilities and want to mainstream one of your students. However, you have some concerns about him generalizing his on-task behavior from the resource room to the regular classroom. Suppose that, through shaping, you get your student to attend to task in the resource room 90% of the time observed. However, your resource room allows the student to work in a relatively distraction-free environment and to earn tokens he may exchange for back-up activity reinforcers if he stays on task. Unfortunately, the real world of the mainstream classroom is filled with distractions and the only payoffs for on-task behavior are receiving passing grades, social reinforcement, avoiding reprimands, and response cost. In the resource room your student is seated facing a wall, with a portable study carrel on his desk that limits visual distractions from the front and the sides. In addition, he is wearing a headset hooked to a tape recorder playing classical music, which limits the distraction of extraneous auditory stimuli in the room. A laminated countoon is taped to the student's desk and he is awarded check marks (to be written on the countoon) on a VI schedule for on-task behavior. Since you have an aide and a smaller number of students than the main-

Figure 5.21. Shaping vs. fading.

stream teacher, you are usually able to provide the student with attention very quickly. He also has "dispatch" material (i.e., busy work) to do if he has to wait for you. Because it is impossible to expect the mainstream teacher to replicate all of this in her classroom, it is therefore necessary to gradually change (i.e., fade) the environmental variables in your room so that it more closely resembles the mainstream classroom. If your student is able to maintain his on-task behavior at or near 90% in the presence of these new environmental variables, he should be ready for his new class. One of the first things you might do is to change the classical music on his headset to class noise from a room with 25 to 30 students. Ask the mainstream teacher if she will tape-record the noise in her room during activity periods. In addition to fading out the classical music, you are providing the student with an audio distraction that he will have to become used to.

The second step might be to remove the headset completely, requiring the student to listen to the class noise directly from the tape recorder in your room. Next, you might remove one or both of the side panels on the desktop study carrel. This will allow your student to learn to deal with peripheral visual distractions. After this you might have him turn his desk around so that he is no longer facing the wall but has visual access to the entire room. Your next step might be to train your student to wait for adult attention for longer and longer periods of time; first with dispatch work, then without. Your goal in this case is to teach patience and the ability to stay out of trouble while waiting without any assigned task. These are skills that the students in the regular class have learned. Continue to use your token economy throughout the fading process described above. Eventually, you will begin to wean your student off of the token economy and use more of the consequences found in the regular classroom, such as grades, reprimands, social reinforcement, and response cost. Finally, when you think he is ready, you could let the student attend the mainstream class for brief periods of time, gradually increasing the duration of each visit until he has been completely mainstreamed. This entire fading process is outlined in Figure 5.22. Notice that it is the environment (stimuli) that gradually changes, while the student's behavior (response) stays the same.

Chaining

The technique of *chaining* may be used to strengthen new responses by helping students to remember to engage in the target behavior. Similarly, chaining may also be used to weaken old maladaptive behaviors that have become so habitual that the student cannot stop engaging in them even if he wants to. Students often have difficulty changing their behavior because they can't remember to behave differently. Their old, unwanted behavior is the result of a *behavior chain* practiced over and over again for years. For example, when my daughter Kim was a child, she would often forget to put her bike away in the garage at the end of each day. It would sit by the front door each night providing a temptation to any would-be bicycle thief. I'm not talking about a little tricycle; this was a relatively expensive ten-speed bike. I tried a number of interventions before I thought about chaining. I put her bike away for her and reminded her to put it away herself next time. I yelled at her to put her bike away. I hid her bike and told her that it was stolen. I took away her bike and/or grounded her for a period of time. On those few occasions when she would remember to put her bike away without being told to do so, I would praise her to the skies. Once, I even woke her up in the middle of night and made her go outside to put her bike away. None of these interventions worked. Kim had practiced this behavior so many times in the past that it had become virtually impossible for her to behave any other way. I needed to come up with a new behavior chain and teach it to her before I could get rid of the old one. The old chain was: ride bike home → stop bike in driveway → get off bike → walk bike to front door → put down kick stand → enter house through front door. Each response in this chain served as a stimulus for the next response. I had to teach her a new chain of behaviors that would end up with the bike in the garage. The new chain was: ride bike home → stop bike in driveway → get off bike → walk bike to garage → open garage door → put bike in garage → close garage door → enter house through garage.

Needless to say, writing a new behavior chain did not automatically change Kim's behavior. First, Kim had to be taught the new chain. Whenever she came home on her bike and left it in front of the house, I would have her get back on it, ride around the block, come home again, stop the bike in the driveway, get off the bike, walk it to the garage, open the garage door, put the bike in the garage, close the garage door, and enter the house through the garage. I continued to do this, and praised Kim for her new behavior, until she was able to go through the new chain by herself (i.e., without being reminded). I can't say that her behavior changed overnight, but eventually it did change.

Problem: Student C. is a handicapped learner currently placed in a resource room. His teacher wants to main-stream him into the regular fifth-grade classroom. However, while C. is able to attend to task in the resource room (on task 90% of time observed), trial placement in the regular classroom indicates that this behavior has not generalized (on task 10% of time observed).

1. *Where to stop:* When C. is able to attend to task 90% of the time observed in the regular fifth-grade classroom without using any of the instructional "supports" operating in the resource room (e.g., headset with music, token economy).

2. *Where to start:* When C. is able to attend to task 90% of the time observed in the resource room while using all of the instructional "supports" (e.g., headset with music, token economy, etc.).

3. *Successive approximations:*

   When C. is able to attend to task 90% of the time in the resource room:

   a. While using all of the instructional "supports" except he will listen to class noise on his headset instead of classical music;

   b. Same as (a) but without wearing headset;

   c. Same as (b) but without side panels to study carrel;

   d. Same as (c) but with desk facing classroom (instead of wall);

   e. Same as (d) but without adult supervision for 1 minute;

   f. Same as (e) but without adult supervision for 2 minutes;

   g. Same as (f) but without adult supervision for 3 minutes;

   h. Same as (g) but without dispatch ("busy") work;

   i. Same as (h) but without token reinforcement.

4. *Criteria for moving to next approximation:* When C. is able to perform satisfactorily (i.e., attend 90% of time observed) for a two-hour interval.

Figure 5.22 Fading program.

Chaining can be used to strengthen new, incompatible (i.e., competing) behaviors in place of old, unwanted behavior chains. The steps in the process are:

1. Identify the responses in the old behavior chain, starting back far enough to include responses that serve as stimuli to the unwanted behavior;

2. write a new behavior chain, again starting well before the target behavior;

3. model the new behavior chain for the student;

4. have the student go through the new chain to demonstrate that she knows what to do;

5. reinforce the student whenever she engages in the new behavior; and

6. should she revert back to the old chain, take her through the new chain right from the beginning again.

In some instances, it may be necessary to employ a self-instruction technique similar to the material discussed in Chapter 12. After telling the student what to do, have her demonstrate each response as she gives herself the direction to do so. At first, have her do this out loud; later, she can merely whisper the directions or silently think them. Eventually the behavior should become automatic and she will not have to think about it at all.

☑ **Checkpoint 5.6**

[pages 156–159]

Fill in the answers to the following items (1–9). Check your responses by referring to the text; relevant page numbers appear in brackets.

Fading should be used when **(1)** _____

_____

_____ [156]

The difference between fading and shaping is **(2)**

_____

_____

_____

_____ [156]

List five successive approximations in a fading program for a student who will stay in his kindergarten class only if his mother sits there with him on her lap (start behavior). The goal is for him to stay in kindergarten without his mother's presence at school (stop behavior). Check your responses against the answers shown following Item 7.

(3) _____

_____

(continues)

CHECKPOINT 5.6, continued

(4) _____

_____

(5) _____

_____

(6) _____

_____

(7) _____

ANSWERS: While your approximations do not have to match mine exactly, they should represent change in the environment (not in behavior) and each should be a closer approximation of the stop behavior *without being the stop behavior.* For example: (3) stays in room with mother sitting next to him holding his hand; (4) stays in room with mother sitting next to him not touching him; (5) stays in room with mother close by (but not next to him); (6) stays in room with mother somewhere (readily visible) in room; (7) stays in room with mother somewhere (not readily visible) in room.

Chaining is **(8)** _____

_____ [157].

Chaining should be used when **(9)** _____

_____

_____ [157]

Redo any items you missed. If you missed more than 2 of the items, reread the material. Otherwise, continue on to the next section.

Contingency Contracting

Another approach to add to your repertoire of behavior management skills is *contingency contracting*. Contingency contracting is based on the Premack principle: If a high-frequency response is made contingent upon a low-frequency response often enough, the low-frequency response is likely to become more frequent in the future (Premack, 1959). For example, if a low-achieving student is left to choose between reading a comic book and a history text, he will probably choose the comic book. We may, therefore, say that the high-frequency (Hi-F) behavior is comic book reading while history-text reading is the low-frequency (Lo-F) behavior. According to the Premack principle, if comic book reading (Hi-F) is made contingent upon reading the history text (Lo-F), chances are the student will be more inclined to read the history text in the future without any prompting from his teacher.

Actually, many teachers and most parents have been using the Premack principle for years without knowing it. My own grandmother, a Russian immigrant with little education, never heard of behavior modification, let alone the Premack principle. Yet she used Premack all the time. Whenever my cousins and I ate at Grandma's house, we were required to drink our milk before we could have soda pop and to finish all of our vegies if we wanted to get our dessert. Knowing that was the rule at Grandma's, we never argued or complained the way we did at home where soda or dessert was sometimes dispensed on a non-contingent basis. We knew we wouldn't get any soda or dessert unless we did what Grandma wanted, so we complied without a fuss. Today, I use Premack on my own behavior whenever I am faced with an aversive task. For example, I do not like grading students' papers at all! However, I do like to watch TV and read fiction or magazines. Therefore, whenever I have a pile of student papers to grade, I make an informal (unwritten) contract with myself that I will do so much paper grading (Lo-F) before I allow myself a certain amount of TV or reading (Hi-F). I might grade five papers and then reward myself with thirty minutes of reading or TV watching. In fact, if it wasn't for Premack, this book might never have been written; writing is a low-frequency behavior for me.

Premack's method can also be used to strengthen a number of Lo-F student behaviors such as staying in seat, studying, completing work assigned, doing homework, coming to class prepared, and sharing work materials with peers, among others. It is not as difficult to find Hi-F student behavior to use as reinforcement. If you watch the student closely during his free time, you will be able to identify something he enjoys doing. As mentioned earlier in this chapter, don't be afraid to use Hi-F behavior which is undesirable in some settings as a payoff for Lo-F behavior, as long as the reward is not harmful. For example, even though one of your students spends more time beating up his peers than he does working on his math, you shouldn't make beating up peers contingent upon working on math. However, if a student spends more time daydreaming than working, there is nothing wrong with using daydreaming as a payoff for working behavior. In this instance, simply tell the student that for every assignment he completes, he will receive two minutes to daydream. For students who are less able, you could incorporate shaping into the program by having them start with two minutes of daydreaming for every example computed or sentence written rather than for completing the entire assignment.

With older or more developmentally able students, you might wish to expand on the Premack principle by actually writing up a contract. A sample set of negotiations might sound like this:

TEACHER: I know you would rather color than practice your cursive writing but we both know that if I let you color now and write later, you probably won't get much writing done without my nagging and we both hate that! So I want you to do your writing first and for every five letters written correctly, you can give yourself one minute of coloring time when you've finished all of the writing.

STUDENT: Five letters for one minute is too hard! I can't do that!

TEACHER: Well, what do you think you could do for the one minute of coloring?

STUDENT: I guess I could do three.

TEACHER: Well, I think you could do the five letters but I'd be willing to let you do only four letters correctly for each minute of coloring. That's the best I can do. You can always sit and do nothing at all. No writing or no coloring. The choice is yours.

Once the teacher and the student agree on the contingency and the payoff, you may write the contract. An example of a simple contract based on these negotiations is shown in Figure 5.23.

The following rules regarding contracts have been suggested by Homme and his associates in their excellent book on contingency contracting (Homme, Csanyi, Gonzales, & Rechs, 1969).

1. Beginning contracts should call for and reward small approximations of the target behavior. In other words, use shaping whenever appropriate.

2. Reward frequently with small amounts rather than with one big reward given later.

3. The contract should call for and reward accomplishment, not blind obedience. Have the student work on adaptive or target behaviors such as assignments completed, coming to class on time and/or prepared, getting along with peers, working independently, and accepting criticism from others.

4. Reward the student's performance only after it occurs. Do not give non-contingent reinforcement.

5. The contract should be fair and written in positive terms. In other words, something good will happen to the student if he engages in desirable behavior. Avoid statements such as "the student will stay after school for one hour if he *fails* to complete his work" or "if the student goes all day *without* fighting, he gets to take home a library book." Instead, write "the student will receive ten minutes of free time during the last hour of the school day for each work assignment *successfully completed,* up to six assignments."

6. The terms of the contract should be clear. Make the student paraphrase the terms to be sure he understands them.

7. The intervention (i.e., the contingency and the payoff) must be used systematically. This means that any changes in the contingency and/or the payoff must be based upon data collected by the teacher, and that decisions regarding the program cannot be made in a haphazard fashion. Be consistent and follow through!

The teacher will _____

_____

_____

_____

if the student_____

will _____

_____

_____

_____

Signed_____

Date _____

Signed_____

Date _____

Witnessed by _____

Date _____

Figure 5.23. Contract used in contingency contracting program.

Contracts may be written for long- or short-term behavior. For example, you may write up a new contract for a student's behavior in your class every day. At the beginning of school or the beginning of the class period, simply take a blank contract form similar to the one shown in Figure 5.23 and fill it in or have the student fill it in, or do it jointly. It then becomes the student's responsibility to live up to his part of the contract for the school day or for the class period and it is your responsibility to "pay up" according to the agreement. If you don't want to

Date	What Student Did (Behavior)	Signature	What Parent Did (Consequence)	Signature

Name _____   Week _____

If found, please return to _____

Example 5.24. Daily report card.

It is understood by all parties (signed below) that the following responsibilities must be attended to:

1. It is the *school's responsibility* to fill out Casey's daily report card regarding tardy and attending behavior. All of Casey's teachers will do so. If the card is not brought to school the parents must be notified.

2. It is the *parents' responsibility* to look at Casey's card daily, initial it, and indicate in writing what consequences occurred. If the card is not brought home, the school should be notified and the consequences agreed upon should occur.

3. It is *Casey's responsibility* to be on time to class, every class, each and every day. It is also his responsibility to bring his card back and forth (home and school) and to see that his teachers and parents sign it.

Signed _____   _____
                    Parent   Date

          _____   _____
                    School   Date

          _____   _____
              Program Manager   Date

          _____   _____
                    Casey   Date

          _____   _____
                                                                Date

Figure 5.25. Contract between student, family, and school.

bother writing up new contracts daily, they can be written for the week, month, term, or even school year, if appropriate.

Contracts can also include other parties in addition to the student and the teacher. For example, you could include the student's parents in a contract in which Hi-F behavior at home such as TV watching, snacking, staying up late, going to movies, sleeping over at a friend's house, and earning allowance, is made contingent upon Lo-F behavior at school (e.g., assignments completed, coming to class prepared or on time, staying on task). Parents can monitor the student's behavior at school via a daily report card such as the one shown in Figure 5.24, which the student takes back and forth between home and school every day. Failure to bring the card home would result in the loss of one or more Hi-F behaviors. This approach requires a great deal of communication and cooperation between parents and the school, but it is well worth the effort because it works! It is especially effective if the parents enter into a contractual agreement in which the school agrees to provide the appropriate consequences for their student's behavior at school (see Figure 5.25). This way, everybody knows what they are responsible for, and the signing of the formal agreement (while not legally binding on any party) results in a more permanent commitment from everyone involved.

Token Reinforcement

A *token economy* is an entire behavior management system that makes use of token reinforcers. Behavior modification itself is often confused with the concept of the token economy, and people often think that behavior modification is nothing more than rewarding desirable student behavior with tokens that are exchanged later for some favored activity, food, or toy. Fortunately, as you know, there is more to behavior modification than just token reinforcement. What you may not know is that there is also more to token reinforcement than just rewarding desirable student behavior with tokens that are exchanged later for a back-up reinforcer. Let's examine all of the questions that must be considered before a token system can be put into use.

1. *What are the contingencies for the tokens?* In other words, what does the student have to do to earn tokens? This should be made clear at the very outset. If more than one student is working on the same contingencies, a list of contingencies should be posted somewhere in the classroom so that everyone will know what they have to do to earn tokens. Figure 5.26 is an example of a list of group contingencies for earning tokens. When an individual student is working on a contingency or a set of contingencies, a list of that student's contingencies should be attached to his or her desk to serve as a constant reminder of what is expected. Figure 5.27 provides an example of a set of individual contingencies for earning tokens.

2. *What are you going to use for tokens?* Check marks? Stamps or stick-ons? A ticket puncher like train conductors use? Play money? Try to use a variety of tokens whenever possible since students tend to get bored with the same type used over and over again. The tokens should appeal to the particular age group with which you are working. Younger students

---

EARN "JOE DOUGH" BY:

$ 1 RAISING HAND FOR TEACHER'S ATTENTION

$ 1 STAYING ON TASK

$ 2 HELPING ANOTHER STUDENT

$ 1 COMING TO CLASS PREPARED

$ 2 PRAISING A PEER

$ 2 BEING ASSERTIVE (LOOK AT PERSON YOU'RE TALKING TO; SAY "NO" WHEN YOU HAVE A GOOD REASON TO DO SO; ASK FOR THINGS DIRECTLY WITHOUT THREATENING PEOPLE)

$ 2 ACCEPTING CRITICISM

Figure 5.26. Group contingencies for earning tokens.

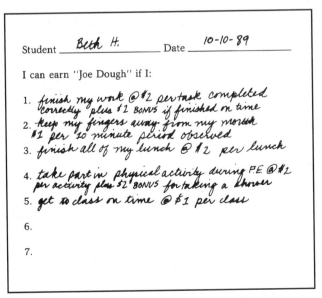

Student _Beth H._   Date _10-10-89_

I can earn "Joe Dough" if I:

1. finish my work @ $2 per task completed correctly plus $1 bonus if finished on time
2. keep my fingers away from my mouth $1 per 10 minute period observed
3. finish all of my lunch @ $2 per lunch
4. take part in physical activity during P.E. @ $2 per activity plus 52 bonus for taking a shower
5. get to class on time @ $1 per class
6.
7.

Figure 5.27. Individual contingencies for earning tokens.

tend to prefer stick-ons (e.g., stars, animals, or hero figures such as cowboys, astronauts, or cartoon characters). Play money, poker chips, or just plain points are popular with older students. You could get your students to make and/or design the tokens themselves, as long as they don't get into the business of "black market" tokens. This situation occurs when students given access to the tokens take advantage of this access by selling tokens to their peers in exchange for favors or a share in the back-up reinforcers. This situation can be easily avoided if you validate each token with a special stamp or your signature and only accept validated tokens from students in exchange for back-up reinforcers. Figure 5.28 is an example of a simple token I have used in the past called "Joe Dough." You can make this type of token in different denominations such as 1s, 5s, 10s, 20s, 50s, and 100s. Older students, especially those in upper elementary and junior high school, seem to enjoy this type of token. It gives them the impression that they are actually earning money, like adults, for their work and behavior. Whatever tokens you decide to use, be sure that they can be given quickly and easily, are cheap and durable, and that it is impossible for the students to give themselves tokens without earning them.

3. *What is the ratio between student behavior and tokens dispensed?* In other words, how much are you going to pay your students, in tokens, for their work and behavior, and what are you going to charge them, in tokens, for the back-up reinforcers?

4. *What are you going to use for back-up reinforcers?* Most token economies use prizes as back-up reinforcers. A prize is something that the average student would not normally get in school, such as a gift certificate to McDonald's. Some token economies use entitlements as back-up reinforcers; these include things that students would normally receive, such as eating lunch in the cafeteria with their peers, attending assemblies, and belonging to school clubs. While entitlements are normally provided to the average student "free of charge," the student in the entitlement token system must "buy" them with tokens earned for appropriate behavior. Whichever system you use, it is unlikely that it will work effectively unless you have back-up reinforcers that are, in fact, reinforcing to your students as well as feasible to dispense. So, unless you know someone in the travel business, don't promise to provide paid vacations to Disneyland or ski trips to Aspen. Be realistic about what students can earn with their tokens and, above all, make sure the prize is something they want. Figure 5.29 is an example of a reinforcing event menu.

Figure 5.28. Token (play money) used in token economy.

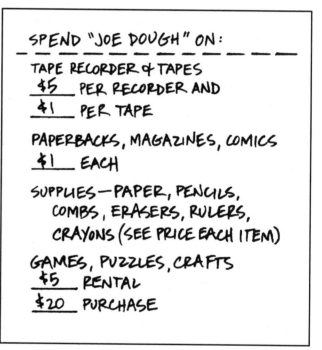

Figure 5.29. Reinforcing event menu for use in token economy.

5. *Who dispenses the tokens?* Tokens are usually dispensed by an authority figure in the student's environment such as a teacher, aide, or peer tutor.

6. *When should they be given?* Tokens should be used when it is not feasible or appropriate to give the student the back-up reinforcer. However, like any reinforcer, tokens should be presented as soon as possible after the contingency for reinforcement is performed. For this reason, the tokens you use should be able to be dispensed quickly and easily

according to whatever reinforcement schedule you may be following with a given student.

7. *How will the tokens be given?* This depends on the type of token used. Check marks can be made by the teacher on her copy of the student's token sheet. Stars and stick-ons can be given to the student for him to paste on his token sheet. (Note that many stick-ons have other reinforcing properties, such as a pleasing smell or taste.) Chips or play money may be given directly to the student or placed in the student's "bank" by the teacher. Two criteria for deciding how the tokens will be dispensed are (a) the method must be reinforcing for the student (i.e., he should be aware that he is going to get a token or tokens) and (b) the method should be as easy as possible for the teacher to use (i.e., she should dispense the tokens so that it won't interfere with her teaching). The teacher probably does not want to become a bookkeeper or an accountant, so keep it simple.

8. *When will the tokens be redeemed (i.e., turned in for the back-up reinforcer)?* This depends on the student's need. Some may be able to wait until the end of the day or even the end of the week before redeeming their tokens. Others may need the back-up reinforcer sooner. Obviously, the longer the student can wait, the better. The selection of a time for the tokens to be redeemed will also depend upon the back-up reinforcer that is being used. For example, if reading comic books is the back-up reinforcer, the student could conceivably turn in his tokens virtually any time during the day. Since comic book reading does not require any elaborate involvement on the part of the teacher, she is free to continue to teach while the student cashes in his tokens for free time reading comics. However, if the back-up reinforcer is teacher attention or a special event such as a class auction or any activity that might disrupt the learning environment, it would be necessary for the teacher to set up a special time for the redemption of tokens. Again, this time would be determined by the teacher's schedule and her students' ability to delay gratification (i.e., wait for the back-up reinforcers).

Implementation

Once you have attended to all of the above, you are ready to implement your token economy. If you have planned accordingly, you should not encounter many problems. However, as a firm believer in Murphy's Law (i.e., if something can go wrong, it will), I would be on the lookout for one or more of the following.

1. *The student who has earned all of the tokens she needs before the school day or class period is over and starts to misbehave.* This student thinks she has nothing to lose since she already has enough points for the back-up reinforcer she wants. All students should be told at the beginning of the program that although they can earn points for appropriate behavior, they can also lose them for inappropriate behavior. This is called *response cost* and will be discussed in more detail in the next chapter. Response cost helps to keep students' behavior under control because they don't want to lose what they have worked so hard to earn. It should be explicitly understood that once response cost is put into effect and tokens are taken away for misbehavior, the student must have the opportunity to earn them back again. If the student feels she doesn't have the opportunity to earn back lost tokens, she may no longer be motivated to behave appropriately. Thus, you have the same situation you had earlier where the student had all of the tokens she needed before the end of the school day and felt that she could afford to misbehave.

2. *The student who complains because he has to do more to earn the same amount of tokens as his peers.* Because your students will vary in terms of their ability, it is likely that two of them might earn the same amount of tokens even though one would be required to do twice the amount of the work as the other. To solve this problem you might try one of the following: First, you could have the "slow" student perform five jobs and if each was done correctly, he would receive ten tokens apiece for a total of fifty tokens for the day. In the meantime, you could have the "fast" student be responsible for completing ten jobs at a rate of ten tokens per job or one hundred tokens for the day. This way, you would not be penalizing the fast student for his greater ability and you would be providing incentive for the slow student to work harder and faster so that he too could add more jobs (and more tokens) each day. A second option would be to limit both the fast and slow student to the same number of jobs per day but agree to pay the fast student more for his work because his jobs are more difficult. Again, this would provide the slow student with an incentive to work harder in order to get more difficult assignments and the opportunity to earn higher pay.

3. *The student who uses extortion to get tokens or back-up reinforcers from peers.* While this sounds more ominous than it actually is, extortion can make your token system fail. What usually happens is that one student who is bigger or tougher than the other students extorts tokens or back-up reinforcers from them under threat of physical harm. This usually occurs when the extortionist is not getting enough

tokens in the classroom, either because he fails to participate in the token economy or because the teacher has made it too difficult for him to earn as many tokens as his peers. To avoid extortion in your classroom make sure that all of your students have the opportunity to earn as many tokens as they feel they need. Sit down and contract with them at the beginning of the program to determine the contingency required, tokens received, back-up reinforcers available and cost for each. Contracting in the classroom can be similar to contracts between employer and employee in the business world. When the employee perceives this agreement as fair and the payoffs as equitable and attainable, he is less likely to take advantage of his employer or his colleagues. You can also discourage extortion in your classroom by keeping close track of the tokens earned by your students. If one or more of them feel that they need to extort tokens from their peers, don't let his behavior lead to a payoff. You can stop this simply by knowing how many tokens each of your students should have. Unfortunately, there is little that you can do to discourage the extortion of back-up reinforcers outside of the classroom if you are using tangible or primary reinforcers such as books, toys, or granola bars. Unless one of your students lets you know what is happening, you may not even find out any extortion has occurred. This is one good reason for avoiding the use of tangible items as back-up reinforcers. If you stick with social reinforcement as well as activity reinforcers awarded during school hours, keep close track of the tokens your students have earned, and make sure that everyone has ample opportunity to share in the "wealth," extortion should not be a problem.

4. *The student who refuses to go off the token economy.* What student in his right mind would voluntarily give up Big Macs, comic books, and model airplanes for pats on the back, smiling faces, and passing grades? What do you say to your students when you feel that they no longer need prizes for behaving properly? If you simply tell them that they no longer need prizes because their behavior is so good, won't they revert back to their old ways in order to get the prizes again? (See Figure 5.30.) I don't know about your students, but I certainly would! The message you are communicating to them is that crime does pay: If you are bad in school, you get tokens; if you are good in school, no tokens. While I'm not suggesting that this situation is inevitable, it does occur and you should take some necessary precautions to avoid it. First of all, the problem is not weaning students off the tokens as much as it's getting them off the back-up reinforcers.

Figure 5.30. Avoid setting yourself up for failure. Be sure to take into account things that typically go wrong with token economies, and plan accordingly.

It's not that the student doesn't want to give up the tokens; he doesn't want to give up what he can buy with them. One way to avoid this situation is to have your students redeem tokens for back-up reinforcers that the average student gets for "free." Instead of using junk food, toys, or trips to the local pizza parlor or skating rink as prizes for work and good behavior, have your students earn entitlements such as eating lunch with their peers in the school cafeteria, attending school assemblies, joining school clubs, participating in intramural or interscholastic athletic programs, and going on field trips, for example. There are two precautions you should be aware of when you use entitlements as back-up reinforcers. First of all, you cannot use access to non-academic classes such as music, PE, art, or shop as a back-up reinforcer, because this would be a violation of Constitutional rights. Second, I would only use entitlements as back-up reinforcers after consulting with the student's IEP team. If it is determined that it is in the student's best interests that he participate in a school experience typically considered an entitlement, it would be unethical (not to mention illegal) to require him to earn this experience.

If you must use prizes, you can still wean students off your token economy if you remember to keep increasing the contingencies for earning tokens. Make it more and more difficult for the student to earn the same amount of tokens as she improves. If she had to stay in her seat 10 minutes in order to earn ten tokens before, when her behavior changes, have her stay in her seat 15 minutes to earn the same amount. Then 20 minutes, 30, and so on. If she balks at having to do more things or work harder to earn the same amount of tokens, tell her she has other options, and list them for her. For example, she can always go off the token economy and work for "nothing." She can stay on the token economy and buy entitlements instead of prizes. She can stop working altogether and watch her peers earn and spend their tokens. She can become disruptive and be punished every day instead of being rewarded. Make it clear that the decision is hers to make. I would also try very hard to convince her that although tokens are a crutch she needs now to help her change her behavior, by working for longer and longer periods of time without receiving tokens, she will eventually be able to work without them and she should take a great deal of satisfaction in that accomplishment.

Also remember to keep giving the student social reinforcement in liberal amounts even though you are cutting back on the tokens. Make sure your praise focuses on her behavior (i.e., the contingency for the tokens). Don't praise her for the amount of tokens she earned but for the work completed or the behavior change that led to the token reinforcement. Make her more aware of the change in her behavior and less aware of the tokens she has earned as a result of that change. Your goal is to make her value her new behavior more than the tokens she receives for it. If you accomplish this goal, weaning her off the token economy should become less difficult.

(*Checkpoint 5.7 follows, on p. 168*)

✔ Checkpoint 5.7

[pages 160–167]

Fill in the answers to the following items (1–16). Check your responses by referring to the text; relevant page numbers appear in brackets.

The Premack principle is **(1)** _____

_____

_____

_____ [160].

Three rules for writing contracts with students are:

(2) _____

_____

(3) _____

_____

(4) _____

_____[161]

There are a number of factors to consider in designing a token economy. They are:

(5)_____

_____

(6)_____

_____

(7)_____

_____

(8)_____

_____

(9)_____

_____

(10)_____

_____

(continues)

CHECKPOINT 5.7, continued

(11) _____

_____

(12) _____

_____ [163–165]

There are several things that can go wrong in a token economy. These are listed below. State a solution for each problem.

Student has all tokens she needs for back-up reinforcer and begins to misbehave.

(13)_____

_____

_____

_____[165]

Student complains about having to do more to earn same number of tokens as peers.

(14)_____

_____

_____

_____[165]

Student extorts tokens from peers.

(15)_____

_____

_____

_____[165–166]

Student refuses to go off token economy.

(16)_____

_____

_____

_____[166–167]

Redo any items you missed. If you missed more than 3 of the items, reread the material. Otherwise, continue on to the next section.

Level Systems

A *level system* is another way to wean students off of the contrived extrinsic reinforcement programs typically used in special education settings. Each level in the system is a closer approximation of the mainstream classroom in terms of the reinforcement dispensed, who dispenses it, and when. For example, in the level system displayed in Figure 5.31, all students at level one ("freshman") receive poker chips awarded by the teacher every fifteen minutes. The contingencies (i.e., expectations) for earning the poker chips are relatively low-level behaviors the students need to survive in the special education setting. Students at the "senior" level receive grades from the teacher on a report card at the end of the week, contingent upon engaging in relatively high-level behaviors they need to survive in the mainstream setting. Seniors are not only able to purchase a wide variety of reinforcers, they are entitled to the reinforcers that students at lower levels must purchase with tokens. Another way level systems help to wean students off of extrinsic reinforcement programs is to gradually make the students themselves the primary change agents. This way, the environment has less and less control over the student's behavior. In the level system displayed in Figure 5.32, students assume more and more responsibility for their behavior as they move from level to level. In Level 1, the teacher is the primary change agent, responsible for targeting, evaluating, consequating, and monitoring student behavior. In Level 2, the stu-

Level One:	Each student begins the school year in Level One where tokens such as poker chips are given approximately every 15 minutes for appropriate academic and social behavior. Every morning and afternoon each student is allowed to rent games, materials, or activity privileges during a 15-minute free time period. Prices of rentals vary according to demand. Upon reaching a specified level of successful performance (e.g., 90% academic success for 10 consecutive days with no major rule infraction), a student may move to Level Two.
Level Two:	In Level Two, tokens are replaced with a card which is marked with checks for correct academic and social behavior every half hour. The checkmarks are exchanged at the end of the day for listed classroom privileges for the following day (e.g., office messenger, paper passer, teacher assistant, media operator). In addition, students on Level Two can use previously purchased activity, material, or game items from Level One free of charge. In effect, it becomes attractive to attain Level Two because more privileges are available but the frequency of reinforcement is decreased and the "concreteness" of tokens (e.g., poker chips) is reduced to checkmarks. Upon reaching another specified criterion of successful performance (e.g., 90% academic success for 10 consecutive days with no major rule infraction) a student may move to Level Three.
Level Three:	In Level Three, checkmarks are replaced by contracts which cover each morning and afternoon. At the end of each session, the teacher reviews each student in Level Three and determines if the contract was met. The students meeting criterion earn schoolwide privileges such as library pass, study hall pass, special period with another class such as P.E. or other appropriate privileges involving increased responsibility. Level One and Level Two privileges are now free for students at Level Three.
Level Four:	Following another successful 10 days, students at Level Three may attain Level Four, in which weekly report cards determine whether goals are met. In Level Four, special responsibilities are encouraged such as school patrol, cafeteria monitors, tutoring others.
Summary:	Each level contains a minimum performance criterion for academic and social behavior. As the student advances in level, a failure to meet the minimum criterion at the advanced level causes the student to move back one level and necessitates working back through demonstrated success. This criterion for backward movement enables those who need more help to be identified quickly and returned to an appropriate level.

Figure 5.31. Illustration of a level system with a token economy. (From "Suggestions for Phasing Out Token Economy Systems in Primary and Intermediate Grades," by L. J. La Nunziata, Jr., K. P. Hunt, and J. O. Cooper, 1984, *Techniques, 1,* pp. 153, 155. Copyright 1984 by *Techniques.* Reprinted by permission.)

Level	Expectations	Incentives
1	attends school 90% of the time compliance at 100% follows established classroom rules at 90%	buys items from class store

[Teacher is change agent solely responsible for evaluating, consequating, and monitoring student behavior listed under expectations; student advancement contingent upon meeting expectations for not less than 20 days.]

Level	Expectations	Incentives
2	same behaviors as level 1 *plus* prosocial interactions with peers and teacher at 90%	same as level 1 *plus* class jobs (e.g., peer tutor playground equipment monitor, paper monitor, homework monitor, peer tutor, etc.)

[Teacher is responsible for evaluating student behavior and student is responsible for consequating and monitoring own behavior listed under expectations; student advancement contingent upon meeting expectations for not less than 20 days *plus* demonstrated competence at consequating and monitoring own behavior.]

Level	Expectations	Incentives
3	same behaviors as levels 1 and 2 *plus* completes assigned work with 80% accuracy and 90% completion rate	same as level 2 *plus* school jobs (e.g., peer tutor in other classrooms; assistant to maintenance, office, cafeteria staff, etc.)

[Student is change agent solely responsible for evaluating, consequating, and monitoring own behaviors listed under expectations; student advancement contingent upon meeting expectations for not less than 20 days plus demonstrated competence at self-management.]

Level	Expectations	Incentives
4	same behaviors as levels 1–3 *plus* behaviors of student's own choosing	same as level 3 *plus* access to more school jobs (e.g., hall or traffic patrol, etc.)

[Student is change agent solely responsible for managing his/her own behavior; exit from system contingent upon meeting expectations for not less than 20 days and continued demonstrated competence at self-management.]

Figure 5.32. Example of level system featuring increased responsibility of student as change agent.

dent is given responsibility for monitoring his own behavior. In Level 3, the student is responsible for evaluating, consequating, and monitoring his behavior, and in Level 4, he begins targeting new behaviors he wants to add to his repertoire.

Several level systems have been described in the literature (Barbetta, 1990; Bauer & Shea, 1988; Braaten, 1979; Gersten, 1984; Grumley, 1984; Klotz, 1987; Mastropieri, Jenne, & Scruggs, 1988; McCullough, 1989). Most have the same characteristics in common. First and foremost, they all have *a similar*

number of levels. Less than two is obviously not a level system and more than five or six tends to be unwieldy. Each level has a set of *expectations* or contingencies for reinforcement. These typically increase in number and/or sophistication along with the levels. For example, the lowest level may simply require that the student attend school without hurting himself or others. He doesn't have to do any work or interact with peers. As he progresses through the levels, he will be required to engage in more sophisticated behavior such as accurately completing assigned work and interacting with others in a pro-social manner.

The *types of reinforcement given, who gives it,* and *when it is given* also differ from level to level. Usually the most artificial or contrived reinforcement is used at the lowest level while the highest level uses more naturally occurring reinforcers. In the beginning level(s), the teacher acts as the primary change agent and the sole dispenser of reinforcement. In the upper levels, the student takes on the responsibilities of the primary change agent and reinforces himself. Students at the upper levels also receive reinforcement for their behavior less frequently than students at the lower levels. This doesn't necessarily mean they get less reinforcement, it just means they are required to wait longer to get it.

Since students are expected to do more and wait longer for reinforcement at each ascending level, *incentives* for moving from one level to the next must be built in. An example of an incentive is getting reinforcers for "free" at a higher level. For instance, students at Level 1 have to "purchase" unstructured activity time with tokens earned for meeting the expectations at their level, while students at Level 2 receive unstructured activity time automatically, without having to "pay." Students at Level 2 also have available to them a wider variety of reinforcers to choose from and/or purchase. Other less tangible incentives include prestige and relative freedom (albeit with more responsibility) at the higher levels.

Another important component of any level system are the *criteria required* for movement (up or down) through the system. This includes not only the CAP for each expectation (e.g., "completes 90% of assignments with 80% accuracy") but the minimum number of days the student must stay at a given level as well. Although the CAP for each expectation can be easily determined by using students who have already met the expectation, time spent at a given level appears to be determined in a more arbitrary fashion. Time spent at a given level typically increases with each level as the quantity (and quality) of expectations increases from level to level.

While level systems provide a relatively painless means of weaning students off of contrived extrinsic reinforcement, they are not without their critics. After a comprehensive review of the research literature on level systems, Smith and Farrell (1993) concluded that although level systems *appear* to be effective, there is little empirical data to support their efficacy at either changing behavior or facilitating the generalization of behavior change. As for the legality of level systems, Scheuermann, Webber, Partin, and Knies (1994) wrote that certain components of level systems may be in violation of the Individuals with Disabilities Education Act (IDEA). I recommend that you read both articles before designing and/or implementing a level system and, at the very least, observe the following guidelines:

1. Student expectations should be individualized and based primarily upon the objectives provided in each student's Individualized Education Plan (IEP). Why bother writing IEPs for students if you are going to require all of them to meet the same expectations whether they need them or not?

2. Access to mainstream classes and other relevant school activities should be available to students *at all levels* unless otherwise determined by the student's IEP team. Making access to general education experiences contingent upon achieving levels is in violation of students' rights mandated by the IDEA (Scheuermann et al., 1994).

3. Movement through the system should be based on current objective assessment data and not solely on time spent or peer review. Failure to do so is in violation of Section 504 of the Vocational Rehabilitation Act of 1973 (Scheuermann et al., 1994).

Designing a level system

The first step in designing a level system is to generate a list of expectations or requirements for each level. As I mentioned earlier, these expectations should originate from the objectives in each student's IEP. You may wish to add to this list from a list of generic survival behaviors for your classroom and/or from a less-restrictive setting such as a mainstream classroom. The second step is to arrange the expectations on your list in a hierarchy. My recommendation is to arrange the expectations in terms of how important each is for the student to meet. For example, attending school takes priority over completing work assigned since the student can't complete work unless he comes to school. By the same logic, interacting with peers without verbal or physical aggression is more important than being on task.

The third step is to arbitrarily divide your list of expectations into groups of 2 to 4 levels. While you won't be using a statistical procedure such as a factor analysis, you can always group expectations into categories according to need, such as "critical" (the student can't be in school without meeting this expectation), "essential" (the student can't be in the special education class without meeting this expectation), and "desirable" (the student can't excel in the special education class without meeting this expectation). The fourth step requires that you determine where each student is currently functioning and place him in one of the levels based on the expectations he needs to meet.

Last, but not least, you add the rest of the components for each level including incentives and CAP for advancement. I should mention that a level system is not merely a descriptive table of levels and components. It should also include a detailed account of how the system operates. For instance, when and how will the students' status be reviewed? Who will participate in the review? How will the students' behavior be monitored? How long will the students stay at each level? What happens if students need to return to a lower level or to a disciplinary level? How will the operation of the system be communicated to students, staff, and parents? Answers to these and related questions can be found in *Development and Implementation of Leveled Behavior Management Systems* by Sugai and Colvin (1989a).

☑ Checkpoint 5.8

[pages 169–172]

Fill in the answers to the following items (1–14). Check your responses by referring to the text; relevant page numbers appear in brackets.

A level system is typically used to **(1)** _____

_____

_____[169]

Five components of a level system are:

(2) _____

_____

(3) _____

_____

(4) _____

_____

(5) _____

_____

(6) _____

_____ [170–171]

Three precautionary guidelines to follow in designing and implementing a level system are:

(7) _____

_____

_____

(8) _____

_____

_____

(continues)

CHECKPOINT 5.8, continued

(9) _____

_____

_____

_____[171].

The steps to follow in designing a level system are:

(10) _____

_____

_____

_____

(11) _____

_____

_____

(12) _____

_____

_____

(13) _____

_____

_____

(14) _____

_____

_____

_____[171–172].

Redo any items you missed. If you missed more than 3 of the items, reread the material. Otherwise, continue on to the next section.

TROUBLESHOOTING

What should you do if your reinforcement program isn't working? The first thing to do is to find out why. This is called troubleshooting. It's not unlike that section in the operator's manual for a dishwasher or stereo.

1. *Does the student have all the essential prerequisites for the target behavior?* Did you do a diagnostic workup on the student before you designed and implemented your reinforcement program? If not, it must be done now. If you did do a diagnostic workup and concluded that the student had all of the prerequisites for the target behavior, take another look at your diagnostic process. Did you leave out any prerequisites in your task analysis? Were you in error about the status of any of these prerequisites? Were any of your assessments invalid? If you are convinced that your diagnostic workup was valid and that the student has all of the essential prerequisites for the target behavior, go on to another area.

2. *Are you using the correct schedules of reinforcement, and, if so, are you using them correctly?* Did you stay on one schedule too long, or not long enough? Did you use any schedules of reinforcement at all? Did you have the correct schedules written on paper but fail to implement them correctly?

3. *Are you presenting your reinforcers appropriately?* Is the latency between the student's behavior and the reinforcer too long? Are you being enthusiastic enough in your use of social reinforcement so that the student perceives it as sincere? Are you overdoing the use of the reinforcer to the point where it is beginning to lose its reinforcing properties?

4. *Are you using the right reinforcer?* How did you decide to use this particular reinforcer? Observation? Interview? How many people did you interview and how well do they know the student?

5. *Should you have used a shaping program?* Are you expecting too much from the student too soon? If you did use a shaping program, did you make too great a jump between successive approximations? Did you wait until the student

was engaging in an approximation on a variable schedule for a period of time before moving on to the next one?

6. *Are you or anyone else in the student's environment modeling a behavior that is incompatible with the target behavior?* In other words, if you wanted to reinforce staying on task or being in seat, is off-task behavior or out-of-seat behavior being modeled by the student's peers? If not by all of his peers, is it being modeled by a peer considered important enough to emulate?

7. *Are the reinforcers themselves interfering with the target behavior?* Is he spending time playing with his earned tangibles when he should be doing his work?

8. *If you are using a shaping program, did you remember to use differential reinforcement or did you accidentally reinforce old approximations instead of (or in addition to) new approximations?*

9. *If the behavior has been learned (i.e., reinforced) but has not generalized to other settings, have you taken the time to program for generalization through fading?*

NEGATIVE REINFORCEMENT

Although I spend a considerable amount of time at the beginning of this chapter arguing against the use of negative reinforcement, I am in fact a pragmatist, and I know there will be times when you are going to have to use whatever works even if it is not much fun for you or your students. Assuming that you may be called upon to use negative reinforcement in your classroom, you should at least know how to use it effectively. Here are some simple guidelines to follow.

First, use negative reinforcement (R–) when you want to strengthen desirable behavior and there is little or no behavior to reward. You can't reward being in seat or on task if the student is seldom in his seat or on task. If it's too difficult to catch the student being "good," catch him being "bad" and use R– (e.g., "If you don't sit down, you're going to lose _____ of the points you've earned" or "If you don't finish your math by dismissal, you will have to finish it after school"). There is nothing wrong with using R– in this situation. You can't use R+ because there isn't enough appropriate behavior to reinforce. You could always punish his out-of-seat and off-task behavior, but punishment has so many disadvantages (see Chapter 6) that you would be better off using R–.

Another rule is to always make sure you can do what you say you will do. If you tell the student he will have to stay after school if he doesn't sit down, you had better be able to back that up. If you know ahead of time that you will be responsible for Joey if he stays after school, you should be able to stay as long as he does. The point is, don't make any threats you can't keep.

Finally, always make sure that all avenues of retreat are closed for the student. In other words, the only way Joey can avoid detention is to sit down. He can't avoid it by being quiet (and still out of his seat) or by running an errand for you or by going back to his seat and not sitting in it. If you make sitting down the only way he can avoid detention and he wants to avoid it, he will sit down. The only time you might want to leave some room for negotiation or flexibility is when you anticipate a power struggle. If Joey refuses to sit down (in his seat) and you anticipate a power struggle, give him a choice such as "You can either sit down in your seat or find another seat of your choice but you must sit down now." A psychologist friend of mine has suggested that teachers use this strategy, and they have met with some success. It seems that being given a choice makes the student feel as if he is more in control of the situation and this makes him more likely to choose.

☑ Checkpoint 5.9

[pages 174–175]

Fill in the answers to the following items (1–9). Check your responses by referring to the text; relevant page numbers appear in brackets.

Assume that you have implemented a reinforcement program with one of your students and it is not working. Six troubleshooting questions you might ask are:

(1) _____

_____

(2) _____

_____

(3) _____

_____

(4) _____

_____

(5) _____

_____

(6) _____

_____ [174]

Three guidelines to follow in the use of negative reinforcement are:

(7) _____

_____

_____

_____

(8) _____

_____

_____

_____

(9) _____

_____

_____

_____ [174–175].

Redo any items you missed. If you missed more than 2 of the items, reread the material. Otherwise, continue on to the next section.

MODELING

Before Albert Bandura's pioneering work in social learning theory, most behaviorists assumed the only way to strengthen behavior was through reinforcement. The behavior was emitted and was consequated by presenting a pleasing stimulus (as in positive reinforcement) or by removing an aversive stimulus (as in negative reinforcement). The primary focus of the change agent was on consequent events; that is, what happened *after* the behavior occurred. Bandura's research on observational learning (also known as modeling) demonstrated that antecedent events—what happened *before* the behavior occurred—can be just as effective in strengthening behaviors as what happens afterward (Bandura, 1965, 1971; Bandura, Ross, & Ross, 1963).

Modeling is actually one of the driving forces behind consumerism in our society. People we believe are special, such as entertainment and sports stars, go on TV and tell us about the products they use—gee, if Michael Jordan drinks that stuff, it must be good; or, I'll be like Mike if I drink it. Even people we don't know can be effective models. Actors in TV commercials model beer-drinking behavior and we go running to the fridge or the store in an effort to imitate them. Monkey see, monkey do. Those of us who teach know firsthand about the power of modeling: We learned to teach by watching other teachers during our practicum and student teaching experiences. While there is, unfortunately, no student teaching experience generally available for university instructors, one learns how to teach at the university level by watching professors in college and graduate school.

To be sure, modeling is more effective if the imitated behaviors are reinforced by the environment. My infant daughter learned how to say "Poppa" after I modeled it for her and gave her lots of reinforcement (e.g., smiles, hugs, and kisses) after she said anything that sounded remotely like "Poppa." The question is, would she have leaned to say "Poppa" if I hadn't combined modeling with reinforcement? Probably not; but without modeling, there would not have been *any* behavior to reinforce.

The two most important procedures in using modeling successfully are selecting a model and promoting imitation of the model's behavior. According to Sulzer-Azaroff and Mayer (1991), the following criteria should be considered in selecting models: similarity, competence, previous experience, and prestige. Let's examine each.

Selecting a Model

The more characteristics the model has in common with the target student, the more powerful the model will be. Think about it. When companies want to sell things to children, they use other children in their commercials. When they want to sell things to the elderly, they do not use adolescent actors. Age is only one of the characteristics the model should have in common with the target student. Other characteristics include grade, sociocultural background, physical appearance, and talents, as well as deficiencies. Research does suggest that children are more powerful models for other children than are adults (Sulzer-Azaroff & Mayer, 1991). Friends are also more likely to be imitated than are nonfriends.

People who are competent (i.e., accomplish what they set out to do) are the most likely to be imitated (Sulzer-Azaroff & Mayer, 1991). This is probably why we are so eager to run out and spend $100 on a pair of basketball sneakers that Michael Jordan wears; he's about as competent as you can get—maybe it *is* the shoes.

Another important criterion in selecting a model is previous experience. This refers to the quantity and quality of experience the observer has had with the behavior being modeled. In general, observers who have (a) experienced failure at the task being modeled and/or (b) participated in a cooperative learning experience with the model are more likely to imitate the modeled behavior (Sulzer-Azaroff & Mayer, 1991). Let's say you are one of a group of learners who are learning a particular skill. If you get it right the first time, you will probably ignore the other learners in your group unless they solicit your help. If you have difficulty learning the skill, you will probably look to your peers for help and you will choose the most successful learner in the group to imitate. This is what makes cooperative learning and small group instruction such powerful learning experiences.

Prestige of the model should not to be confused with simple competence. The model should not simply be good at the behavior to be imitated. She needs to be perceived by the imitator as having influence or credibility. Competent students who also receive a great deal of reinforcement from peers are more likely to be imitated than those who are competent but, for whatever reason, are not as highly regarded (Bandura et al., 1963).

Promoting Imitation

Once you have selected the model, you need to turn your attention to promoting the imitation of the model's behavior. Sulzer-Azaroff and Mayer (1991) present a number of important procedures for promoting effective modeling.

1. *Highlight the similarity between the model and the observer.* For example, when I teach my graduate students at the university, I tell them about my past experience as a classroom teacher. I want them to know I spent ten years of my professional life in the classroom teaching children and youth with learning and behavioral problems. If my students can identify with me, they are more likely to imitate me.

2. *Encourage role play.* Most social skills programs require that students role play the skills to be learned. They don't merely provide a model for students to imitate—they have students practice imitating the model in a controlled setting where they receive feedback on their performance.

3. *Provide verbal instructions and rules.* This can be especially effective if you follow the self-instructional training format described in Chapter 12.

4. *Keep it simple.* If you want your students to imitate a complex social behavior such as being assertive, imitation is likely to be more successful if the behavior is broken down into small parts and learned as a behavior chain.

5. *Reinforce the model. Vicarious reinforcement* is said to occur when the observer sees the model being reinforced for the behavior to be imitated (Bandura et al., 1963). If the observer sees you reinforce the model for raising a hand (instead of calling out), he is more likely to raise his hand when he wants your attention.

6. *Reinforce the imitator.* When the observer imitates the modeled behavior by raising his hand to get attention, you should reward him as soon as possible.

☑ Checkpoint 5.10

[pages 176–177]

Fill in the answers to the following items (1–11). Check your responses by referring to the text; relevant page numbers appear in brackets.

Modeling is another way to strengthen behavior. The major difference between modeling and reinforcement programs is

(1)_____ [176].

Four criteria for selecting a model are:

(2) _____

(3)_____

(4)_____

(5)_____[176].

Six procedures for promoting effective modeling are:

(6)_____

(7)_____

(8)_____

(9)_____

(10)_____

(11)_____[177].

Redo any items you missed. If you missed more than 2 of the items, reread the material. Otherwise, continue on to the next section.

GENERALIZATION

Short of having students internalize their newly learned behavior, here are some rules to follow if you want to increase the probability that generalization will occur.

First, try to teach behaviors that are likely to be reinforced in a variety of settings. Examples of behaviors that all teachers tend to reinforce are compliance, attending to task, work completion, and engaging in prosocial behavior. Behaviors that are not always reinforced across settings are raising hand for teacher attention, staying in seat, making eye contact, asserting self with peers or teacher, and speaking spontaneously.

Second, try to expose the student you are working with to more than one preceding stimulus or cue. If he learns to respond to the same cue all the time, he will be less likely to respond appropriately to a different cue in another environment. For example, one teacher might place her index finger next to her lips as a cue for her students to stop talking and listen. Another might raise his hand in the air or simply say, "Attention!" It is easier to teach the student to respond to as many different attention cues as possible than it is to try to get all of his teachers to use the same cue.

Third, enlist the support and cooperation of as many change agents in the student's total environment as possible. This includes other teachers, parents, peers, siblings, school staff (e.g., maintenance, cafeteria, office), and bus drivers. While you cannot expect to have everyone's cooperation, it is worth the effort to get as many as possible to try to replicate your reinforcement program, at least at the most basic level.

Fourth, before sending the student to another environment (e.g., another class), find out what behaviors she will need in order to receive positive reinforcement in that environment. One of the reasons students with emotional/behavioral problems have difficulty succeeding in general education settings is that they are mainstreamed with new, improved social behaviors but their academic level of functioning is still much lower than that of their mainstream peers. Because of this, many of them have less opportunity to receive positive reinforcement in the regular classroom and they revert back to their old maladaptive behavior.

Fifth, use the technique of fading to enhance the generalization of newly learned behavior. This is particularly important when you want the student to emit the behavior in a particular setting or situation.

Finally, teach your students self-management skills. A student who knows how to manage his own behavior won't have to count on a different change agent from each and every environment he is in to appropriately consequate his behavior. He can do it himself.

Remember, generalization will occur only if (a) the student has internalized the newly learned behaviors enough to engage in the behavior without extrinsic consequences, or (b) you have programmed specifically for generalization to take place.

✔ Checkpoint 5.11

[page 178]

Fill in the answers to the following items (1–17). Check your responses by referring to the text; relevant page numbers appear in brackets.

Generalization refers to

(1) _____

_____

_____

_____ [178]

Six ways to enhance the generalization of newly learned behaviors are:

(2) _____

_____

(3) _____

_____

(4) _____

_____

(5) _____

_____

(6) _____

_____

(7) _____

_____ [178]

Redo any items you missed. If you missed more than 1 of the items, reread the material. Otherwise, continue on to the Chapter Assessment.

ASSESSMENT / CHAPTER 5 ▐█████████

A list of acceptable responses appears following the Assessment.

Design an intervention for each of the cases below. Try to be specific in describing all of the components, as if you were explaining them to another person (e.g., substitute or student teacher, or instructional assistant).

1. You have a student named PJ who presently will stay on task (i.e., read or write his in-seat assignment) as long as you or your instructional assistant stand over him and provide constant encouragement (e.g., "That's good, PJ. You're doing fine. Keep it up."). Unfortunately, this practice takes too much time away from other students. Write a FADING program that will enable PJ to stay on task at least 90% of the time without anyone (other than PJ) providing encouragement. List at least five successive approximations and explain when you would move from one approximation to the next.

2. Addie needs to learn to raise her hand and wait to be called on when she wants your attention. Design a reinforcement program using secondary reinforcers (e.g., calling on her and/or social praise) to strengthen hand-raising and waiting behavior. Explain how and when you would use each SCHEDULE OF REINFORCEMENT (continuous, fixed, and variable) and whether you would use a ratio or interval schedule.

3. Write a SHAPING program for Arthur who, when teased, looks at the ground and says "No" once in a weak little voice. Your target objective for Arthur is that he establish eye contact and say, "Stop that. I don't like it," in a firm voice and repeat it when necessary.

4. You want to strengthen homework-completing behavior in your son or daughter. Right now, he/she arrives home from school and after entering the house, goes immediately to the room with the TV, sits down on the couch, and turns on the set and watches until dinner in ready. Design a CHAINING program that results in the completion of homework before dinner.

5. You have a student with learning disabilities in your class named Max, who acts hyperactive and impulsive and is constantly getting out of his seat. Write a TOKEN ECONOMY for Max that will enable him to stay in his seat when it is appropriate to do so. Include a contract between you and Max.

6. You are a new teacher in a class of 12 SED students, ages 7–11. Based on current objective assessment data and their IEP objectives, your list of student expectations is as follows:

- attends school on regular basis
- follows teacher directives
- interacts with peers in prosocial manner (w/o physical or verbal aggression)
- completes assigned work
- uses socially appropriate language
- accesses and uses property of others in prosocial manner

Design a LEVEL SYSTEM with a minimum of three levels including expectations, incentives, and CAP for advancement for each level.

7. Describe how you might use MODELING to strengthen socially interactive behavior (e.g., eye contact, smiling, greeting) in a shy student who seldom interacts with his peers.

8. You have a student who seldom, if ever, completes assigned work. Having tried positive reinforcement unsuccessfully, explain how you might use NEGATIVE REINFORCEMENT to strengthen work completion.

9. Describe how you might use the PREMACK PRINCIPLE ("Grandma's Rule") to strengthen on-task behavior (looks at and listens to teacher) in a student who spends much of his time daydreaming.

ACCEPTABLE RESPONSES

The following interventions are merely offered as suggestions; you need not have written the exact same intervention to be considered correct. Check the notes inside brackets for information specific to each item.

1. *PJ / on task / fading program.* [Probably the best way to fade out adult encouragement is to *make the latency between giving encouragment longer and longer;* the important thing to remember is that you are *gradually changing the environment while PJ's behavior stays the same;* each approximation must be more like the stop point than the preceding approximation; also indicate when you would shift from one approximation to the next.]

Example

Stop: When PJ is able to stay on task at least 90% of the time *without anyone providing encouragement.*

Start: When PJ is able to stay on task at least 90% of the time *with teacher or instructional assistant providing constant encouragement.*

a. when PJ is able to stay on task at least 90% of the time with teacher or IA providing encouragement at *fixed intervals* of 1 minute

b. same as (a), for 2 minutes

c. same as (a), for 3 minutes

d. same as (a), for 4 minutes

e. same as (a), for 5 minutes

f. with teacher or IA providing encouragement *on random basis* (variable intervals; e.g., 1 minute, then 5 minutes, then 3 minutes, etc.)

Shift from one approximation to next when PJ is able to function satisfactorily (i.e., stay on task 90% of the time) over a two-day period.

2. *Addie / handraising / schedules of reinforcement.* [The important thing to remember here is that you *begin with a continuous (1:1) schedule, then move to fixed, and finally, variable;* you should also indicate when you would move from one schedule to the next.]

Example

a. When Addie raises her hand and waits to be called on, say "Good handraising, Addie"; do so each and every time she raises her hand and waits;

b. when the data indicate Addie is raising her hand and waiting at least as frequently as she is calling out, shift to fixed-ratio schedule with 2:1 arrangement; don't praise Addie unless she raises her hand and waits to be called on two consecutive times;

c. when data indicate Addie is raising her hand and waiting more frequently than before, shift to fixed-ratio schedule with 3:1 arrangement; don't praise Addie unless she raises her hand and waits to be called on three consecutive times;

d. when data indicate Addie is raising her hand and waiting to be called on with little or no calling-out behavior, shift to variable-ratio and schedule and praise Addie on random basis (when you can remember to do so).

3. *Arthur / assertiveness / shaping.* [You can begin by changing what Arthur says or how he says it or how often he says it, or you can begin by changing his eye contact; this is up to you. What you must have is *change in Arthur's behavior* (and not in the environment) and each approximation must be closer to or more like the stop point; *make sure your last approximation is an approximation and not the stop point.* Also indicate when you would shift criterion for reinforcement; this can be according to trials to competence or schedules of reinforcement used.]

Example

Stop: When Arthur establishes eye contact and says, "Stop that. I don't like it," in a firm voice as many times needed.

Start: When Arthur says "No" in weak voice without eye contact (looking at ground).

a. same as start;

b. when Arthur says "No" in weak voice *looking at subject's chest;*

c. when Arthur says "No" in weak voice *looking at subject's mouth;*

d. when Arthur says "No" in weak voice *with eye contact (1-second glance);*

e. when Arthur says "No" in weak voice *with eye contact (3-second look);*

f. when Arthur says "No" *in a stronger voice with eye contact;*

g. when Arthur says "No" *in a firm voice with eye contact;*

h. when Arthur *says "Stop that" in a firm voice with eye contact;*

i. when Arthur *says "Stop that. I don't like it," in a firm voice with eye contact.*

Shift criterion for reinforcement when Arthur can perform an approximation with reinforcement on a variable schedule (or when he can perform an approximation satisfactorily in ten consecutive trials).

4. *son or daughter / chaining / homework.* [Make sure you include both the old and new behavior chains.]

Example

Old Chain: arrives home from school → enters house → goes immediately to room with TV → sits down on the couch → turns on TV

New Chain: arrives home from school → enters house → goes to room without TV → works on homework

Model new chain for child and reinforce him/her as he/she goes through it.

5. *Max / token economy / in seat.* [Be sure you include all of the components of the token economy; e.g., contingencies, tokens, arrangement, etc.]

Example

a. Max must stay in his seat to receive tokens;

b. tokens used will be play money;

c. Max will receive one "dollar" per 5 minutes in-seat behavior;

d. dollars may be turned in for free time at a rate of one dollar per minute;

e. dollars are dispensed by the teacher at five-minute intervals; if Max has been in his seat for the entire interval, he is handed five dollars in tokens;

f. Max may purchase free time between 2 and 3 PM by giving dollars earned to the teacher who will give him a "promissory note" for the amount of free time purchased.

CONTRACT

The teacher _____**(your name)**_____ will give the student _____**Max**_____ one dollar for every five minutes of in-seat behavior. Dollars may be turned in for free time at a rate of one dollar per minute between 2 and 3 PM daily.

Signed _____Date_____

Signed _____Date_____

6. *students / level system / behaviors.* [Include (at least): levels, expectations, CAP for advancement, and incentives.]

Example

Level	Expectations [CAP for advancement]	Incentives
I	• attends school on regular basis [75% attendance rate over 20 days] • follows teacher directives [90% of the time over 20 days] • interacts with peers in prosocial manner [80% of time over 20 days]	earns tokens to be used to purchase items in class store
II	• attends school on regular basis [90% attendance over 20 days] • follows teacher directives [100% of the time over 20 days] • interacts with peers in prosocial manner [90% of time over 20 days] • uses socially appropriate language [80% of time over 20 days] • completes assigned work [75% of assignments given over 20 days]	same as above, *plus* tokens may be used to purchase items in school store
III	• attends school on regular basis [100% of time over 20 days—no unexcused absences at all] • follows teachers directives [100% of time over 20 days] • interacts with peers in prosocial manner [100% of time over 20 days]	

7. *shy student / modeling / socially interactive behaviors.* [No example or product necessary. Simply describe how you would use modeling to achieve your objective for the student. Your description should include information regarding the selection of the model and the promotion of imitation.]

a. Identify a few students who have the skills you want the target student to imitate; they should be approximately the same age and/or grade, come from the same sociocultural background and, if not friends of the target student, must be able to work with him in a non-aversive manner (i.e., not tease him about his shyness).

b. Pair the target student and the model students, whenever possible, in class activities (e.g., group activities, cooperative projects, classroom jobs, work assignments, etc.).

c. Reinforce the model students (and the target student) whenever you see them engaging in the target behaviors (e.g., greeting, smiling, eye contact) with each other.

8. *student / negative reinforcement / completes work assignments.* [No example or product necessary. Simply describe how you would use negative reinforcement to achieve your objective.]

a. Be sure you use an aversive from which the only escape is to complete work assignments; for example, assuming the student finds detention aversive, tell him he must stay after school to finish all work assignments not completed by dismissal. Other possibilities include the threat of response cost—"If you don't finish your work, you will lose X points from your point bank," or the loss of a privilege such as recess.

b. If the student does not work on his assignments, make sure he does not escape from the aversive (e.g., keep him in after school to finish his work). If the student does work on his assignments, remove the aversive.

9. *student / Premack / on task.* [Again, no example or product is necessary. Simply describe how you would use the Premack principle to achieve your objective. Make sure the high-frequency behavior is contingent upon the emission of the low-frequency behavior; have the student spend X amount of time on task *before* he can spend Y amount of time off task.]

CHAPTER SIX

Weakening Behaviors

Upon successful completion of this chapter, the learner should be able to: design interventions utilizing behavior reduction procedures such as differential reinforcement of alternative behavior, differential reinforcement of incompatible behavior, differential reinforcement of the omission of behavior, extinction, redirection, reprimands, response cost, overcorrection, time-out, and the hierarchy of escalating consequences.

BEHAVIOR REDUCTION PROCEDURES

When teachers want to weaken student behavior, the first thing they usually think of is punishment. Currently, the use of punishment has generated a great deal of controversy among behaviorists (see Braaten, Simpson, Rosell, & Reilly, 1988; Skiba & Deno, 1991). Even in cases where the maladaptive behavior is life-threatening (e.g., violence directed toward self or others) and the only remaining treatment is some form of punishment, there is debate over its use. Much of this debate is centered around the idea that punishment gives behaviorism a bad name.

> Behaviorism is not the antithesis of humanism. . . . But the fact that behavior analysts use techniques of punishment, and do so more effectively than has been done hitherto, may be one reason why behaviorism is still not as widely supported as it might be . . . No person of good will is interested in more efficient ways of making people suffer. (Yulevich & Axelrod, 1983, p. 366)

One way behaviorists have dealt with this identity crisis is to deemphasize punishment as the treatment of choice for weakening behavior. In fact, they no longer use the term *punishment*. The new terminology is *behavior reduction procedure* (BRP). Some might consider this change cosmetic, as though BRP is merely a euphemism for punishment, much like behavior management is perceived as a code for

behavior modification. This is not the case. BRPs are strategies used to weaken behavior. Some of these strategies are considered punishment because they involve the presentation of an aversive stimulus. But not all BRPs are punishment. Some of them, such as differential reinforcement of incompatible or alternative behavior, or zero rates of behavior, are actually positive reinforcement. Others, like extinction and redirection, are neither positive nor negative. BRPs that are actually considered punishment are reprimands, response cost, time-out, and overcorrection. I will discuss each of these strategies in detail.

In addition to changing the terminology and emphasizing the use of positive and benign strategies over the traditional negative approaches, behaviorists have also begun to pay more attention to ethical and legal issues regarding the weakening of behavior. This concern within the field has led to the development of guidelines for the ethical and legal use of BRPs. The following is a compilation of some guidelines taken from a position paper by the Council for Children with Behavioral Disorders (1990) and an article by Yell (1990) on the use of BRPs with students with behavioral disorders. I recommend this material to anyone who plans on using BRPs—especially the punitive variety—in their classroom.

1. *Follow due process and obtain informed consent from parents and administrators prior to using BRPs.* This also means you should provide warnings to students. Before you remove something from a student (response cost) or remove a student from something (time-out) you should let him know what to expect

(e.g., "Do that again and you are going to have to take a time-out."). The parent(s) of the student(s) with whom you plan to use the BRP cannot (or should not) give their consent unless and until they are informed about it. You should provide them with the following information: (a) description of the intervention you plan on using as well as a rationale for its use; (b) what you anticipate the outcomes to be; (c) what the positive and negative side effects are; and (d) how effective the intervention has been. In other words, you need to familiarize yourself with the research literature regarding the efficacy of whatever BRPs you plan on using.

2. *Apply the So what? test to determine whether or not the behavior is maladaptive and needs to be weakened in the first place.* Using a BRP—particularly a punitive strategy—is serious business and should not be undertaken unless the behavior you want to weaken is definitely maladaptive. You need to demonstrate that the behavior change is in the student's best interest and not merely in your best interest. For more on this, go back to Chapter 4.

3. *Use BRPs in a hierarchy from least aversive, restrictive, and intrusive to most aversive, restrictive, and intrusive.* Aversive BRPs are those techniques which produce emotional and/or physical pain or discomfort and escape and avoidance behavior. Examples of BRPs that would definitely be considered aversive are corporal punishment (e.g., paddling), the use of noxious stimulants (e.g., electric shock or lemon juice squirted in the mouth), and contingent exercise (e.g., doing push-ups or running laps as punishment). All of these produce some degree of physical as well as emotional pain. Other BRPs, while not producing any physical pain, may produce emotional pain. These include exclusion time-out (being physically separated and isolated from the group for a predetermined period of time), response cost (having to give up one's earnings or privileges), and reprimands (drawing attention to one's maladaptive behavior through a warning or verbal punisher, e.g., "Stop that!"). All aversive BRPs produce escape and avoidance behavior. Students will lie, cheat, or sneak or run away rather than submit to an aversive consequence.

The term *restrictive* refers to the controlling aspects of a BRP—the degree to which the BRP limits the physical movement of the student. Examples of restrictive BRPs include time-out or physically restraining a child by holding him or using a restraining device. A BRP may be considered intrusive if its purpose is to stop ongoing activity (i.e., the maladaptive behavior). All of the BRPs discussed in this chapter may be considered intrusive because they

are all designed to stop maladaptive behavior. Some, however, are more intrusive than others. Putting a student who is teasing his peers in time-out where he can no longer see or talk to them is more intrusive than using a reprimand (e.g., "Stop that teasing!"). Everything is relative. While less intrusive than time-out, that same reprimand is more intrusive than a redirect (e.g., interrupting the student's teasing by asking him if he needs help with his work). Although the redirect, like the reprimand, is used to stop the ongoing activity of teasing, it is less intrusive because it does not call any negative attention to the maladaptive behavior. It is more subtle. The BRPs discussed in this chapter are presented in the order of their aversiveness, restrictiveness, and intrusiveness *from least to most.* Whenever possible, try to begin your intervention with the least aversive, restrictive, and intrusive BRP. (See Figure 6.1.) Obviously, there are exceptions to this rule. If two students are fighting, don't wait until one student stops choking the other student so you can reinforce him for engaging in incompatible behavior! When safety is an issue, you may need to begin with time-out after you get the combatants separated. When safety is not a concern, always use the least restrictive/intrusive strategy first.

Figure 6.1. Avoid using aversive, intrusive, or restrictive behavior reduction procedures.

4. *Try to use a BRP in combination with a strategy for strengthening a target behavior.* If you are using extinction to weaken calling-out behavior, use positive reinforcement to strengthen instances of hand-raising behavior. Together they are more effective than when used in isolation. All of the BRPs covered in this chapter are going to be more effective when used in combination with positive reinforcement of an incompatible or competing response than when used alone.

5. *Use BRPs for which there is empirical evidence of efficacy at weakening the behaviors you wish to weaken.* It is unethical to use a BRP for which there is no demonstrated efficacy. You may have faith in sticking pins in student effigies to weaken certain behaviors but unless you have some hard data to support the efficacy of this approach, you really shouldn't use it. Using an ineffective (or at best, untested) approach can be a waste of time. While you are using it, the student's behavior either remains the same or gets worse and you have wasted valuable time in which you could have been using a tested, effective approach. A rule to follow is: The more intrusive and restrictive the approach, the more important it is to have empirical evidence of its efficacy.

6. *Use only BRPs for which you have been trained.* For example, if you know nothing about the use of time-out procedures, you should not use them. For any of these procedures to be effective, they have to be used correctly.

7. *Collect data.* Be accountable for the efficacy of whatever BRP you use. Some teachers use the same BRPs (e.g., reprimands or response cost) over and over again regardless of whether they effectively weaken student behavior or not. This is highly unethical and unprofessional.

8. *Make sure your BRP does not interfere with a student's educational rights.* For example, seclusion (a physical time-out for more than 50 minutes), expulsion, serial suspensions (i.e., repeated suspensions of less than ten days duration), and prolonged in-school suspensions are all in violation of a student's educational rights. Each of these constitute a change in the student's educational placement and, according to the IDEA, cannot be undertaken without consent of the student's IEP team.

9. *Use BRPs that are reasonable.* A BRP is considered reasonable if (a) it is used to punish a student for breaking a rule that is reasonable, (b) the punishment is appropriate to the crime and the student's age, and (c) the punishment is delivered without malice. For example, sending a ten-year-old to time-out for 20 minutes is unreasonable because the

Figure 6.2. Use BRPs that serve a legitimate purpose. Follow guidelines for responsible selection and use of BRPs, such as those discussed in this chapter.

number of minutes a student spends in time-out should not exceed his age in years. Taking points earned away from a student (response cost) and gloating over his loss is unreasonable because it is punishment delivered in a malicious manner. Punishing a student for not addressing you as "Sir" is unreasonable because the rule itself is unreasonable (unless you and your students are in the armed forces).

10. *Use BRPs that serve a legitimate purpose, with clear guidelines for when and how each is to be used.* Putting a student in time-out simply to get rid of him because you have a headache and are, therefore, less tolerant of his behavior, is not a legitimate purpose. You are better off taking an aspirin. Each and every BRP you use in your program should have a protocol that describes its purpose (i.e., the behaviors it can be used for) and the procedure for its use. These protocols should be made available to students, staff, administrators, and parents. (See Figure 6.2.)

(Checkpoint 6.1 follows, on p. 188.)

☑ Checkpoint 6.1

[pages 185–187]

Fill in the answers to the following items (1–15). Check your responses by referring to the text; relevant page numbers appear in brackets.

There is currently a debate over the use of punishment because

(1) _____

_____

_____

_____[185]

The term punishment has been replaced by the term

(2) _____

_____

_____[185]

This development represents more than a mere name change. BRPs now include all strategies for weakening behavior and not just punishment. BRPs that are least aversive, least restrictive, and least intrusive should be used first.

The aversiveness of a BRP refers to

(3) _____

_____

_____[186]

The restrictiveness of a BRP refers to

(4) _____

_____

_____[186]

The intrusiveness of a BRP refers to

(5) _____

_____

_____[186]

(continues)

CHECKPOINT 6.1, continued

Guidelines have been developed for using BRPs in an ethical and legal manner. These include:

(6) _____

_____

(7) _____

_____

(8) _____

_____

(9) _____

_____

(10) _____

_____

(11) _____

_____

(12) _____

_____

(13) _____

_____

(14) _____

_____

(15) _____

_____ [185–187]

Redo any items you missed. If you missed more than 3 of the items, reread the material. Otherwise, continue on to the next section.

POSITIVE AND BENIGN STRATEGIES

The strategies listed in this section are not considered punishment. Differential reinforcement of alternative behavior (DRA), differential reinforcement of incompatible behavior (DRI), and differential reinforcement of the omission of behavior (DRO) are reinforcement-based, or positive, BRPs. Extinction and redirection are considered benign strategies since they do no harm.

Differential Reinforcement of Alternative (DRA) or Incompatible (DRI) Behavior

The underlying principle of DRA and DRI is that you can weaken a maladaptive behavior by strengthening an alternative behavior in its place. The alternative behavior cannot be just any behavior. You are not going to weaken talk-outs by reinforcing in-seat behavior, nor are you likely to weaken swearing by strengthening hand raising. The alternative behavior you strengthen has to be either incompatible with the maladaptive behavior or must compete with it. *Incompatible* behaviors are mutually exclusive in that engaging in one keeps a person from engaging in the other; for example, a student can't be in his seat and out of his seat at the same time. Notice that by strengthening in-seat behavior, you automatically weaken out-of-seat behavior. Other examples of incompatible behaviors are compliance and noncompliance; assertive behavior and aggressive (or passive) behavior; being punctual and being late; telling the truth and telling lies; making bowel movements in toilet and making them in pants; and doing one's work by oneself and copying the work of others.

Alternative or *competing* behaviors are not mutually exclusive; although one behavior may compete with the other, it is not impossible to engage in both at the same time. For example, doing a math assignment is not incompatible with listening (or even talking) to a peer. It does, however, compete with—or make it more difficult to engage in—talking without permission. Therefore, strengthening on-task (doing math assignment) behavior can result in the weakening of the maladaptive behavior. Other examples of alternative or competing behaviors are raising hand and waiting for eye contact with teacher instead of shouting out, watching teacher while she talks instead of looking out the window, walking away from peers when teased instead of fighting when teased, asking peers questions about themselves (e.g., "do you have any brothers or sisters?") instead of insulting them, and using a handkerchief to blow your nose instead of picking your nose.

Differential reinforcement of incompatible behavior is the strengthening of a behavior that is incompatible with the maladaptive behavior, while differential reinforcement of alternative behavior is the strengthening of a behavior that competes with the maladaptive behavior. The strategy for using either BRP is simple. First find a behavior that either competes with or is incompatible with the behavior you wish to weaken. Ideally, this competing or imcompatible behavior should be a behavior that is already in the student's response repertoire. If not, you will have to teach it to the student. It should also be a behavior that is likely to be maintained by the environment—a practical behavior that is apt to be maintained through natural consequences. Whenever you catch the student engaging in the competing or incompatible (target) response, reinforce it. If you don't see a change in the student's maladaptive behavior after a while, you may have to punish the maladaptive behavior, as long as you remember to continue to reinforce the target behavior, too.

The following is an example of how I used DRI to weaken a maladaptive behavior. I once worked with a severely retarded young woman I'll call Rhonda, who constantly sucked on the backs of her hands until the upper layer of skin came off. Fearing infection, the hospital staff where Rhonda lived wrapped her hands in sterile gauze bandages every day. However, this didn't stop her from sucking on her hand through the gauze. At first we tried reinforcing Rhonda for hand-out-of-mouth behavior. Whenever Rhonda had her hand out of her mouth, someone rewarded her with a primary reinforcer (piece of cookie), rubbed her head and said, "Good girl!" Unfortunately, the patient–staff ratio did not allow us to keep an aide next to Rhonda at all times. Since her hand-out-of-mouth behavior was so infrequent, it was next to impossible for us to catch her being "good" on a continuous basis. We had to create a situation where Rhonda would be inclined to keep her hands out of her mouth more often. When we thought about the reinforcement she was getting out of sucking on her hands, we concluded that the sensation of the sucking (the tactile pressure of the skin) plus the warmth and wetness from her mouth and her saliva was all part of what she liked about the activity. At first we tried to simulate these reinforcing qualities by giving her a doll to "bathe" in a bowl of warm water. The idea was to keep her hands on the doll in the bath water as often and as long as possible, so that we would have more opportunities to reinforce her with the primary and social reinforcement. We quickly discovered that the warm bath water was doing as much damage to Rhonda's hands as her sucking was. Our next intervention was to give her a hot water bottle with a doll painted on it to simulate a "baby," and a baby bottle. The hot water bottle was tied with string to a rod attached to the tray on her wheelchair. The rod was attached to the tray in a position that made it impossible for Rhonda to hold the hot water bottle and suck on her hands at the same time. Rhonda liked sucking on the bottle (even when there was nothing in it) and holding the "baby." From time to time, an adult would walk by her wheelchair and if she was sucking on the bottle and holding the "baby," the adult would gently rub the back of her head and say, "Good girl!" By strengthening an incompatible behavior (or set of behaviors), we managed to weaken a maladaptive behavior.

Both DRI and DRA have a number of advantages. They are positive approaches to behavior reduction without any of the negative side effects of the punitive approaches. They are popular with change agents. It is much more desirable to spend your day rewarding students than punishing them. Teachers tell me they feel like shrews telling kids to stop this and stop that; they became teachers so they could teach, not yell at kids all day. DRI is also educationally sound. It makes more sense to teach a student what he should do instead of merely telling him what he should not do.

Both DRI and DRA are effective. Some of the maladaptive behaviors they have been used to reduce include out-of-seat behavior (Friman, 1990); self-stimulating (Jones & Baker, 1989); off-task behaviors (Deitz & Repp, 1983); highly disruptive behavior (Ayllon & Roberts, 1974); anti-social behavior (Forehand & Baumeister, 1976); incessant screaming and self-injurious behavior (Mayhew & Harris, 1979); severe hyperactivity (Twardosz & Sajwaj, 1972); self-injurious behavior (Tarpley & Schroeder, 1979; Underwood, Figueroa, Thyer, & Nzeocha, 1989; Young & Wincze, 1974); and aggression directed toward others (Pinkston, Rees, LeBlanc, & Baer, 1973).

Differential Reinforcement of the Omission of Behavior (DRO)

In DRO, the student earns reinforcement simply for not engaging in the maladaptive behavior for a specified interval of time. This is different from DRI or DRA, where the student earns reinforcement for engaging in an incompatible or competing target behavior. There are two types of DRO. In *momentary DRO* (MDRO), reinforcement is earned if the student is not engaging in the maladatpve behavior at the end of a given interval. Let's say you want to weaken self-stimming behavior in one or more of your students. Using MDRO, you set a timer to ring at certain intervals. Each time it rings you look at the target students to see whether or not they are self-stimming. You reward the students who are not self-stimming when the timer rings and either ignore or redirect the others. Your students don't have to be engaging in an incompatible or competing behavior in order to earn the reward. They just can't be engaging in the maladaptive behavior when the timer rings. You can combine shaping with MDRO by making the reinforcer contingent upon a gradually increasing number of intervals in which the student refrains from engaging in the maladaptive behavior. An example of a shaping program used with MDRO may be seen in Figure 6.3.

The other type of DRO is *whole-interval DRO* (WDRO), in which reinforcement is contingent upon the student not engaging in the maladaptive behavior for an entire interval of time. For example, you want to weaken disruptive behavior (i.e., shouts out obscenities) in one of your students, so you set a timer for 10-minute intervals. If the student has not engaged in any disruptive behavior for *the entire 10-minute interval* you reward him. If he has been disruptive during the 10 minutes, you don't reward him. Again, he doesn't have to engage in an incompatible or competing behavior to earn the reward. He simply has to refrain from engaging in the disruptive behavior. Again, shaping can be combined with WDRO by requiring the student to refrain from engaging in the maladaptive behavior for longer and longer intervals. Figure 6.4 shows an example of a shaping program combined with WDRO.

Research regarding the efficacy of MDRO and WDRO has generated conflicting reports. Some studies indicate efficacy (Barton, Brulle, & Repp, 1986; DeCatanzo & Baldwin, 1978; Deitz, Repp, & Deitz, 1976; Dwinell & Connis, 1979; Repp, Barton, & Brulle, 1983; Repp, Deitz, & Speir, 1975; Tarpley & Schroeder, 1979) while others do not (Corte, Wolf, & Locke, 1971; Foxx & Azrin, 1973; Harris & Wolchik, 1979).

(*Checkpoint 6.2 appears following Figures 6.3 and 6.4; see p. 192.*)

MDRO (basic procedure):

1. set timer and teach class;

2. when timer rings, observe S;

3. if S self-stimming (e.g., rocking in seat or shaking hands in front of face), ignore or redirect;

4. if S is not self-stimming, reward;

5. reset timer and repeat procedure

Shaping Program

Stop: when S is observed for ten consecutive intervals without self-stimming during a 1-hour period

Start: when S is observed for one interval without self-stimming during a 1-hour period

Reward: social praise (e.g., "John, I like the way you're not _____")

Approximations:

1. Reward *each* interval S is observed not engaging in self-stim behavior;

2. reward contingent upon *two consecutive* intervals of no-stim behavior;

3. reward contingent upon *three consecutive* intervals of no-stim behavior;

4. reward contingent upon *four consecutive* intervals of no-stim behavior;

5. reward contingent upon *five consecutive* intervals of no-stim behavior;

6. reward contingent upon *six consecutive* intervals of no-stim behavior;

7. reward contingent upon *seven consecutive* intervals of no-stim behavior;

8. reward contingent upon *eight consecutive* intervals of no-stim behavior;

9. reward contingent upon *nine consecutive* intervals of no-stim behavior.

Shift criterion for reinforcement when S can perform an approximation satisfactorily for 2 consecutive days.

Figure 6.3. Example of shaping program combined with MDRO.

WDRO (basic procedure):

1. set timer and teach class;

2. when timer rings, begin interval by resetting timer for desired interval;

3. monitor student during this interval to determine whether or not he self-stims;

4. when the timer rings (indicating the end of the interval), if S refrained from self-stimming the entire interval, reward him;

5. if S did not refrain from self-stimming during the interval, do not reward;

6. reset timer and repeat above procedure

Shaping Program

Stop: when S can refrain from self-stimming for 30-minute intervals

Start: when S can refrain from self-stimming for 1-minute intervals

Reward: social praise (e.g., "John, that's very good. You didn't _____ for _____ minutes")

Approximations:

1. when S refrains from self-stimming for 1-minute interval;

2. when S refrains from self-stimming for 2-minute interval;

3. when S refrains from self-stimming for 4-minute interval;

4. when S refrains from self-stimming for 7-minute interval;

5. when S refrains from self-stimming for 10-minute interval;

6. when S refrains from self-stimming for 15-minute interval;

7. when S refrains from self-stimming for 20-minute interval;

8. when S refrains from self-stimming for 25-minute interval.

Shift criterion for reinforcement when S can perform satisfactorily at an approximation for 2 consecutive days.

Figure 6.4. Example of shaping program combined with WDRO.

☑ Checkpoint 6.2

[pages 189–191]

Fill in the answers to the following items (1–22). Check your responses by referring to the text; relevant page numbers appear in brackets.

DRA stands for

(1) _____

_____ [189]

DRI stands for

(2) _____

_____ [189]

The underlying principle of DRA and DRI is

(3) _____

_____

_____

_____ [189]

The difference between DRI and DRA is

(4) _____

_____

_____

_____ [189]

The difference between incompatible and competing behaviors is

(5) _____

_____

_____

_____ [189]

Write an incompatible or competing behavior for each of the following items (6–15). Check your responses against the answers shown following Item 15.

(6) is out of seat/_____

_____

(continues)

CHECKPOINT 6.2, continued

(7) bites self when frustrated/_____

_____

(8) hits peers when angry/_____

_____

(9) calls out without raising hand/_____

_____

(10) takes things from others without asking/

_____

(11) is off task (i.e., looks around room)/_____

_____

(12) leaves room without permission/_____

_____

(13) swears for attention/_____

_____

(14) refuses to comply with request/_____

_____

(15) comes to class late/_____

_____

ANSWERS (6–15): (6) is in seat; (7) touches self when frustrated (or communicates frustration through verbalization or signing); (8) tells peers when angry; (9) raises hand and waits to be called on; (10) asks to handle things from others and waits for permission to do so; (11) is on task (looks at work); (12) only leaves room with permission; (13) asks for attention (using prosocial language); (14) complies with request; (15) comes to class on time

Three advantages of DRI and DRA are:

(16) _____

_____

(17) _____

_____

(continues)

CHECKPOINT 6.2, continued

(18) _____
_____ [190]

DRO stands for
(19) _____
_____ [190]

WDRO stands for
(20) _____
_____ [190]

MDRO stands for
(21) _____
_____ [190]

The difference between WDRO and MDRO is
(22) _____
_____
_____
_____
_____ [190]

Redo any items you missed. If you missed more than 4 items, reread the material. Otherwise, continue on to the next section.

Extinction

As stated earlier in the text, extinction occurs when you withhold or remove the CSE that is reinforcing the student's maladaptive behavior. If you find a student engaging in a behavior you wish to weaken, ask yourself if that behavior is being reinforced by something in the environment. For example, Ronnie engages in behavior I will refer to as "personal narratives." He is constantly telling the teacher how he feels, what he is doing, what is happening in the room or outside the window. At first, Ronnie's teacher would come to his desk and put her hand on his shoulder and her finger to her mouth to indicate that he should be silent. However, when the teacher found herself doing this at a rate of once every 5 minutes, she realized that something had to be done about Ronnie's behavior. By collecting some baseline data on what occurred in the environment immediately after Ronnie's narratives, she was able to see that her attending behavior was actually reinforcing the problem behavior instead of weakening it. By recognizing what was reinforcing Ronnie's behavior, his teacher was able to withhold this reinforcer and extinguish the personal narrative behavior.

However, sometimes the known reinforcer is not under the teacher's control. For example, B.J. spends a great deal of time acting as class clown. He does this because the other students laugh at him and B.J. likes the attention he gets from them. His teacher recognizes this but feels that she has little control over his peers' attending behavior. B.J. does some outrageous things, and although she has tried to get them to stop laughing at him and just ignore him, his peers simply find his antics too funny to ignore. She even tried to reinforce any student who could ignore B.J; unfortunately, as much as his peers liked the reinforcement from the teacher, they just couldn't help themselves when B.J. started his act—he was a born comedian. In desperation, B.J.'s teacher removed him from the class to a special time-out room near the school's office where he would receive none of the peer attention that reinforced his behavior.

Keep in mind that the known reinforcer is not always attention; there are many other potential reinforcers in the environment. For example, I once worked with a young blind student who, when given a puzzle or form board to work with, would drop the pieces on the floor or table top because the sound they made was very stimulating for her. If you took the puzzles away from her, she would sit and rock back and forth on her chair, make a banging sound on the wooden floor, and screech like an animal. After an hour of this, the rest of the students were so stimulated that they would begin a chorus of sounds until the room seemed to quake with the sound track of a Tarzan movie! Time-out didn't help to weaken the student's behavior in the classroom because in time-out she could screech all she wanted. For her, time-out wasn't punishing, it was actually reinforcing! I suggested to the teacher that since the sound of the dropped puzzle pieces was reinforcing the student's behavior, we would have to devise a way of removing this reinforcer without removing the puzzles. The teacher had an ingenious idea. She placed a padded tablecloth on the top of the student's table and a piece of rug remnant under the table. After dropping several puzzle pieces on the table and on the floor and not hearing any sound, the student stopped dropping them. I wish I could report that she then put the puzzles together; unfortunately, her next behavior was to throw the pieces across the room. We finally wound up punishing this behavior (since it was considered potentially harmful to her peers) while at the same time reinforcing her for putting a piece where it belonged. I mention this case only because it serves to illustrate a situation where extinction occurred by withholding a known reinforcer other than attention.

Here are some things you should know about extinction:

1. When using extinction, the maladaptive behavior often gets worse before it gets better. This is referred to as an *extinction burst*. It is usually the result of the student getting frustrated at not receiving the known reinforcer. Be aware of this and do not give up too soon. Extinction may also produce a brief period of aggression in the early stages. This is also related to the frustration surrounding the discontinuation of reinforcement. Again, if you are aware of it, you will be better able to "tough it out."

2. Extinction, of all the methods in this text, probably requires the most patience. It takes a long time to see results. Collect data; even the smallest of changes in behavior can reinforce your effort to stay the course.

3. Extinction, like punishment, should be combined with the positive reinforcement of an adaptive behavior that is incompatible with the behavior you wish to weaken (i.e., DRI). Extinction used in combination with a reinforcement program is much more effective than extinction used alone.

4. Sometimes it is difficult to identify and/or control reinforcers in the environment. For example, let's say you have a class clown whose behavior is reinforced by peer attention. Unfortunately, this fellow is so funny, his peers can't help themselves. No matter how much you reinforce (or punish) their behavior, someone in the room is laughing and reinforcing the clown's behavior. Extinction is inappropriate in this situation because you are unable to withhold the known reinforcer.

5. Do not use extinction with aggressive behaviors, particularly in group situations. Aggressive behavior witnessed by nonaggressives leads to less inhibition in the latter. In other words, students watching a fight tend to lose their inhibitions about fighting and are more likely to engage in aggressive behavior themselves. This is why you often see pushing and shoving around the periphery of a fight.

6. Ask yourself if you are able to tolerate the maladaptive behavior temporarily. If not, extinction is inappropriate to use. Let's say you have a student who curses for any type of adult attention and you have reinforced that behavior in the past by scolding him. Let's also say that you can't stand to hear him curse. It would be foolish to attempt to weaken this student's cursing behavior with extinction since you probably wouldn't be able to ignore the behavior for very long.

7. Also ask yourself if you are able to tolerate the worsening of the behavior. Suppose the cursing escalates in response to your planned ignoring. Would you be able to tolerate the escalation? If not, extinction is inappropriate to use.

8. Determine, if you can, how long the student has been reinforced for his behavior. The longer he has been reinforced for it, the longer it will take for extinction to weaken it. A child whose tantrums have been reinforced for 3 or 4 years is not likely to give up tantrumming so quickly as one whose behavior has been reinforced for 3 or 4 weeks.

9. Also try to determine what type of reinforcement schedule has been used in the past. For example, behavior that has been reinforced on a variable schedule is more resistant to extinction than behavior reinforced on a continuous schedule or even a predictable intermittent schedule.

10. Another factor that influences the effectiveness of extinction is the level of deprivation in student. How badly does the individual need the known reinforcer? The class clown who only receives attention from her peer group when she misbehaves is more needy than the student who has other sources of attention in his life.

11. You should also consider the effort needed to engage in the maladaptive behavior. The more effort required, the more likely the student is to give it up. For example, a student might be more likely to give up tantrumming than to give up talk outs since tantrums require much more effort than simply shouting out.

The advantages of extinction are that it is effective in weakening behavior and the results tend to maintain over time. Research indicates extinction is effective in reducing a wide variety of behaviors including behaviors related to sleep disorders (Durand & Mindell, 1990); compulsive reassurance-seeking behavior (Francis, 1988); negative behaviors related to food refusal (Singer, Nofer, Benson-Szekely, & Brooks, 1991); self-injurious behaviors (Iwata, Pace, Kalsher, Cowdery, & Cataldo, 1990; Luiselli, 1988); disruptive classroom behavior (O'Leary & Becker, 1967; Zimmerman & Zimmerman, 1962); and tantrums (Carlson, Arnold, Becker, & Madsen, 1968). In addition to being effective, extinction is also a benign BRP, and it is nonpunitive and less intrusive and restrictive than most other BRPs.

This is not to say extinction is without any disadvantages. It is probably the most difficult BRP to implement, especially when planned ignoring is involved. Planned ignoring requires that you not attend to the student's behavior in *any way*. Some teachers think that "ignoring" means they should not *directly* consequate the student's behavior. For example, a student continues to talk out in class because his teacher has attended to him by responding to his questions or comments (e.g., "Oh, that's a good question" or "I'm sorry but that's not the answer"). The rule in this teacher's classroom is to raise your hand if you have something to say. Hoping to weaken the student's talking-out behavior, the teacher tries planned ignoring but her idea of ignoring is to substitute one verbal response for another. When the student calls out, instead of focusing on what he says, she tells him to raise his hand. If he says "but I need you now" or "you never call on me," she responds with "please raise your hand." When he raises his hand, she calls on him. The resulting sequence is (a) student calls out without raising his hand, (b) teacher attends to him ("please raise your hand"), (c) student raises his hand, (d) teacher calls on him, and so on and so on. This teacher is not practicing extinction. First of all, the behavior has not been weakened. Second, she has not withheld atten-

tion (the known reinforcer). She has merely changed the *content* of her attention. I have also seen other teachers substitute nonverbal attention for verbal attention. They may not say anything to the student, but they still look at him and/or make some gesture (e.g., finger to mouth or shaking head "No"). This is still attention, and it can serve to strengthen (or, at the very least, maintain) the student's behavior. *Planned ignoring means no attention at all*. This can be extremely difficult to achieve, especially when the behavior escalates or it takes a very long time for the behavior to weaken. If you are working with another person in the classroom, such as an instructional assistant, it is a good idea for you to reinforce each other for ignoring student behavior. Otherwise, it is very easy to convince yourself to give in to student attempts to get attention. If and when you give in, you not only teach the student that persistance pays, you also teach him to start the maladaptive behavior at a higher level next time.

Redirection

Redirection is another benign form of BRP. I have been using it a lot since my daughter Hannah came on the scene a few years ago. When we go to a restaurant and Hannah starts banging chopsticks or silverware on the metal tray of her high chair, we don't say "No" because it doesn't work. We don't simply take the objects away, because she then cries and makes more noise. We use redirection. We offer her another (quieter) object from the table such as a brightly colored napkin, a straw, or the menu. Invariably, she takes the new object and surrenders the offending objects quite readily. She still wants to bang on the tray top but paper and cloth don't make as much noise.

Redirection is simply a nonpunitive interruption of the maladaptive behavior. For example: A student is talking to a peer instead of doing his work. A redirect, in this situation, can be something as simple as asking the student if he needs help with his assignment or if he has any questions about it. You can always ask him to show you his work. If this isn't effective, you can be more direct and tell him "Please get back to work." Redirection is not the same as a reprimand because it is non-punitive. You are not threatening the student (as you would be if you said something like, "You'd better get back to work or else!"). You are not warning the student (as you would be if you said, "If you don't stop talking and get back to work, you're going to lose points."). You are not showing any disapproval of the student. You can even smile at him and use your most pleasant tone of voice. You are not saying "NO." What you are doing is interrupting undesirable behavior, *without drawing any negative attention to it,* by redirecting him to more desirable behavior. Redirection is not the same as DRI or DRA because you are not rewarding the student for any behavior. Redirection is more of a prompt or cue. Sometimes it works alone. While you may interrupt the student's off-task behavior

and get him back to work, it is likely that he will eventually be off task again. You can continue to redirect him, or you can combine redirection with DRI by reinforcing him when he is on task.

There is very little written about redirection in the research literature, especially research that focuses exclusively on the efficacy of redirection. Considering that redirection is so much less intrusive and restrictive than most other BRPs, I feel safe in recommending its use regardless of the lack of supportive data.

☑ Checkpoint 6.3

[pages 193–196]

Fill in the answers to the following items (1–11). Check your responses by referring to the text; relevant page numbers appear in brackets.

Extinction is **(1)** _____

_____

_____[193]

An "extinction burst" is **(2)** _____

_____

_____[194]

Four factors that influence the efficacy of extinction are:

(3) _____

_____

(4) _____

_____

(5) _____

_____

(6) _____

_____[194–195]

(continues)

CHECKPOINT 6.3, continued

Two advantages of extinction are:

(7) _____

_____

(8) _____

_____[195]

A major disadvantage of extinction is **(9)**_____

_____

_____[195]

Redirection is **(10)** _____

_____

_____[195]

Redirection differs from DRI and DRA because

(11) _____

_____

_____

_____

_____[196]

Redo any items you missed. If you missed more than 2 of the items, reread the material. Otherwise, continue on to the next section.

NEGATIVE STRATEGIES

Negative BRPs—that is, punishment—should only be used when positive and benign strategies have failed. There are several reasons for this. For one thing, punishment can lead to avoidance and/or escape behavior such as sneaking, stealing, cheating, lying, running away, and truancy. Here are a few examples. Mrs. X always yells at her students if she catches them talking in class. The children have gotten around this by whispering when her back is turned or by passing notes. Bobby knows he's going to be punished for not being prepared for gym class so he "borrows" Rafael's sneakers from his locker without Rafael's permission. Katy didn't study for the big test in math and her Dad is going to ground her if she gets one more failing grade. To avoid this, she copies from Aletia's paper during the exam. Shelly knows she will be sent to the office if she confesses her part in some vandalism in the girl's lavatory, so she lies and blames it on someone else. Ralph knows he is going to be reprimanded for not doing his homework so he tells his mother he is sick and doesn't go to school. All of these students have one thing in common: They are all trying to avoid or escape punishment. Unfortunately, the only way they can think of to accomplish this end is to engage in behavior that is often just as undesirable as the behavior the teacher wants to punish. (See Figure 6.5.)

Another reason for not using punishment as the strategy of choice in weakening undesirable behavior is that the punisher is often perceived by the student as a model of aggression. It is not uncommon for a student to be paddled for fighting or ridiculed for teasing. Children pay more attention to what we do than to what we say. Telling a student not to fight because he might be hurt or because he might hurt someone else makes no sense if you are proffering this wisdom while you are paddling him. You are really teaching the student, by your actions, that it is all right to hurt others. You are also teaching him to be careful not to get caught in an act of physical aggression—if he was sneakier about it, he wouldn't have to endure the paddling. Of course, if he got caught again, he could always try to lie his way out.

One of the best reasons for not using punishment is the lack of supportive data regarding its long term efficacy. Because punishment does not have a long-lasting effect on behavior, it is used again and again. Behaviors that are no longer punished and/or replaced by incompatible or competing behavior tend to return to their pre-punished state. True, the immediate effect of punishment is to weaken the response that it follows. Tell a student who is out of

Figure 6.5. Byproducts of punishment: stealing, lying, cheating.

his seat to sit down, and assuming he finds the reprimand aversive, he will comply. Out-of-seat behavior has been weakened. Punishment has occurred. However, unless you reinforce in-seat behavior, it is likely that the student will get out of his seat again in the very near future. The problem with this chain of events is that the teacher often believes the punisher (i.e., the reprimand, "Sit down!") is working. Because of its short-term effectiveness, punishment tends to reinforce the teacher's expectation that it always works. This is commonly referred to as the "criticism trap" (Becker et al., 1971). The teacher uses criticism to "punish" out-of-seat behavior. The immediate effect of her criticism makes her think that it works. Because the criticism is only a stopgap measure, the student continues to get out of his seat. Because the teacher has been rewarded (negatively) in the past (for criticizing out-of-seat behavior) when the student sat down, she will continue to use criticism as a punisher. The cycle repeats itself over and over again, day after day. If you showed the teacher some data indicating the frequency of the student's out-of-seat behavior in relation to her criticizing behavior, she would realize that her reprimands do not have the desired effect of weakening the behavior over time and, technically, punishment has not occurred.

There can also be emotional side effects with punishment. Many teachers use it for their own benefit, rather than the student's. Punishing becomes a release for frustrations pent up due to mounting professional and/or personal stress. When this happens, it is often difficult to punish without showing some emotion; and while such venting may aid the teacher emotionally, it often can produce anger, fear, or hurt feelings in the student. These feelings are counterproductive to learning and to the establishment of a positive, trusting relationship between teacher and student. I am not suggesting that all teachers who punish their students will necessarily give them a psychological trauma. I am simply saying that punishment delivered in a highly emotional state often leads to undesirable emotional side effects in the student. The result of all this is that the person doing the punishing often becomes an aversive stimulus to the student. Not only does the punisher become an aversive stimulus, the setting in which the punishment occurs, the subject matter being taught, and the peer group witnessing the punishing event can all become aversive stimuli.

Put simply, if punishment occurs often enough during the school day and across enough settings in the school, students tend to view the entire school experience as aversive and, seeking to escape from these aversive stimuli, may become truant or just drop out.

When to Use Punishment

Although punishment should be avoided because of the above-mentioned effects, there are two situations in which punishment may be necessary. One situation in which punishment may be unavoidable is when the maladaptive behavior is so intense or severe that someone might get hurt, including the child himself. A second situation is when you have tried everything else without success. Remember that it is your responsibility to weaken and, if possible, hopefully eliminate maladaptive behavior as long as the punishment used doesn't create problems for the student and/or those in his environment that are worse than the problem currently caused by the maladaptive behavior.

How to use punishment effectively

Let's assume you are facing one of two situations described above and you have to use punishment. While it is bad enough to have to use it, you don't want to become one of the millions of teachers who use punishment incorrectly. Follow the rules provided here:

1. To be effective, punishment must prevent avoidance and escape from the source of the punishment. If the student can successfully escape from the punishment through sneaking, hiding, cheating, lying, or stealing, punishment will lose much of its potency.

2. Minimize the need for future punishment by positively reinforcing adaptive behaviors that are incompatible or in competition with the maladaptive behaviors you punish. Don't simply punish out-of-seat behavior; positively reinforce in-seat behavior as well. Don't simply punish hitting behavior; positively reinforce gentle touching behavior as well. If the student doesn't know how to touch gently, teach her. Don't simply punish cursing and abusive or aggressive language; positively reinforce the use of appropriate assertive language. Again, if the student doesn't know how to speak in an assertive, nonaggressive manner, teach her.

3. Never be a model of aggressive behavior. Don't attack students verbally or physically when you punish them.

4. Never hold a grudge. It is not healthy for you or your students. If the student feels that you have a grudge against him he will be less inclined to try and change his behavior. Why should he bother, if your feelings toward him prevent you from rewarding him when he's behaving properly?

5. Punishment, like reinforcement, should be administered immediately. The longer the latency, the less likely learning will take place.

6. Communicate to the student, in terms she can understand, exactly how she may earn back whatever reinforcers you might have taken away from her.

7. Try to use a warning signal of some kind before punishing a student. Even a stern look is better than nothing. Give the student one, and only one, opportunity to change her behavior before you punish her. If she doesn't stop, punish her.

8. Always do what you say you will do. Never make a threat if you can't back it up. Don't tell a student she is "going to have to leave school if she doesn't behave" if you don't know whether or not her parent is available to come and get her. Don't threaten detention on any day when you have to leave school early.

9. Try to carry out your punishment in a calm manner, without losing your temper. Besides making you look foolish, weak, scared, immature, and/or insecure, losing your cool can teach the student that self-control is impossible. If an adult can't attain it, how can she be expected to?

10. Be consistent and always punish the same behavior. The student who can't remember her own name somehow always manages to remember who gets punished for what and when.

11. Make sure that the intensity of the punishment is high enough to ensure that the behavior is weakened. At the same time, try not to gradually increase the intensity of the punishment; this may cause the child to develop a tolerance for the punishment.

12. Use a variety of punishers. Just as a student can become satiated from the use of the same reinforcer over and over again, so can he become desensitized to continuous use of the same punisher.

✔ Checkpoint 6.4

[pages 197–199]

Fill in the answers to the following items (1–14). Check your responses by referring to the text; relevant page numbers appear in brackets.

Four reasons for using punishment only as a last resort are:

(1) _____

(2) _____

(3) _____

(4) _____ [197–198]

Two situations in which you might have to use punishment are:

(5) _____

(6) _____ [198]

(continues)

CHECKPOINT 6.4, continued

Eight ways to use punishment effectively are:

(7) _____

(8) _____

(9) _____

(10) _____

(11) _____

(12) _____

(13) _____

(14) _____ [198–199]

Redo any items you missed. If you missed more than 3 of the items, reread the material. Otherwise, continue on to the next section.

Types of Punishment: Reprimands, Response Cost, Overcorrection, Time-out

There are basically four types of punishment covered in this text: reprimands, response cost, overcorrection, and time-out. Let's examine each.

Reprimands

A *reprimand* is a simple word or statement the teacher says to the student to get him to stop doing whatever behavior she objects to. Examples are "No," "Stop," "Don't do that," and "I want you to stop _____." Reprimands are typically the first punisher a teacher uses when she wants to weaken a behavior. Reprimands are different from redirects in that they typically draw negative attention to the student's behavior. Because of this, reprimands are considered more intrusive than redirects. While both reprimands and redirects interrupt ongoing practice, reprimands—because of their punitive nature—tend to produce emotional side effects in the student, whereas redirects do not. Think about it. Which would you rather hear all day long: "Do you have a question? Can I help you?" or "No! Stop that!"?

To be effective in using reprimands, try to follow these guidelines:

1. Get as close to the student as possible, without being threatening, so that your physical presence will help get the student's attention. Don't shout across the room and further disrupt the learning environment. A "private" reprimand is less likely to result in face-saving defiance in front of the student's peer group.

2. If you cannot get close to the student, use an attention signal such as calling her name before giving the reprimand. Sometimes the attention signal ("Amy!") is aversive enough to the student to punish her behavior.

3. Look directly at the student while talking to him, even if he's not looking at you. Eye contact is important in asserting yourself.

4. Make the reprimand as short and succinct as possible, using one or two sentences at the most.

5. Use simple vocabulary. A student can't follow a directive unless she understands it. "Stop procrastinating" is not simple. Instead, say "Stop putting off doing your work," or "Stop daydreaming."

6. Specify the behavior you want the student to stop (or start) engaging in. Don't use terms that are open to interpretation. Don't say "Stop bothering him." "Bothering" is open to interpretation. Instead, say, "Stop talking to him." The stranger test applies to the use of reprimands the same way it does to pinpointing behaviors.

7. Under no circumstances should you use sarcasm. Some students won't understand you, and you also serve as an aggressive model for students who enjoy making fun of others.

8. Use an if–then statement when reprimanding the student. Specify what you want the student to do and let him know exactly what the consequences will be if he doesn't do it. Don't say "Stop talking," or "If you don't stop talking, you are going to be punished." Instead, say "If you don't stop talking to Pete, you'll lose ten points."

9. Deliver the reprimand in your normal teaching voice. Speak too softly and the student might not hear you or may think you don't mean what you say. Speak too loudly and, aside from disrupting the entire class, you may also communicate anxiety, fear, or loss of self-control. Speaking too loudly may stimulate the student (i.e., make her anxious) to the point where she can't respond appropriately even if she wants to, or it might reinforce her maladaptive behavior if she thinks she has managed to annoy you. It is also ludicrous to expect a student to demonstrate self-control in the presence of an adult who has lost hers.

10. Try to finish what you have to say to one student before addressing another. Students can manipulate your verbal behavior and reduce the effectiveness of your reprimands. Don't let yourself be distracted.

11. Students are also good at reading body language and facial expressions. Never fold your arms across your chest when reprimanding a student, because this conveys aggression (or at the very least, defensiveness) and tends to make some students anxious, while others perceive it as a challenge. Pointing, especially when up close, and standing with hands on hips may also convey the same aggressive or hostile message. Try to communicate as little of your feelings as possible through facial expression. Students tend to focus on the way you speak to them rather than on what you actually say. If

your mouth says one thing and your body says something else, students will pay attention to your body. Force them to focus on your words rather than reading your expression or posture. Remember that a low-key, calm demeanor will be more effective in the long run than immediately blowing off steam. The latter approach will make you feel better for the moment but it may serve to prolong and/or escalate the student's disruptive behavior.

12. Give the student enough time to comply with the request. Try to determine what constitutes "enough" time based upon (a) your past experiences with the student, (b) how upset she is now, and (c) how difficult your request is for her to comply with. Compliance time will vary from student to student and from situation to situation. Whatever you do, never repeat a request unless you are certain that the student did not hear you the first time. You will only be teaching her not to pay attention to you and that she doesn't have to comply the first time because you will repeat the directive. Ignore back talk such as "Whattaya pickin' on me for?" or "I'm not doin' nothin'." Compliance is the important thing. As long as the student does as she is told, it doesn't make any difference whether she does it with or without comment. However, in cases where profanity is used, you may wish to punish this with response cost; when other provocative language is used, such as threats to you and/or other students, you may wish to consequate this with something more severe, such as a time-out. (Response cost and time-out strategies are discussed later in this chapter.)

13. If the student has complied with your request within a reasonable amount of time, thank him for his actions and remember to praise him for behavior that is incompatible with his maladaptive behavior. If the student continues to engage in his maladaptive behavior and does not comply with your request (i.e., your reprimand doesn't work), proceed to a more severe consequence; do not continue to use reprimands over and over again if they prove to be ineffective.

Reprimands get mixed reviews regarding their effectiveness. In many instances, they can serve to strengthen rather than weaken maladaptive behavior by providing students with the attention many of them crave but don't get unless they misbehave (see Madsen, Becker, Thomas, Koser, & Plager, 1970). This doesn't mean that reprimands should never be used. It means they should not be *overused.* Kazdin (1994) reports on the high rates of disapproval observed among elementary and secondary teachers in regular education classrooms (Thomas, Presland, Grant, & Glynn, 1978; White, 1975) and suggests that it is the overuse of reprimands that contributes to their long-term ineffectiveness. I agree. The problem is how to change this. It is so easy to use a reprimand instead of a less punitive BRP that requires more work such as DRI or extinction. Remember what I said about the criticism trap: Because reprimands are an easy way to quickly punish a student's behavior, the teacher believes they are effective and continues to use them over and over again even though they have minimal long-term efficacy. I believe the long-range effect of reprimands is not to weaken student behavior but to damage relationships between teacher and student. After using reprimands over and over again, the teacher becomes associated with his reprimands to the extent that he, himself, becomes an aversive stimulus. I also believe that in addition to ruining relationships between teacher and student, excessive use of reprimands has a negative effect on teachers to the extent that it contributes to the escalating rate of burnout among teachers. Think about spending 5 to 7 hours, 5 days per week, at a job where you spend a good deal of your time making negative and punitive comments to people. Depressing, isn't it?

Response cost

Response cost is sometimes referred to as *cost contingency.* It involves the removal of a potentially rewarding event (e.g., leaving school at dismissal) or the removal of an earned reinforcer (e.g., tokens earned for past behavior) contingent upon an undesirable behavior. Grounding a teenager for coming home late from a dance is an example of response cost used to punish staying out late or disobeying rules. Paying a fine for a parking violation is an example of response cost used to punish "bad" driving behavior. Any time you take something away from a student that she has or expects to have, in order to weaken a behavior, you may say you are using response cost.

Do not confuse response cost with extinction. In using extinction strategies, you are withholding or removing the object or event that is reinforcing the student's maladaptive behavior. For example: Joey is distracting a peer by talking to him during independent seatwork. Joey's talking-to-peer behavior is reinforced by his peer's listening behavior. If you withhold the known reinforcer (peer attention) by

Situation 1: Child is blowing bubbles in his milk with a straw at the dinner table for the amusement of his siblings.

In RESPONSE COST, parent takes away straw (or milk).

In EXTINCTION, parents asks siblings to ignore child.

Situation 2: Student curses in class for adult attention.

In RESPONSE COST, teacher takes away points student has earned contingent upon cursing.

In EXTINCTION, teacher withholds all attention from student contingent upon cursing.

Situation 3: Student watches peers at recess through window in classroom instead of doing seatwork.

In RESPONSE COST, teacher takes away student's recess (he should be getting in 20 minutes).

In EXTINCTION, teachers pulls down window shade so student can't see peers outside.

Situation 4: Student uses verbally abusive language (threats and swears) to coerce the teacher into giving him back his recess.

In RESPONSE COST, teacher takes away student's activity period (he should be getting during the last half hour of school).

In EXTINCTION, teacher talks to the student about the problem but does not give in to his demands.

Figure 6.6. Examples of response cost contrasted with extinction.

separating the two students or reinforcing the peer for ignoring Joey, you may say that you are trying to weaken Joey's talking-to-peer behavior with extinction. On the other hand, if you remove tokens from Joey's token bank for each instance of talking to peer, you may say that you are trying to weaken his behavior with response cost. Figure 6.6 has more examples of response cost contrasted with extinction.

Response cost is probably most useful in a token economy. Students need to know that "bad" behavior can result in the subsequent loss of points. The situation where a student is tempted to stop working because he knows he already has enough points for the backup reinforcer should be avoided, and stopping-work behavior needs to be discouraged. If you are not using a token economy and don't have the option of removing tokens earned, there are still some other potentially rewarding events or earned reinforcers you can remove. Unfortunately, you may run out of reinforcers to remove before you weaken the student's behavior. How many times in one day can you tell a student he's going to miss recess or get detention? If you remove recess or give him detention for days on end, you will be defeating your purpose in the long run. The student, knowing that he's "bankrupt" for the next week, may decide that he has nothing to lose as far as his behavior is concerned.

For this reason, I advocate more parent–teacher agreements for the consequation of a student's school behavior *at home*. There are many potential reinforcers available in the home which the parents might remove as a consequence of maladaptive behavior at school. TV privileges, staying up late, eating favored desserts, having snacks, having friends sleep over, going out to play after school, using the family car, going out on dates, going on family outings, going to the movies or sporting events with the family, getting an allowance, and using the stereo are just a few of the potentially reinforcing events that a parent might remove through a response cost program. Don't get me wrong—I still prefer to use a positive program of reinforcement rather than a negative program of punishment to change a student's behavior. However, as I have stated before, when all else fails, punishment may be your only hope.

Should you decide upon a strategy of response cost, make sure you follow these rules:

1. Remove whatever you told the student he would lose as quickly and as quietly as possible. Do this without any dramatics. Do not communicate to the student that you are glad that he is losing something he wants, even if you actually feel this way.

2. Let the student know what she is losing, why she is losing it, how she might earn it back, and what will happen if she continues to misbehave. You might say, for example, "Tina, I'm taking away ten of the points you have earned, because you are still talking to Rudy. If you stop talking and get back to work, you can start earning those points back. If you continue talking to Rudy, you will have to go to time-out and you won't be able to earn any points for 5 minutes no matter how hard you try."

3. Because response cost is so convenient to use, teachers tend to use it too often. Overuse, however, may limit its effectiveness.

4. Collect data ahead of time to determine the severity of the cost or fine. You don't want the fine to be too heavy, because this might result in the student completely giving up and not trying to earn back with adaptive behavior what he has lost through maladaptive behavior. It might also provoke an emotional reaction (e.g., anger) in the student that could exacerbate the situation. On the other hand, if the fine is too light, it will not have the desired effect of weakening the maladaptive behavior. If you have initially settled on a fine that is too light, by all means increase it. However, do not increase it gradually or you may find that the student adapts to it and it will not serve to weaken the maladaptive behavior. Either return to baseline for a while or implement a much heavier fine immediately. For example, Harriet's teacher wants to weaken her swearing behavior through the use of response cost. Since Harriet participates in a token economy, the teacher decides to fine Harriet a certain number of tokens for each swearing episode. At first she fines Harriet 10 tokens for each episode.

This doesn't seem to have any effect, so she immediately moves to a fine of 25 tokens per episode. This fine produces the desired effect and Harriet starts to limit her swearing.

5. If the student become upset at the fine, try to ignore any emotional outbursts. If they become serious, you might consider fining the student for these reactions. You could even begin charging students for the privilege of a tantrum in the same way you would charge for listening to a rock and roll tape. On the other hand, if the student behaves in an accepting and responsible manner, you might consider returning a portion of the fine you assessed.

Response cost has demonstrated efficacy with a number of behaviors including off task (DuPaul, Guervremont, & Barkley, 1992; Gordon, Thomason, Cooper, & Ivers, 1991; Iwata & Bailey, 1974; Salend, Tintle, & Balber, 1988); disruptive behavior (Colozzi et al., 1986; Proctor & Morgan, 1991; Rapport, Murphy, & Bailey, 1982); test-taking errors (Neenan & Routh, 1986); articulation errors (Mowrer & Conley, 1987); noncompliance (Little & Kelley, 1989); multiple sleep problems (Piazza & Fisher, 1991); aggression (Forman, 1980; Wesolowski & Zencius, 1992); classroom interruptions (Sprute, Williams, & McLaughlin, 1990); and persistent nosepicking (Pianta & Hudson, 1990). Like most BRPs, response cost has demonstrated greater efficacy when combined with reinforcement programs such as a token economy than when used in isolation (Bierman, Miller, & Stabb, 1987; Walker, Hops, & Figenbaum, 1976). A special bonus is that response cost is less likely to result in imitative aggression than are other forms of punishment (Bandura, 1973).

(*Checkpoint 6.5 follows, on p. 204.*)

✔ Checkpoint 6.5

[pages 197, 200–203]

Fill in the answers to the following items (1–19). Check your responses by referring to the text; relevant page numbers appear in brackets.

Four types of punishment are:

(1) _____,

(2) _____,

(3) _____,

(4) _____[200]

Seven rules to follow in using reprimands are:

(5) _____

_____

(6) _____

_____

(7) _____

_____

(8) _____

_____

(9) _____

_____

(10) _____

_____

(11) _____

_____ [200–201]

(continues)

CHECKPOINT 6.5, continued

Explain what reprimands have to do with the criticism trap:

(12) _____

_____

_____

_____

_____

_____

_____

_____ [197]

Response cost is

(13) _____

_____ [201]

Response cost differs from extinction because

(14) _____

_____

_____

_____

_____ [201–202]

Five guidelines for using response cost are:

(15) _____

_____

(16) _____

_____

(17) _____

_____

(18) _____

_____

(19) _____

_____[202–203]

Redo any items you missed. If you missed more than 4 of the items, reread the material. Otherwise, continue on to the next section.

Situation 1: Student insults peers.

In RESTITUTION, student writes a letter to peer(s) apologizing for his behavior and saying something nice about peer(s).

In POSITIVE PRACTICE, student pays at least one compliment to each classmate per day for 5 consecutive days.

Situation 2: Student makes a mess of his work area (desk and floor).

In RESTITUTION, student cleans his work area until it is the cleanest in the class.

In POSITIVE PRACTICE, student is given responsibility of cleaning the work areas of a given number of students each day for a week.

Situation 3: Student steals items (e.g., food, crayons, books) from peers.

In RESTITUTION, student returns all items stolen and/or money for consumed items.

In POSITIVE PRACTICE, student is required to voluntarily share his own items with peers a given number of times per day.

Situation 4: Student bullies smaller, younger students.

In RESTITUTION, student apologizes to victims.

In POSITIVE PRACTICE, student is required to serve as peer tutor and/or "big brother" for one or more younger students over an extended period of time.

Figure 6.7.   Examples of overcorrection applied to common behavior problems.

Overcorrection

This is one of the oldest methods used to punish maladaptive behavior in school children. Remember how you were made to write a misspelled word over and over until you learned it? That's overcorrection. So is making students write "I will come to class prepared" 100 times. Other examples are requiring students with messy desks to clean up their own desks *and* everyone else's desk in the classroom, and requiring students caught writing on school walls or furniture to wash all of the walls in the school or refinish all of the desks in their classroom.

Overcorrection has two basic components:

1. *restitution,* which requires the individual to restore the environment to its original state prior to the maladaptive behavior; and

2. *positive practice,* the repeated practice of a positive behavior incompatible with the maladaptive behavior

Here is an example: Jane gets angry and sometimes throws her or another student's desk over, scattering materials everywhere. In applying the restitution component of overcorrection, Jane's teacher makes her pick up the overturned desk(s) as well as the spilled materials. As for the positive practice component of overcorrection, Jane is required to stack all classroom furniture (i.e., put chairs on desks) for the maintenance crew prior to dismissal for one week. Figure 6.7 includes examples of the use of overcorrection in reducing a number of different maladaptive behaviors.

I should mention that although overcorrection always involves a positive practice phase, it does not always require restitution. Having a child who engages in self-injurious behavior (e.g., face and head punching) practice gentle self-touching over and over again is an example of overcorrection without restitution.

Overcorrection has been used successfully to reduce such disparate behaviors as excessive drooling (Trott & Maechtlen, 1986); oral reading errors (Singh & Singh, 1986); disruptive behavior (Sisson, Van Hasselt, Hersen, & Aurand, 1988); stereotypic behavior in severe populations (MacFarlane, Young, & West, 1987); self-injurious behavior (Carter & Ward, 1987; Cipiani, Brendlinger, McDowell, & Usher, 1991); and aggression (Charlop, Burgio, Iwata, & Ivancic, 1988). Despite its demonstrated efficacy, I would be cautious about using overcorrection as a

Figure 6.8. Time-out should be devoid of all reinforcement.

behavior reduction procedure. First of all, it is one of the more restrictive and intrusive interventions and should not even be considered until after you have considered and/or tried other more positive and benign BRPs. Second, it may be too labor intensive for you to use in your classroom. The positive practice component often requires close adult supervision to ensure compliance. If you don't have the time or personnel to commit to the strategy, it won't work.

Time-out

Technically speaking, time-out (TO) is closer to extinction than it is to punishment. You might say that TO is extinction in the extreme. Instead of withholding one reinforcer for one particular response, you withhold all reinforcement for all behavior. For example: Sandy curses at the rate of 5 curses every 10 minutes. In the past, this behavior has gotten her all the attention she wanted, even though most of it was negative. Now, her peers and the teacher ignore her cursing but they attend to her whenever she uses appropriate language. Eventually, Sandy's cursing becomes extinguished because the known reinforcer, attention, is withheld. In this case a specific reinforcer is withheld for a specific response. However, reinforcement is presented for other

behavior, e.g., appropriate language. Let's suppose that Sandy's cursing behavior gets worse and eventually becomes so disruptive to the learning environment that she has to be removed from it. Once Sandy is removed from the environment, she receives no reinforcement for cursing or appropriate language or any other behavior. TO means *time-out from all reinforcement for all behavior.*

I don't want to give the impression that TO always means placing a student behind a partition so he can't see the rest of the class. Sometimes you may simply tell the student to put his head down on his desk as you remove his point card. This would alert the student to the fact that, for a pre-specified period of time, he will not be earning points regardless of what he does. In this case, TO is like being laid off from work—no matter what you do, you aren't going to earn any money from your employer.

For TO to be effective, it is necessary for the teacher to observe the following rules:

1. Be sure to put the student into an environment that is essentially free of reinforcement. (See Figure 6.8.) Putting a student out into the hall, where there are lots of other rooms to look into and lots of hallway traffic, is not my idea of a reinforcement-free environment; there are too many opportunities to interact with peers and

engage in more mischief. Sending a child to his room where he can play with his toys is also not appropriate. Try to set up a TO space in your classroom or somewhere in the school building where a student will receive no reinforcement for any behavior, but where he can be observed from time to time. This may be difficult but it will save you grief later on. And please remember that sticking a child in the cloak room or walk-in closet of a classroom is not only cruel, it's downright risky business; students have been forgotten in closets and some have developed real psychological traumas as a result of such treatment. You should also be aware that a student sent to the hall for TO can inflict some serious physical damage on one or more of his peers who happen to walk by. He might also be the object of physical abuse himself. Aside from the obvious damage to the student, the teacher in this situation is wide open to litigation from the student's parents. In the past, I have simply put a student in a chair facing the corner in my classroom and set a timer so he would know when he would be free to leave TO and return to his desk. This way, I could see him but he could not see the rest of the class. He may still hear us and we may still hear him. Should he attempt to take advantage of this situation, I can always reinforce his peers for ignoring him and/or add more time on the timer. An ideal setup for the classroom would be to place a chair behind a screen in the back of the room. Here, the student would not be able to see his peers and, as long as their seats were facing the front of the room, they would not be able to see him. The teacher, however, would be able to monitor the student even though he was behind the screen by installing a wide-angle mirror above the TO area. If this item is too expensive, there are also wide-angle stick-on mirrors sold in auto parts and recreational vehicle shops that do the job for much less money.

2. In addition to making sure that the student is going to a reinforcement-free environment in TO, you need to be sure that he is leaving an environment that is reinforcing to him. Let's say that Joey dislikes reading group. He is the worst reader in the lowest group and he is embarrassed to read in front of his peers. One day, Joey becomes disruptive in reading group and is arbitrarily given a TO by his teacher. While the TO is a relatively reinforcement-free environment, Joey considers it less aversive than his reading group and continues to engage in disruptive behavior in order to escape to TO. If the student considers himself to already be in an aversive situation or, at the very least, in a reinforcement-free environment, it will not be aversive for him to leave this environment to go to TO.

3. The student should not stay in TO for more than 1 minute for each of his chronological years. In other words, a 10-year-old should not stay in TO for more than 10 minutes. The student should always know how long he is in for. You might have to add time on for disruptive behavior in TO, but I have found that longer time spent in TO results in more disruptive behavior later on. It then becomes a vicious cycle. The student in TO for more than 5 minutes usually becomes restless and agitated. He manifests this by attempting to communicate with the teacher ("How much longer do I have to stay here?" "When can I go back to my desk?"). Although this behavior is ignored by the teacher, it can eventually become disruptive to the other students, causing the teacher to add more time to the TO in order to punish the student's calling-out behavior. The more time she adds on, the more restless and agitated the student becomes and the more disruptive behavior he is likely to engage in.

4. TO should not be used unless the student's behavior is disruptive to the learning environment. If the student's peers cannot learn and the teacher cannot teach as a direct result of his maladaptive behavior, he should be placed in TO, assuming that other less intrusive and restrictive interventions have not been effective.

5. The student should go to TO under her own power. Do not attempt to move her physically unless she is in danger of being physically hurt or is hurting someone else. If she refuses to go, start a stopwatch in her presence and tell her that from now on, the time she takes to go to TO will be added to the time she already has to spend there. If and when she does go to TO, stop the watch and tell her how long it took her to comply and how much total time she has to spend in TO. If she can tell time, she probably won't be asking you every minute how much longer she has to stay there.

6. Should the student leave TO for any reason without your permission before her time is up, she should be told to return to TO and her time begun from zero again.

Maladaptive Behavior: student is disruptive (e.g., talks to peers) during math lesson while teacher is teaching class

Target Behavior: student quietly attends to (i.e., looks at and listens to) teacher during math lesson

1. *Differential Reinforcement of Incompatible (DRI) or Alternative (DRA) Behavior:* Wait until student is quietly attending to teacher during math lesson and reinforce him for attending.

2. *Differential Reinforcement of the Omission of Behavior (DRO):* Reinforce the student if he is not talking to peers at the moment a timer signals the end of an interval (MDRO), or reinforce the student for not talking to peers for the entire duration of an interval (WDRO).

3. *Extinction:* (assuming peer attention is reinforcing disruptive behavior) Reinforce peers for ignoring student when he talks to them or separate students to make it less likely they will attend to him.

4. *Redirection:* Ask student if he has a question about the material being covered.

5. *Reprimands:* Tell student, "If you don't stop talking and start listening, ..."

6. *Response Cost:* Take away points student has earned (or recess or some other entitlement) and tell him how he can earn them back (e.g., by attending to lesson).

7. *Overcorrection:* Have student apologize to you and to peers for disrupting lesson (restitution) and require him to (a) take notes during future math lessons, and (b) make these notes available to any of his peers who might want them (positive practice).

8. *Time-out:* Have student go to time-out (i.e., leave the math lesson and his peer group) for a predetermined time during which he receives no reinforcement for any behavior.

Figure 6.9. Behavior reduction procedures listed from least to most aversive/intrusive/restrictive.

7. Should the student engage in any disruptive behavior while in TO, try to ignore it and reinforce those students who ignore it. If it becomes disruptive to the learning environment, add more time to the timer and let the student know what is happening and why. Don't get into an argument or a dialogue with him, just tell him and go on with whatever you were doing before.

8. Finally, it goes without saying that after the student returns from TO and engages in appropriate behavior, he should be reinforced immediately.

I am not a big TO fan. First of all, what does anyone learn while they are sitting behind a screen contemplating their navel? Where is Joey going to learn how to read better—in TO or in reading group? Where is he going to learn how to deal with his embarrassment better—in TO or in reading group? Every time you send a student to TO you take him away from an opportunity to learn an alternative behavior to the behavior that got him sent to TO in the first place. When does he get the opportunity to practice this alternative behavior if you keep sending him to TO? In all fairness to TO, it certainly does not result in as much lost instructional time as suspension or truancy (Skiba & Raison, 1990).

I also believe that TO can be abused to the point where it ceases to be TO and becomes seclusion. Seclusion is the isolation of an individual for long periods of time (at least 50 minutes). It is used in a non-systematic (i.e., inconsistent and arbitrary) manner. Seclusion is also used without any steps to

ensure accountability. Nobody seems to care whether or not seclusion changes behavior, so no one monitors its efficacy. The bottom line is that seclusion is more for the teacher's benefit than it is for the student's benefit. If you want to avoid having your use of TO evolve into a form of seclusion, you need to observe the following precautions:

1. Use TO systematically. In other words, use it consistently with the same students, for the same behaviors, and purposefully.

2. Keep it brief. Again, follow the 1:1 ratio between student age in years and time spent in minutes.

3. Be accountable. Collect data on the behavior you are using TO to weaken. If the data show that TO is working, continue to use it. If the data show otherwise, you should consider discontinuing its use.

With regard to its efficacy, TO has successfully reduced a number of maladaptive behaviors including aggression (McGuffin, 1991; Olson & Roberts, 1987; Timmons-Mitchell, 1986); noncompliance (Handen, 1992); disruptive behavior (White & Bailey, 1990); and temper tantrums (Wolf, Risley, & Mees, 1964).

To help you better understand the differences between each of these strategies for weakening behavior, I have included examples of the application of each to the same behavior problems; see Figure 6.9.

✔ Checkpoint 6.6

[pages 205–208]

Fill in the answers to the following items (1–16). Check your responses by referring to the text; relevant page numbers appear in brackets.

The two basic components of overcorrection are (list and describe):

(1) _____

_____

_____

_____

(2) _____

_____

_____

_____[205]

Two disadvantages of overcorrection are:

(3) _____

_____

_____

_____

(4) _____

_____

_____

_____[206]

Time-out is

(5) _____

_____

_____

_____[206]

Time-out differs from extinction because

(6) _____

_____

_____

_____

(continues)

CHECKPOINT 6.6, continued

_____

_____[206]

Six rules for using time-out effectively are:

(7) _____

_____

(8) _____

_____

(9) _____

_____

(10) _____

_____

(11) _____

_____

(12) _____

_____[206–208]

The author's primary objection to time-out is

(13) _____

_____

_____[208]

Three ways to keep time-out from turning into seclusion are:

(14) _____

_____

(15) _____

_____

(16) _____

_____[208]

Redo any items you missed. If you missed more than 3 items, reread the material. Otherwise, continue on to the next section.

HIERARCHY OF ESCALATING CONSEQUENCES

When I go into classrooms I find teachers using the same strategies over and over again with all of their students regardless of the behavior. For example, most of the teachers I observe tend to use punitive BRPs such as reprimands or response cost to weaken maladaptive behavior. Negative reinforcement of alternative behavior is also widely used. It is bad enough that teachers choose to use these negative BRPs before trying a positive or benign strategy, even worse if they use them over and over again whether they work or not. Nag, nag, nag. Threaten, threaten, threaten. Yell, yell, yell. Scold, scold, scold. Students become desensitized to the same consequences when they are being used over and over again. This greatly inhibits the efficacy of the consequences being used. I recommend that you use more than one strategy and that you use it in a structured and systematic manner. A format I have found effective is the hierarchy of escalating consequences.

The hierarchy can include any number of consequences in ascending order from least to most aversive. The following is an example of the hierarchy being used by a teacher with a disruptive student.

Response *(what the kid does)*	*Consequence* *(what the teacher does)*
1. Johnny talks to Pete during a math lesson and keeps him from doing his work. Pete listens and laughs at Johnny but does not talk to him. In between Johnny's talking, Pete works on his math. Johnny does not work on his assignments at all.	
	2. Having decided that Johnny's behavior is maladaptive (it is harmful to his and Pete's academic well-being), the teacher decides to intervene. First, she looks for any incompatible or competing behavior in Johnny that she can reinforce. Unfortunately, Johnny is not doing any

Response *(continued)*	*Consequence* *(continued)*
	work so she has nothing to reinforce. She assumes that Pete's attention is reinforcing Johnny's off-task behavior and tries to remove this reinforcer by strenthening Pete's on-task behavior. She begins awarding points to students who are doing their work. When Pete makes an effort to be on task, the teacher awards him points.
3. Despite Pete's new-found resolve to stay on task, Johnny continues to talk to him and it soon becomes apparent to the teacher that Pete is becoming disturbed by Johnny's talking.	
	4. Although the teacher continues to reinforce Pete for being on task (and ignoring Johnny), she sees how difficult it is for him to concentrate and decides to intervene directly with Johnny. She tries to redirect Johnny's behavior by asking him questions regarding his work assignment ("Johnny, how many examples have you completed?"; "Do you need some help?"; "Let me know if you need help.")
5. Johnny indicates he has done a few of the problems and that he does not need help. He looks at his workbook and begins to write but, after a short while, he starts talking to Pete again.	

Response (continued)	Consequence (continued)	Response (continued)	Consequence (continued)
	6. The teacher tries one more redirect. She goes to Johnny's desk and asks to see his work.	13. Johnny complains loudly about losing his points (e.g., "That's not fair!").	
7. Johnny refuses to show the teacher his work and protests ("I'll do it. I'll do it!").			14. The teacher ignores Johnny's complaining until she sees that it's disrupting the rest of the class. Then she quietly tells Johnny she is taking away five more points for arguing. She reminds Johnny that at the rate he is losing points, he will not have enough to spend during free activity time at the end of the day.
	8. Not wanting to get involved in a power struggle, the teacher says, "Good. I'm glad you're going to do it. I want you to get good grades."		
9. Johnny opens his workbook and starts working on one of the problems. After a few minutes he starts talking to Pete again.			
	10. This time, the teacher walks to Johnny's desk and quietly reprimands him ("Johnny, if you don't stop talking and start working, I'm going to have to take away some of the points you've earned today").	15. After a while, Johnny stops complaining and puts his head down on the desk. After a few minutes, he reluctantly begins doing his math.	
11. Johnny starts working again but this lasts only a few minutes. Soon he's talking to Pete again.			16. After watching Johnny do his work for a few minutes, the teacher awards him points and praises him for his efforts. She continues to praise and award points to all of the students who are on task.
	12. The teacher walks to Johnny's desk and quietly tells him she's taking away ten points. She tells him why, and explains how he can earn them back. She also reminds him that he will continue to lose points if he doesn't start working.		

(Text continues on p. 212.)

In the preceding example, Johnny finally stopped talking to Pete and began doing his seatwork after the teacher used response cost. If response cost had not worked and Johnny continued his maladaptive behavior, the teacher could have moved on to the next (more severe) consequence. This might be time-out, or it might be a contingent observation where Johnny is required to move his desk away from his peers. The teacher could also have tried DRO (either WDRO or MDRO) after DRI and/or extinction. You may ask, If response cost is effective in weakening Johnny's behavior, shouldn't the teacher use it all the time and not bother using the less severe consequences? Good question. I would remind you of the ethical and legal guidelines discussed at the beginning of this chapter. While response cost may be effective in reducing Johnny's off-task behavior, it is still a punitive consequence. At the very least, Johnny deserves the opportunity to respond to positive and benign consequences. Wouldn't it be more pleasant for the teacher and Johnny if he eventually responded to redirects or even to the reinforcement of an incompatible behavior? By going through the hierarchy, the teacher is giving Johnny the opportunity to respond to consequences other than response cost.

You will also notice that Johnny's teacher did not return to the least severe consequence each time he resumed his maladaptive behavior. Instead, she moved to the next (more severe) consequence. If a teacher starts over with the first, or least severe, consequence in the hierarchy each time the student resumes his disruptive behavior, it is conceivable that a student will engage in disruptive behavior all day long with the teacher using the same (least severe and ineffective) consequences over and over again. This situation is unsatisfactory for teachers and for students.

Knowing when to start over again or go on to the next (more severe) consequence is not always so obvious. However, the following guidelines will provide you with some basis for making this decision.

1. When a student engages in disruptive behavior where there is the potential for physical harm to another person, begin your intervention with time-out (i.e., isolation and removal from environment of peers).

2. When a student engages in in disruptive behavior (that is not potentially physically harmful) on an intermittent basis several times during the same class period, begin your intervention with the least severe consequence (e.g., DRI and/or

extinction) for the first incident, and progress through the other consequences without starting over at any time.

3. When a student engages in disruptive behavior (that is not potentially physically harmful) on an intermittent basis several times during the school day, begin your intervention with the least severe consequence each time. Students are less likely to remember consequences from hour to hour or class period to class period than from minute to minute.

One last caveat regarding the hierarchy concerns the use of extinction. You will recall that the major disadvantage of extinction is how long it takes to produce results. It therefore has questionable value as a BRP to be used in a hierarchy of BRPs that changes from day to day or from period to period. I recommend including extinction in the hierarchy only if: (a) You know the reinforcer that is maintaining the maladaptive behavior; (b) you are able to control (i.e., remove or withhold) it; and (c) the reinforcer is relatively new (i.e., it has not been maintaining the maladaptive behavior for a prolonged period).

Teachers who have used the hierarchy of escalating consequences over the years have told me that it has two major benefits. First, they don't get as anxious or angry as they used to when they only used one or two strategies over and over again. The reason for this is simple. When you use the same strategies over and over again and they don't always work, you get frustrated and angry, and when you don't have anything else you can think of to do, you get scared. With the hierarchy you are certain to find something that works; and even if it takes a while, you are less likely to panic because you know that if plan A doesn't work, there is always plan B, and so on. The result is that students tend to show more respect for their teachers, especially when the teachers consequate student misbehavior in a calm, matter-of-fact manner rather than showing fear or anger.

Another benefit of the hierarchy is that teachers and students become more reflective (and less reflexive) in terms of their behavior. Both students and teachers are less likely to behave automatically and are more likely to reflect on the consequences of their actions. The old behavior chains such as *teacher yells* → *student yells back or teacher nags* → *student tunes teacher out* are replaced by new behavior chains. If nothing else, the hierarchy can get you out of the rut of using the same old strategies over and over again.

✔ Checkpoint 6.7

[pages 210–212]

Fill in the answers to the following items (1–16). Check your responses by referring to the text; relevant page numbers appear in brackets.

According to the author, you should not use the same BRPs over and over again for the same behaviors and same students because:

(1) _____

_____

_____

(2) _____

_____

_____

_____ [210]

Instead, the author recommends using the hierarchy of escalating consequences, which is:

(3) _____

_____

_____

_____

_____ [210]

Assume you are using a hierarchy of escalating consequences in your classroom and list the following BRPs in the order in which you would use them in your hierarchy—time-out, reprimands, redirection, overcorrection, extinction, DRI/DRO/DRA, response cost:

(4) _____,

(5) _____,

(6) _____,

(7) _____,

(8) _____,

(9) _____,

(10) _____ [210–211]

(continues)

CHECKPOINT 6.7, continued

You use the hierarchy of escalating consequences and eventually find a punitive consequence that works. Explain why the author believes you should not always use this consequence even though it is effective.

(11) _____

_____

_____

_____

_____ [212]

Two benefits of the hierarchy of escalating consequences are:

(12) _____

_____

_____

(13) _____

_____

_____ [212]

Three guidelines to follow in deciding whether to start the hierarchy over again from the beginning or move on to the next (more severe) consequence are:

(14) _____

_____

_____

(15) _____

_____

_____

(16) _____

_____

_____

_____ [212]

Redo any items you missed. If you missed more than 3 items, reread the material. Otherwise, continue on to the Chapter Assesment.

ASSESSMENT / CHAPTER 6

A list of acceptable responses appears following the Assessment.

For each of the following cases, describe your intervention as if you were leaving notes for a substitute or student teacher.

    1. Design an intervention using *DRI or DRA* to weaken noncompliance behavior (i.e., refusal to follow direction first time given) in a student.

    2. Design an intervention using *DRO* (specify WDRO or MDRO) to weaken out-of-seat behavior (i.e., bottom not touching seat) in a student.

3. Design an intervention using a combination of *extinction and DRI* (or DRA or DRO) to weaken cursing in a student who uses four-letter obscenities (e.g., F - - K, S - - T) on a regular basis. You have reinforced this behavior in the past by verbally attending to it (e.g., "Where did you learn to use such language?").

4. Design an intervention using a combination of *redirection and DRI* (or DRA or DRO) to weaken a student's "visiting" behavior (i.e., talking with peers) during quiet independent seatwork sessions.

5. Design an intervention using a combination of *reprimands and DRI* (or DRA or DRO) to weaken disruptive behavior (i.e., tapping pencil on desk, singing, or making animal sounds) in a student.

6. Design an intervention using a combination of *response cost and DRI* (or DRA or DRO) to weaken a student's teasing behavior (i.e., makes insulting comments to peer).

7. Design an intervention using a combination of *overcorrection and DRI* (or DRA or DRO) to weaken a student's destructive behavior. He takes other students' work assignments and scribbles on them or tears them up.

8. Design an intervention using a combination of *time-out and DRI* (or DRA or DRO) to weaken a student's physically aggressive behavior (i.e., unprovoked hitting of peers).

9. Describe how you would use a hierarchy of escalating consequences to weaken a student's off-task behavior (i.e., looks away from work on desk). Include time-out, at least one reinforcement-based strategy, redirection, extinction, reprimands, and response cost in the correct sequence. Assume that you have to use all of the strategies before you find one that works.

ACCEPTABLE RESPONSES

1. *DRI or DRA/noncompliance* [The behavior you are reinforcing should be incompatible with, or at least compete with, noncompliance.]

   Example

   Reinforce the student when he complies with a directive and do not reinforce him when he does not comply.

2. *DRO (WDRO or MDRO)/out-of-seat*

   Example (WDRO)

   a. Set a timer for a fixed amount of time (e.g., 5 minutes);

   b. watch the student to determine if she engages in any out-of-seat behavior;

   c. when the timer rings, indicating the end of the interval, reinforce the student if she did not engage in any out-of-seat behavior during the interval;

   d. do not reinforce her if she engaged in out-of-seat behavior during the interval.

   Example (MDRO)

   a. Set a timer to ring at random intervals;

   b. when the timer rings, observe the student to see if she is engaging in any out-of-seat behavior;

   c. reinforce her if she is not engaging in any out-of-seat behavior when the timer rings;

   d. do not reinforce her if she is engaging in any out-of-seat behavior when the timer rings.

3. *Extinction and DRI (or DRA)/cursing*

   Example (extinction)

   When student curses in front of you, do not say anything or do anything to indicate you have heard him.

   Example (DRI)

   Reinforce the student when he uses socially appropriate language without cursing.

4. *redirection and DRI (or DRA)/"visiting"*

   Example (redirection)

   When student talks to peers during quiet time, interrupt her behavior without calling attention to it directly (e.g., ask her if she needs help, give her an errand or chore to do, ask her to show you her work).

   Example (DRI)

   Reinforce the student when she is in seat doing her work or (DRA) when she is engaged in any behavior that is an acceptable alternative to visiting.

5. *reprimands and DRI (or DRA)/disruptive behavior*

   Example (reprimands)

   a. When student is disruptive, move close to him so you can reprimand him without an audience;

   b. look directly at him and use an "if–then" statement (e.g., "If you don't stop making those noises, you are going to lose some of the points you've earned");

   c. be careful that your voice and body language convey neither aggression nor passivity;

   d. do not repeat the reprimand and do not attend to any backtalk; if the reprimand does not effectively weaken the student's behavior, do what you said you would (i.e., remove his points);

   e. if the reprimand works, thank the student.

   Example (DRI/DRA)

   Be sure to reinforce him for any incompatible or competing behavior such as writing with his pencil (instead of tapping it), talking to you or to peers (instead of singing or making animal noises), or working or sitting quietly.

6. *response cost and DRI (or DRA)/teasing*

   Example (response cost)

   a. When student continues to tease peer(s) after being warned about response cost (e.g., "If you don't stop calling _____ names, you are going to lose _____ points"), take points away;

   b. tell student, "I am taking away _____ points from your point bank because you did not stop teasing when I told you to";

   c. "if you want to earn back your points, you need to talk to _____ without teasing her";

   d. if student continues to tease, try increasing the fine (be careful not to increase it gradually nor in small increments);

   e. if the student objects to the fine and acts abusive (e.g., yells or curses or threatens), take away more points ("I am taking away _____ more points because of what you just said; remember, cursing costs you points; we can discuss this as long as you don't curse or yell or threaten me; otherwise, you will lose more points";

   f. if the student accepts the fine without incident or objects to the fine without acting abusive, you have the option of reducing the fine.

   Example (DRI)

   Reinforce the student when she interacts with (i.e., talks or listens to) peers without teasing.

7. *overcorrection and DRI (or DRA)/destructive behavior*

Example (overcorrection)

a. For *restitution,* have student redo the other student's work (i.e., copy it over or do it from scratch) and apologize to student;

b. for *positive practice,* have student serve as class work assignment monitor and be responsible for collecting other students' work and taking care of it until teacher asks for it (1 week).

Example (DRI)

Reinforce student when he handles peers' work without purposely trying to damage it.

8. *time-out and DRI (or DRA)/physical aggression*

Example (time-out)

a. When student acts in physically aggressive manner towards peers (e.g., unprovoked hitting), tell him to go to time-out;

b. tell him why he is going and for how many minutes;

c. if he balks at going, start a stopwatch and add time it takes him to get there to his TO.

Example (DRI)

Reinforce the student when he interacts with peers without unprovoked hitting.

9. *hierarchy of escalating consequences/off task*

Example

a. Reinforce student when you catch him looking at or actively doing work;

b. if his behavior does not improve with DRI or if you have difficulty implementing DRI because you seldom catch the student on task, look for environmental stimulus controlling student's off-task behavior (e.g., looks at peers, looks out of window, talks with and/or listens to peers, daydreams, focuses attention on materials/objects other than work [e.g., comic book, drawing, listens to radio, plays with toy]);

c. if possible, remove/withhold environmental stimulus (e.g., set up study carrel or turn student's seat in opposite direction, move student to another seat, reinforce peers for ignoring student, pull down window shade, or remove comic book, etc.);

d. try to use in combination with DRI;

e. if student's behavior does not improve with extinction and DRI, try redirecting him by asking him questions about his work (e.g., "Do you need help?", "Are you finished?", "How much more do you have to do?", "Can I see what you've done so far?");

f. if redirection does not improve student's off-task behavior, use a reprimand (e.g., "If you don't stop looking around the classroom and get back to work, I'm going to have to take away _____ points from your points-earned card");

g. if student's off-task behavior continues, take away points (response cost); tell him how many points he is losing, why he is losing them, and how he can earn points back; follow procedure outlined above (see #6);

h. if response cost does not improve student's off-task behavior, try time-out; set a timer for _____ minutes and tell him he will not earn any points for that amount of time (even if he is on task).

CHAPTER SEVEN

Measuring Change

Data Collection

Upon successful completion of this chapter, the learner should be able to design a formative measurement system to measure student progress.

ON BEING ACCOUNTABLE

Responsible change agents hold themselves accountable for the efficacy of their interventions by measuring student progress. Progress may be defined as how quickly the student moves from point A, *where he is now,* to point B, *where you want him to be.* The faster the student moves from A to B, the more progress we may say he is making. The more progress the student is making, the more effective we may say the intervention is. Conversely, the slower the student moves from A to B, the less progress and, therefore, the less effective the intervention. If an intervention does not result in sufficient progress, the responsible change agent revises it—and keeps revising it—until an effective intervention is found. In my opinion, the primary responsibility of teachers is the design and implementation of interventions that move students from point A to point B as quickly as possible. Unless you have psychic powers or a crystal ball, it is often difficult, if not impossible, to determine the efficacy of interventions without measuring student progress.

FORMATIVE VERSUS SUMMATIVE MEASUREMENT

There are two basic approaches to measuring student progress. The more traditional of the two is called *summative measurement* because it requires that the teacher wait until *after* the intervention to measure student progress. In other words, the teacher measures the *sum* of his or her labors, or the end product of the intervention. In the summative approach, data are typically collected at the begin-

ning and end of the intervention. These pre- and post-intervention data are then compared to determine if sufficient change (i.e., progress) has occurred.

The second approach to measuring student progress is called *formative measurement* because it requires that the teacher measure student progress *during* the intervention while the student's behavior is still in a changing, or formative, state. Data are collected at the beginning of the intervention and each day of the intervention thereafter.

Formative measurement has two distinct advantages over the summative approach. First, formative measurement provides more data than summative measurement and the more data you have, the easier it is to determine how much progress the student is making. Also, the more data you have, *assuming it is collected accurately,* the more confidence you can have in its accuracy. A second advantage of formative measurement is that it allows you to make changes in your intervention sooner than you could using summative measurement. This means you waste less time finding the most effective intervention. Consider the following example.

Let's say you are working with a special education student who is often off task. You design an intervention you hope will move her from point A ("looks at work on desk 10% of time observed") to point B ("looks at work on desk 80% of time observed"). Let's also say you want her to reach point B in 4 weeks (20 school days). Using a summative approach to measure progress, you observe her on-task behavior at the beginning of the intervention, use the intervention for *4 weeks* and then observe her on-task behavior again. Comparing the two sets of data, you find the student has gone from 10% on task to 30% (see Figure 7.1). Not exactly what you wanted.

Now let's suppose you use a formative approach to measure student progress. You know where the student is now (10%) and where you want her to be (80%). You also know when you want her to arrive at point B, 80% (4 weeks). Drawing a line from point A (10%) to point B (80% in 4 weeks) shows you how much progress the student needs to make (see Figure 7.2). As long as the data you collect on your student's on-task behavior stays on or above this line, you know she is making sufficient progress. But let's assume your intervention is not working. Since you discover this after only 8 days (compared with 20 days in the summative approach), you are able to make revisions in your intervention much sooner and, therefore, find an effective intervention much sooner.

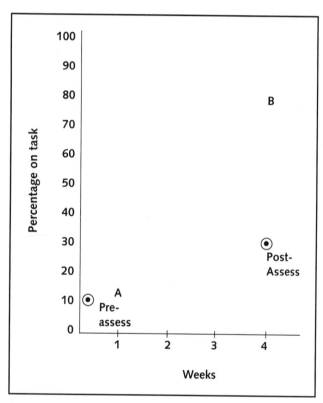

Figure 7.1. Summative approach to measuring student progress.

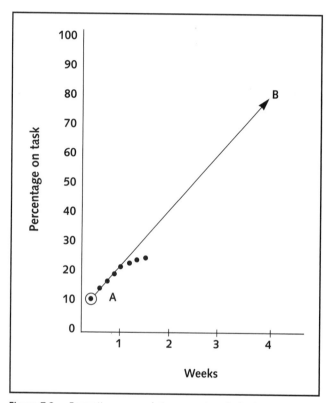

Figure 7.2. Formative approach to measuring student progress.

✔ Checkpoint 7.1

[pages 223–224]

Fill in the answers to the following items (1-5). Check your responses by referring to the text; relevant page numbers appear in brackets.

Responsible change agents are accountable for the efficacy of their interventions. The best way to determine the efficacy of an intervention is to

(1) _____

_____ [223].

Progress may be defined as

(2) _____

_____

_____ [223].

An effective intervention is

(3) _____

_____

_____ [223].

An ineffective intervention is one in which little or no student progress is evident. In this case, the change agent should

(4) _____

_____

_____ [223].

Two basic approaches to measuring student progress are

(5) _____

_____

_____ [223].

Label each of the following characteristics (Items 6–12) **S** (for summative) or **F** (for formative). Check your responses by referring to the answers following Item 12.

(6) _____ Provides more data than the other approach to measuring student progress.

(continues)

CHECKPOINT 7.1, continued

(7) _____ Requires that the teacher measure student progress during the intervention while the student's behavior is still changing.

(8) _____ Data are typically collected at the beginning and end of the intervention.

(9) _____ Allows the teacher to make revisions in his or her intervention sooner than the other approach to measuring student progress.

(10) _____ Data are collected at the beginning of the intervention and each day of the intervention thereafter.

(11) _____ Requires that the teacher wait until after she finishes her intervention before she measures student progress.

(12) _____ Measures the end product of the intervention.

ANSWERS (6–11): (6) F, (7) F, (8) S, (9) F, (10) F, (11) S, (12) S

Redo any items you missed. If you missed more than 3 of the items, reread the material. Otherwise, continue on to the next section.

EXCUSES, EXCUSES

Formative measurement, done right, requires that you collect data daily on student behavior and use the data to make decisions about your interventions. Unfortunately, data collection has never been a popular activity among teachers. While there are teachers who collect data daily and make data-based instructional decisions, these teachers tend to be exceptions. My personal experience, as well as the research I have read on the subject, leads me to believe that the vast majority of teachers, including special educators, fall into one of the following categories:

1. teachers who collect data daily but seldom, if ever, use it in the decision-making process;

2. teachers who collect some data but not consistently and not on a daily basis; or

3. teachers who do not collect any data at all (Burney & Shores, 1979; Farlow & Snell, 1989; Haring, Liberty, & White, 1980; Walton, 1985).

Why don't more teachers collect data daily and use it to make decisions regarding instruction? There are many reasons. The following is a sampler of excuses I have heard over the years.

1. *"I don't need to collect data. I know my methods work."* (See Figure 7.3.) This excuse often comes from teachers who are so ego-invested in their methods that they refuse to believe the methods might not work for every student in their class. While this often sounds like simple self-confidence, it can be misleading. I believe many teachers actually find data collection threatening. They are afraid the data will not support the efficacy of their methods— sometimes the truth hurts. Still, I don't see how you can be an effective teacher by playing it safe. Teaching anybody anything requires that you be courageous and take risks, especially the risk that they might not learn. This does not necessarily mean that the learner or the teacher is at fault. It simply means that the instruction/intervention is inappropriate and needs changing, anywhere from a minor adjustment to an entirely new method. I know from my experiences as a parent and a teacher that parents appreciate and respect teachers who are willing to share their failures as well as their successes. I also believe that students appreciate and respect teachers who are not afraid to take a chance and to admit a mistake.

2. *"Data collection is too hard."* I have heard this excuse from teachers who honestly believe they can't teach and collect data at the same time. Unfortunately, I have also heard it from teachers who

wish to do the least work possible. All I can say is that teaching, done right, is extremely demanding and teachers who meet the demands of the job are typically more effective than teachers who do only whatever is necessary to just get by. Data collection may seem hard at first, but with practice it becomes easy.

3. *"Data collection is not required by my school (or district)."* I would offer the same rebuttal here as I did in Number 2 above. These are probably the same teachers who expect students to be intrinsically motivated to behave responsibly, but have no such expectations for themselves. It could be said that this is an instance of a double standard.

4. *"I don't have enough time to collect data."* Unfortunately, the reason many teachers don't seem to have enough time is because they waste so much of it using ineffective methods to discipline their students. If they took the time to do formative measurement, they would be using effective methods more often and would spend less time on discipline, thereby saving themselves time in the long run. As I've said before, you either pay now or you pay later.

5. *"I don't know how to collect data."* Some teachers have not been taught how to do formative measurement in their preservice programs. Others feel it is too hard to learn how to do formative measurement. A number of the graduate students I have worked with at the university tend to be math illiterate and/or math phobic. They lack a basic understanding of elementary arithmetic concepts and operations such as average, percentage, and rate. I can certainly empathize with them. I remember scoring at the 16th percentile on the Graduate Record Exam (GRE) when I was attempting to enter graduate school. That meant 84% of the males in the stan-

Figure 7.3.   What a fool believes, he or she sees.

dardization sample of the GRE scored higher than I did! Not exactly what you would call an Albert Einstein. Still, as a doctoral student at the University of Oregon, I recognized the importance of formative measurement and persevered until I had mastered it. My message to you is: If I can master formative measurement, anybody can.

6. *"I don't like collecting data."* Some teachers are philosophically opposed to the idea of formative measurement because they think data collection makes them behaviorists (God forbid!). I believe that school is for the students, not for the teachers, and that professionals are willing to put the best interests of their students ahead of their own. Besides, collecting data daily does not make you a behaviorist. (If I'm not mistaken, the Book of Behaviorism states that a behaviorist is someone with a behaviorist mother who observes high holy days such as B. F. Skinner's birthday, March 20.)

7. *"I tried data collection and it didn't work."* Teachers who try formative measurement and give it up tend to fall into two categories: those who do too much or those who do too little. Teachers who do too much either have too broad a focus and attempt to collect data on multiple students for multiple behaviors (see Figure 7.4), or they have too narrow a focus and monitor several specific behaviors when they should simply monitor one class of behaviors. Teachers who have too broad a focus need to prioritize, pick the most critical behaviors in the most needy students, and use formative measurement with them. Teachers with too narrow a focus need to consolidate. It's not necessary to spend all your time collecting data on several different behaviors (e.g., out of seat, talking out, talking back, object throwing, etc.) when you could simply monitor "disruptions."

Teachers who do *too little* tend to take shortcuts that invalidate their data and actually make their data collection a waste of time. For example, instead of monitoring a student's behavior, they monitor the consequences of the behavior. If a student receives tokens for appropriate behavior and/or loses tokens

Figure 7.4. Try to keep it simple.

for inappropriate behavior, the teacher measures student progress not by monitoring the number of times the student engaged in a given behavior but by the number of tokens he winds up with at the end of the day. What these teachers are doing is trying to measure student progress by monitoring teacher behavior. The problem with this approach is that teachers don't always consequate student behavior appropriately. For example, they might give or remove tokens or points depending on their mood, or the amount of time available, or how easy it is to reward or punish the behavior. When this happens, the total number of tokens or points earned does not accurately reflect the change in a student's behavior and therefore should not be used to measure progress.

(Checkpoint 7.2 follows, on p. 228.)

✔ **Checkpoint 7.2**

[pages 225–227]

Provide a rebuttal for each of the excuses below (Items 1–7). Check your responses by looking at the text; relevant page numbers appear in brackets.

(1) "I don't need to collect data. I know my methods work." [226]

(2) "Data collection is too hard." [226]

(3) "Data collection is not required by my school or district." [226]

(continues)

CHECKPOINT 7.2, continued

(4) "I don't have enough time to collect data." [226]

(5) "I don't know how to collect data." [226]

(6) "I don't like collecting data." [227]

(7) "I tried data collection and it didn't work." [227]

Redo any items you missed. If you missed more than 1 of the items, reread the material. Otherwise, continue on to the next section.

MONITORING

Data collection, which I prefer to call *monitoring*, involves the direct observation and recording of student behavior on a daily basis. Designing a monitoring system requires careful consideration of what, when, and how you are going to observe and record behavior as well as how you are going to summarize the data.

What to Monitor

Before you begin monitoring, you need to decide what you are going to monitor. For example, are you going to monitor only what the target student does, or what somebody else does in addition to the target student? Are you going to monitor the maladaptive pinpoint or the target pinpoint, or both? What dimension of the student's behavior are you going to mon-

itor—how often it occurs, or how long it lasts? Let's examine each question more closely.

Whose behavior?

Since one person's behavior is often controlled by the behavior of another, it is sometimes necessary to monitor both persons' behavior. This brings up the question of whether you are monitoring a free operant or a controlled operant. *Free operants* are behaviors that occur without any readily observable antecedent. They seem to occur on their own. Some examples of free operants are unprovoked hitting, asking questions, self-stimulating or self-injurious behaviors, and getting out of seat. While there might be some stimulus that elicits any one of these responses (e.g., a thought or feeling), it is not readily observable and, therefore, is not easily monitored. If a student shouted out whether you asked a question or not, this would be considered free operant behav-

Operant	Type	Behaver/Behaviors to Monitor
Benny hits peers when teased	controlled	peers/tease Benny Benny/hits peers
Joey shouts out when teacher asks question	controlled	teacher/asks question Joey/shouts out
Ross curses	free	Ross/curses
Kim runs out of room	free	Kim/runs out of room
Nicole self-stims	free	Nicole/self-stims
Betsy bites self	free	Betsy/bites self
Mark complies with directive given by teacher	controlled	teacher/gives directive Mark/complies with directive
Hannah answers questions correctly	controlled	teacher/asks questions Hannah/answers questions correctly
Martha completes assignments given	controlled	teacher/gives assignments Martha/completes assignments given
Perry gives compliments	free	Perry/gives compliments
Julio says "Thank you" to other person when they compliment him	controlled	other person/gives Julio compliment Julio/says "Thank you"

Figure 7.5. What to monitor in controlled and free operants.

ior and you would only need to monitor the student's behavior and not your own.

Controlled operants are behaviors that occur only in response to a readily observable antecedent. Most of the time this antecedent is something that another person says or does. Examples of controlled operants include answering questions (asked by another person), hitting (when provoked by another person), complying with requests (made by another person), saying "thank you" (when another person gives you something), and completing assignments (given by another person). Each of these behaviors is a direct response to a readily observable antecedent. They are called controlled operants because they are controlled by an antecedent. For example, the number of times a student calls out an answer to a question or raises her hand and waits to be called on are controlled, to some extent, by the number of questions you ask of the class. Since the number of questions you ask is likely to change from day to day, you not only need to monitor the student's responding behavior, you also need to monitor your question-asking behavior. Figure 7.5 includes a number of examples of free and controlled operants and the behavers and behaviors you should monitor for each.

Maladaptive or target behaviors?

Many teachers tend to focus on the negative behavior of their students. They use behavior reduction procedures to weaken maladaptive behavior instead of strengthening fair-pair target behaviors through reinforcement. This negative focus is carried over to their monitoring. Instead of collecting data on the target behavior, they monitor change in the maladaptive behavior. If you are going to monitor only one behavior, it should be the target behavior. Monitoring the target behavior is much more positive for you and for the student, who should always have access to his data display.

There are times when you will need to monitor both the maladaptive and target behaviors. For example, many teachers write performance objectives with percentages as criteria for acceptable performance (CAP). This is perfectly fine. Just remember that if you use percentage as CAP, you need to summarize your data as percentage, and if you summarize your data as percentage, you will need to monitor two behaviors. For example, if you write a performance objective that states "Kirsten will raise her hand and wait to be called on without shouting out the answer 80% of the time she

---

The student will attend school on school days 100% of the time over a 4-week period unless he has an excused absence. [Need to monitor (a) days attended and (b) unexcused absences to compute percentage of days attended.]

The student will be on task (i.e., eyes directed toward work) 90% of the times observed over a 5-day period. [Need to monitor (a) on task (looking at work) and (b) off task (not looking at work) to compute percentage of on task.]

The student will follow 100% of directives given over a 2-week period. [Need to monitor (a) directives given and (b) student follows, or (a) student follows directives and (b) student does not follow directives, to compute percentage of directives followed.]

The student will be in his seat (i.e., buttocks touching chair) during study hall 90% of the times observed over a 1-week period. [Need to monitor (a) in seat and (b) out of seat (buttocks not touching chair) to compute percentage of in-seat behavior.]

The student will complete 80% of assignments given over a 3-day period. [Need to monitor (a) assignments completed and (b) assignments not completed, or (a) assignments given and (b) assignments completed, to compute percentage of assignments completed.]

The student will raise his hand and wait to be called on without shouting out during recitation and independent seatwork sessions. He will do so 80% of the time over a 3-day period. [Need to monitor (a) raises hand and waits to be called on and (b) shouts out to compute percentage of raising hand and waiting behavior.

Figure 7.6. What to monitor in performance objectives where CAP is expressed as percentage.

attempts to answer a question," the whole point in monitoring this behavior is to determine how quickly Kirtsten is moving from point A (14% hand raising and waiting) to point B (80%). Therefore, you need a monitoring system that allows you to measure change in the *percentage* of hand-raising and waiting behavior. Since you cannot compute a percentage unless you have two behaviors (handraising and calling out), you will have to monitor both. In Kirsten's case, you divide the sum of the total raises hand and waits and the total talk outs into the total raises hand and waits in order to calculate percentage of raises hand and waits behavior. Figure 7.6 is a list of performance objectives with percentage as CAP and the corresponding behaviors to monitor for each.

Which dimension?

In addition to the above, you need to know which dimension of the behavior you are going to measure change in. I use the term "dimension" to refer to the *way* in which a behavior changes. There are many ways a behavior can change. For example, a behavior can occur more or less often. This dimension of a behavior is referred to as *frequency*. Behaviors that occur with high frequency, that are of short duration, and have a readily observable beginning and ending should be observed according to their frequency. Examples of such behaviors are cursing, telling lies, destroying property of others, calling out, teasing or criticizing peers, making self-deprecating remarks, smiling, complying with requests, paying compliments, completing assignments, and coming to class on time and/or prepared.

A behavior can also change by lasting longer or less long as a result of the intervention. This dimension is called *duration*. Some behaviors are more appropriate to monitor in terms of duration because they don't occur often but they do last a long time at each occurrence, and they do not necessarily have a readily observable beginning and end. Behaviors you may want to monitor according to duration include daydreaming, being in (or out of) seat, being on (or off) task, thumb sucking, self-stimming (e.g., rocking in seat or shaking one's hands), tantrumming, and maintaining eye contact.

A third dimension of a behavior that might change as a result of an intervention is *intensity*. When a behavior's intensity changes, the behavior can get louder or quieter, stronger or weaker, harder or softer. Examples of behaviors you would be likely to monitor for intensity are tantrums, a student's speaking voice (audible to inaudible), and self-injurious behavior.

Sometimes teachers don't care how long the behavior lasts or how often it occurs or how intense it is—they simply want to know how the behavior "looks." For example, you may be more interested in the kinds of funny faces a student makes than how many times he makes them, or you may be more interested in what his voice sounds like than in how loud it is or how long he speaks. This dimension of a behavior is referred to as *topography*. Some examples of what you might monitor with regard to topography include facial expressions, tone of voice, body language, and personal hygiene, among others.

Let's suppose that you are not interested so much in what the student does as in how long it takes him to do it. For example, in compliance situations, you might want to know how long it takes a student to at least begin to comply with a directive. This dimension of a student's behavior is referred to as *latency*, the time that elapses between two events (e.g., being told what to do and doing it). Behaviors that lend themselves to latency monitoring include compliance with directive, time spent completing a task, and time spent responding to a question.

Sometimes it is difficult to decide which dimension of a behavior to monitor. Other times you know which dimension to monitor but you don't have the time or the help you need to do it. In some situations it is unethical to monitor a behavior according to a particular dimension. For example, sitting with a stopwatch and monitoring the duration of off-task, out-of-seat, self-stimming, or self-injurious behavior without intervening can be considered unethical. When in doubt, or when the logistics won't work out, or when you start feeling guilty about just watching, remember that you can always monitor the frequency of a behavior. When you think about it, even though some behaviors are more suitable to monitoring a particular dimension, every behavior has a beginning and an ending and at least the potential for occurring more than once. Therefore, a general rule to follow with regard to which dimensions of behavior to monitor is: *when in doubt, monitor frequency.* More about this later.

How to Monitor

Frequency data are the easiest type of data to collect. When you want to know how often a behavior occurs, simply record each instance of it as you see it. For example, each time a student shouts out in class, record it. Shouting-out behavior typically occurs often, doesn't last long (how long does it take for a student to shout out an answer or your name?), and has a readily observable beginning and end. But what about a behavior like off task (i.e., looks away from work on desk)? While one student might shout out 20 times in the space of a minute, another student may be looking away from his desk for an entire minute—one behavior occurs often but doesn't last long, and the other lasts long but occurs infrequently. Remember, I said you could always monitor *any* behavior according to its frequency. Here's how—let's use off task as an example. If you change off-task behavior so that it has a readily observable beginning and ending, it follows that the behavior will occur often and not last long. For example, redefining off task as "looks away from work on desk for 10 seconds" allows you to count each discrete occurrence of the behavior. Simply watch your student, and when he looks away from the work on his desk, count to yourself "One-Mississippi, two-Mississippi . . ." until you reach ten. If he is still looking away from the work on his desk by the time you get to ten, make a mark (/) and begin counting seconds to yourself again. Each time he is off task for 10 seconds, record it. When you are finished, the number of marks will tell you the frequency of his off-task behavior. Your next question should be: How long do you have to watch the student to count the frequency of each discrete 10-second off task? That depends on how much time you have available to watch—more about this later. An example of frequency data may be seen in Figure 7.7.

If you need to know how long a behavior lasts, monitoring duration usually requires that you use a stopwatch. For example, to monitor the duration of off-task behavior, you would have to watch the target student, start the stopwatch when he looks away from the work on his desk, and stop the watch when

he looks back at the work on his desk. If all you want to monitor is total duration of off-task behavior, you don't need to reset your watch back to zero. At the end of the day, use the total time showing on your watch as duration data for the day (see Figure 7.8). Sometimes a behavior can last for a shorter time at each occurrence but also be increasing in frequency; if you only monitored total duration, you might not discover this. If you want to combine frequency and duration monitoring, you need to write down the *time elapsed* (minutes and/or seconds) each time your student sits back down, and reset your watch to zero. By resetting the watch each time and recording the duration for each separate out-of-seat behavior, you can obtain duration data as well as frequency data (see Figure 7.9). This method of collecting duration data is recommended only if you have the time to record the duration of each separate behavior and wish to observe the frequency aspect as well.

Latency is similar to duration in that you are monitoring time elapsed. For example: Immediately after giving the student a directive, start your stopwatch; when the student complies or begins to comply, stop your stopwatch and record the amount of elapsed time. It makes more sense to record each instance and reset the stopwatch each time, so that you will have a record of the number (frequency) of directives given as well as the time of latency between the issuing of the directive and the beginning of compliance. If you don't want to use a stopwatch, count to yourself ("One-Mississippi, two-Mississippi, . . ."). Latency data are displayed in Figure 7.10.

A fourth, less common, dimension of behavior you might want to monitor is *intensity:* the quality (or

Behaver		(student)
Monitor		(teacher)

Counted out of seat (bottom not in contact with chair)

Date	Duration	Totals
2-14-95	5:40	5'40"
2-15-95	7:17	7'17"
2-16-95	9:09	9'09"

(') = minutes; (") = seconds

Figure 7.8. Example of duration data.

Behaver		(student)
Monitor		(teacher)

Counted talk outs (calling out w/o raising hand)

Date	Frequency	Totals
2-14-95	~~HHH~~ //	7
2-15-95	~~HHH~~ ~~HHH~~	10
2-16-95	~~HHH~~ ///	8

Figure 7.7. Example of frequency data.

Behaver (student)

Monitor (teacher)

Counted out of seat (bottom not in contact with chair)

Date	Duration/Frequency					Totals	
						F	D
2-14-95	5'17" 6'01"	7'04"	6'30"	2'11"	4'40"	6	31'43"
2-15-95	3'09"	4'50"	2'22"	8'25"	10'10"	5	28'56"
2-16-95	1'34" 4'15"	6'27" 7'09"	8'02"	7'11"	9'15"	7	43'53"

(´) = minutes; (˝) = seconds

Figure 7.9. Example of frequency and duration data combined.

Behaver (student)

Monitor (teacher)

Counted latency of compliance (time elapsed between directive given and student begin to comply)

Date	Latency								Average (# seconds)
2-14-95	17" 23"	24" 20"	13" 15"	18" 12"	20" 8"	12" 30"	13" 14"	10" 25"	17"
2-15-95	19" 18"	17" 21"	24" 11"	26" 13"	12" 17"	20" 30"	15"	9"	18"
2-16-95	23" 24"	24" 19"	20" 15"	17"	19"	12"	23"	22"	20"

(˝) = seconds

Figure 7.10. Example of latency data.

Behaver _____ (student) _____

Monitor _____ (teacher) _____

Counted _____ tantrums (see below) _____

Date	Level of Intensity (LOI)	Average LOI
2-14-95	1 1 1 2 3 1 2 1	1.5
2-15-95	2 2 2 2 1 1 1 2 1 1 1	1.45
2-16-95	1 2 1 1 1 1 2 1 1	1.22

Key: (1) *mild* tantrum (cries)
   (2) *moderate* tantrum (lies on floor, cries, shakes head)
   (3) *severe* tantrum (lies on floor, screams, bangs head)

Figure 7.11   Example of intensity data.

Behaver _____ (student) _____

Monitor _____ (teacher) _____

Counted _____ topography of depression (facial affect) _____

Date	Level of Affect (LOA)	Average LOA
2-14-95	1 1 1 1 1 1 1 1 2 1 1 1 1 1 1	1.06
2-15-95	1 2 2 1 1 1 2 1 1 1 1 2 1	1.30
2-16-95	2 2 1 1 1 1 2 1 2 2 2 1 1 2	1.5

Key: (1) depressed affect (no expression; staring into space; appears "out of it" or drugged)
   (2) sad affect (some facial expression; eyes averted, oriented downward; mouth curved downward; appears sad)
   (3) interested affect ("normal" facial expression; mouth curved upward or relaxed; eyes focused; appears interested in environment)
   (4) happy affect (animated expression; smiling/laughing; eye movement; appears happy)

Figure 7.12.   Example of topography data.

force) of a behavior, as opposed to the quantity (i.e., how many times it occurs). Data for intensity are collected in the same manner as frequency. But instead of marks (/) that tell you only the number of *times* a behavior occurs, you record *a number that represents a given level* of intensity. For example: Suppose you want to monitor the intensity of a student's tantrum behavior. Let's say that the student's tantrums include loud screaming, lying on the floor, and banging his head. The behavior can't get much worse than this, so let's call this level "severe" and give it an intensity rating of 3. Let's arbitrarily say that the next-lower level of intensity includes crying, lying on the floor with head shaking, but no head banging. We'll call this "moderate" and give it a rating of 2. Finally, the lowest level of tantrum behavior is crying (no lying on the floor or headbanging or shaking); let's call it "mild" and give it an intensity rating of 1. Each time the student engages in tantrum behavior, observe it and decide whether its intensity level is one, two, or three and record the number. An example of this is shown in Figure 7.11.

Topography data can be collected in one of two ways. The first is similar to intensity monitoring. For example, let's say you have a student who appears to be depressed. One of the symptoms of depression is "flat affect," or facial expression. You can arbitrarily identify three or four facial expressions ranging in animation from (1) depressed affect to (4) happy affect. Next, observe the student's expression periodically during the day and record a level of animation, from 1 to 4, for each observation (see Figure 7.12). A less cost-efficient (more time consuming) method of monitoring topography is to *describe* the behavior as it occurs: You write down (or tape record) what you see. By comparing your recorded impressions over time, you will be able to measure any change that might be occurring.

☑ **Checkpoint 7.3**

[pages 229–235]

Fill in the answers to the following items (1–7). Check your responses by referring to the text; relevant pages numbers appear in brackets.

The author uses the term *monitoring* synonymously with

(1) _____

_____ [229].

Behaviors can change according to their frequency, duration, intensity, latency, and topography. To monitor frequency, you would

(2) _____

_____

_____ [231].

To monitor duration, you would

(3) _____

_____

_____ [232].

To monitor frequency and duration at the same time, you would

(4) _____

_____

_____ [232].

To monitor intensity, you would

(5) _____

_____

_____ [232].

To monitor latency, you would

(6) _____

_____

_____ [235].

(continues)

CHECKPOINT 7.3, continued

To monitor topography, you would

(7) _____

_____

_____ [235].

Identify what you would monitor [i.e., behaver(s), behavior(s), and dimension(s)] for each of the following items (8–17). Check your responses by referring to the answers following Item 17.

(8) Joey hits peers when provoked.

behaver(s) _____

behavior(s) _____

dimension(s) _____

(9) When her teacher asks a question of the class, Darlene will raise her hand and wait to be called on without shouting out 90% of the time over a 5-day period.

behaver(s) _____

behavior(s) _____

dimension(s) _____

(10) Pedro asks the same questions (e.g., "what time is it?", "Is it time for lunch yet?") over and over again.

behaver(s) _____

behavior(s) _____

dimension(s) _____

(11) Savannah bites herself.

behaver(s) _____

behavior(s) _____

dimension(s) _____

(12) Tess daydreams (i.e., stares out the window) for long periods.

behaver(s) _____

behavior(s) _____

dimension _____

(continues)

CHECKPOINT 7.3, continued

(13) Tran speaks when spoken to.

behaver(s) _____

behavior(s) _____

dimension(s) _____

(14) Tony complies with request.

behaver(s) _____

behavior(s) _____

dimension(s) _____

(15) When called by name, Carlos will respond by looking at the teacher 90% of the time over a 3-day period.

behaver(s) _____

behavior(s) _____

dimension(s) _____

(16) Manny will be in seat when late bell rings 90% of the time over a 5-day period.

behaver(s) _____

behavior(s) _____

dimension(s) _____

(17) Claire will raise hand and wait to be called on without shouting out when she wants the teacher's attention 80% of the time over a 3-day period.

behaver(s) _____

behavior(s) _____

dimension(s) _____

ANSWERS (8–17): (8) frequency of peer provocations and Joey's hitting in response; (9) frequency of teacher's question-asking behavior and Darlene's hand-raising behavior (or frequency of Darlene's hand-raising behavior and calling-out behavior); (10) frequency of Pedro's question-asking behavior; (11) intensity of Savannah's self-biting behavior; (12) duration of Tess' stares-out-window behavior; (13) frequency of other person speaking to Tran and Tran speaking in response; (14) frequency of teacher making request of Tony and Tony complying in response; (15) frequency of teacher calling Carlos by name and Carlos looking at teacher in response; (16) frequency of Manny's in-seat behavior and not-in-seat behavior when late bell rings; (17) frequency of Claire's hand-raising behavior and shouting-out behavior

Redo any items you missed. If you missed more than 3 of the items, reread the material. Otherwise, continue on to the next section.

When to Monitor

Knowing *when* to monitor is as important as knowing what or how to monitor. For example, are you going to monitor the behavior(s) whenever it occurs, or only at predetermined times? If you want to monitor behavior the entire time the student is with you, use a continuous sample. If you want to monitor behavior only at special, predetermined times, use an interval sample. To determine which sample to use, ask yourself if you will be able to teach your class and monitor the behavior *at the same time*. If the answer is yes, use the continuous sample. If the answer is no, use an interval sample. Here are some examples.

Continuous samples

Suppose you want to monitor the following behaviors: talk outs, fights, raising hand and waiting to be called on, noncompliance, completes and hands in assignments, tantrums, makes bowel movements in pants, tells truth to teacher, speaks in audible voice to teacher, curses at teacher, and gives correct response to teacher questions. Are you able to monitor these behaviors and teach at the same time? Unless your job responsibility is extraordinarily complicated, the answer is probably yes. Since all of the above behaviors easily come to your attention, it is possible for you to teach your class and monitor at least one of these behaviors at the same time. Behaviors that are loud or graphic or are directed at you are easy to monitor and can be monitored continuously. Try to monitor behavior continuously whenever possible, because a continuous sample provides you with more data than an interval sample. The more data you have, the more confidence you can have in its reliability.

Interval samples

Examples of behaviors that do not come to your attention so easily include: sucks thumb, talks to peers, out of seat, makes disparaging remarks to peers (e.g., "you're stupid"), curses at peers, is off task (looks away from work), smiles, is on task (looks at work), talks to peers without cursing, stays in seat. To continuously monitor these behaviors, you must stop teaching and do nothing but watch the target student. You could ask an instructional assistant or a peer tutor or one of your students to do nothing but observe these behaviors, but it is not necessary to do so; you can monitor these behaviors by using an *interval sample*.

Let's use the student who is off task (i.e., looks away from work for 10 seconds) as an example. You do not want to have to watch this student all day and count the frequency of discrete 10-second off-task behaviors. In addition to not getting much teaching done, you might lose your sanity! A more cost-effective approach is to set a timer to ring on a random basis (e.g., after 30 minutes, after 10 minutes, after 60 minutes, etc.). When the timer rings, reset it to ring in 2 minutes. Then watch the student for a full 2 minutes. Each time he looks away from the work on his desk for 10 seconds, record it (/). When the timer rings, reset it to cue you to begin your next 2-minute interval of monitoring. Continue the procedure until you want (or have) to stop monitoring. At the end of the day, count up the total number of times the student was off task for 10 seconds and use this as your frequency score. If you keep the number of 2-minute intervals constant, each day you can monitor the student's behavior in 20 separate intervals. This is a total of 40 minutes of monitoring (20 intervals times 2 minutes per interval) per day.

If you can't spare 40 minutes from your teaching time, consider using the *momentary time sample* (MTS). Instead of watching the student for 2 minutes during an interval, simply glance at him and record if he is on or off task. Reset your timer to remind you when to glance at him next. You will probably want to double the number of intervals when using the MTS method, since a glance won't tell you if the student is off task for 10 seconds or more. Still, the entire procedure of glancing, deciding, recording, and resetting the timer will take you no more than 5 seconds per interval. Even with 50 intervals during the course of the day, total monitoring time is less than 5 minutes! The MTS is an ideal method to use for monitoring behaviors that are quiet and/or last long. You get reliable data with minimal loss of teaching time.

Recording data

For the most part, I have been discussing the observing or watching component of monitoring. But let's not forget the recording component. Here are some helpful hints.

Recording should immediately follow observing. Don't think that you can remember what you observe, especially if there is a lot of behavior occurring. Write it down *now*. Since you are probably going to be teaching and monitoring at the same time, you want to keep the recording process simple so that you can record right away without interrupting your teaching.

Keep the paperwork to a minimum. You know you are going to have to plot the data on some sort of chart. There is no getting around that, so you already have one piece of paper to deal with. An observation-and-recording form only adds more paper. Why bother with two pieces of paper, when you can get by with one? Instead of a fancy form to record your data on, any one of the following suggestions will provide you with a simple but sure way to record data.

Put a piece of masking tape on your wrist and write on it. If you are collecting frequency data, simply make a mark (/). If you are collecting frequency and duration data, write the time (in minutes and seconds) on the tape each time you stop your watch. If you are collecting duration data only, you don't need a wrist tape. Simply take the total time elapsed (in minutes and seconds) that shows on your watch and plot it directly on your chart. If you are collecting latency data, follow the same procedure as for frequency and duration, above. If you are collecting intensity data, simply write the number (for example, 1 for mild, 2 for moderate, and 3 for severe) of the intensity level on your wrist tape. Follow the same procedure if you are collecting topography data.

If masking tape sounds too painful, try one of the following alternatives. If you are collecting frequency data, move beans or pennies from one pocket to another, or use a golf counter. Or use a grease pencil to mark on a piece of mylar taped to cardboard. The mylar/cardboard can be used over and over again each day after you have transcribed the data to your data display. Tape the mylar/cardboard to your arm or wear it around your neck.

Special Monitoring Conventions

Most of the time your monitoring will be basic and straightforward—single behaviors in single subjects. In case you need to do something exotic, here are some examples of monitoring conventions for special situations.

Monitoring multiple subjects

On occasion, your intervention may involve more than one student or an entire class of students. In such cases, determining the efficacy of your intervention requires that you monitor the behavior of multiple students. Here is how you can do it. Let's say you have a class of students who all engage in inappropriate talking behavior; they talk when they are not supposed to. In order to measure the

progress of more than one student, you may wish to focus on the few students who are the greatest offenders. Finding out who these students are requires that you monitor the behavior of the entire class. Taking baseline data on one student each day takes too much time. Therefore, just monitor the talking behavior of the entire class for 1 day.

Using an interval sample technique, monitor the talking behavior of the entire class during a 1-minute sample every half hour. By looking at a different student every 2 seconds, you are able to record whether he or she is engaged in talking (or listening to someone talking). Record the data on a seating chart attached to a clipboard (see Figure 7.13). Moving from student to student, record a plus (+) for talking or listening to someone talking, or a minus (–) for not talking or not listening to someone talk, in a box representing each student's seat. To help you keep track of the time, use a small tape recorder with an earplug that emits a recorded beeping sound every 2 seconds. The sound, discernible only to you, tells you when to move from one student to the next. Actually, use 2 seconds to observe and 2 seconds to record, 2 to observe and 2 to record, and so on. Keep in mind that you only watch one student for 2 seconds. You have to be disciplined and not allow yourself to be distracted. If you watch Student A for 2 seconds and he is not talking, you record it and move on to Student B. If, while you are watching Student B, Student A starts talking, you cannot go back and record this. You must ignore Student A's behavior and concentrate on Student B.

Monitoring multiple behaviors

On occasion, you may wish to monitor more than one behavior in a single student. For example, a student may have a number of behavior problems and you may wish to monitor all of them to determine which one is most in need of change. You may also wish to modify more than one behavior in a student and need to monitor the effects of more than one intervention. Whatever the reason, monitoring multiple behaviors is not as difficult as it sounds.

Figure 7.14 shows the data collected by a teacher who monitors three different behaviors in one student. This child makes loud noises by clapping his hands together or banging them on the desk, and he asks the same questions over and over again. He also stimulates himself by rocking in his seat and waving his hands in front of his face. The teacher wants to monitor all three behaviors. Using an interval sample, she monitors all of the behaviors for a 5-minute period a minimum of 6 times during each school day.

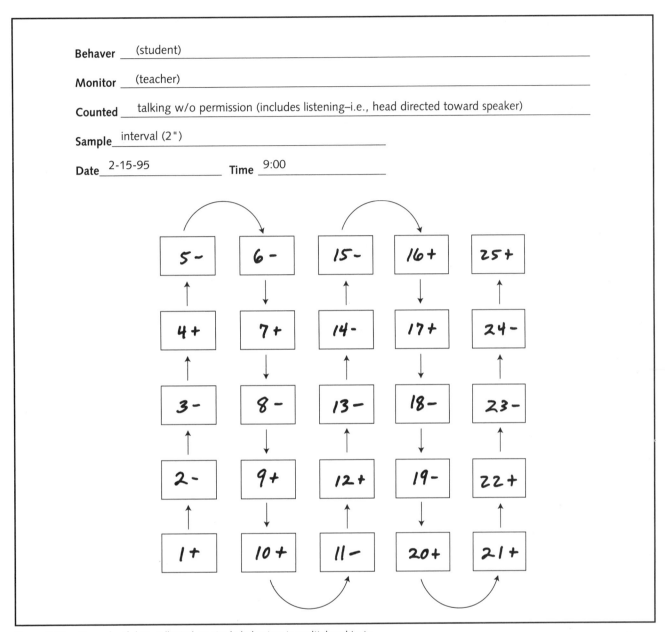

Behaver _____(student)_____

Monitor _____(teacher)_____

Counted _____talking w/o permission (includes listening–i.e., head directed toward speaker)_____

Sample__interval (2")_____

Date__2-15-95_____ Time ___9:00_____

Figure 7.13. Example of data collected on single behaviors in multiple subjects.

Using a recording form such as the one shown in Figure 7.14, she simply circles the code for a behavior each time it occurs.

Monitoring reciprocal behaviors

By *reciprocal* I mean what one person does and what a second person (or persons) does in response. Remember Bandura's theory of reciprocal determinism (1974, 1977, 1986)? Our students shape our behaviors as surely as we shape theirs. They also shape each other's behaviors. For example, Fig-

ure 7.15 shows the data collected by a teacher who is monitoring the reciprocal relationship between a student's physically aggressive behavior and the responses of his peers. Specifically, she wants to see if he is selective in his punching and slapping classmates or if he is acting impulsively. The impulsive student acts before he thinks, and the selective student acts only upon reflection. The impulsive student tends to get into trouble more readily because he doesn't take time to consider the consequences. The teacher in this example wants to find out if the target student is consistently and impulsively hit-

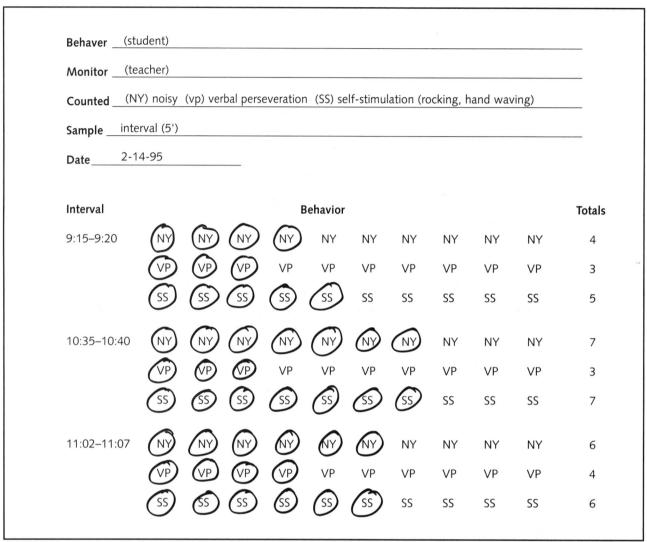

Behaver ___(student)___

Monitor ___(teacher)___

Counted ___(NY) noisy (vp) verbal perseveration (SS) self-stimulation (rocking, hand waving)___

Sample ___interval (5')___

Date___2-14-95___

Interval	Behavior										Totals
9:15–9:20	(NY)	(NY)	(NY)	(NY)	NY	NY	NY	NY	NY	NY	4
	(VP)	(VP)	(VP)	VP	VP	VP	VP	VP	VP	VP	3
	(SS)	(SS)	(SS)	(SS)	(SS)	SS	SS	SS	SS	SS	5
10:35–10:40	(NY)	(NY)	(NY)	(NY)	(NY)	(NY)	(NY)	NY	NY	NY	7
	(VP)	(VP)	(VP)	VP	VP	VP	VP	VP	VP	VP	3
	(SS)	(SS)	(SS)	(SS)	(SS)	(SS)	(SS)	SS	SS	SS	7
11:02–11:07	(NY)	(NY)	(NY)	(NY)	(NY)	(NY)	NY	NY	NY	NY	6
	(VP)	(VP)	(VP)	(VP)	VP	VP	VP	VP	VP	VP	4
	(SS)	(SS)	(SS)	(SS)	(SS)	(SS)	SS	SS	SS	SS	6

Figure 7.14. Example of data collected on multiple behaviors in a single subject.

ting all of his peers, even though many of them are bigger and tougher and often hit him back harder. Using a continuous sample, she records each instance of hitting by the target student by writing the initials of the peer he hits as well as the reaction of that peer. Each box on the 3" × 5" card she uses as a recording form represents one separate instance of a hit by the target student. By using a simple code, the teacher is able to quickly record which peer is hit and what his or her response is. At the end of the monitoring period it becomes obvious that the target student is selective in his attacks, avoiding those peers who previously responded by hitting him back and seeking out those who do not assert themselves physically. This indicates that the student's hitting behavior is reflective rather than impulsive and helps the teacher decide upon an appropriate inter-

vention. Since the data also show how the peer group behaves, the teacher is able to plan an intervention that will include their needs as well.

Self-monitoring

Self-monitoring is important for two reasons. First, letting students monitor their own behavior relieves the teacher of much of the burden of data collection. Second, self-monitoring can make your students more aware of their behavior—how often they are "bad" and how often they are "good." As I mentioned in Chapter 4, awareness of one's behavior is an essential prerequisite for learning to engage in target behaviors.

While much of the specific methodology for self-monitoring is discussed in detail in Chapter 9, now is

Behaver ___(student)_____

Monitor ___(teacher)_____

Counted ___student hits/peer response_____

Date _____2-16-95_____

MJ/I	BR/AG	MJ/I	SL/AG	MJ/AS	ET/AG
MJ/AS	TS/AG	SK/AG	MJ/AS	MJ/I	DL/AG
MJ/AS	MJ/I	PT/AG	MJ/AS	MJ/AS	DK/AG

Key: peer initials/peer response
       (I) = ignores, (AS) = asserts, (AG) = aggresses

Figure 7.15.   Example of data collected on reciprocal behaviors.

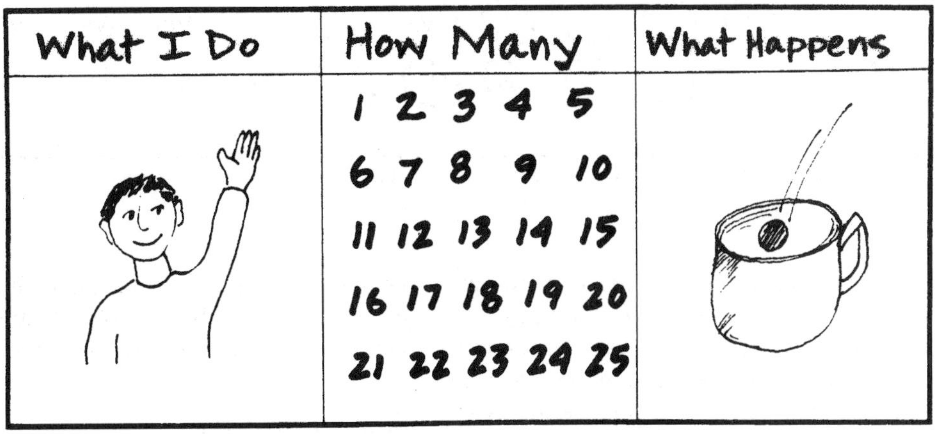

What I Do	How Many	What Happens
	1 2 3 4 5 6 7 8 9 10 11 12 13 14 15 16 17 18 19 20 21 22 23 24 25	

Figure 7.16.   Example of a countoon.

a good time to look at the countoon. The word *countoon* combines this device's two major components: a number line on which behavior can be **count**ed and a car**toon** showing the behavior being counted. For example, Figure 7.16 shows a countoon used to monitor the frequency of hand-raising behavior. The first frame of the countoon ("What I Do") is a drawing of the target behavior being counted. The second frame ("How Many") is a number line on which the student can record the frequency of the target behavior. The third frame ("What Happens") is a drawing of the consequences of the student's behavior.

The countoon can be used in one of two ways. Either the teacher tells the student what to mark on the countoon, which would save her the trouble of recording the data, or the student is completely on his own and decides what to mark and when. If the data on the countoon are left overnight, they serve as a reminder the next morning of what the student needs to do during the day. He may wish to set a new goal for himself based on the preceding day's data. This goal can be marked on the number line of the countoon as a reminder and/or motivator. As the day progresses, the student has a constant reminder of where he is in relation to his goal. The countoon not only helps relieve the teacher of the burden of data collection and develops awareness in the student, it serves as a reminder and motivator for the student.

✔ Checkpoint 7.4

[pages 237–242]

You are a teacher with 30 students and no instructional assistants. Label each of the following items (1-15) **CS** (for continuous sample) or **IS** (for interval sample) based on the sample you would use to monitor each. Check your answers against the responses shown following Item 15.

(1) _____ fist fights

(2) _____ sucks thumb

(3) _____ looks at work on desk

(4) _____ calls out to get teacher attention

(5) _____ completes assignments

(6) _____ copying (looks at peers' work)

(7) _____ complies with request from teacher

(8) _____ makes bowel movements in pants

(9) _____ talks to peer(s)

(10) _____ sleeps in class

(11) _____ gives correct answer to teacher question

(12) _____ tantrums when criticized by teacher

(continues)

CHECKPOINT 7.4, continued

(13) _____ is out of seat (buttocks not touching chair)

(14) _____ masturbates (rubs groin area)

(15) _____ self-stims (rocks in chair and shakes hands)

ANSWERS (1–15): (1) CS, (2) IS, (3) IS, (4) CS, (5) CS, (6) IS, (7) CS, (8) CS, (9) IS, (10) IS, (11) CS, (12) CS, (13) IS, (14) IS, (15) IS

Fill in the correct answers to the items below (16–18). Check your responses by referring to the text; relevant page numbers appear in brackets.

The steps you follow using a momentary time sample (MTS) to monitor the frequency of self-stimming behavior are

(16) _____

_____

_____

_____ [237].

The steps you follow using an interval sample to monitor the frequency of talks-to-peers behavior are

(17) _____

_____

_____

_____ [237].

The steps you follow using a continuous sample to monitor the frequency of complies-with-request behavior are

(18) _____

_____

_____

_____ [237].

Redo any items you missed. If you missed more than 4 of the items, reread the material. Otherwise, continue on to the next section.

SUMMARIZING THE DATA

After recording a day's worth of data, you must summarize it. Data may be summarized as raw score, percentage, rate, or average. For those of you who, like me, have a mental block when it comes to math, a little refresher course is in order.

Raw scores are the total numbers you get before you do anything to them. If you are monitoring the frequency of a student's behavior, *raw score* is the total number of times the student engaged in that behavior. If you are monitoring the duration of a student's behavior, raw score is the total number of minutes and/or seconds the student engaged in that behavior. Calculating raw score is quite simple. Just count the number of times and/or minutes (or seconds) the student engages in the behavior you are monitoring.

I assume you understand what *percentage* is in the general sense. If not, look it up in a basic arithmetic text before you read any further. When you collect data on the frequency of a student's behavior and you need to use percentage, divide the total number of opportunities the student had to engage in the behavior into the total number of times he actually engaged in it. In this case you are dividing behavior (how many opportunities he had to behave) into behavior (how many times he actually engaged in the behavior). For example, Ned's teacher asks 40 questions of the class during a math lesson and Ned calls out the answer to 25 of the questions. To compute the percentage of Ned's calling-out behavior, divide the total number of opportunities he had to call out (the number of questions asked = 40) into the total number of times he called out (25). Twenty-five divided by 40 equals .625. Multiply this decimal fraction by 100 to get the percentage of call outs (62½ percent).

When you are monitoring the duration of a student's behavior and you need to use percentage, divide the total number of minutes you observed the student into the total number of minutes you observed her engaging in that behavior. In this case, you are dividing time (how long you watched the student) into time (how long she engaged in the behavior). For example, Susan is monitored for off-task behavior (looking away from her work) for a total of 82 minutes. During that time she is observed to be off task a total of 39 minutes. To compute the percentage of Susan's off-task behavior, divide the total number of minutes you observed her (82) into the total number of minutes you observed her engaging in off-task behavior (39). Thirty-nine divided by 82 equals .475. Multiply this decimal fraction by 100 to get the percentage of off-task behavior (47½ percent).

Rate may be defined as the average number of times (i.e., frequency of response) a student engages in a particular behavior during a given amount of time (e.g., minutes). It is calculated by dividing the total number of minutes you observed the student into the total number of times she engaged in the behavior. For example, Betsy swears 17 times in 30 minutes (see Figure 7.17). To compute her rate of swearing per minute, divide the total number of minutes you observed her (30) into the total number of

Behaver _____ Betsy _____

Monitor _____ (teacher) _____

Counted _____ swear words spoken ("F--K", "S--T", "D--N") _____

Date	Frequency of Swear Words Spoken	Minutes Observed	Rate
2-14-95	HHT HHT HHT II (17/30 = 0.56 swears per minute)	30	.56
2-15-95	HHT HHT (10/5 = 2 swears per minute)	5	2

Figure 7.17. Frequency data summarized as rate.

times she said a swear word (17). Notice I said "number of *times*" she said a swear word; I did not say "time." You are not dividing time into time; nor are you dividing behavior into behavior. You are *dividing time into behavior.* Seventeen swear words divided by 30 minutes equals 0.56. Although this is a decimal fraction, it is not a percentage. I repeat, it is *not* a percentage. It is a rate, or average number, of behaviors per minute. Therefore you do not treat it as a percentage. Don't multiply it by 100 to get rid of the decimal point. 0.56 is the average number of swear words Betsy says per minute. When communicating this to others (e.g., teachers, parents, Betsy), you can read this rate as "zero point five six" swear words per minute or as "approximately one-half swear word per minute." Another, more meaningful, way to read it is to say that Betsy swears at a rate of

"fifty-six swear words per hundred minutes" or "almost six swear words per ten minutes." Unlike percentage, rate may also be expressed as a whole number. For example, one day Betsy swears 10 times but is only observed for 5 minutes. Ten (number of behaviors) divided by 5 (number of minutes) equals 2. On this day, Betsy's rate of swearing is 2 swear words per minute. Figure 7.18 lists a number of sample rates and how to read each.

Average is typically used to summarize intensity data. It is calculated by dividing the total number of intensity levels (i.e., the number of 1s, 2s, and 3s you recorded) into the sum of these values. For example, in Figure 7.19, the student has a total of 5 tantrums on the first day (2-14-95). This number represents the frequency of his tantrum behavior. The intensity levels of his tantrums are all 3s ("severe"). His average level of intensity is 3. On the fourth day (2-17-95), he has more tantrums (6) than the first day, but his average level of intensity is better. Two plus 2 plus 1 plus 2 plus 1 plus 1 equals 9. Nine divided by 6 (the number of tantrums) equals an average intensity level of 1.5.

Choosing the correct data summarization is a relatively simple matter if you observe the following guidelines:

1. *If you monitor the frequency of free operant behavior for the same amount of time each day, you may summarize the data as raw score.* Suppose you monitor the frequency of talk outs on Monday, Tuesday, and Wednesday for *1 hour each day.* Let's say you record 10 talk outs on Monday, 12 on Tuesday, and 15 on Wednesday. You are correct if you say the behavior is getting worse because the total number of talk outs is increasing *in the same amount of time.* All you need, to summarize the data in this case, is the number of responses.

2. *If you monitor the frequency of free operant behavior for a different amount of time each day, you must summarize the data as rate.* Sometimes it is not possible to monitor a student's behavior for the same amount of time each day. Maybe his schedule changes daily and he doesn't spend the same amount of time with you each day. Or maybe you just don't have the same amount of time available each day to monitor the student's behavior even though he is with you the same amount of time. In either case, you must use rate (average number of behaviors per time observed) to summarize the data. Consider the following example. Suppose you monitor the fre-

.001	is 1 response per 1000 minutes
.01	is 1 response per 100 minutes
.1	is 1 response per 10 minutes
1	is 1 response per 1 minute
10	is 10 responses per 1 minute
100	is 100 responses per 1 minute
1000	is 1000 responses per 1 minute
.007	is 7 responses per 1000 minutes
15	is 15 responses per 1 minute
150	is 150 responses per 1 minute
.15	is 15 responses per 100 minutes or 1½ responses per 10 minutes
.025	is 25 responses per 1000 minutes or 2½ per 100 minutes
32	is 32 responses per 1 minute
6	is 6 responses per 1 minute
.6	is 6 responses per 10 minutes
.08	is 8 responses per 100 minutes
.2	is 2 responses per 10 minutes
.72	is 72 responses per 100 minutes or approximately 7 responses per 10 minutes
.003	is 3 responses per 1000 minutes
.9	is 9 responses per 10 minutes

Figure 7.18. Sample rates (average number of behaviors per 1, 10, 100, or 1000 minutes).

Behaver ___(student)___

Monitor ___(teacher)___

Counted ___bites self___

Date	Level of Intensity (LOI)	Average LOI
2-14-95	3 3 3 3 3 (3 + 3 + 3 + 3 + 3 = 15 / 5 = 3.0)	3.0
2-15-95	2 3 2 2 2 3 (2 + 3 + 2 + 2 + 2 + 3 = 14 / 6 = 2.3)	2.3
2-16-95	2 2 2 2 2 (2 + 2 + 2 + 2 + 2 = 10 / 5 = 2)	2.0
2-17-95	2 2 1 2 1 1 (2 + 2 + 1 + 2 + 1 + 1 = 9 / 6 = 1.5)	1.5

Key: (1) *mild* tantrum (cries)
(2) *moderate* tantrum (lies on floor, cries, shakes head)
(3) *severe* tantrum (lies on floor, screams, bangs head)

Figure 7.19. Intensity data summarized as average.

quency of talk outs on Monday for 1 hour, on Tuesday for 45 minutes, and on Wednesday for 30 minutes. Let's say you record 10 talk outs on Monday, 7 on Tuesday, and 5 on Wednesday. If you summarize these data using raw score, it appears that the talk-out behavior is decreasing in frequency because the total talk outs are down (from 10 to 5). However, if you summarize these data as rate (by dividing the number of minutes into the number of responses), the student's average number of talk-outs per minute is 0.16, 0.15, and 0.16 on Monday, Tuesday, and Wednesday respectively. This means the student engaged in talk-out behavior an average of 16 times per 100 minutes on each of the 3 days data were collected. The student is not getting better. He is staying the same. IMPORTANT: In order to summarize frequency data as rate, you need to record the total number of minutes you observed the student in addition to the number of responses.

3. *If you monitor the frequency of controlled operant behavior, and the number of antecedents (i.e.,*

opportunities to behave) varies, you must summarize the data as percentage. The number of antecedents such as directives given, questions asked, and peer provocations typically changes from day to day. Teachers do not ask their students the same number of questions daily, nor do they give the same number of directives. Likewise, students do not experience exactly the same number of peer provocations each day. As long as these antecedents change on a daily basis, we must summarize the data for operants that are controlled by these antecedents as percentage. Consider the following. Let's say that you count instances of "complies with directives given" and on Wednesday you count 5 instances, on Thursday you count 8, and on Friday you count 12. If you use raw score to summarize these data, it appears that the student is becoming increasingly compliant. However, if you give 7 directives on Wednesday, 12 on Thursday, and 22 on Friday, the student's respective percentages are 71, 66, and 55, which means that she is actually becoming decreasingly compliant! IMPORTANT: In order to summarize frequency data as percentage, you need to record the number of antecedents (opportunities to respond) in addition to the number of responses.

4. *If you monitor the duration of free operant behavior for the same amount of time each day, you may summarize the data as raw score.* Suppose you use a stopwatch to monitor the duration of out-of-seat behavior on Monday, Tuesday, and Wednesday for a total of *5 hours each day.* If the student is out of his seat for a total of 1 hour on Monday, 1½ hours on Tuesday, and 1 hour 47 minutes on Wednesday, you can say that his behavior is getting worse because he is increasingly out of seat. All you need to summarize duration data as raw score is the total number of minutes the student engaged in the behavior being monitored.

5. *If you monitor the duration of free operant behavior for a different amount of time each day, you must summarize the data as percentage.* Let's say you have your instructional assistant do nothing but monitor the duration of out-of-seat behavior of a student on Wednesday for 3 hours, on Thursday for 4 hours 30 minutes, and on Friday for 5 hours. Let's also say that total observed duration for out-of-seat behavior is 60 minutes on Wednesday, 90 minutes on Thursday, and 100 minutes on Friday. Does this mean the student's behavior is getting worse? No. Raw score makes it appear that she is out of seat for increasingly longer periods of time. If you use percentage to summarize your data you see that the student is actually staying the same (out of seat 33% of the time observed). The point is, summarizing the data as raw score in this case does not provide an accurate picture of the student's progress. IMPORTANT: In order to summarize duration data as percentage, you need to record the total number of minutes you observed the student in addition to the number of minutes you observed him engaging in the behavior.

6. *If you are monitoring the intensity, topography, or latency of free operant behavior, you must use*

average regardless of the time observed or opportunities given. Refer to Figures 7.10–7.12 for examples.

Don't give up if you find the above guidelines too confusing. You can always summarize data as raw score *if you take the following precautions.* When you are monitoring the frequency of free operants and you don't want to summarize the data as rate, keep the amount of time you observe the student each day constant. The same applies if you are monitoring the duration of free operants and you don't want to summarize the data as percentage. For example, if the student is with you for a minimum of 30 minutes on Monday and Friday, 45 minutes on Tuesday and Thursday, and 60 minutes on Wednesday, monitor the student's behavior for exactly 30 minutes each day, no more, no less. If you are monitoring frequency, record the number of times the student engages in the behavior during 30 minutes *each day.* No more, no less. If you are monitoring duration, record how long the student engages in the behavior during 30 minutes *each day.* No more, no less. As long as you keep the total number of minutes you monitor the student's behavior each day constant, you may summarize the data as raw score and not have to compute rate or percentage.

When monitoring controlled operants, keep the number of antecedents for the behavior each day constant. This allows you to summarize the data as raw score instead of percentage. For example, if you monitor compliance and the number of directives changes daily, but you know you always give the student a *minimum* of 20 directives per day, simply monitor the student's compliance for the first 20 directives each day. This doesn't mean that you only give him 20 directives each day. It means that you only monitor his response (comply or not comply) to *the first 20* directives. This can easily be done by making 20 boxes on a piece of masking tape used as a wrist counter (see Figure 7.20). Each time you give the student a directive and he complies, mark a plus sign (+) in a box. If he does not comply, mark a zero (0) in the box. When all 20 boxes are filled, stop monitoring.

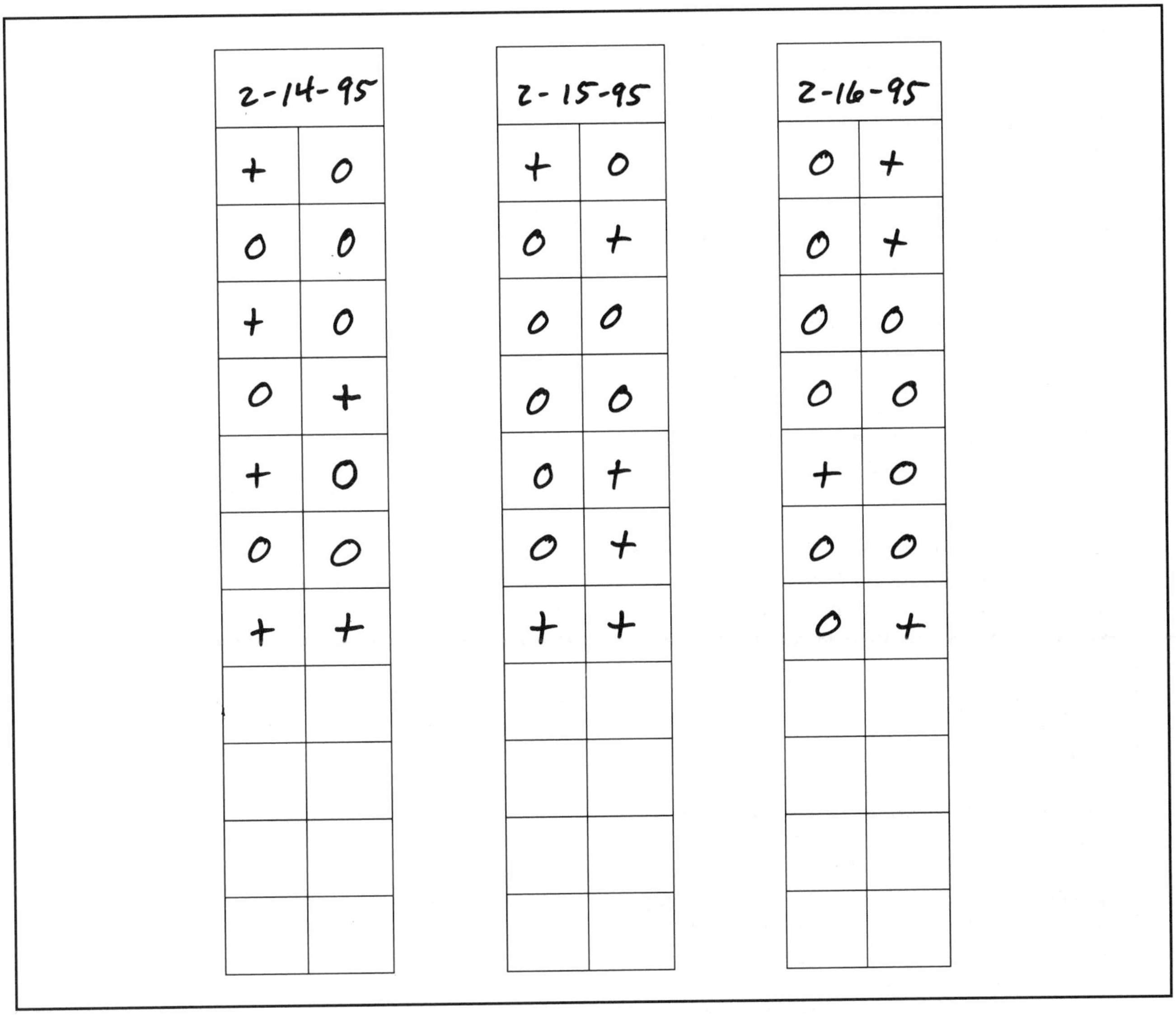

2-14-95	
+	O
O	O
+	O
O	+
+	O
O	O
+	+

2-15-95	
+	O
O	+
O	O
O	O
O	+
O	+
+	+

2-16-95	
O	+
O	+
O	O
O	O
+	O
O	O
O	+

Figure 7.20. Data recorded on adhesive tape "wrist counters."

Do the same thing when you use MTS. By keeping the number of glances each day constant, you are able to summarize the data as raw score instead of percentage. For example, suppose you monitor a quiet behavior such as out of seat with an MTS and you know the number of glances will change from day to day. Let's also suppose that you know the minimum number of glances you make each day is 12. Take a piece of tape and mark 12 boxes on it. Set your timer and, when it rings, observe the behavior and make a mark in a box. Repeat the process until all 12 boxes are filled. If you glance at the student 12 times every day, you may summarize the data as raw score and not bother with percentage.

✔ Checkpoint 7.5

[pages 243–247]

Fill in the correct answer for the items below (1–5). Check your responses by referring to the text; relevant page numbers appear in brackets.

Data may be summarized as raw score, percentage, rate, or average.

To calculate raw score, you

(1) _____

_____

_____ [243].

To calculate percentage (for frequency), you

(2) _____

_____

_____ [243].

To calculate percentage (for duration), you

(3) _____

_____

_____ [243].

To calculate rate, you

(4) _____

_____

_____ [243].

To calculate average (for intensity), you

(5) _____

_____

_____ [244].

(continues)

CHECKPOINT 7.5, continued

Label each of the following items (6–18) **RS** for raw score, **P** for percentage, **RT** for rate, or **A** for average, based on how you would summarize the data. Check your responses by referring to the answers following Item 18.

(6) _____ Frequency of head-banging, and the time observed is constant.

(7) _____ Frequency of question-answering, and the number of questions asked varies.

(8) _____ Frequency of unprovoked hitting, and time observed varies.

(9) _____ Duration of out-of-seat behavior, and time observed is constant.

(10) _____ Intensity of tantrum behavior, and time observed varies.

(11) _____ Frequency of compliance, and number of directives is constant.

(12) _____ Frequency of swear words used, and time observed is constant.

(13) _____ Frequency of assignments completed, and number of assignments given is constant.

(14) _____ Duration of off task (looks away from work), and time observed varies.

(15) _____ Frequency of thumb sucking, and number of glances in MTS varies.

(16) _____ Intensity of self-injurious behavior, and time observed is constant.

(17) _____ Frequency of self-stimming (rocks in seat and waves hand in front of face), and number of glances in MTS is constant.

(18) _____ Frequency of talk outs, and time observed varies.

ANSWERS (6–18): (6) RS, (7) P, (8) RT, (9) RS, (10) A, (11) RS, (12) RS, (13) RS, (14) P, (15) P, (16) A, (17) RS, (18) RT

Redo any items you missed. If you missed more than 4 of the items, reread the material. Otherwise, continue on to the next section.

There is a great deal of material to digest in this chapter. The flowchart in Figure 7.21 is offered as a quick and easy reference to help you make some sense of it. Photocopy the flowchart and use it as a handy dandy checklist of important factors to consider when you design your monitoring system. Write the student's name and the performance objective at the top of the sheet and read through the flowchart, circling the boxes as you go. Then use the information in the boxes to put together a monitoring system.

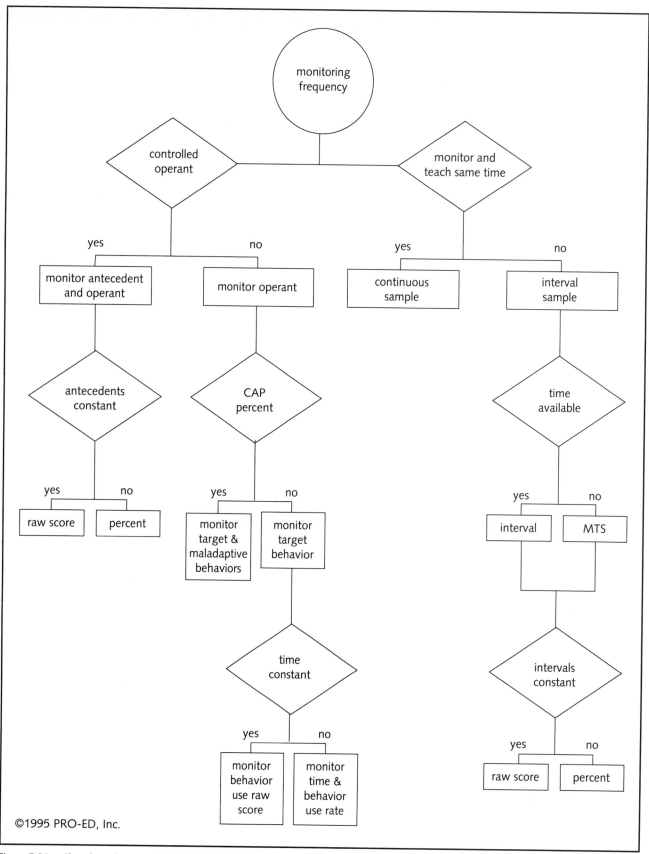

Figure 7.21. Flowchart showing steps in designing a monitoring system.

ASSESSMENT / CHAPTER 7

A list of acceptable responses appears following the Assessment.

Describe how to monitor (collect data) for each of the behaviors described in the performance objectives below. Be sure to include:

    a. the pinpointed behavior(s) you would monitor

    b. the sample (continuous, interval, or MTS) you would use and explain why

    c. a detailed *step-by-step* account of how you would collect the data written as if you were leaving notes for a substitute teacher to follow; also include an explanation of how you would summarize the data (raw score, percentage or rate)

1. Given work at his desk, Andres will be on task (i.e., eyes looking at work on desk) 80% of the times observed over a 3-day period.

2. Given a directive the first time, Lucinda will comply 95% of the time over a 5-day period.

3. When he wishes to speak in class, Joey will raise his hand and wait to be called on 85% of the time over a 3-day period.

4. When communicating with others, Katy will establish eye contact (i.e., look them in the eye and hold for at least 3 seconds) at a rate of 10 eye-contacts per minute over a 5-day period.

5. When observed in the classroom, Saul will engage in spontaneous speech (e.g., asking questions or making comments) when appropriate at a rate of not less than 1 verbalization per 10 minutes (0.1 vpm) over a 5-day period.

ACCEPTABLE RESPONSES

1. *Andres.* Should use MTS since behavior is quiet; must summarize as percentage since CAP in performance objective is expressed as percentage and number of opportunities (i.e., glances) are likely to vary from day to day.

Example (monitoring instructions)
Use the following procedure throughout the day at those times when Andres is expected to be working on assignment at desk.

a) Place tape on wrist;

b) set timer to ring at random intervals (not more than 10 minutes or less than 1 minute apart);

c) when timer rings, glance at Andres; if he is off task (head turned away from work on desk), mark 0 on tape; if he is on task (head turned toward work on desk), mark + on tape;

d) reset timer and repeat procedure throughout the day (at those times when Andres is expected to be on task);

e) at end of day, compute percentage of on-task behavior by dividing total number of +s by sum of +s and 0s.

2. *Lucinda.* Should use continuous sample since behavior can be monitored while teaching; must summarize as percentage since CAP in performance objective is expressed as percentage and behavior is a controlled operant and antecedent (directives given) controlling compliance is likely to vary from day to day.

Example (monitoring instructions)
Use the following procedure throughout the day as long as Lucinda is with you.

a) Place tape on wrist;

b) each time you give Lucinda a directive, count to 5 (e.g., "one-Mississippi, two-Mississippi, three-Mississippi," etc.);

c) if Lucinda follows a directive within 5 seconds, mark a C on tape; if Lucinda does not follow directive within 5 sec., mark NC on tape;

d) at end of observation period, compute percentage of compliance behavior by dividing sum of C and NC into C.

3. *Joey.* Should use continuous sample since behaviors (handraising and/or calling out for your attention) can be monitored while teaching; must summarize as percentage since CAP in performance objective is expressed as percentage.

Example (monitoring instructions)
Use the following procedure throughout the day as long as Joey is with you and is required to raise his hand to access teacher attention.

a) Place tape on wrist;

b) each time Joey calls out without raising his hand and waiting to be called on, mark a T (for talk out) on the tape; each time Joey raises his hand and waits to be called on before speaking, mark an H on the tape;

c) at end of observation period compute percentage of handraising and waiting by dividing sum of Ts and Hs into Hs.

4. *Katy.* Should use interval sample since you can't teach and watch Katy's eyes at same time; must summarize data as rate since CAP in performance objective is expressed as rate and the amount of time you will be observing Katy's behavior will vary daily.

Example (monitoring instructions)
Use the following procedure at those times when you are interacting with Katy on a one-to-one basis.

a) Use a mechanical counting device (since it will be difficult to look away and make a mark on wrist tape);

b) record time you begin working with Katy on one-to-one basis;

c) each time Katy looks at you for 3 sec. (count to yourself "one-Mississippi," etc.), use counting device to record;

d) if Katy looks at you for less than 3 sec., do not record; if Katy looks at you for 6 *consecutive* seconds before looking away, count as 2 looks; if she looks at you for 5 *consecutive* seconds before looking away, count as 1 look.

e) record time you stop working with Katy;

f) compute rate of 3-second looks by dividing total minutes you worked with Katy into the total number of 3-second looks you recorded during that time; if the total time is minutes plus seconds (e.g., 8 minutes 26 seconds), convert total time to seconds, divide into behavior and multiply by sixty to convert back to rate per minute (e.g., 8 minutes 26 seconds = 506 seconds; divided into twenty 3-second looks = .039 looks per second; x 60 = 2.3 3-second looks per minute).

5. *Saul.* Use continuous sample if you are only monitoring Saul's spontaneous verbalizations with you; if you are monitoring all of Saul's spontaneous verbalizations (i.e., with anyone in the class), you will have to use an interval sample since many of these verbalizations may not always come to your attention and you can't sit and watch Saul all day long without taking time from your teaching; summarize data as rate since it is used as CAP in performance objective and the amount of time you will be monitoring Saul's behavior will vary daily.

Example (monitoring instructions)
Use following procedure if you are monitoring Saul's spontaneous verbalizations only with you.

a) Put tape on wrist;

b) write down time you being monitoring;

c) each time Saul asks question of you or makes non-elicited comment, record (/) on tape;

d) continue in this manner throughout the observation period;

e) write down time you end monitoring;

f) compute rate of spontaneous speech by dividing total number of minutes you observed Saul into the total number of times he engaged in spontaneous speech.

Use following procedure if you are monitoring Saul's spontaneous verbalization with *anyone*.

a) Put tape on wrist;

b) set timer to ring at random intervals to cue you when to start monitoring;

c) when timer rings, set for amount of time you wish to monitor Saul (e.g., 1 minute, 5 minutes, 10 minutes; whatever time you can afford);

d) observe Saul during this period and record each instance of spontaneous (i.e., unsolicited) speech;

e) when timer rings indicating end of monitoring interval, stop recording and write down amount of time observed;

f) reset timer to cue you for next monitoring interval and continue same procedure outlined above;

g) at end of day compute rate by dividing total number of minutes you observed Saul (e.g., if you monitored Saul's behavior for fifteen 2-minute intervals, total minutes observed equals 30 minutes) into the total number of spontaneous-speech behaviors.

CHAPTER EIGHT

Measuring Change

Data Display and Analysis

Upon successful completion of this chapter, the learner should be able to:

1. Display data using equal-ratio charts

2. Interpret data displays

TO CHART OR NOT TO CHART

Now that you have collected your data, what do you do with it? Stick it in a drawer and forget about it? Hardly. The main reason for collecting data is to measure student progress, and you can't measure student progress unless you analyze your data. The question is: What is the best way to analyze your data? Do you examine each number one by one like the data displayed on a card in Figure 8.1 or do you display it as dots on a chart like the one in Figure 8.2? Obviously, the chart makes it easier to recognize a trend or pattern. The sooner you can estimate a trend, the sooner you can determine whether or not the intervention is working. This is particularly important when you have several interventions operating at the same time. So, what is the best way to analyze your data? No contest: Charts.

Words Read Correctly (per minute)	
Day	*Rate*
M	50
T	42
W	52
TH	48
F	60
M	65
T	60
W	70
TH	75
F	65

Figure 8.1. Data displayed on a card.

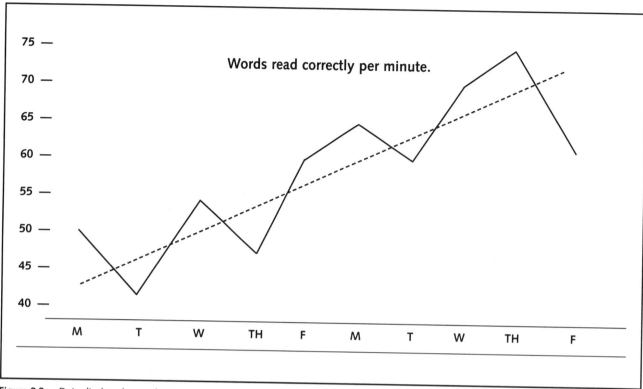

Figure 8.2. Data displayed on a chart.

This leads us to the next question: What is the best type of chart to use? The chart that is used most often is the *equal-interval chart* (see Figure 8.3). It also goes by the names *linear* and *arithmetic* chart. All it takes to make an equal-interval chart is a piece of graph paper. You can display data as dots with connecting lines (see Figure 8.4) or as a simple bar graph (see Figure 8.5). Although perfectly acceptable, the equal-interval chart is not the best chart to use.

THE KING OF CHARTS

The best chart to use in a formative evaluation is the equal-*ratio* chart commonly used by precision teachers. Precision Teaching, developed by Ogden Lindsley (1971), is a formative evaluation system designed specifically to measure student progress. While precision teaching doesn't dictate what or how to teach your students, it does tell you how effective your teaching methods are. Although it is not my intent to discuss precision teaching per se, I do want to describe the precision teaching chart as well as some of the trend estimation and interpretation techniques used in precision teaching since they have

important applications for evaluating the efficacy of interventions for behavioral problems.

The Standard Chart

The heart of the precision teaching system is an equal-ratio chart known as the *standard* chart, shown in Figure 8.6. It looks intimidating but you needn't respond like the people shown in Figure 8.7. It's really quite a wonderful invention. Let's take a quick look at it to familiarize ourselves with some of its features.

Display more data

The lines that go up and down are the day lines. There are 140 of them. This means you can plot 140 days of data on the standard chart. Even though you can only plot data for one particular behavior on each chart, you would only need two charts to record data on a student for the entire school year. The heavy day lines are Sunday lines. Since data are not usually plotted on the weekend, you need to be careful to skip Saturday and Sunday. The horizontal lines on the standard chart are frequency lines. Most people use the standard chart to plot rate data but

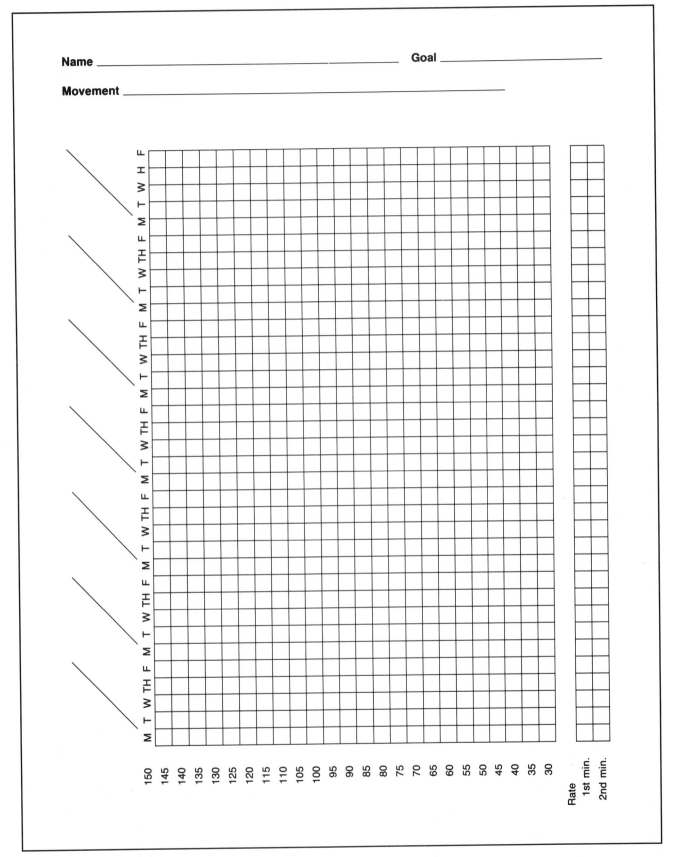

Figure 8.3. Equal-interval chart.

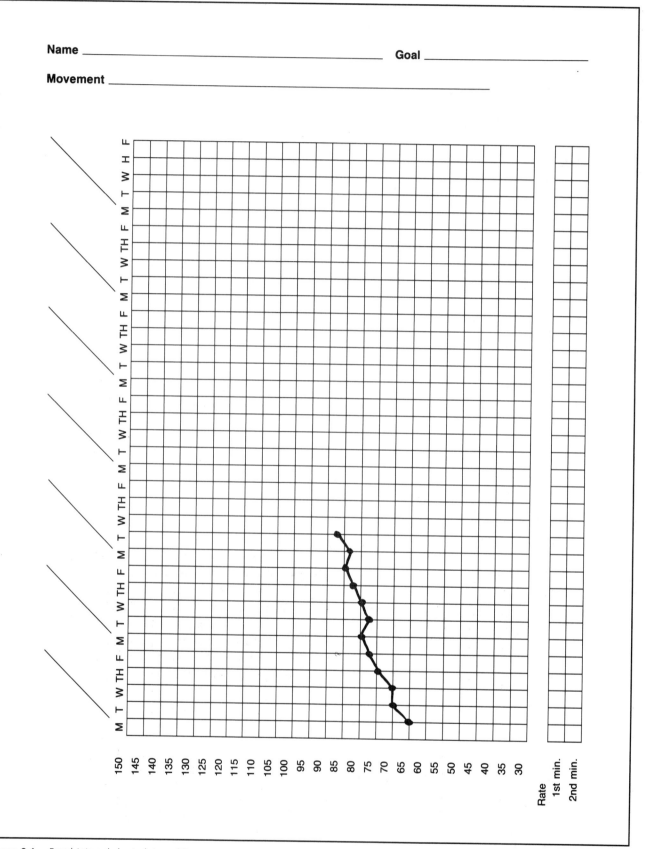

Figure 8.4. Equal-interval chart: dots and lines.

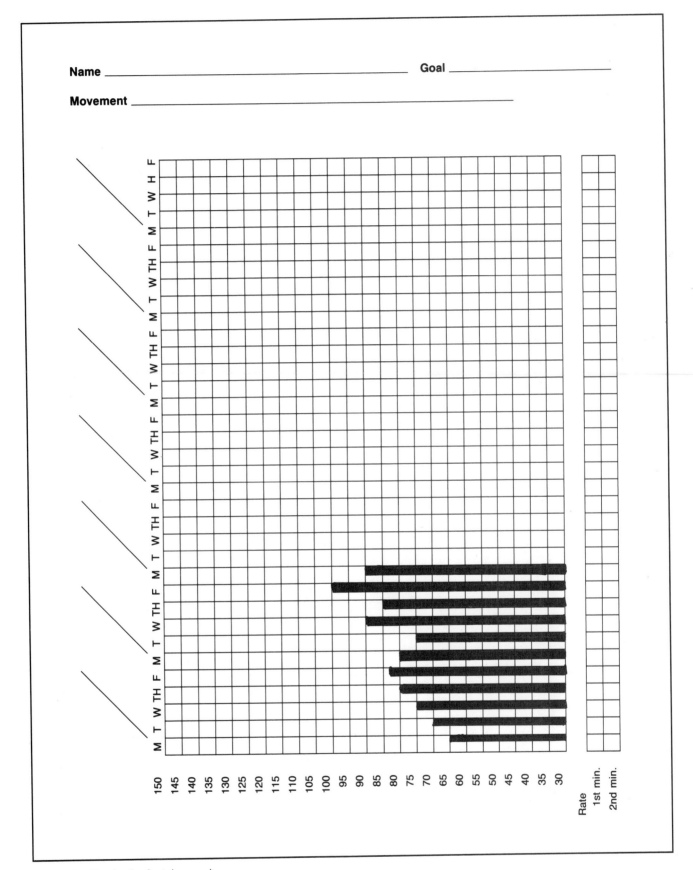

Figure 8.5. Equal-ratio chart: bar graph.

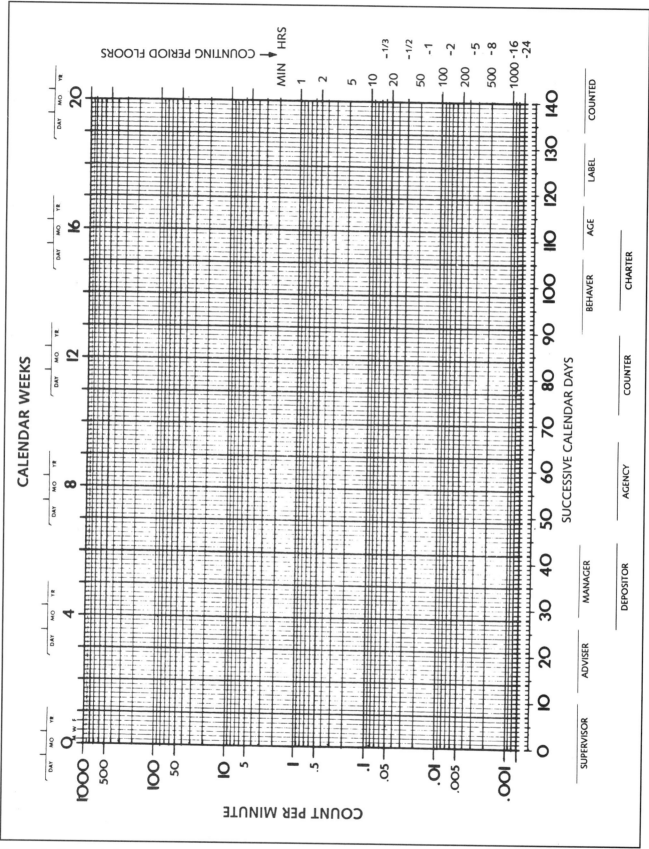

Figure 8.6. The standard (six-cycle) equal-ratio chart.

Figure 8.7. Don't be afraid of the equal-ratio chart!

you can also plot raw scores on it. There is also an equal-ratio chart for use with percentage data. More about this later.

Display all kinds of data

The standard chart is also referred to as the "six-cycle" chart because it has six cycles, or areas, in which to record frequency of response. Figure 8.8 shows each cycle. Knowing about the cycles is important because the number of cycles on an equal-ratio chart tells you how many different kinds of behaviors can be displayed on it. As you can see, Cycle 1 includes frequency lines for behaviors that occur at a rate of 1 per 1,000 minutes up through 9.9 behaviors per 1000 minutes. .001 is read as "one

behavior per thousand minutes," .002 as "two behaviors per thousand minutes," .003 as "three behaviors per thousand minutes," and so on. Cycle 1 on the standard chart is where you plot rate data for those behaviors that occur infrequently. An example is the case of a student who tantrums 3 times in 6 hours (360 minutes). Three (behavior) divided by 360 (time) equals .008 tantrums per minute, which is read as "eight tantrums per thousand minutes." Let's suppose this behavior occurred on Monday of the first week. You plot this rate where the first Monday line and the .008 line converge (see Figure 8.9). Since this is a behavior you want to weaken, it is marked by an X. Behavior you want to strengthen is marked by a dot.

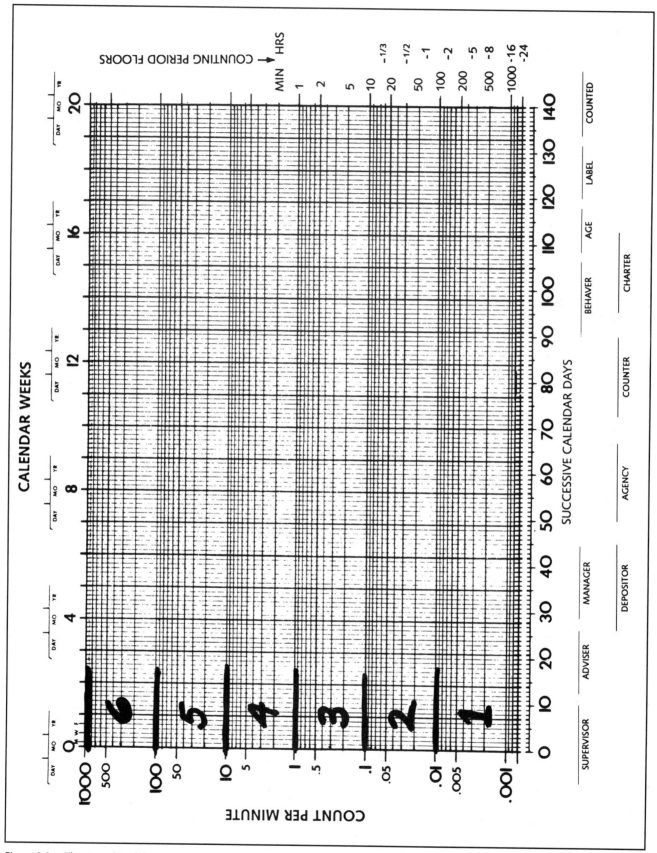

Figure 8.8. The six cycles of the standard chart.

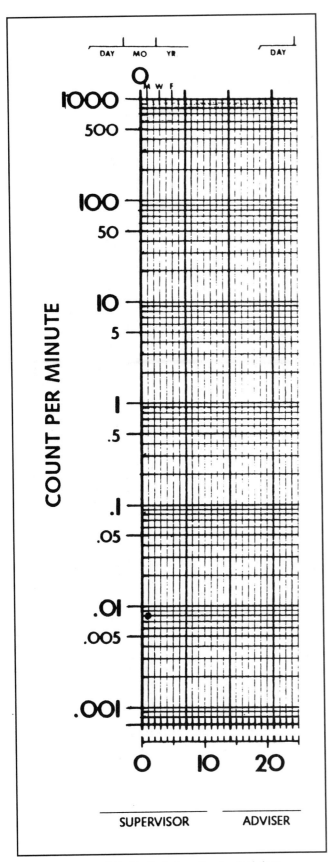

Figure 8.9. Data plotted in Cycle 1 on the standard chart.

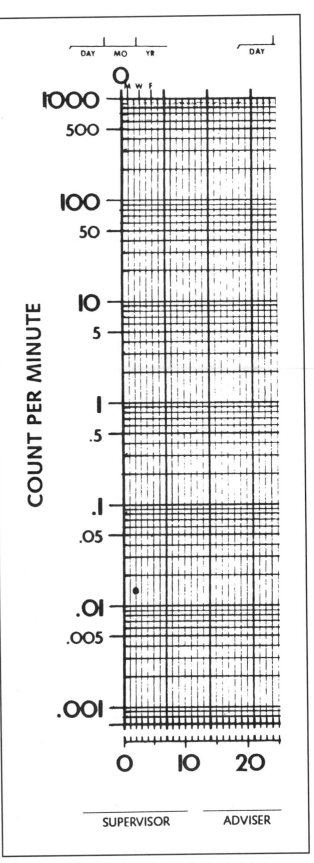

Figure 8.10. Data plotted in Cycle 2 on the standard chart.

Cycle 2 includes frequency lines for behaviors that occur at a rate of 1 per 100 minutes up through 9.9 behaviors per 100 minutes. .01 is read as "one behavior per hundred minutes," .02 as "two behaviors per hundred minutes," etc. Cycle 2 is another area on the chart for behaviors that do not occur often. Let's suppose you have a student who runs out of the room 5 times in 300 minutes on Tuesday of the first week. Five (behaviors) divided by 300 (time) is .016 behaviors per minute, which can be read as "approximately one and a half behaviors per hundred minutes" or rounded up to "two behaviors per hundred minutes." This rate is plotted on the chart in Cycle 2 where the first Tuesday line and the .016 (or .02) line converge (see Figure 8.10).

Behaviors that occur at a rate of 1 per 10 minutes up through 9.9 behaviors per 10 minutes are charted in Cycle 3. You read .1 as "one behavior per ten minutes," .2 as "two behaviors per ten minutes," and so on. Cycle 3 is the area on the chart for behaviors that occur more frequently than those found in Cycles 1 and 2. For example, Figure 8.11 shows where you plot frequency data for a student who speaks spontaneously 100 times in 3 hours (180 minutes). One hundred (behavior) divided by 180 (time) equals .55 behaviors per minute. This is read as "five-and-a-half behaviors per ten minutes," or rounded off to "six behaviors per ten minutes." Assuming it occurred on Friday of the first week, you plot this rate on the first Friday line between the .5 and .6 frequency lines (i.e., on the .6 line). You use a dot because it is behavior you want to strengthen.

Cycles 4 through 6 are for frequencies from 1 behavior per minute through 1,000 behaviors per minute. These are obviously behaviors that occur more frequently than those plotted in Cycles 1 through 3. Figures 8.12, 8.13, and 8.14 show where you plot data for a student who speaks without cursing 100 times in 20 minutes, or 5 behaviors per minute (Cycle 4) on the first Monday; another who self-stims (touches self) 72 times per minute (Cycle 5) on the first Thursday; and a third student who reads at a rate of 140 words correct per minute (Cycle 6) on Wednesday of the first week.

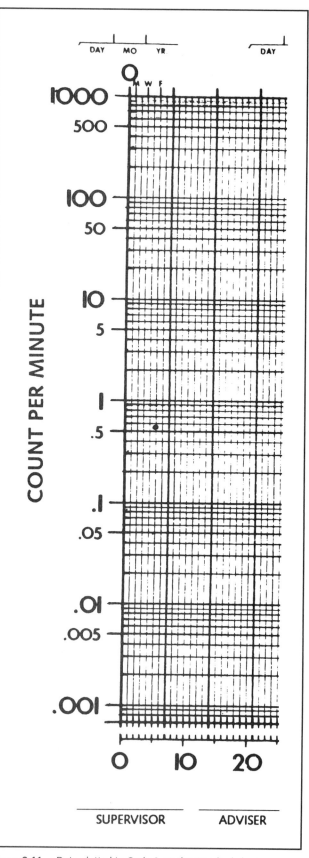

Figure 8.11. Data plotted in Cycle 3 on the standard chart.

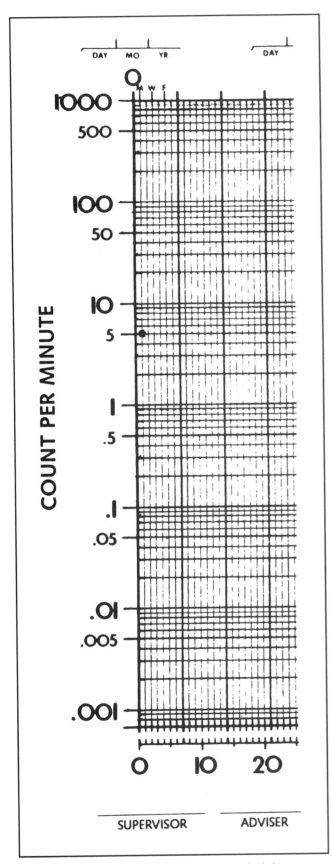

Figure 8.12. Data plotted in Cycle 4 on the standard chart.

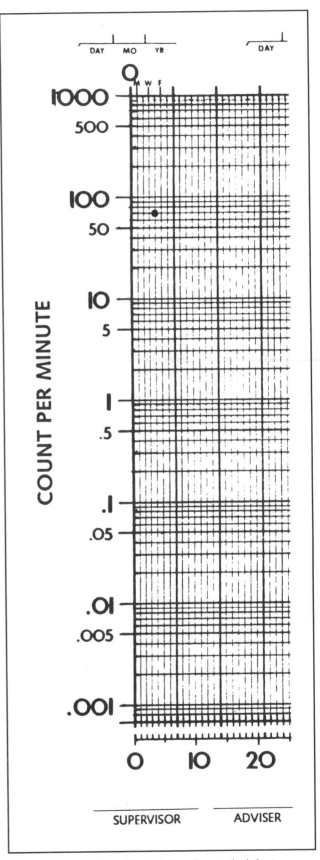

Figure 8.13. Data plotted in Cycle 5 on the standard chart.

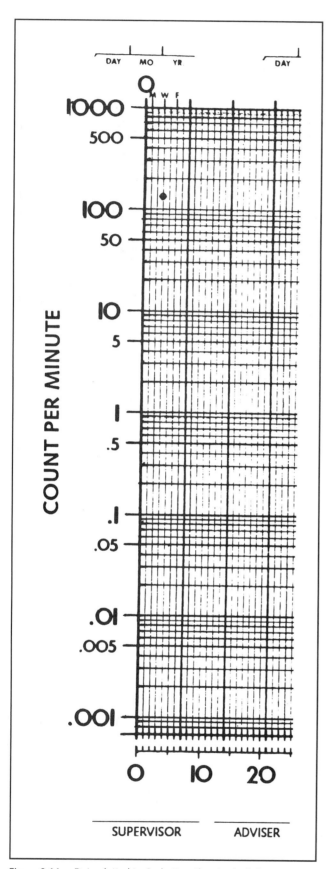

Figure 8.14. Data plotted in Cycle 6 on the standard chart.

Make predictions—amaze your friends

By far the biggest advantage ratio charts have over interval charts is that they not only show you the direction in which the behavior is going, they also show you how fast the behavior is changing. It is not enough to look at lines on a chart and see that they are going up or down. Knowing *how fast* these lines are rising or descending enables you to predict approximately when the student will reach the objective (CAP) set for him. Consider the following analogy. Let's say that you are taking a trip by automobile and your destination is north of your starting point. You know which direction you are heading because the signs on the freeway say north and you have a compass in the car. There is only one problem; your speedometer is broken. You know you are going in the right direction, but without a speedometer it's difficult to predict an estimated time of arrival (ETA). Are you making sufficient progress? Maybe; maybe not. Using an equal-interval chart is like driving a car without a speedometer: You may know where you are going, but it's difficult to predict your ETA. The equal-ratio chart, on the other hand, has a built-in "speedometer." You not only know the direction you are moving, you know your ETA. This information not only helps you decide whether or not you should revise your intervention, it helps you decide what kind of revision to make. And it does all this with a minimum amount of data.

Cut decision-making time in half

The ratio chart is able to do all this because it shows *proportion*. The frequency lines on the ratio chart are not equidistant from one another as are the lines on the interval chart. If you look at the equal-ratio chart in Figure 8.15, you will see that the distance between Frequency Lines 1 and 2 is the same as the distance between Frequency Lines 2 and 4, 3 and 6, 4 and 8, 10 and 20, and 50 and 100—each represents a *times two* ratio or proportion; this is why the ratio chart is referred to as an *equal*-ratio chart. It does something the *equal*-interval chart cannot do. It shows proportion of growth. It is the ratio chart's ability to show proportion that makes it possible to determine student growth with a minimum of data, certainly far less than you need with an interval chart. The advantage is obvious. If you can accurately determine the trend of a student's progress with half the data, you can make revisions in your interventions in half the time. This means you can find the most effective interventions much faster, thus moving your students from Point A to Point B much faster.

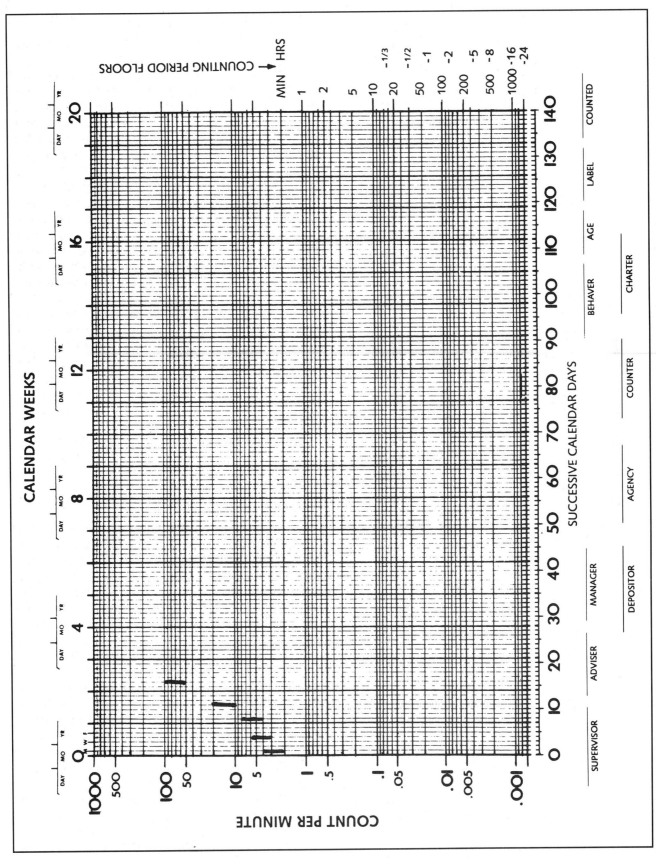

Figure 8.15. Equal-ratio chart shows proportion.

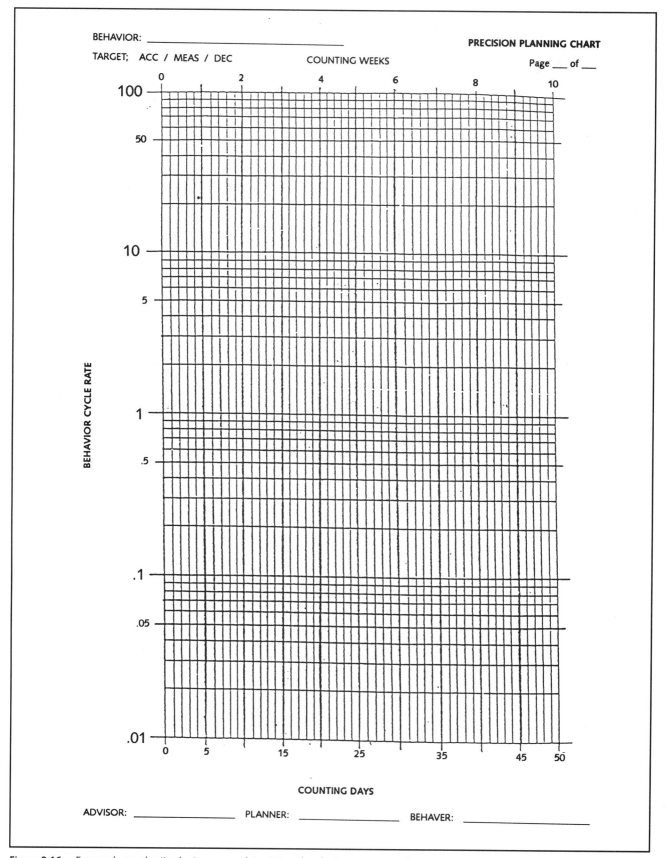

Figure 8.16. Four-cycle equal-ratio chart accommodates 10 weeks of rate or raw score data.

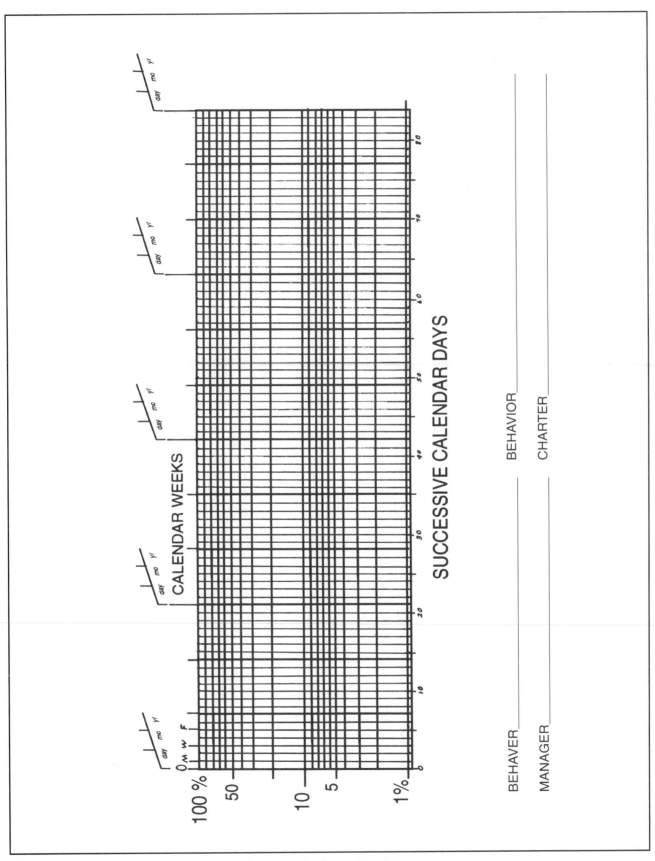

Figure 8.17. Two-cycle equal-ratio chart accommodates 12 weeks of percentage data.

But wait . . . there's more

Equal-ratio charts come in all sizes. If you find the standard chart a bit daunting, you can always use equal-ratio charts with fewer cycles and less days. It is likely that most behaviors you want to chart can be plotted anywhere from Cycle 3 through Cycle 5. The chart in Figure 8.16 is a four-cycle chart. It can accommodate data for behaviors that occur at a rate of 1 per 100 minutes up to 100 behaviors per minute. You can plot either rate or raw score data on this chart. Figure 8.17 is an example of an equal-ratio chart used especially for percentage data. It has two cycles (1–10 and 10–100). Since both of these charts show proportion, they have the same advantage of the standard chart in that they can be used to make predictions about student performance with a minimum amount of data.

✔ Checkpoint 8.1

[pages 257–272]

Fill in the answers to the following items (1–9). Check your responses by referring to the text; relevant page numbers appear in brackets.

The advantage of displaying summarized data on a chart rather than simply keeping a written record of the data is

(1) _____

_____

_____ [257].

The chart most often used to display data is called

(2) _____

_____ [258].

Precision teaching is

(3) _____

_____

_____ [258].

(continues)

CHECKPOINT 8.1, continued

The chart used by precision teachers is called

(4) _____

_____ [258].

It gets its name because it (5) _____

_____ [268].

The advantages of the equal-ratio chart over the traditional equal-interval chart are:

(6) _____

_____

(7) _____

_____

(8) _____

_____

(9) _____

_____ [258–272].

Identify the cycle you would use on the standard (six-cycle) chart for each of the following raw score and rate data (p/m is *per minute*). Check your responses by referring to the answers below.

	Data	Cycle
(10)	6 hits p/m	_____
(11)	18 words spoken	_____
(12)	150 self-stims p/m	_____
(13)	.009 runs away p/m	_____
(14)	45 smiles	_____
(15)	.08 talk outs p/m	_____
(16)	.005 fights p/m	_____
(17)	.2 raises hand p/m	_____
(18)	8 people spoken to	_____
(19)	.03 compliments p/m	_____

ANSWERS (6–15): (10) Cycle 4; (11) Cycle 5; (12) Cycle 6; (13) Cycle 1; (14) Cycle 5; (15) Cycle 2; (16) Cycle 1; (17) Cycle 3; (18) Cycle 4; (19) Cycle 2

Redo any items you missed. If you missed more than 4 of the items, reread the material. Otherwise, continue on to the next section.

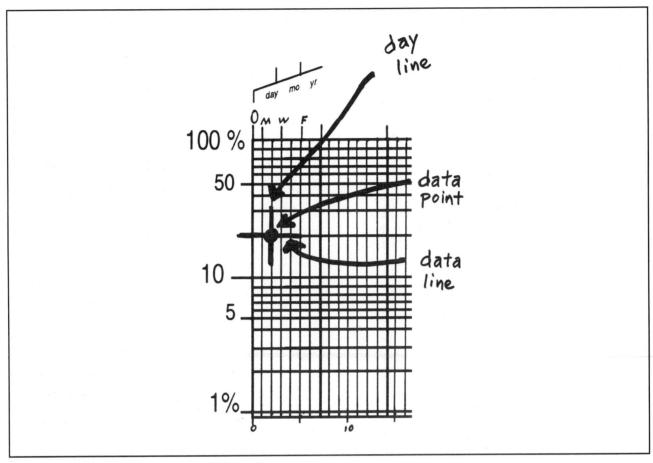

Figure 8.18. Plotting data.

CHARTING

Now that I've thoroughly sold you on the equal-ratio chart, I'd be remiss if I didn't explain how to use it. Using equal-interval charts is easy. Elementary students make bar graphs all the time. The equal-ratio chart, on the other hand, requires some getting used to. Just remember that the time and effort you put into mastering the equal-ratio chart will be repaid over and over again. Because the chart enables you to evaluate the efficacy of your interventions in half the time it would take using conventional data displays, you will spend less time on discipline and more time on teaching. It just takes practice.

Getting Started

Before you begin plotting data, make sure you have all of the necessary identifying information on your chart. First of all, be sure to identify the target student, referred to as "behaver" on all of the equal-ratio charts. Second, identify the behavior you are plotting on the chart. On the standard (six-cycle) chart, behavior is referred to as "counted." On the

four-cycle chart, it is referred to simply as "behavior." It is also important that you identify the person(s) responsible for the intervention, especially if there is more than one. "Manager" refers to the person responsible for implementing the intervention; in other words, the primary change agent. The "charter" is the person responsible for plotting the data. In some instances, the student may be responsible for all of these tasks.

Plotting Data

As I indicated earlier, correct (i.e., target behavior) data appear as dots, and incorrect (i.e., maladaptive behavior) data as X's. Each data point is plotted at the point where the day (vertical) lines and the frequency (horizontal) lines converge (see Figure 8.18). Reading the percentage chart is easy. Most of you of will probably want to start with the four-cycle chart because it is larger and easier to read and you will probably only need four cycles to plot your data. Figure 8.19 shows some rate data plotted on the four-cycle chart. Use your finger on

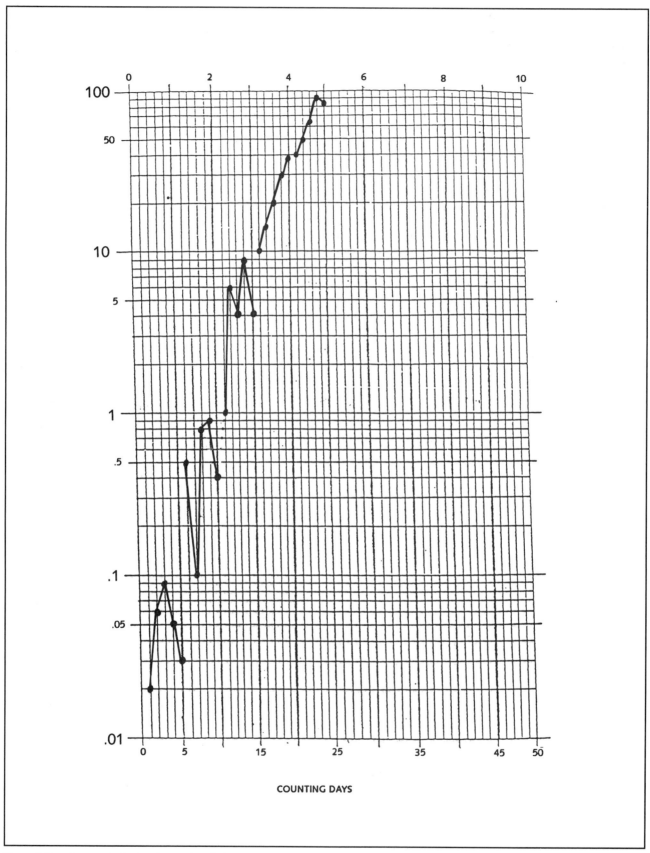

Figure 8.19. Four-cycle chart with rate data (behaviors per minute).

the chart and read along with me. Remember, these are rates. So that we are synchronized, find the heavy vertical line that is numbered as the Friday line indicating the end of a school week. The first data point is .02 (2 behaviors in 100 minutes) on Monday of the *first week*. The next data point is .06 (6 behaviors in 100 minutes) on Tuesday of the first week. The rest of the first week's data are .09 (9 behaviors in 100 minutes) on Wednesday, .05 (5 behs per 100 minutes) on Thursday, and .03 (3 behs per 100 minutes) on Friday. *Second-week* data are .5 (5 behaviors per 10 minutes) on Monday, .1 (1 beh per 10 minutes) on Tuesday, .8 (8 behs per 10 minutes) on Wednesday, .9 (9 behs per 10 minutes) on Thursday, and .4 (4 behs per 10 minutes) on Friday. *Third-week* data are 1 behavior per minute on Monday, 6 behaviors per minute (bpm) on Tuesday, 3 bpm on Wednesday, 9 bpm on Thursday, and 5 bpm on Friday. *Fourth-week* data are 10 bpm on Monday, 15 bpm on Tuesday, 20 bpm on Wednesday, 30 bpm on Thursday, and 48 bpm on Friday. *Fifth-week* data are 50 bpm on Monday, 60 bpm on Tuesday, 75 bpm on Wednesday, 90 bpm on Thursday, and 85 bpm on Friday.

To see if you understand how to read the chart, look at the data in Figure 8.19 and try reading each data point without looking at the text in the preceding paragraph. Try to read 1 week at a time before checking yourself. If you are able to read the chart in Figure 8.19 correctly, try plotting the data. Take a piece of paper and cover the data I plotted for the first 5 weeks. Then try plotting the data cited in the preceding paragraph for the last 5 weeks of the chart. Be sure to connect the data points within each week as I did. After you finish, remove the paper covering the first 5 weeks and see if you plotted the data correctly.

Raw scores are plotted on the four-cycle chart. The only difference is, instead of using all four cycles, you only use Cycles 3 (from 1 to 10) and 4 (from 10 to 100). To plot a raw score of zero, use the frequency line immediately below the "1" line (.9). Figure 8.20 shows the following raw scores plotted on a four-cycle chart: During the *first week*—1 on Monday, 7 on Tuesday, 2 on Wednesday, 5 on Thursday, and 0 on Friday; during the *second week*— 16 on Monday, 19 on Tuesday, 13 on Wednesday, 12 on Thursday, and 15 on Friday; during the *third week*—20 on Monday, 25 on Tuesday, 30 on Wednesday, 42 on Thursday, and 36 on Friday; during the *fourth week*—50 on Monday, 60 on Tuesday, 75 on Wednesday, 100 on Thursday, and 80 on Friday.

Plotting zero-rate data

Since rate data can be expressed as a whole number or a decimal, all six cycles on the standard chart and all four cycles on the 10-week chart are used to plot rate data. This makes it somewhat difficult to find zero on the chart if you are plotting rate data. Most of the time you will be plotting the rates of (target) behaviors you want to strengthen on the chart. Therefore, you really don't have to worry about zero or the record floor. Still, if your baseline data show the student engages in the behavior at a rate of zero per minute, you need to know how to plot this on your chart. If you have a rate of zero behaviors per minute to plot on the chart, do not use the frequency line immediately below 1. You must use the frequency line immediately below what is referred to as the *record floor*. The record floor is the rate of response representing the student's lowest level of performance *other than zero*. For example, what would be the least number of responses other than zero a student could make in any given amount of time? The answer is *one*. Let's say you watch a student for 300 minutes and monitor his talk-out behavior. The lowest number of talk outs he can emit in 300

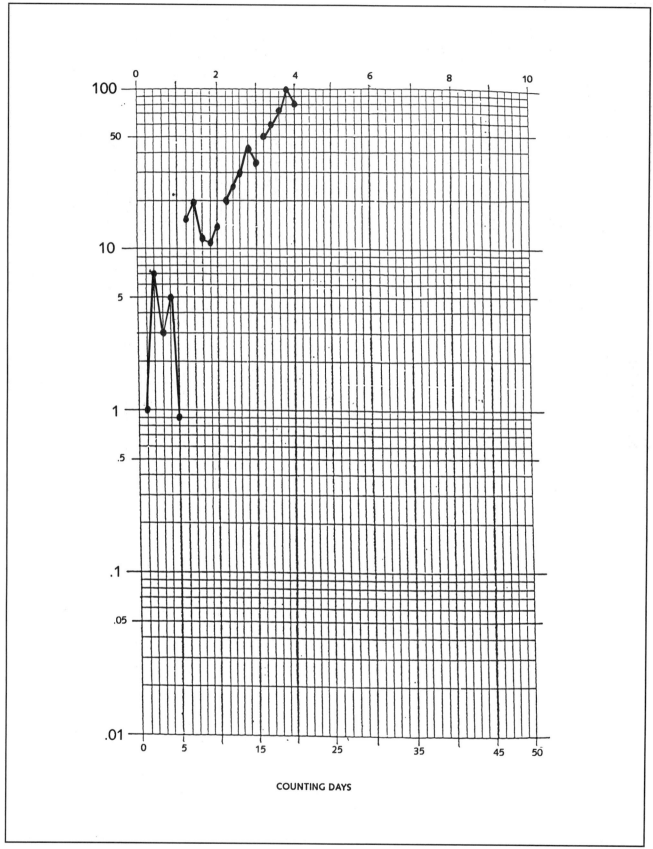

Figure 8.20. Four-cycle chart with raw score data.

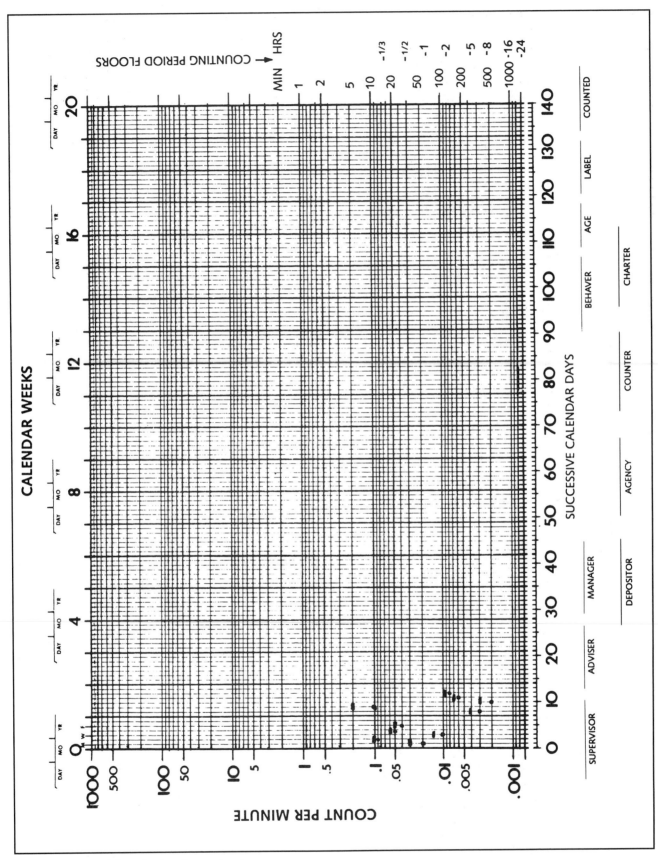

Figure 8.21. Record floors (–) and zeroes (•).

minutes *other than zero* is one talk out. If you divide one talk out (behavior) by 300 minutes (time), you get a rate of .003 talk outs per minute (3 talk outs per 1000 minutes). This is the record floor for that behavior for the amount of time you observed the student. If you monitor the same student's talk outs the next day for 60 minutes, the record floor would change. One talk out divided by 60 minutes equals .016 talk outs per minute (roughly $1\frac{1}{2}$ talk outs per 100 minutes). Whatever behavior you are monitoring, the formula for computing record floor is the same: One divided by the number of minutes you observed the behavior. Why is the record floor important? The record floor tells you where to plot zero on the chart; *wherever the record floor is, "zero" is plotted on the line immediately below it.* The record floor is marked on the chart by a dash (–). Figure 8.21 shows the record floors and rates of zero plotted on the chart for the following data:

Week	Day	Minutes
1	M	30
1	T	10
1	W	60
1	Th	15
1	F	20
2	M	240
2	T	5
2	W	300
2	Th	142
2	F	77

✔ Checkpoint 8.2

[pages 273–278]

Use the blank equal-ratio charts on pp. 311 and 313 to plot the data listed below. Use the four-cycle chart (Chart A) to plot the raw score and rate data and the two-cycle chart (Chart B) to plot the percent data. USE A PENCIL. Connect the data points for each week and check your accuracy using the Answer Keys on pp. 315 and 316.

RAW SCORE

Week	Day	Data
1	M	25
	T	95
	W	13
	Th	0
	F	36
2	M	100
	T	5
	W	11
	Th	43
	F	17
3	M	0
	T	60
	W	1
	Th	2
	F	7
4	M	58
	T	77
	W	0
	Th	10
	F	80

(continues)

CHECKPOINT 8.2, continued

RATE

Week	Day	Data
7	M	.5 bpm
	T	.05 bpm
	W	25 bpm
	Th	0 bpm*
	F	100 bpm
8	M	.09 bpm
	T	.2 bpm
	W	15 bpm
	Th	.02 bpm
	F	52 bpm
9	M	.4 bpm
	T	.01 bpm
	W	.9 bpm
	Th	9 bpm
	F	1 bpm
10	M	5 bpm
	T	.07 bpm
	W	.7 bpm
	Th	90 bpm
	F	2 bpm

*record floor = .3

(continues)

CHECKPOINT 8.2, continued

PERCENT

Week	Day	Data
1	M	30%
	T	1%
	W	5%
	Th	15%
	F	2%
2	M	9%
	T	100%
	W	4%
	Th	20%
	F	7%
3	M	55%
	T	13%
	W	70%
	Th	33%
	F	5%
4	M	42%
	T	4%
	W	0%
	Th	10%
	F	85%

Redo any missed data points. If you made more than 5 plotting errors, reread the material Otherwise, continue on to the next section.

ANALYZING DATA

Now that you have mastered the fine art of "dot dropping" (O. R. White, personal communication, 1994), you are ready to stand back and analyze the data. Remember, this is all about measuring student progress. You collect data and display it on a chart so that you can determine the efficacy of your intervention. If it's working, leave it alone. If it's not working, revise it.

The best way to determine whether or not you should revise your intervention is to compare the progress a student *does* make with the progress she *should* make. The progress a student actually does make is represented by the data you collect each day and plot on her chart. The progress a student should (or needs to) make is represented by a line drawn between Point A—where the student is now, and Point B—where you want her to be in a given amount of time. In the precision teaching literature, this line is referred to as the *minimum 'celeration line* (White & Haring, 1976). I prefer to call it the *should-do* line. Simply put, if you want to know whether or not your intervention is working, compare the student's daily data with the should-do line on her chart. If they are both going in the same direction, you know the program is working; if they are going in different directions, you will probably have to revise it. Before I show you how to draw the should-do line, let me tell you more about Points A and B.

Point A

Point A is where the student is now—what she currently does and how often she does it. You already know what the student does; you wrote a pinpoint describing her behavior (e.g., "hits peers when teased" or "uses swear words"). How often she does it is usually determined by collecting some *baseline data*. Baseline data are data typically collected before any new or different intervention is implemented. To be sure your data are reliable, you need to collect baseline data until a trend, or pattern, emerges. This may take you 3 to 5 days but it is worth the effort. You won't be able to accurately measure student progress unless you know precisely where Point A is. Collecting baseline data is not always necessary. Some students simply do not engage in the target behavior at all. For example, a student may never comply with a request or never complete a work assignment; you don't need to col-

lect baseline data in this instance. Just be careful you are not jumping to conclusions. Sometimes it *seems* like a student never does what you want her to or is always misbehaving. However, when you collect baseline data, you are surprised to see that even though it seems like she is always misbehaving, there actually are times when she does what you want her to. When in doubt, collect baseline data.

Here is an example of how you can precisely determine Point A. Let's say you have a student we'll call Kirsten who is disruptive in class and you want to change her behavior. Pinpointing her behavior provides you with information about *what* she does (e.g., "shouts out in response to a question asked of the class without raising her hand and waiting to be called on"). To find out *how much* she does it, you collect some baseline data. When you ask questions of your students, you record whether Kirsten shouts out (no hand raising) or raises her hand (no shouting). At the end of each day, you compute the percentage of hand raising (no shouting) by dividing the total number of "attempts to answer" (i.e., shout-outs plus instances of raising hand and waiting) into the total number of instances of raising hand without shouting. After 3 days you notice the following trend: The student raised her hand and waited 10%, 20%, and 10% of the times she attempted to answer a question, for an average of approximately 14%. Point A (where the student is now) may therefore be defined as, "Kirsten raises her hand and waits 14% of the time she attempts to answer a question."

Point B

Point B is where you want the student to be, and by when. To determine Point B, you need two pieces of information: Where you want the student to be at the end of your intervention, and the estimated time of arrival (ETA). To determine the former, simply use your performance objective. For example, let's say that after checking with the mainstream teachers and observing in a mainstream classroom, you decide that in order for Kirsten to survive in the mainstream, she needs to increase her hand-raising behavior from 14% to 80% or more. Your performance objective is, "When attempting to answer a question in class, Kirsten will raise her hand and wait to be called on without shouting out the answer 80% of the time." This tells you where you want the student to be at the end of your intervention. Now you need to determine when she will reach 80%.

Precision teachers refer to the ETA as the *aim date*. It is the estimated day in the future when you want your student to reach the CAP in your performance objective. You could always determine the aim date the "easy" way, like the teacher in Figure 8.22. Or you could do it the "hard" (scientific) way, by considering a number of factors that might influence the aim date.

One factor is *time*. How much time do you have in which to change the student's behavior? If your student is being mainstreamed in 2 weeks and reaching Point B will help her succeed in the mainstream setting, your aim date should probably be set 2 weeks from the start of the intervention. If you only have access to your student 3 days per week instead of 5, you will probably require more than 2 weeks for your intervention to succeed. In this case, you should set a later aim date.

A second factor is the *behavior*. Maladaptive behaviors such as fights with peers, runs out of room, makes bowel movements in pants, and does not comply with directives need to be changed more quickly than other behaviors such as off task, out of seat, talk outs, and so forth. You must realize, of course, that setting an earlier aim date alone will not necessarily make the behavior change any faster. I wish it *could* be that easy! Setting an earlier aim date forces you to make more revisions in less time and, in so doing, enables you to find the most effective intervention more quickly.

A third factor to consider is *distance*. How far do you have to go? Taking a student from 10% on-task behavior to 80% on task will most likely require more time than taking the same student from 50% on task to 80%.

A fourth consideration is the *student* and what she brings to the intervention. Does she have all of the prerequisites discussed in Chapter 4? How long has she engaged in the maladaptive behavior and what kind of reinforcement has she received for this behavior in the past? If she lacks one or more of the prerequisites for engaging in the target behavior, you will probably need a later aim date. A later aim date is also indicated if she has a long history of engaging in the maladaptive behavior and/or has been reinforced on a variable schedule of reinforcement.

A fifth factor to consider is the *intervention* you are planning to use. Remember, extinction takes longer than other interventions. Extinction and DRI takes less time than extinction alone. How powerful are the rewards (or aversives) at your disposal? Will they be immediate or delayed? Is there any research that supports the efficacy of your intervention of choice? If you are able to use a combination of interventions with demonstrated efficacy, you will proba-

Figure 8.22. Determining the aim date the "easy" way.

bly be able to set an earlier aim date.

A sixth factor to consider in setting the aim date is you, the *teacher*. Have you used the intervention before? With what success? Do you have all of the essential prerequisites to implement the intervention in an effective manner? Have you had experience in dealing with this behavior in the past? How successful have you been? If you have had little or no experience with a particular intervention, you may wish to give yourself more time and set a later aim date.

Again, using Kirsten as an example, let's assume the following: a) Time is not a factor, because Kirsten is not going anywhere in the next month or two; b) while Kirsten's behavior is disruptive, it presents no threat to life or limb; c) there is a considerable distance between Points A and B; d) Kirsten appears to have all of the prerequisites needed to engage in the target behavior; e) you plan on using extinction (i.e., planned ignoring of her talk outs) plus positive rein-forcement of hand raising and waiting to be called on; and f) you have used both strategies success-fully in the past. Let's say that you have been able to change a variety of attention-seeking behaviors using extinction and DRI in as little as 4 and as many as 20 school days. Given all of the above plus the fact that Kirsten's last teacher reinforced her disruptive behavior on a variable schedule, you decide to set the aim date as Friday of the third week (15 days). The aim date is not set in stone, nor does it have to be precise. With your daily data plotted on your equal-ratio chart, you will be able to see very quickly (within 5 to 6 days) whether or not your aim date is accurate and appropriate.

One last word regarding the aim date. We teach-ers are often impatient about change in our students. If an intervention doesn't work right away, we toss it. Other times we settle for whatever progress we can get no matter how little or late it is. When in doubt, give yourself more time rather than less. A later date is better than an early date and any date is better than no date at all. The rule of thumb is: While you should try not to change your destination (CAP), it is okay to change your estimated time of arrival (aim date).

✔ Checkpoint 8.3

[pages 280–282]

Fill in the answers to the following items (1–11). Check your responses by referring to the text; rele-vant page numbers appear in brackets.

The best way to determine whether or not you should revise your intervention is

(1)_____

_____

_____[280].

The should-do line is

(2)_____

_____

_____[280].

To identify Point A (where the student is now) you need to:

(3)_____

_____

_____

_____[280].

To identify Point B (where you want the student to be) you need to:

(4)_____

_____

_____

_____[280].

Baseline data are:

(5)_____

_____

_____[280].

Six factors to consider in setting the aim date are:

(6–11) _____

_____

_____

_____

_____

_____

_____[281].

Redo any items you missed. If you missed more than 2 of the items, reread the material. Otherwise, con-tinue on to the next section.

The Should-Do Line

Now that you know how to determine Points A and B, you are ready to learn how to draw the should-do line on your chart. The should-do line is actually drawn on your chart before you begin your intervention and plot intervention data. Again, this line tells you how much progress the student *needs to make* in order to move from Point A to Point B. It is called the "should-do" line because it shows what the student *should* do (or what you want the student to do) while the intervention data show what the student actually *does* do. According to Bohannon (1975), the should-do line can significantly improve the chances that decisions regarding program revision will be made in a timely fashion and that these decisions will result in greatly improved pupil progress. I will first show you how to draw the should-do line, and then how to use it to determine whether or not an intervention revision is necessary.

Drawing the should-do line

To draw the should-do line, you need to:

1. Plot at least 3 days of baseline data on your chart

2. Find the mid-day line on the chart for the baseline data (assuming you have 3 days of data, this would be the second day)

3. Find the mid-data line on the chart for the baseline data; again, assuming you have 3 days of data, this would be the second data point from the bottom (or top); it is the median data point

4. Where the mid-day and mid-data lines converge, make a circle (see Figure 8.23); this is called the *start mark*—it represents Point A, where the student is now

5. Next, find the day line on the chart that represents the aim date

6. Find the frequency line on the chart that represents the CAP in the performance objective

7. Where the day line for the aim date and the frequency line for the CAP converge, draw an aim star (✦) (see Figure 8.24); the aim star represents Point B, where you want the student to be and by when

8. Connect the start mark **O** and the aim star ✦ with a straight line (see Figure 8.25); this line is the should-do line.

Figures 8.26 and 8.27 are examples of charts ready for intervention data.

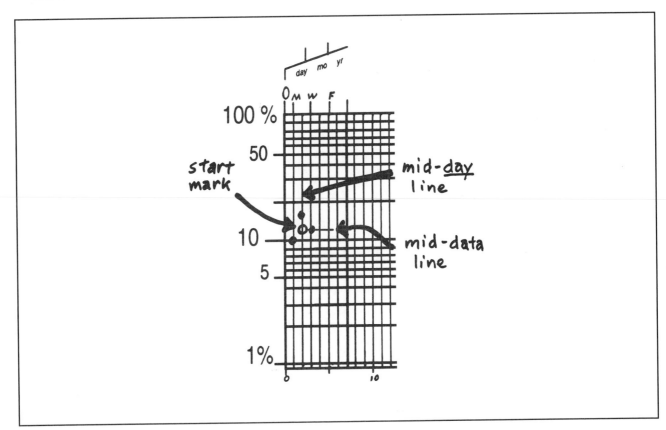

Figure 8.23. Drawing the start mark.

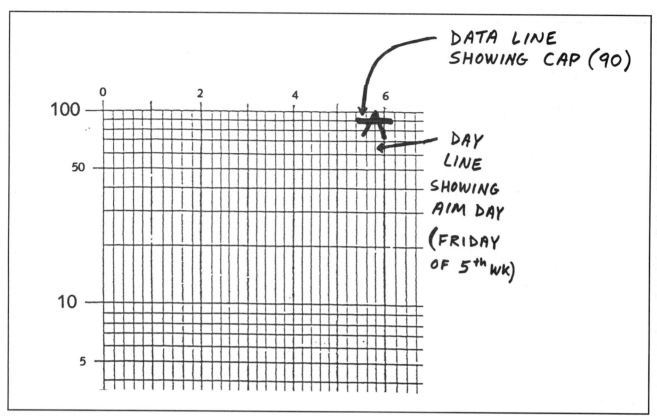

Figure 8.24. Drawing the aim star.

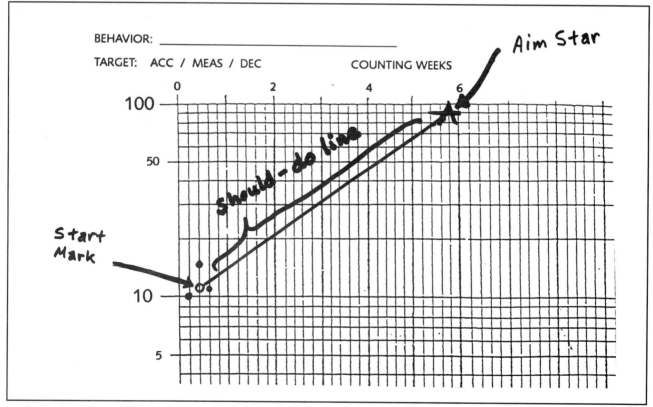

Figure 8.25. Drawing the should-do line.

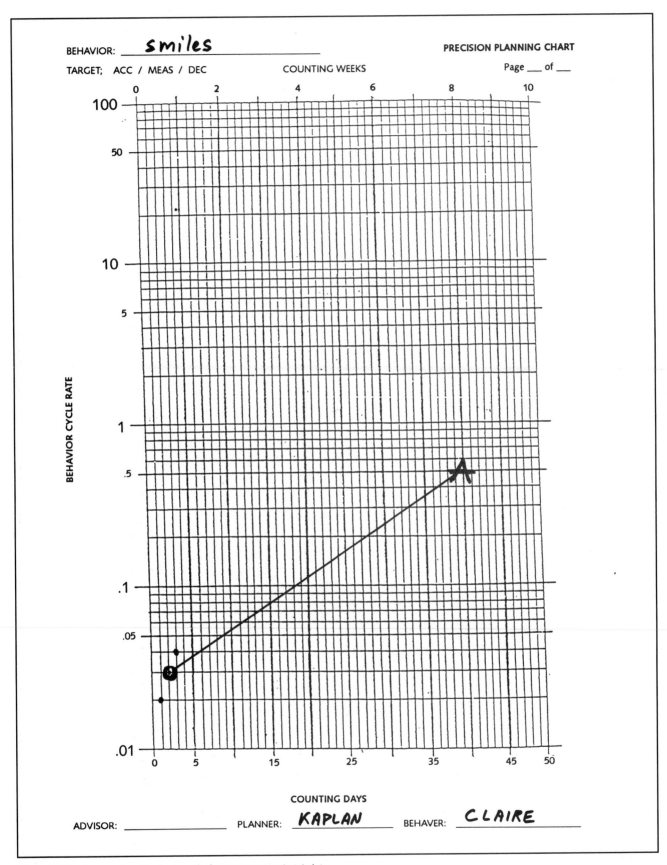

Figure 8.26. Four-cycle ratio chart ready for intervention (rate) data.

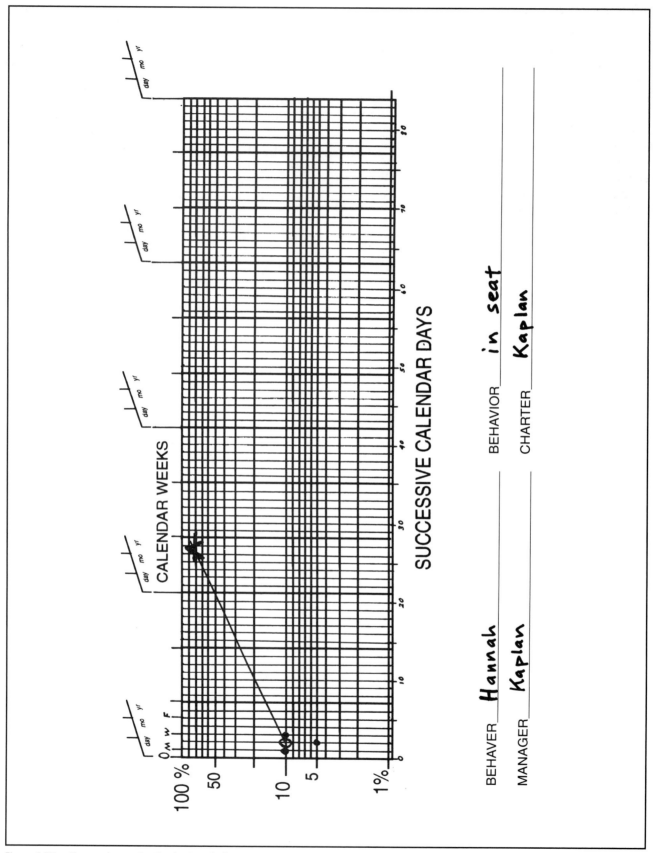

Figure 8.27. Two-cycle equal-ratio chart ready for intervention (percentage) data.

Using the should-do line

OK—you have plotted 3 days of baseline data on your equal-ratio chart and have drawn your should-do line. Now what? Now you begin your intervention, and collect daily data and plot it on your chart. As long as the student's dots are on or above the should-do line for the target pinpoint (see Figure 8.28) and/or the Xs are on or below the should-do line for the maladaptive pinpoint (see Figure 8.29), you will not have to revise the intervention. Just keep plugging away. When the dots fall below the line (Figure 8.30) and/or the Xs are above the line (Figure 8.31), consider revising the intervention.

Let's assume that most of the time you are going to be charting data on target behaviors. This means that you want the data points to stay on *or above* the should-do line. What happens if the data go below the should-do line? A rule of thumb precision teachers use is: Consider making changes in an intervention if the student has *three consecutive* data points that are under the should-do line (see Figure 8.32). Research has shown that although a student may fall below the should-do line for 1 or even 2 days in a row, he will usually still reach the aim on time. However, if he falls below the line for 3 consecutive days, there is only a 6% chance that he will reach the aim on time unless a change is made in the program of intervention (Liberty, 1972; White & Liberty, 1976).

(Text continues on p. 293.)

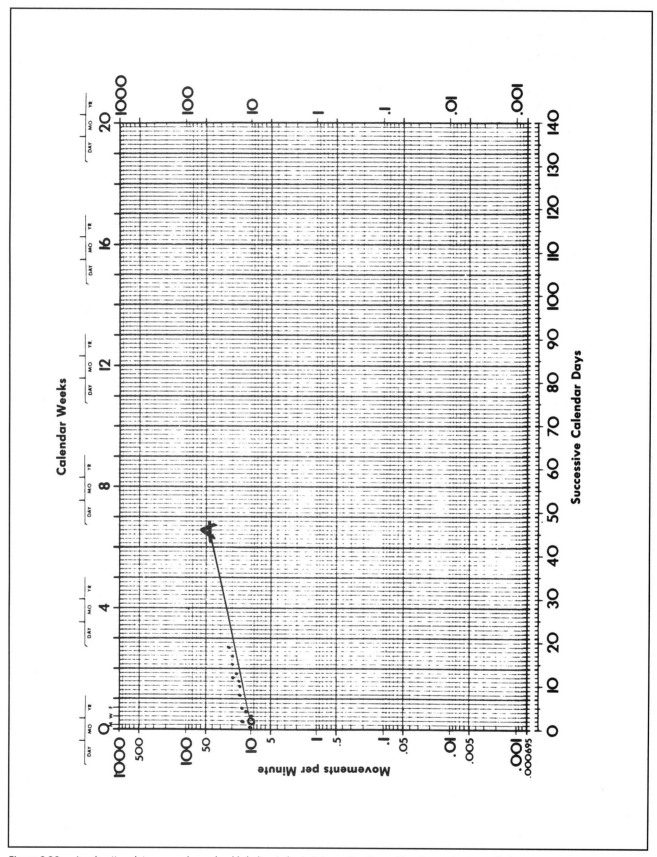

Figure 8.28. Acceleration data on *or above* should-do line indicate intervention is working (increasing target behavior).

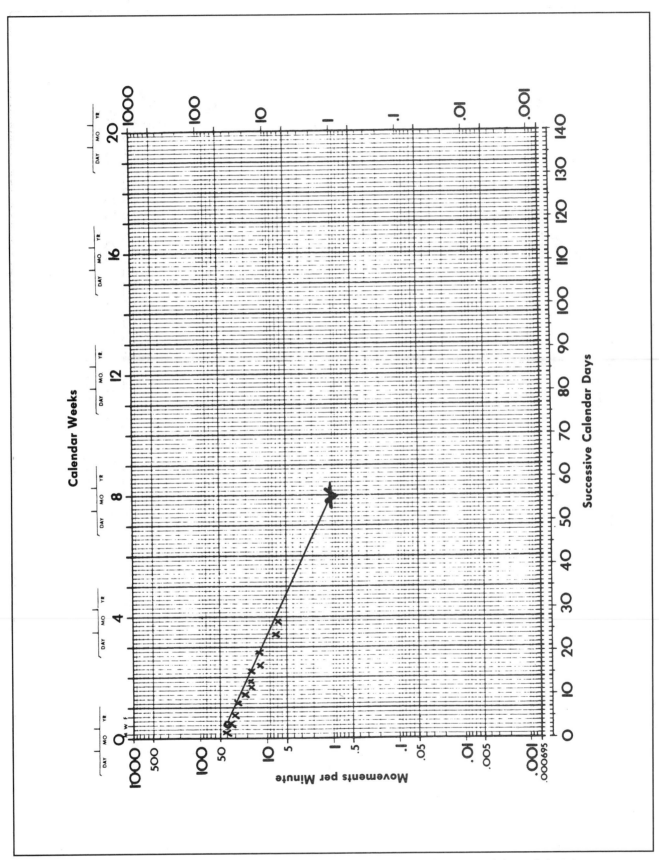

Figure 8.29. Deceleration data on *or below* should-do line indicate intervention is working (decreasing maladaptive behavior).

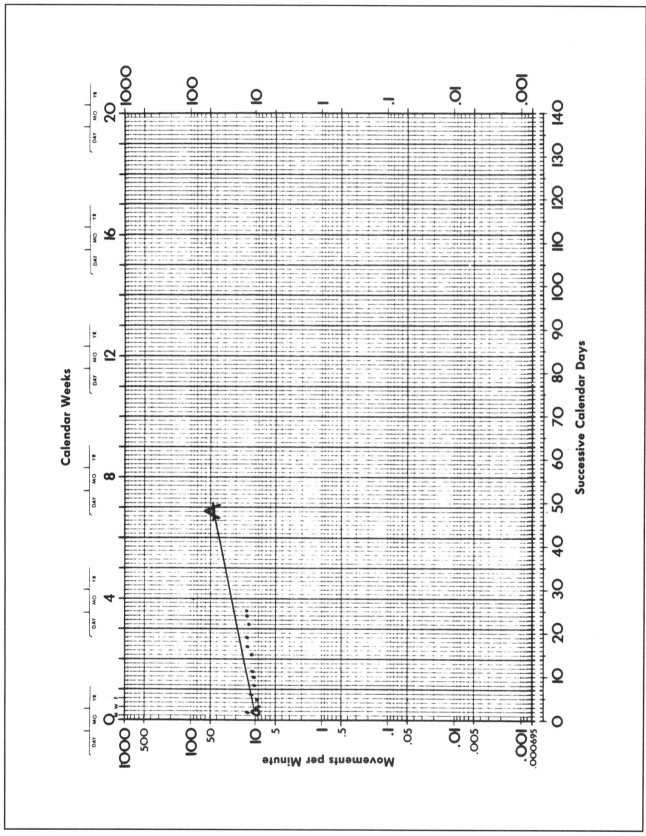

Figure 8.30. Acceleration data *below* should-do line indicate intervention is *not* working (target behavior not increasing fast enough or not increasing at all).

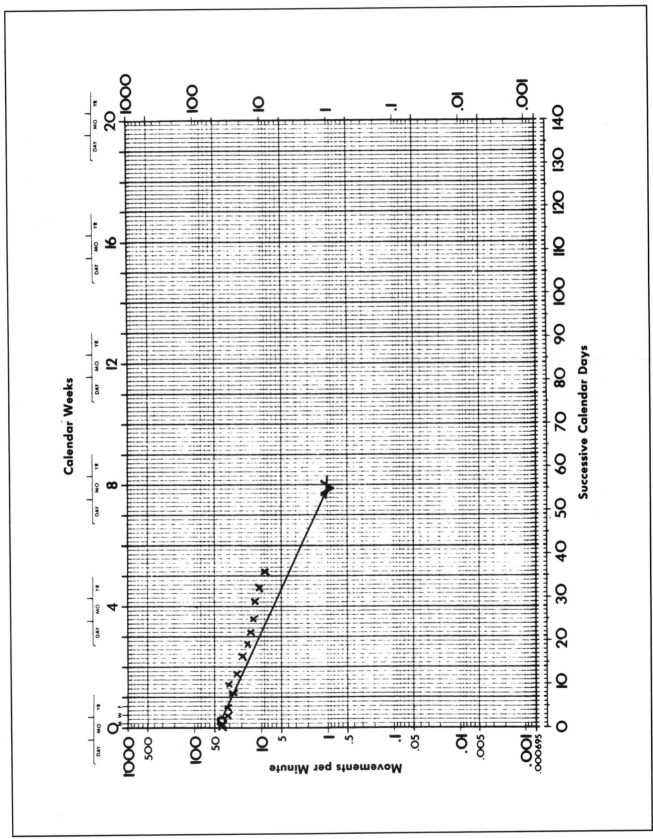

Figure 8.31. Deceleration data *above* should-do line indicate intervention is *not* working (maladaptive behavior not decreasing fast enough or not decreasing at all).

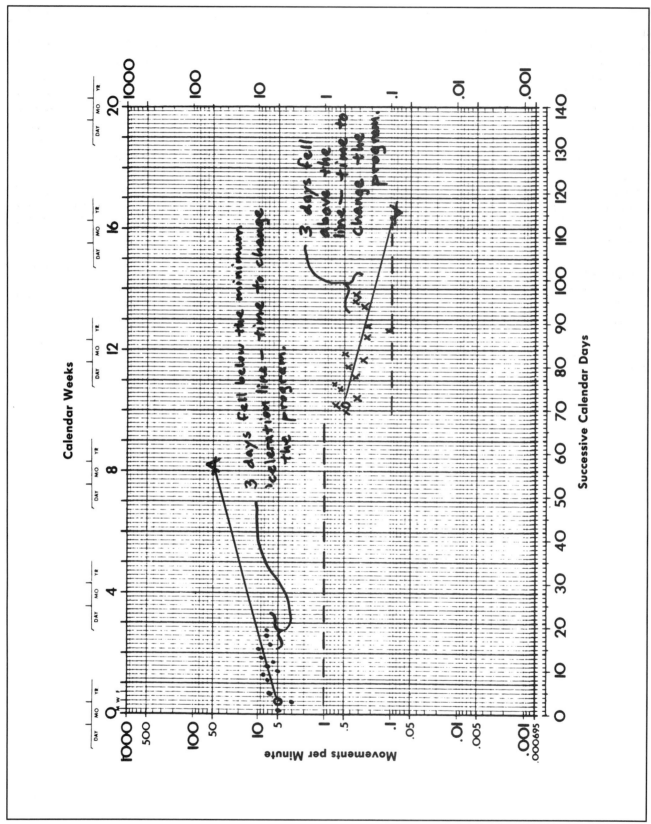

Figure 8.32. Time to change the program of intervention. *Note.* Adapted from *Exceptional Teaching: A multimedia training package* (p. 260), by O. R. White and N. G. Haring, 1976, Columbus, OH: Merrill. Copyright 1976, 1995, by O. R. White and N. G. Haring. Reprinted with permission.

Sounds too easy? You're right. Nothing is that simple. There are exceptions to the "three-data-point" rule. The first type is seen in Figure 8.33, where the student starts out like a house on fire but soon peters out and his data level off. It is obvious that if the student continues at his current rate of progress, he is not going to reach Point B on time (if ever). In this case, I would not wait until he goes below the should-do line 3 consecutive days. I would revise the intervention *now.* Another exception to the three-data-point rule is seen in Figure 8.34. This student starts off with three consecutive data points below the should-do line but his data do show an upward trend. In this case, since there is some evidence of progress, I would recommend waiting until you have at least six data points before considering a program revision. However, if you have a student like the one in Figure 8.35 whose first three data points are below the should-do line and there is no evidence of progress, I would make a change immediately.

Assuming that the three-data-point revision criterion has been met, revise the intervention and implement the modifications as quickly as possible.

A change in the program should be noted on the chart by drawing a heavy vertical line just before the day when the new intervention is implemented. Since the student has failed to meet the old should-do line, draw a new one. If the aim date can be changed to a later date, the new should-do line is drawn from the middle of the last three data points, *parallel with the old should-do line,* to the frequency line on the chart that represents the CAP in the performance objective (see Figure 8.36). However, if you cannot extend the aim date, draw your new should-do line from the middle of the last three data points to the old aim star (see Figure 8.37). Use the modified intervention, and continue collecting data using the new should-do line as a reference point in the same manner as before.

The good news about the should-do line is it tells you *when* you need to make revisions in your intervention. The bad news is it doesn't necessarily tell you *what* revisions to make. To do that you need the does-do line.

(Checkpoint 8.4 follows Figures 8.33–8.37, on p. 299.)

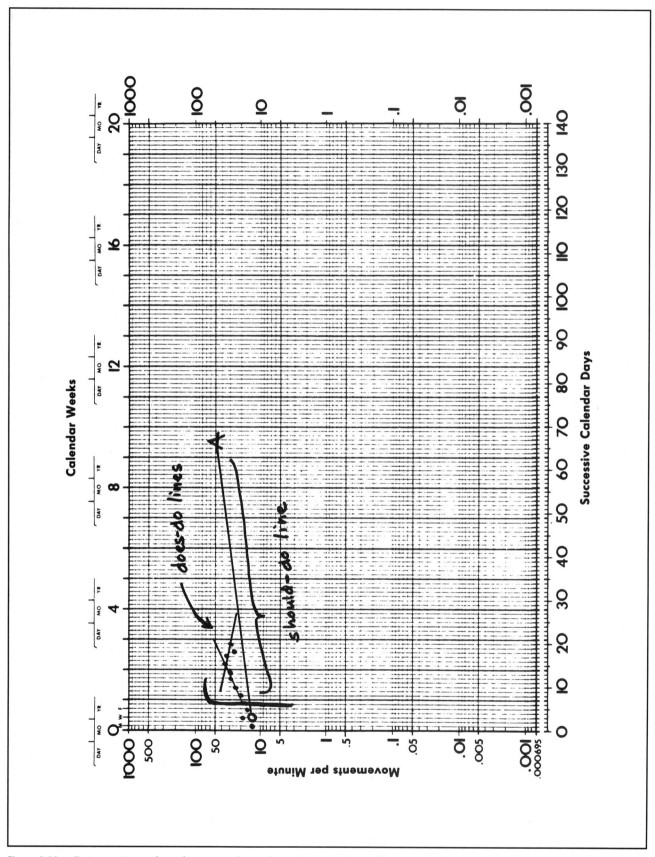

Figure 8.33. First exception to three-data-point rule—make revision even though there are not three data points below should-do line.

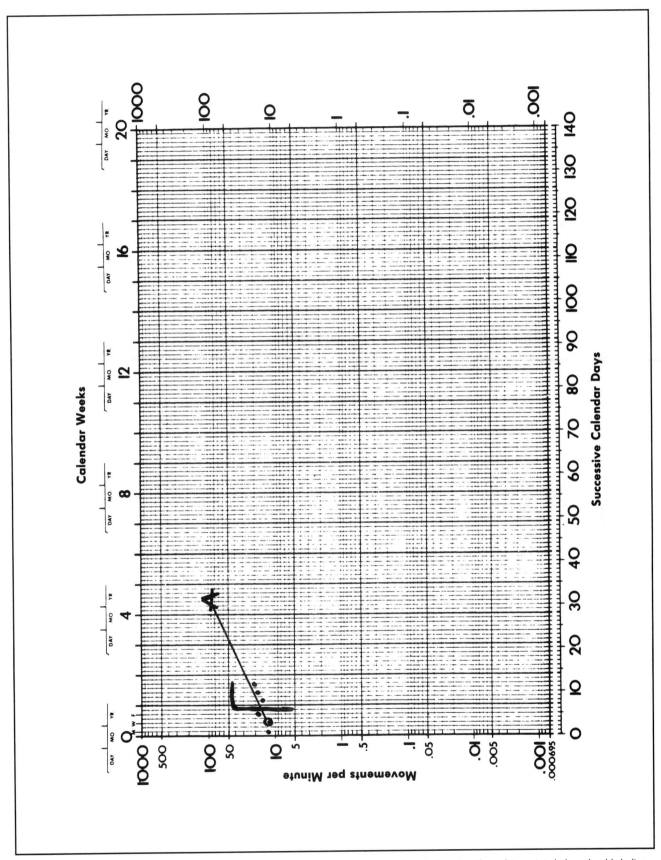

Figure 8.34. Second exception to three-data-point rule—do not make revision even though there are three data points below should-do line.

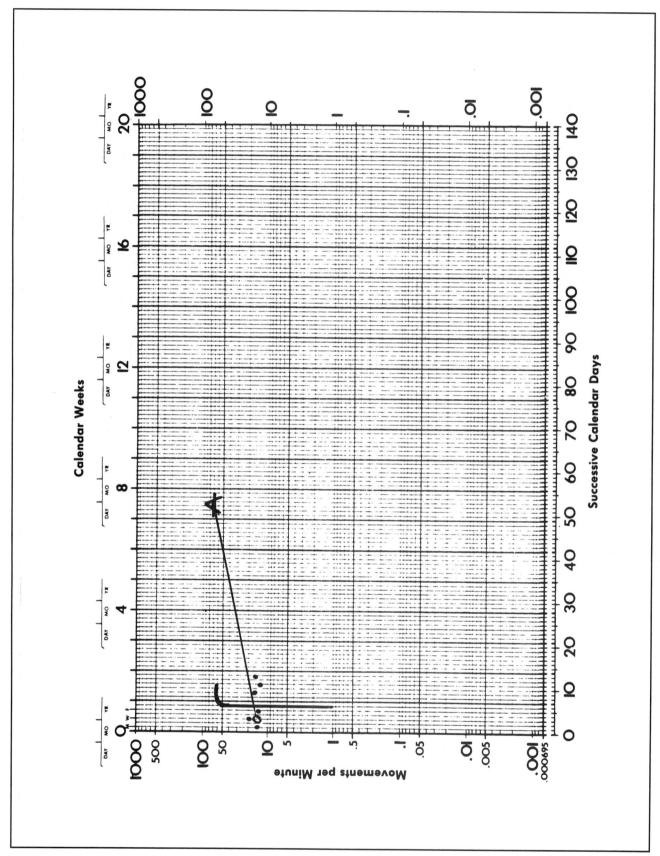

Figure 8.35. Third scenario: Observe the three-data-point rule and make revision immediately.

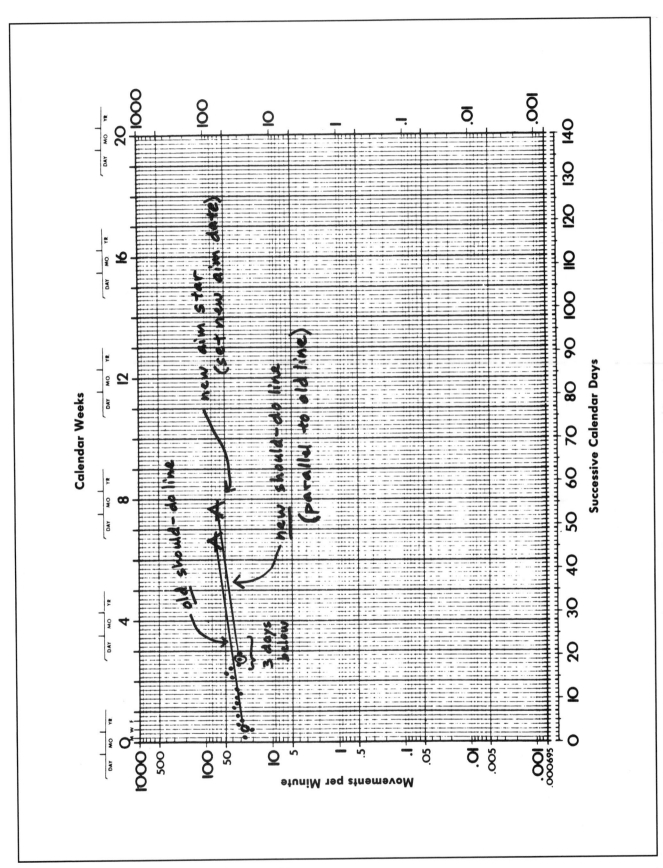

Figure 8.36. Drawing new should-do line with *new* aim date.

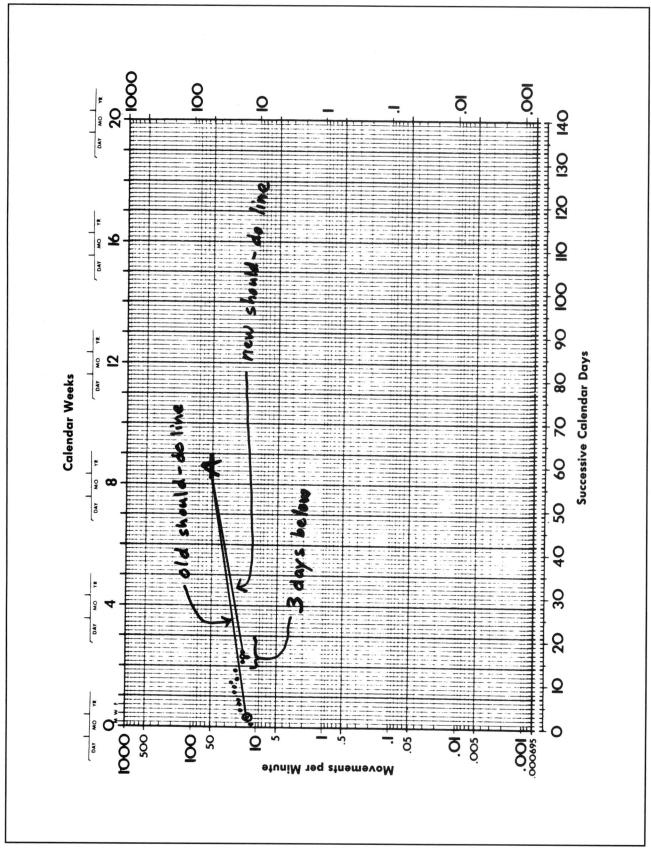

Figure 8.37. Drawing a new should-do line using old aim date.

✔ Checkpoint 8.4

[pages 283–298]

Use the following information to draw should-do lines on the chart on page 317. USE A PENCIL. Check your responses by using the Answer Key on p. 319. If you did not draw a should-do line accurately, erase it and redraw it.

Target Behavior **(1)**

baseline:	.05 bpm (Tu/wk 1);
	.07 bpm (Wed/wk 1);
	.05 (Th/wk 1)
CAP:	10 bpm
Aim Date:	Fri/wk 4

Maladaptive Behavior **(2)**

baseline:	25 bpm (Mon/wk 5);
	20 bpm (Tu/wk 5);
	27 bpm (Wed/wk 5)
CAP:	0 bpm (record floor = 1)
Aim Date:	Fri/wk 8

Fill in the answers to the following items (3–9). Check your responses by referring to the text; relevant page numbers appear in brackets.

The three-data-point rule for behavior you want to strengthen is:

(3) _____

_____

_____ [293].

The three-data-point rule for behavior you want to weaken is:

(4) _____

_____

_____

_____ [293].

(continues)

CHECKPOINT 8.4, continued

Three exceptions to the three-data-point rule are:

(5) _____

_____

(6) _____

_____

(7) _____

_____ [293].

When you make a revision in your intervention, you need to draw a new should-do line. When you can change (extend) the aim date, a new should-do line is drawn by:

(8) _____

_____

_____

_____ [293].

When you cannot extend the aim date, a new should-do line is drawn by:

(9) _____

_____

_____

_____ [293].

Redo any items you missed. If you missed more than 2 of the items, reread the material. Otherwise, continue on to the next section.

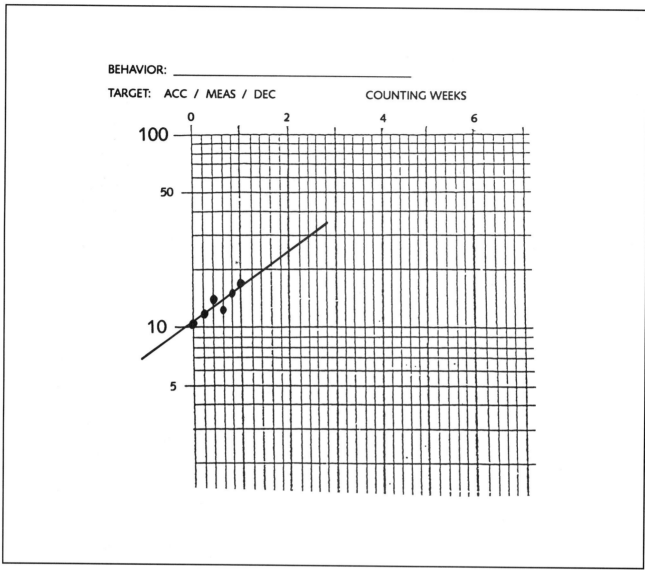

Figure 8.38. The does-do line.

The Does-Do Line

The does-do line is the trend line drawn through the intervention data plotted on your chart. It shows the *trend,* or direction in which the student is actually moving. To draw a does-do line, you must have at least six data points. After plotting 6 days of intervention data on your chart, draw a line through the data as I have done in Figure 8.38. Much of the time you can draw the does-do line using the "eyeball"

method by simply drawing a line through the data as if to divide the data in half. For example, you can use the eyeball method to draw does-do lines for the data shown in Figure 8.39. Other times your data will be too variable to use the eyeball method. For some students, such as those with emotional/behavioral disorders, variability of data is quite common. When your data are too variable to eyeball a does-do line, you can do one of two things.

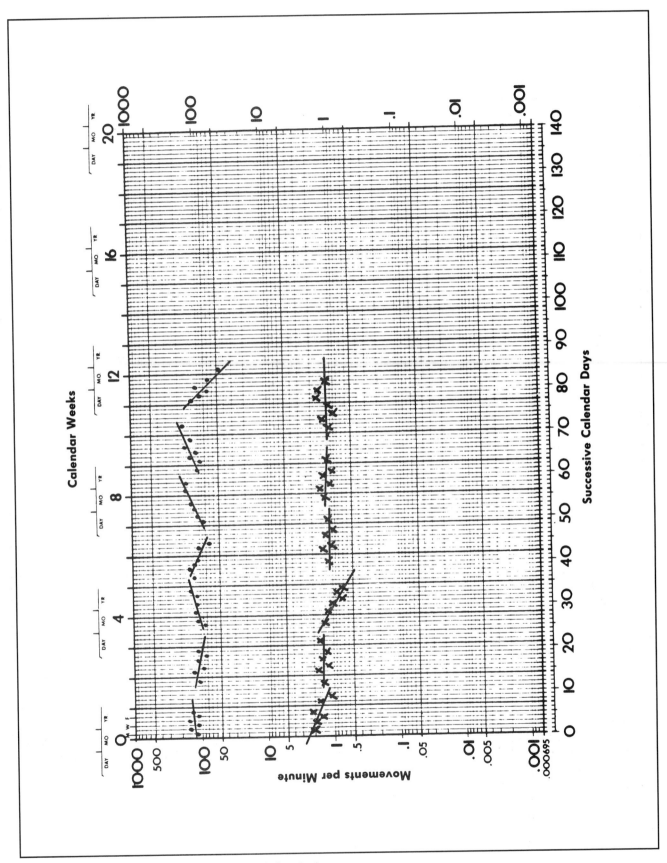

Figure 8.39. Examples of does-do lines drawn by eyeball method.

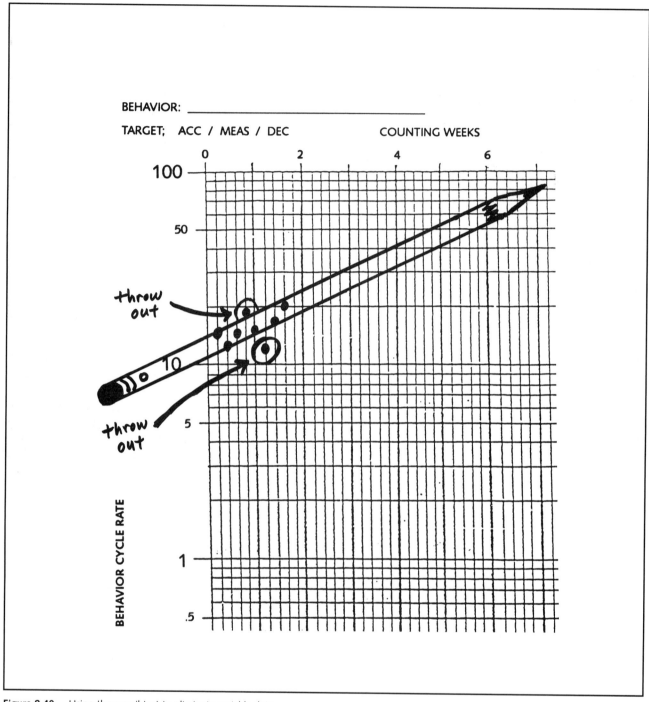

Figure 8.40. Using the pencil test to eliminate variable data.

The pencil test

First, you can eliminate one or more of the variable data points by employing the "pencil test." Lay a pencil over the data in the manner illustrated in Figure 8.40 and throw out any data points the pencil doesn't cover. Keep in mind that you still need a minimum of six data points to draw your does-do line. If, after employing the pencil test, you are left with less than six data points, you will need to collect more data. Once you have eliminated the variable data and you have at least six data points that are fairly linear, you can use the eyeball method to draw your does-do line.

The split-middle method

Sometimes your data may be too variable and the pencil test may eliminate too many data points. You may have to collect data for another week or more to get the six you need. Since the purpose of the equal-ratio chart is to save time, you are defeating the purpose if you wait until you get data free of variability. You don't have to wait—you can use a technique known as the *split-middle method of trend estimation* (White, 1971). The split-middle method is based on a powerful statistic known as the median slope (White, 1972). It provides you with an accurate does-do line with as few as six data points, no matter how variable. Here's how to use it.

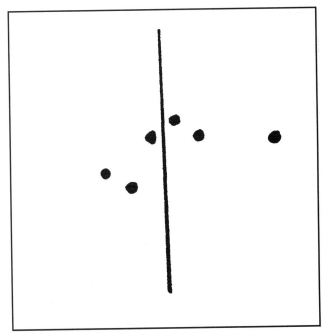

Figure 8.41. Divide data in half.

First, count out the number of data points you wish to include in your does-do line. There must be at least six. These data are allowed to be variable, so don't bother using the pencil test to get rid of any. Next, divide the data points in half by drawing a vertical line between them (see Figure 8.41). Then find the mid-day line for each half and draw a vertical line dividing the data in half again (see Figure 8.42). Next,

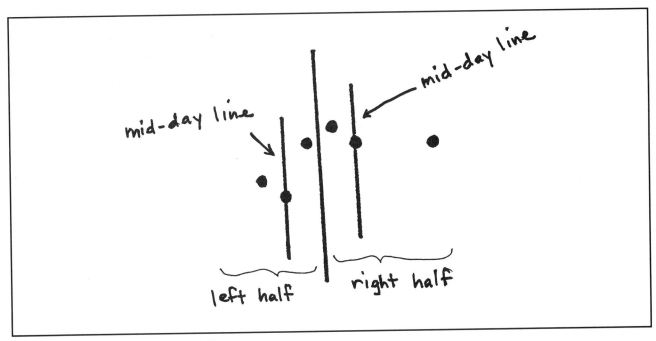

Figure 8.42. Find mid-day line for each half.

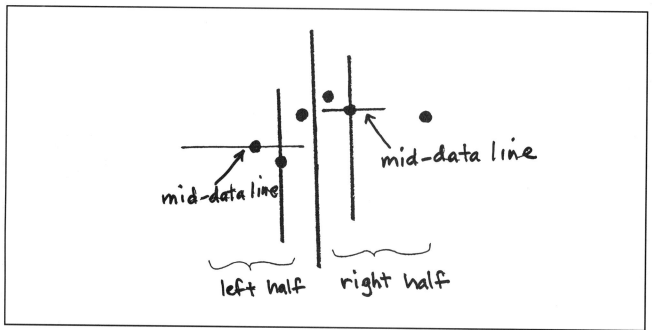

Figure 8.43. Find mid-data line for each half.

find the mid-data line for each half and draw a horizontal line dividing the data in half (see Figure 8.43). Where the mid-day line and the mid-data point line converge, make an X (see Figure 8.44). Finally, draw a line through the two Xs (see Figure 8.45). This is the does-do line.

If you have an odd number of data points (such as 7 or 9) through which to draw your trend line, follow the same procedure but with the following variations. When you divide your data in half, you must draw a vertical line through the middle day's data. Once you do this, consider that data point "dead" and do not use it to determine your trend line. You may now proceed as in the even-number-of-points example, and then draw your does-do line through the Xs in each half (see Figure 8.46).

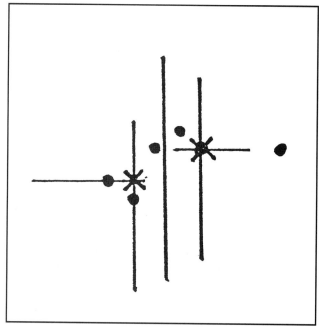

Figure 8.44. For each half, mark X at point where mid-day and mid-data lines converge.

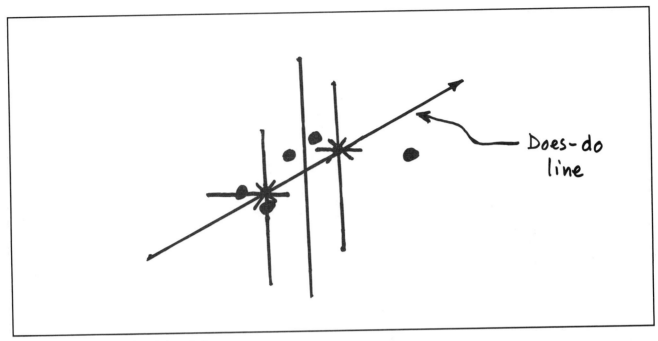

Figure 8.45. Connect Xs to get does-do line.

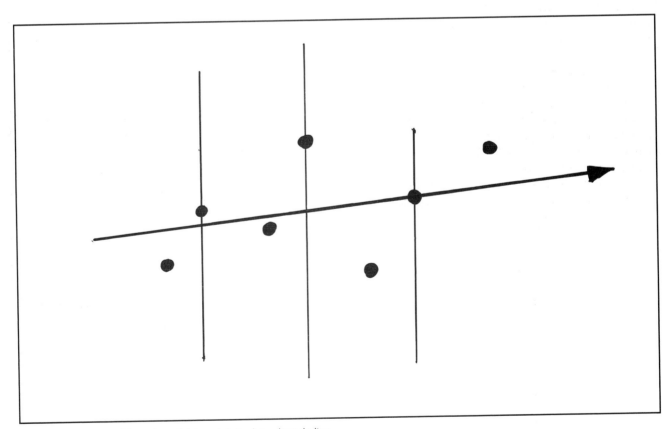

Figure 8.46. Using odd number of data points to draw does-do line.

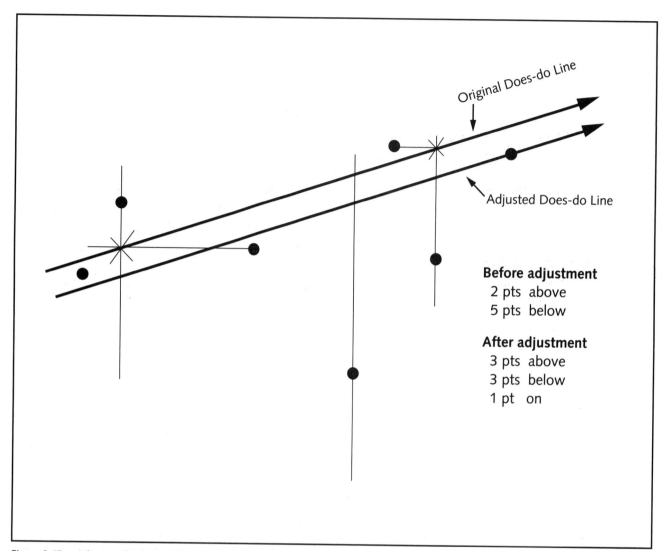

Before adjustment
  2 pts above
  5 pts below

After adjustment
  3 pts above
  3 pts below
  1 pt   on

Figure 8.47.   Adjusting the does-do line to split data in half.

Ideally, the does-do line divides the data in half. In other words, there should be approximately the same number of data points above and below the trend line. If this is not the case, you will need to "move" the line by drawing a parallel line above it or below it so that it splits the data in half (see Figure 8.47).

✔ Checkpoint 8.5

[pages 300–306]

Fill in the answers to the following items (1–6). Check your responses by referring to the text; relevant page numbers appear in brackets.

The does-do line is **(1)** _____

_____

_____

_____ [300].

You need a minimum of **(2)** _____ data points to draw the does-do line. Often, you will be able to draw a does-do line by eyeballing the data.

When your data are too variable to eyeball a does-do line, you can always **(3)**_____

_____ [303]

or you can **(4)** _____

_____ [303]

or you can **(5)** _____

_____[303].

The split-middle method is a technique used to

(6) _____

_____

_____[303].

Use the *eyeball method* to draw does-do lines for items **(7–12)** on the chart on page 321. Use the pencil test to eliminate any variable data. Check your responses by using the Answer Key on page 325.

Use the *split-middle method* to draw does-do lines for items **(13–15)** on the chart on page 323. Make sure you adjust your lines so they split the data in half as closely as possible. Check your responses by using the Answer Key on page 326.

Redo any items you missed. If you missed more than 3 of the items, reread the material. Otherwise, continue on to the next section.

Making Revisions

The slope of the does-do line can indicate what is wrong with an intervention and suggest what changes to make. For example, a flat does-do line, such as the one in Figure 8.48, usually indicates any one or a combination of the following:

a. You are using ineffective rewards since they don't seem to have any effect on the student's behavior (assuming you are using a reinforcement program);

b. the student has a skill deficit and doesn't know how to engage in the behavior (even if he wanted to);

c. you are using the wrong antecedents (cues or reminders) or not giving the student enough information about what he is supposed to be doing; as a result, he is confused about what to do and/or when to do it.

I recommend completing a Pre-Mod analysis to identify exactly what the problem is and work on the missing prerequisite(s) before returning to your original intervention. The student may lack awareness, not know the rule, be unable to control his behavior, not know how to engage in the behavior, and/or not be motivated by the consequences.

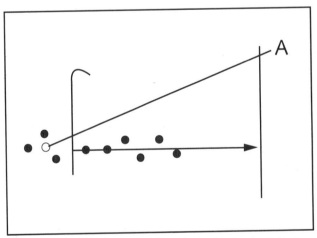

Figure 8.48. Flat slope of does-do line indicates no growth at all.

A does-do line that shows steady but slow progress, such as the one shown in Figure 8.49, usually means you are using the right reinforcers (since the student's behavior is getting stronger) but the student isn't getting enough of them. You need to give him more opportunities to earn reinforcement and/or change the schedule of reinforcement.

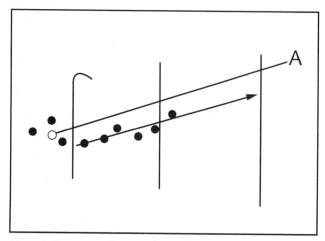

Figure 8.49. Data indicate progress—steady, but slow.

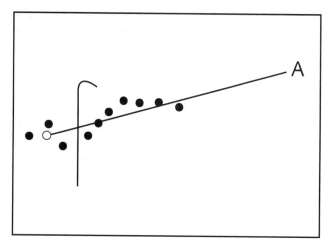

Figure 8.50. Data indicate initial progress followed by leveling off.

Does-do lines like the one in Figure 8.50, where the student's initial progress levels off or reverses, can mean one of two things. Either the student is getting too much reinforcement and is becoming satiated, or he is getting too little reinforcement and you have managed to extinguish his behavior. If he is becoming satiated, you may have had him on a continuous schedule too long or made it too easy for him to get the reward. Either move immediately to a fixed schedule of reinforcement (2:1), or return to a brief baseline phase to establish a state of deprivation in the student and then begin again with a continuous schedule. This time, watch the data carefully and as soon as you see the data start to level off, begin a fixed schedule of reinforcement. If you are using a shaping program, move on to the next higher approximation. If the student is getting too little reinforcement and extinction has occurred, you must begin all over again with a continuous schedule of reinforcement and stay on it until you see it start to level off.

☑ **Checkpoint 8.6**

[pages 307–308]

Fill in the answers to the following items (1–6). Check your responses by referring to the text; relevant page numbers appear in brackets.

A does-do line that shows no progress at all usually means (list at least three interpretations)

(1–3) _____

_____

_____

_____

_____

_____[307].

A does-do line that shows slow but steady progress usually means

(4) _____

_____

_____[307].

A does-do line that shows leveling off or regression after initial progress usually means (list two interpretations)

(5, 6) _____

_____

_____

_____

_____[308].

Redo any items you missed. If you missed more than 1 of the items, reread the material. Otherwise, continue on to the next section.

PUTTING IT ALL TOGETHER

Let's recap the process of charting and analyzing data. Assuming you have already collected some baseline data and are going to use an equal-ratio chart, this is the procedure you need to follow:

1. Fill out the identifying information (e.g., the behaver, behavior charted, the manager and charter) on the chart;

2. plot the baseline data on the chart and draw a start mark to indicate Point A;

3. establish an aim date;

4. use the aim date and the CAP from the student's performance objective to locate Point B on the chart and mark it with an aim star;

5. draw a should-do line by connecting the start mark (A) and the aim star (B);

6. implement your intervention and monitor the student's behavior;

7. plot the intervention data on your chart and apply the three-data-point rule to determine if and when an intervention revision is necessary (be aware of any exceptions to the rule);

8. draw a does-do line through a minimum of six of the most recent data points to determine what kind of intervention revision is necessary; if the data are variable, use the pencil test to determine which data to keep and eliminate or use the split-middle method to draw a does-do line.

This may seem like a long, complicated procedure—but with practice, you will be able to keep charts and analyze intervention data on several students with a minimal amount of time and effort. As I have said before, the practices outlined in this chapter will result in a decrease in the time you currently spend on ineffective discipline. These practices can also be mastered by your students. At the very least, they can learn to chart data, draw a should-do line, and apply the three-data-point rule, and you don't have to get involved unless it becomes necessary to decide on an intervention revision. The charts also serve as a powerful motivator for students because attention is focused on growth (how fast they are changing) instead of performance (where they are on a given day).

While I would love to see more teachers collect, chart, and analyze data on their behavioral (and academic) interventions, I have been an educator too long to expect change overnight. A shaping procedure is probably the best way to get yourself started. If you currently don't collect data at all, start collecting it. First on one student, then another. Nothing fancy. Keep it simple. Then start charting the data you collect. Try using simple arithmetic charts first—maybe some bar graphs. Then move on to a four-cycle equal-ratio chart . . . and before you know it, you'll be on your way.

(Chapter 8 Assessment begins on p. 327.)

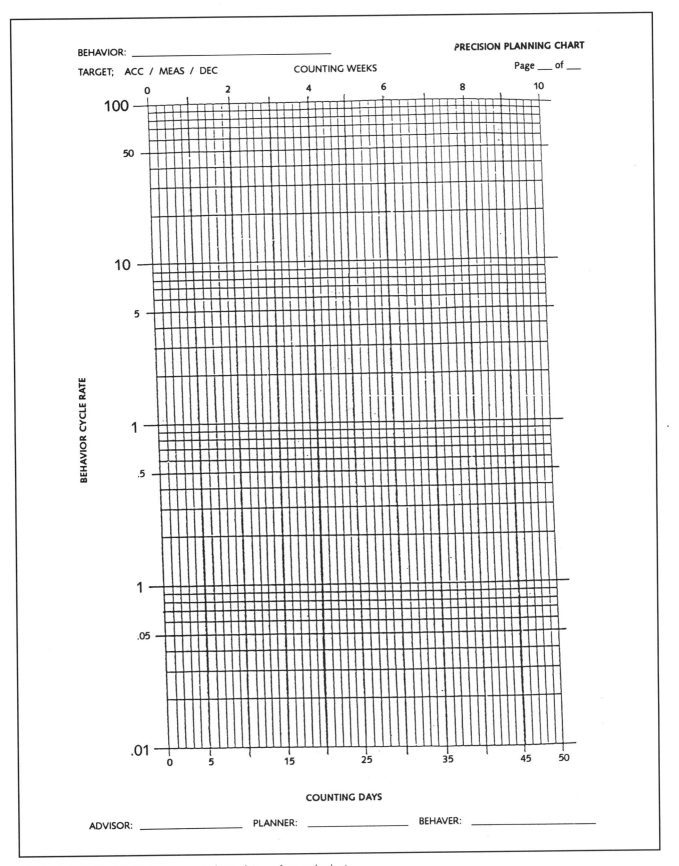

Checkpoint 8.2, Chart A: Plot raw score and rate data on four-cycle chart.

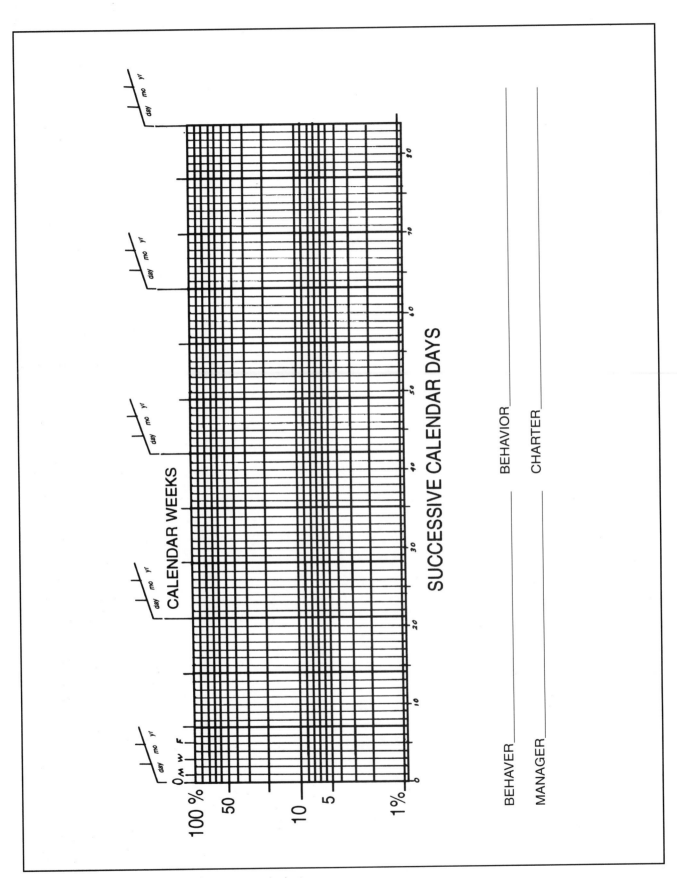

Checkpoint 8.2, Chart B: Plot percent data on two-cycle chart.

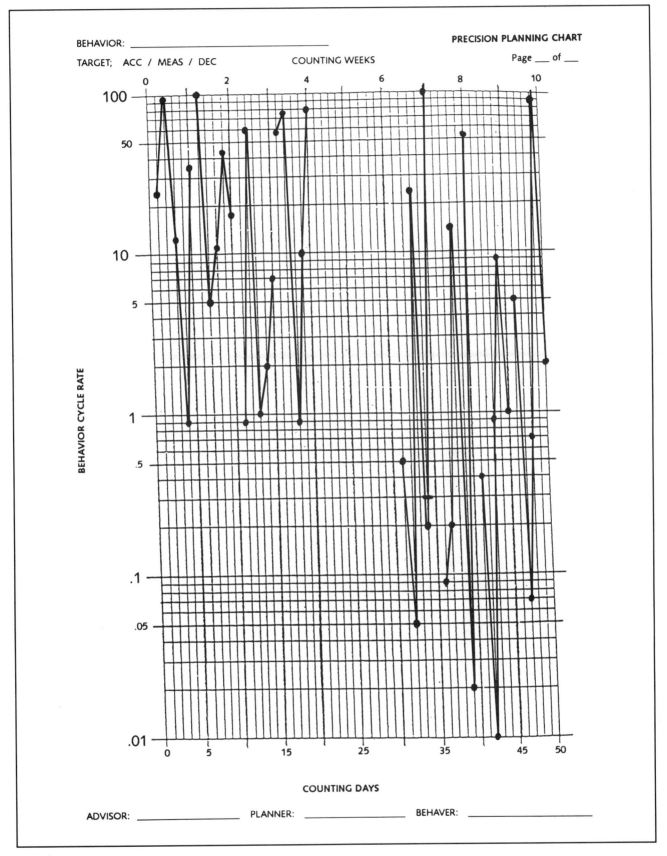

BEHAVIOR: _____

PRECISION PLANNING CHART

TARGET; ACC / MEAS / DEC

COUNTING WEEKS

Page ___ of ___

BEHAVIOR CYCLE RATE

COUNTING DAYS

ADVISOR: _____   **PLANNER:** _____   **BEHAVER:** _____

Answer Key for Checkpoint 8.2, Chart A.

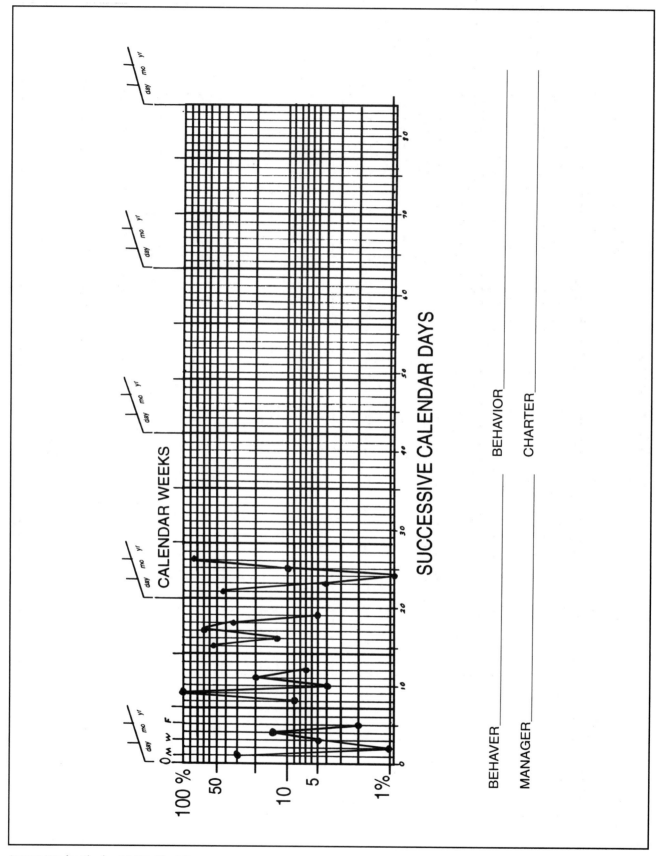

Answer Key for Checkpoint 8.2, Chart B.

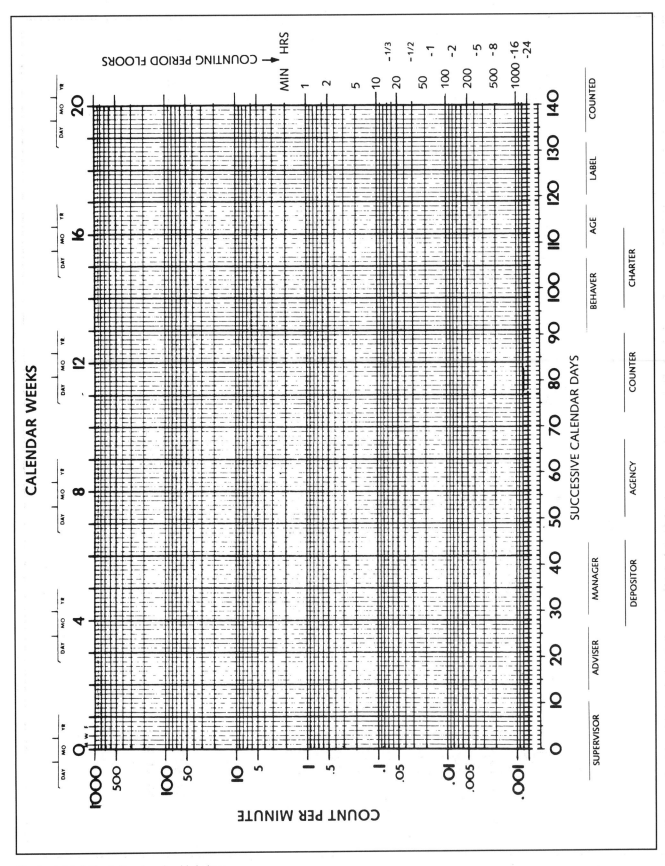

Checkpoint 8.4 Chart: Drawing should-do lines.

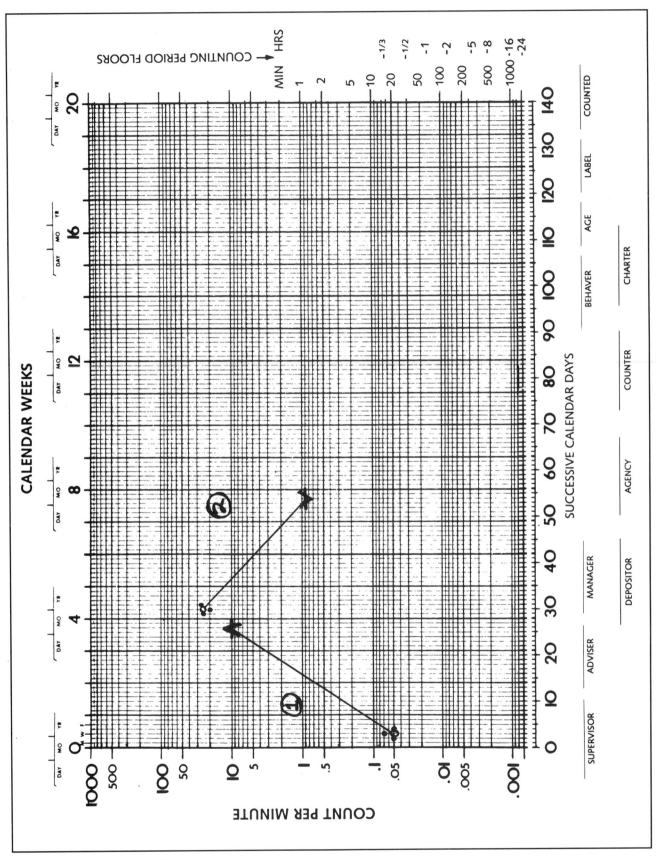

CALENDAR WEEKS

Answer Key for Checkpoint 8.4 Chart.

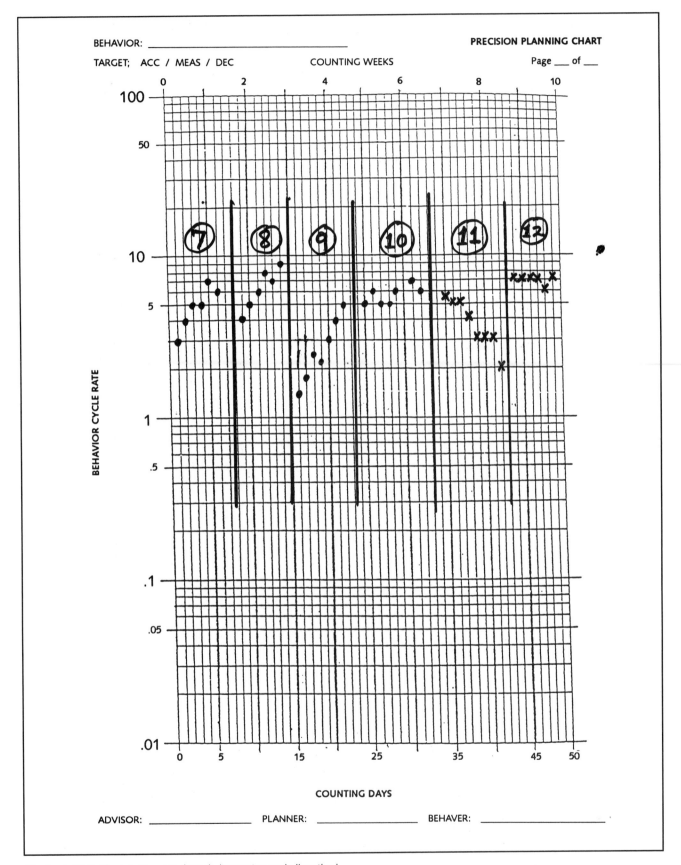

Checkpoint 8.5, Chart A: Drawing does-do lines using eyeball method.

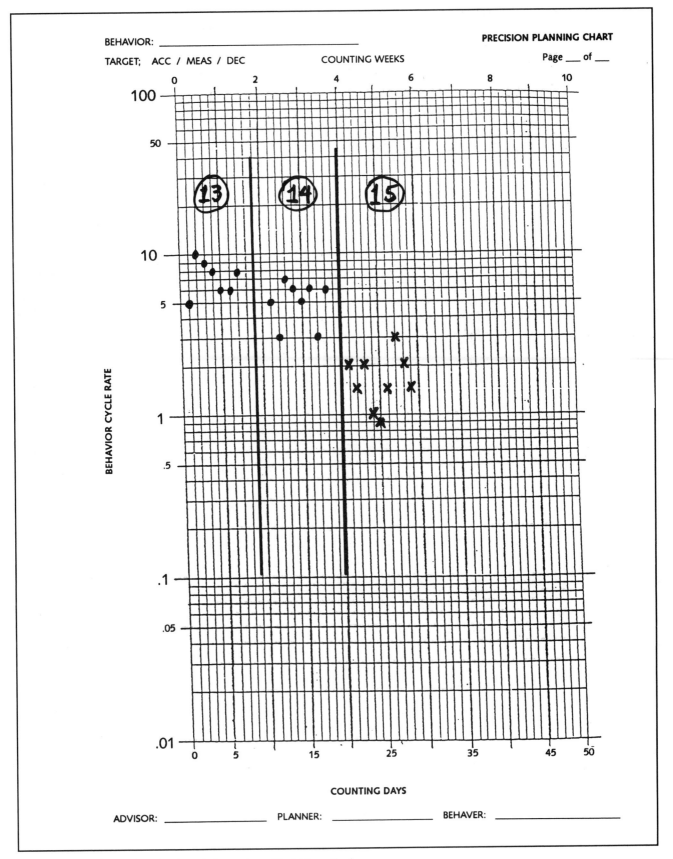

Checkpoint 8.5, Chart B: Drawing does-do lines using split-middle method.

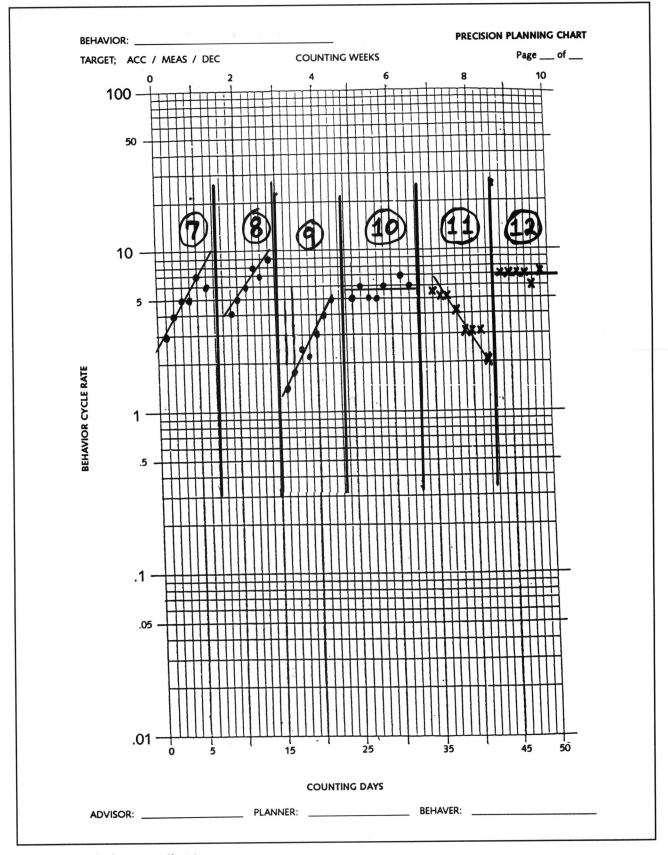

BEHAVIOR: _____

TARGET; ACC / MEAS / DEC

COUNTING WEEKS

PRECISION PLANNING CHART

Page ___ of ___

BEHAVIOR CYCLE RATE

COUNTING DAYS

ADVISOR: _____ **PLANNER:** _____ **BEHAVER:** _____

Answer Key for Checkpoint 8.5, Chart A.

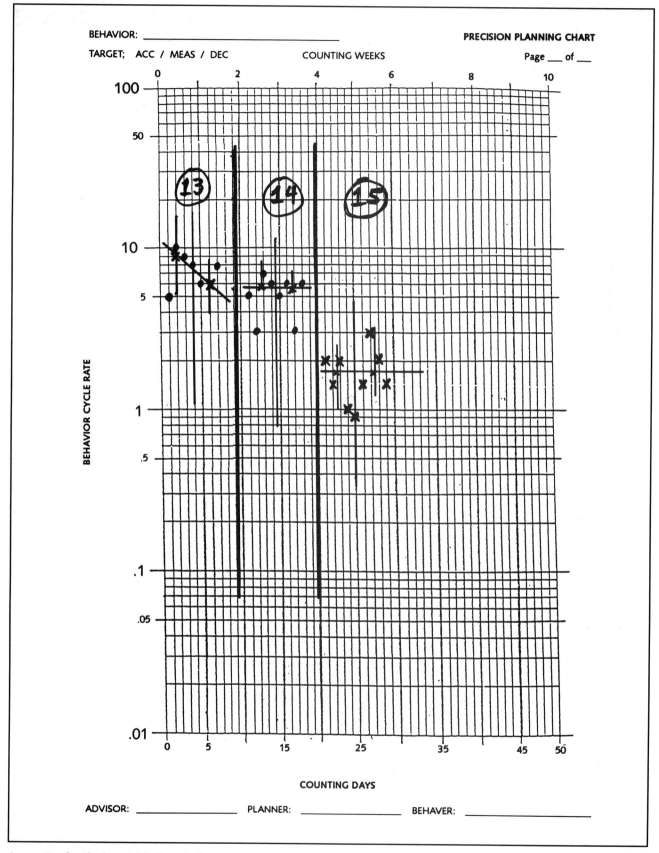

Answer Key for Checkpoint 8.5, Chart B.

ASSESSMENT / CHAPTER 8 ▮▮▮▮▮▮

A list of acceptable responses appears on p. 328; answer keys for Charts A, B, C, and D appear on pp. 337–340.

Use the blank equal-ratio charts on pp. 329–335 to:

1. Display the data listed below;

2. draw should-do lines;

3. when necessary, draw does-do lines;

4. write an interpretation of what is happening in each case; your interpretation should include a) whether or not the intervention is working, b) what action you need to take, and c) why.

Chart A: on task

> **baseline:** 5% (Mon/wk 1); 6% (Tue/wk 1); 5% (Wed/wk 1)
>
> **CAP:** 80%
>
> **Aim Date:** Fri/wk 5
>
> **intervention:** 6% (Thu/wk 1); 7% (Fri/wk 1); 8% (Mon/wk 2); 10% (Tue/wk 2)

Chart B: eye contacts

> **baseline:** .2 bpm (Mon/wk 1); .3 bpm (Tue/wk 1); .3 bpm (Wed/wk 1)
>
> **CAP:** 10 bpm
>
> **Aim Date:** Fri/wk 8
>
> **intervention:** .4 bpm (Thu/wk 1); .5 bpm (Fri/wk 1); .5 bpm (Mon/wk 2); .6 bpm (Tue/wk 2); .7 bpm (Wed/wk 2); .7 bpm (Thu/wk 2)

Chart C: in seat

> **baseline:** 5% (Mon/wk 1); 10% (Tue/wk 1); 8% (Wed/wk 1)
>
> **CAP:** 70%
>
> **Aim Date:** Fri/wk 4
>
> **intervention:** 15% (Thu/wk 1); 20% (Fri/wk 1); 25% (Mon/wk 2); 35% (Tue/wk 2); 40% (Wed/wk 2); 35% (Thu/wk 2); 40% (Fri/wk 2); 35% (Mon/wk 3); 35% (Tue/wk 3); 40% (Wed/wk 3)

Chart D: compliance

> **baseline:** 5% (Mon/wk 1); 4% (Tue/wk 1); 6% (Wed/wk 1)
>
> **CAP:** 90%
>
> **Aim Date:** Fri/wk 4
>
> **intervention:** 5% (Thu/wk 1); 6% (Fri/wk 1); 6% (Mon/wk 2)

ACCEPTABLE RESPONSES

Chart A (on task): Although the data is not on the should-do line, the behavior is moving in the right direction; should give it 2 to 3 more days before considering any program revision.

Chart B (eye contacts): No change is necessary; intervention is working.

Chart C (in seat): Although first five data points show significant progress, does-do line for last six or seven data points indicates virtually no progress; need to make exception to three-data-point rule and revise intervention now; assuming a reinforcement program is being used, reinforcer may be losing its power to reinforce through overuse (satiation); need to make it more difficult to get reinforcer by moving to next highest schedule (if 1:1, move 2:1; if 2:1, move to 3:1) or if using shaping program, use next highest approximation as contingency for reward; another possibility is that you went through schedules of reinforcement or approximations too quickly and student is not getting enough reinforcement (extinction); need to move back (i.e., make it easier to get reinforcer).

Chart D (compliance): Data show no progress at all; need to make program revision immediately; conduct Pre-Mod analysis to determine if problem is skill deficit or using wrong reinforcer, or not giving student enough or correct antecedents.

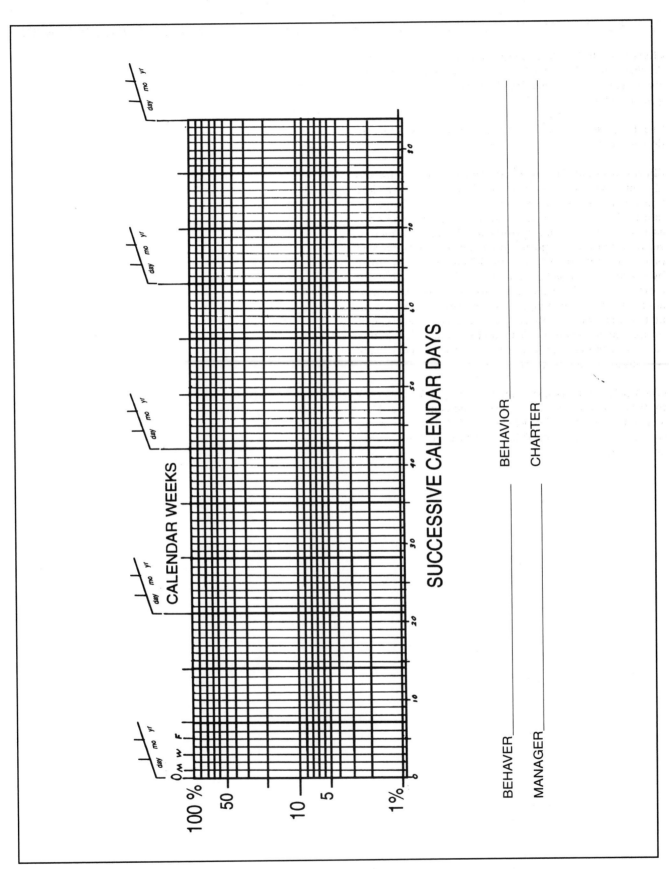

Assessment Chart A: On Task.

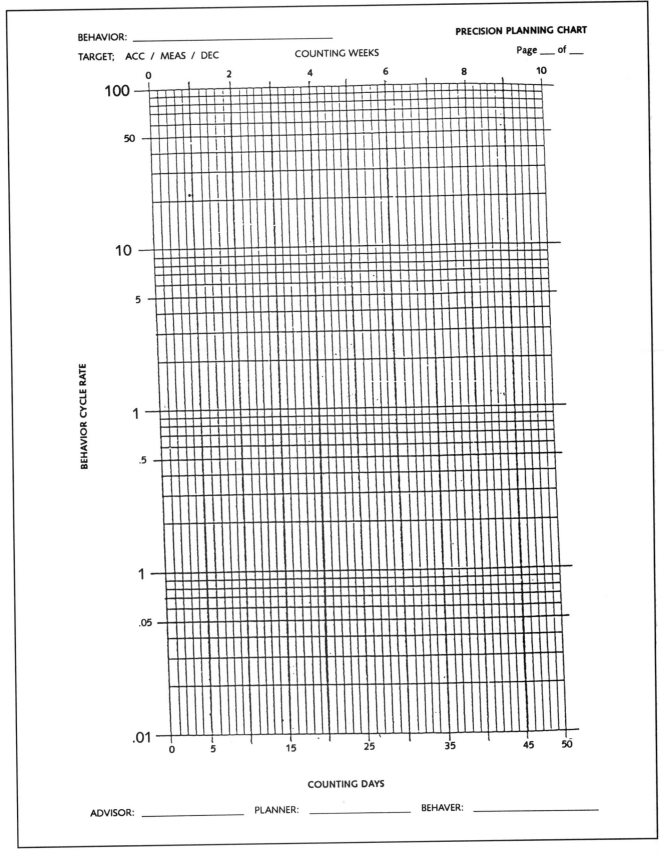

BEHAVIOR: _____

TARGET; ACC / MEAS / DEC

COUNTING WEEKS

PRECISION PLANNING CHART

Page ___ of ___

BEHAVIOR CYCLE RATE

COUNTING DAYS

ADVISOR: _____ PLANNER: _____ BEHAVER: _____

Assessment Chart B: Eye Contacts.

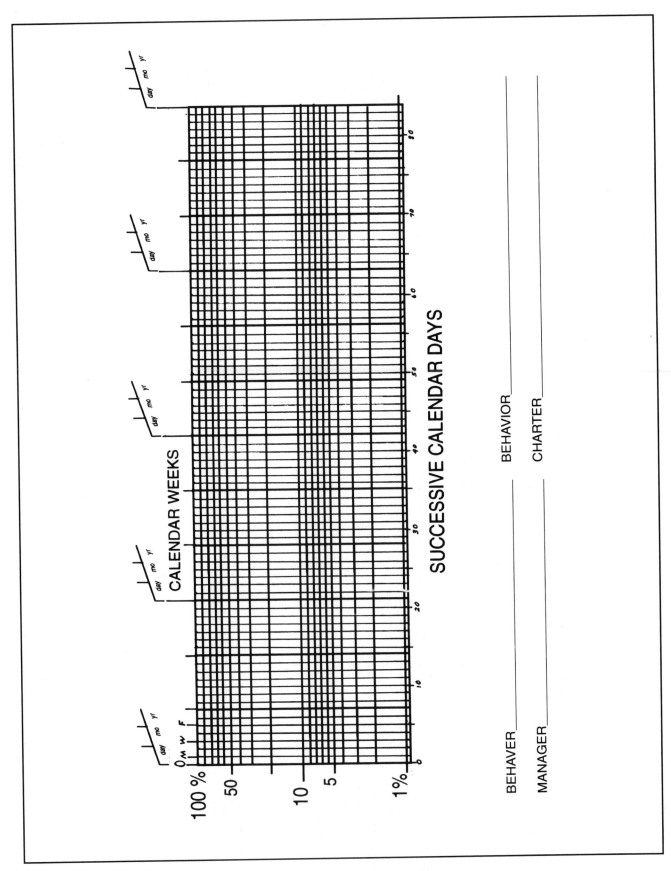

Assessment Chart C: In seat.

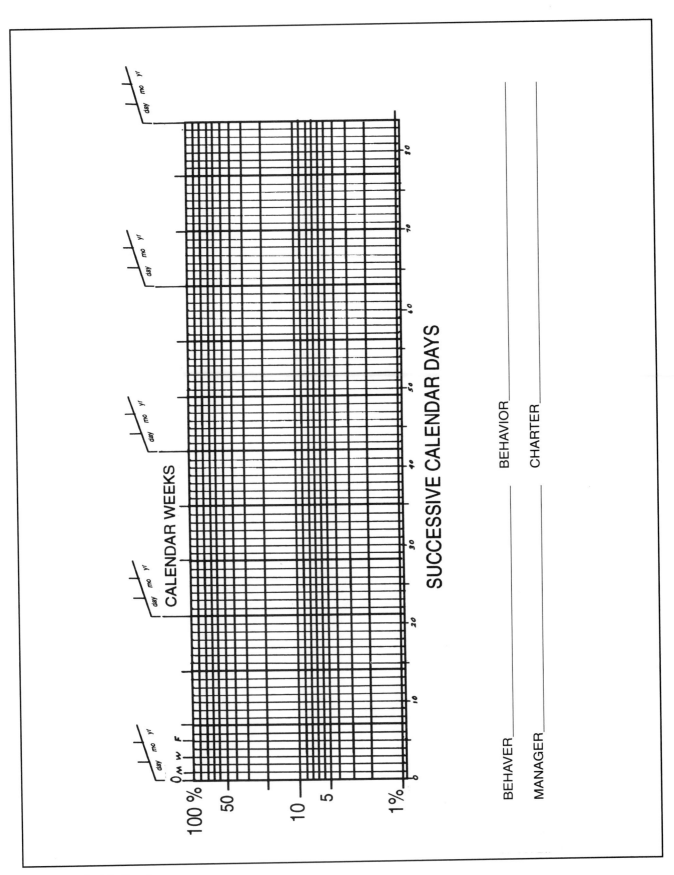

SUCCESSIVE CALENDAR DAYS

CALENDAR WEEKS

BEHAVER

MANAGER

BEHAVIOR

CHARTER

Assessment Chart D: Compliance.

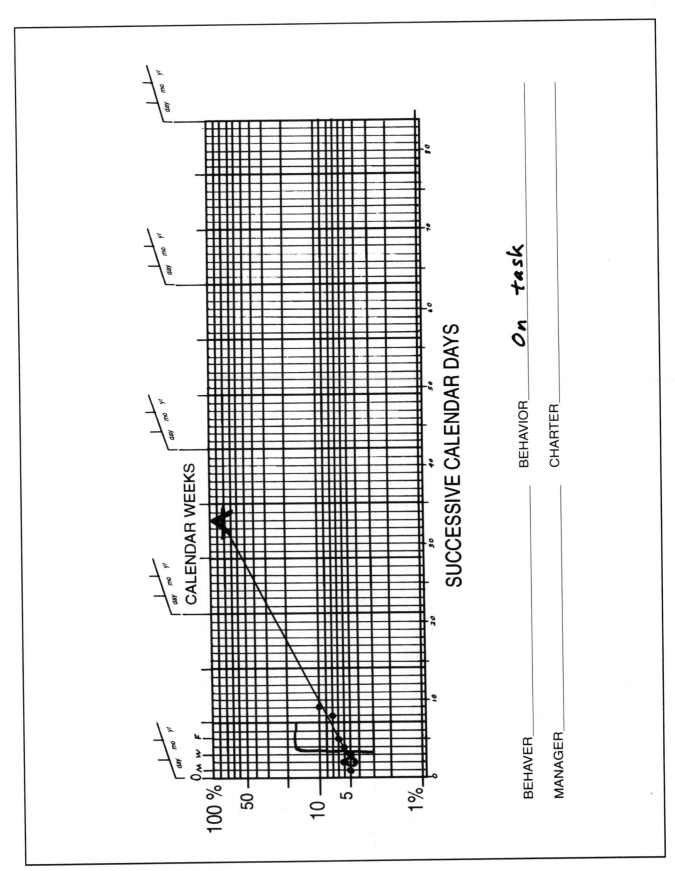

Answer Key for Assessment Chart A (on task).

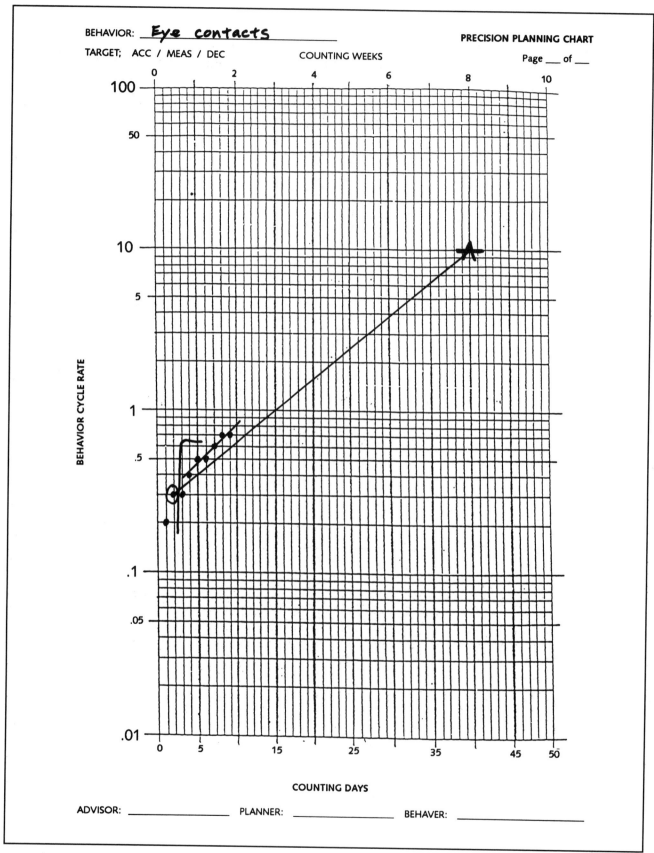

BEHAVIOR: **Eye contacts**

PRECISION PLANNING CHART

TARGET; ACC / MEAS / DEC

COUNTING WEEKS

Page ___ of ___

BEHAVIOR CYCLE RATE

COUNTING DAYS

ADVISOR: _____ PLANNER: _____ BEHAVER: _____

Answer Key for Assessment Chart B (eye contacts).

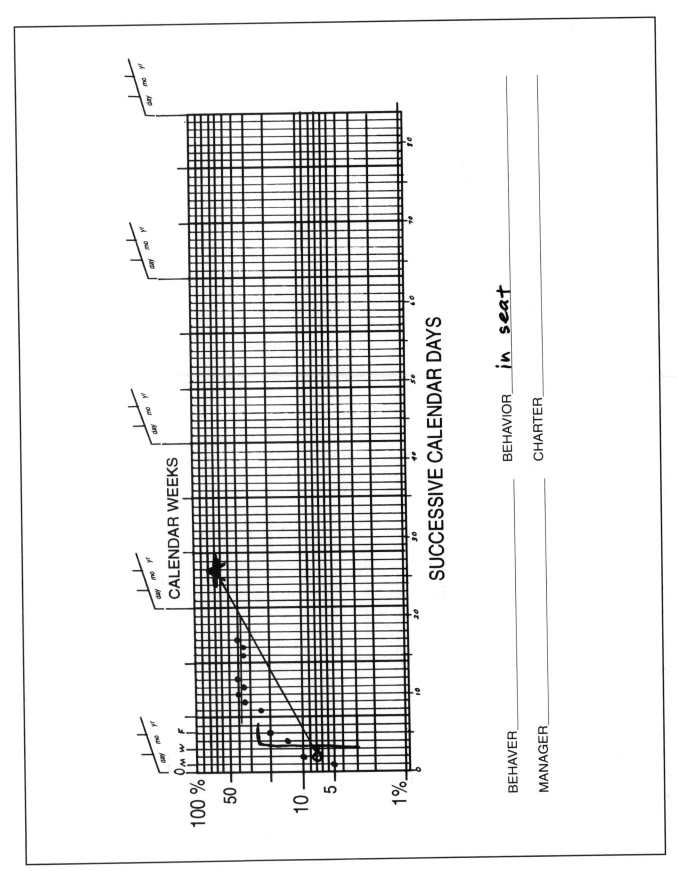

Answer Key for Assessment Chart C (in seat).

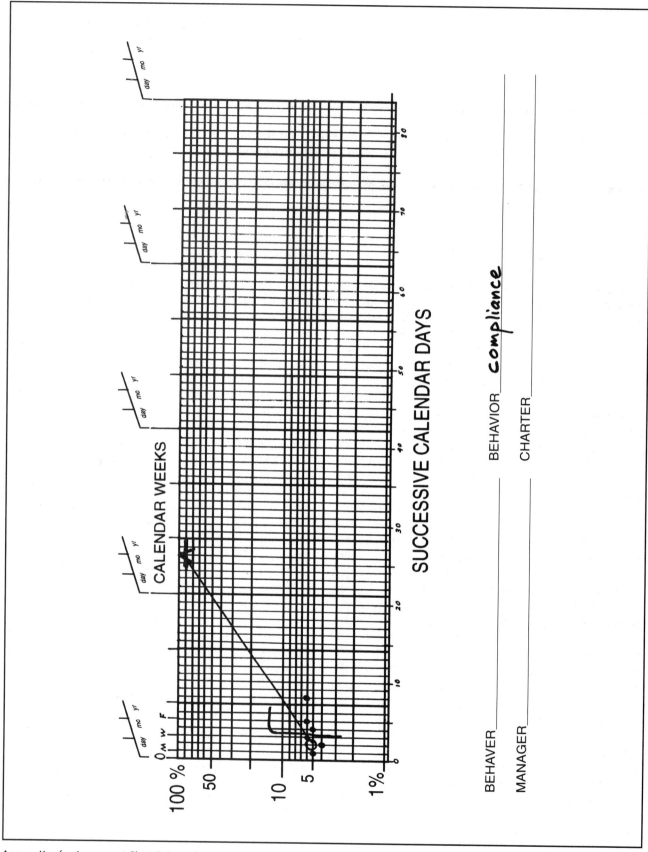

Answer Key for Assessment Chart D (compliance).

Self-Management

Upon successful completion of this chapter, the learner should be able to design self-management programs for various behavior problems.

A RATIONALE

So far, we have been discussing strategies for behavioral interventions in which the teacher is the primary change agent. At some point in time, extrinsic control of student behavior needs to be faded out and responsibility for change given over to the student. There are several reasons for teaching students how to manage their own behavior.

1. *First of all, self-management works.* Research indicates that self-management strategies are effective in changing a wide range of academic and social behaviors among students of varying ages and disabilities (Bolstad & Johnson, 1972; Bowers, Clement, Fantuzzo, & Sorensen, 1985; Brigham, Hill, Hopper, & Adams, 1980; Carr & Punzo, 1993; Drabman, Spitalnik, & O'Leary, 1973; Epstein & Goss, 1978; Felixbrod & O'Leary, 1974; Glomb & West, 1990; Glynn, Thomas, & Shee, 1973; Humphrey, Karoly, & Kirshenbaum, 1978; Kapadia & Fantuzzo, 1988; Kneedler & Hallahan, 1981; Lovitt, 1984; Mahoney & Mahoney, 1976; McKenzie & Rushall, 1974; Minner, 1990; Moletzky, 1974; Neilans, Israel, & Pravder, 1981; Nelson, Lipinski, & Boykin, 1978; Nelson, Smith, Young, & Dodd, 1991; Rhode, Morgan, & Young, 1983; Robertson, Simon, Pachman, & Drabman, 1979; Santograssi, O'Leary, Romanczyk, & Kauffman, 1973; Seymour & Stokes, 1976; Smith, Young, West, Morgan, & Rhode, 1988; Turkewitz, O'Leary, & Ironsmith, 1975; Workman, Helton, & Watson, 1982).

2. *Since students can be successful at changing their own behaviors, it certainly makes good sense for teachers to encourage student-operated interventions, given the obvious savings in time and energy.* A special education teacher with 12 to 15 students in his class could conceivably have *at least* 12 to 15 interventions going on simultaneously. Add to this the time and energy involved in teaching curriculum, plus the bookkeeping (e.g, IEPs, attendance, lunch money, assessment reports, etc.), and you can see

what a boon it would be to have students take over responsibility for their interventions.

3. *Teaching students self-management may lead to enhanced generalization and maintenance of newly learned behavior.* Notice I said "may lead to." The research on the efficacy of self-management in producing generalization and maintenance has yielded mixed results—some positive, others negative (Baer, Stokes, Holman, Fowler, & Rowbury, 1981; Drabman et al., 1973; Rhode et al., 1983; Robertson et al., 1979; Turkewitz et al., 1975). For the most part, maintenance occurs more regularly than does generalization. The latter effect typically does not occur spontaneously and, as in the case with teacher-operated interventions, requires systematic programming. Another typical finding is that self-management programs are more effective when combined with other more conventional approaches such as token reinforcement. Regardless of the equivocal research findings, I still believe that self-management may be a solution to the age-old problem of generalization. Theoretically, once the student becomes the primary change agent in his own intervention, he has, at the very least, the potential to provide whatever is needed to use his newly learned behaviors across settings. From a behavioral standpoint, anything that promises to improve the generalization of behavior is worth trying.

4. *Self-management provides a bridge or transition between extrinsic control and self-control.* Walker (1979) has suggested that the typical two-stage behavior management program illustrated in Figure 9.1 be replaced by the three-stage program shown in Figure 9.2. The current two-stage model has the teacher monitoring and consequating the student's behavior in Stage 1. Assuming the intervention in Stage 1 is successful, what follows is the natural control of student behavior through consequences in the natural environment. The latter would include grades and report cards, teacher and/or peer

PHASE	BASELINE Ø	1	2
Student Behavior	Maladaptive 😈	Target 😇	Target 😇
Management (structured program)	None (or ineffective)	Teacher Operated (e.g., behavior modification program)	None Naturally occurring consequences (e.g., praise, grades, enjoyment of task)

Figure 9.1. Traditional two-phase approach to behavior management.

PHASE	BASELINE Ø	1	2	3
Student Behavior	Maladaptive 😈	Target 😇	Target 😇	Target 😇
Management (structured program)	None (or ineffective)	Teacher Operated (e.g., behavior modification program)	Student (i.e., self) Operated (e.g., behavior modification program)	None Naturally occurring consequences (e.g., praise, grades, enjoyment of task)

Figure 9.2. Walker's three-phase approach to behavior management.

approval, satisfying activities, etc. In the three-stage model, advanced by Walker, a transition phase is inserted between Stages 1 and 2. In the transition phase, the student is made responsible for management of his own behavior. Figures 9.1 and 9.2 illustrate the differences between the two models applied to a hypothetical case. Walker suggests that adding the new Stage 2 (i.e., self-management) would

enhance the probability of success at Stage 3 and improve the overall chances for maintenance and generalization of the newly learned behavior.

5. *There is also some empirical evidence (Bradley & Gaa, 1977; Pawlicki, 1976) that teaching students self-management skills can change their locus of control* (see Figure 9.3). Since so many students with behavior problems have been conditioned to rely on

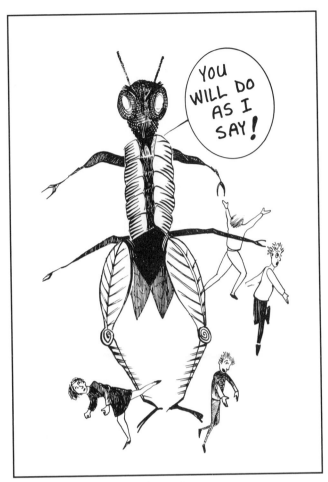

Figure 9.3. The "locus(t)" of control.

external controls such as medication or token economies for much of their school life, it is not surprising that, as a group, they tend toward externality. Educators and learning theorists such as John Dewey (1936) and Robert Gagne (1965) have touted self-reliance as the ultimate goal of education. What better way to teach self-reliance than to train students to manage their own behavior? With self-reliance comes responsibility for one's actions and, consequently, a more internal locus of control.

6. *Finally, it can be argued that training in self-management skills is actually more relevant than many of the other skills we teach our students.* When was the last time you had an occasion to use the Pythagorean Theorem or any of those dates you learned in history class? On the other hand, self-management skills can be used in countless situations during a student's life, both in and out of school.

☑ Checkpoint 9.1

[pages 341–343]

Fill in the answers to the following items (1–6). Check your responses by referring to the text; relevant page numbers appear in brackets.

The six reasons for teaching students self-management skills are:

(1) _____

_____

_____

_____

(2) _____

_____

_____

_____

(3) _____

_____

_____

_____

(4) _____

_____

_____

_____

(5) _____

_____

_____

_____

(6) _____

_____

_____

_____

_____

Redo any items you missed. If you missed more than 1 of the items, reread the material. Otherwise, continue on to the next section.

COMPONENTS

Self-management is also referred to in the literature as "behavioral self-control," "self-regulated behavior management," and "self-directed behavior." Occasionally, the strategy of self-instruction is referred to as self-management. While self-instruction does require the student to act as the primary change agent in changing his behavior and may therefore technically be considered self-management, I prefer to categorize self-instruction as a form of cognitive behavior modification. Regardless of what you call it, self-management typically includes three basic skills: self-assessment (SA), self-monitoring (SM), and self-reinforcement (SR). These skills are not very different from those used in traditional (teacher-operated) behavior modification programs. Instead of the teacher assessing the student's behavior to determine whether or not it should be reinforced, in SA the student assesses his or her own behavior and makes that decision. In SM, the student, not the teacher, monitors his or her progress. Instead of the teacher reinforcing the student as a consequence of his or her behavior, SR requires that the student do it.

For example, let's suppose a student we'll call Hannah is off task 90% of the times observed and is put on a token economy which, initially, is run by her teacher. Since Hannah's teacher is the primary change agent responsible for assessing, rewarding, and monitoring Hannah's on-task behavior, this is a teacher-operated intervention. Hannah is given work she can successfully complete and is told the teacher is going to look at her at different times during the day to see if she is on task. If she is on task, the teacher records a plus in a box on a card in her pocket. *On task* is defined as any one or combination of the following: a) looking at the task, b) doing the task, and/or c) talking about the task with the teacher or a peer. If Hannah is not engaging in any of these behaviors, she is considered off task and her teacher records a zero in a box on the card. At the end of a designated period of time (e.g., class period or school day), the teacher computes Hannah's percentage of on-task behavior; if she has reached the designated goal for the day, she receives a predetermined amount of time to engage in a favored activity. Hannah's on-task behavior improves quickly and a new goal is set for each day until she reaches the overall (IEP) goal of 80%. Eventually, Hannah's teacher finds she no longer has time to run the program. There are too many other students in Hannah's class who are more in need of the teacher's attention. At this point, many teachers stop the teacher-

operated intervention and hope that the student's behavior maintains over time and transfers across settings. Hannah's teacher decides not to risk a relapse and keeps the token economy in place, but gives responsibility for running the program to Hannah. This frees the teacher to work with other students in the class and also increases the chances of maintenance and generalization.

In a student-operated intervention, the student can start out being responsible for all three components (i.e., SA, SM, and SR) or she can take on responsibility for the components one at a time. For example, Hannah's teacher can continue to assess and monitor on-task behavior and only give Hannah the responsibility for dispensing reinforcement. If this situation works out satisfactorily, Hannah can then be given the responsiblity of assessing as well as reinforcing her own behavior while the teacher continues to monitor it. Finally, Hannah can take over all three components. Let's assume Hannah's teacher gives her the responsibility for all three components at the outset. The first thing the teacher does is make sure Hannah understands exactly what constitutes on- and off-task behavior so that she is able to accurately assess whether or not she is engaging in one or the other. Again, on task is defined as any one or combination of a) looking at the task, b) doing the task, c) talking about the task with the teacher or peers; and since Hannah is able to assess her thoughts as well as her behavior, we may include d) thinking task-related thoughts. To help Hannah remember what on- and off-task behavior is, her teacher provides her with a form (see Figure 9.4) to keep on her desk that graphically depicts examples of each type of behavior.

Hannah uses the same signal system as her teacher when she assesses her behavior. A tape recorder on the teacher's desk plays a tape of music. When the music stops, that is the signal for Hannah to assess her current behavior as on- or off-task. Let's say Hannah is signaled approximately 2 minutes after starting work on her math assignment. At that time, Hannah looks at the pictures of on- and off-task behaviors and asks herself if she is on or off task. She decides she is engaging in at least one of the behaviors and marks a plus on her rating sheet (see Figure 9.5). Hannah continues to assess her behavior each time she is signaled by the tape recorder to do so. At the end of the period (or day), she counts the total number of boxes marked and the total number of pluses and computes her percentage of on-task behavior for that period of time (see Figure 9.6). She then compares her attained percentage of on-task behavior with her designated goal. Being at or over

Figure 9.4.   Hannah's "cheat sheet."

NAME _____ DATE _____

ON TASK = +   OFF TASK = O

TOTAL INTERVALS = ____

TOTAL ON TASK (+) = ____

PERCENTAGE ON TASK = ____ %

Figure 9.5.   Hannah's rating sheet (blank).

this goal earns Hannah minutes of free time with a favored activity at the end of the school day. If necessary, a self-punishment component is added in the form of response cost where Hannah loses minutes earned earlier in the day if she begins to slack off during the afternoon. Again, she is responsible for computing the deductions.

Hannah then uses the data from her self-rating form to monitor her progress. She marks the percentage from the form on a chart (see Figure 9.7). This not only helps her and the teacher see how she is progressing, it helps keep her motivated to stay on task.

Cheating

At this point you are probably wondering what would keep students you wouldn't normally turn your back on from cheating. First of all, there is some empirical evidence that contradicts the assumption that students can't be trusted to reinforce themselves without cheating (Workman & Hector, 1978).

In some instances, students responsible for their own behavior management programs were either not giving themselves enough reinforcement or were being too rigorous in their self-assessment (again, see Workman & Hector). Still, if you feel it is necessary, there are ways to keep students honest. You can practice random surveillance and periodically assess student behavior or check the student's records against the amount of reinforcement given. In other words, do an audit—check the books from time to time. When you find discrepancies in the student's favor, fine him. On the other hand, when you find that he has been running an honest program, give him a bonus. Show him honesty pays. If you don't have the time to practice this surveillance you

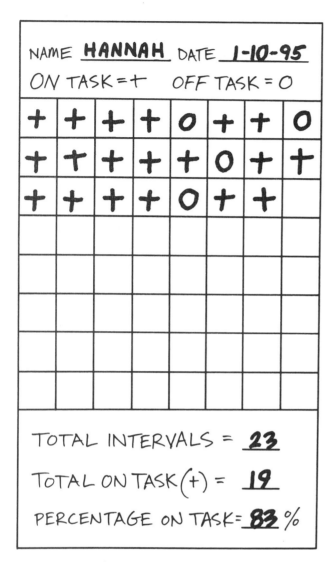

NAME **HANNAH** DATE **1-10-95**

ON TASK = +   OFF TASK = 0

+	+	+	+	0	+	+	0
+	+	+	+	+	0	+	+
+	+	+	+	0	+	+	

TOTAL INTERVALS = __23__

TOTAL ON TASK (+) = __19__

PERCENTAGE ON TASK = __83__ %

Figure 9.6. Hannah's rating sheet (completed).

dent's data shows he made 15 compliments during a given period of time but your data shows he made only 10 compliments. Simply divide the big number (15) into the little number (10) to get the percentage of "interobserver" agreement. In this case, the interobserver agreement is 67 percent. This is not very good, especially since the student's data shows him giving more compliments than he actually gave. In this case, you should "fine" the student for his overrecording. On the other hand, if the student counts 10 compliments and you count 15, you need to find out why he underrecorded. Did he forget to monitor his behavior? Is he starting to internalize his behavior to the extent that he no longer needs extrinsic rewards? Is he confused about what constitutes a compliment? Don't penalize the student, but do try to find out why there is a discrepancy between your data and his. I would not be overly concerned about discrepancies of 20% or less; with everything that goes on in a classroom, you can expect to miss one or two behaviors. If you want to be absolutely accurate, you cannot simply compare data totals. You have to compare individual recordings. This requires that you record the frequency of behaviors within specified intervals. For example, you observe the student for ten 1-minute intervals and record the number of compliments he gives in each interval. Have the student do the same and then compare each of your intervals with each of his. Figure 9.8 illustrates this process. The teacher recorded one compliment given in the first, third, seventh, ninth, and tenth intervals. The student recorded one compliment given in the first, second, third, sixth, tenth, twelfth, and fifteenth intervals. If you only look at the data totals, both the teacher and the student recorded the same total number of compliments given: five. That's 100% agreement. Not bad. On the other hand, if you compare individual recordings, you get a very different picture of interobserver reliability. As you can see from Figure 9.8, the teacher's data and the student's data agree on the first, third, fourth, fifth, eighth, and tenth intervals, but disagree on the second, sixth, seventh, and ninth. If you add the total agreements (6) to the total disagreements (4) and divide that sum (10) into the total agreements (and multiply by 100), you get 60% interobserver reliability. The student may not be cheating, since his total for compliments recorded is the same as yours, but he certainly isn't recording data accurately. On two occasions it appears that he did not record compliments he made. Yet on two other occasions, he recorded compliments he apparently did not make. Did he do this on purpose? Was he confused? Did he forget? It's your job to find out.

might merely suggest that you are going to do it. Planting the idea that Big Brother (or Sister) is watching can be just as effective as actually watching (Hundert & Bastone, 1978).

To determine whether or not your student is being honest, you need to monitor his behavior and compare your data with his. For example, let's suppose the student is monitoring his complimenting behavior. Each time he says something to another person that meets the criteria for a compliment, he makes a mark on a piece of tape on his wrist. At the end of the day, he counts the number of compliments given and charts it as raw score. If you want to make sure he wasn't cheating (i.e., marking compliments he did not make), *you* need to count the number of compliments he makes and compare your data at the end of the day with his data. Let's suppose the stu-

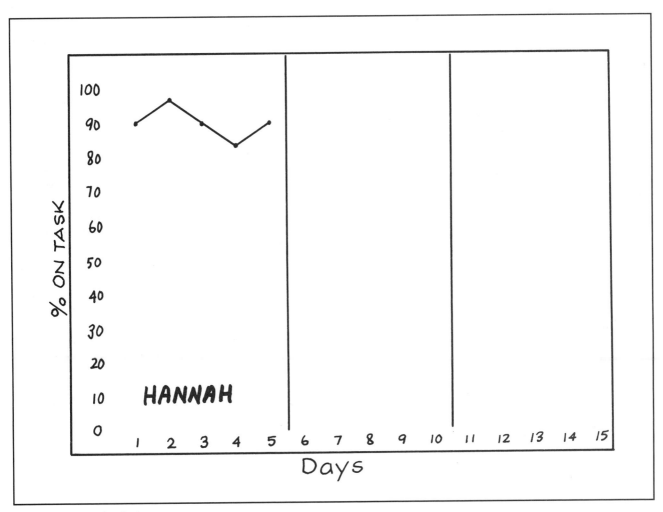

Figure 9.7. Hannah's chart.

Minutes	1	2	3	4	5	6	7	8	9	10	Total C
Teacher	C	0	C	0	0	0	C	0	C	C	5
	+		+	+	+			+		+	
Student	C	C	C	0	0	C	0	0	0	C	5

Key: C = *gives compliment*; 0 = *gives no compliment*; + = *agreements*

$$\frac{\text{agreements}}{\text{agreements} + \text{disagreements}} \quad = \quad \frac{6}{10} \quad = \quad .60 \times 100 = 60\%$$

Figure 9.8. Interobserver reliability.

✔ Checkpoint 9.2

[pages 344–347]

Fill in the answers to the following items (1–6). Check your responses by referring to the text; relevant page numbers appear in brackets.

Name and describe each of the three components of self-management.

(1) _____

_____

_____

_____ [344].

(2) _____

_____

_____

_____ [344].

(3) _____

_____

_____

_____ [344].

Three ways you can keep students from cheating in a self-management program are:

(4) _____

_____

_____

(5) _____

_____

_____

(6) _____

_____

_____[345–346]

Redo any items you missed. If you missed more than 1 item, reread the material. Otherwise, continue on to the next section.

OPERATION

Although the following self-management skills are not listed in any special order, I recommend that you a) introduce (i.e., teach and let the student use) them one at a time, and b) introduce first the skill you believe the student would have the least difficulty learning and using, and introduce last the skill he might have the most difficulty with.

Self-Assessment

In self-assessment (SA), the first step is to *select a target behavior*. In other words, sit down with the student and identify and specify the maladaptive and fair-pair target behavior. If the student-operated intervention follows a teacher-operated intervention, this will already have been done. It is important that the student be involved in the process, especially when the so what? test is applied. The student should understand why her behavior is maladaptive and why it is in her best interests to engage in the target behavior. The behavior should also be pinpointed so that it passes the stranger test and so that the student has no problem recognizing the behavior when she engages in it. If necessary, use pictures as examples of appropriate and inappropriate behaviors. These may be drawn by the student, or you can use some Polaroid snapshots.

The second step in teaching the student how to self-assess his behavior is to *devise a rating system*. The rating system refers to the process by which the student will assess, evaluate and/or rate her behavior. It must include a description of what she does and how and when she does it. Be sure you involve the student in the process. She is the one who is going to have to use the system. Getting the student's input in devising the system, or any other component in the program, will improve the chances of her understanding how it works as well as her willingness to cooperate and use it. Again, if you are following a teacher-operated intervention, don't "reinvent the wheel"; simply use the rating system already in place. If it is too complex for the student to use, don't dump it—simply make some modifications in it until the student can use it and you can still have confidence in its reliability.

The third step in the process of SA is to *design and produce any of the rating forms (or other materials)* the student may be required to use. An excellent source for rating forms is Workman (1982). In addition to pencil and paper forms, you may need to produce a signal that will cue the student to assess her behavior. One idea is to make a tape recording of a sound (e.g., a beep) emitted at varying intervals. I have had good success using the hold timer signal on a microwave oven. The obvious advantage of using a prerecorded signal is that the student can't predict when it will be emitted.

Next, *list all of the steps* the student will follow in assessing her own behavior. This is essentially an operationally defined task analysis. What she does first, second, third and so on. Finally, *explain and model* these steps for the student. This is probably the most critical part of the process. If the student does not understand when and how she is to assess her own behavior, she will either do it incorrectly or not at all. Make sure you use vocabulary that the student can understand. Use a direct teaching approach. Get feedback from the student to make sure that she heard you, understood what you said, and can do what you want her to.

Self-Monitoring

The first step in self-monitoring (SM) is to *pinpoint the target behavior*. Use the same procedure here as you do in a teacher-operated intervention. Describe the behavior you want the student to monitor so that it passes the stranger test. Make sure the student understands what aspect of his behavior he is recording. In most instances, it will be less complicated if the student simply records frequency of response. So, even if you want him to spend more time engaged in a target behavior such as in seat or on task, you can have him record the number of times (i.e., intervals) he rated his behavior as in seat or on task when cued to do so. If the number of intervals change daily, make sure he understands he will need to summarize his data as percentage. Make sure he knows how to compute percentage. Don't take anything for granted. He won't cooperate if he doesn't understand what to do or how to do it.

Next, *set the intervention goals*. What percentage of the time should he be in seat or on task? What percentage of assignments should he complete? What percentage accuracy should he strive for? How many times should he use "socially appropriate" language (i.e., without using threats or swear words) in communicating with the teacher or a peer? These may be the same as you used in your teacher-operated intervention or they may be renegotiated with the student. It is important that the student know what he is aiming for so that he can monitor his progress daily.

Next, *design and produce the necessary forms,* such as the observation and recording (O & R) form and the data display or chart. In many instances, the O & R form could be the same as the rating form on which he assesses his behavior. Check Workman (1982) for examples of O & R forms and data displays. Finally, *list the steps* that the student will follow in monitoring his own behavior and *explain and model them* for him.

Self-Reinforcement

The first step in self-reinforcement (SR) is to *determine the reinforcer*. Again, if your student-operated intervention follows a teacher-operated program, you might simply continue using the same reinforcer. The process for determining a reinforcer is no different than that used in the teacher-operated intervention (i.e., interview, observation, interest inventory). Next, *determine the contingencies*. In other words, how much of the target behavior must the student engage in to earn X amount of reinforcement? Again, this can be negotiated with the student. Finally, *list the steps* in the process and *explain and model* for the student.

Self-reinforcement does not always have to involve a tangible reinforcer. There is some evidence that covert positive reinforcement can be effective in self-management programs with students (Krop, Calhoun, & Verrier, 1971). Most of us have used covert reinforcement at one time or another. When we are tired of running we push ourselves to run one more mile or one more lap by thinking of how good we will feel when we finish, or fantasizing finishing or even winning an upcoming race, or imagining ourselves slim, trim, and fit and all the admiring glances and comments we will receive from others. Your students can use covert reinforcement to strengthen their behavior. Have your students think of a fantasy that is particularly pleasing to them that is tied to the behavior they want to strengthen. For example, a student who is failing in school and is using self-management to strengthen task completion might fantasize himself earning passing grades in school, bringing home a good report card, and getting some tangible reinforcement from his family such as an increased allowance or some long-coveted privilege(s). Another student who is shy and using self-management to strengthen spontaneous speaking might fantasize herself enjoying the company of new friends. In each case, the fantasy serves as the reward and is contingent upon the attainment of a prespecified goal. The failing student only gets to indulge in his fantasy if he completes a prespecified number of assignments. The shy student only gets to indulge in her fantasy if she engages in spontaneous speaking a prespecified number of times. The fantasy does not always have to be tied to the target behavior. A student who enjoys thinking about baseball, or fishing, or being in a favorite place, or just daydreaming about nothing in particular can use covert reinforcement to strengthen his behavior as long as the visual imagery is made contingent upon the emission of the target behavior. A student could actually have a number of fantasies and choose one from a "menu" of reinforcing fantasies. Actually, the student doesn't have to use a fantasy. He can use positive self-talk as a covert reinforcer. These not only reinforce but function as affirmations that lead to new thinking. For example, the failing student can repeat "This task was hard but I did it," "I can succeed if I try," and "I'm smart" several times upon completing a task. The shy student might use phrases such as "It was hard but I did it—I spoke first," "I didn't sound afraid—I sounded good!" or "They liked it—They smiled at me," after she engages in spontaneous speech with another person.

☑ Checkpoint 9.3

[pages 348–350]

Fill in the answers to the following items (1–15). Check your responses by referring to the text; relevant page numbers appear in brackets.

Describe each of the steps in the self-management process. Provide enough detail so that someone not familiar with the process (e.g., parent or substitute teacher) could use it.

Self-Assessment (SA)

(1) _____

_____

_____

_____

(2) _____

_____

_____

_____

(3) _____

_____

_____

_____

(4) _____

_____

_____

_____

(5) _____

_____

_____

_____ [348–349].

Self-Monitoring (SM)

(6) _____

_____

_____

_____

(7) _____

_____

_____

_____

(continues)

CHECKPOINT 9.3, continued

(8) _____
_____
_____
_____

(9) _____
_____
_____
_____

(10) _____
_____
_____
_____ [349].

Self-Reinforcement (SR)

(11) _____
_____
_____
_____

(12) _____
_____
_____
_____

(13) _____
_____
_____
_____

(14) _____
_____
_____
_____

(15) _____
_____
_____
_____ [349–350].

Redo any items you missed. If you missed more than 3 items, reread the material. Otherwise, continue on to the next section.

TEACHING SELF-MANAGEMENT

Just as teacher-operated interventions require some basic competencies of the teacher (e.g., monitoring, assessing, and reinforcing behavior), student-operated intervention requires the student to acquire the same competencies if he or she is to operate a successful intervention. How do students learn these competencies? The same way teachers learn—someone teaches them. In the case of the students, that "someone" is you, the teacher. Self-management competencies should be taught the same way you would teach the student reading, writing, or arithmetic competencies. Here are some specific guidelines to follow.

1. *Teach in small amounts.* Don't teach self-assessment, self-monitoring, and self-reinforcement all at the same time. If necessary, break down a component and teach parts of it. For example, if you were going to teach self assessment, you might break it down into small steps, such as:

a. set timer without looking and place in pocket or desk

b. begin work on assigned task

c. when timer rings, decide if you are on task (e.g., looking at task, thinking about task, talking about task, doing task) or off task (e.g., not looking, thinking, or talking about or doing task)

d. if yes (on task), mark a + (plus) on score card; if no, mark a 0 (zero) on card

When you teach the student to do self-assessment, you would first teach Step A, setting the timer without looking at how much time it is set for. If the student has difficulty learning Step A, break it down into even smaller parts, such as: setting the timer while looking at it, and *then* setting the timer without looking at it.

2. *Teach to the fluency level.* Most learning in schools occurs at the acquisition level. Students are taught content and are required to demonstrate learning by giving accurate responses to structured questions. For example, we teach the child his "plus ones" (e.g., 4 + 1 = 5) and then test him to see how much he has learned. If he is accurate, despite being slow, we assume he has learned the content and then move on to new content. Students who are taught content at the fluency level, where they are accurate *and fast*, retain more of what they have learned, transfer what they have learned to other settings and situations, and choose to use what they have learned

to a much greater extent than do students merely taught at the acquisition (accurate but slow) level (White, 1986). This is especially important when you are teaching complex (i.e., multi-step) tasks such as self-assessment, self-monitoring, and self-reinforcement. Teach one step at a time and do not move on to the next step until the student has demonstrated fluency at the preceding step. For example, you might give the timer to the student and give him directions to "set the timer" on three separate occasions. If the student is able to set the timer without looking at it and place it in his pocket or desk within an acceptable period of time (e.g., 5 seconds) on each of the three trials, I would assume that he has mastered this step and would move on to Step B.

3. *Use chaining.* Remember the discussion of chaining in Chapter 6? Chaining is particularly useful when you are teaching tasks with multiple steps. Using the example above (#1), you would teach your student Step A; and when he can perform at the fluency level, move on to Step B. However, before you introduce Step B, have your student perform Step A. Teach Step B, and when your student can perform it at the fluency level, move on to Step C. Before you introduce Step C, have your student perform Steps A and B in sequence. Teach Step C, and when your student is able to perform it at the fluency level, move on to Step D. Before introducing Step D, have your student perform Steps A through C in sequence. Teach Step D, and when your student can perform it

at the fluency level, have him go through all of the steps, A through D, in sequence. This method of teaching will help the student remember all of the steps in the sequence since each step (i.e., link) in the behavior chain will serve as a stimulus for the next step.

4. *Always request feedback.* Don't assume that the student understands you, or is even listening to you, just because he is looking at you and shaking his head. Request feedback. Ask questions. "How do you know if you are paying attention?" Have the student model the behavior you have just demonstrated. "Show me how you mark your rating form." Provide lots of stimulus–response units. Stimulus–response units are composed of a preceding stimulus (e.g., "Show me how you compute the percentage of on-task behavior.") followed by a response (e.g., student computes percentage correctly) followed by a consequence (e.g., "That's right!"). Research on effective instruction shows that the more task-specific stimulus–response units you provide the student during instruction, the more learning (i.e., higher achievement) takes place.

5. *Watch your vocabulary.* Either use vocabulary you know the student has heard before and understands, or teach and/or review vocabulary ahead of time. Terms you might wish to teach or substitute for include *self-management, self-assessment, self-monitoring, self-reinforcement, graph* or *chart, plot, rating form, goal, reinforcer* or *reward,* and *compute,* among others.

✔ Checkpoint 9.4

[pages 351–352]

Fill in the answers to the following items (1–5). Check your responses by referring to the text; relevant page numbers appear in brackets.

State and explain each of the guidelines to follow in teaching a student how to manage his or her own behavior. Use examples.

(1) _____

_____

_____

_____

(2) _____

_____

_____

_____

(3) _____

_____

_____

_____

(4) _____

_____

_____

_____

(5) _____

_____

_____

_____

Redo any items you missed. If you missed more than 1 item, reread the material. Otherwise, continue on to the next section.

GRANDMA'S RULE

So far, we have been talking about self-management in the context of a transitional phase between teacher-operated interventions and the internalization (and maintenance) of behavior. This is not the only way to use self-management. For years, parents and teachers have been telling children they could change their behavior if they just had more will-power. No wonder kids give up! We parents and teachers have made it sound as if the only way one can change is to have been blessed (i.e., born) with some magical trait—a blessing obviously not bestowed on these particular children. These students don't need *will*power; they need *skill*power. They need to *know how* to change. One simple self-management skill you can teach them is how to apply "Grandma's rule." Grandma's rule (see Figure 9.9) says "children who don't eat their vegetables don't get any dessert" (or words to that effect). Grandmas understand that for most children, eating vegetables is a low-frequency activity while eating dessert is a high-frequency activity. In other words, left on their own, children will spend more time eating desserts than they will eating vegetables. However, when children are required to eat their vegetables in order to get their dessert, vegetable-eating behavior increases in frequency. If Grandma's rule sounds familiar, it should. It's based on the Premack principle discussed in Chapter 5: When a high-frequency behavior is made contingent upon the emission of a low-frequency behavior, the low-frequency behavior increases in frequency (Premack, 1959). Your goal is to get your students to use Grandma's rule by themselves to modify their own behavior (i.e., to increase low-frequency responses). You want them to start making high-frequency behaviors (e.g., TV watching) contingent upon low-frequency behaviors (e.g., doing homework) so that the low-frequency behaviors will increase in frequency.

How can you get students to voluntarily use Grandma's rule? First, explain what Grandma's rule is. The rule may be stated any number of ways, depending on the age and cognitive ability of your students. For example, it might be expressed as, "When I do something I *don't* like doing, then I may do something I *do* like doing," or it could be stated simply as "Business before pleasure" or "Work before play." Relate specific examples of how people have used Grandma's rule to change their behavior. Use yourself as an example—you've probably used Grandma's rule at least once in your life to change a behavior; maybe some of your students have, too.

Figure 9.9. Grandma's rule.

Even if you have used Grandma's rule, it's possible that you've never heard of David Premack or heard the rule formally stated before. It's a good bet your students haven't heard of David Premack. Still, that need not preclude either you or them from using the Premack principle. What you want to do in this first stage is to get your students to know the rule and understand how it works.

Second, have your students brainstorm high- and low-frequency activities. Try to limit these to school-related activities. For example, a student-generated list of *low-frequency* school-related activities might include reading, doing classwork, sitting at desk, answering questions, having to share, doing math, doing homework, typing, practicing music, having to read aloud, taking group showers, going to science class, doing what the teacher says, etc. Examples of high-frequency school-related activities might include going to recess, eating lunch, doing silent reading, talking with friends, playing video games, shooting baskets in PE, listening to music, being a messenger or doing errands, etc.

Third, when your students have generated a list of high- and low-frequency behaviors, have them choose one behavior from the low-frequency list they would like to change into a high-frequency behavior. Some of your students might want to increase the frequency of completing assignments or answering questions or time spent studying for tests. Next, have them pick a behavior from the high-frequency list that they are willing to use as a payoff for engaging in the low-frequency behavior. For example, students might use an easy task (e.g., reading) as a reward for doing a difficult task (e.g., math). You can take it one step further and have them contract with themselves (see Figure 9.10).

The final stage, of course, is to get your students to actually implement Grandma's rule. You can keep them accountable by having them relate to you and their peers on a daily basis how they used Grandma's rule in your class, in school, or outside of school. In the beginning, you might want to use some extrinsic reinforcement to strengthen their use of Grandma's rule, at least until they realize how effective it is in changing their own behavior and they experience the intrinsic thrill of being able to perceive the changes they have brought about in themselves.

I, _Jerry Jones_ promise that before I _go outside to recess today (at 11 AM)_,
    (Student)   (Hi-F behavior)

I will _finish my assignments in math and reading_.
        (Lo-F behavior)

Signed _Jerry Jones_   Date _5/1/95_

Witnessed by _Mr. Augustine_   Date _5-1-95_

Figure 9.10. Student contract for use in self-management program.

☑ Checkpoint 9.5

[pages 353–354]

Fill in the answers to the following items (1–16). Check your responses by referring to the text; relevant page numbers appear in brackets.

Grandma's rule (the Premack principle) is:

(1) _____

_____

_____

_____ [353].

Examples of high-frequency behaviors in students are

(2–6): _____

_____

_____

_____

_____

_____

_____

_____

_____

Examples of low-frequency behaviors in students are

(7–11): _____

_____

_____

_____

_____

_____

_____

(continues)

CHECKPOINT 9.5, continued

List and describe the steps in using the Premack principle as if you were describing them for another person (e.g., instructional assistant, student teacher, substitute, parent) who would be using it.

(12) _____

_____

_____

_____

(13) _____

_____

_____

_____

(14) _____

_____

_____

(15) _____

_____

_____

(16) _____

_____

_____ [353–354].

Redo any items you missed. If you missed more than 3 of the items, reread the material. Otherwise, continue on to the Chapter Assessment.

ASSESSMENT / CHAPTER 9

A list of acceptable responses appears following the Assessment.

Design a student-operated intervention for each of the cases described in the following items. Be sure to include all three of the essential components as well as all of the necessary materials.

1. You have a student who interrupts you whenever you are talking with or helping another student. She demands to have your attention immediately. You implement a teacher-operated intervention that is successful in getting her to wait until you are ready to attend to her. However, you realize that you are not always going to be around to help her engage in appropriate attention-seeking behavior. Design a student-operated intervention that will enable her to help herself in this area.

2. You have a student who constantly teases and makes fun of his peers, saying things such as "That's stupid" and "You're retarded." You successfully implement a teacher-operated intervention that results in his making five times as many positive comments (e.g., "That's a good idea," "You're good at that stuff") as negative comments to his peers. Design a student-operated intervention that will enable this student to maintain the change in his behavior even when you are not around to help him with it.

3. Design a student-operated intervention, using the Premack principle, to help a student who procrastinates and seldom turns in assigned work to complete his assignments on time.

ACCEPTABLE RESPONSES

The following examples of self-management programs are presented as possible ideas. It's OK if your programs don't match mine; the important thing is that you include all of the necessary components, your steps are simple, and they make sense.

1.0 student who interrupts

EXAMPLE

1.1 *Self-assessment (SA)*

1.1.1   Target behavior: Student will wait until teacher is not engaged with (i.e., talking or listening to) a person or persons other than the student before trying to verbally and/or physically engage the teacher.

1.1.2   Rating system: Student self-assesses by asking herself two questions: (1) Is teacher already engaged? (i.e., is she talking or listening to someone; she is listening to someone if she is looking at a person who is speaking to her), and (2) Did I wait until she was not engaged before trying to engage her?

1.1.3   Rating form: Piece of masking tape on student's wrist.

1.1.4   Steps:
 a) When you want teacher attention, locate teacher
 b) Decide if she is engaged (talking or listening to person or persons)
 c) If she is not engaged, you may try to engage her by speaking; do not record on tape
 d) If she is engaged, mark circle on tape
 e) If you try to engage teacher while she is already engaged, mark "I" inside of circle (for "interrupt")
 f) If you wait until she has disengaged before you try and engage her, mark "W" inside of circle (for "waits")

1.2 *Self-monitoring (SM)*

1.2.1   Pinpoint: *Waits* for teacher to disengage with another person (i.e., teacher is looking at a person who is speaking to her or she is speaking to another person); *interrupts* teacher (i.e., talks to and/or touches teacher while she is engaged with another person)

1.2.2   Intervention goals: 80% waits (20% interrupts)

1.2.3   Forms: Use wrist tape (see above) and data display

1.2.4   Steps:
 a) Mark circle on tape if teacher is already engaged
 b) If you wait until she has disengaged before trying to engage teacher, mark "W" inside circle
 c) If you try to engage teacher before she has disengaged, mark "I" inside circle
 d) Compute percentage of "waits to engage" by dividing total Ws by sum of total Ws and total Is
 e) Plot percentage on data display

1.3 *Self-reinforcement (SR)*

1.3.1   Determine reinforcer (whatever you want)

1.3.2   Determine the contingencies (e.g., 80% waits)

1.3.3   Steps:
 a) Decide on goal (percentage) for the day and use as contingency for reward;
 b) At end of observation period, decide if goal met;
 c) If yes, give self-reward; if no, withhold reward

2.0 student who teases

EXAMPLE

2.1 *Self-assessment (SA)*

2.1.1 Target behavior: Student will make positive comments to peers (e.g., "That's a good idea," "You're good at that stuff")

2.1.2 Rating system: Student will mark + (plus) for each positive comment and – (minus) for each negative comment he makes to peer

2.1.3 Rating form: Masking tape on student's wrist

2.1.4 Steps:
   a) Student makes comment to peer;
   b) Student decides if comment is compliment (i.e., student says something positive about peer) or insult (i.e., student says something negative about peer);
   c) Student marks + (plus) on tape if compliment and – (minus) on tape if insult

2.2 *Self-monitoring (SM)*

2.2.1 Pinpoint: Student makes complimentary statement to peer (e.g., "That's a good idea," Or "You're good at that stuff") or insulting comment to peer (e.g., "That's a dumb idea," or "You're stupid")

2.2.2 Intervention goals: Ratio of compliments to insults is five to one

2.2.3 Forms: Use wrist tape (see above) and data display

2.2.4 Steps:
   a) When communicating with peers, mark + (plus) on tape if compliment given and – (minus) if insult given;
   b) At end of counting period, compute percentage of compliments given by dividing sum of + (plus signs) and – (minus signs) into total + (plus signs);
   c) Plot percentage on data display

2.3 *Self-reinforcement (SR)*

2.3.1 Reinforcer: Whatever

2.3.2 Contingencies: Percentage of negatives should not exceed 20% of total positive and negative statements

2.3.3 Steps:
   a) Decide on goal for day and use as contingency for reward;
   b) At end of observation period, decide if goal is met;
   c) If yes, give self-reward; if no, withhold reward

3.0 student who procrastinates
Choose any program in which the student uses low-frequency behavior (e.g., completing school work) as the contingency for engaging in high-frequency behavior (e.g., watching TV, engaging in hobby, playing outside).

CHAPTER TEN

Social Skills Training

by Jane Carter

Upon successful completion of this chapter, the learner should be able to:

1. Identify the seven steps in the social skills training sequence;

2. Understand the purpose of each step in the sequence;

3. Identify tasks associated with each step; and

4. Understand the types of social skills problems and interventions associated with each problem type.

Numerous studies have presented compelling evidence regarding long-term negative effects of social incompetence. Results suggest that children displaying social skills deficits experience school failure as youngsters as well as other interpersonal problems which persist into adulthood (Goldstein, 1988; Jensen, Sloane, & Young, 1988). Most educators have witnessed the peer rejection experienced by those children who fail to develop adequate social competence. In fact, educators often respond to social incompetence in students by referring them for psychological evaluation and eventual placement into special programs. Therefore, it can be argued that appropriate social skills development is a condition for school success and remaining in general education environments (Knoff, 1988).

Due to the relationship between social competence and school success, effective social skills interventions may ultimately affect the student's educational placement as well as improve the student's academic and interpersonal success (Gresham, 1981). In particular, for those students placed in special education programs, developing effective social skills should increase their success in mainstreaming and facilitate reintegration into general education settings. Adequate prosocial skills may also facilitate transition of at-risk preschool children into public school settings. Therefore, all special education students as well as children at risk for school failure should receive direct and systematic interventions designed to enhance social competence and develop prosocial behaviors.

UNDERSTANDING SOCIAL COMPETENCE

The professional literature continues to debate the distinction between *social competence* and *social skills*. However, sufficient similarity exists between various authors' arguments to allow us to draw some conclusions that are helpful to educators. Social competence is best described as an individual's global, comprehensive ability to effectively select and successfully apply social skills in social situations (Knoff, 1988). Social skills, on the other hand, are the discreet social behaviors or processes that combine to make up one's social competence (see Figure 10.1). As educators, our ultimate goal should be to promote not only specific social skills but to emphasize the individual's ability to apply social skills, which is the expression of social competence.

Michelson, Sugai, Wood, and Kazdin (1983) describe social skills as a) skills that are learned through observation, modeling, rehearsal, and feedback; b) discreet verbal and nonverbal behaviors; c) including both initiation and response skills; d) behaviors that result in positive social outcomes and reinforcement; e) skills that are interactive by their

Figure 10.1. Examples of social skills.

attempting to provide social skills interventions, educators often rely upon commercially available social skills curriculum materials. Unfortunately, relying on curriculum materials alone may result in implementation of training designed to meet recommendations of the publishers rather than specific needs of socially deficient learners.

A teaching model based on applied behavior analysis is applicable to social skills training (Wolery, Bailey, & Sugai, 1988). Steps in this model include a) identification of an overall objective, b) assessment of the problem, c) development of specific learning goals, d) planning and implementing the intervention, e) monitoring student progress or performance, and f) evaluating student performance. This chapter has been designed to expand on each step in an applied behavior analysis teaching model and apply the steps specifically to social skills training. By implementing the step-by-step social skills training sequence presented here, educators will be able to efficiently develop and implement effective, comprehensive social skills training programs. The process described here includes multimethod and socially valid techniques for assessment of deficient skills that draw upon information from others in the child's environment. Social skills interventions described here include direct instruction, which provides learners with specific information on how and when to use a certain skill. Finally, strategies for systematic evaluation that validate socially important changes in behavior are presented.

nature; f) behaviors that are situationally specific or are influenced by the characteristics of the immediate environment; and g) skills that may be successfully and systematically influenced by social skills interventions.

Once we understand and agree that social skills problems may be ameliorated through teacher-directed interventions, the interventionist must determine the most effective and efficient means to employ. Time can be an enemy to children displaying insufficient social competence. Children and educators have limited time available, in terms of hours during a school day as well as years of schooling, with which to intervene. Therefore, the strategies presented in this chapter, which are designed to enhance effectiveness and efficiency, should be of assistance to educators.

SOCIAL SKILLS INTERVENTIONS

Many educators recognize the importance of targeting and improving children's prosocial behavior. In

SOCIAL SKILLS TRAINING SEQUENCE

Social skills are generally defined as those behaviors an individual engages in which produce predictable, positive outcomes for the individual, such as positive adult regard and peer acceptance (Jensen et al., 1988; Kerr & Nelson, 1989). Social competence refers to an individual's general ability to employ prosocial behaviors in specific situations using social judgment (Hops, 1983; Kerr & Nelson, 1989; Knoff, 1988). Our goal as educators should be to go beyond discrete skill development. We should endeavor to develop and implement training strategies that result in socially competent individuals. It should be our ultimate goal that the students we work with will be able to use the skills they learn in novel and demanding situations, just as we might teach reading in a manner so that children can apply their reading skills to a variety of situations from reading books to reading signs. Therefore, all social skills interventions should result in socially valid changes in child behavior. Socially valid changes in behavior will enable children to function competently in a variety of social situations and in a variety of settings.

Various authors suggest that educators employ methods which are similar to academic instruction when teaching social skills (Carter & Sugai, 1988; Rathjen, 1984). For example, the applied behavior analysis teaching model (Wolery et al., 1988) suggests that educators begin by identifying an overall goal that describes either a problem statement (e.g., the student needs to develop peer interaction skills), or a statement describing inappropriate behaviors that interfere with prosocial behavior (e.g., the student will reduce aggressive behavior toward peers). Once a general problem statement or description has been generated, the educator needs to gather assessment information regarding the student's actual performance. When an educator has identified a goal statement and determined the present level of performance, a specific learning objective should be developed (e.g., the student will use age-appropriate greeting skills toward peers). Analysts of applied behavior suggest that teaching strategies should be implemented after the educator has identified specific skills to teach. When the intervention has been developed and implemented, teachers should assess student learning over time to determine a student's rate of learning or progress, as well as to determine whether to modify an instructional intervention. Applied behavior analysis is particularly helpful as a model when teaching social skills, because social skills trainers, like behavior analysts, should be concerned not only with developing specific skills but also with ensuring functional use of skills by children as they interact with their environment.

When the applied behavior analysis teaching model is expanded to include social skills training, a similar process emerges. Specifically, steps in the social skills training sequence are: a) describe the problem behavior, b) determine the problem type, c) develop a teaching plan, d) identify curriculum materials and learning activities, e) identify relevant role-play topics, f) develop measurement strategies, g) implement teaching strategies, and h) evaluate effectiveness. (See Figure 10.2.)

Describing the Problem Behavior(s)

Unfortunately, in anticipation of developing a social skills training program, some practitioners turn first to selecting curriculum materials. Social

---

SOCIAL SKILLS TRAINING SEQUENCE

Step One: Describe the problem behavior(s)

Step Two: Determine the problem type

Step Three: Develop a teaching plan

Step Four: Identify curriculum materials and learning activities

Step Five: Identify relevant situations for teaching and role plays

Step Six: Develop measurement strategies

Step Seven: Implement teaching strategies

Figure 10.2. Social skills training sequence.

---

skills training packages may appear at first glance to be quite comprehensive and thoroughly prepared, and, therefore, effective. However, experienced teachers of academic skills recognize the importance of matching student needs to curriculum materials. In fact, many teachers often begin a program of academic skill remediation by identifying student strengths and weaknesses. Effective teachers will assess student skills and subsequently develop and implement a remediation program. Likewise, more effective social skills training programs begin by evaluating the student's social skills strengths and weaknesses and developing an objective description or statement of the problems identified.

A large variety of social skills assessment procedures have been described in the professional literature (Strain, Guralnick, & Walker, 1986) that will assist teachers as they attempt to specify and quantify inadequate social development in children. Assessment strategies include direct observation, sociometrics, self-reports, analog, and behavior rating scales. (Some of these strategies are described in this chapter.) Practitioners should become familiar with the advantages of each assessment method before selecting any particular one.

Social skills assessment has three purposes. First, the educator should determine the type of learning error that is occurring (Lewis, 1992). For example, children who engage in a prosocial behavior occasionally, but not consistently, may have a performance deficit. Individuals who never engage in a specific social skill have an acquisition deficit. Second, the assessment process should identify problem behaviors which may interfere with the development and effective use of prosocial behaviors. Finally, the assessment strategy should facilitate the development of a problem statement or description. The assessment strategies selected should, therefore, be specific to social behavior and result in objective descriptions of behaviors which may in turn be used to plan social skills interventions.

Assessment strategies

Direct observation techniques offer teachers the advantage of watching a student during periods of the day when behaviors are of concern, observing interaction skills, environmental influences, frequency of behaviors, and other dimensions related to social skills use (Lewis, 1992). While direct observation provides educators an opportunity to observe social behavior in a natural context, it may be time consuming (Jensen et al., 1988).

Sociometric strategies include techniques such as peer nominations, peer ranking, and peer ratings (Shapiro & Kratchowill, 1988). Peer nominations require children to nominate or select peers based on specific dimensions, such as who they would prefer to play a game with. Peer rankings ask children to rank order other children along a specific dimension, for example, most friendly to least friendly. Finally, peer ratings ask children to assign a rank (e.g., 1–5) to each classmate based on how much they would like to play with the particular classmate. Peer assessment strategies have been presented in the literature for years, but the interpretation of these measures is not always clear. For example, the assessment will not tell an educator why a particular child received a low ranking from peers, only that the child has a lower status (Shapiro & Kratchowill, 1988). Also, peer nominations tend to have poor reliability and are particularly problematic with very young children. Sociometric strategies do not provide specific information regarding skill deficits but are often useful as part of a multimethod assessment package (Kerr & Nelson, 1989).

Self-report, as the name implies, provides an assessment strategy which requires the child to report his or her own perceptions of a problem. Often implemented by means of an interview process, self-report allows children to describe events, relate information, and interpret situations (Witt, Cavell, Heffer, Carey, & Martens, 1988). While self-report methods are frequently used by psychologists, these data are by definition based upon

Problem Behavior	Descriptive Statement (in terms of social skills)
Sandi grabs toys during free time	Sandi does not ask to borrow toys during free play time with peers
Sam yells and screams in the classroom at his teachers	Sam does not respond affirmatively when giving tasks by adults
Jose slaps and hits peers when he is angry	Jose does not demonstrate age-appropriate anger control strategies
Maggie looks down at the floor and won't speak when adults or peers talk to her	Maggie does not use conversation skills or eye contact when others talk to her

Figure 10.3. Examples of statements that describe problem behavior in terms of social skills.

perceptions and interpretations of the children providing the information and are, therefore, inherently biased. However, self-report methods provide information not available through other assessment strategies (Witt et. al., 1988).

Behavior rating scales offer one of the more cost- and time-efficient methods (Merrell, Stein, & Jantzsch, 1992) of assessing prosocial behavior. Social competence rating scales such as the Walker–McConnell Scale of Social Competence and School Adjustment (Walker & McConnell, 1988) and the Social Skills Rating Scale (Gresham & Elliott, 1990) allow the practitioner to distinguish between types of social skills problems in a reliable, time-efficient manner. The multidimensional nature of rating scales provides an opportunity to compare across raters and environments. When numerous raters are involved in assessing a student, the practitioner should look for agreements across raters. Skills rated as nonexistent in more than one area should be targeted for instruction. Other skills rated as occurring in some settings, or with some raters but not others, should be targeted for interventions designed to maintain or generalize emerging skills. More information on intervention development is presented later, in the section on developing a teaching plan.

The goal of assessment during this first phase is to develop a succinct, objective description of the problem behavior that will direct planning and delivery of training. When the trainer develops problem statements, the use of "observable" language, which includes action verbs, to describe behavior is most helpful. For example, assessment of a student named Ben may reveal that he does not greet peers or adults at the appropriate times. A problem statement for this deficit might be, "Ben does not use verbal greetings and eye contact when a peer or adult approaches." Other examples are presented in Figure 10.3. Once a problem statement has been generated, the next task is to identify what type of problem the student has.

☑ Checkpoint 10.1

[pages 363–367]

Fill in the answers to the following items (1–11). Check your responses by referring to the text; relevant page numbers appear in brackets.

How is the concept of *social competence* different from *social skills*?

(1) _____ [363].

Social skills may be defined as

(2) _____ [363].

(continues)

CHECKPOINT 10.1, continued

The six steps of the teaching model based on applied behavior analysis include:

(3) _____

(4) _____

(5) _____

(6) _____

(7) _____

(8) _____ [364].

When developing a social skills training program, the teacher's first step should be

(9) _____ [365].

What purpose(s) does social skills assessment serve?

(10) _____ [365].

What is the teacher's objective during the assessment phase of social skills planning?

(11) _____ [366].

Redo any items you missed. If you missed more than 2 of the items, reread the material. Otherwise, continue on to the next section.

Determining the Problem Type

The primary focus of the assessment phase of this social skills training sequence is to describe problem behaviors; next the trainer must identify the problem type. That is, social skills deficits may be identified when the student has never been observed engaging in a specific social skill (*acquisition deficit*). Conversely, if the student engages in the prosocial skill occasionally or under some circumstances but not others, the skill should be categorized as a *performance deficit*. Item-by-item analysis of social skills rating scales should indicate the frequency of occurrence of specific behaviors as reported by the rater. The relative frequency "never" probably indicates an acquisition deficit, while skills rated as occurring "sometimes" indicates a performance deficit (Merrell et al., 1992). For example, a rater may report that a child never engages in sharing materials with peers by noting "never" on a behavior rating scale; such a rating may indicate an acquisition deficit. Similarly, a rater may report that the child "sometimes" engages in cooperative play with peers; this may indicate a performance deficit because the child engages in cooperative play sometimes but not all of the time.

If there are discrepancies between the reports of multiple raters, the trainer may need to confirm the type of problem through direct observation of the child. The trainer will want to observe occurrence vs. nonoccurrence (i.e., frequency count) of the social skill in question. Therefore, targeting times of the day when the social skill is most likely to be used probably will be more efficient than simply observing the student for long periods of time.

The ability to distinguish types of social skills problems (acquisition vs. performance) will be of great importance to practitioners when they design interventions to remediate social skills problems. The following section describes the different interventions which a practitioner might develop to address an acquisition deficit as opposed to an intervention designed to mediate a performance deficit.

Developing a Teaching Plan

Once a teacher has developed a description of the problem behavior and identified the specific skill problem type, efforts should focus on identifying and planning effective social skills intervention strategies. For example, if assessment methods reveal that an individual uses prosocial skills (e.g., conversation skills) in some settings, but not in all situations, strategies to promote generalization should be identified and implemented. By employing an applied behavioral approach, the teacher could improve generalization of social skills by manipulating setting events, antecedent events, and consequent events (Wolery et al., 1988).

Setting events include all components of the training environment that are also present in the generalization environment. If the training environment and generalization environment are both classrooms, they have many components in common, for example, people, furniture, and blackboards. If the training environment (e.g., classroom) is very different from the generalization environment (e.g., playground), the trainer may need to incorporate stimuli from the generalization setting into the training setting to enhance gneralization.

Antecedent events comprise all components of instruction including examples, prompts, directions, and instructions provided by the teacher. A critical antecedent manipulation in social skills training is *example selection*. Examples used for demonstration and role plays have a great impact on both acquisition and generalization of social skills. Situations selected to be demonstrated or to be role played should be examples of situations that students are most likely to encounter. Very often, authors of social skills curricula will provide trainers with suggested situations for use during training; but if the goal is generalization, trainers should be careful to identify and use situations common to the student's daily routine. For example, if a trainer were practicing peer communication skills with a young child, the topic of the conversation would be different than the topic used if the trainer were practicing with an adolescent. Or if the trainer were teaching joining in an activity, the example role plays would be different for a very young child who might be taught to join in a game of four-square while a young adolescent might be taught to join in a conversation.

Assessment data may indicate that a child engages in greeting peers on some days but not on others. In this instance, the teacher may need to implement a consequent manipulation strategy such as positive reinforcement or shaping. For example, the teacher may implement a plan in which the student receives stickers and positive adult attention for each observed prosocial greeting. Another youngster may greet adults but fail to make eye contact during the greeting; this child may benefit from a positive reinforcement program designed to increase frequency of eye contact during greetings. For a complete discussion of antecedent and consequent manipulation strategies, consult a text which describes applied behavior analysis techniques (e.g., Wolery et al., 1988). Assessment data may indicate an acquisition deficit; that is, an individual has never demonstrated a specific skill. For example, a child who does not engage in conversations with peers would be described as having an acquisition deficit because she never uses the skill of peer conversation. In this instance the trainer needs to develop learning activities which directly teach conversation skills. Direct instruction is required to remediate an acquisition deficit and a complete lesson plan should be developed by the trainer.

An integrated, comprehensive social skills training lesson should include direct instruction on the skill targeted for intervention, modeling or demonstrations of the skill, behavioral rehearsal and feedback, and generalization strategies such as homework assignments (Goldstein, 1988; Knoff, 1988). A lesson planning form such as the one in Figure 10.4 will assist the trainer in identifying and planning for each component of an effective social skills lesson. The lesson plan format includes: the social skill rule, skill sub-steps, demonstration or modeling, role plays or rehearsal and feedback, and generalization (Goldstein, 1988; Lewis, 1992).

Each portion of the lesson plan has a specific purpose and should be thoroughly planned before instruction begins. For example, providing a short name for the skill being taught will facilitate clear communication of the desired behavior or concept.

SOCIAL SKILLS LESSON PLAN

Name of Skill

_____

Critical Rule

_____

Description of Skill and Skill Components

_____

Model/Demonstration

_____

Role Play

_____

Review/Test

_____

Homework Assignment

Figure 10.4. Social skills lesson planning form. *Note.* From "Essential features of a social skills instructional program," by T. Lewis, 1992, *Oregon Conference Monograph,* p. 38. Copyright 1992 by the University of Oregon. Reprinted with permission.

A simple word like "sharing" will be easier for most young children to remember and talk about than a more complicated title such as "positive peer interaction skills."

The lesson plan also includes rule development. Social skills rules, or guidelines, should communicate when a skill should be used. Knowing when to use specific skills is a critical discrimination in developing social competence. The trainer should keep in mind that the name of the skill and the component skills tell the child "what," while the rule tells "when." For example, a rule about sharing might say, "When you're playing with other children at recess, you need to share."

Skill components are the subskills or task-analyzed skills which make up the prosocial response. Nearly all social skills may be task analyzed or broken into a set of sequential subskills. The teacher must identify these subskills prior to teaching so that they may be discussed and practiced with the child. Many social skills curricula are available to assist teachers with identifying these subskills. However, if a certain skill is not in a commercially available material, the teacher must examine the specific social skill and extract from it the subskills and their sequence. For example, accepting feedback from your supervisor may be an important skill to develop for an adolescent entering the work force. In this instance, "accepting feedback" is the skill name; the rule is, "When a supervisor talks to you, you need to accept the feedback." The skill components might include: Look at the person who is talking, listen carefully, tell the person what you will do to improve, thank the person.

Teachers also need to plan example situations to use during the lesson. Modeling requires a competent individual to demonstrate the steps in the skill being taught. The model could be a capable peer or an adult. Teachers should keep in mind that the first example should be correct use of the skill; skill components should be identified as they are being modeled, and a review of the rule and skill components should follow each demonstration. It may be helpful to teach discrimination of applying the rule by having a negative example of the skill demonstrated. If a negative example is used, an *adult* should model the unacceptable behavior rather than allowing children to practice unacceptable behavior. Also, negative examples should be quickly followed by positive examples so children see the correct use of the skill before they are expected to practice the skill in a role play.

Role plays are opportunities for children to practice the prosocial skill and its component skills in an instructional setting and receive feedback about their performance. Many commercially available social skills curricula provide trainers with specific instructions regarding setting up role plays and providing descriptive, evaluative feedback. It is critical that the teacher select role play scenarios for each lesson that are drawn from situations in the student's daily life. Using example situations from real life will promote generalization of the skill beyond the training setting, which is, of course, the goal of social skills interventions. Trainers usually can find examples for role plays by observing children in various environments. For example, observing elementary-aged children during recess or adolescents in the hallways during break should provide scenarios for practicing various age-appropriate situations. Again, most curriculum materials will suggest role play topics but it is crucial that the topics and situations selected closely match those that students will actually encounter.

As with any other lesson, a review of information presented will enhance student learning. Following the role plays and feedback, the teacher should briefly review the skill and its component skills. Testing for student understanding may involve brief questions such as, "What skill did we practice today?", "Where will you use this skill?", and "What are the steps in the skill?" The test may also include a novel role play situation in which the students practice the skill from the lesson.

The homework portion of the lesson is also critical to application and generalization of the skill beyond the training setting. The goal of the homework assignment is to require children to use the practiced skill in nontraining situations. This may be accomplished in a variety of ways. For example, verbal contracts may be formed. That is, the teacher asks children where and when they could use the skill and then encourages them to do so. Written contracts should require the student to name the skill, identify possible times of the day and locations where the skill might be used, and sign the contract agreeing to use the skill. Also, homework assignments could require that students get an adult to sign their contract when they successfully use the targeted skill. Motivational strategies might also be used to encourage children to use their new prosocial skill. A variety of token systems (e.g., tickets, stars, coupons) are helpful in promoting skill use. The emphasis in social skills training must be helping children remember to use the skills beyond the training setting. Motivation systems that are effective in academic skill development will often be effective in promoting social skill development.

✔ Checkpoint 10.2

[pages 368–370]

Fill in the answers to the following items (1–17). Check your responses by referring to the text; relevant page numbers appear in brackets.

Name and define the two types of social skills problems:

(1) _____

_____

(2) _____

_____ [368]

It is important for a teacher to distinguish between the two because:

(3) _____

_____ [368].

The type of problem displayed when an individual uses a social skill in some situations but not in others is **(4)** _____

_____ [368].

In this situation, the intervention the teacher should select is **(5)** _____

_____ [368].

Example selection is important in teaching social skills because **(6)** _____

_____ [368].

It would be helpful to implement consequent manipulations in a social skills training program when **(7)** _____

_____

_____ [368].

(continues)

CHECKPOINT 10.2, continued

The intervention suggested for students with acquisition deficits is **(8)** _____

_____

_____ [369].

The components of a comprehensive social skills training lesson are:

(9) _____

_____

(10) _____

_____

(11) _____

_____

(12) _____

_____ [369]

A teacher should use the lesson planning form to plan social skills lessons because **(13)** _____

_____ [369].

Role plays are **(14)** _____

_____

and they are important in developing prosocial behavior because **(15)** _____

_____

_____ [370].

Homework is **(16)** _____

_____

and it is important because **(17)** _____

_____

_____ [370].

Redo any items you missed. If you missed more than 3 of the items, reread the material. Otherwise, continue on to the next section.

Identifying Curriculum Materials and Learning Activities

Fortunately, many comprehensive social skills curricula are commercially available to educators and trainers today. A representative sample may be found in Appendix D. Generally, a social skills curriculum should include sufficient information for the trainer regarding modeling and demonstration strategies, role plays or behavioral rehearsal strategies, assessment strategies and instruments, and generalization strategies, and should be cost-effective (Carter & Sugai, 1988). It will also be helpful to use curricular materials which offer trainers flexibility. That is, trainers should be able to select lessons and activities targeted to remediate specific skill deficits identified during the assessment phase. As mentioned earlier, training will be most effective if specific skills are targeted for teaching, rather than simply selecting lessons suggested by the author of the curricular material.

Curricular material should be appropriate to the age of the targeted children; for example, it should be designed for elementary-aged children rather than adolescents if the children in the training group are elementary age. Young children may also require more practice and expansion activities during social skills learning than older students, just as they would during academic skills instruction. It may even be helpful to draw items from more than one curricular material, if necessary.

Social skills often fail to generalize to novel situations (Berler, Gross, & Drabman, 1982). Activities designed to promote generalization and maintenance of social skills—such as prompting and coaching in the actual setting where the skills should be used, positive reinforcement for using skills, and various self-management strategies—should be identified and incorporated into training activities (Carter & Sugai, 1988; Jensen et al., 1988; Morgan & Young, 1984). Prompting, or providing additional assistance to the student in order to elicit the prosocial response, may be particularly effective when used in settings where the skill is required. For example, the social skills trainer could accompany a student to recess and verbally coach or prompt use of the play skills that were taught during a direct instruction lesson. This type of coaching—telling the student what to do and when—is most effective when applied to actual events.

Adding homework assignments to social skills training groups also expands use of skills beyond the training setting. At the close of each training session, trainers should lead students through a process of: identifying skills covered in class, discussing where a particular skill could be used outside of training (perhaps later in the day), with whom the skill could be used, and when the skill should be used. This process should be followed by either formal or informal contracting with the student. The contract could be as informal as a verbal agreement to "attempt the skill sometime later," or as formal as a written con-

---

HOMEWORK CONTRACT

I agree to practice _____ social skill today.

I will practice the skill when _____.

One place I could practice the skill_____.

If I practice the skill and bring this contract back to class tomorrow, I will earn _____.

Student's Signature_____

Teacher's Signature_____

Figure 10.5. Sample homework contract.

tract such as the one in Figure 10.5.

It is critical that trainers identify activities which will require children to use newly trained skills beyond the training setting. Promoting generalization of new skills should be foremost in the trainer's mind as planning takes place. Generalization strategies such as homework assignments should not be an afterthought; effective generalization is planned for during the early stages of social skills training.

Identifying Relevant Situations for Teaching and Role Plays

Effective social skills training includes opportunities for individuals to observe the appropriate skills as well as to practice skills and obtain feedback from others regarding their performance (Jensen et al., 1988; Knoff, 1988). Models or demonstrations by the trainer or competent peers provide positive examples of the desired behavior. Role plays provide opportunities for students to practice newly acquired social skills in controlled settings and experience reinforcement for appropriate responses. In order to promote acquisition and generalization of skills, situations selected for demonstrations and role plays should be drawn from the student's experiences and be those situations which students are likely to encounter (Lewis, 1992).

Generally, the most efficient way to identify likely role play situations is through direct observation of children. Social skills trainers should spend time observing students in a variety of settings and social situations and make note of the particular situation, who is involved, and the specific social skill required. Trainers should also record age-appropriate variations of social skills such as greeting, conversation topics, body language, duration of behaviors, etc. This information should be incorporated into instruction so that children are practicing social behaviors most similar to those of their peers. Direct observation will also provide evaluative feedback to the trainer once training sessions have begun. It is important to assess training effectiveness by confirming through observation that students are using prosocial skills in nontrained, natural settings. Regular, systematic observation will provide both the trainer and the student with this information.

Developing Measurement Strategies

Teachers as well as students need to evaluate the success of training opportunities. Various options are available, including role plays on novel situations, direct observation of students in natural situations, self-evaluation by participating students, and behavior rating scales. Changes in ratings in a positive direction on standardized behavior rating scales should reflect development of prosocial behavior. Trainers should implement assessment strategies (discussed earlier) to evaluate the success of the intervention.

Regardless of the assessment strategy selected, monitoring student performance should not be an afterthought. Evaluating social skills acquisition provides the teacher with important information regarding the need for additional practice and reinforcement. Further, trainers may discover, after social skills instruction and practice, that the skills which were the focus of direct instruction because of an acquisition deficit have indeed been acquired but performance deficit is now an issue. The interventions selected before training may need to be modified after the reassessment.

Implementing Teaching Strategies

Once planning has been completed, group composition has been determined, logistics arranged, and curricular materials prepared, training should begin. Preplanning group rules and management will facilitate pacing and presentation of the lesson (Lewis, 1992). As with any effective student management system, clear expectations for student behavior should be identified as well as consequences for appropriate and inappropriate behavior. It is also helpful to preplan and teach cues to students regarding when to begin and end role plays, such as "action" (meaning *to begin*) and "cut" (meaning *to stop*). Assigning the audience specific things to watch for during the role plays usually improves attention to the actors as well as acquisition of the skill being demonstrated. For instance, students may be required to watch for different steps in the skill, for example, "Hold up your hand when you see the actors making eye contact." Engaging the audience in feedback following demonstrations of skills also improves attending and acquisition.

Many of the effective teaching principles identified in recent literature apply to social skills training. For example, social skills trainers should focus on brisk pacing of instruction. It is easy to allow social skills lessons to drag or require long periods of waiting during role plays. Trainers need to implement strategies to maintain momentum of the lesson such as using effective questioning techniques, being well prepared for the lesson, having material ready, and monitoring student behavior. Effective monitoring of student behavior during lessons allows the trainer to interrupt unproductive behavior and provide positive reinforcement of appropriate behavior. Furthermore, smooth, quick transitions between activities will also maximize instructional time while minimizing off-task behavior. Trainers may need to practice transitions with children in order to teach expected behavior so that instruction time is not wasted. Effective trainers will also structure the training time by providing review of skills taught earlier, using advance organizers (like agendas), stating expectations for behavior by developing rules that govern student behavior, and explaining why the rules are necessary. Effective trainers also provide corrective feedback when children meet or fail to meet expectations (Berliner, 1985; Evertson, Emmer, Clements, Sanford, & Worsham, 1989; Rosenshine, 1983).

☑ Checkpoint 10.3

[pages 372–374]

Fill in the answers to the following items (1–8). Check your responses by referring to the text; relevant page numbers appear in brackets.

Characteristics a teacher should look for when considering a social skills curriculum include

(1) _____

_____

_____

_____

_____

_____ [372].

What is prompting, and when should it be used?

(2, 3) _____

_____

_____ [372].

The most efficient way to identify role play situations is

(4) _____

_____

_____ [373].

Four strategies for measuring training outcomes are:

(5) _____

_____

(6) _____

_____

(7) _____

_____

(8) _____

_____ [373].

Redo any items you missed. If you missed more than 2 items, reread the material. Otherwise, continue on to the next section.

CONCLUSION

Social skills training must be systematically planned and implemented if the desired outcome—socially competent students—is to be achieved. Inadequate social skills are associated with numerous negative outcomes for children with disabilities, including rejection, isolation, and school failure (see Figure 10.6). Educators must not ignore social skills development, and they should not implement a social skills curriculum simply as a matter of convenience. This chapter described seven steps designed to assist educators concerned with systematic planning of social skills training. The social skills planning sequence may be used with any published curricular material or with teacher-generated training material. Through careful planning and efficient implementation, students and educators are more likely to experience success in their efforts to develop social competence.

Figure 10.6. How (not) to win friends and influence people.

ASSESSMENT / CHAPTER 10 ▰▰▰▰

A list of acceptable responses appears following the Assessment.

1. Identify the seven steps in the social skills training sequence and briefly explain the purpose of each step.

Step 1:

Step 2:

Step 3:

Step 4:

Step 5:

Step 6:

Step 7:

2. What is an acquisition problem, and how should it be remediated?

3. What is a performance problem, and how should it be remediated?

4. Describe the components of an effective social skills lesson.

5. What is the relationship between assessment and intervention when developing social skills training programs?

ACCEPTABLE RESPONSES

1.0 Seven steps in social skills training sequence:

1.1 *Describe the problem behavior.* The purpose of this step is to assess the learner's prosocial behavior and develop an objective description of the problem.

1.2 *Determine the problem type.* The purpose of this step is to distinguish between acquisition and performance problem types.

1.3 *Develop a teaching plan.* The purpose of this step is to develop intervention strategies which match the type of problem identified in Step 2. For example, an intervention plan for acquisition problems should include direct instruction on the unknown skill.

1.4 *Identify curriculum materials and learning activities.* The purpose of this step is to identify and select potential materials and activities that will be effective as part of the intervention.

1.5 *Identify relevant situations for teaching and role plays.* The purpose of this step is to select, usually from real-life situations, role play scenarios.

1.6 *Develop measurement strategies.* The purpose of this step is to preplan how student learning will be evaluated. The results of evaluation activities should indicate the need for further training.

1.7 *Implement teaching strategies.* Once comprehensive social skills training programs have been planned, they must be carefully implemented. Effective teaching practices apply to social skills training.

2.0 Acquisition problem is indicated when the learner never performs a given social skill. Acquisition problems require direct teaching of the absent/deficient social skill.

3.0 Performance problem is indicated when a learner performs a social skill in some situations or with some people but not in all situations. Performance problems require consequent manipulations like positive reinforcement, or antecedent manipulations like coaching, in order to improve student performance.

4.0 An **effective social skills lesson** includes direct instruction on the targeted skill, modeling or demonstrations of the skill, behavioral rehearsal and feedback, and generalization strategies.

5.0 Assessment is an integral part of any social skills program. For example, you cannot develop a social skills program without conducting an assessment to tell you what the problem behavior is (i.e., what specific skills need to be taught) and what the problem type is (acquisition or performance deficit).

CHAPTER ELEVEN

Cognitive Strategies

Changing Beliefs

Upon successful completion of this chapter, the learner should be able to:

1. Design interventions using cognitive behavior modification strategies such as cognitive restructuring to change the belief systems of students

2. Construct and validate belief assessments to identify irrational thinking in students

COGNITIVE BEHAVIOR MODIFICATION

Behaviorists are beginning to realize the importance of focusing their interventions on covert behaviors such as thoughts and feelings. This change in philosophy has come about primarily because of a) the need for behavior management strategies other than (or in addition to) conventional behavior modification for use with older and more developmentally able students, and b) the emergence of effective intervention strategies reported in the literature on cognitive behavior modification (CBM) (Bem, 1967; Bornstein & Quevillon, 1976; Camp, Blom, Herbert, & Van Doorwick, 1976; De Voge, 1977; Di Giuseppe, 1975; Finch, Wilkinson, Nelson, & Montgomery, 1975; Gottman et. al., 1974; Karnes, Teska, & Hodgins, 1970; Knaus & Block, 1976; Knaus & McKeever, 1977; Leon & Pepe, 1983; Meichenbaum & Goodman, 1971; Novaco, 1975; O'Leary, 1968; Palkes, Stewart, & Freedman, 1972; Schneider, 1974; Spivack & Shure, 1974). As you can see, CBM has been around for a number of years; but only recently, with the popularity of social skills training, has it become more widely used by teachers. In 1985, an entire issue of the *Journal of Abnormal Child Psychology* (see Harris, Wong, & Keogh, 1985) was devoted to CBM. To quote from the Foreword of that issue, "CBM is not just another fad" and "in its brief history to date it has evidenced strong links to data and empirical verification" (p. 329).

CBM has five characteristics which distinguish it from other forms of behavior management. First, in CBM programs, the subjects themselves rather than external agents (e.g., the classroom teacher) are the primary change agents; if not at the beginning of the program, certainly by the end. Second, verbalization —on an overt level, then covert—is the primary component. CBM requires that the subject talk to himself, first out loud, then using silent speech. Third, subjects are taught to identify and use a series of steps to solve their problems. Fourth, modeling is used as an instructional procedure, and fifth, most of the CBM literature focuses on helping the individual to gain self-control. More about these characteristics will be described later when we discuss different CBM strategies.

Cognitions

Before we look at CBM strategies I want to define exactly what the concept of *cognition* is, as used in CBM. This concept is referred to often in CBM, as, for example, in discussion of cognitive events, cognitive processes, cognitive structures, and inner speech. *Cognitive events* are the thoughts and images that occur, seemingly of their own volition, in our stream of consciousness. If you have ever tried to meditate, you know about cognitive events—unfortunately, there is very little one can do to modify them. *Cognitive processes* are the ways in which we appraise and transform external stimuli; they are more the *way* we think as opposed to *what* we think. One way to modify cognitive processes is through a CBM strategy known as problem solving or interpersonal

381

cognitive problem solving (ICPS) (Spivack, Platt, & Shure, 1976; Spivack & Shure, 1974). *Inner speech* is a type of cognition also referred to as self-talk, automatic thoughts, and covert self-instructions. Individuals vary in the degree to which they are cognizant of what they are saying to themselves. Inner speech may be modified through two CBM strategies: self-instructional training (Meichenbaum, 1977; Meichen-

baum & Goodman, 1971) and verbal mediation (Blackwood, 1970). *Cognitive structures* are beliefs; we sometimes refer to them as ideas or thinking, as in "he has this idea that everybody is out to get him" or "he thinks he's stupid." The term *cognitive restructuring* (Ellis, 1962) means changing beliefs, in the same sense that behavior modification means changing behaviors.

☑ **Checkpoint 11.1**

[pages 381–382]

Fill in the answers to the following items (1–11). Check your responses by referring to the text; relevant page numbers appear in brackets.

Two reasons why behaviorists have begun to realize the importance of focusing their interventions on thoughts and feelings are

(1) _____

_____

_____ and

(2) _____

_____ [381].

Five characteristics of CBM that distinguish it from other forms of behavior management are **(3–7):**

_____

_____

_____

_____

_____

_____ [381].

(continues)

CHECKPOINT 11.1, continued

Describe each of the following types of cognitions and the CBM strategy used to modify it.

(8) cognitive processes: _____

_____

_____

_____ [381].

(9) cognitive structures: _____

_____

_____

_____ [381].

(10) inner speech: _____

_____

_____

_____ [382].

(11) cognitive events: _____

_____

_____

_____ [382].

Redo any items you missed. If you missed more than 2 items, reread the material. Otherwise, continue on to the next section.

Beliefs and Behavior

Most people assume that what happens to them —the events in their lives—causes them to feel and behave the way they do. A person gets fired from his job and this event makes him depressed, and his depression is manifested by giving up and not doing anything about his situation. Another person gets passed over for a job she wants and this event makes her angry, and she manifests this anger by acting nasty toward her co-workers. In both cases, the cause of the individual's feelings and behaviors is thought to be the event (i.e., getting fired). According to Albert Ellis (1962), it is not the events in our lives that directly influence our feelings and our behavior. Ellis argues that it is what we believe (i.e., think) about these events that produces our feelings and subsequent behavior. To support his argument, Ellis points to the fact that the same event can occur in the lives of several people and each person can react differently. For example, the person who loses his job and gets depressed and ends up doing nothing thinks, "This is awful. I must be incompetent. I'll never get or keep another job. Why bother trying." The second person gets fired and thinks, "This is so unfair. I don't deserve this. I hate these people for doing this." This person gets so angry he goes out, buys a gun, and shoots his boss. A third person gets fired and thinks, "I don't like this but I'm not going to let it get me down. I'm going to find out why I was fired and see if I have any recourse. Maybe I can get my job back. At the very least, I'll know what I need to improve on." This person does not get depressed or angry. He gets disappointed and concerned and takes some productive action. Same event but three different sets of feelings and behaviors.

The idea that thoughts precede feelings and behaviors is not new, nor did it originate with Ellis. There have been many great (and not so great) thinkers, ranging from a first-century philosopher to a twentieth-century baseball player, who—in so many words—expressed the same idea as Ellis. (See Figure 11.1.)

The A-B-C Model

According to Ellis (1962), the sequence is set in motion by an activating event (i.e., something that happens to us). This event, also referred to as A (for "activating"), may be external (e.g., being teased by peers) or internal (e.g., thinking about being teased by peers). The event (A) usually causes the person to think about what happened. This thinking activity (verb) is influenced by the person's belief system (noun) and is referred to as B (for "belief"). It is B, the person's belief about what happened, that produces the strong emotional (feeling) response and the resultant behavior. Since the emotional and behavioral responses are the consequences in this sequence, they are called the consequent affect and consequent behavior, or simply referred to as C (for "consequence"). Once again, the sequence is: Something happens to a person (A) and what he thinks about it (B) causes him to experience strong emotions (C) that are manifested in behavior (C).

The key component in the sequence is, of course, B. Again, according to Ellis (1962), there are two types of beliefs: rational and irrational. Rational beliefs are ideas that are based on logic and/or fact. Conversely, irrational beliefs are either illogical (i.e., they defy reason) or untrue (i.e., there is no physical evidence to support them). Figure 11.2 includes a sample of irrational and rational beliefs. "I must be good at everything I do" is an example of an irrational belief because it is untrue. A person may *want* to be good at everything she does but there is no universal rule or natural law that says she must be. More likely, it is the individual who makes her own rule about personal competence. While there is certainly nothing wrong with wanting to succeed, it is virtually impossible for the average person to achieve success at everything they try, especially on the first attempt. A more rational view of the world is, "While I would *like* to be good at everything I do, I don't *have* to be. I can only try my best." Another example of an irrational belief is, "People who do bad things are bad and must be punished." On the one hand, the person says, "That person hurt me and hurting people is bad." On the other hand, they say, "They must be hurt for hurting me." In other words, "I must act like a bad person because I don't like it when someone else acts like a bad person." This is illogical. A fair-pair rational belief is the statement, "two wrongs don't make a right." According to Ellis, the problem with irrational thinking is that it often causes people to put a negative spin on the events in their lives, which eventually leads to intense emotional states such as anger, fear, depression, and/or maladaptive behavior. Figure 11.3 illustrates the role that irrational thinking plays in the development of maladaptive affect and/or behavior.

When a student misbehaves, we typically focus our intervention on the activating event (A) (e.g., "stay away from him if you don't like being teased"), the consequent affect (C) (e.g., "count to ten if you feel yourself getting angry"), and/or the behavior (C) (e.g., "I'm taking away ten points for hitting"). Instead, we should be focusing our intervention on

Figure 11.1. The idea that thoughts precede feelings and behaviors is not new.

Irrational Thinking	Rational Thinking
I must be good at everything I do.	Few people are good at everything they do. I can only try my best.
Everyone must like me.	You can't please all the people all the time. It's OK if some people don't like me.
If people do bad things, they must be bad people and must be punished.	People are fallible. They don't always do bad things because they are bad. I do bad things sometimes but that doesn't make me a bad person.
Everything must go my way all the time.	It's unrealistic to expect everything to always go my way. Sometimes I'm going to be disappointed.
Everyone must treat me fairly all the time.	It's unrealistic to expect everyone to treat me fairly all the time. For one thing, people are not always going to agree with me about what is and isn't fair.
I never have any control over what happens to me in my life.	While I don't have control over everything in my life, I do have control over many things.
When something bad happens to me, I must never forget it and I must think about it all the time.	Thinking about bad things all the time makes me sad. I'm a nice person. I don't deserve to be sad all the time. Besides, thinking about something bad isn't going to make it better.
I should never have to do anything I don't want to.	There is always going to be someone to tell us what to do and we aren't always going to want to do what they tell us to. We can always refuse but we can't always escape the consequences.

Figure 11.2. Examples of irrational and rational beliefs.

Event (A)	Thinking (B)	Feelings/Behavior (C)
1. Peers tattle on him	"If people do things to me that I don't like, they must be rotten and deserve to be punished."	Anger/verbal and/or physical attacks on peers
2. Asked to do something new and/or difficult	"I must be competent at everything."	Anxiety attack/noncompliance
3. Loses a game at recess	"Things must always go my way."	Anger/tantrum
4. Peers tease her	"Everyone must like me."	Depression/truancy
5. Asked to change his behavior	"I can't help the way I am."	Apathy/negativism/frustration/noncompliance

Figure 11.3. Ellis's A-B-C Model applied to school situations. Irrational thinking plays an important role in the development of maladaptive affect and behavior.

the belief (B) that may be mediating between A and C (e.g., "two wrongs don't make a right; you don't have to hit someone because they call you a name"). Cognitive restructuring has some advantages over traditional behavior modification. First of all, if the student's behavior *is* under the control of a mediating belief, focusing our intervention on the child's behavior is unlikely to be successful. Second, the student has a lot more control over his own beliefs than he does over external events such as antecedents or consequences. Third, the chances that the student's behavior will generalize and maintain across settings and over time are greater if you change his belief than if you simply change his behavior. Finally, in teaching the student cognitive restructuring, you are contributing to his mental health as well as his self-reliance. Many adults I know are either in therapy or in denial because they believe they have little or no control over their own misfortunes.

Learning Beliefs

Before I show you how to do cognitive restructuring with your students, I need to give you some background information regarding belief systems. First of all, we are not born with our beliefs. They are learned, and like behaviors they can be unlearned. According to the Russian psychologist A. R. Luria (1961), the acquisition of a belief system is an integral part of the development of language. Children learn language through a combination of modeling and operant conditioning. For example, the parent points to a book and says "book." The child, observing this, imitates the parent and says an approximation of the word book. The delighted parent says "good girl" and hugs the child. Over time, this event is repeated and the child not only learns the *word* book, she learns the *concept* book. Eventually, she brings a book to her parent, says "book" and crawls into her parent's lap and waits for the parent to read to her. Luria postulated that as children grow older, they learn beliefs in much the same way that they learn language and concepts such as book. Here's how it works.

Let's suppose that the child discussed in the previous praragraph is now learning how to walk. While walking, she falls down. Although falling down is an event, not an object (like book), the parent can give meaning to this event just as she gave meaning to the

object. On one level, she can name the event for the child, by saying something such as, "Oh, baby fall down." Over time, the baby learns the words and the concept of "fall down." However, on another level, the parent can teach the child how to *feel* about falling down. She can get upset (scared) when the child falls and communicate this through her actions and words. For example, if she screams, "Oh, no. Baby fell down. How awful!" and picks up baby in an agitated fashion, she is likely to teach her child that falling down is a terrible thing that should be avoided at all costs. On the other hand, if the parent calmly picks up the child, comforts her and tells her, "It's OK," the meaning conveyed is that falling is one of life's unpleasant but tolerable occurrences. Again, as in learning words or concepts, there must be repeated trials (i.e., opportunities to learn). (See Figure 11.4.)

Here's another example of how an irrational belief is learned. Joey's father likes to drive fast and

Figure 11.4. How beliefs are learned.

gets angry when other drivers, who are observing the speed limit, keep him from driving as fast as he wants to. While riding in his father's car, Joey observes other drivers who are not going as fast as his father wants them to; this is the activating event. Joey's father teaches the meaning of the event by the way he responds to it. Joey's father yells and curses at each driver he passes. Over time, he teaches Joey that "he should get what he wants (a clear road without obstacles) whenever he wants it" and "anybody who does something he doesn't like (drives too slow) is bad and should be punished (cursed at)." This thinking is irrational. First of all, it is not factual; Joey's father does not know the other drivers—how can he judge whether they are good or bad? It is also irrational because it is illogical. The other drivers are observing the speed limit; it is only because Joey's father is speeding that he thinks the other drivers are "bad." People who speed in cars often get into accidents and get hurt, and sometimes die. In this case, just who is behaving badly? It is also illogical because Joey's father does things that other people don't like but nobody yells and curses at him; it doesn't make sense that Joey's father is not perceived as bad when he displeases others, but that they are perceived as bad for displeasing him. It is also illogical to expect a clear road without obstacles whenever one drives. The point is, Joey's father is engaging in irrational thinking, and, by his example, he is teaching Joey the very same irrational thinking. This irrational thinking can be harmful because it can lead to anger whenever Joey doesn't get what he wants or when someone does something he doesn't like. This anger may then be manifested in verbal or physical aggression that could result in someone getting hurt or, at the very least, leave Joey without a friend.

☑ Checkpoint 11.2

[pages 383–387]

Fill in the answers to the following items (1–10). Check your responses by referring to the text; relevant page numbers appear in brackets.

Most people assume that

(1) _____

causes them to feel and behave the way they do.

Psychologist Albert Ellis believes that

(2) _____

_____

causes people to feel and behave the way they do [383].

Explain Ellis's A-B-C model:

(3) _____

_____

_____

_____

_____ [383].

Rational beliefs are

(4) _____

_____ [383].

Irrational beliefs are

(5) _____

_____ [383].

Four advantages cognitive restructuring has over traditional behavior modification are:

(6) _____

_____;

(7) _____

_____;

(continues)

CHECKPOINT 11.2, continued

(8) _____

_____ ;

(9) _____

_____ [386].

Explain where we get our beliefs from and give an example

(10) _____

_____

_____

_____

_____

_____

_____

_____ [386].

Redo any items you missed. If you missed more than 2 of the items, reread the material. Otherwise, continue on to the next section.

Unlearning Beliefs

Irrational beliefs can be unlearned through *cognitive restructuring.* I have broken down the strategy into the six steps listed in Figure 11.5. Although its roots are in psychotherapy and counseling, I firmly believe the most practical (and humanistic) application of cognitive restructuring is to teach people how to use it to change themselves.

One becomes proficient at cognitive restructuring by mastering each of the competencies listed in the scope and sequence in Figure 11.6. As to when to teach these competencies, you can be proactive and teach all of your students all of the competencies beginning the first week of school *before they need them,* or you can be reactive and teach individual students the competencies they need *when the need arises.* While I have no bias toward either approach,

let me show you how you might teach each of the competencies if you were reacting to a specific problem in a given student. Remember our student Rosario, from Chapter 4, who responded aggressively to peer teasing? Our Pre-Mod analysis indicated he endorses beliefs that are incompatible with responding assertively to peer teasing. He believes that people who do things he doesn't like are bad and need to be punished. The recommended intervention is cognitive restructuring. Your goal is to teach Rosario what it is and how to use it to change his own thinking. Let's look at how you might go about teaching each of the competencies listed in the scope and sequence in Figure 11.6.

Since your goal is for Rosario to use cognitive restructuring to change his own thinking, it would be wise to first give him a rationale for learning and using it. You could always use traditional behavior modification such as a token economy to get Rosario to learn, and possibly even use, cognitive restructuring. This has been done before with some success (De Voge, 1977). However, I would suggest that even though you may have to use extrinsic reinforcement in the beginning, eventually your goal should be to get Rosario to want to learn and use cognitive restructuring because he understands and appreciates how it can benefit him. You are not always going to be around to reward Rosario for using it; he needs to do it on his own. To accomplish this, Rosario must learn: a) how strong feelings (e.g., anger and fear) can be harmful while weak feelings (e.g., annoyance, irritation, concern) can be helpful; b) how his feelings (and, subsequently, his behaviors) are often controlled by his thinking (beliefs); and c) how cognitive restructuring can help him change his thinking so that he can gain control over his feelings. Even though Rosario's problem appears to be primarily with anger, I would include references to anxiety as well. Young males in our society often confuse feelings of anger and fear. Since our society teaches its males that it is better to show anger than fear, feelings of fear are often masked by a false show of anger (e.g., yelling, cursing, posturing). Some young males are negatively reinforced for using this false anger because it often serves to intimidate the person or persons whose provocation they find threatening. More about this in Chapter 13.

Competency 1—Understands how strong feelings can be harmful. To teach Rosario how strong feelings can be harmful, communicate the following ideas:

STEP 1—Student recognizes emotional and/or behavioral signal(s) that something is wrong (C)

STEP 2—Student identifies event(s) (A) associated with signals

STEP 3—Student identifies belief(s) (B) that mediate(s) between (A) and (C)

STEP 4—Student attempts to dispute belief(s)

STEP 5—Student generates rational belief(s)

STEP 6—Student develops plan to internalize rational belief(s)

Figure 11.5. Steps in the cognitive restructuring process.

a. All of us are born with feelings. Infants are capable of displaying strong feelings such as fear and anger.

b. Feelings are important because they make life interesting. Life would be pretty dull if we had no emotions (like Mr. Spock in the Star Trek movies).

c. Feelings motivate us to take action when we need to. Getting mad can motivate us to stick up for ourselves and get what we want. Getting scared can keep us out of harm's way. [Give examples.]

d. Strong feelings like anger and fear can be harmful (e.g., they can hurt us physically, they are hard to control, they cause us to say and do things that hurt others or hurt us). [Give examples.]

When you are finished with your lesson, give Rosario an assessment to see if he learned what you wanted him to. Ask him to state all of the reasons why strong feelings such as anger and fear can sometimes be harmful. Acceptable responses should include the ideas that they don't feel good, they are hard to control, and that they cause us to say and do things that are harmful to others and/or ourselves. He should give all of the above responses within 20 seconds without prompting (refer to Objective 1 in Figure 11.6).

Next, give Rosario some examples of how anger and fear can be harmful. Here is a typical example you might use. Joey's clothes aren't cool and he has skin problems, and he gets angry when he's teased about the way he looks. One day he gets so angry at one of the guys for teasing him that he picks a fight and gets a black eye. Not only that, he gets sent to the office and listens while the principal calls his parents. The school has a rule that students caught fighting are sent home right away. Joey's mom has to come to school to pick him up. She is going to lose some pay for leaving work early. Joey feels guilty about that. When Joey's dad finds out about it, he grounds him for a week. Finally, when he does go back to school, Joey gets teased about his black eye. Ask Rosario how anger hurt Joey. Give him other examples, and for each one, see if Rosario can tell you how the person's anger or fear hurt him or her (see Objective 2 in Figure 11.6). Make sure he is able to do this before going on to the next competency.

Competency 2—Understands that his feelings (and subsequently, his behavior) are often controlled by his thinking. To teach Rosario how his feelings, and subsequently his behaviors, are often controlled by his thinking communicate the following ideas:

a. It is possible to control our feelings. We control our anger when we get angry at somebody who can hurt us (like our parents or the principal) but we let ourselves get angry at somebody who can't hurt us (like a younger sib). [Ask Rosario if he has ever controlled his anger.]

b. People think that someone or something—other than themselves—makes them angry or frightened (e.g., "My parents make me angry!" or "Taking a test makes me scared."). Actually, we make ourselves angry and scared.

c. Events are things that happen to us (e.g., being grounded by your parents, or taking a test). Our feelings are not caused by events. They are caused by what we *think* about the events. [At this point, you should explain the A-B-C rule and give examples.]

d. The same thing (event) can happen to more than one person with more than one reaction; for example, one person gets angry, one gets scared, one gets annoyed, one doesn't feel anything. (See Figure 11.7.) [Explain differences in each case; you may wish/need to use illustrations.]

COMPETENCY 1—*Student understands how strong/mild feelings can be helpful/harmful*

(1) The learner will, when asked, state all of the reasons why intense feelings such as anger, fear, and/or depression can be harmful. He should include the ideas that they don't feel good, are hard to control, and cause us to say and do things that are harmful to others or ourselves. This should be done within 20 seconds without prompting.

(2) Given hypothetical cases involving anger, fear, and/or depression, the learner will correctly state how the individual's emotions in each case were harmful. This should be done correctly for each of three cases within a reasonable amount of time without prompting.

COMPETENCY 2—*Student understands how feelings/behaviors are often caused by thinking*

(3) The learner will, when asked, state the A-B-C rule (e.g., "It's not what happens to you that makes you feel the way you do, it's what you think about what happens to you that makes you feel that way.") within 10 seconds without prompting.

(4) Given examples of hypothetical individuals experiencing anger, fear, and/or depression, the learner will correctly explain how each person became angry, anxious, and/or depressed according to the A-B-C rule. This should be done correctly for each of three cases within a reasonable amount of time without prompting.

COMPETENCY 3—*Understands how cognitive restructuring can help modify thinking in order to manage feelings and behavior*

(5) The learner will, when asked, correctly state all of the steps in the cognitive restructuring strategy in the correct sequence. This should be done within 20 seconds without prompting.

COMPETENCY 4—*Student can recognize own feelings/behaviors (C)*

(6) The learner will self-monitor his/her strong feelings (e.g., anger, anxiety, or depression) and the maladaptive behaviors manifested by those feelings on an A-B-C form. This should be done until there is at least 80% inter-rater reliability for data in column C for 2 consecutive days without prompting.

COMPETENCY 5—*Student can identify events (A) associated with feelings*

(7) In addition to his/her strong feelings (e.g., anger, anxiety, or depression) and the maladaptive behaviors manifested by those feelings, the learner will self-monitor the events that immediately precede the feelings and behaviors on an A-B-C form. This should be done until there is at least 80% inter-rater reliability for data in columns A and C combined for 2 consecutive days without prompting.

COMPETENCY 6—*Student can recognize thinking that mediates between (A) and (B)*

(8a) Given written examples of irrational self-talk, the learner will identify (mark) each according to its core belief (i.e., You stink!, I stink, Doomsday, Robot, Namby Pamby, Fairy Tale) with 90% accuracy in 3 minutes (assuming adequate reading skills).

(continues)

Figure 11.6. Scope and sequence of competencies in cognitive restructuring curriculum.

(8b) Given verbal examples of irrational self-talk, the learner will identify (name) each according to its core belief with 90% accuracy taking no more than 10 seconds for each (assuming inadequate reading skills).

(9a) Given written examples of events (A) and consequent affect and behavior (C), the learner will write the irrational core belief (B) that mediates between A and C. This should be done with 90% accuracy taking no more than 5 minutes (assuming adequate reading and writing skills).

(9b) Given pictures (drawings or photos) of examples of events (A) and consequent affect and behavior (C), the learner will write (or name) the irrational core belief (B) that mediates between A and B. This should be done with 90% accuracy taking no more than 15 seconds for each (assuming inadequate reading and/or writing skills).

(10) The learner will self-monitor his/her strong feelings, maladaptive behaviors, events, and the irrational core belief that mediates between them on an A-B-C form. This should be done until there is at least 80% inter-rater reliability for data in columns A, B, and C *combined* over 2 consecutive days without prompting.

COMPETENCY 7—*Student disputes belief*

(11) The learner will, when asked, verbally describe the disputation process including the five questions (i.e., keep me Alive? Feel better? based on Reality? get along with Others? reach my Goals?). This should be done to the satisfaction of the examiner within a reasonable amount of time without prompting.

(12) Given examples of rational and irrational self talk, the learner will attempt to dispute each demonstrating correct use of the A-F-R-O-G disputation process. This should be done to the satisfaction of the examiner within a reasonable amount of time without prompting.

COMPETENCY 8—*Student generates rational belief*

(13) The learner will, when asked, correctly state definitions for rational and irrational beliefs. This should be done within a reasonable amount of time without prompting.

(14a) Given written examples of rational and irrational self-talk, the learner will correctly identify (mark) each with _____% accuracy within _____ minutes (assuming adequate reading skills).

(14b) Given verbal examples of rational and irrational self-talk, the learner will correctly identify (name) each with _____% accuracy within _____ minutes (assuming inadequate reading skills).

(15a) Given written examples of irrational self-talk, the learner will produce (in writing) an acceptable example of rational (fair-pair) self-talk for each. This should be done with _____% accuracy with _____ minutes (assuming adequate reading and writing skills).

(15b) Given verbal examples of irrational self-talk, the learner will produce (verbally) an acceptable example of rational (fair-pair) self-talk for each. This should be done with _____% accuracy taking no more than 20 seconds per example without prompting (assuming adequate reading and writing skills).

COMPETENCY 9—*Student develops plan to internalize rational thinking*

(16) When asked to do so, the learner will correctly describe an acceptable plan for the purposes of internalizing the fair-pair rational thinking. This should be done to the examiner's satisfaction within a reasonable amount of time.

Figure 11.6. *Continued.*

Figure 11.7. Same event . . . different response.

Ask Rosario to state the A-B-C rule (i.e., it's not what happens to you that makes you feel the way you do, it's what you think about what happens to you that makes you feel that way). He should answer correctly within 10 seconds without prompting (see Objective 3 in Figure 11.6). Next, give him some stories about people getting scared or angry and ask him to explain how each person got his or her feelings. For example, a girl was grounded by her parents. She thought that wasn't fair and she got angry at them. Ask Rosario: "What made the girl angry?" Rosario's response should convey the idea that it was not the event—being grounded—that made the girl angry but what she thought about the event (i.e., it was unfair) that made her angry. For another example, a boy was baby-sitting at a house late at night and heard a strange noise coming from outside. He thought it might be someone trying to break into the house and got scared. He called his home on the telephone to ask them what he should do. Ask Rosario: "What made the boy scared?" His response should convey the idea that it was not the noise that scared him but what he thought about the noise (e.g., it might be a burglar) that scared him. In each case, Rosario should be able to correctly identify the event, the belief, and the feelings in sequence and

convey the idea that the belief (rather than the event) caused the feelings (see Objective 4 in Figure 11.6). When he can do this, move on to the next competency.

Competency 3—Understands how cognitive restructuring can help him modify his thinking in order to manage his feelings and behavior. To teach Rosario how cognitive restructuring can help him change his thinking so that he can control his feelings, explain each of the steps in the process. These are:

a. First he should recognize when he is getting angry (or scared);

b. next, he should identify what happened (the event) that is associated with the anger;

c. next, he should identify the thinking that caused his anger;

d. next, he should try to dispute this thinking (i.e., try to prove that his thinking is illogical or false);

e. next, he should identify new logical and true thinking to substitute for the irrational thinking;

f. finally, he should practice the new thinking.

At this point, you don't have to go into detail about how each step is achieved. The important thing is that Rosario understands that a) there is a strategy called cognitive restructuring (you can call it whatever you want to, e.g., "rethink," "think again," "thimk," "saying is believing"), and b) the strategy includes six steps that will help him change his thinking so he can control his feelings. Assess his knowledge of the strategy by asking him to list each step. He should be able to list all six steps in the correct sequence in 20 seconds or less without prompting (see Objective 5 in Figure 11.6). When he is able to do this, move on to the next competency.

After teaching Rosario competencies 1, 2, and 3, he should be relatively motivated (out of curiosity, if nothing else) to try and learn cognitive restructuring.

☑ Checkpoint 11.3

[pages 383–393]

Fill in the answers to the following items (1–16). Check your responses by referring to the text; relevant page numbers appear in brackets.

Using cognitive restructuring in a proactive manner requires that you

(1) _____
_____ [388].

A reactive approach to cognitive restructuring requires that you

(2) _____
_____ [388].

Four key ideas that help students understand how strong feelings can be harmful are:

(3) _____
_____ [389];

(4) _____
_____ [389];

(continues)

CHECKPOINT 11.3, continued

(5) _____
_____ [389];

(6) _____
_____ [389];

Four key ideas that help students understand how their feelings/behaviors are often controlled by their thinking are:

(7) _____
_____ [389];

(8) _____
_____ [389];

(9) _____
_____ [389];

(10) _____
_____ [389];

The six steps in the cognitive restructuring process are:

(11) _____
_____ [389];

(12) _____
_____ [389];

(13) _____
_____ [389];

(14) _____
_____ [389];

(15) _____
_____ [389];

(16) _____
_____ [389];

Redo any items you missed. If you missed more than 3 of the items, reread the material. Otherwise, continue on to the next section.

Name **Rosario**   Date **2-11-95**

Directions: Fill out in the following order: 1. C   2. A   3. B

A—Events (What happened?)	B—Thoughts (What did I think about?)	C—Feelings/Behaviors (How did I feel/act?)
		(10:00) I got angry at R. and told him to shut up.
		(11:00) I got mad at S. and called her a bitch.
		(1:30) I got mad at R. and told him he better stop calling me names or I will kick his butt.
		(2:30) I got mad at T. and called him a dick face.

Figure 11.8. The A-B-C form with feelings/behavior data.

Name **Rosario**   Date **2-17-95**

Directions: Fill out in the following order: 1. C   2. A   3. B

A—Events (What happened?)	B—Thoughts (What did I think about?)	C—Feelings/Behaviors (How did I feel/act?)
(11:00) S. laughed at me when I asked T. a question.		(11:00) I got mad at S. but I didn't do anything about it.
(1:00) T. bumped into my desk when he went by.		(1:00) I got mad at T. and yelled for him to watch his big butt.
(2:00) S. called me a butt.		(2:00) Got mad at S. and flipped her off.

Figure 11.9. The A-B-C form with feelings/behavior and events data.

Competency 4—Is aware of one's feelings. Awareness of one's feelings such as anger or anxiety signals us that something may be wrong and that some type of action is necessary. In Rosario's case, being aware of his anger should cue him to begin his cognitive restructuring. Rosario can't always depend on others to cue him to start doing cognitive restructuring. You aren't always going to be around when he's teased and you certainly can't expect his peers to cue him. Therefore, he must be able to cue himself, and that requires being able to recognize when he is angry. To teach Rosario how to recognize his own feelings, use a form such as the one illustrated in Figure 11.8. Have Rosario monitor his angry feelings by recording them in the feelings/behaviors (C) column each time he gets angry. He should also record what he does when he gets angry. Since Rosario may not always remember to do this, you will have to cue him. Don't cue him when you observe him getting angry. If you do this, he will not develop his own awareness of his feelings; he will learn to depend on others to tell him what he feels and when he's feeling it. Instead, cue him at the end of regular intervals (e.g., every 20 or 30 minutes). Say something like, "Did you get angry at all since the last time I asked you? If you did, write down that you got angry and write what you did when you got angry." Repeat this several times a day, at the end of each 20- or 30-minute interval, *until Rosario is able to do it without being cued.* In the meantime, you should keep your own record of Rosario's feelings and behavior and compare it with his at the end of each day. Compute the percentage of inter-rater reliability by dividing the total number of intervals into the number of intervals you and Rosario agree on his feelings and behavior. When there is at least 80% inter-rater reliability for 2 consecutive days without any cueing on your part (see Objective 6 in Figure 11.6), you may assume that Rosario has this competency and move on to the next one.

Competency 5—Is aware of the event(s) that are associated with one's feelings. Rosario's awareness of his anger serves as a signal that something is wrong. To find out what is wrong he needs to identify two things: What happened to him (A—the event), and what he thinks about it (B—the belief) that might be causing his anger. To help him identify the event he associates with his anger, use the same form you used to teach him Competency Number 4 (see Figure 11.8). This time, have him monitor *two* things: when he gets angry and what he does (recorded in column C), and what happened to him right before he gets angry (written in column A). This may be seen in Figure 11.9. Again, you may have to

cue him until he can remember to do it himself. Be careful not to say "Write what happened that *made* you angry." Remember, the event didn't make Rosario angry; what he *thinks* about the event made him angry. Again, you keep your own record of Rosario's feelings and events and, at the end of the day, compute the percentage of inter-rater reliability. When there is at least 80% inter-rater reliability *for both A and C combined* for 2 consecutive days without any cueing on your part (see Objective 7 in Figure 11.6), you may assume that Rosario has this competency and move on to Competency Number 6.

Competency 6—Can recognize the thinking that mediates between the event and the feelings/behaviors. This is a somewhat complex competency for Rosario or any young person to learn. Before Rosario is able to recognize the thinking (B) that mediates between the event (A) and the feelings and behavior (C), he must first learn what irrational thinking is. Ellis (1962) has identified a number of core irrational beliefs. These are listed in Figure 11.10. The problem with teaching these to young people is that they often find it daunting to try and commit these beliefs to memory. Fortunately, Roush (1984) offers a relatively easy and interesting solution to this problem. In his excellent article on teaching cognitive restructuring to low-functioning students, Roush offers an abridged version of Ellis' core beliefs that is relatively easy (and fun) to learn. This abridged set of irrational beliefs is illustrated in Figures 11.11 and 11.12. Let's take a closer look at each of these six types of irrational thinking.

Students who engage in *"You stink!"* thinking subscribe to the tenet that people who do things they don't like are bad and deserve to be punished (or at least reprimanded). They can't (or won't) separate the behaver from his behavior. They think that a person who does a bad thing is a bad person, and they tend to see things in terms of absolutes with no in-between. They see others as either innocent or guilty and most as guilty. They are extremely judgmental and are quick to assign blame. They find fault with others and focus on the negative. They favor punishment without leniency—an eye for an eye. As you can imagine, they are often angry and engage in a number of aggressive behaviors including, but not limited to, verbal and physical aggression, teasing, noncompliance, destructive vandalism, stealing, and lying.

While "You stink!" thinkers are hard on others, students who engage in *"I stink"* thinking tend to be hard on themselves. "I stink" thinkers believe a) they must have the love, approval, and good will (or, at the very least, the attention) of everyone they meet;

and/or b) they must prove competent or adequate at everything they undertake. Their self-worth is tied directly to their performance and how others view them and behave towards them. They experience a great deal of anxiety and engage in a wide range of maladaptive behaviors including attention seeking (disruptive), noncompliance and not completing assignments (both tied to a fear of failure), and tend towards passivity (when criticized or manipulated).

Students who engage in *"Doomsday"* thinking subscribe to the belief that if something can go wrong it will, and things will never get better. When they experience a threatening event (e.g., peer rejection, failing grade), they spend an inordinate amount of time brooding about it. They are often preoccupied with doom and gloom and look at events from a decidedly negative or pessimistic point of view. They are very good at telling you why things won't work out. They tend to worry a lot and are often depressed. They are often off task, do not complete school work, socially isolate themselves, and are often truant.

"Namby Pamby" thinkers are often confused with "Doomsday" thinkers. To use an analogy, "Namby Pamby" is to "Doomsday" as acute is to chronic. Since "Doomsday" thinkers are preoccupied with doom and gloom, they tend to be depressed much of the time; their condition is more chronic than acute. "Namby Pamby" thinkers can be perfectly happy for long stretches of time until something happens that they perceive as threatening (e.g., being teased by a peer or doing poorly on a test). At such times, they have a tendency to perceive the event as more threatening than it actually is and overreact. They get upset, cry, and/or run to the teacher or peers for support. Their reaction is one of "I can't stand this!" They suffer from self-induced extreme anxiety which, in males, is often masked by anger. Our society teaches males not to show fear, but it is OK to show anger. A display of anger is better than OK, it's macho. Sometimes it is negatively reinforced by get-

---

1. You must have love or approval from all the people you find significant.

2. You must prove thoroughly competent, adequate, and achieving or you at least must have competence or talent in some important area.

3. When people act obnoxiously and unfairly, you should blame and damn them, and see them as bad, wicked, or rotten individuals.

4. You have to view things as awful, terrible, horrible, and catastrophic when you get seriously frustrated, treated unfairly, or rejected.

5. Emotional misery comes from external pressures and you have little ability to control or change your feelings.

6. If something seems dangerous or fearsome, you must preoccupy yourself without it and make yourself anxious about it.

7. You can more easily avoid facing many life difficulties and self-responsibilities than undertake more rewarding forms of self-discipline.

8. Your past remains all-important and because something once strongly influenced your life, it has to keep determining your feelings and behavior today.

9. People and things should turn out better than they do and you must view it as awful and horrible if you do not find good solutions to life's grim realities.

10. You can achieve maximum human happiness by inertia and inaction or by passively and uncommittedly "enjoying yourself."

Figure 11.10. Ellis's core irrational beliefs. *Note.* From *A new guide to rational living* (pp. 88, 102, 113, 124, 138, 145, 158, 168, 177, 186), by A. Ellis and R. A. Harper, 1975, North Hollywood, CA: Wilshire Book Company. Copyright 1975 by Wilshire Book Company.

---

1. Robot thinking ("It's not my fault")

2. I stink thinking ("It's all my fault")

3. You stink! thinking ("It's all your fault")

4. Fairy Tale thinking ("It's just not fair")

5. Namby Pamby thinking ("I can't stand it")

6. Doomsday thinking ("It's never gonna get better")

Figure 11.11. Roush's core irrational beliefs for use with children and youth (Roush, 1984).

Figure 11.12. Six types of irrational thinking.

ting us what we want. One student picks on another and the victim's "Namby Pamby" reaction gets the attention of the teacher who intervenes in his behalf. In addition to being disruptive, the "Namby Pamby" thinker can be verbally and/or physically aggressive when provoked; gives up when frustrated; tantrums easily; impulsively calls out; and can be noncompliant (when threatened).

The student who engages in *"Fairy Tale"* thinking wants things to go his way all the time. He lives in a fairy-tale world that operates by his rules. He must get whatever he wants whenever he wants it. It's "not fair" if he gets detention for not finishing his work; it's "not fair" that he gets grounded for rule infractions at home. Since the real world is far from being fair, the "Fairy Tale" thinker sets himself up for disappointments every day. He also tends to be rigid in his thinking and has difficulty with seeing things from anyone else's perspective. He experiences much righteous anger manifested by a number of maladaptive behaviors including verbal and/or physical aggression and noncompliance (he can be prone to power struggles).

Finally, the *"Robot"* thinker is the student with an external locus of control. She often thinks and says things like "I can't help it," "He (she) made me do it," "I am what I am and can't change it," "It's her (his) fault." "Robot" thinkers blame others (or rotten luck)

for whatever befalls them. Even though they tend to disavow responsibility most of the time, being a "Robot" thinker can be scary. How would you feel if you woke up every morning and went to work or school thinking that you had little or no control over what happened to you? Scary thought, isn't it? This thinking often leads to anxiety and/or depression. Maladaptive behaviors associated with "Robot" thinking include noncompliance, resistance to change, and negativism regarding school and school work.

I should mention that although I keep referring to these students as "I stink" thinkers or "Robot" thinkers, these students rarely use just one kind of irrational thinking. Most of them tend to engage in more than one type of irrational thinking at a time. For example, a student might engage in "Doomsday" thinking and "Robot" thinking at the same time. She not only believes that things are going to go wrong, she also believes that they aren't going to get better because she has little or no control over what happens to her. You might see a combination of "You stink!", "Fairy Tale," and "Robot" thinking in another student. In his fairy tale world, he should not be held accountable for his behavior. When he receives a failing grade from a teacher for not doing his work, he refuses to accept any responsibility for his behavior ("Robot") and blames and damns the teacher ("You stink!") for not playing by his rules ("Fairy Tale"). Now that you know a little bit about each type of thinking, let's get back to Rosario and his problem thinking.

The best way to teach Rosario the six irrational core beliefs is to teach them one at a time. For example, assuming you are teaching "You stink!" thinking, give Rosario a definition and some examples and not-examples and see if he can differentiate between them. Examples and not-examples of "You stink!" thinking may be seen in Figure 11.13. Assess Rosario's knowledge of a core belief by having him label examples and not-examples for that belief. He should be at least 90% accurate within a reasonable amount of time before moving on to the next core belief (see Objectives 8a or 8b in Figure 11.6). Be careful to always review previously learned beliefs each time you introduce a new belief. You also want

to include examples of core beliefs previously taught on each new assessment. For example, let's assume that you teach the core beliefs in the following order: "You stink!", "I stink," "Doomsday," "Fairy Tale," "Robot," and "Namby Pamby." After teaching and assessing "You stink!" thinking, you teach and assess "I stink" thinking. Be sure to review "You stink!" thinking before you introduce examples and not-examples of "I stink" thinking, and when you are ready to assess the latter, be sure you include some examples of "You stink!". And so on and so on. This way, Rosario will be sure to remember all of the irrational core beliefs and not just those most recently taught. Don't forget to emphasize proficiency. Speed *and* accuracy is better than accuracy alone. Proficiency can be attained by using flashcards with an example of self-talk on one side and the core belief it represents on the other side. An example of the assessment used to measure Rosario's knowledge of the core irrational beliefs is seen in Figure 11.14.

After Rosario has mastered the six irrational core beliefs, give him some examples of situations where a person got angry or scared. Be sure to include the event and the consequent feelings and behavior in each situation *but not the mediating belief*. Ask Rosario to provide the mediating belief. For example, a girl is teased by her brother (A) and she gets angry and screams at him, "I hate you!" (C). What kind of thinking (B) do you suppose she is doing that makes her angry?" If you want, you can list all six types of thinking for Rosario and have him choose the right one. In this particular case, the most appropriate response would be "You stink!" thinking. Another way to teach this competency is to use pictures. For example, the pictures in Figures 11.15 through 11.17 show A, B, and C and require the student to write (or state) the irrational or rational mediating belief in the thought balloon over the student's head. If you are unable to use line drawings, use a Polaroid to take posed snapshots of your students and write in the dialogue on "stick-ons" you can purchase from a photography store. Use an assessment similar to the one in Figure 11.18 to see if Rosario can identify the mediating beliefs. He should be about 90% accurate within an appropriate time limit (depending on whether you read or he reads) without prompting (see Objective 9a or 9b in Figure 11.6).

(*Text continues on p. 404.*)

Examples of You stink! thinking

People who do things I don't like are rotten and deserve to be punished.

Anybody who walks away from a fight is a wimp.

One of the worst things a person can do is make fun of another person.

People who tease you (others) are no good.

People who tease you (others) deserve whatever they get.

If somebody gets hurt for bothering others, it serves them right.

Not-Examples of You stink! thinking

I can't help the way I am. (*Robot*)

If people don't like me, there is nothing I can do about it. (*Robot*)

People shouldn't tease or make fun of others. (*Fairy Tale*)

People wouldn't tease me if I was OK (a good person). (*I stink*)

Being made fun of (teased) is scary. (*Namby Pamby*)

I'll never be able to stop others from teasing (making fun of) me. (*Doomsday*)

Figure 11.13. Examples and not-examples of You stink! thinking.

SELF-TALK / Core Beliefs

Name _____ Date _____ Score _____

When the teacher says "Begin," identify each example of irrational self-talk by circling the correct label underneath it. Work as quickly and as carefully as you can. CAP = 100% accuracy in _____ minutes.

1. "What others think about me is more important than what I think about myself."
   You stink!   I stink   Namby Pamby   Robot   Fairy Tale   Doomsday

2. "No matter how hard I try, I can't change the way I am."
   You stink!   I stink   Namby Pamby   Robot   Fairy Tale   Doomsday

3. "I'm no good."
   You stink!   I stink   Namby Pamby   Robot   Fairy Tale   Doomsday

4. "You can't trust teachers."
   You stink!   I stink   Namby Pamby   Robot   Fairy Tale   Doomsday

5. "Things should always go the way I want them to."
   You stink!   I stink   Namby Pamby   Robot   Fairy Tale   Doomsday

6. "People who make fun of others are rotten and deserve whatever they get."
   You stink!   I stink   Namby Pamby   Robot   Fairy Tale   Doomsday

7. "Things are hopeless and they're never going to get better."
   You stink!   I stink   Namby Pamby   Robot   Fairy Tale   Doomsday

8. "Being teased by others is the worst thing that can happen to you."
   You stink!   I stink   Namby Pamby   Robot   Fairy Tale   Doomsday

9. "I can't stand to make mistakes."
   You stink!   I stink   Namby Pamby   Robot   Fairy Tale   Doomsday

10. "If somebody doesn't like you, there isn't much you can do about it."
    You stink!   I stink   Namby Pamby   Robot   Fairy Tale   Doomsday

11. "People should be free to do whatever they want."
    You stink!   I stink   Namby Pamby   Robot   Fairy Tale   Doomsday

12. "If something can go wrong, it will."
    You stink!   I stink   Namby Pamby   Robot   Fairy Tale   Doomsday

Figure 11.14.   Example of assessment used to measure a student's knowledge of core beliefs.

Figure 11.15. Exercise for identifying the mediating belief (rational thinking).

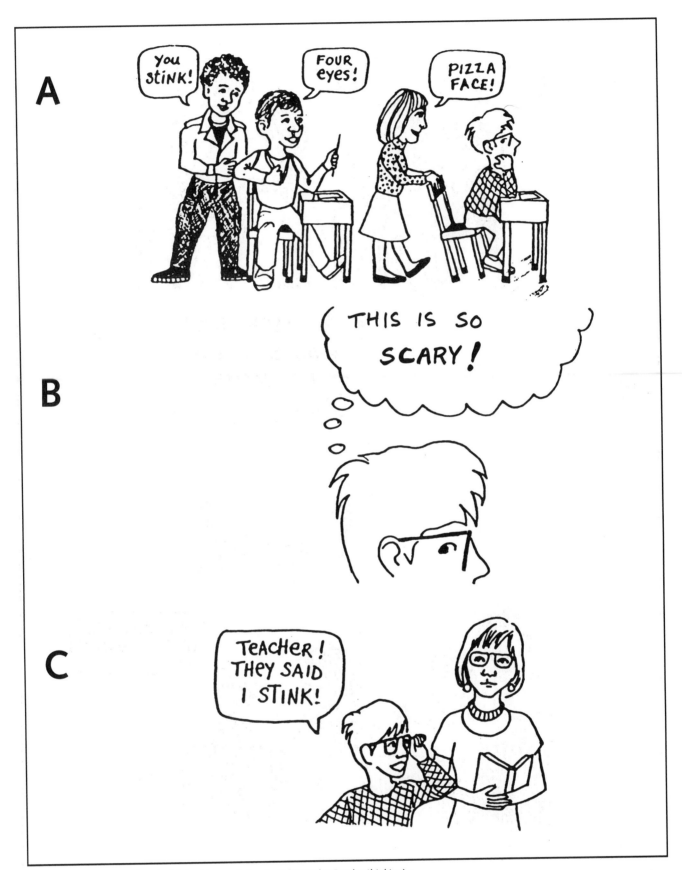

Figure 11.16. Exercise for identifying the mediating belief (Namby Pamby thinking).

Figure 11.17. Exercise for identifying the mediating belief (You stink! thinking).

SELF-TALK / Mediating Beliefs

Name _____ Date _____ Score _____

When the teacher says "Begin," read each case below and write what kind of thinking you are probably doing (You stink!, I stink, Robot, Namby Pamby, Fairy Tale, Doomsday). CAP = 90% accuracy in 3 minutes.

(A) Event	(B) Self-Talk	(C) Feelings/Behavior
1. Your teacher criticizes you for making a mistake		You get angry and call her a name
2. Your teacher criticizes you for making a mistake		You get scared and run out of the room
3. You make a mistake while doing your work		You feel like a dope and give up
4. Your teacher won't let you do what you want to		You get angry and have a tantrum
5. You fail a test		You don't accept any responsibility and tell everyone the test was too hard
6. You fail a test		You keep thinking about it until you get depressed
7. Some students laugh at you when you answer a question		You feel bad and stop answering questions
8. Some students tease you on the playground		You get angry and threaten to beat them up
9. Some students tease you on the playground		You get scared and run to the teacher
10. You don't get chosen by the team you want during recess		You get upset and refuse to play ball
11. You have a test in school		You lie awake the night before and worry about failing it
12. You have a test in school		You cut class so you don't have to take it.

Figure 11.18. Example of assessment used to measure skill at identifying mediating beliefs.

Name **Rosario**   Date **2-21-95**

Directions: Fill out in the following order: 1. C   2. A   3. B

A—Events (What happened?)	B—Thoughts (What did I think about?)	C—Feelings/Behaviors (How did I feel/act?)
(11:00) S. laughed at me.	You Stink I hate her for laughing at me.	(11:00) I got mad at S. and called her retardo woman.
(11:30) T. took my ruler from my desk without asking me.	You Stink I hate it when people steal from me.	(11:30) I got mad at T. and hit him when Mr. B. wasn't looking.
(2:00) T. said I was dopey looking.	You Stink cause he called me names.	(2:00) I got mad at T. and told him to shut up.

Figure 11.19. The A-B-C form with feelings/behavior, events, and thoughts data.

Now for the acid test. Using the form in Figure 11.19, have Rosario monitor his feelings and behaviors in column C, what happens to him in column A, *and* the type of thinking he was engaging in in column B. On a separate sheet, you record *what you observe* in columns A and C (you can't do B unless you are psychic) and then record *what you assume* his thinking was in column B. Compute the percentage of inter-rater reliability for *A, B, and C combined* and discuss with Rosario. When there is at least 80% agreement for 2 consecutive days without cueing (see Objective 10 in Figure 11.6), move on to the next competency.

☑ **Checkpoint 11.4**

[pages 394–404]

Fill in the answers to the following items (1–24). Check your responses by referring to the text; relevant page numbers appear in brackets.

Describe how you would use the A-B-C form to help your students **(1)** become aware of their feelings/behaviors _____

_____

_____ [395];

(2) become aware of the events associated with their feelings/behaviors_____

_____

_____

_____ [395];

and **(3)** identify the mediating belief_____

_____

_____ [404];

Label each of the following irrational beliefs according to its type (i.e., "You stink!," "I stink," "Namby Pamby," "Doomsday," "Fairy Tale," "Robot"). Check your responses by referring to the answers following Item 15.

(4) "I can't stand it when something I don't like (consider threatening) happens."

_____

(5) "People who do things I don't like (consider wrong) are bad and deserving of punishment."

_____

(6) "Things (events) should always turn out the way I want them to."

_____

(7) "I am the way I am and I can't help it."

_____

(8) "If something bad happens to me I should think about it all the time."

_____

(continues)

CHECKPOINT 11.4, continued

(9) "I don't deserve to get what I want."

_____

(10) "Anyone who walks away from a fight is a wimp." _____

(11) "People will either like you or they won't. There isn't much you can do about it."

_____

(12) "Things should come easily to me."

_____

(13) "Things are hopeless and they are never going to get better."

_____

(14) "I must be stupid if I make mistakes."

_____

(15) "When something goes wrong, I always expect the worst." _____

ANSWERS (4–15): (4) Namby Pamby; (5) You stink; (6) Fairy Tale; (7) Robot; (8) Doomsday; (9) I stink; (10) You stink; (11) Robot; (12) Fairy Tale; (13) Doomsday; (14) I stink; (15) Namby Pamby.

List at least one type of irrational thinking (e.g., "You stink!," "Fairy Tale," etc.) that might mediate between the events (A) and consequences (C) in each of the following items. Check your responses by referring to the answers following Item 24.

(16) A Student is provoked by peers

　　B

　　C Student hits peer in anger

(17) A Student is provoked by peers

　　B

　　C Student runs away in fear

(18) A Student is criticized by teacher

　　B

　　C Student gets angry and tantrums

(continues)

CHECKPOINT 11.4, continued

(19) A Student is criticized by teacher

B

C Student is hurt/upset and cries

(20) A Student is ignored by teacher and/or peers

B

C Student engages in chronic attention-seeking behavior

(21) A Student's requests denied by teacher and/or peers

B

C Student gets angry and tantrums

(22) A Student makes mistakes when working

B

C Student gets frustrated and gives up

(23) A Student fails test

B

C Student blames teacher

(24) A Student fails test

B

C Student gets depressed and talks about dropping out of school

ANSWERS (16–24): (16) You stink and/or Fairy Tale; (17) Namby Pamby; (18) You stink and/or Fairy Tale; (19) I stink and/or Namby Pamby; (20) I stink; (21) You stink and/or Fairy Tale; (22) I stink and/or Namby Pamby; (23) Robot; (24) Doomsday

Redo any items you missed. If you missed more than 5 items, reread the material. Otherwise, continue on to the next section.

Competency 7—Can dispute the thinking that mediates between the event and the feelings/behavior. This is, in my opinion, the most difficult competency to teach. Sometimes the student *wants* to keep the irrational belief; even though there is no evidence to support his belief—and, in fact, there is evidence that disputes it—he may refuse to accept this. Sometimes the student *needs* to keep the irrational belief. For example, a student who is small in stature may feel that the only way to keep the bigger belligerent students from hurting him is to initimidate them with out-of-control behavior. When threatened by a peer, this student goes "crazy," picks up the nearest object (rock, stick, or chair), and through wild screaming of threats and obscenities and aggressive posturing convinces the other party to back off. We've all seen this display in nature movies where animals puff themselves up twice their size or run around in circles or change colors to intimidate a predator. While this behavior in animals is instinctive, in humans it is learned. Societies do this when they go to war. Leaders incite people to make them angry at the enemy to help them overcome fear and to make their soldiers fight harder—you must *learn* to hate your enemy. Our small student has learned, through negative reinforcement, that he can escape from harm's way by being as wildly aggressive and intimidating as he can. The problem is, the only way he can overcome his fear in these situations is by making himself angry at his antagonist. To make himself angry he must believe that his antagonist is his enemy and is bad and deserving of punishment. Take away this belief and you deprive him of his anger and leave him with his fear, which may paralyze him (keep him from taking any action to defend himself) or force him to run away. The solution, of course, is to give this student an alternative to his out-of-control behavior. Perhaps if he learned how to be more assertive, he could *talk* himself out of harm's way.

Getting back to Rosario, let's assume that he identifies his irrational belief as, "People who do things I don't like are bad and deserve to be punished." This is classic "You stink!" thinking. Disputing irrational beliefs can be done one of two ways: a) For each irrational belief, you teach the disputations directly; or b) you teach the student a rule or procedure he can apply to any irrational belief to generate the disputations himself. It's analogous to what one does in teaching reading or spelling. You can teach each word to a student directly or you can teach him a rule or procedure he can apply himself to read or spell words he doesn't know. As with reading and spelling, I think it is more effective to do both—to teach him the disputations along with a procedure for disputing irrational beliefs he has not learned disputations for. I would teach Rosario the procedure first and see if he can generate his own disputations. I believe that he will be more inclined to accept his own disputations than those I might give him. If he has trouble learning the procedure or generating his own disputations with it, I would then provide him with some made-to-order disputations.

The procedure I would use to teach Rosario to generate his own disputations is another technique devised by Roush (1984). Borrowing the five disputation questions suggested by Maultsby (1984), Roush has again made them easier and more interesting to learn. The five questions are:

1. Does this thinking keep me *alive*?
2. Does this thinking make me *feel* better?
3. Is this thinking based on *reality*?
4. Does this thinking help me get along with *others*?
5. Does this thinking help me reach my *goals*?

Maultsby teaches his clients to apply each question to their irrational thinking. If the answer is "No" *to each question,* they should consider their thinking irrational and generate rational thinking in its place. If the answer is "Yes" *to at least one question,* they should consider their thinking rational (or at least, of some value to them) and should not give it up. Roush has made these questions easier to remember by sequencing them in such a way that they spell a mnemonic device, the word "AFROG." The letters in this word are taken from the first letter of each of the words italicized in the questions shown in the preceding list. Before teaching Rosario the five questions, you should explain to him that there are five reasons for keeping an idea or belief. One reason is that the belief helps *keep you alive*. Give him some examples of beliefs that might keep him alive (e.g., "Don't play with matches," "HIV can happen to anyone," "Drugs are not cool," "Drinking and driving don't mix," "Speed kills," etc.). Give him a few of these and see if he can come up with some on his own.

A second reason for keeping a belief is that it *makes you feel better*. Examples of ideas that make you feel better are positive affirmations about one-

---

Belief: I believe people who do things I don't like are bad and deserve to be punished.

1. *Does this belief help keep me ALIVE?*

   No. It could possibly lead to my being seriously hurt some day because it makes me angry and when I get angry I get into fights. Someday I might get into a fight with someone with a gun or a knife who could hurt me bad enough that I could die.

2. *Does this belief make me FEEL better?*

   No. When I think this way, I get angry and my anger feels bad.

3. *Is this belief based on REALITY?*

   No. Not everyone who does something I don't like is bad and deserves to be punished. Sometimes my mom does things I don't like but she's not a bad person. Sometimes my sisters and brothers do things I don't like but they are not bad people. Sometimes I do things that other people don't like but I'm not a bad person. And two wrongs don't make a right. Just because somebody does something that hurts me, it doesn't always mean I should do something to hurt them. There are other ways to keep people from hurting me, without punishing them.

4. *Does this belief help me get along with OTHERS?*

   No. It does just the opposite. When I think this way and get angry and fight with my classmates, they won't like me and I won't have any friends.

5. *Does this belief help me reach my GOALS?*

   No. My goals are to be happy, graduate from school, and get a good job. My thinking makes me angry and I can't be happy and angry at the same time. My anger makes me fight and I can't graduate from school if I keep getting in trouble for fighting and I can't get a good job if I don't graduate from school.

Figure 11.20. The A-F-R-O-G procedure—Rosario's "cheat sheet."

self and/or about specific situations or about life in general (e.g., "I'm smart"; "People like me"; "I'm a good person"; "I have lots of friends"; "No matter what happens to me, I can handle it"; "Things may be bad now, but things change"). Again, have Rosario come up with some beliefs on his own after you give him two or three examples. A third reason for keeping a belief is that it is *based on reality*. In other words, there is empirical (experiential) evidence or data that the belief is true. Examples of beliefs that are based on reality are "Most people who finish high school get better jobs and earn more money than people who don't finish"; "If I don't do my school work, I won't get passing grades"; "I'll get into trouble if I curse at teachers." Again, after you give Rosario a few examples, let him generate some. A fourth reason for keeping a belief is that it helps you *get along with others* (e.g., "You should do unto others as you would want them to do unto you," "Two wrongs don't make a right," etc.). A fifth reason for keeping a belief is that it helps you *reach your goals* (examples are "If at first you don't succeed, try, try again," etc.). I would then test Rosario to see if he can explain the disputation process and name each of the five reasons and give you at least one example of a belief for each reason. He should be able to do this to your

satisfaction within a reasonable time limit without prompting (see Objective 11 in Figure 11.6).

Next, ask Rosario to apply the questions to a few beliefs from a list of beliefs that you give him and tell you whether or not each belief is rational or irrational. Make sure he goes through the procedure out loud so you can evaluate his performance and give him feedback (e.g., prompts and corrections). If you are satisfied with his responses for the first two or three items, have him do the rest on his own without any help from you. When he is able to do all of them correctly within a reasonable time and without prompting (see Objective 12 in Figure 11.6), move on to the next competency.

If Rosario has difficulty learning and/or applying the A-F-R-O-G procedure, he may have to use a "cheat sheet" like the one shown in Figure 11.20. He can refer to it in much the same manner as he might refer to a dictionary to look up the pronunciation or meaning of a word. Have Rosario help you write his cheat sheet. With the right prompting, he may be able to come up with some of the disputations himself.

Competency 8—Can produce an alternative (fair-pair) belief. Whether Rosario uses his procedure to dispute a belief without assistance or he uses his "cheat sheet," he will need to replace it with an alter-

Old (irrational) Belief	New (rational) Belief
"People who hurt others deserve to be hurt (an eye for an eye)."	"Two wrongs don't make a right." "Bad behavior doesn't always mean the person is bad."
"When something bad happens to me I should worry about it all the time."	"Don't worry; be happy!"
"I must be good at everything I do."	"Nobody's perfect."
"Everyone must like me."	"You can't please all the people all the time."
"Everything must go my way."	"You can't always get what you want. (But if you try hard enough, you might find you can get what you need.)"
"Everyone must treat me fairly all the time."	"Who said life is fair?"
"I have no control over what happens to me."	"But do I have control over myself."

Figure 11.21. Examples of fair-pair thoughts.

native (fair-pair) belief. To do this on his own, Rosario needs to know that a rational belief is typically one of the following:

a. A belief that has a meaning opposite to the irrational belief (e.g., "It's terrible to make mistakes" and "It's OK to make mistakes"), or

b. a disputation of the irrational belief (e.g., "It's terrible to make mistakes" and "Nobody's perfect").

Before assessing Competency 8, make sure Rosario knows the definitions for rational and irrational beliefs (see Objective 13 in Figure 11.6) and he can differentiate (identify) them (Objective 14a or 14b in Figure 11.6). Next, provide him with some models to go along with the rule, and see if he can apply the rule by giving him some irrational belief statements and having him generate rational belief statements for each. To be correct, each rational statement should either be an opposite of the irrational statement or a disputation of the irrational belief. He should be able to generate at least 9 rational statements out of 10 irrational beliefs. He should do this without prompting and within a reasonable time limit (see Objective 15a or 15b in Figure 11.6). Assuming Rosario has difficulty doing this, you are going to have to provide him with rational statements in the same manner as you provided him with disputations for Competency 7. Refer to Figure 11.21 for fair-pair examples of irrational beliefs and corresponding rational belief statements.

☑ **Checkpoint 11.5**

[pages 406–409, 412]

Fill in the answers to the following items (1–16). Check your responses by referring to the text; relevant page numbers appear in brackets.

Two ways to dispute irrational beliefs are:

(1) _____

_____

(2) _____

_____ [406]

(continues)

CHECKPOINT 11.5, continued

An example of a belief that helps keep you alive is

(3) _____

_____

_____ [407]

An example of a belief that makes you feel better is

(4) _____

_____

_____ [407]

An example of a belief that is based on reality is

(5) _____

_____

_____ [408]

An example of a belief that helps you get along

with others is (6) _____

_____

_____ [408]

An example of a belief that helps you realize your

goals is (7) _____

_____

_____ [408]

Write examples of logical, empirical, and functional disputations (arguments) for the belief, "People who do things I don't like are bad and deserve to be punished."

(8) logical:_____

_____

_____

_____

(9) empirical: _____

_____

_____

_____

(continues)

CHECKPOINT 11.5, continued

(10) functional: _____

_____

_____

_____ [412]

Write a fair-pair target (rational) belief for each of the following irrational beliefs:

(11) "I know I'm OK if others tell me I'm OK."

_____

_____ [409]

(12) "People who do things I don't like are bad and deserve to be punished."

_____

_____

_____ [409]

(13) "It's not fair that I can't get what I want whenever I want it."

_____

_____

_____ [409]

(14) "When bad things happen to me, it is usually the fault of others."

_____

_____

_____ [409]

(15) "If something can go wrong, it will."

_____

_____

_____ [409]

(16) " I can't stand it when something bad happens."

_____

_____

_____ [409]

Redo any items you missed. If you missed more than 3 items, reread the material. Otherwise, continue on to the next section.

Competency 9—Can internalize the alternative (fair-pair) belief. The fact that Rosario is able to dispute his irrational belief and generate an alternative rational belief does not mean that he will automatically internalize, or learn, his new belief or give up his old one. He needs to learn his new belief in much the same manner as he learned the old one, by hearing it repeated over and over again. This time, however, instead of hearing someone else (e.g., a parent, sib, or teacher), he needs to practice saying his new belief to himself over and over again several times a day. He must learn that the act of disputing an old belief and generating a new belief is not the end of cognitive restructuring. He should be taught how beliefs are learned so that he can better understand how he can learn new rational beliefs. Discuss with Rosario different ways he might learn a new belief. Some of these include:

a. listening to a tape recording of him saying his new belief;

b. reading his new belief from a card several times per day;

c. keeping a journal in which he keeps a daily record of the times he experienced events that produced some anger and what he said to himself to keep the anger managable;

d. keeping track of how many times he thinks his new belief (and rewards himself) or how many times he says his new belief to someone (and is rewarded by them).

Assume Rosario knows how to learn a new belief if he can a) explain how beliefs are learned, and b) describe specific activities for learning them (see Objective 16 in Figure 11.6).

OK. So now Rosario has demonstrated mastery of all nine competencies. What do you do now? Now you have Rosario put all of the competencies together and use cognitive restructuring to modify his irrational belief. Give him a little notebook to write in, along with the following assignment: Every time he experiences anger, he is to write down how he feels (e.g., furious, angry, annoyed, irritated); what he does (e.g., fight, talk, nothing); what happened to him (who did what); what he thinks about it ("you stink," "I stink," "fairy tale," etc.); try to dispute that thinking (using A-F-R-O-G questions); generate alternative thinking and a plan for learning the new thinking. If he needs help or encouragement, he can always come to you. Don't lose sight of your original goal: Rosario will use cognitive restructuring to change his own thinking. When you see him actually doing this, and/or check his notebook periodically and find appropriate entries, reward him with social praise and other reinforcement as needed.

Caveat Emptor

There is some evidence that cognitive restructuring is an effective intervention in children and adolescents for anxiety (Albert, 1972; Brody, 1974; DiGiuseppe & Kassinove, 1976; Meyer, 1982; Warren, 1978); low self-esteem (Bernard, 1979; Dye, 1980; Katz, 1974); low frustration tolerance (Brody, 1974); anger (Forman, 1980); and depression (Butler, Miezitis, Friedman, & Cole, 1980). However, beware—cognitive restructuring is not for everyone. There are some limitations you need to know if you are considering using it with your students.

First of all, not all of your students are going to be willing to learn cognitive restructuring. I have already discussed the case of the student who needs to hold on to his irrational behavior because of what it does for him; the student who needs his irrational thinking to fuel his anger because it helps him overcome his fear and survive (literally, in some cases) among his peers; the student who needs his irrational thinking to feed his fear because it helps him act like a victim, getting him sympathy and support from adults who feel sorry for him; the student who needs his irrational thinking to keep him depressed because he can't bear the pain of his other emotions. None of these students are going to give up their irrational thinking without first getting a replacement "crutch" that provides them with whatever they need. The student who has to be angry to keep the wolves at bay needs to learn how to be assertive; the victim needs to learn how to fend for himself and how to get what he wants from others without appearing helpless; and the depressed student may need medication and/or therapy to help him deal with painful emotions. My point is, when students resist the use of cognitive restructuring techniques, pay attention to their protestations and back off.

Another limitation to be aware of is the "personal fable" (Protinsky, 1976) which is sometimes seen in adolescents who believe their thoughts and feelings are unique. The personal fable—that a certain belief may be true for others but not for them because they are different—prevents the adolescent from considering rational ideas. Protinsky reported that group work, particularly sharing their beliefs, is helpful to adolescents in overcoming the personal fable. Another problem that often surfaces with adoles-

cents in cognitive restructuring programs is feeling "phony," that, somehow, "it's not me." Adolescents need to be encouraged and reminded that all new skills feel awkward at first, but with practice they will become comfortable with their new thinking. They (and you) also need to understand that beliefs are not developed overnight. Consequently, they are not going to change overnight; it is a long, gradual process.

Some students may be willing to learn cognitive restructuring but they may not have the cognitive skills necessary to master it. Your students don't have to read or write at grade level in order to use cognitive restructuring, but they must be cognitively able to dispute beliefs. Another of Roush's (1984) suggestions is: If students have difficulty with logical disputations (i.e., the belief is irrational because it doesn't make sense), try an empirical disputation (i.e., the belief is irrational because there is no physical or experiential evidence to support it). If the student still has trouble comprehending this, try a functional disputation where you appeal to the student's basic sense of hedonsim (i.e., the belief is irrational because it results in pain for the student). Examples of logical, empirical, and functional arguments for each of the six irrational core beliefs may be seen in Figure 11.22.

If the student can't understand and generate a functional disputation, you will probably have to look for an alternative to cognitive restructuring. Before you do, you might try a modified form of cognitive restructuring in which *you* dispute the student's irrational thinking for him. You tell him what's wrong with his thinking and you give him a fair-pair rational belief. While this appears to be a simpler, more straightforward approach than teaching students how to use cognitive restructuring, it has certain weaknesses. By not teaching the student how to use cognitive restructuring himself, you must take the time and make the effort to use it with him. *You* will have to be on the lookout for his displays of anger. *You* will have to help him identify the event and mediating belief. *You* will have to help him dispute this belief and generate an alternative belief and reinforce him every time you hear him voice his new belief. He won't have to master any competencies, but *you* will. An excellent example of the inelegant approach to cognitive restructuring may be seen in an article by De Voge (1977). I personally don't like the inelegant approach. To me, it's analogous to painting over wallpaper: You have to get rid of the wallpaper if you want the paint to adhere; likewise, you have to get rid of the irrational thinking if you want the rational thinking to take hold, and you sim-

"You stink!"	*Logical:*	"Do you do bad things (or things others don't like) sometimes? Are you a bad person? Should you always be punished for doing something that others don't like?" Have the student try to give you an example of his doing something to someone that they didn't like or that they thought was bad (e.g., calling someone a name they didn't like or taking something away from them or disappointing another person). The point you want to get across is that people are fallible and we often do things that hurt or disappoint others; if we do such things and we don't consider ourselves bad or deserving of punishment, why should we consider others bad and deserving of punishment?
	Empirical:	Have the student collect data to support (or disprove) his argument. For example, if he believes that *all* of his teachers are *always* picking on him, have him collect data for a few days on positive and negative comments his teachers direct at him; hopefully, these data will show that not all (but some) of his teachers pick on him some (not all) of the time.
	Functional:	Simply ask the student if his thinking makes him feel better or worse: "How do you feel when you think that all of your teachers always pick on you? Does that make you feel good or bad? Do you like feeling bad? Maybe if you changed your thinking you might start feeling better—would you like to feel better?"
"I stink!"	*Logical:*	Where performance anxiety is the issue and the student is reluctant to try new tasks, you can use the argument that everyone makes mistakes; nobody's perfect. Where low self-esteem is the issue and the student is a social isolate, you can use the argument that everyone has value or self-worth simply by virtue of being a person.
	Empirical:	Have the student list all the tasks she learned to do over the years, such as feed herself, dress herself, and learn language. We take many of these for granted but they are not all easy to learn. Have the student list some things she learned to do that not everybody else can do, such as use a personal computer, take her bike apart and put it together, draw, and do well at math. Have the student make a list of all the people who like her including family members, teachers, and peers; if she can't think of people who like her, have her collect data on the number of times people at school (peers or teachers) greet her, compliment her, smile at her, or try to help or "be nice" to her over a 3-day period.
	Functional:	The same as for "You stink!"
"Robot"	*Logical:*	"People are not machines. Look at all the ways you have changed already; therefore, you can't say that it's impossible for you to change the way you are or that you have little or no control over how you behave."
	Empirical:	Have the student monitor his own behavior. Use a behavior that he is changing, such as the number of math facts computed correctly on daily quizzes; have him plot data (e.g., test scores) on a chart and call his attention to the change in his behavior.
	Functional:	The same as for "You stink!"
"Namby Pamby"	*Logical:*	"You can stand it; you're still alive, here, and not crazy. Think of the worst thing that could happen to you—how does this compare?"
	Empirical:	Have the student collect data on events in her life (for 1 week) that are threatening and also write down whether or not the threat ever materialized (i.e., whether it was actually as bad as she thought it would be) and what happened to her (i.e., if she got hurt, sick, died, or whatever she thought would happen to her).
	Functional:	The same as for "You stink!"
"Fairy Tale"	*Logical:*	"Life is not fair, so (logically) you can't expect things always to turn out the way you want them to."
	Empirical:	Have the student collect data on events in his life over a 1-week period that he considers fair (i.e., turned out the way he wanted) or unfair (i.e., didn't turn out the way he wanted).
	Functional:	The same as for "You stink!"
"Doomsday"	*Logical:*	"Bad things are always happening to good people; if they worried about that prospect all the time, they would never experience any joy in their lives. It doesn't pay to worry about things over which you have little control."
	Empirical:	Have the student collect data about good or positive things that happened to her over a 1-week period.
	Functional:	The same as for "You stink!"

Figure 11.22. Sample disputations.

ply cannot do this by using the inelegant form of cognitive restructuring. I especially don't like this approach with "I stink" thinking. Telling someone that his thinking is hurting him and that he needs to think differently can be interpreted by an "I stink" thinker as *validation* that *he* is worth less because his thinking has less worth. A better alternative may be to try an entirely different strategy. For example, in Rosario's case, if he couldn't handle the most basic (functional) disputation, I might instead try some stress management (i.e., relaxation training) to help him with his anger awareness and control. Another alternative might be problem solving, whereby Rosario learns to generate alternative solutions to the problem of peer provocation, makes a plan to help him implement the most promising solution, and then implements the plan.

What if the student is willing and able to dispute his belief but discovers it is rational after all? What if he answers "Yes" to one or more of the five sacred questions? What if his belief is logically sound and/or empirically based? What then? Then he keeps his belief and, with your help, tries an alternative strategy to solve the behavior problem.

Other Applications

I have spent a considerable amount of time and space discussing a reactive approach to cognitive restructuring. You can also use cognitive restructuring proactively by teaching these same competencies to a group of students who may or may not have any behavior problems related to irrational thinking. Simply teach the same competencies in the same sequence with the same content and gear your instruction to a group instead of one student. Some teachers I know like cognitive restructuring so much they use it proactively, whether their students need it or not. They include it as a part of their "social skills" or "affective education" curriculum and spread out the instruction in several lessons over a number of months. I have no problem with this. If somebody had taught me cognitive restructuring at an early age, I could have avoided a lot of self-inflicted pain over the years. I consider it every bit as important to teach as reading, math, science, or anything else in the traditional curriculum.

If you don't have room in your schedule to teach cognitive restructuring on a proactive basis, you will need to know how to determine whether, and when, it has become necessary to teach it on an as-needed basis. This can be done in a number of ways. First,

let's assume you have a student whose behavior problems are not responding to a traditional (i.e., behavioral) intervention and it appears that something more exotic may be required. Conduct a Pre-Mod analysis to determine whether or not the student lacks any of the essential prerequisites such as awareness, self-control, skill competency, etc. Include a beliefs assessment to determine whether or not the student endorses any irrational beliefs that may be contributing to his maladaptive behavior. If the beliefs assessment indicates that the student does, in fact, engage in irrational thinking, consider instituting a cognitive restructuring program in the same manner as described for Rosario.

A second method for determining when and if cognitive restructuring is necessary is to give all of your students a set of beliefs assessments at the beginning of the school year as a screening measure. This way, you may be able to identify those particular students and those specific irrational beliefs you need to work on. This could lead to a proactive program where you could divide those students who need cognitive restructuring into groups according to beliefs and/or cognitive abilities and teach them from day one, before behavior problems arise. Or you could use the information from your screening program to identify students who may be at risk for behavior problems because of their irrational thinking.

A third approach would be to simply watch and listen to your students. What they say and do will tell you a great deal about what they think. Students who get angry and say things like "That's not fair" whenever things don't go their way are probably engaging in Fairy Tale thinking. Students who are afraid to try new things for fear of making mistakes and looking bad are probably engaging in I stink thinking. Students who are always blaming others for their failures and who can't take any credit for their successes are probably Robot thinkers. You stink! thinkers are characterized by their belligerent behavior, while depression is often seen in students who engage in Doomsday thinking. Students who engage in Namby Pamby thinking typically overreact to everything they perceive as threatening and often manifest anxiety. Figure 11.23 includes a list of common maladaptive behaviors and corresponding irrational beliefs. If you find a student or students who engage in any of these behaviors, you can always validate your suspicions by administering a beliefs assessment. You can construct your own assessments by following the instructions given in the next section of this chapter.

"You stink!"

physical and/or verbal aggression when provoked

truancy and/or chronic tardiness

lying, stealing, cheating, swearing

destruction of property; vandalism

off task; doesn't do school work (enjoys spiting others)

teases or makes fun of others (as a form of punishment for something they have done—retribution)

"I stink"

attention seeking/disruptive (needs attention of others to validate her worth)

noncompliant and/or does not complete assignments (performance anxiety; fear of failure)

submissive behavior (allows self to be bullied and/or manipulated)

difficulty handling criticism

teases or makes fun of others (to make herself feel more important)

"Fairy Tale"

noncompliant (if he feels he should not have to follow a given directive or any directive)

physical and/or verbal aggression (directed at any individual who does not behave according to his "rules")

tattling

rule violations ("rules are made to be broken"; "rules are for the other guy"; "I can wear my hat, chew gum, leave my seat, leave the room, talk with peers, etc.")

tantrums (to get his own way)

"Namby Pamby"

tattling

disruptive

off task (too upset to pay attention)

attention seeking (needs to be reassured that things are OK)

noncompliant (some things are too scary to try)

tantrums (to express her anxiety or get assistance)

"Doomsday"

off task (often preoccupied with negative thoughts)

withdrawn; socially isolated (too sad, worried, anxious to interact; peers reject him because he's a "drag")

noncompliant (doesn't want to do it if he thinks something could go wrong)

"Robot"

noncompliant (why bother doing anything—nothing I do makes a difference)

verbally and/or physically aggressive (attributes blame to external source)

doesn't do school work (why bother?)

gives up when frustrated ("If I can't do something, it's because it's too hard")

Figure 11.23. Examples of core irrational beliefs and the maladaptive behaviors often associated with each.

Assessing Beliefs

Before attempting to modify a person's beliefs, you need to determine: a) what the beliefs are; b) whether or not they need changing; and c) if they do, what specific changes are required. How do you find out what another person believes? This is no easy task, but one well worth the effort. The traditional method has been the pencil-and-paper test. This is still an acceptable approach as long as certain guidelines are followed.

1. The testing should be direct. This means it should be a direct measure of the student's beliefs without relying on esoteric interpretations. Projective tests are not direct measures of a person's beliefs. Completing a sentence *can* be a direct measure of a person's beliefs *if* the sentence relates to the beliefs you wish to measure. For example, if you want to ascertain the student's belief about school, you could have him complete the sentence, "I think that school is . . ."

2. The testing should be continuous. In other words, give the test more than once. This helps to ensure reliability or consistency of response. It is a good idea to give your entire class a pencil-and-paper beliefs inventory once a week or once a month. This way, you can see how their thinking changes over time or how persistent they are in their thinking. You can also see how each student's mood affects his thinking.

3. A number of test items should be included for each belief you wish to assess. For example, if you want to determine a student's locus of control, include more than one item such as, "If I get a passing grade on a test, a) it's more likely to be because I studied for it; b) it's more likely to be because I was lucky." Include several items that differentiate between internals and externals. If a student chose "b" (i.e., "because I was lucky") in the only item measuring locus of control, it doesn't prove that his locus of control is external. However, if a student consistently chose the external-oriented responses from a number of locus of control items, you could assume that he does, in fact, have an external locus of control.

4. Always compare the student's performance on the pencil-and-paper assessment with her observable behavior. When there is a discrepancy between the student's behavior and her responses on the pencil-and-paper test, I prefer

to give more weight to behavior. By "behavior," I mean what the student usually says or does at school. If, for example, a student consistently makes negative comments about school, tends to be tardy and/or truant, and is seldom observed being successful or having positive experiences at school, I assume she believes school is aversive. If her responses on a pencil-and-paper test suggested the opposite, I would not be inclined to give them any credence.

5. Try to conduct the pencil-and-paper assessment without being present. If the student has difficulty reading and/or writing, it may be necessary to provide her with a tape-recorded version of the test. She can listen to the items and either mark her responses if they are multiple choice, or tape-record them if necessary. Your presence during the testing session may have some effect on the student's performance. It might inhibit her from responding in a truthful (i.e., valid) manner.

6. Try to use published test instruments that present evidence of validity and reliability whenever possible. Measures of children's locus of control (related to Robot thinking) include the Locus of Control Scale (Nowicki & Strickland, 1973), the Intellectual Achievement Responsibility Ques-

tionnaire (IAR; Crandall, Katkovsky, & Crandall, 1965), the Multidimensional Measure of Children's Perceptions of Control (MMCPC; Connell, 1985) and the Stanford Preschool Internal–External Scale (Mischel, Zeiss, & Zeiss, 1974). Instruments that assess cognitive structures associated with depression and Doomsday thinking in children include the KASTAN (Kaslow, Tanenbaum, & Seligman, 1978), the Attributional Style Questionnaire (Fielstein et al., 1985), the Children's Negative Cognitive Error Questionnaire (CNCEQ; Leitenberg, Yost, & Carroll-Wilson, 1986), and the Hopelessness Scale (Kazdin, Rodgers, & Colbus, 1986). The Children's Self-Efficacy for Peer Interaction Scale (CSPIS; Wheeler & Ladd, 1982), the Self-Efficacy Scale for Social Skills (Ollendick, Oswald, & Crowe, 1986) and the Network of Relations Inventory (Furman & Buhrmester, 1985) assess childrens' beliefs about their ability to influence others or participate in social activities and may be appropriate to use with students who manifest anxiety in social situations related to I stink or Namby Pamby thinking. Two instruments that provide a more global picture of students' beliefs are the Children's Survey of Rational Beliefs: Form B, Ages 7–10; and the Children's Survey of Rational Beliefs: Form C, Ages 10–13; both by Knaus (1974).

Maladaptive Behavior:

When criticized by teachers (i.e., they point out mistake) student gets upset and refuses to respond.

irrational beliefs (iB)

I must be stupid if I make mistakes.

I must be good at everything I do and it's awful if I'm not.

Mistakes are always bad.

What people think or say about is more important than what you think about yourself.

If at first you don't succeed, it's best to give up so you won't be disappointed anymore.

My teachers like it when I'm wrong.

I never make mistakes.

I'm a failure.

I never do anything right.

Target Behavior:

When criticized by teachers (i.e., they point out mistake), student listens to criticism and tries again, w/o getting upset.

rational beliefs (rB)

Everyone makes mistakes.

It's OK to make mistakes.

Mistakes help you learn.

What you think about yourself is more important than what others think about you.

If at first you don't succeed, try, try again.

It's my teacher's job to tell me when I'm wrong.

Nobody's perfect

You can fail at something and still be a good person.

I'm good at lots of things.

Figure 11.24. Constructing a beliefs assessment.

Name _____ Date _____

Directions: Which of the 18 beliefs stated on the following pages do you think are most typical of *a student who is extremely sensitive to criticism from adults?* When criticized by teachers (i.e., when they point out a mistake or something he is doing wrong and/or attempt to correct him), this student gets visibly upset and refuses to cooperate (i.e., he gives up, refuses to try the task again, or refuses to respond altogether). Please indicate *how typical* each belief is by marking (circle) the descriptor underneath each belief.

Descriptor Key:

Very Typical ....the student *definitely believes* this

Somewhat Typical ....the student *probably believes* this

Less Typical ....the student *probably does not believe* this

Atypical.............................the student definitely does not believe this

Don't Know.......................not enough information given about the student to make a decision about whether or not the student believes this

If you are not satisfied with the wording of a statement, please feel free to change it. Also, feel free to make comments regarding any of the items.

1. Nobody's perfect.
   Very Typical   *Somewhat Typical*   *Less Typical*   *Atypical*   *Don't Know*

2. Everyone makes mistakes.
   Very Typical   *Somewhat Typical*   *Less Typical*   *Atypical*   *Don't Know*

3. My teachers like it when I'm wrong.
   Very Typical   *Somewhat Typical*   *Less Typical*   *Atypical*   *Don't Know*

4. I'm a failure.
   Very Typical   *Somewhat Typical*   *Less Typical*   *Atypical*   *Don't Know*

5. What you think about yourself is more important than what others think about you.
   Very Typical   *Somewhat Typical*   *Less Typical*   *Atypical*   *Don't Know*

6. I never make mistakes.
   Very Typical   *Somewhat Typical*   *Less Typical*   *Atypical*   *Don't Know*

(continues)

Figure 11.25. Validation edition of beliefs assessments.

Constructing beliefs assessments

Assuming none of the above-mentioned published assessments are appropriate, you will have to construct your own. The procedure is neither difficult nor time consuming. Your objective in assessing beliefs should be to identify those beliefs a student endorses which might support his maladaptive behavior and/or interfere with his engaging in the target behavior. The best way to achieve this objective is to provide the student with a list of statements reflective of beliefs or ideas and have him indicate which ones he agrees with (or believes to be true) and which he disagrees with (believes to be false).

For example, let's construct and validate a beliefs assessment for use with students who are sensitive to criticism from adults. When a teacher points out a mistake or something the student is doing wrong and/or attempts to correct him, this student gets visibly upset and refuses to cooperate. He gives up, refuses to try the task again or refuses to respond altogether. First, we take a piece of paper and write down the maladaptive behavior the student engages in. Next, we fold the paper in half and, on one side of the fold, we write all of the irrational beliefs (*iB*) we can think of that support the maladaptive behavior. *After we finish writing all of the iB statements,* we write a fair-pair rational belief (*rB*) for

7. You learn by your mistakes.
   Very Typical   *Somewhat Typical*   *Less Typical*   *Atypical*   *Don't Know*

8. Mistakes are always bad.
   Very Typical   *Somewhat Typical*   *Less Typical*   *Atypical*   *Don't Know*

9. I never do anything right.
   Very Typical   *Somewhat Typical*   *Less Typical*   *Atypical*   *Don't Know*

10. If at first you don't succeed, try, try again.
    Very Typical   *Somewhat Typical*   *Less Typical*   *Atypical*   *Don't Know*

11. What others think or say about you is more important than what you think about yourself.
    Very Typical   *Somewhat Typical*   *Less Typical*   *Atypical*   *Don't Know*

12. I must be stupid if I make mistakes.
    Very Typical   *Somewhat Typical*   *Less Typical*   *Atypical*   *Don't Know*

13. It's my teachers' job to tell me when I'm wrong.
    Very Typical   *Somewhat Typical*   *Less Typical*   *Atypical*   *Don't Know*

14. It's OK to make mistakes.
    Very Typical   *Somewhat Typical*   *Less Typical*   *Atypical*   *Don't Know*

15. You can fail at something and still be a good person.
    Very Typical   *Somewhat Typical*   *Less Typical*   *Atypical*   *Don't Know*

16. I must be good at everything I do and it's awful if I'm not.
    Very Typical   *Somewhat Typical*   *Less Typical*   *Atypical*   *Don't Know*

17. I'm good at lots of things.
    Very Typical   *Somewhat Typical*   *Less Typical*   *Atypical*   *Don't Know*

18. If at first you don't succeed, it's best to give up so you won't be disappointed anymore.
    Very Typical   *Somewhat Typical*   *Less Typical*   *Atypical*   *Don't Know*

Figure 11.25. *Continued.*

each one. We try to generate a list of sixteen to twenty iB and rB statements (i.e., approximately eight to ten of each). Now we go over each statement and reword it so it will be easy for our student to understand it. An example of this may be seen in Figure 11.24.

Once we have 18–20 belief statements, we need to validate them. First, we list them randomly on a second sheet of paper leaving room underneath each statement for the descriptors "very typical," "somewhat typical," "less typical," "atypical," and "don't know." Next, we add a set of directions such as those shown in the validation edition in Figure 11.25. Finally, we identify a small sample (N = 3 to 5) of

"experts" to serve as validators. If they are not familiar with the target student, they should at least be familiar with the maladaptive behavior he engages in. They complete our validation edition.

Notice the directions tell the validators to label each belief statement according to how typical it is of a student who is sensitive to adult criticism. The theory is that the iB statements are more typical of this student and the rB statements are less typical. All of the validators should mark the iB statements "very typical" or "somewhat typical" and the rB statements "less typical" or "atypical." Statements for which there is no clear (unanimous) consensus should be discarded or reworded. Statements for

Name _Joey_   Date _2/11/95_   CR

Directions: Read each statement below and decide whether it is true or false. If you believe the statement is true, write the letter "T" next to the number of the statement. If you think that it is false, write the letter "F" next to the number. It is not necessary to think about each one for very long. Be honest. You are not going to be graded on this and no one but you and your teacher will ever see it. Don't answer the way you think your teacher might want you to or the way you think you are supposed to. You won't get into any trouble because of your answers so answer the way you really believe.

__T__ 1. I like school.

__F__ 2. I have lots of friends.

__F__ 3. I'm good at lots of things.

__F__ 4. Nobody's perfect.

__T__ 5. People shouldn't make mistakes.

__T__ 6. You learn by your mistakes.

__T__ 7. What others think or say about you is more important than what you think about yourself.

__F__ 8. It's my teacher's job to tell me when I'm wrong.

__F__ 9. If at first you don't succeed, try, try again.

__T__ 10. People will either like you or not like you. There isn't much you can do about it.

__F__ 11. You can fail at something and still be a good person.

__T__ 12. What you think about yourself is more important than what others think about you.

__T__ 13. If something can go wrong, it will.

__T__ 14. My teachers like it when I'm wrong.

__F__ 15. It's OK to make mistakes.

__T__ 16. You should always treat others the way you would like to be treated.

__T__ 17. I must be stupid if I make mistakes.

__T__ 18. It's important to get an education.

__F__ 19. I must be good at everything I do and and it's awful if I'm not.

__T__ 20. Mistakes are always bad.

__T__ 21. If at first you don't succeed, it's best to give up so you won't be disappointed anymore.

__F__ 22. Everyone makes mistakes.

__T__ 23. I'm a failure.

__T__ 24. I never do anything right.

Figure 11.26. Student (final) edition of beliefs assessment.

which there is a clear consensus that disagrees with our scoring should also be discarded or reworded. For example, the expected response for Item 1 ("Nobody's perfect") is "less typical" or "atypical." The logic is that a student who gets upset when his mistakes are pointed out to him probably doesn't believe that "nobody's perfect"; if he did, he could use it to rationalize his making mistakes and probably wouldn't get so upset about having them brought to his attention. In order for Item 1 to be validated, all of our validators should mark it "less typical" or "atypical." If we do not have a clear consensus, we discard or reword this item. If there is a clear consensus but all of our validators mark Item 1 as "very typical" or "somewhat typical," we discard or reword

this item. We also discard or reword this item if one or more of our validators marks it "don't know."Let's assume our five experts each complete a validation edition of the beliefs assessment and there is a clear consensus for all of the items except for Item 6 ("I never make mistakes"). Rather than losing an item, we reword it as "People shouldn't make mistakes" and use it in our final (i.e., student) edition. To our 18 iB and rB statements, we add 6 neutral items which have little or nothing to do with the maladaptive behavior and serve as distractors so that what we are measuring is less obvious to our subjects. We also add the letters "CR" in the upper right-hand corner to serve as a code for "criticism." If we have a number of beliefs assessments, each for a different

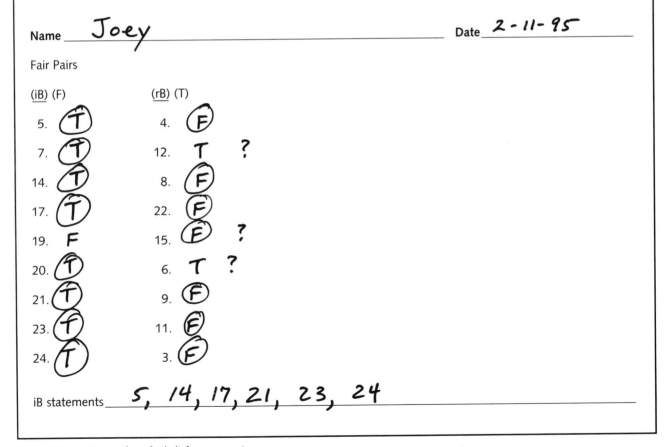

Scoring (CR)

1. Write subject's response (T or F) next to each number below.

2. Circle subject's response if it does not match answer (i.e., all iB statements should be answered *false* and all rB statements answered *true*).

3. Write ? next to all contradictory responses (i.e., when both iB and the fair-pair rB are answered the same).

4. *Being careful not to include any contradictory responses,* write the number of each iB statement answered *true*. These are the irrational ideas the student needs to dispute.

Name _Joey_   Date _2-11-95_

Fair Pairs

(iB) (F)   (rB) (T)

5. Ⓣ   4. Ⓕ
7. Ⓣ   12. T   ?
14. Ⓣ   8. Ⓕ
17. Ⓣ   22. Ⓕ
19. F   15. Ⓕ ?
20. Ⓣ   6. T ?
21. Ⓣ   9. Ⓕ
23. Ⓣ   11. Ⓕ
24. Ⓣ   3. Ⓕ

iB statements _5, 14, 17, 21, 23, 24_

Figure 11.27. Scoring form for beliefs assessment.

maladaptive behavior, we need a code to distinguish each without alerting the student as to what the assessment measures. The directions on our student edition are different from the directions that appear on our validation edition. We want our students to indicate whether or not they agree with the belief statements. An alternative to the true-and-false format would be a Likert scale including "strongly agree," "agree," "disagree," and "strongly disagree."

We administer the student edition shown in Figure 11.26 to a student who has difficulty handling teacher criticism. Using the scoring form shown in Figure 11.27 we find that he has made three pairs of contradictory responses. He answers Items 7 and 12 both true; Items 19 and 15 both false; and 20 and 6 both true. These items are fair pairs. For example, Item 7 is "What others think or say about you is more important than what you think about yourself," and Item 12 is "What you think about yourself is more important than what others think about you." Does the student really believe both of these statements are true? More likely he was careless or he misread them or he put down any old answer. Whatever the reason, I would not count his response on these items. As you can see, the student answered true to six iB statements (Items 5, 14, 17, 21, 23, and 24). I would count these and use them as irrational beliefs in a cognitive restructuring program. Keep in mind that one administration of a beliefs assessment may not be enough. You may have to administer alternate forms (the same items in different order) of the beliefs assessment three or four times before you have any real confidence in the results and/or you stop getting any contradictory responses.

☑ **Checkpoint 11.6**

[pages 410–420]

Fill in the answers to the following items (1–15). Check your responses by referring to the text; relevant page numbers appear in brackets.

Three ways for students to learn new beliefs are:

(1) _____

_____

(2) _____

_____

(continues)

CHECKPOINT 11.6, continued

(3) _____

_____ [410]

Three situations in which you might use cognitive restructuring are:

(4) _____

_____

(5) _____

_____

(6) _____

_____ [413]

Five guidelines to follow in assessing beliefs are:

(7) _____

_____

(8) _____

_____

(9) _____

_____

(10) _____

_____

(11) _____

_____ [414]

Four steps to follow in constructing a beliefs assessment are:

(12) _____

_____

(13) _____

_____

(14) _____

_____

(15) _____

_____ [416]

Redo any items you missed. If you missed more than 3 items, reread the material. Otherwise, continue on to the Chapter Assessment.

ASSESSMENT / CHAPTER 11 ▮

A list of acceptable responses appears following the Assessment.

1. You have a student named Harriet who engages in Fairy Tale thinking to the extent that she consistently finds fault with your discipline practices and complains stridently when she does not get her way. "That's not fair!", she yells for others to hear. The result is several disruptions in the course of a day. Since your traditional behavior management program has not been effective with Harriet, you decide to try a cognitive–behavioral approach. A beliefs assessment indicates Harriet thinks she should be allowed to do whatever she wants since it's her life and she's the one who has to live with the consequences of her actions (e.g., "If I don't study for a test and fail it, it's my problem, not yours."). Explain how you would use cognitive restructuring to help Harriet modify her irrational thinking. Your ultimate goal is for Harriet to use cognitive restructuring to modify her thinking without any assistance from you. Describe each of the steps in your program as if you were explaining it to a student teacher or substitute teacher.

2. Construct a beliefs assessment for the following maladaptive behavior: noncompliance (student does not comply with request unless it is repeated several times). Include directions to your students and to the examiner, as well as an answer key. Include at least 20 items. Describe how you would attempt to validate your assessment.

ACCEPTABLE RESPONSES

1. *Harriet.*

Should include all of the competencies the student would need to modify her own thinking *without assistance;* should also include a brief description of how you would develop each competency and measure student's competence.

1.1   Teach H how strong feelings such as anger can be harmful: a) Provide examples for H of how anger can be harmful; b) ask H to explain how the anger response in each situation is harmful.

1.2   Teach H that her anger (and subsequently, her disruptive and confrontive behavior) are often controlled by her thinking; teach H the A-B-C rule; ask H to state and explain the A-B-C rule; provide examples for H of how anger and maladaptive behavior are controlled by thinking.

1.3   Teach H how cognitive restructuring can be used to change thinking in order to manage anger and maladaptive behavior; ask H to state and explain each of the steps in the cognitive restructuring process.

1.4   Teach H to become aware of her anger; both you and H monitor her anger (C) on an A-B-C form until there is at least 80% agreement between her data and yours and she can monitor her anger without cueing.

1.5   Teach H to become aware of the events associated with her feelings; both you and H monitor her anger (C) and the events associated with her anger (A) on an A-B-C form until there is at least 80% agreement between your data and hers and she can collect data without cueing from you.

1.6   Teach H to recognize the thinking that mediates between the event and feelings/behaviors; teach H the six types of irrational thinking; give H examples of irrational thoughts and ask her to label each according to type; give H examples of events (A) and consequent affect and behavior (C) and ask her to produce the type of irrational thinking (B) that mediates between them; both you and H monitor her anger (C), the events associated with her anger (A), and the beliefs (B) that mediate between A and C on an A-B-C form until there is at least 80% agreement between the both of you and H can monitor without cueing.

1.7 Teach H how to dispute thinking that mediates between the event and the feelings/behavior; teach H how to use the A-F-R-O-G disputation procedure to dispute irrational beliefs; give H examples of rational and irrational beliefs and ask her to attempt to dispute each using the A-F-R-O-G procedure; ask H to attempt to dispute her irrational belief (i.e., that she should be allowed to do what she wants since it's her life and she's the one who experiences the consequences of her actions).

1.8   Teach H how to produce an alternative (fair-pair) belief; give H examples of irrational beliefs and alternative (fair-pair) beliefs; give H examples of irrational beliefs and ask her to produce fair-pair beliefs; ask H to produce a fair-pair belief to replace her irrational thinking.

1.9   Help H internalize fair-pair belief; teach H all of the techniques for internalizing her fair-pair belief; ask H to design a plan for internalizing her fair-pair belief.

2.   Your belief assessment for noncompliance should include items such as those listed below. While your items and mine need not match word for word, they should convey similar ideas. For every irrational belief (iB) you should try to include a fair-pair rational belief (rB). You should also include a few distractor items.

sample iBs [and fair-pair rBs]

Nobody should have to do anything he or she doesn't want to do. [Everybody has to follow the rules sometimes.]

Rules are made to be broken. [Good rules should be obeyed.]

I can't help the way I am. [You can change the way you are if you try hard enough.]

My teachers tell me to do things just because they like to boss students around. They are on a power trip. [My teachers usually ask me to do things that are good for me to do. They want me to do well in school.]

My teachers are not my parents so I don't have to listen to them. [When I'm in school, my teachers are responsible for me in the same way my parents are responsible for me at home.]

Only wimps do what they are told./It's not cool to be good in school./Students should be free to do whatever they want in school./I'm old enough to do what I want. [Everybody has to follow the rules sometimes.]

All of the rules at school are dumb. [Without any rules in school, little would get done and people might get hurt./Learning to follow rules is important.]

It's not fair that adults get to boss kids around. [Even when I'm an adult, there is always going to be somebody telling me what to do, e.g., the person I work for, the government, an officer in the armed services, etc.]

Compare your scoring/answer key with the one in Figure 11.27. Throw out contradictory responses (i.e., when student answers iB and fair-pair rB same) and look for all iBs answered true.

Validate your test items according to the procedure described in the text (see pages 412–420).

CHAPTER TWELVE

More Cognitive Strategies

Problem Solving and Self-Instruction

Upon successful completion of this chapter, the learner should be able to design interventions using cognitive behavior modification strategies including problem solving, self-instructional training, and verbal mediation.

This chapter begins where the last one left off. When it is not necessary or feasible to modify a student's beliefs, or when cognitive restructuring proves ineffective, there are other CBM strategies you can try. These can be just as effective at helping students change their behavior and are much easier to use and take less time than cognitive restructuring. *Self-instructional training* and *verbal mediation* are used to modify automatic self-talk (*what* students think) while *problem solving* focuses on the cognitive processes (*how* students think). Let's look at self-instructional training first.

SELF-INSTRUCTIONAL TRAINING

Self-instruction training (SIT) is based on research in the development of socialization and language in young children by the Russian psychologists Luria (1961) and Vygotsky (1962). Their findings suggested three stages by which the initiation and inhibition of voluntary motor behaviors come under verbal control. In the first stage, the speech of others in the child's environment (e.g., his parents) controls and directs his behavior. In the second stage, the child's own overt speech becomes an effective regulator of his behavior; he begins telling himself out loud what he should or should not do. In the third stage, the child's covert (i.e., inner) speech assumes a self-governing role; he stops telling himself what to do out loud and begins to think about it instead. Eventually, he no longer needs to think about what he should or should not do. He simply does it automatically (Meichenbaum, 1977, pp. 18–19).

This sequence may be experienced by adults as well as children. For example, when I first learned how to drive a manual shift automobile, my Uncle Syd would take me out in his old Chevy convertible and tell me what to do. I would repeat these directions out loud as I followed them. "Push in clutch with left foot. Shift down into first. Ease up on clutch and down on gas until it catches." My driving behavior was being regulated by my uncle. After several trials, I began to regulate my own behavior by telling myself what to do. Again, I spoke the directions out loud. Uncle Syd would simply nod his approval and say things like, "That's the way. Good!" By the time I reached the third stage, my self-instructions had gone "underground." I was thinking out my actions before I acted. Today, of course, I shift from gear to gear automatically and concentrate instead on the traffic, road conditions, and my destination. I no longer have to think about pushing in the clutch and shifting gears.

Borrowing on the theoretical work of Luria (1961) and Vygotsky (1962), Meichenbaum (1977) developed a practical program of self-instruction to help hyperactive, impulsive children bring their behavior under their own control. The first step requires an adult model to perform the task while talking to himself out loud. This step is referred to as *cognitive modeling*. The second step, *overt external guidance*, requires the child to perform the same task under the adult's direction. In *overt self-guidance*, the third step, the child performs the task while instructing himself aloud. The fourth step requires the child to whisper the instructions to himself as he performs the task; this is referred to as *faded, overt self-guidance*. Finally, in the fifth step, *covert self-instruction*, the child performs the task while guiding his performance via inner speech. If you have trouble remembering these steps, think of them as:

1. teacher says/teacher does;

2. teacher says/student does;

3. student says/student does;

4. student whispers/student does; and

5. student thinks/student does.

Meichenbaum's (1977) work in self-instruction eventually led to the development of the Think Aloud

materials, a commercially-available program in self-instructional training (Camp & Bash, 1981). These materials have been used effectively with hyperactive, impulsive, and aggressive students (Camp, 1980), and clearly represent a future trend in behavior management. While much of the research has focused on the effects of SIT on academic behaviors, there is research to suggest that SIT is also effective in improving social behaviors in problem children (Drummond, 1974; Monohan & O'Leary, 1971; O'Leary, 1968) and in prolonging a student's tolerance for resisting temptation (Hartig & Kanfer, 1973). In particular, SIT can be effective in dealing with low

---

Step 1.   Teacher (T.) models and talks out loud while student (S.) watches and listens.

   a. T. imitates S. doing work and starting to get upset; T. says out loud, "My muscles are getting tense and my face feels hot. I must be starting to get upset. What am I supposed to do when I get upset about my work?" T. pauses as if thinking.
   b. T. says out loud, "I know. First, I'm supposed to take a few deep breaths."
   c. T. models diaphragmatic breathing with her hand on her abdomen.
   d. T. says out loud, "That feels better. What should I do next?" T. pauses as if thinking.
   e. T. says out loud, "I know. I'll raise my hand and ask for help."
   f. T. models proper hand-raising and waiting-for-attention behavior.
   g. T. says out loud, "Good! I kept control over my behavior. I can do it!"

Step 2.   S. performs task while teacher gives him instructions out loud.

   a. S. role plays self doing work and starting to get upset; T. says out loud, "My muscles are getting tense and my face feels hot. I must be starting to get upset. What am I supposed to do when I start to get upset about my work?" S. pauses as if thinking.
   b. T. says out loud, "I know. First, I'm supposed to take a few deep breaths."
   c. S. does diaphragmatic breathing with his hand on his abdomen.
   d. T. says out loud, "That feels better. What should I do next?" S. pauses as if thinking.
   e. T. says out loud, "I know. I'll raise my hand and ask for help."
   f. S. models proper hand-raising and waiting-for-attention behavior.
   g. T. says, "Good! I kept control over my behavior. I can do it!"

Step 3.   S. performs task while he repeats steps out loud.

   a. S. role plays self doing work and starting to get upset; S. says out loud, "What am I supposed to do when I get upset while I'm doing my work?" S. thinks.
   b. S. says out loud, "I know. First, I'm supposed to take a few deep breaths."
   c. S. does diaphragmatic breathing with his hand on his abdomen.
   d. S. says out loud, "That feels better. What should I do next?" S. thinks.
   e. S. says out loud, "I know. I'll raise my hand and ask for help."
   f. S. models proper hand-raising and waiting-for-attention behavior.
   g. S. says out loud, "Good! I kept control over my behavior. I can do it!"

Step 4.   S. performs task while he whispers steps. Steps 4a through 4g are the same as steps 3a through 3g.

Step 5.   S. performs task while he thinks them (i.e., says them to himself). Steps 5a through 5g are the same as steps 4a through 4g.

Figure 12.1.   Example of self-instructional training program.

frustration tolerance, personal narrative behavior, helping students listen to directions before acting, and sitting/standing next to peer(s) without engaging in any provocative physical contact. An excellent source regarding research in SIT is Kendall and Braswell (1982)

Figure 12.1 is an example of a SIT program to help a student with low frustration tolerance. By the time the student has gone through Steps 1 through 5, she is able to talk herself through frustrating work situations without external assistance. If necessary, the teacher can provide the student with a card such as the one shown in Figure 12.2. This card not only acts as a reminder to talk through the problem, it also helps remind her what to say and do.

Some helpful hints in using SIT:

1. Whenever possible, use peer teaching by having children cognitively model while performing for another child.

WHEN I HAVE TROUBLE WITH MY WORK, I SHOULD:

① Check the work models and try again,

② ask an adult for help,

③ ask a friend for help, or

④ put it away, try something else, and come back to it later.

Figure 12.2. Alternative self-talk and responses for student who destroys work out of frustration.

2. Facilitate remembering in your students by having them move through the program at their own rate, building up the number of self-statements little by little. You can also use written cues or prompts such as the first few words of a statement on a card at the student's desk.

3. Students should not simply repeat the self-statement in a rote, mechanical fashion but should rehearse meaningful self-talk through paraphrasing. Whenever possible, have them speak the self-statement you have given them in their own words or have them generate the self-statements themselves.

4. In the beginning, when you are first introducing a student to SIT, use it to modify simple psychomotor or academic behaviors such as learning long division or putting a puzzle together. Do not use it to change behaviors associated with intense emotional states (e.g., anger or anxiety). After students have had a successful experience with SIT, use it to modify behaviors in the affective domain.

5. At the beginning of each SIT session, ask the students to recall their self-instructions. Students who cannot should practice their statements while you work with those who can remember. Let your students use scripts and/or tapes, but don't let students become dependent upon them. Eventually, they must memorize their self-talk.

6. Encourage your students to use their self-statements outside of the classroom (for homework). Ask them to remember one instance of when they used self-talk and to describe it at the beginning of the next lesson.

☑ Checkpoint 12.1

[pages 425–427]

Fill in the answers to the following items (1–15). Check your responses by referring to the text; relevant page numbers appear in brackets.

According to the Russian psychologists Luria and Vygotsky, the three stages by which the initiation and inhibition of voluntary motor behaviors come under verbal control are:

(1) _____

_____

(2) _____

_____

(3) _____

_____ [425]

Name and describe the five steps that make up self-instructional training developed by Meichenbaum.

(4) _____

_____

(5) _____

_____

(6) _____

_____

(7) _____

_____

(8) _____

_____ [425]

Three behaviors SIT is particularly helpful for are

(9, 10, 11): _____

_____

_____

_____ [426]

(continues)

CHECKPOINT 12.1, continued

Four helpful hints in using SIT are:

(12) _____

_____

(13) _____

_____

(14) _____

_____

(15) _____

_____ [427]

Redo any items you missed. If you missed more than 3 of the items, reread the material. Otherwise, continue on to the next section.

VERBAL MEDIATION

It has been said that "when a child is tempted to misbehave, he often thinks before, while, and after acting. When he thinks in words, overt or covert, the words mediate between the temptation (i.e., the stimulus situation which tends to evoke the misbehavior) and the target response" (Blackwood, 1970, pp. 251–252). This is essentially what verbal mediation is all about: Teaching students to talk themselves out of "bad" behavior and into "good" behavior. This skill may be particularly important in helping students deal with tempting situations. Consider the following situation. You have a student in your class who is engaging in off-task behavior (e.g., talking to peers) when she should be doing her work. She knows she will have to stay after school to finish her work if it is not finished by dismissal. Although talking to her peers is positively reinforcing, detention is extremely aversive to her. The temptation to talk to her peers, however, occurs in the morning and she doesn't have to experience detention until hours later in the afternoon. If, when tempted to talk to her peers, she was willing and able to use verbal mediation, she could describe the consequences of her off-task behavior to herself. (See

Figure 12.3.) It could serve as a warning strong enough to suppress the misbehavior. In addition, she could describe the consequences of a competing response (e.g., finishing her work, riding home on the school bus at dismissal, and being with her friends). Traditionally, in this type of situation, we would rely on extrinsic controls such as telling the student what will happen if she doesn't stop talking and get back on task, but this would not help the student learn self-control. We need instead to condition the student to produce her own verbal stimulus at the time of the temptation in order for her to eventually bring her behavior under her own control. How can we teach the student to do this? Through the use of mediation essays.

For example, the teacher has the off-task student dictate an essay ahead of time regarding her misbehavior. "Ahead of time" means before the misbehavior occurs. The essay contains the six questions shown in Figure 12.4. When the student misbehaves (i.e., is off task talking to peers), the teacher places a copy of the essay on her desk without any verbal interaction. The student is required to write two copies of the essay by the next day. If she doesn't complain at the time she receives the essay and she stops engaging in the off-task behavior, the assignment is decreased to one copy by the next day. If the student complains and/or the misbehavior continues, the number of copies is increased. If the assignment is not turned in by the following day, it is

doubled. If it is still not done, a detention slip is sent home for the parent(s) to sign. If the student does not stay for detention, detention is doubled. If she still doesn't stay for detention, she is sent to the principal. This is an example of a hierarchy of escalating consequences similar to those discussed in Chapter 6. If the student does the essay and gives it to the teacher upon entering class the following day, the teacher compliments and praises her. If it is not turned in the next day, the teacher waits until she has a chance to discuss the matter privately with the student. Detention is made highly aversive and the student may only leave detention if and when she cooperates by copying the essay.

For the first two misbehaviors, the student is required to copy the essay at home. For the third misbehavior, the student is kept after school to paraphrase the essay, and if she continues to misbehave, she is required to write the essay from memory. Finally, she is required to orally describe the situation that typically stimulates her misbehavior and how she would think (i.e., what she would say to herself) when tempted again.

Does verbal mediation work? It appears to. There have been a number of studies comparing the efficacy of verbal mediation and other traditional behavior modification approaches such as token reinforcement on a wide range of behaviors and subjects, and the findings suggest verbal mediation is more effective (Blackwood, 1970; Miller et. al., 1987).

Figure 12.3. Verbal mediation.

1. *What am I doing (or did I do) that I'm not supposed to do?*

   I'm talking to my friends instead of working on my assignment.

2. *Why shouldn't I be doing this?*

   Because talking to my friends will get me into trouble with the teacher. It will keep them from doing their work. It will keep me from doing my work and if I don't do my work, I will fail in school.

3. *What will probably happen if I continue doing it?*

   I will probably have to stay after school until my work is finished. I'll miss the school bus and my parents will be called to come get me or else I'll have to walk home. My parents will be angry with me if they have to come get me. They might take away my TV and ground me. My friends might be angry with me if they get detention too.

4. *What should I be doing instead?*

   I should be doing my work without talking to anybody.

5. *Why should I be doing it instead?*

   So I won't get into trouble in school or at home. So I won't have to stay after school. So I'll pass my subjects at school and learn something. So my friends can get their work done.

6. *What will probably happen if I do what I'm supposed to?*

   I'll get my work done and leave school at dismissal. I'll be able to take the bus home and not have to walk.

Figure 12.4. Sample essay used in verbal mediation program.

☑ **Checkpoint 12.2**

[pages 428–430]

Fill in the answers to the following items (1–8). Check your responses by referring to the text; relevant page numbers appear in brackets.

Verbal mediation is all about

(1) _____

_____

_____

_____ [428].

This skill may be particularly important in helping students deal with

(2) _____

_____

_____ [428].

(continues)

CHECKPOINT 12.2, continued

Six questions used in a verbal mediation essay are:

(3) _____

_____

(4) _____

_____

(5) _____

_____

(6) _____

_____

(7) _____

_____

(8) _____

_____ [430].

Redo any items you missed. If you missed more than 2 items, reread the material. Otherwise, continue on to the next section.

PROBLEM-SOLVING SKILLS

Students with behavior problems tend not to perceive the same numbers or types of behavioral options perceived by others and are more likely to engage in rigid thinking (Spivack & Shure, 1974). One reason for this may be the *availability heuristic,* the theory that people are apt to select those behavioral options which are easiest for them to remember (Tuersky & Kahneman, 1973). Obviously, the things easiest for them to remember are those events in their lives that most dramatically aroused emotions and/or occurred most frequently. For example, if a student has seen force applied frequently or dramatically to solve problems, he is most likely to recall this "solution" when he is faced with a problem to solve. When he experiences a new situation, he may search for options but because of his specially trained perception, he may only recognize the ones involving force. Because he fails to perceive non-forceful options, he has fewer choices to make and therefore has less freedom to act (Howell & Kaplan, 1980). A student who comes from a home where disagreements are settled by fighting is most likely to perceive fighting as the only viable option available to him when he finds himself in a dispute at school. This may explain why many students persist in engaging in maladaptive behavior such as fighting even though they are repeatedly punished for their actions. They simply can't perceive any other behavioral alternatives. These students need to be taught how to problem solve.

Why? First of all, problem-solving skills are valuable to adjustment. It has been said that "psychological health is related to a problem-solving sequence consisting of the ability to recognize and admit a problem, to reflect on problem solutions, to make a decision, and to take action" (Kendall & Braswell, 1982, p. 116). There is also some research which suggests that improvement in problem solving can lead to improved classroom behavior (Spivack & Shure, 1974).

Second, we need to encourage children and youth to think of their own solutions to their own problems and not always tell them what we think they should do. (See Figure 12.5.) Students are more likely to choose to use an idea if it is their own. Researchers found that when children were allowed to think of their own solutions, they were less likely to resist than when suggestions were offered or demanded by an adult (Spivack & Shure, 1974). We must stop thinking for the child if we want him to think for himself.

Figure 12.5. You can't always depend on others for solutions.

Third, problem solving is a lifetime skill—something the student can use in or out of school, today or five years from today. Problem solving, truly, is probably more important than a lot of the curriculum we currently teach.

What Is Problem Solving?

Problem solving has been defined as "a behavioral process . . . which a) makes available a variety of potentially effective response alternatives for dealing with the problematic situation and b) increases the probability of selecting the most effective response from among these various alternatives" (D'Zurilla & Goldfried, 1971, p. 108). In terms that kids might understand, problem solving is what you do to find the solution to a problem that is most likely to work.

Most of the research in the area of problem solving has been done by George Spivack and his associates (Spivack, Platt, & Shure, 1976). They have divided problem solving into five separate competencies:

1. recognizing a problem,

2. defining the problem and the goal,

3. generating alternative solutions,

4. evaluating the solutions, and

5. designing a plan.

Let's take a look at each.

1. Recognizing a problem.   Not everyone recognizes a problem when it exists. In order to have this competency, a student must be able to differentiate between instances and not-instances of problems. It would help a great deal if your students knew the characteristics of a problem. Kendall and Braswell (1982) define a problem as "a situation to which a person must respond in order to function effectively but for which no effective response alternative is readily available." In simpler terms, you have a problem when you need to do something to get what you want but you don't know what to do or how to do it. Problems can be interpersonal or intrapersonal. The former always involves another person. Having a bigger student extort lunch money from you is an example of an interpersonal problem. On the other hand, an intrapersonal problem does not involve anyone but yourself. An example of this is losing your lunch money.

If you want to assess whether or not your students are able to recognize a problem when they see one you can give them instances and not-instances of problems and see if they can differentiate between them. Consider the following example:

TEACHER: "You get home from school on Monday and find that you left your math book in your desk at school and you have an assignment due on Wednesday. Is that a problem?"

STUDENT: "No."

TEACHER: "Why not?"

STUDENT: "Because there is something you can do to get what you want and you know what it is." [in other words, there is an effective response alternative readily available]

TEACHER: "What is that?"

STUDENT: "You can get the book on Tuesday and still have time to finish the assignment."

TEACHER: "Here's another . . . You get home from school on Monday and find that you left your math book at school, which is locked up for the evening, and you have an assignment due on Tuesday. Your math class meets first period. Is that a problem?"

STUDENT: "Yes, because if you wait until Tuesday to get the book, you won't have time to finish the assignment."

TEACHER: "You get home from school on Monday and find that you left your math book at school, which is locked up for the night, and you have an assignment due on Tuesday. Your math class meets third period after a study hall. Is that a problem?"

STUDENT: "No, because you can get your book on Tuesday and finish the assignment during study hall."

An alternative for younger students might be using pictures of instances and not-instances of problems.

Teaching students to recognize instances of problems can follow the same procedure as assessment. I recommend using a direct instruction approach similar to the following one.

TEACHER: "We have a problem when we need to do something to get what we want but at the time we need to do something, we don't know what to do. What's a problem?"

STUDENTS: [state definition of a problem]

TEACHER: "Good! Now here's an example of a problem. Some bigger kids are picking on you on the playground. You want them to stop but you don't know how to do this. You have a problem because you need to do something to get the kids to stop picking on you but you don't know what to do. Why is this a problem?"

STUDENTS: "Because you want them to stop picking on you but you don't know what to do."

TEACHER: "Good. Here's another example of a problem." [give several more instances of problems and in each case, be sure to ask your students why each one is a problem]

TEACHER: "Here are some examples of situations that are not problems. See if you can tell me why each is not a problem. Your best friend at school stops talking to you. You want to know why so you decide to ask her why. Why isn't this a problem?"

STUDENTS: "Because you want to know why she won't talk to you and you ask her."

TEACHER: "Right. You need to do something to get what you want and you know right away what to do. What did you want?"

STUDENTS: "To find out why she stopped talking to you."

TEACHER: "Good. And did you know right away how to get what you wanted?"

STUDENTS: "Yes."

TEACHER: [continue giving other not-instances of problems and, in each case, ask your students why it is not a problem]

Before moving on to the second competency, be sure your students pass an assessment on identifying (i.e., labeling) instances and not-instances of problems.

2. Defining the problem and stating the goal(s). This competency is especially important since many students who have difficulty with problem solving know that a problem exists but misdefine it. The most common error seems to be leaving themselves out of the problem. Consider the following:

TEACHER: "It's lunch time, you're hungry, and you're on the way to the cafeteria with two of your classmates. The school bully stops you all and asks each of you in turn to give him money. The first classmate is not afraid, refuses the bully, and walks away. The second classmate pulls his pockets inside out, holds up his lunch bag, and tells the bully he's brought his lunch and has no money. The bully looks at you. By this time, he's good and angry. You are afraid of him and you did bring money for lunch. What's the problem?"

STUDENT: "The problem is the bully."

TEACHER: "And what is your goal (or, what would you like to have happen)?"

STUDENT: "That he would leave me alone."

What's wrong with this? The student has misdefined the problem. The problem is not simply the bully. He's only part of the problem. The bully tried to extort money from three students. The first one wasn't afraid of him and refused. Did this student have a problem? No. The second student didn't have any money to give to the bully. Did he have a problem? No. The third student has money that he could lose and is afraid of the bully. Does this student have a problem? Yes. He has a problem. What is the problem? Well, it isn't simply the bully, or the bully extorting money, because the bully wasn't a problem for two other students. Only the third student has a problem. His problem is that the bully is trying to extort money from him, he doesn't want to give the bully his money, and he doesn't know what to do about it. This definition of the problem is different from the original definition which only included the bully and the bully's behavior. By defining the problem only as the bully, the goal becomes one of simply getting rid of him. This goal won't solve the student's problem because it doesn't give him enough information with which to generate a viable alternative solution. It is also very external. It puts the responsibility for what happens to the student on parties or forces outside of him, over which he has no control—maybe his luck will change one day and the bully will die, move to a new neighborhood, take pity on him, or decide to leave him alone. However, learning how to effectively deal with extortion is a more viable solution to this student's problem than wishing that the bully would disappear or spontaneously change his behavior.

In teaching the skill of defining problems and goals, first generate a list of student problems to draw from. This may be done simply by asking your students to brainstorm problems they encounter in (or out of) school. Remember, brainstorming requires no censorship on your part. Once you have this list, take each problem from it and give it to your students to define and then give them each defined problem and have them write a goal for it. Examples of defined problems and their corresponding goals are listed in Figure 12.6.

1. The problem is that you lose your homework assignment by the time you get home from school and you need to turn it in first thing next day. Your goal is to turn in your homework on time.

2. Some bigger kids start picking on you at school; you want them to stop but you don't know what to do to make them stop. Your goal is to get the bigger kids to stop picking on you.

3. You like some girl (boy) at school but she (he) doesn't pay any attention to you. Your goal is to get her (him) to pay attention to you.

4. You are having trouble with an assignment in class and you need (want) to get a good grade on it but you don't know how. Your goal is to successfully complete the assignment.

5. You forget where your next class meets and your name will be sent to the office for cutting class if you don't get there on time. Your goal is to get to class as quickly as possible.

6. Some kids offer you a cigarette (dope, alcohol). You don't want to take it but you're afraid of what they'll think of you if you don't. Your goal is to refuse the offer without losing face.

Figure 12.6. Examples of defined problems and goals.

3. Generating alternative solutions. Spivack and his associates (Spivack et al., 1976) consider this skill the most critical or essential problem-solving skill because knowing what else to do in case of failure is the cognitive skill that best prevents, or at least diminishes, the student's continued frustration and his subsequent need for impulsive behaviors or withdrawal. They consider it a) the single most powerful predictor of maladaptive behavior before training in problem solving; b) the one that is most enhanced by training; and c) the one that, when enhanced, seems to result in concomitant improvement in student behavior (Spivack & Shure, 1974). The ability to turn to another solution may be all the encouragement one needs not to give up. This results in resiliency instead of frustration.

The ability to generate alternative solutions is assessed in much the same way as it is taught, through brainstorming. Simply take a list of defined problems with corresponding goals and present each to a student or group of students and have them brainstorm possible solutions for each. Consider the following:

TEACHER: "I am going to give you a defined problem with a goal and I want you to tell me as many possible solutions as you can. Remember, a solution is anything you do that will get you what you want without causing any new problems for you. Don't bother to think about each solution before you give it to me. It can be anything you want. It might turn out to be silly or wrong or something you wouldn't even try. I still want you to tell me what it is. Any questions? (pause) OK. The problem as defined is: When you come back to your seat after sharpening your pencil, you find another student sitting there and you know you'll get into trouble if you're not in your seat. Your goal is to sit in your seat as soon as possible. Tell me what you could do to solve this problem."

STUDENTS: [the students yell these out one by one and you write them on the board, overhead projector, or easel]:

"pull him out of my seat"

"tell the teacher"

"ask him to get out of my seat"

"find another seat to sit in"

"go sit in his seat"

"share my seat with him"

"sit down on top of him"

"beat him up"

"sit on the floor"

"hide so the teacher won't see you"

"go back to the pencil sharpener and make believe you're still sharpening your pencil (stall)"

"stand there until he moves"

"keep asking him to move until he moves (i.e., broken-record approach)"

[keep encouraging your students to give you more "solutions" until it appears they are dried up]

Spivack and his associates (Spivack et al., 1976) found that the number of different solutions generated by a student considered competent at this skill is at least 3 or 4 and that children as young as 4 years old are considered capable of developing this skill.

4. Evaluating solutions. Once your students are able to generate a number of alternative solutions to a problem, they need to evaluate each solution according to the following criteria: a) Efficacy—will this solution help me reach my goal (i.e., get me what I want) without creating more problems for me? and b) feasibility—will I be able to do it (i.e., take the action cited in my solution). Starting with the list of solutions generated through brainstorming, help your students analyze each solution and evaluate it with regard to efficacy and feasibility. If they think it will help them get what they want without creating new problems for them, instruct them to label the solution "E" for effective. If they aren't certain the solution will help them get what they want without creating new problems, they should label it "e" to indicate their doubt. If they know the solution would definitely not get them what they want, they should cross out (eliminate) the solution. If they think they could definitely do it, they should label the solution "F" for feasible. If they aren't sure, they should label the solution with an "f." If they know they couldn't do it, they should eliminate the solution. When they are all finished with each solution, they should first look for any solutions labeled both "E" and "F." These are the solutions with the best chance of working since they are both effective and feasible. These are the solutions to try first. If there aren't any solutions designated both effective and feasible, you can brainstorm again to see if there was anything you missed, or reevaluate the solutions you have, or try one of the solutions you have some doubts about. The goal is to generate as many possible (i.e., "E" and "F") solutions as you can. The more you have, the more likely it is you will find one that really works. The teacher must act as a facilitator. This means you don't *tell* your students which solutions are effective or feasible and which are not; you ask the students and let them tell you. If it becomes obvious they are having difficulty evaluating solutions, then you should help them, but only *help*—do not give them the answer. They must arrive at the answer themselves. Be prepared to ask pointed questions. For example:

> TEACHER: "OK, let's look at the first solution, 'pull him out of my seat.' Would this work? Would this get you what you want (to sit in your seat as soon as possible) without creating any new problems for you?" [wait for response]
>
> STUDENTS: "Yes, it would get you what you want."

> TEACHER: "It could get you in your seat as soon as possible. Could it also create some new problems for you?"
>
> STUDENTS: "Maybe, maybe not."
>
> TEACHER: "How many of you think it might create some new problems?"
>
> STUDENTS: [a few students raise their hands]
>
> TEACHER: [address question to these students] "OK, why do you think pulling the student out of your seat might make new problems for you?"
>
> STUDENTS: [no response]
>
> TEACHER: "Who can tell me what might happen if you tried to pull the student out of your seat?"
>
> STUDENTS: "He might put up a fight and you could get hurt (or hurt him) and get into trouble for fighting (or hurting him)."
>
> TEACHER: "OK, how many of you still think that the first solution is effective (would get you what you wanted without creating new problems for you?)"
>
> STUDENTS: [no students raise hands]
>
> TEACHER: "Should we label this "E," "e," or should we cross it out?"
>
> STUDENTS: "Cross it out!"
>
> TEACHER: "Why did we get rid of it?"
>
> STUDENTS: " 'Cause it wouldn't help us get what we wanted without making new problems for us."

5. Making a plan. The last step in the problem-solving process is to take the best solution from the list of solutions generated and make a list of things you would have to do to implement that solution. This skill requires the ability to identify obstacles that might have to be overcome as well as the understanding that goal satisfaction may not occur immediately. This can also be accomplished through brainstorming. Consider the following:

> TEACHER: "Now that we have decided to try the solution of being assertive (using broken-record approach) and asking the student in our seat to move over and over again until he does, let's make a plan to help us carry out this

solution. What's the first thing we need to do?"

STUDENTS: "Think about what we're going to say."

TEACHER: "Good [writes it down], and after we decide what to say, what should we do next?"

STUDENTS: "Think about how we are going to say it over and over again."

TEACHER: "Good, in other words, use broken-record approach [writes this down]. What else?"

STUDENTS: "Try to stay calm."

TEACHER: "OK, and what can we do to stay calm?"

STUDENTS: "Do some belly breathing."

TEACHER: "Good [writes this down]. Is there anything else we need to include in our plan?" [pause]

After this first go-round, you might want to look at each of the steps in the plan and ask your students if there are any obstacles that might arise and how long they expect it will take to arrive at goal satisfaction (i.e., get the other student out of their seat). For example:

TEACHER: "Can you think of anything that might keep you from reaching your goal?"

STUDENTS: "Yeh, the kid might get mad and try to hurt you."

TEACHER: "OK, what should you do if that happens?"

STUDENTS: "walk away"; "protect yourself so you don't get hurt"; "tell the teacher"

TEACHER: "Those are all good ideas. How long do you think it might take to reach your goal?"

STUDENTS: "a few seconds"; "two days"; "a week"; "five, ten minutes"

TEACHER: "Why do you think it might take days to get the student out of your seat?" [discuss] "Why do you think it might only take a few seconds?"

✔ Checkpoint 12.3

[pages 431–436]

Fill in the answers to the following items (1–12). Check your responses by referring to the text; relevant page numbers appear in brackets.

The theory of the availability heuristic is

(1) _____

_____

_____

_____ [431].

An example in which the availability heuristic theory determines how problems are "solved" is

(2) _____

_____

_____

_____

_____

_____ [431].

Three reasons for teaching problem-solving skills in school are:

(3) _____

_____

(4) _____

_____

(5) _____

_____ [431].

"Problem solving" has been defined as

(6) _____

_____

_____

_____ [431].

(continues)

CHECKPOINT 12.3, continued

A "problem" may be defined as

(7) _____

_____

_____

_____ [432].

The five competencies of problem solving are:

(8) _____

_____

(9) _____

_____

(10) _____

_____

(11) _____

_____

(12) _____

_____ [432].

Redo any items you missed. If you missed more than 2 of the items, you should probably reread the material. Otherwise, continue on to the next section.

GETTING STUDENTS TO USE CBM STRATEGIES

Throughout the last two chapters I have described ways to teach your students how to use CBM strategies. Although students are often *able* to use these strategies, they are not necessarily *willing* to use them. What good is having any skill if you need to use it and choose not to? The following is a list of helpful hints which may enhance the probability of your students using CBM strategies outside of their CBM lessons.

1. You—the teacher—must be a model for your students. You can use these CBM strategies yourself whenever it is appropriate to do so. Share with your students how you are using (or have used) cognitive restructuring to help you modify your thinking about them, about your job, about teaching, about yourself. Don't be afraid of self-disclosure. It will go a long way toward humanizing you in the eyes of your students. Use problem-solving skills in front of your students. Ask them to help you brainstorm some alternative solutions; let them see how you use it to solve your own problems. Don't worry about making mistakes—you are a coping model, not a mastery model. Nobody learns much from a mastery model. Everyone thinks mastery models are perfect and never make mistakes; people have trouble identifying with them. If there is some bonding between you and your students (i.e., they can identify with you or relate to you or, God forbid, even care about you), they are going to be more likely to do as you do. So—*do.*

2. Teach each skill and subskill in each CBM strategy to the mastery level. You wouldn't teach multiplication tables to your students without assessing whether or not they had learned them. Do the same with CBM skills. Be sure your students have learned them as well as they have learned their times tables. Give assessments and make sure each student has learned a skill sufficiently to be able to use it if he wanted to. When skills or knowledge are learned at the mastery level (i.e., when the student is both fast and accurate), the learner is more likely to choose to use that skill or knowledge than if he learned it only at the acquisition level (i.e., when the student is accurate but slow).

3. Any time you observe a student using any of the CBM skills outside of the CBM lesson, reinforce her. Use that person as a model for her peers. "Janey, do you want to share with the class how you used your problem-solving skills to help you solve a problem you had on the playground today?" Encourage Janey's peers to praise her behavior and encourage them to follow suit. Use more tangible reinforcement if you wish. Set up a token economy system and reward students who use CBM skills outside of the CBM lesson with points or tokens that can be turned in for back-up reinforcers. Ideally, you might try setting up a level system which features expectations based on your students' use of CBM strategies. The system might start with self-management for all students and move on to other CBM or stress management strategies based on individual needs. An example of such a level system is illustrated in Figure 12.7.

Level	Expectations	Incentives
1	Uses self-management with teacher assistance to manage *behaviors targeted by teacher;* will demonstrate competence and willingness to use self-assessment, self-monitoring, and self-reinforcement	Buys items from class store

[Contracted with student; advancement to next level contingent upon meeting expectations for two separate behavior change projects initiated by teacher]

Level	Expectations	Incentives
2	Uses self-management with teacher assistance to manage *behaviors of own choosing*	Same as Level 1 *plus* class jobs (e.g., playground equipment monitor, paper monitor, homework monitor, peer tutor, etc.)

[Contracted with student; advancement to next level contingent upon meeting expectations for two separate behavior change projects initiated by student]

Level	Expectations	Incentives
3	Uses CBM or stress management strategy with teacher assistance to manage *behaviors, cognitions, and/ or emotions targeted by teacher;* will demonstrate competence and willingness to use strategy(ies), e.g., cognitive restructuring, problem solving, SIT, verbal mediation, relaxation	Same as Level 2 *plus* school jobs (e.g., peer tutor in other classrooms; assistant to maintenance, office, cafeteria staff, etc.)

[Contracted with student; advancement to next level contingent upon meeting expectations for one project initiated by teacher]

Level	Expectations	Incentives
4	Uses CBM or stress management strategy with teacher assistance to manage *behaviors, cognitions, and/ or emotions of own choosing*	Same as Level 3 *plus* access to more school jobs (e.g., hall or traffic patrol, etc.)

[Contracted with student; exit from system contingent upon meeting expectations for one project initiated by student]

Figure 12.7. Level system used to reinforce student use of CBM strategies.

4. Be sure you program for generalization by having your students use CBM skills outside of the lesson. Give them homework assignments requiring them to use CBM skills outside of the CBM lesson (e.g., in your classroom, in other classrooms, in other parts of the school, or outside of school). Role play these situations at first. For example, role play how to use verbal mediation to help deal with temptation and in dealing with peer pressure, or using SIT to deal with frustration in trying to master difficult skills or knowledge, or using problem solving to solve a problem with a family member.

5. Discuss the relevance of (i.e., the need for using) each strategy when you teach it. Kids tend to think that much of what we teach them in school is irrelevant—and they are probably right. Remember, it doesn't matter how relevant *we think* our curriculum is. If our students don't see any relevance in what we're teaching them, they probably won't use it outside of our classroom without some form of extrinsic controls. And then we're right back where we were before, with the student learning to rely on his environment rather than on himself.

6. Try teaching self-management skills before you teach CBM strategies. Remember, students with an external locus of control have difficulty accepting responsibility for their behavior and are not likely to assume the role of primary change agent. Success at self-management promotes internality. The more internal your students are, the more willing they may be to assume the role of primary change agent and implement one of the CBM strategies.

7. Provide your students with as many opportunities as possible to practice their new CBM skills. Use "setups" toward this end. Setups are those situations when you purposely create a situation in which the student is required to use a CBM strategy. For example, if you want your students to practice their problem-solving skills, create problems for them on purpose. Create shortages on purpose. If you have twelve students, hand out eleven science texts and see whether or not your target student uses problem solving correctly, if at all. If you want your students to practice their cognitive restructuring skills, set them up by creating a situation which requires that they use these skills. Setups require informed consent, so don't forget to warn your students ahead of time that you "may try some setups

today." They can either say "No, I'm not ready yet," or "Go ahead." Also, be willing to cut back on your control and let your students control themselves. Don't run such a tight ship that your students have little or no opportunity to practice their CBM strategies. If there are no problems, your students can't practice problem solving. Without temptations, they can't practice verbal mediation. If someone is always there to tell them what to do, they can't practice self-instruction. Without adversity, they can't practice their cognitive restructuring.

8. Remember that CBM strategies are fairly complex and sometimes difficult to remember. You can enhance your students' learning of CBM strategies by using SIT. When you teach a strategy, or even one competency for a given strategy, follow the steps of teacher say/teacher do, teacher say/student do, student say/student do, student whisper/student do, and student think/student do.

9. Follow the practice of "each one teach one." When you have one student master a CBM strategy, have her teach that strategy to another student or group of students. Children and youth are more powerful models for other children and youth than are adults. Your students will tend to pay more attention to their peers, and they will also see that learning CBM is not as hard as it might appear—"If he can do it, so can I."

MEASURING STUDENT PROGRESS

In one respect, determining the efficacy of a CBM intervention is no different from determining the efficacy of a traditional behavioral intervention. In both cases, efficacy is determined by measuring student progress; how quickly the student moves from Point A to Point B. After that, the differences between the two approaches become quite apparent. Since the traditional behavioral approach focuses on change in behavior, one must measure student behavior to determine whether or not sufficient progress is occurring. CBM interventions, on the other hand, can result in changes in cognitions and emotions as well as behavior. Therefore, progress in a CBM intervention is best determined by measuring change in cognitions and emotions as well as behavior. In the traditional behavioral intervention, the teacher is the primary change agent and there is usually no question about when or how she uses the intervention strategies. Since CBM strategies require that the student eventually become the primary change agent, student use of the strategies becomes critical. If the student does not use a particular strategy or uses it incorrectly, there is not likely to be any change in his behavior, cognitions, and/or emotions. Therefore, when you attempt to measure student progress in a CBM intervention, you must be sure to measure change in the student's use of the strategy in addition to any behavioral, cognitive, and/or emotional change(s). Here are some ideas to help you determine the efficacy of the CBM strategies covered in the last two chapters.

Cognitive Restructuring

To determine whether or not the student is using cognitive restructuring correctly when needed, have him self-monitor his use of cognitive restructuring. Don't be satisfied with a frequency count of how many times he used it each day. This doesn't tell you if he used it correctly and in an appropriate situation. Require him to keep a log in which he enters a brief description of how he used cognitive restructuring to help him with a particular problem. He should enter the date, the event (A), the mediating belief (B), the consequent affect and behavior (C), the disputation, and the rational (fair-pair) belief. He should also explain how he plans on internalizing his new thinking. If a written log is expecting too much from your student, have him give you this information verbally. He can do this as the need arises or he can report to you at the end of the day. However you do it, it is imperative that you find some way to assess your student's use of cognitive restructuring.

Assuming your student uses cognitive restructuring correctly when needed, the next step is to determine its efficacy. One way to do this is to administer the beliefs assessment originally used to identify the irrational thinking. This can be done on a weekly basis, being careful to use alternate forms of the beliefs assessment. Another approach is the direct observation of the student's verbal behavior. Monitor what the student says and when she says it to see if there is any change in her thinking. This, of course, is based on the premise that what students say reflects what they believe. Still another method involves the student monitoring her own thinking. Have her collect data on the frequency of her irrational thoughts. Obviously, great care must be taken to describe exactly what constitutes an irrational

thought. This can be a difficult undertaking. The most reliable approach to measuring the efficacy of cognitive restructuring requires monitoring change in a student's thinking, emotions, and behavior. Measuring change in student behavior is discussed in Chapter 7 while the measurement of student affect (i.e., anger, depression, anxiety) is covered in Chapter 13. Whenever possible, try to measure change in all three.

Self-Instructional Training and Verbal Mediation

To determine whether or not the student is using either of these strategies correctly when needed, have him self-monitor his behavior. For example, if he needs to use SIT when he is frustrated, have him monitor a) times frustrated and b) times he uses SIT to help him through his frustration. Have him compute the percentage of times he uses SIT when frustrated and look for changes in this percentage to determine progress. Use the same approach with verbal mediation. Have the student self-monitor the number of urges he has to engage in the maladaptive behavior and the number of times he suppresses the urges with mediating self-talk. Then compute the percentage of urges suppressed through verbal mediation. A high percentage (e.g., 80% to 100%) indicates that the student is a) using verbal mediation correctly when needed and b) it is working.

Problem Solving

Determine whether or not your students are using problem solving correctly when needed in the same manner you assessed their use of cognitive restructuring. Have them keep a problem-solving log in which they record the date, the defined problem, a list of possible solutions, the solution of choice, and a plan for implementing that solution. Again, if they have trouble writing this information down, have them report it to you verbally. Take particular note of whether they followed all the steps correctly and in the correct sequence. Also make sure they used the strategy to solve a real problem. To determine the efficacy of their problem-solving intervention, monitor their behavior. There should be a reduction of maladaptive behavior and an increase in adaptive behavior that correlates with an increase in their use of the problem-solving strategy.

✔ Checkpoint 12.4

[pages 437–441]

Fill in the answers to the following items (1–12). Check your responses by referring to the text; relevant page numbers appear in brackets.

Describe six ways to enhance the probability of students using CBM strategies outside of their CBM lessons.

(1) _____

_____

_____

_____

(2) _____

_____

_____

_____

(3) _____

_____

_____

_____

(4) _____

_____

_____

_____

(5) _____

_____

_____

_____

(6) _____

_____

_____

_____ [437–439].

(continues)

CHECKPOINT 12.4, continued

Measuring student progress in a CBM intervention is different than measuring student progress in a traditional behavioral intervention because:

(7) _____

_____

_____

_____

and

(8) _____

_____

_____

_____ [439].

For each of the the following CBM strategies, describe how you would a) determine if the student has used the strategy correctly when needed, and b) whether or not the strategy has been effective.

Cognitive Restructuring (9) _____

_____

_____ [440].

Problem Solving (10)_____

_____

_____ [440].

Verbal Mediation (11)_____

_____

_____ [440].

Self-Instructional Training (12)_____

_____

_____ [440].

Redo any items you missed. If you missed more than 2 of the items, reread the material. Otherwise, continue on to the Chapter Assessment.

ASSESSMENT / CHAPTER 12 ■

A list of acceptable responses appears following the Assessment.

1. Design a self-instruction (SIT) program for the following hypothetical case: Benny is a high school student who impulsively engages in "personal narrative" behavior. He is nicknamed "motormouth" by his peers because he is constantly verbalizing his thoughts and actions out loud. This behavior is often disruptive and brings Benny a great deal of negative attention from his peers. The objective of your SIT program should focus on getting Benny to reflect on *what* is appropriate and *when* it is appropriate to verbalize out loud, and what and when it is not. Describe each of the steps in your SIT program as if you were explaining it to a substitute or student teacher.

2. Design a verbal mediation essay for a student who is off task 70% to 90% of the time during independent seatwork. Instead of working on his assignments, he looks around the room, out the window, or watches whatever activity is going on (e.g., students talking or the teacher helping another student). Describe how you would use the essay as if you were explaining it to a substitute or student teacher.

3. Use the problem-solving strategy discussed in this chapter to solve the following problem: You are a student in a middle school and your teacher does not pay any attention to you when you want/need assistance. She either ignores you when you raise your hand for help, tells you she doesn't have time to help you ("do the best you can"), or tells you she will "be right there" but never follows through on her promise. You are failing her class and your parents will punish you if you get any Fs on your report card. Assume you already recognize you have a problem and work from there.

ACCEPTABLE RESPONSES

1.0 Self-Instructional Training

1.1 Teach Benny *what* information is and is not appropriate to share with peers; it *is appropriate* to share information that others *need or want* either because they have asked for the information (e.g., "what did she say to do?") or because it will help them to know it (e.g., "Your hair is on fire"); it *is not appropriate* to share information that others *do not need* to know (e.g., "I'm wearing new undershorts").

1.2 Given information that is appropriate to share with peers, teach Benny *when* it is appropriate and not appropriate to do so; it *is appropriate* to share information with others when it has something to do with the subject being discussed (e.g., it's OK to tell others you are wearing new undershorts if you are discussing the condition of your underwear); it *is not appropriate* to share information with others when it has nothing to do with the subject being discussed (e.g., it's not OK to tell others you are wearing new undershorts when the teacher is teaching a math lesson).

1.3 Assess Benny's competence at identifying appropriate and inappropriate information sharing by giving him examples of both and have him label each (e.g., Is it OK to tell your classmates you have baloney sandwiches for lunch when the class is talking about lunch?; Is it OK to tell your classmates your family got cable TV during a lesson on the Civil War?).

1.4 Prepare a script for Benny to learn (e.g., "What do I want to share? _____ Do they *need/want* to know this? _____ Does it have anything to do with what's going on now? _____ OK. I'm going to/not going to share it now/later.").

1.5 Teach Benny his script using the SIT sequence of teacher says–teacher does, teacher says–student does, student says–student does, student whispers–student does, and student thinks–student does.

2.0 Verbal Meditation

2.1 *What am I doing now that I shouldn't be doing?*
I'm looking everywhere but at my work.

2.2 *Why shouldn't I be doing this?*
Because looking everywhere but at my work will keep me from finishing my work on time.

2.3 *What will probably happen if I continue doing it?*
I won't get my work done and I will get poor grades. My teacher will tell me to get back to work. This embarrasses me because my classmates laugh at me. They think I'm stupid. When I get poor grades it makes them think they are right.

2.4 *What should I be doing instead?*
I should be looking at my work.

2.5 *Why should I be doing this?*
Because looking at my work will remind me to stay on task.

2.6 *What will probably happen if I do what I am supposed to?*
I will get my work done and get better grades. My teacher won't have to remind me to get back to work and my classmates won't laugh at me. When I get better grades, they will see that I'm not stupid.

  a. Have student dictate verbal mediation essay (e.g., one above);

  b. when student is off task (looking away from work on desk), hand him 2 blank copies of essay and a completed version and have him copy essays for homework;

  c. if behavior persists, repeat homework assignment;

  d. if behavior still persists, have student paraphrase essay during after-school detention;

  e. if still no improvement, have student write essay from memory during after-school detention;

  f. if still not better, have student orally describe classroom situation that precedes his off-task behavior and what he would say to himself to weaken his off-task behavior.

3.0 Problem Solving

3.1 *Define the problem:*

My teacher does not pay attention to me when I want/need her assistance and I want her to attend to me.

3.2 *Generate alternative solutions:*

[Try to have at least 10]

a. Create a disturbance in class so my teacher will have to attend to me

b. Be patient and sit with my hand in the air until she notices me

c. Be more assertive and not take "No" for an answer

d. Meet with my teacher to tell her how I feel about the situation

e. Complain to the principal (and/or school board) about it

f. Complain to my parents about it

g. Give up and accept my "fate"

h. Do the best I can on my work and accept whatever grade I get

i. Cheat (copy classmate's work)

j. Try to get a good (smart) student to help me and forget about getting help from the teacher

k. Intimidate teacher into helping me (threaten her with physical/verbal abuse)

l. Cut her class

3.3 *Evaluate solutions:*

a, i, k, and l are not effective solutions because they would create new problems for me; the same is probably true for e and f; b is not much different from what I'm doing now without success; g and h are the same as doing nothing and I can't afford to do nothing; c, d, and j are my best options; I will try d first, then c, and finally j if I can't get the teacher to help me.

3.4 *Make a plan:*

a. Ask the teacher when I can meet with her; if she says she doesn't know when, I will suggest different dates and times until I get her to commit to one; I should know ahead of time how long the meeting will take; scheduling the meeting shouldn't take more than a few minutes so I'll stop by her classroom first thing in the morning or at the end of the day.

b. Plan what I want to say (i.e., what's been happening, how I feel about it, and what I would like); if she gets mad at me or tells me I'm wrong, I will be assertive and keep asking for what I want; I will try to be positive; I will ask for ideas about how I can get her to help me in class; the meeting should take no more than 20 to 30 minutes.

c. Rehearse what I want to say to her; role play with a friend or imagine the meeting.

CHAPTER THIRTEEN

Stress Management Strategies

Upon successful completion of this chapter, the learner should be able to design a stress inoculation program for students who have problems with anxiety, anger, or depression.

DO KIDS NEED STRESS MANAGEMENT?

No one would deny that stress is a problem for adults. Is it also a problem for children and youth? Do we need to teach stress management strategies to them? The answer is *yes*. Today's young people seem to be more susceptible to stress and are less equipped to handle it than adults. Consider the following.

It has been estimated that 20% of the child population is negatively affected by biological (e.g., chronic disease) and psychological (e.g., parental divorce) stressors (Eisen, 1979). A much greater number of children are negatively affected by stressors that might be termed social, economic, and cultural (e.g., disadvantaged families and disadvantaged or high-pressure schools). One million 12- to 17-year-olds get pregnant each year, and 1 in 5 uses drugs more than once a week. There are more and more runaways, more violent acts committed by adolescents, and more suicides. While suicide rates for adults have remained static, rates for adolescents and young adults 15 to 24 years old began rising in the mid-1950s and had tripled by 1978. Some 5000 adolescents now take their lives each year. Suicide rates for 10- to 14-year-olds have tripled as well, and psychiatrists report increased suicidal behavior—from fantasies and threats to attempts and deaths—in children ages 6 to 12 years old.

What are some of the reasons for these alarming statistics? One reason offered by sociologists pertains to the family unit. Today's family is typically headed by dual-career parents or a single parent or stepparent. In 1950, 24% of wives worked outside of the home. In 1980, more than 50% of wives did so and

21% of families with children were single-parent families, 90% of which were female headed. It has been suggested that, as a result of this change in the family unit, child–mother dependency has been replaced by early independence. We have gone from the "age of protection" to the "age of preparation" (Winn, 1983). Elkind (1981) refers to today's children as "hurried children." They have to achieve success early or they are regarded as losers. "Schools divide the young into winners and losers and then train them to accept their roles" (Sebald, 1981, p. 53). Children suffer from fears and the consequences of failure. Unfortunately, it is predicted that the trend will continue well into the year 2000, which will be marked by an intensification of the pressures and fears that characterize contemporary times.

According to David Elkind (1981), United States society puts emphasis on early achievement. Parents, in turn, require achievement from their children without offsetting these demands with a comparable level of support. This leads to a disequilibrium in the parent–child contract. Parents want and expect more from their children today than parents did 30 years ago, but today's parents are less willing and/or able to help their children cope with the resultant stress.

In summary, we have a situation in which:

1. *The family unit is changing.* Because of several factors (e.g., increase in divorce rates, unemployment and economic inflation, as well as increasing feminist awareness), the two-parent family where dad works and mom stays home to be with the children at least until they begin junior or senior high school (or, in some cases, until they begin college) is becoming the exception rather than the rule.

2. *There is more stress in the home.* Parents are exposed to more and more stress in the workplace

and tend to bring this stress home, where it's "safe" to displace, and thus create more stress for their children. This makes life especially difficult for single parents who have to deal single-handedly with stress at work as well as in the home, usually without the support they need.

3. *Children are being exposed to more stress at an earlier age and are less able to cope with it.* As the family unit of the past (dad the breadwinner and mom the protector) evolves to the family unit of the present (dad or mom is both breadwinner and protector), children in the family are exposed to more stress at an earlier age. And they are not able to cope. Their parent(s) also often serve as negative models. If mom or dad is coping with daily stress by yelling, drinking, being physically aggressive or doing drugs, or withdrawing in front of the TV or behind a newspaper or behind a closed door, children will probably learn to cope with their stress in much the same way. The problem is, adult society doesn't approve of children who yell at their parents or teachers or act physically aggressive or engage in substance abuse or act withdrawn; we tend to label these kids Behavior Disordered or Seriously Emotionally Disturbed.

Through commercialism and the media, society is putting more pressure on today's youth to grow up faster. Madison Avenue doesn't respect the laws of nature when it comes to sheltering youth from potential dangers. When you are young, you are less able to cope with stress by virtue of your limited experiences, cognitive ability, skills, etc., but that's traditionally OK because you are insulated by your family from a great deal of life stress, so you don't have to worry about things like jobs and sex and being assertive with friends and getting a scholarship to college. As you get older, you naturally have more experiences, learn new skills, and develop cognitively, while at the same time your family insulates you from stress less and less; this is the natural order of things. Even during the Middle Ages, when children left their homes in the country to live in the city and work as apprentices at 12 and 14 years of age, they still lived with a family, usually the family of the person they were apprenticed to. They had surrogate parents and surrogate siblings who assumed responsibility for insulating them from the stress of life until they were ready to cope. Today, this is not the case. Many of today's adolescents have learned to expect the freedom they think comes with being an adult but they are unprepared to accept adult responsibilities. This attitude often puts them into direct conflict with the parent or parents who attempt to set limits. The result is more stress.

On the one hand, adolescents are getting messages from a number of sources (e.g., peer group, parents, society, media) telling them to grow up fast (how many times have you told a kid, "Will you just grow up!"?), while on the other hand, they are neither willing nor able to take on the responsibilities of being grown-up and this brings them into conflict with their environment.

What I've presented so far is a broad, sociological view of the problem of stress in children. Now let's look at what this has to do with behavior management. There is evidence that a large number of students with chronic behavior problems have also experienced chronic life stress. For example, in an epidemiological study of the mental health of children in midtown Manhattan, Gersten, Langer, Eisenberg, and Orzek (1974) found that parent ratings of a variety of child adjustment problems was significantly correlated with their reports of stressful life events occurring during the previous year. Felner, Stolberg, and Cowan (1975) found that 20% of students identified by teachers as having adjustment problems had a family history that included either a parental divorce, separation, or death. More specifically, students with a history of parent separation or divorce were high in acting-out behaviors while students with a history of parent death were high in shy–anxious behaviors. Sandler and Block (1979) investigated the relationship between life stress events and adjustment problems perceived in inner-city elementary students. They hypothesized that students identified by teachers as having adjustment problems had experienced more recent stress events than matched controls and that the amount of stress would correlate positively with both parent and teacher ratings of the child adjustment problems. They studied 99 students in kindergarten through the third grade who had been identified by their teachers in four inner-city elementary schools as manifesting some social–emotional adjustment problem in the classroom. Results demonstrated evidence of a relationship between recent life stress events and the adjustment problems of young inner-city elementary students. Both hypotheses were supported by the results.

As further evidence of a link between stress and behavior problems in children and youth, when Johnson and McCutcheon (1980) developed and standardized their Life Events Checklist, they found that negative life stress, particularly among females, correlated significantly with general maladjustment.

There is little doubt that childhood stress is correlated with childhood maladjustment. The question is: Does childhood stress cause maladjustment?

Chandler (1985) argues that much of the maladaptive behavior we see in the schools is the direct result of the life stress events that children experience both in and out of school. In many instances, these behaviors may actually be coping mechanisms, albeit inappropriate and inefficient ones. Most likely, they are coping mechanisms that have been modeled in frequent or dramatic fashion by a significant other (e.g., parent, teacher, peer, or sibling). If this theory is valid, we certainly need to teach our students more appropriate ways of coping with stress. In addition to reducing the deleterious effects of stress, teaching students appropriate and effect stress management may also help eliminate some of their maladaptive behavior.

Other benefits may be derived from teaching students stress management. Most of the stress management skills are also self-management skills. They require that the individual apply the skill to and/or for himself. He can't rely on someone else to apply the skill for him. It's not like going to a counselor or a doctor or a teacher and having them do something to you or for you; you must do it yourself. Therefore, in the process of learning how to manage stress, students also become more self-reliant. The more self-reliant they become, the less external their locus of control and the more responsibility they will ultimately take for their behavior.

✔ Checkpoint 13.1

[pages 449–451]

Fill in the answers to the following items (1–6). Check your responses by referring to the text; relevant page numbers appear in brackets.

Three reasons for the increased stress experienced by today's children are:

(1) _____

_____

_____

(2) _____

_____

_____

(3) _____

_____

_____[449–450]

Three reasons for teaching students self-management strategies are:

(4) _____

_____

_____

(5) _____

_____

_____

(6) _____

_____

_____ [451]

Redo any items you missed. If you missed more than 1 item, reread the material. Otherwise, continue on to the next section.

BASIC CONCEPTS

The following is a list of basic concepts I believe you should teach your students prior to teaching them stress management strategies.

1. First, you need to define terms such as "stress," "stressor," "eustress," and "distress." Most students (like their parents) confuse *stress* with *stressor*. A stressor is an event (e.g., being teased by peers or failing a test) which usually leads to stress. Stress itself is the physiological response we experience depending upon how threatened we are by the stressor and how much control we believe we have over it. For example, some students are likely to feel more threatened by peer teasing than other students and, as a result, will experience more stress than their peers. Students with an external locus of control will probably tend to experience more stress than their more internal peers simply because they believe they have less control over the stressors they encounter in their lives.

2. You also should teach your students that not all stress is bad. The stress we experience in scoring the winning touchdown or seeing our team score the winning touchdown is good stress. It's called "eustress," with the "eu-" meaning "good" or "healthy," as in "euphoria." However, the stress we feel when somebody teases us or when taking a test we are sure we're going to fail is bad stress. It's called "distress" because it is negative or disabling. Students need to learn the difference between the two and also to understand that sometimes distress can actually be helpful. For example, when Jake is confronted by a bully, the distress he feels can produce the necessary changes in his body to help him escape the bully (i.e., run away so fast the bully can't catch him) or fight the bully (i.e., stand up for his rights and not get hurt). What we want to avoid is distress that is so disabling it keeps us from helping ourselves so that we can't escape or fight for our rights.

3. You should also teach your students about the physiological changes that occur during times of stress. The *stress response* is referred to in the literature as the General Adaptation Syndrome (G.A.S., Selye, 1976) and it is particularly important that your students understand the first stage in the G.A.S., the alarm reaction. An analogy often used to explain the alarm reaction describes the response of a primitive hunter

following the trail of a wounded and dangerous predator. As the hunter follows the tracks of the predator, his stress level is high enough to keep him alert but not so high that he will run away or charge ahead at the sound of a broken twig. Finally, the trail ends at the entrance of a dark cave and the hunter's stress level increases, but again, not so high that he will charge into the cave or be frozen with indecision outside. As he enters the cave, he hears a low growling and can see the eyes of the wounded prehistoric cat glowing in the dark. As these eyes seem to move toward him and the growling gets louder, the hunter's stress level rises. He is now experiencing Stage 1 of the G.A.S., the alarm reaction. This stage is commonly referred to as the "fight or flight" stage. The following are some of the changes taking place in the hunter's body: a) His pupils dilate to let in more light so that he can see in the dark better; b) his heart beats faster to pump more blood and life-giving oxygen to his muscles; c) his muscles tense to better serve as armor protecting his vital organs in case of attack and also to better enable him to spring into action (either run away or stay and fight); d) his blood undergoes chemical changes so that clotting time is decreased just in case he is wounded; e) his throat and nasal passages dry up so that more oxygen can be taken in; f) his body stops producing saliva in his mouth, again to allow the easy flow of oxygen; g) his body stops digesting food since it has more important things to do at the moment; h) more blood is sent to the muscles and the brain to help the hunter act more quickly; and i) his breathing becomes quicker and more shallow. All of the above occurs automatically. The hunter doesn't have to think about it; it happens on its own. It is a survival mechanism that helps the hunter in life-or-death situations.

Your purpose in discussing all of this with your students is to communicate the important role stress plays in our lives. From early man to modern man, the fight or flight response has served us well as a survival mechanism when we needed it. However, over the years, the average person in a highly industrialized society hasn't needed the fight or flight response as much as our early ancestors. We don't have to hunt for our food—we can go to the supermarket and buy it. There is usually nothing that happens at the supermarket that is so threatening to us that it evokes the fight or flight response required by the prehistoric hunter in the preceding story.

This is not to say that modern man doesn't need the fight or flight response. The paper boy being chased by a vicious dog shown in Figure 13.1 needs the fight or flight response just as much as the prehistoric hunter. We will always need it whenever we find ourselves in situations where our physical safety is threatened. However, the paper boy does not need the fight or flight response when he is teased by his peer group at school (see Figure 13.2). In this situation, fight or flight actually has a negative effect on the individual because it interferes with his ability to deal with his peers in an assertive manner (e.g., letting them know how he feels about their behavior). Instead, the stress response of the alarm reaction causes him to become verbally and/or physically aggressive and someone gets hurt and/or he gets into trouble, or he becomes passive to the point where he reinforces his peers' behavior and/or feels badly about himself for not standing up to them. While the fight or flight response is instinctive (i.e., we are born with it) in all of us, we can learn to control it so that it doesn't disable us—and learning stress management skills is the way to do this.

4. Another basic concept you should teach your students is that we can't always escape from stress by running away from the stressor. You can't always run away from an angry dog on your paper route; eventually, you will have to talk to the dog's owner. You can't always run away from the school bully; sooner or later, you are going to have to confront your fear and do something about him. You can quit your paper route or fake being sick or play hooky from

Figure 13.2. Example of cognitively mediated stress (irrational fear).

school but, in the long run, these are poor solutions. There are too many angry dogs and bullies in this world. Get rid of one and you'll probably run into another. No matter where you go, you are bound to find similar stressors, and you'd better learn to deal with them or you'll be running all of your life. Some examples of stressors students typically run away from are: teachers ("if only I had a different teacher"); schools ("if only I was in a different school"); authority ("if only I didn't have to do what people tell me to"); and responsibility ("if only I didn't have so much work"). Try to get your students to tell you why these are all unrealistic statements. For example, there is no place they can go where they won't find authority and responsibility and, even if they escaped from teachers and schoolwork by quitting school, they would just have to substitute a boss and work on a job that might be harder. The basic idea you are teaching here is that stressors are everywhere and nobody can escape them.

5. Effective stress management requires a holistic approach. You can't focus on only one thing or keep trying old methods that work only with some stressors. Your students must learn a variety of strategies and when (as well as how) to use them. Your students will need to modify how they feel as well as what they think and how they act (behave). This holistic approach to stress management may be seen in Figure 13.3. The

Figure 13.1. Example of cognitively mediated stress (rational fear).

Means \ Ends	To Create Least Stressful Environment Situations in which potential stressors are kept to a minimum and/or individual is inoculated against deleterious effects of stress.	To Maintain Least Stressful Environment Situations in which stressors are present but individual is coping adequately.	To Restore Least Stressful Environment Situations in which individual has experienced difficulty coping with stressors.
Somatic–Physiological	Exercise Progressive relaxation (PRT) Proper diet Stress inoculation	Diaphragmatic breathing Progressive relaxation (PRT) Stress inoculation	Exercise Diaphragmatic breathing
Cognitive–Psychological	Cognitive restructuring	Self-instruction Problem solving	Cognitive restructuring Thought stopping
Social–Behavioral	Time management	Behavioral self-control Assertiveness training Social skills training	

Figure 13.3. Holistic stress management curriculum for children and youth.

somatic–physiological interventions are used to modify stress directly, and have a direct effect on the stress response. The *cognitive–psychological* interventions are used primarily to modify thoughts, attitudes, beliefs, and self-talk regarding stressors. The *social–behavioral* interventions are used to modify overt responses to stressors. Your students need to learn how to use all three types of interventions. In addition, they need to learn when to use them—before, during, or after encountering stressors. They need to learn that they can't use these strategies away from the stressor or after it "hits the fan," because this tends to create an escapist attitude (e.g., "If only I wasn't here," "I can't wait to get outta here, and smoke some dope," "Beam me up, Scotty.").

6. Your students need to learn that stress is cumulative and that people are often better able to deal with one big stressor than with the cumulative effect of several small stressors. Use the analogy of the straw breaking the camel's back or the boxer using several combinations of punches instead of one knockout punch. You can demonstrate the concept by having your students build a pyramid by trying to pile objects of the same weight and size as high as they can. Eventually, something has to give. This concept is important to understand, because any one stressor that can be eliminated from their daily lives may reduce the total stress they experience; since each stressor is small (rather than large), it should be relatively easy to eliminate just one. Your students need to learn that they are better off working on one stressor at a time, and they should begin by working on the one that is easiest to fix.

7. Also, you should teach the conceptual framework behind cognitively mediated stress using Ellis's A-B-C model to illustrate the idea that events (A) do not produce stress (C); it is what we say to ourselves (B) about the stressors that

produces stress. Use pictures (cartoons) whenever possible to dramatize concepts. An example may be seen in Figure 13.4.

8. Hold a brainstorming session early on to generate a list of as many student stressors as possible. Figure 13.5 is a sample list of stressors commonly experienced by children and youth. Ask your students to identify the two or three stressors that create the most stress for them. This should provide you with enough potential stressors on which to focus during the school year. Once you have identified those stressors your students need to work on, you might have students list, name, or identify their affective (emotional or feeling) and behavioral response(s) to each stressor. You might first have to teach them how to monitor their emotional and behavioral responses to stressors and collect some baseline data. Teach them how to monitor their stress level by subjectively assigning a value (number) to it. One such numbering system is referred to as Subjective Units of Distress, or SUD (Wolpe, 1969). Students are taught that their SUD level can be as low as 1 (very calm and relaxed) or as high as 10 (extremely distressed). They are taught how to calibrate this internal "instrument" so that, at any given time, they can assign a number to their stress level. Sitting around the house at

Figure 13.4. What's wrong with this picture?

death of parent

death of sibling or close friend

death of relative

divorce or separation of parents

sibling leaves home

moving

parent fighting

substance abuse (parent and/or sibling)

illness (of parent, sibling, child)

parent out of work

loss of pet

new school

failure in school

physical appearance problems (complexion, clothes, height, weight, sexual development, etc.)

poverty

victimization by peers

lack of proper nutrition

holidays

loss of friends (moved away)

test anxiety

new sibling (natural or step-sibling)

new parents

sports-related pressure

new job (of parent)

parent away from home often

puberty

injury to self or significant other

placement in special education

dating

learning to drive

peer pressure (drugs, sex, tobacco, alcohol, cheating, stealing, skipping classes or school, etc.)

witnessing traumatic events

graduation

punishment

finding job

control from authority

responsibility for siblings

homework

breaking up of relationship

Figure 13.5. Common stressors experienced by children and youth.

night watching TV might produce a SUD level of 2 or 3 (maybe higher if they're watching something scary or exciting or their parents are fighting in the next room). Being asked to stand up in class and give a report or calling someone up for a date might result in a SUD level of 8 or 9. Have your students keep logs on their SUD levels by writing down the stressor, when it occurred, and the SUD level it produced. They must do this over a period of several days in order to effectively calibrate their subjective measures. Ask them periodically during the day what their SUD levels are. This experience will put them in touch with their bodies and build an awareness of physiological stress, which is a prerequisite for change. In order to reduce your stress you must first become aware of it, and the sooner you become aware of it, the easier it will be to reduce it. Keeping a log will also make your students more aware of the stressors they encounter and which ones produce the most stress for them. More about SUD levels later.

☑ Checkpoint 13.2

[pages 452–456]

Fill in the answers to the following items (1–8). Check your responses by referring to the text; relevant page numbers appear in brackets.

Eight basic concepts students should learn about stress and stress management are:

(1) _____

_____

_____

(2) _____

_____

_____

(3) _____

_____

_____

(4) _____

_____

_____

(5) _____

_____

_____

(6) _____

_____

_____

(7) _____

_____

_____

(8) _____

_____

_____

Redo any items you missed. If you missed more than 2 items, reread the material. Otherwise, continue on to the next section.

STRESS MANAGEMENT STRATEGIES

Somatic–Physiological

Somatic–physiological stress management strategies produce a direct effect on the body. They are the easiest skills to learn and they produce the fastest results. Three examples of somatic–physiological skills your students can learn are diaphragmatic breathing, progressive relaxation training, and exercise. Diaphragmatic breathing and progressive relaxation training may be used before (in anticipation of), during, or after experience with stressors. Exercise can protect you against the harmful effects of stress and it is especially beneficial after experiencing a stressor.

Diaphragmatic breathing

I suggest you begin by training your students in diaphragmatic breathing since it is the easiest technique to learn and requires the least amount of discipline for them to master it. Some of your students may already engage in diaphragmatic breathing. In order to find out how you students breathe, have them close their eyes and put one hand on their chest and the other on their abdomen and breathe naturally for 30 seconds or so. Ask them to notice whether their chest or their abdomen rises and falls when they breathe. Explain that diaphragmatic (i.e., abdominal) breathing is better than thoracic (chest) breathing because they obtain more oxygen by breathing from their diaphragm. If you are working with younger students and they have trouble remembering terms, you might want to refer to diaphragmatic breathing simply as "belly breathing." In belly breathing, the belly rises (i.e., pushes out) when you inhale and falls (i.e., pulls in) when you exhale. Have your students practice this regularly for several minutes during the day. If possible, have them lie on the floor when they do this as it will increase the relaxation produced. Your next step will be to demonstrate how belly breathing can effectively produce relaxation. Put your students in some mild to moderate anxiety-provoking situations such as standing in front of their peers and talking, or talking to someone in class they don't know very well. Have them concentrate on their SUD levels. When they feel their SUD level rising, have your students stop what they are doing and practice their belly breathing as they to continue to monitor their SUD levels. This simple but dramatic exercise demonstrates the efficacy of belly breathing and, more significantly, each stu-

dent's ability to gain control over his or her stress level. Next, have your students make a list of situations when they might use belly breathing, and again have them keep a log over several days that includes stressors, SUD levels, and perceived efficacy in reducing stress and producing relaxation.

Progressive relaxation training

Once they have mastered belly breathing and fully appreciate the effectiveness of relaxation in managing their stress, you can move on to *progressive relaxation training* (PRT; Jacobson, 1929). PRT is more difficult to learn than belly breathing but, once mastered, it produces a deeper and longer-lasting state of relaxation. PRT is much more involved than belly breathing. It is based on the principle of reciprocal inhibition, which simply means that a muscle cannot be in a relaxed state and a tensed state at the same time (Wolpe, 1969). A muscle is *either* relaxed or tense. By alternately making your muscles tense and relaxed, you learn to recognize the sometimes subtle differences between the states and you also learn to relax all of your muscles. As it becomes easier to recognize tension in your body through PRT you are able to achieve a more total and longer-lasting level of relaxation. Naturally, this takes time, and the biggest problem you will have is getting your students to practice it to the point where the benefits of PRT will be enough of a motivation to continue practicing it. I have included a relaxation script in Appendix C for use in teaching students progressive relaxation. Your students should receive 15–20 minutes of supervised practice daily (in class) over a period of several weeks in order to achieve the desired results.

Exercise

Exercise is also an effective stress coping skill. There is some evidence that aerobic exercise (i.e., rhythmic, reciprocal movement that keeps the heart working at a predetermined "training" rate) will not only have a "tranquilizer" effect in reducing stress, it will also lead to a concomitant reduction of maladaptive behaviors (Allen, 1980; Yell, 1988). Exercises such as jogging, roller-skating, cycling, and fast walking can all be done at school. Enlist the cooperation of your school's physical education teachers or go it alone. Make sure you teach your students how to compute and monitor their training heart rate before beginning your exercise program (see Figure 13.6). It's probably a good idea to have the student obtain a medical release before they participate in

1. Begin with the number 220 (don't ask me why, but this is the magic number).

2. Have students subtract their chronological age (CA) from 220. The result is the maximum heart rate (MHR).

3. Have students take their resting pulse. The best way to do this is to use the pulse in the wrist (or the neck) upon awakening in the morning and before getting out of bed. Otherwise, have them take their pulse after sitting quietly for a while and practicing diaphragmatic breathing until they perceive themselves to be relaxed.

4. Have students subtract their resting heart rate (RHR) from their MHR. The result is their resting heart rate reserve (RHR reserve).

5. Have students multiply their RHR reserve by 0.60 (60%) and 0.70 (70%) respectively.

6. Have students add their RHR to the respective products computed in Step 5. This is their training heart rate (THR), lower and upper range. In order to gain the tranquilizing effect of exercise, your students should engage in aerobic exercise with their pulse rate somewhere between the lower and upper range of their THR for a minimum of 20 continuous minutes per day, 3 days per week.

Example: Joey is a 12-year-old student with a resting pulse rate of 72. Subtracting 12 (CA) from 220 = 208 (MHR) minus 72 (RHR) = 136 (RHR reserve) times 0.60 = 81.60 plus 72 (RHR) = 153.60 (rounded off to 154). This is the lower end of Joey's training heart rate (THR). Multiply Joey's RHR of 136 by 0.70 = 95.20 plus 72 (RHR) = 167.20 (rounded off to 167). This is the upper end of Joey's THR. When Joey exercises, he should try to keep his pulse rate somewhere between 154 and 167 in order to achieve the tranquilizing effect. A simple way for Joey to check his pulse during exercise is to take it (in his wrist or neck) for 6 seconds (count beats while looking at a sweep second hand) and multiply the number of beats he gets in 6 seconds by 10 to get his rate per minute. Ideally, it should be somewhere between 154 and 167.

Figure 13.6. Computing training heart rate for use in aerobic exercise program.

any exercise program. Remember what I said earlier about your being a "coping model," and be sure to participate in the belly breathing, PRT, or exercise programs along with your students.

Cognitive–Psychological

Cognitive–psychological stress coping skills are more difficult to learn than the somatic–physiological skills discussed above. They may even be more difficult to learn than many social–behavioral skills. This should not, however, deter you from teaching them to your students. If your stress management program is going to have a long-lasting effect on your students' stress, it is imperative that they learn how to change their minds as well as their bodies. Skills such as cognitive restructuring and problem solving, covered in Chapters 11 and 12, may be applied to the reduction of stress. Students can learn how their beliefs and attitudes (i.e., self-talk) contribute to their high levels of anxiety or anger and how they can modify these debilitating emotions by disputing irrational beliefs and generating rational self-talk. They can also learn that proficiency in problem solving can lead to a reduction in stress levels since problem solvers are less likely to be threatened by stressors (i.e., problems) and more likely to feel in control of the situation or its outcome. Cognitive–psychological skills may be used before, during, or after encountering stressors.

Social–Behavioral Strategies

These stress coping skills include all of the verbal and other overt behaviors required by the student to manage his stress through the manipulation of his environment. These might include some social skills, such as acting assertively in response to criticism (e.g., teasing) or manipulation (e.g., peer pressure). They might also include something as simple as time management. Students can be taught how to determine and set both short- and long-term goals as well as the activities they need to spend time on in order to realize those goals. Students should also be encouraged to monitor the activities they currently engage in as well as the time they spend on each. It may be that they need to reprioritize and spend less time on some activities (e.g., TV watching, socializing on the telephone) and more time on others (e.g., homework, reading, exercising).

☑ **Checkpoint 13.3**

[pages 457–458]

Fill in the answers to the following items (1–9). Check your responses by referring to the text; relevant page numbers appear in brackets.

Name one somatic–physiological stress management strategy that could be used in each of the following situations:

before (in anticipation of) stress: **(1)**_____

_____

during stress: **(2)** _____

_____

after stress: **(3)**_____

_____ [457]

Name one cognitive–psychological stress management strategy that could be used in each of the following situations:

before (in anticipation of stress): **(4)**_____

_____

during stress: **(5)** _____

_____

after stress: **(6)**_____

_____ [458]

Name one social-behavioral stress management strategy that could be used in each of the following situations:

before (in anticipation of) stress: **(7)**_____

_____

during stress: **(8)** _____

_____

after stress: **(9)**_____

_____ [458]

Redo any items you missed. If you missed more than 2 of the items, reread the material. Otherwise, continue on to the next section.

STRESS INOCULATION

Stress inoculation (Meichenbaum, 1985) is a relatively new intervention which appears to be effective in managing anger and anxiety as well as depression in children and youth (Maag, 1988). It is considered an *integrative* strategy because it integrates, or combines, several different skills. Integrative strategies such as stress inoculation are thought to be more effective because they combine a number of techniques rather than using one technique in isolation (Emery, Bedrosian, & Garber, 1983). For example, stress inoculation combines relaxation (somatic–physiological) with cognitive restructuring (cognitive–psychological) and behavioral rehearsal or role play (social–behavioral). The steps, or stages, involved in stress inoculation are:

1. the conceptual framework stage, where the student is taught basic concepts regarding stress and stress management;

2. the relaxation training stage, where the student learns to master some form of relaxation training, usually PRT;

3. the cognitive restructuring stage, where the student disputes any irrational beliefs that might be contributing to his high levels of anxiety or anger;

4. the stress script stage, where the student writes down everything he needs to say and/or do to manage his stress before, during, and after being exposed to the stressor; and

5. the inoculation stage, in which he uses his stress script as he is gradually exposed to larger and larger "doses" of the stressor. (See Figure 13.7.)

Let's go through the stress inoculation strategy using it in an anger management intervention with our old friend Rosario.

Conceptual Framework Stage

This involves teaching Rosario some basic precepts regarding anger as well as Ellis's A-B-C rule and cognitively mediated anger. Figure 13.8 is a list of anger management principles adapted from the work of Novaco (1975). One of the first things Rosario needs to learn is that the goal of an anger management program is not to stifle his anger but to teach him to control it to the extent necessary to allow him to change his behavior when he gets angry. He also

Stage 1: A Conceptual Framework

   a. Teach basic concepts regarding stress and anger (anxiety, depression)

   b. Present an overview of the program

   c. Provide a rationale for learning and using the program

Stage 2: Relaxation

   a. Learning to read body signals (SUD levels)

   b. Learning relaxation skills (e.g., diaphragmatic breathing and/or progressive relaxation)

Stage 3: Cognitive Restructuring

   a. Understanding the A-B-C model

   b. Identifying external (A) and internal (B) triggers of stress

   c. Disputing irrational beliefs

   d. Substituting fair-pair rational beliefs

Stage 4: Stress Scripts

   a. Explaining stress scripts

   b. Writing stress scripts

Stage 5: Inoculation

   a. Covert rehearsal (visualizing using the stress script successfully)

   b. Behavioral rehearsal (role playing the stress script in a hierarchy of stress-provoking situations)

   c. Homework (live application of the stress script in an actual stress-provoking situation)

Figure 13.7. The stress inoculation strategy. *Note.* Adapted from *Cognitive behavior modification: An integrative approach,* by D. Meichenbaum, 1977, New York: Plenum Press. Copyright 1977 by Plenum Press.

1. Anger sometimes is a cover-up for feeling scared. You should ask yourself, "Am I angry or am I anxious (scared)?"

2. Don't take insults personally. Stay on task. Do what you must to get what you want without getting sidetracked. People will sometimes insult you to bait you into a quarrel in order to get you off task.

3. Sometimes we get angry because we don't know what to do. Once you learn other ways to act besides getting angry, you won't have to get angry.

4. Learn to recognize the signs of anger, such as dry mouth, hot skin, or tense muscles, as soon as they start. It will be easier to relax these feelings away if you catch them early.

5. Use your anger to work for you. Like pain, anger is a signal that something is wrong. It could be that your thinking is wrong and needs changing.

6. Sometimes we get angry because we are afraid that we're losing control. Remember, when you give in to your anger, you have already lost control.

7. It's not what happens to you that makes you angry. It's what you say to yourself about what happens that makes you angry. No one has the power to make you angry but you. No one has the power to get rid of your anger but you.

8. Be nice to yourself and others. Anger hurts.

Figure 13.8. Anger management principles for students. *Note.* Adapted from *Anger control: The development and evaluation of an experimental treatment,* by R. Novaco, 1975, Lexington, MA: Heath. Copyright 1975 by Heath.

needs to learn that anger is sometimes a mask for fear. Since public displays of fear are less socially acceptable among males than are displays of anger, young men in our society learn at an early age to mask their fear with anger. This makes it difficult for a young man to identify the irrational thinking that might be at the root of his anger. For example, anger tends to be closely associated with You stink! and Fairy Tale thinking, while Namby Pamby or I stink thinking often is associated with anxiety reactions. If Rosario's anger is actually a cover-up for his feeling scared when he is teased, he needs to reevaluate the type of thinking he engages in.

Rosario needs to examine the motivation behind the peer teasing he is subjected to. In his mind, the teasing is always motivated by malice, a desire to make him suffer. But in reality this is not always the case. Rosario needs to understand that teasing, like most behavior, is motivated by any number of reasons. Some people use criticism to manipulate others into behaving a certain way. For example, when Rosario asks a peer to return a book he let him look at, the peer refuses. When Rosario persists, the peer insults him. This inevitably leads to an aggressive response from Rosario followed by teacher intervention. The result is that Rosario gets sent to time-out or the office and the peer doesn't have to return the book. When Rosario begins to view criticism as a manipulative device, he will not invest it with the power he did in the past. He will be better able to stay focused and get what he wants from the other person. Rosario also needs to learn that sometimes he may get angry out of frustration at not knowing what else to do. By learning alternative responses to teasing, Rosario should experience less frustration and not have to get angry.

Rosario needs to learn to pay attention to his body—that's where the first signals of anger appear. If he becomes aware of these signals early enough, he can begin using his coping skills earlier and they will be much more effective. It is analogous to learning to interpret an early warning system for forest fires: Discover them early enough and they are relatively easy to put out; discover them later and they burn out of control. Rosario needs to learn that his anger is telling him something is wrong and needs changing. He also needs to learn that getting angry sometimes is the result of fear of losing control; this is a Catch-22. He gets angry because he feels he has no control over his peers' teasing, but by allowing himself to get angry he gives up control of himself. He must learn that although most of us have little control over the emotions, thoughts, and behaviors of others, we do have control over ourselves.

Rosario should be taught that he makes himself angry; others don't make him angry. Nobody gives him an anger pill or pushes his "anger button." People can make him behave in different ways, but they have very little control over his thoughts and emotions. If he gets angry, it's because he makes himself angry. He doesn't have to be angry if he doesn't want to. He has the power to be in control!

After discussing the anger management principles with Rosario, move on to a discussion of stress inoculation and a rationale for learning and using it. Describe each of the stages and skills in the program and why it is important for Rosario to master them. Have Rosario help you generate reasons for learning to manage his anger. If the reasons come from him, they are likely to have more credibility than if you simply tell him what's good for him. Use a Socratic method of inquiry and ask him leading questions to help draw reasons out of him. Emphasize the idea of self-empowerment, "power to the person." When you are finished discussing the rationale for learning and using stress inoculation, move on to the relaxation phase.

Relaxation Stage

Before you teach Rosario how to relax, teach him how to monitor the effects of relaxation strategies. The most scientific approach involves the use of biofeedback equipment such as an electromyograph (EMG) machine that monitors changes in muscular tension; the more tension, the more electrical impulses. You can buy a relatively inexpensive EMG machine at Radio Shack. Rosario might enjoy "playing" with it like a "mad scientist." You can also try using Biodots, which are small circles of microencapsulated cholesteric liquid crystals that, worn on the skin, show changes in temperature; the more tension, the darker the color of the dot. These may be purchased, along with a teaching unit on stress, from Biodot International, Inc., PO Box 29099, Indianapolis, IN 46229; 317/637-5776. While electrical

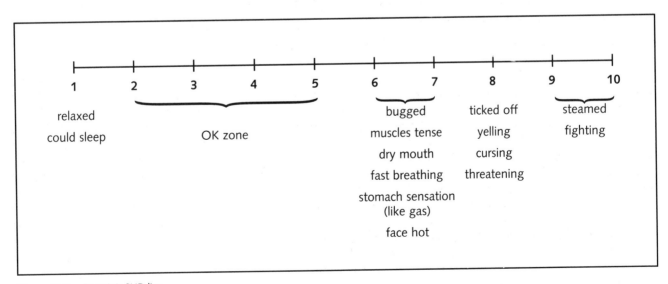

Figure 13.9. Rosario's SUD line.

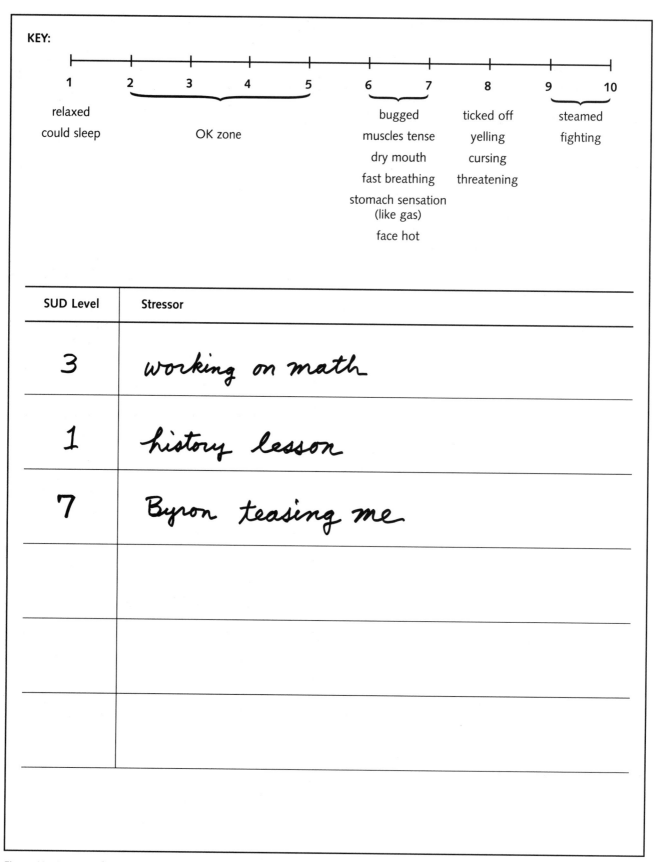

Figure 13.10. Page from Rosario's anger journal.

impulses and skin temperature are fairly accurate sources of tension, you can't expect Rosario to carry an EMG machine around with him all the time, and skin temperature is affected by factors other than tension. A more practical approach is to teach Rosario to monitor his tension/relaxation states using the SUD level discussed above. Here is how you do it.

After discussing the SUD level concept in general, have Rosario draw a horizontal line on a piece of paper and write numbers from 1 to 10 equally spaced along the line. This is Rosario's SUD line. Explain to him that 1 represents calm, peace, and relaxation—a total absence of anger, with an arousal level so low he could actually fall asleep. Have him write some descriptors under these numbers that describe his physical state when he experiences a total absence of anger. Then move to the opposite end of the SUD line and explain that 10 represents rage, fury; a feeling so strong, he would be unable to control himself. Have him write descriptors under 10. Next, explain that 8 and 9 represent being mad—anger, but not as strong as fury or rage. He would still have some ability to control himself but is slowly losing it as he moves toward rage. Have him write descriptors under 8 and 9. Finish the rest of the SUD line, moving from rage down to calm. The finished product might look like the SUD line shown in Figure 13.9. Have Rosario calibrate his SUD line by keeping an anger journal. At the top of each page in the journal is a SUD line that serves as a key. At random times during each day, have Rosario enter his SUD level and describe the environmental events occurring at the time. An example of a page from Rosario's anger journal may be seen in Figure 13.10. The idea is to give him enough practice in attending to his physiological state that he will eventually be able to give accurate and consistent (i.e., reliable) readings much like a biofeedback mechanism. Once Rosario has calibrated his SUD line you can teach him one of the relaxation techniques discussed above. Diaphragmatic breathing is easier and faster to learn, but progressive relaxation provides deeper and longer-lasting levels of relaxation. Let's assume that you teach Rosario progressive relaxation, and after a few weeks he becomes proficient enough to reduce his SUD level to a manageable state. You are now ready to move on to cognitive restructuring, the third stage of stress inoculation.

Cognitive Restructuring Stage

Since I spent the better part of Chapter 11 discussing cognitive restructuring, I won't bother to explain it in detail here. Rosario needs to a) identify beliefs that fuel his anger response, b) attempt to dispute them, c) generate fair-pair rational beliefs that don't make him angry, and d) internalize the rational beliefs. When he has at least generated some rational self-talk, Rosario will be ready for the fourth stage of stress inoculation: writing the stress script.

Stress Script Stage

The stress script consists of everything Rosario says and/or does before, during, and after encountering the anger-provoking stressor. Figure 13.11 is

---

The following is an example of a stress script that might be used to help a student manage her or his anger in the face of peer teasing (e.g., name-calling such as "retard," "faggot," "stupid").

Before (confrontations with peers):

"What do I have to do? Take a few belly breaths to get ready. This is going to be hard but I can do it. I just have to remember to take deep breaths and keep telling myself the magic words, 'saying it doesn't make it so.' Here they come. I'm ready for them."

During (confrontation):

"Stay cool. Saying it doesn't make it so. Take some deep breaths. Watch my SUD level. Saying it doesn't make it so. Just ignore them. Look away. Saying it doesn't make it so. Saying it doesn't make it so."

After (confrontation):

"I did it! I kept myself from getting angry. It worked. I can control myself. They didn't tease me as much as they usually do. Pretty soon they won't tease me at all. Now let's see . . . was there anything I could improve on for next time?"

Figure 13.11. Example of stress script for use in anger management (stress inoculation) program.

First Situation:

Students call me names but I get to choose the students and the names they call me.

I write the names on a list and they can't call me any names that aren't on the list.

They can't do this for more than 1 minute; if I say stop before the minute is up, they must stop.

Second Situation:

Students call me names; teacher chooses the students but I still get to choose the names they call me.

I write the names on a list and they can't call me any names that aren't on the list.

They can't do this for more than 1 minute; they don't have to stop before the minute is up even if I tell them to.

Third Situation:

Students call me names; teacher chooses the students and they get to choose the names they call me.

They write the names on a list and clear them with the teacher; they can't call me any names that aren't on the list.

Fourth Situation:

Students call me names; teacher chooses the students and they get to choose the names they call me.

They don't have to clear the names with the teacher ahead of time.

Fifth Situation:

(This is the same as the fourth situation, but it lasts longer.)

Figure 13.12. Example of a hierarchy of anger-provoking role-playing situations for use in a stress inoculation program.

an example of a stress script Rosario might use to help him cope with anger provoked by peer teasing. The stress script is to be written by Rosario in collaboration with his teacher.

Inoculation Stage

The fifth and final stage in stress inoculation is to actually use the stress script in an anger-provoking situation. A preliminary step, called *covert rehearsal*, has Rosario imagining himself using his stress script successfully in an anger-provoking situation. He visualizes himself using the script before, during, and after the situation. He should visualize the script helping him control his anger. This step helps Rosario memorize the script and gives him confidence in actually using it. The next step, *behavioral rehearsal*, has Rosario actually using his script in a "safe" role-playing situation simulating the anger-provoking event. Assuming Rosario is able to use his script to keep his SUD level down during several of the role plays, he can then be given the green light to use his script in a live situation. During the behavioral rehearsal, various elements and/or conditions can change gradually so that the role-play situation more closely resembles the actual situation which produces anger. For example, Rosario might be exposed to a progressively larger group of peers who tease him or he might be exposed to a progressively longer period of teasing or an increase in the number of phrases (i.e., insults) used in teasing. Another gradual change can be the types of insults used. Rosario might be given the opportunity ahead of time to preview and censor the insults used. As he gets better at controlling his anger, he might be given less (or no) opportunity to censor insults. Rosario should be encouraged to work with his teacher in developing a hierarchy of stress- (e.g., anger-) provoking situations, such as the one illustrated in Figure 13.12.

Stress inoculation, such as the preceding program in anger management for Rosario, is a long and demanding process. However, it can be an effective intervention for problems involving anger, anxiety, and depression. As I have said before, you either pay now or you pay later.

✔ Checkpoint 13.4

[pages 459–464]

Fill in the answers to the following items (1–11). Check your responses by referring to the text; relevant page numbers appear in brackets.

List and describe each of the five stages in stress inoculation.

(1) _____

_____

_____

_____

(2) _____

_____

_____

_____

(3) _____

_____

_____

_____

(4) _____

_____

_____

_____

(5) _____

_____

_____

_____ [459]

(continues)

CHECKPOINT 13.4, continued

The goal of an anger management program is

(6) _____

_____

_____ [459]

Five anger management principles that students need to learn are:

(7) _____

_____

(8) _____

_____

(9) _____

_____

(10) _____

_____

(11) _____

_____ [460]

Redo any items you missed. If you missed more than 2 of the items, reread the material. Otherwise, continue on to the next section.

MEASURING STUDENT PROGRESS

There are a number of ways to measure the efficacy of a stress management program. Assuming the stress is manifested in a maladaptive behavior, you can monitor the student's *behavior*. For example, to measure the efficacy of Rosario's anger management program, you could monitor Rosario's fighting in response to teasing. The problem here is that Rosario could conceivably change his behavior but still be angry. A better approach is to monitor both the operant and respondent behavioral correlates of Rosario's anger. These are listed on Rosario's SUD line and include dry mouth, muscle tension, face gets hot, breathing gets rapid and shallow, yelling, voice changes to high pitch, swearing, making threats, and fighting. You can always monitor Rosario's operant behavior because it is easily observed, and Rosario himself can monitor his respondent behavior (e.g., dry mouth, muscle tension, etc.) using his SUD line to record his SUD levels.

Another way to measure the efficacy of a stress management program involves the use of pencil and paper self-report measures. These include the Child Anxiety Scale (Gillis, 1980); the Children's Depression Inventory (CDI; Kovacs, 1983); the Child Depression Scale (Reynolds, 1988); Reynolds's Adolescent Depression Scale (RADS; Reynolds, 1987); Beck Depression Inventory (Beck, Ward, Mendelson, Mock, & Erbaugh, 1961); the Test Anxiety Scale for Children (TASC; Sarason, Davidson, Lighthall, & Waite, 1960); the Revised Child Manifest Anxiety Scale (RCMAS; Reynolds & Richmond, 1978); the School Anxiety Scale (SAS; Phillips, 1978); the Children's Inventory of Anger (Nelson & Finch, 1978); State–Trait Anger Expression Inventory (Spielberger, 1988); and the State–Trait Anxiety Inventory for Children (Spielberger, 1973). These self-report measures are completed by the student at the beginning and end of a stress management intervention. Since it is a summative form of measurement (pre and post), the self-report measure is not the ideal way to determine the efficacy of your intervention. Still, used in conjunction with the formative approach described above, it can provide you with some valuable data.

ASSESSMENT / CHAPTER 13

A list of acceptable responses appears following the Assessment.

Design a stress inoculation program for each of the cases described below. Include the following components:

a. a list of irrational self-talk and fair-pair rational self-talk (at least five of each for each case)

b. a stress script (before, during, and after the stressor) to include what the subject says and does

c. a hierarchy of behavioral rehearsal (role-play) situations (at least five)

1. A student who gets depressed and gives up when he makes mistakes or receives poor grades on his assignments.

2. A student who loses his temper when he is criticized by his teachers.

3. A student who is afraid of his peers and is easily coerced into doing things he doesn't want to do.

ACCEPTABLE RESPONSES

1. **stress inoculation/depressed student**

   a. *self-talk* Since this student is depressed, he is probably engaging in some "doomsday" (hopelessness and dire consequences) and "I stink!" (helplessness and low self-esteem) thinking; you should have examples of one or both

   irrational: "This is hopeless. I'm never going to learn this stuff. I'm going to fail. I'm not going to graduate. If I do, I probably won't get into college. I'll never get a decent job. I'll probably wind up being homeless on the streets. I'm a loser. I'm a failure. I'm stupid. I'm worthless."

   rational: "This is disappointing but it's not hopeless. If at first you don't succeed, try, try again. I'm OK. I'm not stupid. I can learn. I've learned lots of things. Some things take a little longer to learn than others. It's not the end of the world."

   b. *stress script* Your script should be divided into three phases: waiting to get his work back; getting his work back and examining it; and after examining his work.

   before getting work back He needs to run through a mental checklist of things to do if he gets a disappointing grade; he also needs to set a positive mood—that things will work out regardless of the grade he gets.
   Example: "What do I need to do to prepare myself? I need to think positively. I need to wait and see how I did before I start thinking negative thoughts. Maybe I did better than I think. Think positively. I did my best and that's all I can do. Whatever grade I get, things will work out."

   getting work back (with low grade) and examining it The emphasis is on thinking positive thoughts; relaxation is not necessarily a factor here.
   Example: "Think positively. This is disappointing but it's not hopeless. I'm OK. It's disappointing but it's not hopeless. Think positively. This doesn't mean I'm dumb. Think positively. Now, what do I need to do to improve my grade? First, I'll look over my work and then ask the teacher to discuss it with me. I'm smart, and with her help, I'll get through this. The important thing is not to get into a funk about it."

   after getting work back He changes his focus from the paper and grade to his emotional state; how did he do in handling his disappointment? Is he sad, unhappy, sorrowful, depressed? After evaluating his feelings, he looks at what he can do to improve. This is also a time to reward himself.

   Example: "How do I feel? I'm not happy but I'm not in a funk about this. That's good. Not being depressed is more important than my grade in this class. I'm doing OK. I may not be getting good grades but at least I'm doing a good job of managing my feelings. As long as I don't get depressed, I'll have the energy to work on my grades."

   c. *hierarchy*

   1st situation: Student turns in "fake" assignment to teacher (e.g., a blank piece of paper with only the student's name on it); he practices using his stress script (before) while teacher spends several minutes "grading" his paper; after getting his paper back with a low grade on it, the student practices using his stress script while he looks at it; finally, he practices his stress script after putting his paper away.

   2nd situation: Student turns in real assignment; these assignments are relatively easy (e.g., he has already completed them before with some success); he gets a passing grade on it but the teacher marks his mistakes; he practices using his stress script before, during, and after examining his graded paper.

   3rd situation: Same as 2nd situation, with student given progressively more difficult assignments that he is less successful with; he practices using his stress script before, during, and after examining his graded paper.

2. **stress inoculation/angry student**

   a. *self-talk* Since this student is angry, he is probably engaging in fairy tale thinking (life isn't fair) and you stink! thinking (an eye for an eye); you should have examples of one or both.

   irrational: "Why is he telling *me* to stop talking? Other students are talking. He's not telling them to stop talking. It's not fair! He's always picking on me. He doesn't like me. If he's mean to me, I can be mean to him. I hate him!"

   rational: "I don't like it when he tells me to stop doing something but I'm not the only one he criticizes. It's the teacher's job to criticize students. You can dislike what a person does without disliking him. He doesn't like what I'm doing but that doesn't mean he dislikes me. Besides, two wrongs don't make a right."

b. *stress script*

before being criticized   Review and prepare.

Example: "Sometimes I get criticized in this teacher's class. What do I have to do? Stay relaxed. Practice taking deep breaths. Pay attention to my SUD level. Do a reality check: Do I deserve to be criticized? If yes, grin and bear it. If no, be assertive but respectful. Don't take it (criticism) personally."

during criticism   Think positive thoughts; attend to SUD level; practice relaxation.

Example: "He's criticizing me. Telling me to stop talking. Do I deserve it? I was talking without permission. Just grin and bear it. What's my SUD level? Take deep breaths. Don't take it personally."

after criticism   Changes focus from what teacher says to how he (student) handled it.

Example: "That wasn't so bad. I didn't lose my cool. I *can* control myself when I want to. All right!"

c. *hierarchy*

1st situation: Student tells teacher what he can (and cannot) say to him; student can stop teacher anytime he wants; 1 minute role play.

2nd situation: Teacher decides what he will say to student; student can still stop role play anytime he chooses; 1 minute role play.

3rd situation: Same as 2nd situation except student cannot stop teacher.

4th situation: Same as 3rd situation except it can go on as long as teacher wants it to.

3.   **stress inoculation/passivity with peers**

a. *self-talk*   Since this student is anxious, he is probably engaging in "namby pamby" thinking (overreaction; perceives threat as greater than it actually is) and some "I stink!" thinking (perceives self as impotent in dealing with peers—he's at their mercy); should include examples of one or both.

irrational: "This is so scary I can't stand it. I don't want to do what they want me to but if I don't, they might hurt me. I'm afraid. I'd better give in and do what they want. They're going to get what they want from me. They always do. There's nothing I can do about it."

rational: "This is scary but I can stand it. I don't have to do what they want me to. They can't make me. I'll just keep saying 'no,' and if they keep bothering me, I'll walk away."

b. *stress script*

before coercion   Review and prepare.

Example: "Here come those guys that always bother me. What do I need to do? Got to stay relaxed. Take deep breaths. Watch my SUD level. Use broken-record approach. No, no, no. I can do it."

during coercion   Pay attention to body; practice relaxation; watch thinking; encouragement.

Example: "Take deep breaths. What's my SUD level? If I can control my fear, I can control my behavior. Use broken-record approach. If it gets too scary, I'll just walk away. I can do it. I'm doing it. I'm controlling my fear. I'm saying 'no.'"

after coercion   Evaluate his performance.

Example: "I did it! I said 'no' and they stopped bugging me. It was scary but I managed my fear. I kept it under control by watching my SUD level, taking deep breaths and not thinking scary thoughts. I controlled my behavior by controlling my fear. I'm proud of myself."

CHAPTER FOURTEEN

Changing

Teacher Behavior

Upon successful completion of this chapter, the learner should be able to design interventions for teacher-behavior problems.

INTRODUCTION

Given the reciprocal nature of behavior problems, I would be remiss if I did not include a chapter on changing teacher behavior. Remember the case of the disruptive student in Chapter 1 who shouted out in class to get the teacher's attention? The student learned that shouting relieved the anger she felt when her teacher didn't pay attention to her. She also learned that by shouting she could get attention from the teacher. Meanwhile, her teacher learned that scolding relieved the anxiety he felt when his student started shouting. He also learned that by scolding he could get rid of the student's shouting, albeit briefly. The point is, the student and the teacher shaped *each other's behavior.* This makes the teacher part of the problem and, optimistically, part of the solution. It means that teachers should not focus their interventions exclusively on students. They have to include themselves as well. This won't be easy—changing your own behavior can sometimes be harder than changing someone else's.

There are a few important points I'd like to make before going any further. First and foremost, this is not a chapter about self-help for teachers in the general sense. I am not going to teach you how to become a self-actualized human being or even how to love your job. I am going to focus specifically on those teacher behaviors, cognitions, and emotions that tend to influence the success (or failure) of students in school. Should you wish to make some changes in your life that extend beyond your teaching, there are several fine textbooks devoted exclusively to self-management (see Mahoney, 1979; Mahoney & Thoresen, 1972; Schmidt, 1976; Watson & Tharp, 1981).

Second, this material is not for everyone (see Figure 14.1). It is not for teachers who are unaware that something needs changing. Nor is it for teachers who know what needs changing and are unwilling to change. It is for those of you who are aware that something needs changing and are willing to change but *don't know how to change.*

Third, whether you use self-management or stress management or cognitive restructuring, or any intervention strategy covered in this text, you may consider its application the same whether it is used

Figure 14.1. Saints need not read this chapter.

by teachers to change students or by teachers to change themselves. Therefore, I will not describe those previously discussed strategies in any detail in this chapter. I will, however, provide several examples of how teachers might apply those strategies to their own behavior problems.

PROACTIVE VERSUS REACTIVE

As in dealing with the behavior problems of students, you can either take a proactive approach or wait until a teaching-behavior problem surfaces and react to it. Let's begin with the proactive approach.

Proactive Approach

One way to prevent teaching-behavior problems from occurring is to use the research on effective instruction to identify those classroom and/or behavior management competencies you might be lacking, and do something about them before they create (or maintain) student behavior problems. An excellent place to start is the Englert, Tarrant, and Mariage (1992) article on effective teaching in special education programs. Figure 14.2 is an observation checklist taken from Englert (1984). It lists all of the teacher competencies that effective classroom managers should have. Look over this list and identify any competencies you feel you need to work on and proceed accordingly.

For example, let's say room scanning is one of the teaching behaviors you feel you need to work on. The first thing you need to do is pinpoint room scanning as "looks at entire classroom, from wall to wall, pausing to observe all student activity." Next, you design your monitoring system and field test it by collecting some baseline data. Keep the process simple by making time and opportunities constant so all you have to monitor is the behavior pinpointed above. Since you can monitor and teach at the same time, you can use a continuous sample. Assuming that the total time you monitor varies from day to day, you need to keep track of the time you begin and end as well as the frequency of room scans. At the end of the day, you record the rate of room scans per minute on your equal-ratio chart.

After collecting baseline data, write a performance objective for each behavior and decide what you want your CAP to be. This can be done by a) identifying one or more teachers whom you know to be effective at classroom and behavior management, and b) monitoring their room-scanning behavior.

Let's say, for argument's sake (since I don't know for sure), during a 20 minute period, teachers competent in classroom and behavior management room scan at a rate of not less than 3 scans per minute. Given these data, your performance objective can be stated as: "When I am in the classroom, I will room scan at a rate of not less than 3 scans per minute for 3 consecutive days."

Your next step is to design an intervention. In this case, I would combine a self-management (i.e., reinforcement) program with antecedents to serve as reminders. Here's how it might look:

1. Decide on goal for the day (i.e., rate of room scanning you want to reach) and mark it on chart;

2. place tape on wrist;

3. set wrist chronograph to beep at 60-second intervals;

4. write down time you begin collecting data on tape;

5. at the sound of the beep, scan room (look at entire classroom, wall to wall, pausing to observe all students);

6. mark S on wrist tape;

7. write down time you stop collecting data on tape;

8. at end of day, compute rate (total minutes data collecting divided into total room scans) and plot on equal-ratio chart;

9. if goal for day is reached, self-reward; if goal for day is not reached, consider reasons and possible changes.

I have included an example of a data display you might use with some hypothetical data (see Figure 14.3). As you can see, it looks like your intervention is working. Congratulations!

In addition to (or instead of) the literature on effective instruction, you can use a list of maladaptive teaching behaviors such as the one in Figure 14.4 to identify behaviors you might need to work on. Since you are following a proactive approach, you need to identify and remediate maladaptive teaching behaviors *before* they contribute to teaching problems with your students. For example, if you know you have a tendency to lecture students until they tune you out, take too long to praise (or punish) behavior, or you attend to student maladaptive behavior when it is more appropriate to ignore it, you need to work on these behaviors *now*—not later.

Observation Checklist for Classroom Management

Teacher _____ Observer _____
School & District_____ Class/Subj./Grade _____
Date _____Beginning of Observation: Time _____to _____
Observer _____Number of Students in Instruction _____Number of Students in Seatwork _____
This self or observer checklist shows what was and was not observed during the time noted.

Instructional, Interactional sequences	Excel-lent		Satis-factory		Needs Work	Notes
Arranges physical space to maintain minimally disruptive traffic patterns and procedures	5	4	3	2	1	
Creates rules and procedures for non-instructional events (e.g., movement about room, student talk, distributing materials, bathroom use, etc.)	5	4	3	2	1	
Creates rules and procedures related to instructional events (e.g., getting ready for lessons, expected behavior of the instructional group, obtaining help, seatwork procedures, out-of-seat procedures, etc.)	5	4	3	2	1	
Establishes rules that involve respect for other members of the class and provides verbal reminders to students about how to treat others	5	4	3	2	1	
Clearly states in advance what behavior will be tolerated and what will not	5	4	3	2	1	
Introduces rules, procedures, and consequences (e.g., states rules, posts rules, gives rationale for rules, provides discussion of rules, defines specific contexts within which rules apply, states consequences in advance)	5	4	3	2	1	
Demonstrates what behavior is acceptable by presenting examples and non-examples of the target behavior	5	4	3	2	1	
Requires student rehearsal of rules and procedures; monitors rule compliance, and provides feedback during rehearsal	5	4	3	2	1	
Consequates rule noncompliance quickly; cites rule or procedure in responding to disruptive behavior	5	4	3	2	1	
Positions self in the room to provide high degree of visibility (e.g., can make eye contact with all students)	5	4	3	2	1	
Scans class frequently	5	4	3	2	1	
Uses nonverbal signals whenever possible to direct students in a nondisruptive manner when teaching other groups of students	5	4	3	2	1	
Administers praise contingently, and uses specific praise statements	5	4	3	2	1	
Includes students in the management of their own behavior and cues self-regulation (e.g., self-monitoring, self-charting, self-evaluating)	5	4	3	2	1	
Provides behavioral corrections to students that indicate how they can control themselves	5	4	3	2	1	

Figure 14.2. Teacher competencies in classroom/behavior management. *Note:* Adapted from *Teacher Education and Special Education (TESE)*, Vol. 15, No. 2, Spring 1992. Copyright *TESE* 1992. Reprinted by permission.

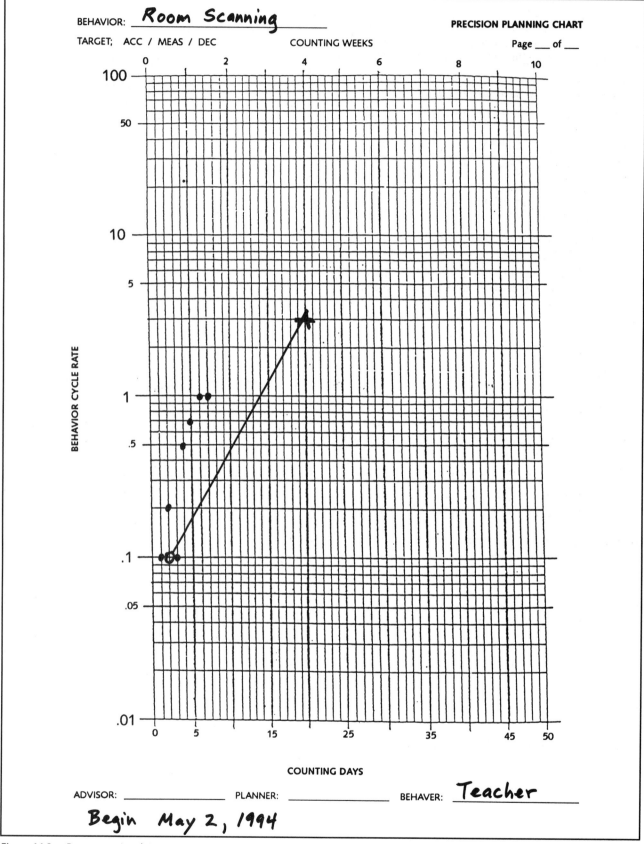

Figure 14.3. Room scanning data.

1. Overreacting to student maladaptive behavior (e.g., losing temper, using abusive–provocative language, or getting physical with students).

2. Lecturing students (or "preaching" or talking too much) until they tune you out.

3. Forgetting to praise students when it is appropriate to do so.

4. Not praising with any enthusiasm, so that the praise is perceived by the student as insincere.

5. Praising inconsistently (i.e., not according to schedule) or praising one student (or group of students) more than others.

6. Punishing inconsistently or punishing one student (or group of students) more than others.

7. Taking too long to praise (or punish) a student (i.e., the latency between the student's behavior and the teacher's consequence is too long to be of any value).

8. Attending to student maladaptive behavior when it is more appropriate to ignore it.

9. Being unassertive with students when it is more appropriate to be assertive.

10. Consistently being negative with students (i.e., using "put-downs" and negative comments, pointing out negative behavior, and ignoring positive behavior).

11. Failing to collect data on student behavior when it is desirable to do so.

12. Allowing oneself to be manipulated by students.

Figure 14.4. Examples of maladaptive teaching behaviors.

✔ Checkpoint 14.1

[pages 473–477]

Fill in the answers to the following items (1–13). Check your responses by referring to the text; relevant page numbers appear in brackets.

The author believes it is important for teachers to be able to modify their own behavior, cognitions, and emotions in the classroom because

(1) _____

_____

_____

_____

_____

_____

_____ [473]

Two ways to prevent teaching-behavior problems from occurring are:

(2) _____

_____

_____

_____ [474]

(3) _____

_____

_____

_____ [474]

Five classroom/behavior management competencies from the teaching effectiveness literature are:

(4) _____

_____

(5) _____

_____

(6) _____

_____

(continues)

CHECKPOINT 14.1, continued

(7) _____

_____

(8) _____

_____ [475]

Write a fair-pair target behavior for each of the maladaptive teaching behaviors listed below.

lecturing students (or "preaching," or talking too much) until they tune you out

(9) _____

_____

taking too long to praise (or punish) a student

(10) _____

_____

attending to student misbehavior when it is more appropriate to ignore it

(11) _____

_____

not attending to student misbehavior when it is more appropriate to attend to it

(12) _____

_____

not praising students when it appropriate to do so

(13) _____

_____ [477]

Redo any items you missed. If you missed more than 2 items, reread the material. Otherwise, continue on to the next section.

Reactive Approach

So far we have been talking about changing maladaptive teacher behavior *before* it contributes to a specific student-behavior problem. Let's turn our attention to what you should do when a student (or students) engages in maladaptive behavior and you

suspect your behavior is contributing to the problem. I'll use a personal experience as an example.

For several years, the primary instructional format I have used in my university teaching is the lecture. I recognize that lecture can be deadly boring, but I am vain enough to believe that this only applies to other lecturers and not me. My lectures are so entertaining, my students follow every word on the edge of their seats. . . . Not! At some point in time, I had to admit that many of my students were not paying attention during my lectures. One clue was the vacant look in their eyes. My students are not stupid; most of them are bright, and yet they managed to look stupid during my lecture. A second clue was the questions they asked. Either I had already answered the same question, asked by another student, 10 minutes earlier, or I had already given them this information in the lecture. Also, whenever I asked a question of them (which was extremely rare), they couldn't answer it even when I had just given them the answer. Some of them couldn't even repeat the question. Was it time to do something drastic like stop lecturing? Nah! Too drastic. Instead, I decided to increase the frequency with which I asked questions, reasoning that the more questions I asked, the more attentive my students would be to my lectures. This made good sense, but there was one problem . . . I kept forgetting to ask questions. It was time for a self-management project on question asking.

I pinpointed the target behavior as: "Joe asks questions of his students during a lecture session," and the performance objective as: "When lecturing students, Joe will ask questions at a rate of 1 every 2 minutes (.5 questions per minute) for ten consecutive lecture sessions." I determined the CAP arbitrarily.

My self-management project was quite simple. First, I hung 3" × 5" yellow cards around the room with a large black question mark drawn on each. This served as a cue to remind me to ask questions. Whenever I asked a question, I recorded it on a golf counter worn on a belt loop on my trousers. Since lecture time varied from class to class, I decided to summarize the data as rate and was careful to record the time I began and ended each lecture. Immediately after class, I computed my rate of question-asking behavior and plotted it on the equal-ratio chart shown in Figure 14.5. My intervention consisted simply of a reminder to ask questions (the yellow cards) and the self-monitoring of the target behavior. I also received reinforcement from plotting my own data and seeing my behavior improve. Reinforcement also came from seeing the concomitant change in my students' attending behavior.

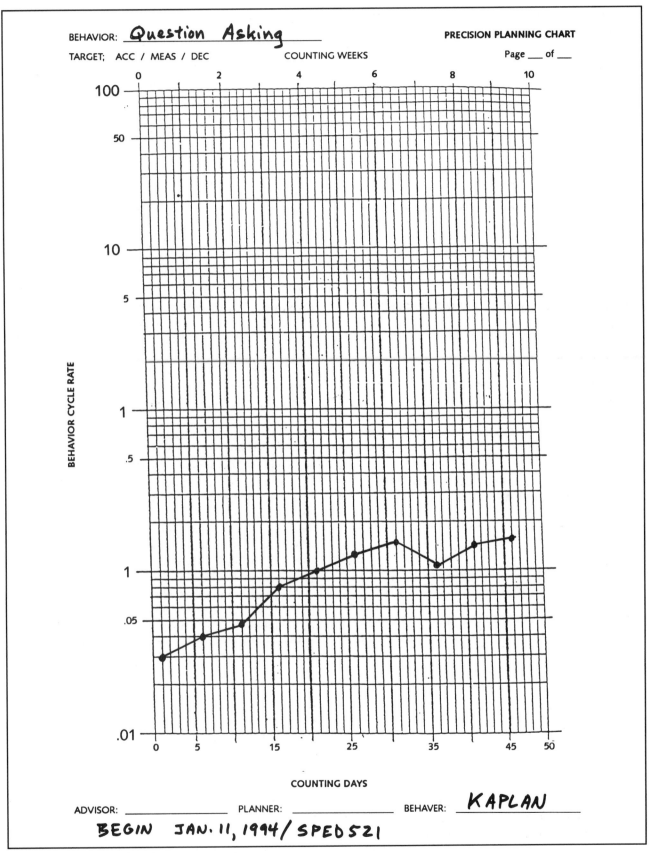

Figure 14.5. Question-asking data.

While I have no hard data to support this, it appeared to me that the number of vacant stares decreased and students were more involved in the sessions. They appeared to answer (and ask) more questions. The only problem has been with maintenance. Whenever I stop using the intervention, I notice my question-asking behavior drops to baseline levels and my students' vacant stares return. I now realize I may have to use the intervention indefinitely. Still, considering how simple it is and the difference it makes in my students' attending behavior, it is well worth the effort.

In my case, I was able to recognize what I was doing that was contributing to the off-task behavior of my students. Sometimes this is not so obvious. If you are having difficulty dealing with a student-behavior problem and want to determine whether or not your teaching behavior might be contributing to that problem, I suggest you do a functional analysis. Simply follow the procedure outlined in Chapter 4. Write down what happens in the environment before and after the *student's* maladaptive behavior occurs. Look for any behaviors on your part that might be contributing to (i.e., exacerbating, or at least maintaining) the maladaptive behavior. These might include not giving enough cues, giving the wrong cues, not consequating the behavior soon enough, or using the wrong consequences, to name a few. For example, let's suppose a student frequently engages in out-of-seat behavior that the teacher typically consequates with reprimands (e.g., "Sit down now!"). Frustrated by her inability to weaken the student's behavior for any length of time, the teacher completes a functional analysis which indicates she is actually reinforcing the student's behavior by attending to it. The S-R-S form may be seen in Figure 14.6. Knowing what is causing the problem allows the teacher to take steps to remediate it. She embarks on a program of planned ignoring and DRI. When the student is out of his seat, she ignores him; when he is in his seat, she attends to him.

The teacher in the example discussed in the previous paragraph only needed to know what she was doing wrong to be able to fix it. She was willing and able to change her behavior. But what if the teacher can't stop attending to the student's out-of-seat behavior? When this happens, the teacher must try to find out *why* she can't stop attending. Again, diagnosis begins with a functional analysis—only this time, the functional analysis focuses on the teacher's behavior, not the student's behavior. The teacher writes down what happens in the environment before and after she reprimands the student for being out of his seat. Actually, all she has to do is

take the first S-R-S form and rewrite it with her attending behavior as the response instead of the consequence (see Figure 14.7). This time she also considers the setting events more closely. For example, her reprimanding behavior occurs during a class lesson taught late in the day. Class lessons require that all students be in seat attending to the teacher. The S-R-S form shows that an immediate consequence of the teacher's attending behavior is student compliance (i.e., he sits down). All teachers like to feel they are effective. If the student sits down immediately after being reprimanded, this serves to reinforce (albeit negatively) the teacher's behavior. What does all of this mean? We have a teacher who reprimands a student when he is out of seat even though she knows her reprimands serve to maintain his behavior. She reprimands him during a class lesson when students are supposed to be quiet and in their seats. His behavior is probably more provocative for the teacher at these times than at other times because it is a blatant rule violation that is easily observed by the entire class. What if the others decide to imitate his behavior? It also occurs at a time in the day when the teacher's energy and patience are both in short supply. The student's immediate response of sitting down also negatively reinforces the teacher's reprimanding. She is caught in a criticism trap, believing her consequence is working when it's not. All of the above mitigates against the teacher's efforts to modify her reprimanding behavior.

Using information from the functional analysis, the teacher can do a number of things to help herself. First, she can change her schedule so that she teaches all class lessons early in the day when she still has lots of patience and energy. Or, if possible, she can give herself a short respite from teaching immediately before the last class lesson in order to "recharge her batteries." She can also take some pressure off herself and her students by stretching the out-of-seat rule during class lessons (e.g., out of seat is OK as long as it is not more than one person at a time). If this is not practical, she can set up a reinforcement system to keep her students from imitating the behavior of the target student. She can hang a sign or signs at eye level around the room reminding her of the criticism trap (e.g., "Beware the criticism trap!"). She can also use a behavior reduction procedure such as WDRO to help her weaken her reprimanding behavior. She can set a timer to ring at gradually longer intervals and if she hasn't reprimanded the student for out-of-seat behavior during an interval, she can reward herself with tokens, real money, self-praise, or praise from a stu-

Student: Joey	Teacher: Ms. K.	Date: March 1995

Behavior: out of seat (stands up, or leaves seat and stands in aisle)

Setting Events: during class lesson in P.M.

S	R	S
T. teaches lesson	J. stands up	T. says, "Sit down, Joey"
C	J. sits down	T. teaches lesson
C	J. leaves seat to stand in aisle	T. says, "Sit down, Joey"
C	J. sits down	T. teaches lesson
C	J. leaves seat to stand in aisle	T. yells, "Sit down now!"

Figure 14.6. S-R-S form completed for functional analysis of Joey's out-of-seat behavior.

Student: __Joey_____ Teacher: __Ms. K._____ Date: __March 1995__

Behavior: __attends to student's out-of-seat behavior (i.e., tells Joey to sit down)__

Setting Events: __during class lesson in P.M.__

S	R	S
J. stands up	T. says, "Sit down, Joey"	J. sits down
C	T. teaches lesson	J. leaves seat to stand in aisle
C	T. says, "Sit down, Joey"	J. sits down
C	T. teaches lesson	J. leaves seat to stand in aisle
C	T. yells, "Sit down now!"	J. sits down

Figure 14.7. S-R-S form completed for functional analysis of teacher's attending-to-student behavior.

dent or instructional assistant. Any combination of the above might effectively help the teacher ignore out-of-seat behavior. Since she will also be monitoring the effect of her ignoring on her student's out-of-seat behavior, she will also receive reinforcement from plotting data on the student's chart, assuming his behavior improves. Remember, all of this is possible because of the functional analysis the teacher does on her own behavior.

But what if the teacher still has difficulty ignoring the student's behavior? This probably means there are other factors (in addition to the environmental factors) that are contributing to the problem. Remember the concept of reciprocal determinism? Environment, behavior, and personal variables all interact to produce behavior. The teacher needs to identify the personal variables she brings to the situation that make it difficult for her to ignore the student's out-of-seat behavior. She does this by completing a Pre-Mod analysis on her own behavior.

The teacher begins by identifying her own maladaptive and target behaviors. Notice I said *her own* maladaptive and target behavior. She needs to complete a Pre-Mod analysis to determine what, if any, prerequisites she is lacking that make it difficult for her to ignore the student's out-of-seat behavior. Figure 14.8 is the completed analysis. Let's take a look at each prerequisite.

Prerequisite 1. Some teachers get a little confused about what they are supposed to do. For example, this teacher might equate "ignoring" out-of-seat behavior with not punishing (reprimanding) it. In her mind, it's OK to look at or even talk to the student when he's out of seat as long as she doesn't reprimand him. The problem here, of course, is that *any* form of attention—a reprimand, a frown, eye contact, or *any* attempt at verbal communication—serves to strengthen the student's out-of-seat behavior. This is why it is important that the teacher understand exactly what it is she is supposed to do when the student is out of seat. To assess this understanding, the teacher pinpoints her target behavior (i.e., "I will not look at, gesture toward, or speak to _____ when he is out of his seat") and shares it with a colleague to see if it passes the stranger test. They both agree that, given the circumstances, the teacher has the correct interpretation of "ignore." She understands that she is supposed to withhold all attention of any kind from the student when he is out of seat.

Prerequisite 2. This teacher must also be aware of when she is ignoring the student and when she is not. Don't confuse this with Prerequisite 1. A teacher lacking Prerequisite 1 does not know what to call what she is doing but knows when she is doing it; a teacher lacking Prerequisite 2 knows what to call what she is doing but does not know when she is doing it. In this particular case, the teacher knows intellectually that ignoring means no attention of any kind. She needs to determine if she is aware of when she is attending to the student and when she is not. I remember years ago supervising a graduate student teacher who hardly ever smiled at her students even though she knew, intellectually, that smiling at students was expected of her. When I mentioned this to her, she couldn't believe it. Did she know what smiling was? Yes. When I asked her to show me what she was supposed to do with students, she smiled. The problem was, her lack of awareness was such that she thought she was smiling much more than she was. She continued to dispute me until I showed her a videotape of her interacting with students and asked her to monitor her smiling behavior. Her rate of smiles was something like 2 every 10 minutes! Until she saw herself on tape and monitored her behavior, she was totally unaware of it. The teacher profiled in Figure 14.8 should assess her awareness of ignoring versus attending the same way she would assess a student's awareness. She self-monitors ignoring and attending while a colleague monitors her at the same time. As you can see, there is nothing wrong with her level of awareness. So far, she understands what behavior is expected of her and is aware of her behavior.

Prerequisite 3. The teacher must also be able to control her attending to out-of-seat behavior. If she acts out of impulse or emotion (e.g., anger or anxiety), it will be difficult for her to ignore the student's behavior until she learns self-control. To assess this, the teacher measures her SUD level several times during the day, including those times when the student is out of seat. In addition to recording her SUD level, she writes down what is happening at the time. At the end of the day, she discovers her high SUD levels occur during student misbehavior, with the highest levels occurring at those times when the target student is out of his seat. Given the behavioral, psychological, and physiological symptoms of her distress, she accurately labels it as an anxiety reaction. To make matters worse, she has little or no competence in stress management. So far, the teacher understands she is supposed to withhold *all* attention for out-of-seat behavior and is aware of when she is and is not doing so. Unfortunately, she has an extreme anxiety reaction to the student's behavior and the only way she currently knows how to relieve her distress is to yell at the student.

Prerequisite 4. Knowing how to ignore her student's behavior is also critical. Many teachers imple-

Subject: **Teacher**   Evaluator: **Teacher**   Date: **March 1995**

Maladaptive Pinpoint: **Attends to (yells at) Student X when out-of-seat**

Target Pinpoint: **Ignores (no look, no talk, no gesture) Student X when out-of-seat**

Prerequisites	Status	Assessments	Results
1. Understand I am supposed to ignore X and that "ignore" means no look/ no talk/ no gesture	Y	will write pinpoint of target behavior and share with peer; should pass stranger test	shared with two colleagues; both agree PASS
2. Aware of when I am ignoring and attending to X	Y	will self-monitor ignoring/attending; have peer monitor me; should be 80% agreement	90% agreement PASS
3. Able to control impulses and emotions in order to ignore X	N	will monitor SUD level; should not be significantly higher for out-of-seat behavior	SUD level consistently higher for out-of-seat; no known coping strategies NO PASS
4. Know how to ignore X	Y	explain to expert how I would ignore; should agree	school psychologist agrees PASS
5. Consider consequences of ignoring X more rewarding (or less aversive) than consequences of attending to X	N	cue sort; all consequences of ignoring should be more rewarding than consequences of attending	all consequences of attending more rewarding than consequences of ignoring NO PASS
6. Only hold beliefs compatible with ignoring X	N	brainstorm beliefs; should not endorse any incompatible w/ ignoring	endorses several beliefs incompatible with ignoring NO PASS

Figure 14.8. Pre-Mod analysis of teacher's attending-to-student behavior.

ment behavior management techniques incorrectly. They simply don't know how to operate a token economy or a level system or monitor behavior or give contingent praise. In this case, the teacher may not know how to ignore the student's behavior. To assess her knowledge of planned ignoring, the teacher tells the school psychologist (an expert in behavior management) how she would use planned ignoring to extinguish out-of-seat behavior. The school psychologist decides that the teacher knows how to do it. The teacher also has Prerequisites 1 and 2 but lacks Prerequisite 3.

Prerequisite 5. In order to ignore the student's behavior, the teacher should consider ignoring or its consequences more rewarding than attending to the student (or its consequences). (Some teachers actually enjoy catching students being "bad" and punishing them.) The teacher uses the cue-sort method to assess this prerequisite. First, she lists all of the consequences of ignoring and attending to (reprimanding) the student's behavior on 3" × 5" cards. The consequences are:

Attending	*Ignoring*
J sits down	J won't sit down
I feel less stress	I feel more stress
peers less likely to imitate	peers will imitate J
if model is punished	will lose control of class
students will respect me	students won't respect me
will keep my job	could lose my job
and my self respect	lose my self respect
feel like I'm asserting myself	feel like I'm letting him get away with something

Then she sorts the cards into two piles: consequences she considers rewarding and those she doesn't consider rewarding. Unfortunately, all of the consequences of attending are those she considers rewarding, and she considers all of the consequences of ignoring as aversive. So far, she knows what to do, is aware of what she is doing, knows how to do it; but has trouble controlling her behavior and considers her attending to the student less aversive than ignoring him.

Prerequisite 6. Of course, the teacher's beliefs can influence her behavior in the classroom as surely as her students' beliefs influence their behavior in the classroom (see Figure 14.9). Rather than assess this prerequisite with a beliefs assessment, the

Figure 14.9. Keep self-talk positive.

teacher simply brainstorms her beliefs about the student, herself, and the situation. The following is a sample of her thinking on the subject:

> Ignoring a student's misbehavior is the same as letting him get away with it.
>
> Ignoring student behavior only makes it worse.
>
> If my students misbehave, it means I'm a bad teacher.
>
> If one student misbehaves, the others will surely follow.
>
> A good teacher maintains order in her classroom.
>
> Teachers who do not maintain order in their classrooms get fired.
>
> Order in the classroom means students follow the rules.

As you can see, the teacher endorses a number of beliefs that are incompatible with her ignoring out-of-seat behavior. In order for her to effectively practice extinction with her student, she must believe that a) extinction is a consequence; b) extinction may take some time but it can work; and c) by using it, she will not lose control of her classroom or get fired.

Having completed the Pre-Mod analysis, the teacher designs an intervention to remediate the following prerequisite deficits: (3) experiences high-level anxiety states whenever the student is out of seat, and lacks effective stress-coping skills; (5) considers reprimanding out-of-seat behavior less aversive (since it relieves her stress) than ignoring it; and (6) believes that ignoring out-of-seat behavior will lead to a student revolt and the loss of her job. On the basis of this information, the teacher selects stress inoculation as her primary intervention strategy because it addresses all three of the prerequisite deficits. Figures 14.10 and 14.11 are examples of a stress script and hierarchy of role plays the teacher uses in her stress inoculation program.

APPLYING STUDENT STRATEGIES TO TEACHER-BEHAVIOR PROBLEMS

Whether you use a proactive or reactive approach to modify your teaching behaviors, the strategies in this text that work with student-behavior problems also work with teacher-behavior problems. The CBM strategies in Chapters 11 and 12 can be particularly useful. For example, you can use problem solving to

---

First Situation:
Role play after school hours with assistant acting as out-of-seat student and no students present.

Second Situation:
Role play with a designated student acting as out-of-seat student. All students present including target student. I decide who the student is and signal him/her to get out of seat.

Third Situation:
Same as second situation except designated student is signaled to get out of seat by assistant so I can't anticipate when they will get out of seat.

Fourth Situation:
Same as third situation except different students are designated by assistant so I can't anticipate who will be out of seat and when they will do so.

Fifth Situation:
I signal target student to get out of seat so I can anticipate.

Sixth Situation:
Assistant signals target student to get out of seat so I can't anticipate.

Figure 14.11. Hierarchy of anxiety-provoking situations for use in stress inoculation program.

BEFORE
take deep breaths
what am I supposed to do (if he gets out of seat)?
no look, no talk, no gesture
ignoring is the right thing to do
it will probably get worse before it gets better but I can handle it
He doesn't control me. I control me.

DURING
take deep breaths
no look, no talk, no gesture
stay on task—keep teaching
scan room and reward peers for ignoring
ignoring is the right thing to do

AFTER
I did it! I went the entire lesson without attending to him.
I can control myself.
What did I do (or not do) that I need to work on for next time.

Figure 14.10. Stress script for use in stress inoculation program.

---

generate alternative solutions to your behavior management problems. Self-instructional training (SIT) can be useful in learning the steps in some of the more complex CBM or stress-management strategies. SIT can be used to help manage maladaptive teaching behaviors related to impulsivity. You can change from a REACT NOW! mode of operating to a wait-and-reflect mode. Regulate your teaching behaviors through verbal mediation. Figure 14.12 is an example of a verbal mediation essay used to modify a maladaptive teaching (i.e., consequating) behavior.

I believe irrational thinking is the root cause of a number of teaching-behavior problems. Figure 14.13 is a list of irrational beliefs common to teachers. I must admit that I, too, have endorsed more than one of them at some point in my teaching career. Some are still there, lurking in the corners of my mind, waiting to pop into consciousness at the right moment. I still wish I could have the love and approval of *all* my students and colleagues. I don't handle rejection very well. (So please don't sell this

What am I doing that I'm not supposed to do?

I'm yelling at my students again when they misbehave.

Why shouldn't I be doing this?

I feel guilty and frustrated after I yell at students.

Yelling gets their attention but it doesn't weaken their behavior.

Yelling serves as a model for aggressive behavior.

What will probably happen if I continue doing it?

My students will become desensitized to my yelling.

My students will not like me or respect me.

I will continue to feel guilty and frustrated.

They will imitate my behavior.

What should I be doing instead?

I should use other BRPs such as DRI or DRO, extinction, redirection, etc., and use them in a hierarchical order from least to most intrusive, aversive, and restrictive.

Why should I be doing this?

Because this is a more ethical way to weaken behavior than to only use yelling over and over again whether it works or not. It is also more effective.

What will probably happen if I do what I'm supposed to?

I will be able to effectively weaken maladaptive behavior in my students without feeling guilty or frustrated.

My students will like (or at least respect) me more.

Figure 14.12. Verbal mediation essay for use with teacher-behavior problem.

book back to the bookstore unless you're starving!) The sad thing is, I'm only *half* joking, and I know there are thousands of teachers out there who are just as needy for approval as I am. We are "I stink" thinkers. We need the goodwill of our students and colleagues to validate our worth. The problem with this type of thinking is it often causes us to do things we shouldn't do, in order to keep our students' goodwill. Letting our students get away with "murder" in order to gain their approval, or avoid being rejected by them, is acting in our own best interests—not theirs. Some of us are also "namby pamby" thinkers because we are frightened by confrontations and

avoid them by not holding students accountable for their actions. Those of us who engage in "You stink!" thinking are likely to get angry a lot and consequate student behavior too harshly. We become models of aggression for our students to emulate. Teachers who engage in "robot" thinking don't take any responsibility for their actions—it's all the student's fault, and if he would only go away, everything would be OK. "Robot" thinkers don't really do much behavior management. They would prefer that somebody else do something with the student. . . . Send him to a psychologist or give him a pill; what do you expect *me* to do about it? "Doomsday" thinkers are so worried and depressed, they have neither the energy or the inclination to be positive with students. Finally, "fairy tale" thinkers tend to spend an inordinate amount of time railing about the injustices in their classrooms. "After all I've done for you, this is how you repay me?" "It's just not fair that a kid like that can get away with it!" "When I was a student, nobody praised me when I behaved and I turned out OK." If you discover that you engage in some irrational thinking that might interfere with your teaching, put yourself on a cognitive restructuring program. Follow the same procedure outlined for students in Chapter 11.

Strategies from Chapter 5 that can be used to remediate teaching-behavior problems include chaining (to help you break away from old behavior chains and establish new ones), shaping (to help you establish new behavior in a slow but steady progression), and fading (to help you generalize newly learned behaviors). Contingency contracting can be used to help motivate you toward change. An example of a self-contract might read, "For each week I increase my rate of contingent praise by 10% (over the preceding week), I get to purchase either a book or a CD (purchases not to exceed $15)." Contracts are a way of making a commitment to change. When you state your intention to change in writing, it often makes it easier to stick with the program.

Also, don't be shy about using someone other than (or in addition to) yourself for reinforcement. Include a data display of your behavior(s) on the classroom bulletin board along with data displays from your students' behavior projects. Arrange to have your students reward you for appropriate teaching behavior. Students can be effective change agents when it comes to modifying the behavior of their teachers (Graubard, Rosenberg, & Miller, 1971). While you are using others in your reinforcement program, don't underestimate the power of self-praise. Self-praise helps you to internalize your new behavior by constantly reminding you that your

1. I must have the love or approval of all my students, parents of students, and co-workers and it's terrible if I don't.

2. I must prove thoroughly competent as a teacher and it's awful if I don't.

3. When students, parents of students, or co-workers act obnoxiously and unfairly, I must blame and damn them, and see them as bad, wicked, or rotten individuals.

4. When I get seriously frustrated, am treated unfairly, or experience rejection on the job, I must view things as awful, terrible, horrible, and catastrophic.

5. All of my job-related stress is the result of external pressures and events and there is little or nothing I can do about it.

6. When things happen at work that I consider dangerous or fearsome, I must preoccupy myself with these things and make myself anxious about them.

7. It's terrible when my students don't learn, and I should consider myself a failure as a teacher.

8. My students should have the same values that I do, and it's terrible if they don't.

9. It's awful if my students don't learn what I want them to right away.

10. It's terrible if my students misbehave and I must take it personally.

11. It's just not fair when my classes are over-crowded, when my students are not all bright and polite, when I don't have any or enough planning periods, when I don't have the teaching supplies I need, and when I don't get paid what I think I'm worth.

12. It's better for me not to take my teaching too seriously so that in case something goes wrong, I won't be disappointed.

13. Because of my training in college or the early experiences I've had in teaching, I can't help being as I am today and I'll always be this way.

14. It's terrible when my students experience problems and I must be upset about this.

Figure 14.13. Irrational thinking by teachers.

prize is the change in your behavior rather than some gift you might buy for yourself—knowing you can change your behavior is the greatest gift you can ever hope to give yourself. As Mahoney and Thoresen (1972) said, self-management means "power to the person." In addition to self-praise, you might want to use fantasizing as a payoff for a change in your behavior. Fantasize yourself in a week or a month or a year as an extremely effective and successful teacher, all because of your newfound self-management skills. Think of expanding these skills into other aspects of your life where you feel change is warranted.

Even certain behavior reduction procedures from Chapter 6 can be used to modify teacher behavior. For example, MDRO or WDRO can be used to help you reduce or eliminate maladaptive teacher behaviors such as overdwelling, yelling, making negative statements, being off task, and talking too much, among others. Either you set the timer and control the number and length of the intervals, or have your assistant or your students do it. If the timer rings and you are not engaging in the maladaptive behavior at that moment (MDRO) or you have not engaged in it for the length of the interval (WDRO), reward yourself or have someone else reward you.

✔ Checkpoint 14.2

[pages 478–489]

Fill in the answers to the following items (1–17). Check your responses by referring to the text; relevant page numbers appear in brackets.

Explain how you might use a functional analysis to determine whether or not your teaching behavior was contributing to a student-behavior problem.

(1) _____

_____

_____

_____

_____

_____ [480]

The six generic Pre-Mod prerequisites applied to teacher-behavior problems are:

(2) _____

(3) _____

(4) _____

(5) _____

(6) _____

(7) _____ [483]

(continues)

CHECKPOINT 14.2, continued

Briefly state how each of the following strategies might be used to help you with a teacher-behavior problem.

shaping **(8)** _____

_____

chaining **(9)** _____

_____

fading **(10)** _____

_____

WDRO or MDRO **(11)** _____

_____

SIT **(12)** _____

_____

verbal mediation **(13)** _____

_____

cognitive restructuring **(14)** _____

_____

problem solving **(15)** _____

_____

stress inoculation **(16)** _____

_____

contingency contracting **(17)** _____

_____

Redo any items you missed. If you missed more than 3 items, reread the material. Otherwise, continue on to the next section.

PUTTING IT ALL TOGETHER: A STRATEGY OF STRATEGIES

There are so many strategies covered in this text I could not end it without first providing a strategy for using the strategies. This metastrategy is represented by the flowchart seen in Figure 14.14. Let's walk through it.

First, always try to prevent behavior problems. Work hard to increase the on-task behavior of your students by making your curriculum intrinsically rewarding. Teach relevant content in a stimulating manner and program for success. Use classroom management styles such as those described by Kounin (1970) that correlate highly with on-task student behavior. Understand that despite your best proactive efforts, you will still encounter maladaptive student behavior requiring a reaction on your part. Reactive behavior management isn't always a token economy or a level system, nor is it necessarily instruction in social skills or cognitive restructuring. Reactive behavior management can be something as simple as using the positive and benign BRPs in the hierarchy of escalating consequences. Look for incompatible, or at least alternative, behavior to reinforce. At the same time, keep an eye out for reinforcers from the environment. The most obvious are usually peer and/or teacher attention. Try withholding these if you can. Failing this, try a redirection. If the behavior persists, I do not advocate using any of the negative BRPs in the hierarchy (e.g., reprimands, response cost, time-out) without first doing some sort of formal analysis of the problem. Do a simple functional analysis to get a better understanding of the relationship between the student's behavior and the environment. If the functional analysis does not yield sufficient information with which to formulate an intervention, try doing a Pre-Mod analysis. Consider Bandura's (1974, 1977, 1986) concept of maladaptive behavior based on reciprocal determinism: Behavior and environment are only two pieces of the puzzle. The third piece—personal variables—is just as important. The Pre-Mod analysis will help you identify any personal variables (e.g., skills, knowledge, emotions, cognitions) that might be influencing the student's behavior. Assuming you determine the cause of the behavior problem, design your intervention. If it requires a significant change in your behavior, you may need to complete another Pre-Mod analysis to determine whether or not there are any personal variables you need to work on. If so, incorporate into the intervention a strategy for changing your behavior as well as the student's. Design a formative evaluation strategy for measuring the efficacy of the intervention and proceed. If the intervention is working, continue using it. If your evaluation indicates changes are necessary, make them as needed and proceed until you reach your objective.

In conclusion, I must confess that writing this text has been for me the greatest test of self-management. Writing, whether textbooks or a letter to a friend, has always been one of my low-frequency behaviors. I consider it a triumph of self-management that this text ever got written; willpower had very little to do with it. So take heart, O ye of little faith. What one can conceive, one can achieve. Power to the person!

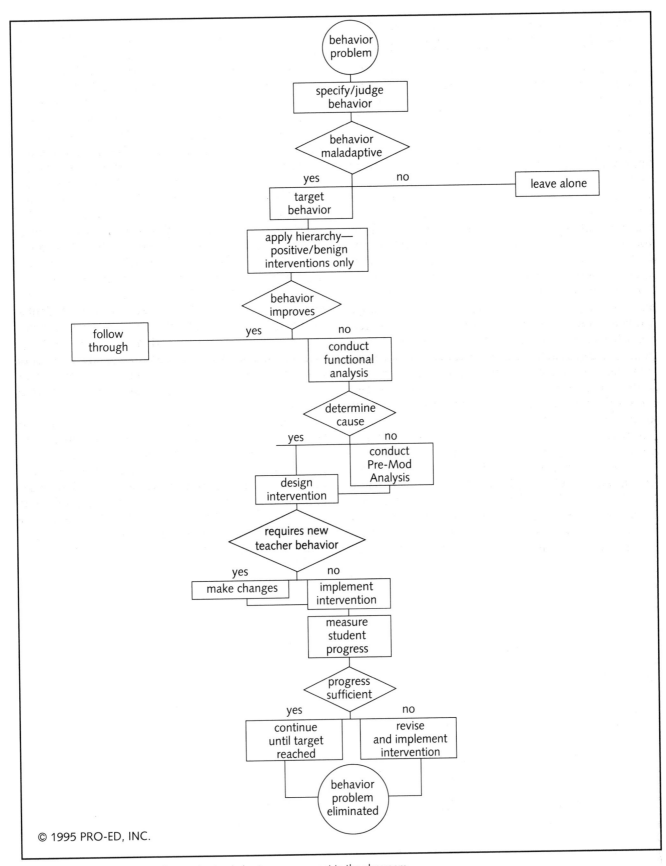

Figure 14.14. A metastrategy for conducting behavior management in the classroom.

ASSESSMENT / CHAPTER 14 ▄▄▄▄▄▄▄▄

A list of acceptable responses appears following the Assessment.

1. You are a teacher in a classroom of students with learning and behavior problems, and you are evaluated by your supervisor. Although her report is generally positive, she is critical of your use of positive feedback to students. According to her baseline data, the ratio of positive to negative comments you make to your students is 1 positive to 4 negative. She wants you to change this to 4 positive to 1 negative. Design an intervention utilizing self-management (see Chapter 9) to help you reach this objective.

2. You have a tendency to use the same BRP over and over again whether it works or not. Whenever one of your students misbehaves, you typically reprimand them. Since the immediate effect of the reprimand is to weaken the student's behavior, you believe it works. After looking at data that show otherwise, you decide to abandon the practice and try using other BRPs instead. However, this proves more difficult than you imagined, because you have been using reprimands for so long. Design an intervention utilizing SIT (see Chapter 12) and DRI (see Chapter 6) to help you change your behavior.

3. You use a token (point) system with a response cost component in your classroom. When students misbehave, they lose points they have earned. Normally, the system works fine. Unfortunately, there are a few students who try to take advantage of your lack of assertiveness by coercing you into smaller fines than they deserve. The sequence is: a) They misbehave; b) you warn them about losing points; c) they continue to misbehave; d) you take away points; e) they give you a hard time ("that's not fair," "you're a bitch"); and f) instead of fining them for their coercive behavior, you give them most of their points back. The fact is, you are intimidated by their verbal aggression. Something needs to change if your token system is to succeed. Design an intervention using stress inoculation (see Chapter 13) to help you overcome your anxiety in dealing with coercive students.

ACCEPTABLE RESPONSES

1. strengthen positive comments/self-management

Example:

Self-Assessment (SA)

Target behavior: makes positive comments to students

Rating system:

a. Define the behavior; positive (and negative) comments are statements made to a student or students; their purpose is *not necessarily to strengthen or weaken* any behavior but merely to communicate to the student(s) what the teacher thinks about them at any given time; they can be both free and controlled operants since they are not necessarily contingent upon anything students say or do; examples are "I like the way _____ is working" (controlled); "_____, you look nice today" (free); "_____ is not very good at math" (free); "You're making too much noise" (controlled); positive comments convey that you like what the student or students are doing (or not doing) while negative comments convey a dislike.

b. Establish competence at discriminating between positive and negative comments by listening to tape recording of your own teaching; mark + (plus) and – (minus) on wrist tape; have independent observer (instructional assistant) discriminate same material; should be at least 90% agreement.

c. Put into practice; evaluate comments made to students during several brief (5- to 10-minute) intervals during the course of the school day; if positive comment made, mark + (plus) on wrist tape; if negative comment made, mark – (minus).

    Rating form: see above (wrist tape)

    Steps: see above (rating system)

Self-Monitoring (SM)

Pinpoint: see above (define the behavior)

Goal(s): 4 to 1 ratio, positive statements to negative

Forms: wrist tape and chart

Steps: At end of day, count total number of positive statements and total number of negative statements and plot both on same chart (use different colors or solid line–broken line to discriminate); calculate ratio of positives to negatives; if 4:1 is reached, indicate on chart with star.

Self-Reinforcement (SR)

Reinforcer: Praise from students; display chart on classroom bulletin board.

Contingencies: Gradually increasing number of consecutive days reaching goal (2 days in succession, 3 days in succession, 4 days in succession, and so on).

Steps: Check chart on display at end of each day; when contingency (number of consecutive days reached goal) is met, students provide with verbal praise/support.

2. weaken reprimands/SIT and DRI

Example:

SIT

Content: "The student is misbehaving again. What do I need to do?"

Stop and think: "What behavior do I want to weaken? What have I done before? Has it worked? What else can I do?"

Process: (1) Start with teacher says–teacher does using cue card; (2) move to teacher whispers–teacher does using cue card (only if necessary); (3) move to teacher thinks–teacher does using cue card (only if necessary); eventually, fade out cue card

DRI

Reinforce yourself for use of any BRP with students other than reprimand (e.g., DRI, DRA, DRO, extinction, redirection, etc.).

3. build assertiveness/stress inoculation

a. Identify irrational thinking (most likely namby pamby, I stink, or robot).

Namby Pamby: "This is scary. I could look bad, lose control of the class, lose my job, or get hurt!"

I stink: "I'll never be assertive with students (or anyone), so why should I even try."

Robot: "I have no control over what my students say or do."

b. Practice relaxation technique (e.g., progressive relaxation or diaphragmatic breathing).

c. Generate rational (fair-pair) thinking.

"This situation makes me uncomfortable but I can tolerate it. It's not going to kill me."

"This is a good opportunity to practice being assertive. If I keep at it, I can become assertive in the classroom and, perhaps, in other areas of my life."

"I have less control over what my students say and do than I do over myself but I can certainly influence their behavior."

d. Write stress script.

before confrontation:
"What do I need to do? Watch my SUD level. Take deep breaths. Think positively. I can do it."

during confrontation:
"What's my SUD level? Take deep breaths. You're not going to die. Be assertive—eye contact; voice—quiet and firm; posture—nonthreatening. You're not going to die. Here comes the intimidation. Use broken-record approach. SUD level? Deep breaths. Not going to die. Eyes, voice, posture. Keep it up."

after confrontation:
"How did I do? Pretty good! I asserted myself with a student. It was hard but I did it. Is there anything I could improve on next time? This isn't easy, but with practice, I can master it. I'm proud of myself!"

e. Behavioral rehearsal using hierarchy:

first situation: with instructional assistant
second situation: with "safe" students (volunteers from mainstream class) using scripted response (able to anticipate)
third situation: with "safe" students—unscripted responses (unable to anticipate)

Interest Inventory

Note: While the following material would probably be suitable for use with students of any age, read it carefully beforehand and make any changes in content and/or vocabulary you deem necessary.

Student _____ Age _____ Grade _____

School _____ Teacher _____

Interviewer _____ Date _____

1. What do you like to do in your spare time? _____

   What do you usually do right after school? _____

   In the evening? _____

   On the weekend? _____

   With whom do you like to (play, hang out; spend time)? _____

   _____

2. How many brothers and sisters do you have? _____

   How old are they? _____

   Do you (play, hang out, spend time with) them? _____

3. What kind of work do your parents do? _____

   Are there any (jobs, chores) you are expected to do at home? _____

   Which do you prefer? _____

4. Do you belong to any (clubs, groups, organizations)? _____

   Why do you belong? _____

5. Do you take lessons in anything (e.g., swimming, piano, gymnastics, horseback riding)? _____

   _____

How long have you taken these lessons? _____

What are your hobbies? _____

6. Do you (receive an allowance, earn any money)?_____

For doing what? _____

What do you usually spend your money on?_____

If you had money of your own, what would you spend it on? _____

_____

7. How often do you go to the movies? _____

With whom do you usually go?_____

Which are the two best movies you ever saw? _____

Which of these movies do you like the best? Comedy, Melodrama, Western, Romance, Musical, Adventure, Fantasy, Cartoon, Science Fiction, Murder, Horror, Other?

_____

Who is your favorite actor? Actress?_____

Why? _____

8. What are your favorite television programs?_____

How much time do you spend watching television? _____

9. What are your favorite radio stations? _____

How much time do you spend listening to the radio? _____

10. Do you or your family have a pet? _____

11. What subjects do you like best at school? _____

Least? _____

12. Do you enjoy reading?_____

Do you like to have someone read to you?_____

How much time do you spend just reading? _____

Do your parents encourage you to read at home? _____

What are some books you read lately? _____

Do you have a library card?_____

How often do you use it? _____

Do you get books from the school library? _____

How many books of your own do you have? _____

What are some books you would like to own? _____

How many books are in your home? _____

What kind of reading do you like best? Adventure, Science, Animal Stories, Fantasy, Science Fiction, Plays, History, Novels, Poetry, Mysteries, Biographies, Fairy Tales, Other?

_____

What newspapers do you read? _____

Which part do you read first? _____

Do you get any magazines at your house? _____

Do you read them?_____

What is your favorite magazine?_____

13. What would you like to do when you (grow up, finish or graduate from school)? _____

_____

14. If you had free time right now to do anything you wanted, what would you most like to be doing?

 Name five things. _____

_____

Legal Rights Checklist

Note: The following is presented as an example of a legal rights checklist that might be used in the public schools. Many of the items originated from material in *Legal Challenges to Behavior Modification* (Martin, 1975). It is suggested that: (1) the checklist be used only in cases where changes in student behavior are substantial enough to necessitate changes in his or her individualized education program (IEP), (2) a copy of the checklist be kept on record in the student's file, and (3) the party completing the checklist do so under the guidance of an administrator such as the building principal.

Student _____ Age _____ Grade _____

School _____ Teacher _____

Maladaptive Behavior _____

Target Behavior _____

Party Completing Checklist _____ Date_____

Directions: Make all necessary comments directly after each of the following items.

1. *Maladaptive Behavior*

   a. The student's maladaptive behavior is presently or potentially interfering with his or her (and/or his or her peers') physical, emotional, social, and/or academic growth:

   b. The maladaptive behavior is actually occurring (or the target behavior is failing to occur) regularly enough to justify intervention:

   c. The school initiating the intervention and in which the intervention will take place has a legitimate interest in the behavior that it is attempting to modify:

2. *Target Behavior*

    a. The target behavior is in the best interests of the student and will benefit him or her more than it will benefit the school and/or the persons initiating the intervention:

    b. The target behavior is written as an objective complete with measurable criteria for acceptable performance. The latter should have been established through appropriate procedures (e.g., an analysis of ecological baseline data):

    c. The target behavior reflects a positive change (i.e., a strengthening of an adaptive behavior) rather than a negative change (i.e., weakening of a maladaptive behavior):

    d. The student's problem could not be solved by changing someone else's behavior instead of his or hers:

    e. The intervention does not involve changing a behavior that is actually constitutionally permissible:

    f. It has been determined through a diagnostic procedure that the student has all of the essential prerequisites for the target behavior:

3. *Intervention*

    a. The intervention does not call for one group of students to be treated significantly differently from another group to the extent that the distinction may be considered illegal:

    b. The intervention does not call for the student to lose a constitutionally protected right or privilege:

    c. That which the student is legally entitled to will not be used as a reward for desirable behavior:

    d. There are efficacy data available on the use of the strategy or strategies employed in the intervention with subjects similar to the student to warrant its use with the student:

    e. The intervention is available to all students who might benefit from it in addition to the target student:

    f. No student who might benefit from the intervention will be denied access to it because he or she has been assigned to a "control" group:

    g. Should it become necessary to employ aversive strategies in the intervention, this will not occur until less drastic alternatives have been tried first and it has been demonstrated that (a) the less drastic measures were not effective and (b) the aversive strategies are effective:

h. The student will not be needlessly isolated from others during the intervention unless his or her behavior becomes disruptive to the learning environment:

i. Should it become necessary to use time-out as part of the intervention, safeguards will be in place to assure that it can only be used for a few minutes:

4. *Monitoring and Evaluation*

The student's progress will be reviewed continuously or at least at reasonably short enough intervals so that a change in the intervention may be implemented quickly if no progress is evident:

5. *Due Process*

a. A meeting has been held to discuss the intervention with the student and his or her parents:

b. All concerned parties have consented to participate in the intervention:

Relaxation Script for Children*

In order for you to get the best feelings from these exercises, there are some rules you must follow. First, you must do exactly what I say, even if it seems kind of silly. Second, you must try hard to do what I say. Third, you must pay attention to your body. Throughout these exercises, pay attention to how your muscles feel when they are tight and when they are loose and relaxed. And, fourth, you must practice. The more you practice, the more relaxed you can get. Does anyone have any questions?

Are you ready to begin? Okay. First, get as comfortable as you can in your chair. Sit back, get both feet on the floor, and just let your arms hang loose. That's fine. Now close your eyes and don't open them until I say to. Remember to follow my instructions very carefully, try hard, and pay attention to your body. Here we go.

Hands and Arms

Pretend you have a whole lemon in your left hand. Now squeeze it hard. Try to squeeze all the juice out. Feel the tightness in your hand and arm as you squeeze. Now drop the lemon. Notice how your muscles feel when they are relaxed. Take another lemon and squeeze it. Try to squeeze this one harder than you did the first one. That's right. Real hard. Now drop your lemon and relax. See how much better your hand and arm feel when they are relaxed. Once again, take a lemon in your left hand and squeeze all the juice out. Don't leave a single drop. Squeeze hard. Good. Now relax and let the lemon fall from your hand. (Repeat the process for the right hand and arm.)

Arms and Shoulders

Pretend you are a furry, lazy cat. You want to stretch. Stretch your arms out in front of you. Raise them up high over your head. Way back. Feel the pull in your shoulders. Stretch higher. Now just let your arms drop back to your side. Okay, kittens, let's stretch again. Stretch your arms out in front of you. Raise them over your head. Pull them back, way back. Pull hard. Now let them drop quickly. Good. Notice how your shoulders feel more relaxed. This time let's have a great big stretch. Try to touch the ceiling. Stretch your arms way out in front of you. Raise them way up high over your head. Push them way, way back. Notice the tension and pull in your arms and shoulders. Hold tight, now. Great. Let them drop very quickly and feel how good it is to be relaxed. It feels good and warm and lazy.

Shoulder and Neck

Now pretend you are a turtle. You're sitting out on a rock by a nice, peaceful pond, just relaxing in the warm sun. It feels nice and warm and safe here. Oh-oh! You sense danger. Pull your head into your house. Try to pull your shoulders up to your ears and push your head down into your shoulders. Hold in tight. It isn't easy to be a turtle in a shell. The danger is past now. You can come out into the warm sunshine, and, once again, you can relax and feel the warm sunshine. Watch out now! More danger, hurry, pull your head back into your house and hold it tight. You have to be closed in tight to protect yourself. Okay, you can relax now. Bring your head out and let your shoulders relax. Notice how much better it feels to be relaxed than to be all tight. One more time, now. Danger! Pull your head in. Push your shoulders way up to your ears and hold tight. Don't let even a tiny piece of your head show outside your shell. Hold it. Feel the tenseness in your neck and shoulders. Okay. You can come out now. It's safe again. Relax and feel comfortable in your safety. There's no more danger. Nothing to worry about. Nothing to be afraid of. You feel good.

---

*From "Relaxation Training for Children" by A. S. Koeppen, 1974, Oct. *Elementary School Guidance and Counseling, 9,* pp. 16–20. Published by American School Counselor Association, a division of American Association for Counseling and Development, 5999 Stevenson, Avenue, Alexandria, VA 22304.

Jaw

You have a giant jawbreaker bubble gum in your mouth. It's very hard to chew. Bite down on it. Hard! Let your neck muscles help you. Now relax. Just let your jaw hang loose. Notice how good it feels just to let your jaw drop. Okay, let's tackle that jawbreaker again now. Bite down. Hard! Try to squeeze it out between your teeth. That's good. You're really tearing that gum up. Now relax again. Just let your jaw drop off your face. It feels so good just to let go and not have to fight that bubble gum. Okay, one more time. We're really going to tear it up this time. Bite down. Hard as you can. Harder. Oh, you're really working hard. Good. Now relax. Try to relax your whole body. You've beaten the bubble gum. Let yourself go as loose as you can.

Face and Nose

Here comes a pesky old fly. He has landed on your nose. Try to get him off without using your hands. That's right, wrinkle up your nose. Make as many wrinkles in your nose as you can. Scrunch your nose up real hard. Good. You've chased him away. Now you can relax your nose. Oops, here he comes back again. Right back in the middle of your nose. Wrinkle up your nose again. Shoo him off. Wrinkle it up hard. Hold it just as tight as you can. Okay, he flew away. You can relax your face. Notice that when you scrunch up your nose that your cheeks and your mouth and your forehead and your eyes all help you, and they get tight, too. So when you relax your nose, your whole face relaxes too, and that feels good. Oh-oh. This time that old fly has come back, but this time he's on your forehead. Make lots of wrinkles. Try to catch him between all those wrinkles. Hold it tight, now. Okay, you can let go. He's gone for good. Now you can just relax. Let your face go smooth, no wrinkles anywhere. Your face feels nice and smooth and relaxed.

Stomach

Hey! Here comes a cute baby elephant. But he's not watching where he's going. He doesn't see you lying there in the grass, and he's about to step on your stomach. Don't move. You don't have time to get out of the way. Just get ready for him. Make your stomach very hard. Tighten up your stomach muscles real tight. Hold it. It looks like he is going the other way. You can relax now. Let your stomach go soft. Let it be as relaxed as you can. That feels so much better. Oops, he's coming this way again. Get ready. Tighten up your stomach. Real hard. If he steps on you when your stomach is hard, it won't hurt. Make your stomach into a rock. Okay, he's moving away again. You can relax now. Kind of settle down, get comfortable, and relax. Notice the difference between a tight stomach and a relaxed one. That's how we want it to feel—nice and loose and relaxed. You won't believe this, but this time he's really coming your way and no turning around. He's headed straight for you. Tighten up. Tighten hard. Here he comes. This is really it. You've got to hold on tight. He's stepping on you. He's stepped over you. Now he's gone for good. You can relax completely. You're safe. Everything is okay and you can feel nice and relaxed.

This time imagine that you want to squeeze through a narrow fence and the boards have splinters on them. You'll have to make yourself very skinny if you're going to make it through. Suck your stomach in. Try to squeeze it up against your backbone. Try to be as skinny as you can. You've got to get through. Now relax. You don't have to be skinny now. Just relax and feel your stomach being warm and loose. Okay, let's try to get through that fence now. Squeeze up your stomach. Make it touch your backbone. Get it real small and tight. Get as skinny as you can. Hold tight, now. You've got to squeeze through. You got through that skinny little fence and no splinters. You can relax now. Settle back and let your stomach come back out where it belongs. You can feel really good now. You've done fine.

Legs and Feet

Now pretend that you are standing barefoot in a big, fat mud puddle. Squish your toes down deep into the mud. Try to get your feet down to the bottom of the mud puddle. You'll probably need your legs to help you push. Push down, spread your toes apart, and feel the mud squish up between your toes. Now step out of the mud puddle. Relax your feet. Let your toes go loose and feel how nice that is. It feels good to be relaxed. Back into the mud puddle. Squish your toes down. Let your leg muscles help push your feet down. Push your feet. Hard. Try to squeeze that mud puddle dry. Okay. Come back out now. Relax your feet, relax your legs, relax your toes. It feels so good to be relaxed. No tenseness anywhere. You feel kind of warm and tingly.

Conclusion

Stay as relaxed as you can. Let your whole body go limp and feel all your muscles relaxed. In a few minutes I will ask you to open your eyes, and that will be the end of this session. As you go through the day, remember how good it feels to be relaxed. Sometimes you have to make yourself tighter before you can be relaxed, just as we did in these exercises. Practice these exercises every day to get more and more relaxed. A good time to practice is at night, after you have gone to bed and the lights are out and you won't be disturbed. It will help you get to sleep. Then, when you are a really good relaxer, you can help yourself relax here at school. Just remember the elephant, or the jawbreaker, or the mud puddle, and you can do our exercises and nobody will know. Today is a good day, and you are ready to go back to class feeling very relaxed. You've worked hard in here, and it feels good to work hard. Very slowly, now, open your eyes and wiggle your muscles around a little. Very good. You've done a good job. You're going to be a super relaxer.

Commercially Available Programs and Materials

The following is a partial listing of commercially available programs and other materials that can help students learn many of the strategies covered in this text. I have included a sentence or two describing each item to give you some idea of what each covers and what level student each item is appropriate for. If you are particularly interested in cognitive restructuring programs and materials, I suggest you send for the Institute of Rational Emotive Therapy catalog. Catalogs are also available from other publishers.

Address information for the Institute of Rational Emotive Therapy and other publishers mentioned in this section appears following the list of programs and materials.

LIST OF PROGRAMS AND MATERIALS

Anderson, J. (1981). *Thinking, changing, rearranging: Improving self esteem in young people.* Eugene, OR: Timberline Press.

A program in *cognitive restructuring* for use with students "from about 10 upward." Consists of a paperback book for student use with reading and writing activities.

Anderson, J. (1987). *Pumsy in pursuit of excellence.* Eugene, OR: Timberline Press.

Teaches self-esteem to elementary-age students through *cognitive restructuring* and positive thinking skills.

Bedford, S. (1974). *Instant replay.* New York, NY: Institute for Rational Living.

A *cognitive restructuring* storybook for elementary-age students. Can be used as a supplement to other materials.

Biofeedback, biodots and stress. Indianapolis, IN: Biodot International.

Biodots are temperature-sensitive dots which, when placed on the skin, serve as simple instruments for biofeedback measures and allow children (and adults) to monitor their *stress* levels. Comes with teacher's manual and lesson on stress. Appropriate mainly for elementary age students.

Camp, B. W., & Bash, M. A. (1981). *Think aloud: Increasing cognitive skill, a problem-solving program for children.* Champaign, IL: Research Press.

Combines training in *verbal mediation, self-instruction,* and *problem solving* for elementary students. Available as a small group program, designed for use with 6- to 8-year-olds; and three classroom programs, for Grades 1–2, 3–4, and 5–6. Heavily researched and field-tested on hyperactive and aggressive students.

Cautela, J. R., & Groden, J. (1978). *Relaxation: A comprehensive manual for adults, children, and children with special needs.* Champaign, IL: Research Press.

Includes descriptions of *relaxation* techniques for varied populations as well as procedures for teaching these techniques.

Elias, M. J., & Clabby, J. F. (1989). *Social decision-making skills: A curriculum guide for the elementary grades.* Rockville, MD: Aspen.

Well-researched program in *problem solving* for elementary-age students.

Garcia, E. J., & Pellegrini, N. (1974). *Homer the homely hound dog.* New York, NY: Institute for Rational Living.

Another *cognitive restructuring* storybook for elementary-age students. Best used as a supplement to other materials.

Gerald, M., & Eyman, W. (1981). *Thinking straight and talking sense*. New York, NY: Institute for Rational Living.

A comprehensive program in *cognitive restructuring* for students "above the fifth grade." Includes activities, exercises, stories, and information for students, all in a student workbook format. Notes for teachers are included in the workbook.

Goldstein, A. P. (1988). *The prepare curriculum*. Champaign, IL: Research Press.

A comprehensive "social skills" program in textbook form. It includes methods and samples of materials for training in *problem solving, interpersonal (social) skills, anger control,* moral reasoning, and *stress management,* among others. Also includes material on classroom management and transfer and maintenance. Designed for youth (i.e., adolescents and younger children) who are deficient in prosocial skills.

Goldstein, A. P., & Glick, B. (1987). *Aggression replacement training: A comprehensive intervention for aggressive youth*. Champaign, IL: Research Press.

A textbook on aggression replacement training (ART), a comprehensive research-based program for juvenile offenders. It includes methods and samples of materials for behavioral *(social skills),* affective *(anger management),* and cognitive (moral education) components.

Goldstein, A. P., Sprafkin, R. P., Gershaw, N. J., & Klein, P. (1980). *Skillstreaming the adolescent: A structured learning approach to teaching prosocial skills*. Champaign, IL: Research Press.

A comprehensive *social skills* curriculum for secondary-level students. Based on the Structured Learning approach, which involves modeling, role playing, performance feedback, and transfer training. Covers 50 prosocial skills. For students who display aggression, immaturity, or withdrawal.

Hazel, J. S., Schumaker, J. B., Sherman, J., & Sheldon-Wildgen, J. (1982). *Asset: A social skills program for adolescents*. Champaign, IL: Research Press.

For group instruction. Videotaped material providing models of appropriate and inappropriate *social interaction skills* are available, as are lesson plans, training procedures, and skill sheets. Covers skills such as giving and accepting negative feedback, resisting peer pressure, problem solving, negotiation, etc.

Jackson, N. F., Jackson, D. A., & Monroe, C. (1983). *Getting along with others: Teaching social effectiveness to children*. Champaign, IL: Research Press.

For students of elementary and middle school age as well as mildly retarded people between the ages of 18 and 35. Comes with program guide and skills lessons and activities for the 17 core *social skills* taught. Color videotapes are available.

Kaplan, J. S. (in press). *Kid Mod: An instructional program in behavior modification for children and youth*. Austin, TX: PRO-ED.

Teaches the fundamental principles of *positive reinforcement* and *extinction* to students from upper elementary through middle school. Encourages students to use these principles to modify their own behavior and the behavior of their peers, teachers, and family members. Combines a direct instruction and structured learning (role play) approach. Includes performance objectives and criterion-referenced assessments for measuring student progress.

Knaus, W. (1974). *Rational emotive education: A manual for elementary school teachers*. New York, NY: Institute for Rational Living.

A comprehensive program in *cognitive restructuring*. Uses the format of a teacher's manual, with descriptions of several student activities for working on specific types of irrational thinking (e.g., mistake-making, catastrophizing, stereotyping, etc.).

Mannix, D. S. (1986). *I can behave: A classroom self-management curriculum for elementary students*. Austin, TX: PRO-ED.

An illustrated storybook comprising 10 stories and 125 full-page drawings. Each story focuses on a specific classroom problem such as not taking turns or talking too loud. Storybook comes with manual and lesson plans. Field-tested.

McGinnis, E., & Goldstein, A. P. (1984). *Skillstreaming the elementary school child: A guide for teaching prosocial skills*. Champaign, IL: Research Press.

A comprehensive *social skills* curriculum for elementary-age students. Covers 60 specific prosocial skills including asking for help, apologizing, etc.

McGinnis, E., & Goldstein, A. P. (1990). *Skillstreaming in early childhood: Teaching prosocial skills to the preschool and kindergarten child.* Champaign, IL: Research Press.

Similar to other Skillstreaming programs; focuses on younger students.

Merrifield, C., & Merrifield, R. (1979). *Call me RET-man and have a ball.* New York, NY: Institute for Rational Living.

An introduction to rational emotive therapy (RET) in comic book form. For secondary-level students and adults. Use as a supplemental material.

Platt, J. J., & Spivack, G. (1976). *Workbook for training in interpersonal problem solving thinking.* Philadelphia, PA: Philadelphia Department of Mental Health Sciences, Hahnemann Medical College and Hospital.

Heavily researched and field-tested program in *problem solving* skills. Write to the authors for availability information.

Sheinker, J., & Sheinker, A. (1988). *Metacognitive approach to social skills training: A program for grades 4 through 12.* Rockville, MD: Aspen.

Focuses on *self-management.* Appears to work best with students who display no overt antisocial behavior. Teacher acts as a facilitator (rather than teacher) for each 40 minute lesson. Multimodal—incorporates art and music into lessons.

Shure, M. B. (1992). *I can problem solve.* Champaign, IL: Research Press.

Teaches problem-solving skills to students in the intermediate elementary grades.

Vernon, A. (1989). *Thinking, feeling, behaving: An emotional education curriculum for children.* Champaign, IL: Research Press.

Available for Grades 1 through 6. Contains 90 activity lessons that use *cognitive restructuring* to help students modify their faulty thinking.

Vernon, A. (1989). *Thinking, feeling, behavior: An emotional education curriculum for adolescents.* Champaign, IL: Research Press.

See preceding entry; similar program, geared for older students.

Waksman, S. A., & Messmer, C. L. (1986). *The Waksman social skills curriculum: An assertive behavior program for adolescents.* Austin, TX: PRO-ED.

For children and adolescents. Focuses on teaching *assertive skills.* Can be taught in 20 minute lessons. Comes with teacher's manual and worksheets for students.

Walker, H. M., McConnell, S., Holmes, S., Todis, B., Walker, J., & Golden, N. (1983). *The Walker social skills curriculum: The ACCEPTS program.* Austin, TX: PRO-ED.

Designed for use with students in Grades 1 through 6. Uses a direct instruction approach. Comes with video, teaching scripts (for 28 skills), and behavior management procedures.

Walker, H. M., Todis, B., Holmes, S., & Horton, G. (1985). *The Walker social skills curriculum: The ACCESS program.* Austin, TX: PRO-ED.

Similar to the ACCEPTS program but geared toward the middle and high school student. Covers skills in three basic areas: relating to peers, to adults, and to yourself.

Waters, V. (1979). *Color us rational.* New York, NY: Institute for Rational Living.

An RET coloring book for elementary-age students. Supplemental material.

Waters, V. (1980). *Rational stories for children.* New York, NY: Institute for Rational Living.

Another *cognitive restructuring* storybook for elementary-age students. Supplemental material.

Wells, R. H. (1986). *Personal power: Succeeding in school* (Vol. I). Austin, TX: PRO-ED.

Consists of three volumes: (1) succeeding in school, (2) succeeding with others, and (3) succeeding with self. Text consists of 90 lesson plans (20–30 minutes each). For secondary-level students.

ADDRESSES OF PUBLISHERS/SOURCES

Aspen Publishing, Inc.
1600 Research Boulevard
Rockville, MD 20850

Biodot International, Inc.
PO Box 46229
Indianapolis, IN 46229
(317) 637-5776

Institute for Rational Emotive Therapy
    (formerly Institute for Rational Living)
45 East 65th St.
New York, NY 10021-6593

PRO-ED, Inc.
8700 Shoal Creek Blvd.
Austin, TX 78757
(512) 451-3246; (800) 397-7633

Research Press
2612 Mattis Avenue
Champaign, IL 61820

Timberline Press
Box 70071
Eugene, OR 97401

aim date   The estimated point in time when the student is expected to reach the CAP for the target behavior described in the performance objective. It may be expressed simply as "Friday of the fifth week" (after the intervention begins).

aim star   The point on the data display where the aim date (e.g., "Monday of the fourth week") converges with the frequency line that represents the CAP in the performance objective (e.g., "80%"). It may also be referred to as "Point B" (where you want the student to be and by when). It is represented on the chart as follows: ✦ . The should-do line is drawn by connecting the aim star to the start mark with a straight line.

alarm reaction   The first stage in Selye's (1976) General Adaptation Syndrome. It is sometimes referred to as the "fight or flight response."

antecedent stimulus event (ASE)   Any environmental stimulus that elicits a response. Examples in the classroom are cues, prompts, questions, or commands from the teacher and negative or positive attention from peer group (e.g., insults, compliments, greetings).

arrangement   In a schedule of reinforcement, the number of consecutive correct or desirable responses the student has to make before being reinforced.

availability heuristic   Psychological theory that suggests people are apt to select those behavioral options that are easiest for them to remember. Such options tend to be those that occurred most frequently in their lives and/or those that most dramatically aroused emotions. The availability heuristic can influence a student's ability to problem solve since it tends to limit his choices of possible solutions to those options he has had the most experience with (see Tuersky & Kahneman, 1973).

aversion therapy   A type of behavior therapy in which an unwanted behavior (e.g., smoking, alcoholism) is weakened by pairing it with an aversive stimulus (e.g., a nausea-inducing drug).

baseline   That phase in a behavior change program when there is no change in what the teacher does to modify the student's behavior. It doesn't necessarily mean that she does nothing to modify the behavior; it means she continues to do whatever she has been doing (which could be nothing). Data collected during the baseline phase will be compared with data collected during the intervention phase to see if there is any change in the student's behavior. Also known as the "before" phase.

behavior, maladaptive   Any behavior a student engages in which is considered currently or potentially harmful to the student's or another person's social, emotional, physical, or academic well-being. Any behavior considered to be maladaptive passes the So what? test and should be modified.

behavior management   A term loosely used to describe any direct attempt to modify a student's behavior. However, it is often used synonymously with behavior modification.

behavior modification   A model of behavior change based on the laboratory findings of B. F. Skinner (1938). It involves the systematic application of principles or rules of learning called *operant conditioning.*

behavior reduction procedure (BRP)   Those strategies whose primary purpose is to weaken maladaptive behavior. Some of these strategies involve the use of positive reinforcement (e.g., DRA, DRI, DRO). Others, such as extinction and redirection, are considered benign (i.e., neither positive nor negative). Aversive (i.e., negative) BRPs that may be considered a type of punishment include reprimands, response cost, time-out, and overcorrection. BRPs are typically used in a hierarchy with the least aversive, intrusive, and restrictive used first.

behavior, target That behavior required of the student at the successful termination of the intervention. This change in the student's behavior has to be in his best interest in order to pass the So what? test. NOTE: In much of the research literature, the term *target behavior* is used to denote the maladaptive behavior (i.e., the behavior you wish to change).

behavior therapy A form of behavior modification which includes techniques such as aversion therapy and systematic desensitization, it is used primarily by psychologists and psychiatrists in clinical settings or in private practice. Refer to Wolpe (1969).

behavioral setting A physical setting; a specific time and place with a particular set of activities and inhabitants.

chaining A technique used to strengthen new behaviors. It involves the identification of a set (i.e., chain) of stimulus–response links and having the subject perform them from the beginning of the chain to the end, over and over again.

change agent(s) In a behavior modification program, the person responsible for changing the behavior of another (e.g., teacher, peer, parent).

chart, equal-interval Also known as *linear,* or *arithmetic,* chart. A type of chart in which the interval (i.e., distance between data lines) is always the same; hence, the name "equal-interval."

chart, equal-ratio A chart in which, unlike the equal-interval chart, the distance between data lines differs. However, the distance between data lines *representing the same ratio* is the same. For example, the distance between the data lines 1 and 2 is the same as the distance between 10 and 20, and 50 and 100; they each represent a ratio of 2:1. Also known as *logarithmic* chart. The standard six-cycle chart used by precision teachers is an example of an equal-ratio chart.

cognitions Refers to mental activity engaged in by human beings. It includes (but is not limited to) cognitive events (i.e., one's stream of consciousness), cognitive structures (e.g., beliefs or attitudes), cognitive processes (i.e., the mental machinations or system one uses to solve problems), and inner speech (i.e., "self-talk").

cognitive-behavior modification (CBM) An offshoot of behavior modification, CBM is the label given to a number of strategies designed to indirectly modify one's behavior by first modifying one's cognitions. Examples of such strategies include self-instruction and verbal mediation (to change self-talk), problem solving (to change cognitive processes), and cognitive restructuring (to change beliefs or attitudes). Refer to Meichenbaum (1977) and Harris et al. (1985).

cognitive restructuring A type of CBM strategy that is used to modify a person's beliefs or attitudes. The term is often used synonymously with *rational emotive therapy* (see Ellis, 1962). It involves identifying negative beliefs that trigger strong negative emotions and attempting to dispute them and replace them with positive beliefs that would produce less intense (and more productive) emotions.

consequent stimulus event (CSE) The effect produced by the operant on the environment. It is what happens after a behavior occurs that serves to strengthen or weaken the operant.

contingency The conditions under which a CSE occurs. For example, the teacher who tells her class that only students who finish their work may go to the movie in the assembly is using work completion as a contingency, or condition, for the CSE (seeing the movie in the assembly).

contingency contracting A comprehensive behavior modification program popularized by the work of Lloyd Homme and based on the earlier research of David Premack. In some instances, it is called *contingency management* and is used synonymously with *behavior modification.* It involves the use of contracts between teachers and students with the latter contracting, or agreeing, to perform low-frequency behaviors (e.g., completing assignments) in return for engaging in high-frequency behaviors (e.g., free time at a favored activity) as a reward. Refer to Homme et al. (1969).

continuous sample A method of data collection in which the behavior is monitored as long as it occurs and the teacher is present to record it. It is used with behaviors which can be monitored without interfering with the teacher's instruction (e.g., compliance, attention seeking, question asking or answering, fighting). It is the most reliable method of data collection because it yields the greatest amount of data.

countoon An observation and recording form used by the student to monitor her own behavior. It is usually in the form of a card taped to the student's desk, and it includes three components: a) a cartoon drawing of what the student does (usually the target behavior); b) a number chart on which the student counts each instance of the behavior being monitored; and c) a cartoon drawing of what happens (i.e., the CSE) if the student reaches a prespecified number.

criteria for acceptable performance (CAP) That portion of the performance objective that states how well the student must perform the target behavior. For example, "The student will raise her hand and wait to be called on (behavior) *80% of the time* (CAP) she attempts to answer a question in class (conditions)."

data, duration Information regarding a person's behavior that *shows how long the behavior lasts*. It is usually collected on behaviors that last a long time (e.g., daydreaming) or occur so fast and/or frequently that they don't have a readily observable beginning and ending (e.g., waving one's hand back and forth in self-stimming).

data, frequency Information regarding a person's behavior that *shows how often the behavior occurs*. It is usually collected on behaviors that don't last long and do occur frequently, and which have a readily observable beginning and ending (e.g., hitting peers, telling lies, or noncompliance).

data, intensity Information regarding a person's behavior that *shows how forceful the behavior is*. It is usually collected on behaviors ranging in force from soft to hard, quiet to loud, restrained to wild. Examples are temper tantrums, speaking (volume), and self-injurious behaviors (e.g., self-biting).

data, intervention That phase in a behavior-change program when the teacher implements an intervention that is different from that which was used during baseline. Data collected during the intervention phase will be compared with baseline data to see if there is any change in the student's behavior. Also known as the "during" phase.

data, latency Information regarding a person's behavior that *shows the amount of time passing between two events*. An example is the amount of time it takes a student to comply with a directive.

data, topography Information regarding a person's behavior that *shows what a particular behavior looks like*. An example is the facial expression a student makes.

dead man's test The test applied to a target behavior to make sure it is a *fair pair*. If a dead man cannot engage in the target behavior, it is a fair pair. If a dead man can engage in the target behavior, it is not a fair pair.

deprivation A state of need in the student that must exist for reinforcement to occur.

deviant behavior Dysfunctional behavior; also known as *maladaptive behavior*.

diaphragmatic breathing A simple stress management technique used to relax the body by breathing through the diaphragm. Also known as *abdominal* or *belly breathing*, it is performed by forcing the abdomen out when inhaling and in when exhaling.

differential reinforcement of alternative behavior (DRA) A behavior modification technique used to weaken a maladaptive behavior by strengthening a fair pair target behavior in its place. In DRA, the target behavior and the maladaptive behavior need not be mutually exclusive. The target behavior need only compete with the maladaptive behavior it is supposed to replace. An example of DRA is rewarding a student, who typically calls out without raising her hand, for raising her hand and waiting; the purpose is to weaken calling-out behavior by strengthening a competing behavior (hand raising and waiting).

differential reinforcement of incompatible behavior (DRI) Same as DRA, except the target and maladaptive behaviors must be mutually exclusive; you can't engage in both at the same time. An example of DRI is rewarding a student, who is often out of seat, for being in his seat. The purpose is to weaken out-of-seat behavior by strengthening an incompatible behavior (in seat).

differential reinforcement of the omission of the behavior (DRO) A behavior modification technique used to weaken a maladaptive behavior by rewarding the student for not engaging in that behavior. One type of DRO is whole-interval (WDRO), in which the student is rewarded for not engaging in a maladaptive behavior for a given interval of time (e.g., going 5 minutes without self-stimming). A second type of DRO is momentary (MDRO), in which the student is rewarded for not engaging in a maladaptive behavior at a specific moment in time (e.g., not self-stimming when the teacher looks at him).

disputing irrational beliefs (DIBs) One of the techniques used in cognitive restructuring; it requires the student (with or without the teacher's help) to evaluate the validity of his belief(s). Although there is no established rule about how one proceeds, a typical approach is to apply several questions to the belief (e.g., Does it help keep me alive? Does it make me feel better? Is it based on reality? Will it help me get along with others? Will it help me realize my goals?). If the answers to all questions are "No," the belief may be considered irrational and in need of replacement with a fair-pair rational belief. If one or more of the questions can be answered "Yes," the belief may not be irrational and need not be replaced.

distress Physiological responses (e.g., tense muscles, sweating, shaking, change in voice, raised pulse) which are associated with negative emotions such as anger and anxiety.

does-do line The line drawn through the data displayed on a chart that represents what the student *does* (i.e., his actual progress). It requires a minimum of six data points in order to be reliable. Typically drawn on equal-ratio charts, it can also be used (albeit with less confidence) on equal-interval charts. Also known as *line of progress*.

ecobehavioral analysis Applied behavioral analysis that incorporates an environmental perspective on behavior. The basic assumption is that maladaptive behavior is the result of "poor fit" between the child and the environment. Therefore, the goal of the analysis is to identify both the student and environmental characteristics that contribute to the poor fit and the resultant maladaptive behavior.

eustress Physiological responses associated with positive emotions such as joy.

extinction The weakening of an operant by withholding a known reinforcer contingent upon the emission of the operant. For example, a known reinforcer for hand-raising behavior is teacher attention. When a student raises her hand, the teacher usually calls on her. Calling on the student tends to reinforce hand-raising behavior. In extinction, the teacher may forget to call on the student who raises her hand, with the result that hand-raising behavior is weakened. In planned extinction, the teacher deliberately withholds the known reinforcer in order to weaken the behavior.

fading The process of gradually changing the environmental (i.e., antecedent or consequent) events surrounding a student's response. For example, token reinforcement or a certain stimulus or cue might be faded out to get the student to perform without it. This differs from shaping primarily in that shaping requires the gradual change of the student's response.

fair pair When the strengthening of a target behavior directly leads to the weakening of a maladaptive behavior, the two behaviors may be referred to as a fair pair. Examples are strengthening in-seat behavior to weaken out-of-seat behavior and strengthening on-task behavior to weaken off-task behavior. Change agents are encouraged to use fair pairs when attempting to modify student behavior.

formative measurement An approach to measuring student progress in which data are collected on the student's behavior during the intervention while the behavior is still changing. Data are collected at the beginning of the intervention and for each day of the intervention.

functional analysis A procedure used to diagnose behavior problems based on the principles underlying applied behavioral analysis. The teacher conducts a "research" project by first recording all instances of the student's maladaptive behavior as well as the antecedents that precede it and the consequences that follow it; then using this information to generate a testable explanation or hypothesis as to which (if any) antecedents and/or consequences might be causing the behavior; and finally testing this hypothesis by changing the suspected causative agents and looking for any concomitant change in behavior. The functional analysis will only identify external (i.e., environmental and behavioral) factors that contribute to maladaptive behavior.

general adaptation syndrome (G.A.S.) The three-stage model of stress first described by Hans Selye (1976). It includes a) the alarm reaction ("fight or flight response," which doesn't last very long); b) the stage of resistance (which may last years and is characterized by physical evidence of stress, e.g., gastrointestinal or sleep disorders); and c) the stage of exhaustion (when the body breaks down and disease may appear).

generalization   In behavior modification, the transfer of learning from one environment or situation to another. For example, we may say that generalization has occurred if a student's newly-acquired hand-raising behavior in one class is also demonstrated in other classes whether or not the same ASEs and CSEs are occurring in all of the classes.

hierarchy of escalating consequences   Refers to the technique of using several consequences to weaken a student's behavior. Consequences are presented from least to most aversive, intrusive, and/or restrictive.

internalization   In behavior modification, that state in which a person engages in a behavior without the use of extrinsic antecedents (e.g., reminders) or consequences (e.g., rewards). In other words, the person engages in the behavior because he believes it is appropriate to do so. This requires a change in attitude as well as behavior.

interval sample   Used when monitoring student behavior that is "quiet" or does not easily come to the teacher's attention so that it is difficult or impossible to monitor the behavior and teach at the same time (e.g., off task, quiet out of seat, quiet talking, quiet self-stimming). It is accomplished by monitoring the student at predetermined intervals (e.g., for 5- or 10-minute intervals every 30 minutes).

level system   A system whereby students, usually in a token economy, are "promoted" from one level to the next based upon their improved behavior. Since each level is another step away from the token system, it is often used to wean students off of a token economy.

locus of control (LOC)   The degree to which an individual perceives the events in his life to be under his control. Refer to Rotter (1966).

maintenance   In behavior modification, it refers to the length of time the behavior change lasts once attained.

modeling   The process of providing a person with a visual, verbal, and/or manual representation of the behavior you want him or her to engage in. Also known as *observational learning* (Bandura, 1965).

monitoring   Observing and recording behavior.

momentary time sample (MTS)   A type of interval sample in which the teacher observes the student at a specific moment in time. An example is glancing at a student to see if he is in or out of his seat whenever a timer rings. The momentary time sample is used when the student's behavior is difficult or impossible to monitor while teaching and the teacher does not have the time to use a whole interval sample.

operant   Any voluntary behavior that produces an effect on the environment. Examples are walking, talking, reading, writing, etc.

operant conditioning   A form of learning popularized by B. F. Skinner (1938), it forms the basis of behavior modification.

operants, controlled   Behaviors which are controlled by (or dependent on) the behaviors of others. Examples are questions answered (controlled by questions asked), hits when provoked (controlled by provocations), and complies with commands (controlled by commands given).

operants, free   Behaviors that do not appear to be controlled by (or dependent upon) any observable behavior of another person. Examples are questions asked, hits (without provocation), and gets out of seat.

overcorrection   A form of punishment in which the person is required to a) make restitution by restoring the situation to its former state, and b) practice an exaggerated form of behavior that is incompatible with the behavior you want to weaken. For example, if the student insulted a peer, she would make restitution by apologizing to the peer and then paying a compliment to every student in her class.

performance objectives   Statements which describe the student's behavior after a successful intervention. They not only describe what the student will do but under what conditions and how well he will perform. By attending to the performance objective the teacher will know when the student no longer needs instruction/intervention.

pinpoint   The name given to the brief statement that describes the student's maladaptive or target behavior. To be considered a pinpoint, the statement must pass the stranger test. Examples of pinpoints are: "is in seat before the late bell rings," "does not complete assignments," "hits peers without provocation," and "speaks in a voice audible to everyone in the room."

pinpointing The act of writing a pinpoint.

precision teaching A behavioral approach to instruction pioneered by Ogden Lindsley, it involves a) pinpointing the academic or social behavior to be modified, b) preparing and implementing the instructional plan, c) evaluating student progress through direct and continuous measurement, d) plotting the test data on ratio (logarithmic) charts, e) estimating and interpreting the learning trend (i.e., how fast the student is learning); and f) making instructional decisions based on these trends. Refer to White (1986).

Premack principal Based on research conducted by David Premack (1959), who found that when high-frequency behavior is made contingent upon low-frequency behavior, the low-frequency behavior tends to increase in frequency. Also known as *Grandma's rule*: "Children who eat their vegetables get dessert."

Pre-Mod analysis An abbreviation for "prerequisite modification," it is a diagnostic procedure used to determine the cause of behavior problems. Based on the task anlytical model, its underlying premise is that the student misbehaves because she is lacking one or more of the prerequisites (e.g., skills, knowledge, beliefs) needed to engage in the target behavior. Once the prerequisite deficits are remediated, the misbehavior can be readily changed.

problem solving A type of CBM strategy in which students are taught how to solve intra- and interpersonal problems.

progressive relaxation training (PRT) The name usually given to the tense–release system of deep-muscle relaxation developed by Edmund Jacobson (1929). It may be used by itself as a somatic–physiological stress management skill or integrated with other skills as in stress inoculation.

punishers These are CSEs that serve to weaken the operants they follow. Punishers may range in severity from a reprimand (e.g., "Stop that!") to corporal punishment such as paddling. Whether or not a CSE is a punisher depends entirely on the effect it has on the operant it follows. It makes no difference whether or not the person presenting the CSE thinks it is a punisher. If the CSE weakens the operant it follows, it is a punisher; if the CSE strengthens the operant it follows, it is actually a reinforcer.

punishers, learned These are aversive CSEs that have to be paired with other aversive CSEs before they can effectively weaken the operants they follow. Examples include failing grades, abusive-provocative language (e.g., teasing, threats, sarcasm), and rejection.

punishers, unlearned Aversive CSEs that can effectively weaken the operants they follow without first having to be paired with other aversive CSEs. In other words, they can weaken an operant on their own. An example would be anything that causes physical pain.

punishment The act of weakening an operant by following it with the presentation of an aversive CSE. For example: If a student is talking without permission and the teacher tells him to stop, and this served to weaken his talking behavior, we could say that punishment of talking behavior has occurred.

rational emotive therapy (RET) Pioneered by Albert Ellis (1962), this is a form of cognitive therapy in which the individual is taught that it is not what happens to her that makes her upset and causes her to behave in a counterproductive manner, but rather what she thinks about what happens to her. A form of RET called Rational Emotive Education is used with children and youth. See Knaus (1974).

reactivity Refers to the change in a person's behavior brought about solely by monitoring his own behavior. This occurs during the baseline phase when the individual is not using any (new) intervention. It is usually attributed to the increased awareness in the individual as a result of self-monitoring.

reciprocal determinism The cornerstone of social learning theory, reciprocal determinism explains behavior as the reciprocal relationship (i.e., mutual interaction) between a) an individual's personal variables (e.g., emotions, perceptions, cognitions, skills, knowledge), b) his behavior, and c) the environment. See Bandura (1971).

record floor The lowest rate of response in a student other than zero. It is used to find zero on an equal-ratio chart. Wherever the record floor is on the chart, zero is the frequency line immediately below it. The record floor is computed by dividing one (the least number of behaviors the student can emit other than zero) by the time in minutes the student is observed. For example, if the student is observed for 30 minutes, the record floor is .033 (1/30 = .033, or $3\frac{1}{3}$ behaviors per 100 minutes). With a record floor of .033, zero is plotted on .03.

redirection A benign form of behavior reduction procedure. It involves the nonpunitive interruption of maladaptive behavior. An example is asking a student who is off task and talking to a peer how he is doing on his assignment.

reinforcement The act of strengthening an operant by following it with the presentation of a CSE the person likes, wants, or values, or by removing a CSE the person considers aversive. The two kinds of reinforcement are *positive* and *negative*.

reinforcement, differential Reinforcing a behavior you want to strengthen and not reinforcing a behavior you do not want to strengthen. It is a very important component of a *shaping program*.

reinforcement, extrinsic Strengthening an operant with external CSEs. In other words, the reinforcement comes from the environment, such as a token or verbal praise. When a student engages in a low-frequency behavior such as doing a difficult homework assignment, he will probably need extrinsic reinforcement to keep him on task.

reinforcement, instrinsic Strengthening an operant with internal CSEs. In other words, the reinforcement comes from engaging in the behavior. When a student engages in high-frequency behavior such as comic book reading, he is usually getting intrinsic reinforcement; nobody needs to give him tokens or verbal praise for this behavior; he does it because of the pleasure he derives from it.

reinforcement, negative The strengthening of an operant by following it with the removal of an aversive CSE contingent upon the occurrence of the operant. For example, if a student doesn't like school work and also doesn't like detention, her teacher can negatively reinforce (strengthen) her school work behavior by either threatening her with detention if she doesn't do her work or by actually keeping her in detention until she does it.

reinforcement, noncontingent Presenting a reward to the student without making it contingent upon some positive behavior. For example, letting a student leave class early whether or not he has completed his work.

reinforcement, positive The strengthening of an operant by following it with the presentation of a CSE the person likes, wants, or values. For example, if a student likes praise but doesn't like school work, the latter may be strengthened by praising him for each assignment he completes. If the student does more school work, we may say that positive reinforcement has occurred. If the student does not do more school work, all we can say is that we presented a CSE that had no effect on the desired behavior.

reinforcement, shifting criteria for The conditions under which you will move from one successive approximation to another in a shaping program. Typically, one waits until the student can perform an approximation on a variable schedule of reinforcement before moving to the next approximation.

reinforcers CSEs that serve to strengthen the operants they follow. Examples are listening to a person speaking, laughing at someone's joke, and complimenting a person's behavior or appearance.

reinforcers, activity CSEs that allow the student to engage in a favored activity contingent upon performing the desired operant. Examples are doing work from another class, taking over as teacher, reading comic books or magazines, listening to music, and working on arts and crafts projects.

reinforcers, learned CSEs that have to be paired with other CSEs before they can strengthen the operants they follow. Examples are smiles and verbal praise, passing grades, and money. Also called *secondary reinforcers*.

reinforcers, social CSEs that meet a person's psychosocial needs. Examples are smiles, eye contact, handshakes, pats on the back, and compliments and other verbal praise.

reinforcers, tangible CSEs that are physical objects (e.g., toys, coloring books, pocket combs, and crayons).

reinforcers, unlearned CSEs that do not have to be paired with other CSEs to strengthen the operants they follow. Examples include anything that provides physical comfort or pleasure (e.g., being held) or helps the individual meet a biological need (e.g., being fed). Also called *primary reinforcers*.

reprimand A form of punishment, usually administered verbally, such as "Stop that!" Facial expressions and posturing can also function as a reprimand. Reprimands differ from redirection in that they usually draw negative attention to the student's behavior. The objective is to cause the student enough discomfort that he will cease engaging in the maladaptive behavior.

respondent Refers to behaviors controlled by the autonomic nervous system such as the heartbeat, salivating, and the eyeblink reflex.

respondent conditioning A form of learning pioneered by the Russian psychologist Pavlov (1897). Also known as *classical conditioning*.

response cost An aversive behavior reduction procedure that is also known as *cost contingency*. It involves the removal of something the student prizes (e.g., tokens earned) contingent upon the student's behavior.

satiation This occurs when a known reinforcer loses its reinforcing properties due to overuse. For example, a child who formerly complied with directives if given peanuts becomes *satiated* on them; the result is that he is no longer willing to comply with directives if given peanuts.

schedules of reinforcement These tell the change agent when to reinforce the student. There are three basic schedules: continuous, fixed, and variable.

schedule, continuous A schedule of reinforcement used when you want to condition a response that is new to the student. The student is reinforced for every correct response he makes or is reinforced continuously over time.

schedule, fixed A schedule of reinforcement used when moving from a continuous schedule to a variable schedule of reinforcement. The student is reinforced for so many consecutive desired responses he makes or units of time he engages in the desired behavior. Examples of fixed schedules of reinforcement are reinforcing the student for every 2 consecutive correct responses or for every 4 consecutive minutes he is on task.

schedule, interval A schedule of reinforcement based on the amount of time the student engages in the behavior. For example, a student on a fixed-interval schedule of 2:1 would be reinforced once every 2 consecutive minutes she was on task. A student on a variable-interval schedule of 3:1 would be reinforced on the average of every 3 minutes that he was in his seat.

schedule, ratio A schedule of reinforcement based on the number of responses a student makes. For example, a student on a fixed-ratio schedule of 4:1 would be reinforced once for every four consecutive directives he complies with. A student on a variable-ratio schedule of 2:1 would be reinforced on the average of every two times she raises her hand to get teacher attention.

schedule, variable A schedule of reinforcement used when a student has learned a new response and you want to maintain that response. You reinforce him for an unpredictable number of desirable responses or over an unpredictable amount of time. For example, a variable-ratio (VR) schedule with a 5:1 arrangement would mean that the student was being reinforced on the average of every fifth desirable response. A variable-interval (VI) schedule with a 2:1 arrangement would mean that the student was reinforced for engaging in desirable behavior on the average of every 2 minutes.

self-instructional training (SIT) A CBM strategy used to help students control their impulsivity and learn new (and complex) tasks. It involves several steps, beginning with the teacher modeling and verbalizing the target behavior for the student and ending with the student modeling the target behavior while she thinks through the steps. See Meichenbaum (1977).

self-management A set of skills used by students (or teachers) to manage their own behavior. These include: a) self-assessment, in which the individual evaluates his own behavior and decides whether or not he is behaving appropriately; b) self-reinforcement, in which the individual determines how much he should be reinforced for his behavior and dispenses the reinforcer; and c) self-monitoring, in which the individual collects daily data on his behavior and evaluates the efficacy of the intervention. Also known as *behavioral self-control, self-directed behavior, self-regulated behavior*. See Workman (1982).

shaping The process of gradually changing a person's behavior by reinforcing progressively closer approximations of the target behavior. This differs from fading primarily in that fading requires changing the environmental (i.e., antecedent and consequent) events surrounding a student's behavior as opposed to shaping, where changes are made in the behavior itself. For example, in a shaping program, a student who is seldom in her seat more than 2 minutes at a time might be reinforced for progressively closer approximations of the target behavior (e.g., stays in seat for 15 minutes at a time); first, she would be reinforced for being in her seat for 2 minutes, then 3 minutes, then 4, 5, and so on, until the target behavior is performed.

should-do line The line drawn on a chart to represent the least amount of progress a student *should* make in order to be successful. It is drawn between Point A (the start mark) and Point B (the aim star). Typically drawn on equal-ratio charts, it can also be used (albeit with less confidence) on equal-interval charts. Also called the *minimum-'celeration line.*

social skills training The term used to describe instruction in a number of interpersonal skills (e.g., being assertive, sharing, giving and receiving criticism) that many students with behavior disorders seem to be lacking. The trend now is to make social skills training a regular part of the curriculum, along with reading, writing and arithmetic, in classes for students with behavior disorders.

So what? test An informal test applied to the maladaptive and target behaviors to determine whether or not the behavior change is necessary and appropriate. A negative or undesirable behavior would pass the So what? test if it met the criteria for being maladaptive. A positive or desirable behavior would pass the So what? test if it could be shown that the change in the student's behavior (i.e., the target behavior) would result in the weakening of the maladaptive behavior and would be in the student's best interest.

split-middle method A technique used to accurately estimate the trend of variable data displayed on a chart. It produces an accurate does-do line when it is difficult to do so via the eyeball method. Based on a powerful statistic known as the *median slope.*

start mark Also referred to as "Point A" (where the student is now), it is the point on the chart where the mid-data point of the baseline data and the mid-day of the baseline data converge. It is represented as a circle on the chart **○** . The should-do line is drawn by connecting the start mark to the aim star with a straight line.

stranger test An informal test applied to maladaptive and target behaviors to determine whether or not they have been stated as pinpoints. If a stranger can derive the same meaning from such statements as the person who made them, they are said to pass the stranger test and may be considered pinpoints. For example, "is hostile" would not pass the stranger test because a stranger might have a different interpretation of "hostile" than the person making the statement. However, "kicks peers when teased" would pass the stranger test because it is highly unlikely that a stranger would derive a different meaning from this than the person making the statement.

stress Those physiological changes experienced in the presence of stressors from the environment (or from thinking about them). For a more technical definition, see Selye (1976).

stress inoculation An integrative stress management strategy used to cope with anger and/or anxiety. It includes several stages: a) conceptual framework, or teaching basic concepts regarding stress (anger or anxiety) and stress management; b) training in PRT; c) identifying and disputing irrational beliefs; d) writing stress scripts; and e) using stress scripts in graduated stress situations. See Meichenbaum (1985).

stressors Those events in an individual's life that tend to produce stress. Examples of stressors in children and youth include parental divorce, illness in family, failing in school, being rejected by peers, moving to a new community, and entering a new school.

stress management Includes a wide range of skills used to help the individual cope with the stressors and stress in his life. To be effective, a stress management strategy should be holistic; in other words, it should be preventative as well as restorative and it should have benefits that are psychological and behavioral as well as physical.

summative evaluation A procedure for measuring student progress in which data are collected on the student's behavior only at the beginning (pretest) and end (posttest) of the intervention. This way, the teacher measures the sum of her labors, that is, the end product of the intervention.

successive approximations Those steps in the shaping process which tell the change agent when to reinforce the student. Each step describes behavior that is a closer approximation of the target behavior. For example, if the target behavior was to complete 100% of his assignments and the student currently only completed 10%, his successive approximations might be 20%, 40%, 60%, and 80%. Although none of these steps is the target behavior, each is a closer approximation of the target behavior than the preceding step.

symptom substitution A criticism of behavior modification based on the idea that behavioral interventions won't work because they only treat the symptoms (i.e., behavior) and don't get at the underlying cause of the problem. The weakened symptom is thought to be replaced by another, different, symptom.

subjective units of distress (SUD) A subjective way of monitoring stress in the individual. The student is taught to monitor her own stress by periodically gauging her stress level on a scale of 1 (calm) to 10 (distressed). It is one of the ways to evaluate the efficacy of stress management programs. See Wolpe (1969).

task analysis The breaking down of a task into its smaller parts. See Howell et al. (1979).

task analytical model Based on the concept of task analysis, the task analytical model provides a set of guidelines for assessing learning problems for both academic and social behaviors. See Howell et al. (1979).

time-out (TO) Technically, a behavior reduction procedure that involves the removal of all reinforcement for all behavior for a period of time (ideally, not to exceed 1 minute per year in student's age). Practically speaking, TO has been used as a form of punishment in which the person is isolated from his peers for an undetermined amount of time (e.g., "Go to the office!").

token economy A comprehensive behavior modification program popularized by the work of Nathan Azrin and Teodoro Ayllon (1968) in a state mental hospital. It involves the use of secondary reinforcers such as tokens (i.e., points, chips, stars, play money) contingent upon prespecified target behaviors. The tokens are then turned in at a later time for back-up reinforcers such as food, favored activities, or other tangible items. The advantage of the token economy is that because the tokens act as substitutes for the back-up reinforcers, they may be given at times when it would be inappropriate to give a back-up reinforcer. Also, because the tokens are generalized reinforcers, like money, they can be given again and again without likelihood of satiation.

verbal mediation A type of CBM, it involves self-talk in which the individual asks himself a series of questions including a) What am I doing?; b) Why shouldn't I do it?; c) What should I be doing instead?; and d) Why should I be doing it? Initially, students respond to these questions in writing. The goal of the program is to get students to automatically think through these questions on their own. See Blackwood (1970).

References

Adler, A. (1962). *Understanding human nature*. New York: Humanities.

Albert, S. (1972). *A study to determine the effectiveness of affective education with fifth grade students*. Unpublished master's thesis, Queens College New York.

Algozzine, R. (1992). *Problem behavior management: Educator's resource service* (2nd ed.). Gaithersburg, MD: Aspen.

Allen, J. (1980) Jogging can modify disruptive behaviors. *Teaching Exceptional Children, 12,* 66–70.

Argulewicz, E., Elliott, S., & Spencer, D. (1982). Application of cognitive-behavior modification for improving classroom attention. *School Psychology Review, 11,* 90–95.

Ayllon, T., & Azrin, N. H. (1968). *The token economy.* New York: Appleton-Century-Crofts.

Ayllon, T., & Roberts, M. (1974). Eliminating discipline problems by strengthening academic performance. *Journal of Applied Behavior Analysis, 7,* 71–76.

Azrin, N., & Lindsley, O. (1956). The reinforcement of cooperation between children. *Journal of Abnormal and Social Psychology, 52,* 100–102.

Baer, D. M., Stokes, T. F., Holman, J., Fowler, S. A., & Rowbury, T. G. (1981). Uses of self-control techniques in programming generalization: In S. W. Bijou & R. Ruiz (Eds.), *Behavior modification: Contributions to education.* Hillsdale, NJ: Erlbaum.

Bandura, A. (1965). Behavioral modification through modeling practices. In L. Krasner & L. Ullman (Eds.), *Research in behavior modification* (pp. 310–340). New York: Holt, Rinehart & Winston.

Bandura, A. (1969). *Principles of behavior modification.* New York: Holt, Rinehart & Winston.

Bandura, A. (1971). *Social learning theory.* Englewood Cliffs, NJ: Prentice-Hall.

Bandura, A. (1972). Modeling theory: Some traditions, trends, and disputes. In R. D. Parke (Ed.), *Recent trends in social learning theory* (pp. 35–61. New York: Academic Press.

Bandura, A. (1973). *Aggression: A social learning analysis.* Englewood Cliffs, NJ: Prentice-Hall.

Bandura, A. (1974). Behavior theory and the models of man. *American Psychologist, 29,* 859–869.

Bandura, A. (1977). Self-efficacy: Toward a unifying theory of behavioral change. *Psychological Review, 84,* 191–215.

Bandura, A. (1986). *Social foundations of thought and action: A social cognitive perspective.* Englewood Cliffs, NJ: Prentice-Hall.

Bandura, A., Ross, D., & Ross, S. A. (1963). Imitation of film-mediated aggressive models. *Journal of Abnormal and Social Psychology, 66,* 3–11.

Barbetta, P. (1990). GOALS: A group-oriented adapted levels system for children with behavior disorders. *Academic Therapy, 25,* 645–656.

Barton, L. E., Brulle, A. R., & Repp, A. C. (1986). Maintenance of therapeutic change by momentary DRO. *Journal of Applied Behavior Analysis, 19,* 277–282.

Bauer, A. M., & Shea, T. M. (1988). Structuring classrooms through level systems. *Focus on Exceptional Children, 21,* 1–12.

Beck, A. T., Ward, C., Mendelson, M., Mock, J., & Erbaugh, J. (1961). An inventory for measuring depression. *Archives of General Psychiatry, 4,* 53–63.

Becker, W. C., & Engelmann, S. (1973). Summary analyses of five-year data on achievement and teaching progress with 14,000 children in 20 projects. (Tech. Rep. No. 73). Eugene: University of Oregon Follow-Through Project.

Becker, W. C., Engelmann, S., & Thomas, D. R. (1971). *Teaching: A course in applied psychology.* Chicago: Science Research Associates.

Bem, S. (1967). Verbal self-control: The establishment of effective self-instruction. *Journal of Experimental Psychology, 74,* 485–491.

Berler, E. S., Gross, A. M., & Drabman, R. S. (1982). Social skills training with children: Proceed with caution. *Journal of Applied Behavior Analysis, 15,* 41–53.

Berliner, D. C. (1985). Effective classroom teacher: The necessary but not sufficient condition for developing exemplary schools. In G. R. Austin & H. Garber (Eds.), *Research on exemplary schools* (pp. 127–154). Orlando, FL: Academic Press.

Bernard, M. E. (1979, April). *Rational-emotive group counseling in a school setting.* Paper presented at the American Educational Research Association's Annual Meeting, San Francisco.

Bierman, K. L., Miller, C. L., & Stabb, S. D. (1987). Improving the social behavior and peer acceptance of rejected boys: Effects of social skills training with instructions and prohibitions. *Journal of Consulting and Clinical Psychology, 55,* 194–200.

Birnbrauer, J., & Lawler, J. (1964). Token reinforcement for learning. *Mental Retardation, 2,* 275–279.

Blackwood, R. (1970). The operant conditioning of verbally mediated self-control in the classroom. *Journal of School Psychology, 8,* 251–258.

Bohannon, R. (1975). Direct and daily measurement procedures in the identification and treatment of reading behaviors of children in special education. Unpublished doctoral dissertation, University of Washington, Seattle.

Bolstad, O., & Johnson, S. (1972). Self-regulation in the modification of disruptive classroom behavior. *Journal of Applied Behavior Analysis, 5,* 443–454.

Bornstein, P., & Knapp, M. (1981). Self-control desensitization with a multi-phobic boy: A multiple baseline design. *Journal of Behavior Therapy and Experimental Psychiatry, 12,* 281–285.

Bornstein, P., & Quevillon, R. (1976). The effects of a self-instructional package on overactive preschool boys. *Journal of Applied Behavior Analysis, 9,* 179–188.

Bowers, D. S., Clement, P. W., Fantuzzo, J. W., & Sorensen, D. A. (1985). Effects of teacher-administered and self-administered reinforcers on learning disabled children. *Behavior Therapy, 16,* 357–369.

Braaten, S. (1979). The Madison School program: Programming for secondary level severely emotionally disturbed youth. *Behavioral Disorders, 4,* 153–162.

Braaten, S., Simpson, R., Rosell, J., & Reilly, T. (1988, Winter). Using punishment with exceptional children. *Teaching Exceptional Children,* 79–81.

Bradley, R., & Gaa, J. (1977). Domain specific aspects of locus of control: Implications for modifying locus of control orientation. *Journal of School Psychology, 15,* 18–24.

Brigham, T. A., Hill, B., Hopper, C., & Adams, J. (1980). Self-management training as an alternative to expulsion. *Progress Report ESEA Title NC.*

Brody, M. (1974). The effect of the rational-emotive affective education approach on anxiety, frustration tolerance and self-esteem with fifth-grade students. Unpublished doctoral dissertation, Temple University.

Brophy, J. E. (1979). Teacher behavior and its effects. *Journal of Educational Psychology, 71,* 733–750.

Brophy, J. E., & Evertson, C. M. (1977). Teacher behavior and student learning in second and third grades. In G. D. Borich (Ed.), *The appraisal of teaching: Concepts and process.* Reading, MA: Addison-Wesley.

Brophy, J., & Good, T. L. (1986). Teacher behavior and student achievement. In M. C. Wittrock (Ed.), *Handbook of Research on Teaching* (3rd ed., pp. 328–375). New York: Macmillan.

Burney, J. P., & Shores, R. E. (1979). A study of relationships between instructional planning and pupil behavior. *Journal of Special Education Technology, 2,* 16–25.

Butler, L., Miezitis, S., Friedman, R., & Cole, E. (1980). The effect of two school-based intervention programs on depressive symptoms in preadolescents. *American Education Research Journal, 17,* 111–119.

Camp, B. (1980). Two psychoeducational treatment programs for young boys. In C. Whalen, & B. Henler (Eds.), *Hyperactive children: The social ecology of identification and treatment.* New York: Academic Press.

Camp, B. W., & Bash, M. S. (1981) *Think aloud: Primary Level.* Champaign, IL: Research Press.

Camp, B., Blom, G., Herbert, F., & Van Doorwick, W. (1976). *Think aloud: A program for developing self-control in young aggressive boys.* Unpublished manuscript, University of Colorado School of Medicine, Boulder.

Carlson, C. S., Arnold, C. R., Becker, W. C., & Madsen, G. H. (1968). The elimination of tantrum behavior of a child in an elementary classroom. *Behavior Research and Therapy, 6,* 117–120.

Carr, S. C., & Punzo, R. P. (1993). The effects of self-monitoring of academic accuracy and productivity on the performance of students with behavioral disorders. *Behavioral Disorders, 18,* 241–250.

Carter, J., & Sugai, G. M. (1988). Teaching social skills. *Teaching Exceptional Children, 20* (3), 68–71.

Carter, M., & Ward, J. (1987). The use of overcorrection to suppress self-injurious behavior. *Australia and New Zealand Journal of Developmental Disabilities, 13,* 227–242.

Chandler, L. A. (1985). *Assessing stress in children.* Praeger.

Charlop, M. H., Burgio, L. D., Iwata, B. A., & Ivancic, M. T. (1988). Stimulus variation as a means of enhancing punishment effects. *Journal of Applied Behavior Analysis, 21,* 89–95.

Christensen, C. (1974). *Development and field testing of an interpersonal coping skills program.* Toronto, Canada: Ontario Institute for Studies in Education.

Cipiani, E., Brendlinger, J., McDowell, L., & Usher, S. (1991). Continuous vs. intermittent punishment: A case study. *Journal of Developmental and Physical Disabilities, 3,* 147–156.

Cohen, H. L., & Filipczak, J. (1971). *A new learning environment.* San Francisco: Jossey-Bass.

Colozzi, G. A., Coleman-Kennedy, M., Fay, R., Hurley, W., Magliozzi, M., Schackle, K., & Walsh, P. (1986, September). Data-based integration of a student with moderate special needs. *Education and Training of the Mentally Retarded,* 192–199.

Connell, J. P. (1985). A new multidimensional measure of children's perceptions of control. *Child Development, 56,* 1018–1041.

Corte, H. E., Wolf, M. M., & Locke, B. J. (1971). A comparison of procedures for eliminating self-injurious behavior of retarded adolescents. *Journal of Applied Behavior Analysis, 4,* 201–213.

The Council for Children with Behavioral Disorders. (1990). Position paper on use of behavior reduction strategies with children with behavioral disorders. *Behavioral Disorders, 15,* 243–260.

Crandall, V. C., Katkovshy, W., & Crandall, V. J. (1965). Children's beliefs in their own control of reinforcement in intellectual-academic achievement situations. *Child Development, 36,* 91–109.

DeCatanzo, D. A., & Baldwin, G. (1978). Effective treatment of self-injurious behavior through a forced-arm exercise. *American Journal of Mental Deficiency, 82,* 433–439.

Deitz, S. M., & Repp, A. C. (1983). Reducing behavior through reinforcement. *Exceptional Education Quarterly, 3,* 34–46.

Deitz, S. M., Repp, A. C., & Deitz, D. E. D. (1976). Reducing inappropriate classroom behavior of retarded students through three procedures of differential reinforcement. *Journal of Mental Deficiency Research, 20,* 155–170.

De Voge, C. (1977). A behavioral approach to RET with children. In A. Ellis & R. Grieger (Eds.), *Handbook of rational-emotive therapy.* New York: Springer.

Dewey, J. (1938). *Experience and education.* New York: Macmillan.

Di Giuseppe, R. A. (1975). The use of behavior modification to establish rational self-statements in children, In A. Ellis & R. Grieger (Eds.), *Handbook of rational-emotive therapy.* New York: Springer.

DiGiuseppe, R., & Kassinove, H. (1976). Effects of a rational-emotive school mental health program on childrens' emotional adjustment. *Journal of Community Psychology, 4,* 382–387.

Drabman, R. S., Spitalnik, R., & O'Leary, K. D. (1974). Teaching self-control to disruptive children. *Journal of Abnormal Psychology, 82,* 10–16.

Dreikurs, R. (1968). *Psychology in the classroom* (2nd ed.). New York: Harper & Row.

Dreikurs, R., Grunwald, B., & Pepper, F. (1971). *Maintaining sanity in the classroom.* New York: Harper & Row.

Drummond, D. (1974). *Self-instructional training: An approach to disruptive classroom behavior.* Unpublished doctoral dissertation, University of Oregon, Eugene.

Dunlap, L. (1942). Technique of negative practice. *American Journal of Psychology, 55,* 270–273.

DuPaul, G. J., Guervremont, D. C., & Barkley, R. A. (1992). Behavioral treatment of Attention-Deficit Hyperactivity Disorder in the classroom: The use of the Attention Training System. *Behavior Modification, 16,* 204–225.

Durand, V. M., & Mindell, J. A. (1990, January). Behavioral treatment of multiple childhood sleep disorders: Effects on child and family. *Behavior Modification,* 37–49.

Dwinell, M. A., & Connis, R. T. (1979). Reducing inappropriate verbalizations of a retarded adult. *American Journal of Mental Deficiency, 84,* 87–92.

Dye, S. O. (1980). *The influence of rational-emotive education on the self-concept of adolescents living in a residential group home.* Unpublished doctoral dissertation, University of Virginia.

D'Zurilla, T. J., & Goldfried, M. R. (1971). Problem solving and behavior modification. *Journal of Abnormal Psychology, 78,* 107–126.

Eisen, P. (1979). Children under stress. *Australia and New Zealand Journal of Psychiatry, 13,* 193–207.

Elkind, D. (1981). *The hurried child: Growing up too fast, too soon.* Reading, MA: Addison-Wesley.

Ellis, A. (1962). *Reason and emotion in psychotherapy.* New York: Lyle Stuart Press.

Ellis, A., & Harper, R. A. (1975). A new guide to rational living. N. Hollywood, CA: Wilshire.

Emery, G., Bedrosian, R., & Garber, J. (1983). Cognitive therapy with depressed children and adolescents. In D. P. Cantwell & C. A. Carlson (Eds.), *Affective disorders in childhood and adolescence: An update* (pp. 445–471). Spectrum.

Englert, C. S. (1984). Measuring teacher effectiveness from the teacher's point of view. *Focus on Exceptional Children, 17*(2), 1–15.

Englert, C. S., Tarrant, K. L., & Mariage, T. V. (1992). Defining and redefining instructional practice in special education: Perspectives on good teaching. *Teacher Education and Special Education, 15,* 62–86.

Epstein, R., & Goss, C. (1978). A self-control procedure for the maintenance of nondisruptive behavior in an elementary school child. *Behavior Therapy, 9,* 109–117.

Evans, W. H., Evans, S. S., Schmid, R. E., & Pennypacker, H. S. (1985). The effects of exercise on selected classroom behaviors of behaviorally disordered adolescents. *Behavioral Disorders, 11,* 42–51.

Evertson, C. M., Emmer, E., Clements, B., Sanford, J., & Worsham, M. (1989). *Classroom management for elementary teachers.* Englewood Cliffs, NJ: Prentice-Hall.

Farlow, L. J., & Snell, M. E. (1989). Teacher use of student performance data to make instructional decisions: Practices in programs for students with moderate to profound disabilities. *Journal of the Association for the Severely Handicapped, 14,* 13–22.

Feindler, E. L., & Fremouw, W. J. (1983). Stress inoculation training for adolescent anger problems. In D. Meichenbaum & M. E. Jaremko (Eds.), *Stress reduction and prevention.* New York: Plenum Press.

Felixbrod, J. J., & O'Leary, K. D. (1974). Self-determination of academic standards by children: Toward greater freedom from external control. *Journal of Educational Psychology, 66,* 845–850.

Felner, R. D., Stolberg, A., & Cowan, E. L. (1975). Crisis events and school mental health referral patterns of young children. *Journal of Consulting and Clinical Psychology, 43,* 305–311.

Fielstein, E., Klein, M. S., Fischer, M., Hanon, C., Koburger, P., Schneider, M. J., & Leitenberg, H. (1985). Self-esteem and causal attributions for success and failure in children. *Cognitive Therapy and Research, 9,* 381–398.

Finch, A., Wilkinson, M., Nelson, W., & Montgomery, L. (1975). Modification of an impulsive cognitive tempo in emotionally disturbed boys. *Journal of Abnormal Child Psychology, 3,* 45–52.

Fleming, C. (1983). Evaluation of an anger management program with aggressive children in residential treatment. *Dissertation Abstracts International, 43,* (12-B), 4143.

Forehand, R., & Baumeister, A. A. (1976). Deceleration of aberrant behavior among retarded individuals. In M. Hersen, R. M. Eisler, & P. M. Miller (Eds.), *Progress in behavior modification (Vol. 2).* New York: Academic Press.

Forman, S. G. (1980), A comparison of cognitive training and response cost procedures in modifying aggressive behavior of elementary school children. *Behavior Therapy, 11,* 594–600.

Foxx, R. M., & Azrin, N. H. (1973). The elimination of autistic self-stimulatory behavior by overcorrection. *Journal of Applied Behavior Analysis, 6,* 1–14.

Francis, G. (1988). Childhood obsessive-compulsive disorder: Extinction of compulsive reassurance-seeking. *Journal of Anxiety Disorders, 2,* 361–366.

Freud, S. (1938). *A general introduction to psychoanalysis.* New York: Doubleday.

Friman, P. C. (1990, September). Nonaversive treatment of high-rate disruption: Child and provider effects. *Exceptional Children,* 64–69.

Fuller, P. (1949). Operant conditioning of a vegetative human organism. *American Journal of Psychology, 62,* 587–590.

Furman, W., & Buhrmester, D. (1985). Children's perceptions of the personal relationships in their social networks. *Developmental Psychology, 21,* 1016–1024.

Gagne, R. (1965). *The conditions of learning.* New York: Holt, Rinehart & Winston.

Garrison, S. R., & Stolberg, A. L. (1983). Modification of anger in children by affective imagery training. *Journal of Abnormal Child Psychology, 11,* 115–130.

Gersten, L. (1984). University of Northern Colorado severe ED demonstration project. In H. L. Swanson & H. R. Reinert (Eds.), *Teaching strategies for children in conflict* (2nd ed; pp. 343–360). Saint Louis: Times-Mirror/Mosby.

Gersten, J. C., Langer, T. S., Eisenberg, J. G., & Orzek, L. (1974). Child behavior and life events. In B. S. Dohrenwend & B. P. Dohrenwend (Eds.), *Stressful life events: Their nature and effects.* New York: Wiley.

Gewirtz, J. L., & Baer, D. M. (1958). Deprivation and satiation or social reinforcers as drive conditioners. *Journal of Abnormal Psychology, 57,* 165–172.

Gillis, J. S. (1980). *The Child Anxiety Scale.* Champaign, IL: Institute for Personality and Ability Testing.

Glass, C. (1974). Response acquisition and cognitive self-statement modification approaches to dating behavior training. Unpublished doctoral dissertation, Indiana University, Bloomington.

Glomb, N., & West, R. P. (1990). Teaching behaviorally disordered adolescents to use self-management skills for improving the completeness, accuracy and neatness of creative writing homework assignments. *Behavioral Disorders, 15,* 233–242.

Glynn, E. (1970). Classroom applications of self-determined reinforcement. *Journal of Applied Behavior Analysis, 3,* 123–132.

Glynn, E., Thomas, J., & Shee, S. (1973). Behavioral self-control of on-task behavior in an elementary school classroom. *Journal of Applied Behavior Analysis, 6,* 105–113.

Goldfried, M. (1973). Reduction of generalized anxiety through a variant of systematic desensitization. In M. Goldfried & M. Merbaum (Eds.), *Behavior change through self-control.* New York: Holt, Rinehart & Winston.

Goldstein, A. P. (1988). *The Prepare Curriculum: Teaching prosocial competencies.* Champaign, IL: Research Press.

Good, T. L. (1979). Teacher effectiveness in the elementary school. *Journal of Teacher Education, 30,* 52–64.

Gordon, M., Thomason, D., Cooper, S., & Ivers, C. L. (1991). Nonmedical treatment of ADHD/hyperactivity: The Attention Training System. *Journal of School Psychology, 29,* 151–159.

Gottman, J., Gonso, J., & Rasmussen, B. (1974). Social interaction, social competence and friendship in children. Unpublished manuscript, Indiana University, Bloomington.

Goyette, C., Conners, K., & Ulrich, R. (1978). Normative data on revised Conners Parent and Teacher Rating Scales. *Journal of Abnormal Child Psychology, 6,* 221–236.

Graubard, P. S., Rosenberg, H., & Miller, M. B. (1971). Student applications of behavior modification to teachers and environments or ecological approaches to social deviancy. In E. A. Ramp & B. L. Hopkins (Eds.), *A new direction for education: Behavior analysis.* (pp. 80–101). Lawrence, KS: University of Kansas Press.

Gresham, F. M. (1981). Social skills training with handicapped children: A review. *Review of Educational Research, 51,* 139–176.

Gresham, F. M. (1985). Utility of cognitive-behavioral procedures for social skills training with children: A critical review. *Journal of Abnormal Child Psychology, 13,* 411–423.

Gresham, F., & Elliott, S. (1990). *Social skills rating system.* Circle Pines, MN: American Guidance Service.

Grumley, L. (1984). *Day treatment program agreement.* Jeffersonville, IN: Clark County Special Education Cooperative.

Hall, R. V., Panyan, M., Rabon, D., & Broden, M. (1968). Instructing beginning teachers in reinforcement procedures which improve classroom control. *Journal of Applied Behavior Analysis, 1,* 315–322.

Handen, B. L. (1992). Using guided compliance versus time out to promote child compliance: A preliminary comparative analysis in an analogue context. *Research in Developmental Disabilities, 13,* 157–70.

Haring, N. G., Liberty, K. A., & White, O. R. (1980). Rules for data-based strategy decision in instructional programs. In W. Sailor, B. Wilcox, & L. Brown (Eds.), *Method of instruction for severely handicapped children* (pp. 159–192). Baltimore: Paul H. Brookes.

Harris, A., & Kapche, R. (1978). Behavior modification in schools: Ethical issues and suggested guidelines. *Journal of School Psychology, 16,* 25–33.

Harris, S. L., & Wolchik, S. A. (1979). Suppression of self-stimulation: Three alternative strategies. *Journal of Applied Behavior Analysis, 12,* 185–198.

Harris, H. R., Wong, B. Y. L., & Keogh, B. K. (Eds.). (1985). Cognitive-behavior modification with children: A critical review of the state of the art [Special issue]. *Journal of Abnormal Child Psychology, 13,* 329–476.

Hartig, M., & Kanfer, F. (1973). The role of verbal self-instructions in children's resistance to temptation. *Journal of Personality and Social Psychology, 25,* 259–267.

Hewett, F. (1964). Teaching reading to an autistic boy through operant conditioning. *Reading Teacher, 17,* 613–618.

Hinshaw, S. (1984). Self-control in hyperactive boys in anger-inducing situations: Effects of cognitive-behavioral training and of Methylphenidate. *Journal of Abnormal Child Psychology, 12,* 55–77.

Hobbs, N. (1966). Helping the disturbed child: Psychological and ecological strategies. *American Psychologist, 21,* 1105–1115.

Homme, L. E., with Csanyi, A. P., Gonzales, M. A., & Rechs, J. R. (1969). *How to use contingency contracting in the classroom.* Champaign, IL: Research Press.

Hops, H. (1983). Children's social competence and skill: Current research practices and future directions. *Behavior Therapy, 14,* 3–18.

Howell, K. W., Fox, S., & Morehead, M. K. (1993). *Curriculum-based evaluation: Teaching and decision making* (2nd ed.). Pacific Grove, CA: Brooks/Cole.

Howell, K. W., & Kaplan, J. S. (1980). *Diagnosing basic skills: A handbook for deciding what to teach.* Columbus, OH: Merrill.

Howell, K. W., Kaplan, J. S., & O'Connell, C. Y. (1979). *Evaluating exceptional children: A task analysis approach.* Columbus, OH: Merrill.

Hren, C., Mueller, K., Spates, C. R., Ulrich, C., & Ulrich, R. E. (1974). The learning village elementary school. In R. E. Ulrich, T. Stachnik, & J. Mabry (Eds.), *Control of human behavior (Vol. 3) Behavior modification in education.* Glenview, IL: Scott, Foresman.

Humphrey, L., Karoly, P., & Kirshenbaum, D. S. (1978). Self-management in the classroom. Self-imposed response cost versus self-reward. *Behavior Therapy, 9,* 592–601.

Hundert, J., & Bastone, D. (1978). A practical procedure to maintain pupils' accurate self-rating in a classroom token program. *Behavior Modification, 2,* 93–112.

Iwata, B., & Bailey, J. S. (1974). Reward versus cost token systems: An analysis of the effects on students and teacher. *Journal of Applied Behavioral Analysis, 7,* 567–576.

Iwata, B. A., Pace, G. M., Kalsher, M. J., Cowdery, G. E., & Cataldo, M. F. (1990). Experimental analysis and extinction of self-injurious escape behavior. *Journal of Applied Behavior Analysis, 23,* 11–27.

Jacobson, E. (1929). *Progressive relaxation.* Chicago: University of Chicago Press.

Jensen, W., Sloane, H., & Young, R. (1988). *Applied behavior analysis in education: A structured teaching approach.* Englewood Cliffs, NJ: Prentice-Hall.

Johnson, J. H., & McCutcheon, S. (1980). Assessing life stress in older children and adolescents: Preliminary findings with the Life Events Checklist. In I. G. Sarason & C. D. Spielberger (Eds.), *Stress and anxiety.* (Vol. 7). New York: Hemisphere.

Jones, M. C. (1924). The elimination of children's fears. *Journal of Experimental Psychology, 7,* 382–390.

Jones, V. F. (1992). Integrating behavioral and insight-oriented treatment in school-based programs for seriously emotionally disturbed students. *Behavioral Disorders, 17,* 225–236.

Jones, R. S. P., & Baker, L. J. V. (1989). Reducing stereotyped behaviour: A component analysis of the DRI schedule. *British Journal of Clinical Psychology, 28,* 255–266.

Kagan, J. (1966). The generality and dynamics of conceptual tempo. *Journal of Abnormal Child Psychology, 71,* 17–24.

Kapadia, S., & Fantuzzo, J. (1988). Teaching children with developmental disabilities and severe behavior problems to use self-management procedures to sustain attention to preacademic/academic tasks. *Education and Training in Mental Retardation, 23,* 59–69.

Kaplan, J. S., & Kent, S. (1986). *PRE-MOD II: A computer-assisted program in behavioral analysis.* Austin, TX: PRO-ED.

Karnes, M., Teska, J., & Hodgins, A. (1970). The effects of four programs of classroom intervention on the intellectual and language development of 4-year-old disadvantaged children. *American Journal of Orthopsychiatry, 40,* 58–76.

Kaslow, N. J., Tanenbaum, R. L., & Seligman, M. E. P. (1978). *The KASTAN: A children's attributional styles questionnaire.* Unpublished manuscript, University of Pennsylvania.

Katz, S., (1974). *The effects of emotional education on locus of control and self-concept.* Unpublished doctoral dissertation, Hofstra University.

Kaufman, K. F., & O'Leary, K. D. (1972). Reward, cost, and self-evaluation procedures for disruptive adolescents in a psychiatric hospital school. *Journal of Applied Behavior Analysis, 5,* 293–309.

Kazdin, A. (1973). Covert modeling, model similarity and reduction of avoidance behavior. *Journal of Abnormal Psychology, 81,* 87–95.

Kazdin, A. E. (1994). *Behavior modification in applied settings* (5th ed.). Pacific Grove, CA: Brooks/Cole.

Kazdin, A. E., Rodgers, A., & Colbus, D. (1986). The Hopelessness Scale for Children: Psychometric characteristics and concurrent validity. *Journal of Consulting and Clinical Psychology, 54*, 241–245.

Kendall, P., & Braswell, L. (1982). Cognitive-behavioral self-control therapy for children. A components analysis. *Journal of Consulting and Clinical Psychology, 50*, 672–689.

Kendall, P., & Wilcox, L. (1979). Self-control in children: Development of a rating scale. *Journal of Consulting and Clinical Psychology, 47*, 1020–1029.

Kennedy, R. (1982). Cognitive-behavioral approaches to the modification of aggressive behavior in children. *School Psychology Review, 11*, 47–55.

Kerr, M. M., & Nelson, C. M. (1989). *Strategies for managing behavior problems in the classroom.* (2nd Ed.). Columbus, OH: Merrill.

Kettlewell, P. W., & Kausch, D. F. (1983). The generalization of the effects of a cognitive-behavioral treatment program for aggressive children. *Journal of Abnormal Child Psychology, 11*, 101–114.

Klotz, M. E. B. (1987). Development of a behavior management level system: A comprehensive school-wide behavior management program for emotionally disturbed adolescents. *The Pointer, 31*, 5–11.

Knaus, W. (1974). *Rational-emotive education: A manual for elementary school teachers.* New York: Institute for Rational Living.

Knaus, W., & Block, J. (1976). *Rational-emotive education with economically disadvantaged inner-city high school students: A demonstration study.* Unpublished manuscript.

Knaus, W. J., & McKeever, C. (1977). Rational-emotive education with learning disabled children. *Journal of Learning Disabilities, 10*, 10–14.

Kneedler, R. D., & Hallahan, D. P. (1981). Self-monitoring of on-task behavior with learning disabled children: Current studies and directions. *Exceptional Education Quarterly, 2*, 73–81.

Knoff, H. M. (1988). Effective social interventions. In J. L Graden, J. E. Zins, & M. J. Curtis (Eds.), *Alternative educational delivery systems: Enhancing instructional options for all students* (pp. 431–453). Washington, DC: National Association of School Psychologists.

Koeppen, A. S. (1974, October). Relaxation training for children. *Elementary School Guidance and Counseling, 9*, 16–20.

Kounin, J. S. (1970). *Discipline and group management in classrooms.* San Francisco: Holt, Rinehart & Winston.

Kovacs, M. (1983). *Children's Depression Inventory.* (Available from Maria Kovacs, University of Pittsburgh School of Medicine–Western Psychiatric Institute.)

Krop, H., Calhoun, B., & Verrier, R. (1971). Modification of the "self-concept" of emotionally disturbed children by covert self-reinforcement. *Behavior Therapy, 2*, 201–204.

La Nunziata, L. J., Hunt, K. P., & Cooper, J. O. (1984). Suggestions for phasing out token economy systems in primary and intermediate grades. *Techniques: A Journal for Remedial Educational and Counseling, 1*, 151–156.

Lazarus, A. (1959). The elimination of children's phobias by deconditioning. *South Africa Medical Proceedings, 5*, 161–165.

Leitenberg, H., Yost, L. W., & Carroll-Wilson, M. (1986). Negative cognitive errors in children: Questionnaire development, normative data, and comparisons between children with and without self-reported symptoms of depression, low self-esteem, and evaluation anxiety. *Journal of Consulting and Clinical Psychology, 54*, 528–536.

Leon, J. A., & Pepe, H. J. (1983, September). Self-instructional training: Cognitive behavior modification for remediating arithmetic deficits. *Exceptional Children*, 54–60.

Lewis, T. (1992). Essential features of a social skill instructional program. *The Oregon Conference Monograph,* University of Oregon, Eugene, OR.

Liberty, K. A. (1972). *Decide for progress: Dynamic aims and data decisions.* Working paper, Regional Resource Center for Handicapped Children, University of Oregon, Eugene.

Lindsley, O. R. (1964). Direct measurement and prosthesis of retarded children. *Journal of Education, 147*, 62–81.

Lindsley, O. R. (1971). From Skinner to precision teaching: The child knows best. In J. B. Jordan & L. S. Robins (Eds.), *Let's try doing something else kind of thing: Behavior principles and the exceptional child.* Reston, VA: The Council for Exceptional Children.

Little, L. M., & Kelley, M. L. (1989). The efficacy of response cost procedures for reducing children's noncompliance to parental instructions. *Behavior Therapy, 20*, 525–534.

Long, N. J., Morse, W. C., & Newman, R. G. (Eds.). (1965). *Conflict in the classroom.* Belmont, CA: Wadsworth.

Lovaas, O. I., Schaeffer, B., & Simmons, J. Q. (1965). Building social behavior in autistic children by use of electric shock. *Journal of Experimental Research in Personality, 1*, 99–109.

Lovitt, T. (1973). Self-management projects with children with behavioral disabilities. *Journal of Learning Disabilities, 6*, 15–28.

Luiselli, J. K. (1988). Comparative analysis of sensory extinction treatments for self-injury. *Education and treatment of children, 11*, 149–156.

Luria, A. R. (1961). *The role of speech in the regulation of normal and abnormal behaviors.* New York: Liveright.

Maag, J. (1988). *Treatment of adolescent depression with stress inoculation.* Unpublished doctoral dissertation, Arizona State University, Tempe.

MacFarlane, C. A., Young, K. R., & West, R. P. (1987, September). An integrated school/home overcorrection procedure for eliminating stereotypic behavior in students with severe multiple handicaps. *Education and Training in Mental Retardation*, 156–166.

Madsen, C. H., Becker, W. C., Thomas, D. R., Koser, L., & Plager, E. (1970). An analysis of the reinforcing function of "sit down" commands. In R. K. Parker (Ed.), *Readings in educational psychology* (pp. 265–278). Boston: Allyn & Bacon.

Mager, R. F. (1962). *Preparing instructional objectives.* Belmont, CA: Fearon.

Mahoney, M. J. (1979). *Self-change: Strategies for solving personal problems.* New York: Norton.

Mahoney, M. J., & Mahoney, K. (1976). Self-control techniques with the mentally retarded. *Exceptional Children, 42,* 338–339.

Mahoney, M. J., & Thoresen, C. E. (1972). Behavioral self-control: Power to the person. *Educational Researcher, 1,* 5–7.

Marholin, D., & Steinman, W. (1977). Stimulus control in the classroom as a function of the behavior reinforced. *Journal of Applied Behavior Analysis, 10,* 465–478.

Martin, R. (1975). *Legal challenges to behavior modification.* Champaign, IL: Research Press.

Mastropieri, M. A., Jenne, T., & Scruggs, T. E. (1988). A level system for managing problem behaviors in a high school resource program. *Behavioral Disorders, 13,* 202–208.

Maultsby, M. C. (1984). *Rational behavior therapy.* Englewood Cliffs, NJ: Prentice-Hall.

Mayhew, G., & Harris, F. (1979). Decreasing self-injurious behavior: Punishment with citric acid and reinforcement of alternative behavior. *Behavior Modification, 3,* 322–336.

McCullough, L. L. (1989). The Garden Springs phase system. In M. M. Kerr & C. M. Nelson (Eds.), *Strategies for managing behavior problems in the classroom* (2nd ed.; pp. 385–390). Columbus, OH: Merrill.

McGuffin, P. W. (1991). The effect of timeout duration on frequency of aggression in hospitalized children with conduct disorders. *Behavioral Residential Treatment, 6,* 279–288.

McKenzie, T. L., & Rushall, B. S. (1974). Effects of self-recording on attendance and performance in a competitive swimming training environment. *Journal of Applied Behavior Analysis, 7,* 199–206.

Meichenbaum, D. (1977). *Cognitive behavior modification: An integrative approach.* New York: Plenum Press.

Meichenbaum, D. (1985). *Stress inoculation training.* New York: Pergamon Press.

Meichenbaum, D., Gilmore, B., & Fedoravicius, A. (1971). Group insight vs. group desensitization in treating speech anxiety. *Journal of Consulting and Clinical Psychology, 36,* 410–421.

Meichenbaum, D., & Goodman, J. (1971). Training impulsive children to talk to themselves: A means of developing self control. *Journal of Abnormal Psychology, 77,* 115–126.

Merrell, K. W., Stein, S., & Jantzsch, (1992). Using behavior rating scales to assess social competence with children and youth. In J. Marr & G. Tindal (Eds.), *The Oregon Conference Monograph 1991* (pp. 10–18). Eugene, OR: College of Education, University of Oregon.

Meyer, D. J. (1982). *Effects of rational-emotive group therapy upon anxiety and self-esteem of learning-disabled children.* Unpublished doctoral dissertation, Andrews University.

Michelson, L., Sugai, D. P., Wood, R. P., & Kazdin, A. E. (1983). *Social skills assessment and training with children: An empirically-based handbook.* New York: Plenum Press.

Mikulas, W. L. (1978). *Behavior Modification.* New York: Harper & Row.

Miller, S. R., Osborne, S. S., & Burt, E. (1987). The use of mediation essays in modifying inappropriate behavior of three behaviorally disordered youth. *Teaching: Behaviorally Disordered Youth,* 18–27.

Minner, S. (1990, August). Use of a self-recording procedure to decrease the time taken by behaviorally disordered students to walk to special classes. *Behavioral Disorders, 15,* 210–216.

Mischel, W., Zeiss, R., & Zeiss, A. (1974). Internal-external control and persistence: Validation and implications of the Stanford Preschool Internal-External Scale. *Journal of Personality and Social Psychology, 29,* 265–278.

Moletzky, B. (1974). Behavior recording as treatment: A brief note. *Behavior Therapy, 5,* 107–111.

Monohan, J., & O'Leary, D. (1971). Effects of self-instruction on rule breaking behavior. *Psychological Reports, 79,* 1059–1066.

Morgan, D. P., & Young, K. R. (1984). *Teaching social skills: Assessment procedures, instructional methods, and behavior management techniques.* Logan, UT: Utah State University Press.

Mowrer, O. H., & Mowrer, W. M. (1938). Enuresis—A method for its study and treatment. *American Journal of Orthopsychiatry, 8,* 436–459.

Mowrer, D. E., & Conley, D. (1987). Effect of peer administered consequences upon articulatory responses of speech-defective children. *Communication Disorders, 20,* 319–326.

Neenan, D. M., & Routh, D. K. (1986). Response cost, reinforcement, and children's Porteus maze qualitative performance. *Journal of Abnormal Child Psychology, 14,* 469–480.

Neilans, T. H., Israel, A. C., & Pravder, M. D. (1981). The effectiveness of transition to a self-control program in maintaining changes in children's behavior. *Child Care Quarterly, 10,* 297–306.

Nelson, W. M., III, & Finch, A. J., Jr. (1978). *The children's inventory of anger.* Unpublished manuscript, Xavier University.

Nelson, R. O., Lipinski, D. P., & Boykin, R. A. (1978). The effects of self-recorders' training and the obtrusiveness of the self-recording device on the accuracy and reactivity of self-monitoring. *Behavior Therapy, 9,* 200–208.

Nelson, J. R., Smith, D. J., Young R. K., & Dodd, J. (1991, May). A review of self-management outcome research conducted with students who exhibit behavioral disorders. *Behavioral Disorders, 16,* 169–179.

Novaco, R. (1975). *Anger control: The development and evaluation of an experimental treatment.* Lexington, MA: Heath.

Nowicki, S., & Strickland, B. (1973). A locus of control scale for children. *Journal of Consulting and Clinical Psychology, 40,* 148–154.

O'Leary, K. D. (1968). The effects of self-instruction on immoral behavior. *Journal of Experimental Child Psychology, 6,* 297–301.

O'Leary, K. D., & Becker, W. C. (1967). Behavior modification of an adjustment class: A token reinforcement program. *Exceptional Children, 33,* 637–642.

O'Leary, K. D., Becker, W. C., Evans, M. B., & Sandargas, R. A. (1969). A token reinforcement program in a public school: A replication and systematic analysis. *Journal of Applied Behavior Analysis, 2,* 2–13.

Ollendick, T. H., Oswald, I., & Crowe, H. P. (November, 1986). *The development of the Self-Efficacy Scale for Social Skills in children.* Paper presented at the annual meeting of the Association for the Advancement of Behavior Therapy, Houston.

Olson, R. L., & Roberts, M. W. (1987). Alternative treatments for sibling aggression. *Behavior Therapy, 18,* 243–250.

O'Neill, R., Horner, R., Albin, R., Storey, K., & Sprague, J. (1990). *Functional analysis of problem behavior: A practical assessment guide.* Sycamore, IL: Sycamore.

Palkes, H., Stewart, M., & Freedman, J. (1972). Improvement in maze performance on hyperactive boys as a function of verbal training procedures. *Journal of Special Education, 5,* 337–342.

Patterson, G. R. (1965). An application of conditioning techniques to the control of a hyperactive child. In L. P. Ullmann, & K. Krasner (Eds.), *Case studies in behavior modification.* New York: Holt, Rinehart & Winston.

Patterson, G. R. (1969). Behavioral intervention procedures in the classroom and in the home. In A. E. Bergin & S. L. Garfield (Eds.), *Handbook of psychotherapy and behavior change.* New York: Wiley.

Patterson, G. R. (1973). *Emotional development: Aggression.* CRM Educational Films.

Pavlov, I. P. (1897). *Lectures on the work of the principal digestive glands.* St. Petersburg.

Pawlicki, R. (1976). Effects of self-directed modification training on a measure of locus of control. *Psychological Reports, 39,* 319–322.

Pearl, R. (1985). Cognitive-behavioral interventions for increasing motivation. *Journal of Abnormal Child Psychology, 13,* 443–454.

Phillips, B. N. (1978). *School stress and anxiety: Theory, research, and intervention.* New York: Human Sciences Press.

Phillips, E. L., Phillips, E. A., Fixsen, D., & Wolf, M. (1971). Achievement Place: Modification of behavior of predelinquent boys within a token economy. *Journal of Applied Behavior Analysis, 4,* 45–61.

Pianta, M., & Hudson, A. (1990). A simple response cost procedure to reduce nosepicking by a 7-year-old boy. *Behaviour Change, 7,* 58–61.

Piazza, C. C., & Fisher, W. (1991). A faded bedtime with response cost protocol for treatment of multiple sleep problems in children. *Journal of Applied Behavior Analysis, 24,* 129–140.

Pinkston, E. M., Rees, N. M., LeBlanc, J. M., & Baer, D. M. (1973). Independent control of a preschool child's aggression and peer interaction by contingent teacher attention. *Journal of Applied Behavior Analysis, 19,* 93–98.

Premack, D. (1959). Toward empirical behavior laws: 1. Positive reinforcement. *Psychological Review, 66,* 219–233.

Proctor, M. A., & Morgan, D. (1991). Effectiveness of a response cost raffle procedure on the disruptive classroom behavior of adolescents with behavior problems. *School Psychology Review, 20,* 97–109.

Protinsky, H. (1976, March). Rational counseling with adolescents. *The School Counselor,* 241–246.

Rapport, M. D., Murphy, H. A., & Bailey, J. S. (1982). Ritalin vs. response cost in the control of hyperactive children: A within-subject comparison. *Journal of Applied Behavior Analysis, 15,* 205–216.

Rathjen, D. P. (1984). Social skills training for children: Innovations and consumer guidelines. *School Psychology Review, 13,* 302–310.

Redl, F. (1959). The concept of a therapeutic milieu. *American Journal of Orthopsychiatry, 29,* 721–734.

Redl, F., & Wineman, D. (1952). *Controls from within.* New York: Free Press.

Renne, C. M., & Creer, T. L. (1976). Training children with asthma to use inhalation therapy equipment. *Journal of Applied Behavior Analysis, 9,* 1–11.

Repp, A. C., Barton, L. E., & Brulle, A. R. (1983). A comparison of two procedures for programming the differential reinforcement of other behavior. *Journal of Applied Behavior Analysis, 16,* 435–445.

Repp, A. C., Deitz, S. M., & Speir, N. C. (1975). Reducing Stereotypic responding of retarded persons through the differential reinforcement of other behavior. *American Journal of Mental Deficiency, 79,* 279–284.

Reynolds, W. M. (1987). *Reynolds Adolescent Depression Scale*. Odessa, FL: Psychological Assessment Resources.

Reynolds, W. M. (1988). *Child Depression Scale*. Odessa, FL: Psychological Assessment Resources.

Reynolds, W. M., & Richmond, B. O. (1978). What I Think and Feel: A revised measure of children's manifest anxiety. *Journal of Abnormal Child Psychology, 6,* 271–280.

Rhode, G., Morgan, D. P., & Young, K. R. (1983). Generalization and maintenance of treatment gains of behaviorally handicapped students from resource rooms to regular classrooms using self-evaluation procedures. *Journal of Applied Behavior Analysis, 16,* 171–188.

Rhodes, W. C. (1967). The disturbing child: A problem of ecological management. *Exceptional Children, 33,* 449–455.

Rimland, B. (1964). *Infantile autism*. New York: Appleton-Century-Crofts (Prentice-Hall).

Robertson, S. J., Simon, S. J., Pachman, J. S., & Drabman, R. S. (1979). Self-control and generalization procedures in a classroom of disruptive retarded children. *Child Behavior Therapy, 1,* 347–362.

Rogers-Warren, A. K. (1984). Ecobehavioral analysis. *Education and treatment of children, 7,* (4), 283–303.

Rosenshine, B. (1978). *Instructional principles in direct instruction*. Paper presented at the annual meeting of American Educational Research Association, Toronto.

Rosenshine, B. (1983). Teaching functions in instructional programs. *Elementary School Journal, 83,* 335–352.

Rosenshine, B., & Stevens, R. (1986). Teaching functions. In M. C. Wittrock (Ed.), *Handbook of Research on Teaching* (3rd ed., pp. 376–391). New York: Macmillan.

Rotter, J. B. (1966). Generalized expectancies for internal versus external control of reinforcement. *Psychological Monographs, 80* (Whole No. 609.).

Roush, D. (1984). Rational-emotive therapy and youth: Some new techniques for counselors. *Personnel and Guidance Journal, 62,* 414–417.

Salend, S. J., Tintle, L., & Balber, H. (1988). Effects of a student-managed response cost system on the behavior of two mainstreamed students. *The Elementary School Journal, 89,* 89–97.

Sandler, I. N., & Block, M. (1979). Life stress and maladaptation of children. *American Journal of Community Psychology, 7,* 425–440.

Santograssi, D. A., O'Leary, K. D., Romanczyk, R. G., & Kauffman, K. F. (1973). Self-evaluation by adolescents in a psychiatric hospital school token program. *Journal of Applied Behavioral Analysis, 6,* 227–287.

Sarason, I. (1973). Test anxiety and cognitive modeling. *Journal of Personality and Social Psychology, 28,* 58–61.

Sarason, S., Davidson, K., Lighthall, F., & Waite, R. (1960). A test anxiety scale for children. *Child Development, 29,* 105–113.

Scheuermann, B., Webber, J., Partin, M., & Knies, W. C. (1994). Level systems and the law: Are they compatible? *Behavioral Disorders, 19,* 205–220.

Schlesser, R., & Thackwray, D. (1982). Impulsivity: A clinical developmental perspective. *School Psychology Review, 11,* 42–46.

Schlicter, K. J., & Horan, J. J. (1981). Effects of stress inoculation on the anger and aggression management skills of institutionalized juvenile delinquents. *Cognitive Therapy and Research, 5,* 359–365.

Schmidt, J. A. (1976). *Help yourself: A guide to self-change*. Champaign, IL: Research Press.

Schneider, M. (1974, Fall). Turtle technique in the classroom. *Teaching Exceptional Children,* 22–24.

Schwitzgebel, R. (1964). *Streetcorner research: An experimental approach to the juvenile delinquent*. Cambridge, MA: Harvard University Press.

Sebald, H. (1981). *Adolescence: A social psychological analysis* (revised ed.). Englewood Cliffs, NJ: Prentice-Hall.

Selye, H. (1976). *The stress of life*. New York: McGraw-Hill.

Seymour, F. W., & Stokes, T. F. (1976). Self-recording in training girls to increase work and evoke staff praise in an institution for offenders. *Journal of Applied Behavior Analysis, 9,* 41–54.

Shapiro, E., & Kratchowill, T. R. (1988). Analogue assessment: Methods for assessing emotional and behavioral problems. In E. S. Shapiro & T. R. Kratchowill (Eds.), *Behavioral assessment in schools: conceptual foundations and practical applications* (pp. 290–321). New York: Guilford Press.

Sheehan, J. (1951). The modification of stuttering through non-reinforcement. *Journal of Abnormal and Social Psychology, 46,* 51–63.

Shipman, W. M. (1984). Emotional and behavioral effects of long-distance running on children. In M. L. Sachs & G. W. Buffone (Eds.), *Running as therapy: An integrated approach*. Lincoln, NE: University of Nebraska Press.

Shmurak, S. (1974). Design and evaluation of three dating behavior training programs utilizing response acquisition and cognitive self-statement modification techniques. Unpublished doctoral dissertation, Indiana University, Bloomington.

Singer, L. T., Nofer, J. A., Benson-Szekely, L. J., & Brooks, L. J. (1991). Behavioral assessment and management of food refusal in children with cystic fibrosis. *Journal of Developmental and Behavioral Pediatrics, 12,* 115–120.

Singh, N. N., & Singh, J. (1986). Increasing oral reading proficiency. A comparative analysis of drill and positive practice overcorrection procedures. *Behavior Modification, 10,* 115–130.

Sisson, L. A., Van Hasselt, V. B., Hersen, M., & Aurand, J. C. (1988). Tripartite behavioral intervention to reduce stereotypic and disruptive behaviors in young multihandicapped children. *Behavior Therapy, 19,* 503–526.

Skiba, R., & Deno, S. (1991). Terminology and behavior reduction: The case against "Punishment." *Exceptional Children, 57,* 298–313.

Skiba, R., & Raison, J. (1990). Relationship between the use of timeout and academic achievement. *Exceptional Children, 57,* 36–45.

Skinner, B. F. (1938). *The behavior of organisms: An experimental analysis.* New York: Appleton-Century.

Skinner, B. F. (1971). *Beyond freedom and dignity.* New York: Knopf.

Smith, D. J., Young, R., West, R. P., Morgan, D. P., & Rhode, G. (1988). Reducing the disruptive behavior of junior high school students: A classroom self-management procedure. *Behavioral Disorders, 13,* 231–239.

Smith, S. W., & Farrell, D. T. (1993). Level system use in special education: Classroom intervention with prima facie appeal. *Behavioral Disorders, 18,* 251–264.

Spielberger, C. D. (1973). *Manual for the State–Trait Inventory for Children.* Palo Alto, CA: Consulting Psychologists Press.

Spielberger, C. D. (1988). *State–Trait Anger Expression Inventory: Research Edition.* Odessa, FL: Psychological Assessment Resources.

Spivack, G., Platt, J. J., & Shure, M. (1976). *The problem-solving approach to adjustment.* San Francisco: Jossey-Bass.

Spivack, G., & Shure, M. (1974). *Social adjustment of young children: A cognitive approach to solving real-life problems.* San Francisco: Jossey-Bass.

Sprick, R. (1981). *The solution book: A guide to classroom discipline.* Chicago: Science Research Associates.

Sprick, R. (1985). *Discipline in the classroom: A problem-by-problem survival guide.* West Nyack, NY: The Center for Applied Research in Education.

Sprute, K. A., Williams, R. L., & McLaughlin, T. F. (1990). Effects of a group response cost contingency procedure on the rate of classroom interruptions with emotionally disturbed secondary students. *Child and Family Behavior Therapy, 12,* 1–12.

Staats, A. W., Staats, C. K., Schutz, R. E., & Wolf, M. (1962). The conditioning of textual responses utilizing "extrinsic reinforcers." *Journal of the Experimental Analysis of Behavior, 5,* 33–40.

Stephenson, W. (1980). Newton's fifth rule and Q methodology application to educational psychology. *American Psychologist, 35,* 882–89.

Strain, P., Guralnick, M., & Walker, H. (Eds.) (1986). *Children's social behavior: Development, assessment, and modification.* Orlando, FL: Academic Press.

Sugai, G., & Colvin, G. (1989a). *Development and implementation of leveled behavior management systems.* Eugene, OR: Behavior Associates.

Sugai, G., & Colvin, G. (1989b). *Environmental explanations of behavior: Conducting a functional analysis* (2nd ed.). Eugene, OR: Behavior Associates.

Sulzer-Azaroff, B., & Mayer, G. R. (1991). *Behavior analysis for lasting change.* San Francisco: Holt, Rinehart & Winston.

Tarpley, H., & Schroeder, S. (1979). Comparison of DRO and DRI on rate of suppression of self-injurious behavior. *American Journal of Mental Deficiency, 84,* 188–194.

Thomas, J. D., Presland, I. E., Grant, M. D., & Glynn, T. L. (1978). Natural rates of teacher approval and disapproval in grade-seven classrooms. *Journal of Applied Behavior Analysis, 11,* 91–94.

Thorndike, E. L. (1921). *The psychology of learning.* New York: Teachers College, Columbia University.

Timmons-Mitchell, J. (1986). Containing aggressive acting out in abused children. *Child Welfare, 65,* 459–468.

Trott, M. C., & Maechtlen, A. D. (1986). The use of overcorrection as a means to control drooling. *The American Journal of Occupational Therapy, 40,* 702–704.

Tuersky, A., & Kahneman, D. (1973). Availability: A heuristic for judging frequency and probability. *Cognitive Psychology, 5,* 207–232.

Turkewitz, H., O'Leary, K. D., & Ironsmith, M. (1975). Generalization and maintenance of appropriate behavior through self-control. *Journal of Consulting and Clinical Psychology, 43,* 577–583.

Twardosz, S., & Sajwaj, T. (1972). Multiple effects of a procedure to increase sitting in a hyperactive, retarded boy. *Journal of Applied Behavior Analysis, 5,* 73–78.

Underwood, L. A., Figueroa, R. G., Thyer, B. A., & Nzeocha, A. (1989). Interruption and DRI in the treatment of self-injurious behavior among mentally retarded and autistic self-restrainers. *Behavior Modification, 13,* 471–481.

Vygotsky, L. (1962). *Thought and Language.* New York: Wiley.

Walker, H. (1979). *The acting-out child.* Boston: Allyn & Bacon.

Walker, H. M., & Buckley, N. (1972). Programming generalization and maintenance of treatment effects across time and across settings. *Journal of Applied Behavior Analysis, 5,* 209–224.

Walker, H. M., Hops, H., & Figenbaum, E. (1976). Deviant classroom behavior as a function of combination of social and token reinforcement and cost contingency. *Behavior Therapy, 7,* 76–88.

Walker, H. M., & McConnell, S. R. (1988). *The Walker–McConnell scale of social competence and school adjustment: A social skills rating scale for teachers.* Austin, TX: PRO-ED.

Walton, W. T. (1985). Educators' responses to methods of collecting, storing, and analyzing behavioral data. *Journal of Special Education Technology, 7,* 50–55.

Warren, L. R. (1978). *An evaluation of rational emotive imagery as a component of rational-emotive therapy in the treatment of interpersonal anxiety in junior high school students.* Unpublished doctoral dissertation. University of Oregon, Eugene.

Watson, D. L., & Tharp, R. G. (1981). *Self-directed behavior: Self-modification for personal adjustment.* Monterey, CA: Brooks/Cole.

Watson, J. B. (1913). Psychology as a behaviorist views it. *Psychological Review, 20,* 158–177.

Watson, J., & Raynor, R. (1920). Conditioned emotional reactions. *Journal of Experimental Psychology, 3,* 1–14.

Webster's New World Dictionary of the American Language: College Edition. (1958). New York: World.

Wesolowski, M. D., & Zencius, A. H. (1992). Treatment of aggression in a brain injured adolescent. *Behavioral Residential Treatment, 7,* 205–210.

Wheeler, V. A., & Ladd, G. W. (1982). Assessment of children's self-efficacy for social interaction with peers. *Developmental Psychology, 18,* 795–805.

White, A. G., & Bailey, J. S. (1990). Reducing disruptive behaviors of elementary physical education students with sit and watch. *Journal of Applied Behavior Analysis, 23,* 353–359.

White, M. A. (1975). Natural rates of teacher approval and disapproval in the classroom. *Journal of Applied Behavior Analysis, 8,* 367–372.

White, O. R. (1971). *The "split-middle": A "quickie" method of trend estimation.* Working Paper No. 1, University of Oregon, Regional Center for Handicapped Children.

White, O. R. (1972). *A manual for the calculation and use of the median slope—A method for progress estimation and prediction in the single case.* Working Paper No. 16, University of Oregon, Regional Resource Center for Handicapped Children.

White, O. R. (1986). Precision teaching—precision learning. *Exceptional Children, 52,* 522–534.

White, O. R., & Haring, N. G. (1976). *Exceptional teaching: A multimedia training package.* Columbus, OH: Merrill.

White, O. R., & Liberty, K. A. (1976). Evaluation and measurement. In N. G. Haring & R. Schiefelbusch (Eds.), *Teaching special children.* NY: McGraw-Hill.

Williams, C. (1959). The elimination of tantrum behavior by extinction procedures. *Journal of Abnormal and Social Psychology, 59,* 269.

Wilson, R. (1984). A review of self-control treatments for aggressive behavior. *Behavioral Disorders, 9,* 131–140.

Winn, M. (1983). *Children without childhood.* New York: Pantheon Books.

Witt, J. C., Cavell, T. A., Heffer, R. W., Carey, M. P., & Martens, B. (1988). Child self-report: Interviewing techniques and rating scales. In E. S. Shapiro & T. R. Kratchowill (Eds.), *Behavioral assessment in schools: Conceptual foundations and practical applications* (pp. 384–454). New York: Guilford Press.

Wolery, M. R., Bailey, D. B., & Sugai, G. M. (1988). *Effective teaching: Principles and procedures of applied behavior analysis with exceptional students.* Boston: Allyn & Bacon.

Wolf, M. M., Risley, T. R., & Mees, H. (1964). Application of operant conditioning procedures to the behavior problems of an autistic child. *Behavior Research and Therapy, 1,* 305–312.

Wolpe, J. (1969). *The practice of behavior therapy.* New York: Pergamon Press.

Wong, B. Y. L. (1985). Issues in cognitive-behavioral interventions in academic skill areas. *Journal of Abnormal Child Psychology, 13,* 425–442.

Wood, R., & Flynn, J. (1978). A self-evaluation token system vs. an external token system alone in a residential setting with predelinquent youth. *Journal of Applied Behavior Analysis, 11,* 503–512.

Workman, E. (1982). *Teaching behavioral self-control to students.* Austin, TX: PRO-ED.

Workman, E., & Dickinson, D. (1979). The use of covert positive reinforcement in the treatment of a hyperactive child: An empirical case study. *Journal of School Psychology, 17,* 67–73.

Workman, E., & Hector, M. (1978). Behavior self control in classroom settings: A review of the literature. *Journal of School Psychology, 16,* 227–236.

Workman, E., Helton, G., & Watson, P. (1982). Self-monitoring effects in a four year old child: An ecological behavior analysis. *Journal of School Psychology, 20,* 57–64.

Yell, M. (1988, August). The effects of jogging on the rates of selected target behaviors of behaviorally disordered students. *Behavioral Disorders, 13,* 273–279.

Yell, M. (1990). The use of corporal punishment, suspension, expulsion, and timeout with behaviorally disordered students in public schools: Legal considerations. *Behavioral Disorders, 15,* 100–109.

Young, J. A., & Wincze, J. P. (1974). The effects of the reinforcement of compatible and incompatible alternative behaviors on the self-injurious and related behaviors of a profoundly retarded female adult. *Behavior Therapy, 5,* 614–623.

Yulevich, L., & Axelrod, S. (1983). Punishment: A concept that is no longer necessary. *Progress in Behavior Modification, 14,* 355–382.

Zakay, D., Bar-El, Z., & Kreitler, S. (1984). Cognitive orientation and changing the impulsivity of children. *British Journal of Educational Psychology, 54,* 40–50.

Zimmerman, E. H., & Zimmerman, J. (1962). The alteration of behavior in a classroom situation. *Journal of the Experimental Analysis of Behavior, 5,* 59–60.

Author Index

Subject Index